BATTLE OF THE BULGE

This map details the area of Hitler's Ardennes Offensive, December, 1944 through January, 1945. All of the towns and villages depicted here were involved in the Battle of the Bulge. This map serves as a basis for the Situation Maps in the book that show extensive troop movements.

BATTLE OF THE BULGE

Hitler's Ardennes Offensive, 1944-1945

Danny S. Parker

Combined Publishing
Pennsylvania

For my late friend
Charles B. MacDonald.

Paperback edition, 1999
First published in the United States of America in 1991 by
Combined Books, Inc.

Copyright © 1991 by Danny S. Parker

For information, address:
Combined Publishing
P.O. Box 307
Conshohocken, PA 19428
Web: www.combinedpublishing.com
E-mail: combined@combinedpublishing.com
Orders 1-800-418-6065

Library of Congress Cataloging-in-Publication Data
Parker, Danny S.
   Battle of the Bulge: Hitler's Ardennes Offensive,
1944-1945 / Danny S. Parker.
         p.   cm.
   Includes index.
   ISBN 1-58097-023-0 (pbk)
   1. Ardennes, Battle of the, 1944-1945. I. Title.
D756.5.A7P368   1991
940.54'21431 – dc20   91-26173

Layout: Lizbeth Nauta, Leigh Schofield
Cartography: Robert L. Pigeon, III

Printed in Hong Kong

Acknowledgement is given to the following authors and publishers for so graciously allowing me to quote from published works:
Bloody Clash at Sadzot by William B. Breuer, Zeus Publishers, 1981.
War by Gwynne Dyer, Crown Publishers, 1985.
Six Months to Oblivion, by Werner Girbig, Hippocrene Books, 1975.
"The Honorable Mr. Moyne," oral story told by Ernest Hemingway, reprinted from the *Letzebuerger Land*, December 1, 1972.
Another Bridge Too Far, Another Longest Day, by E.V.D. Hoeven, C.R.I.B.A., 1987.
The Men of Company K, by Harold P. Leinbaugh and John D. Campbell, William and Morrow, 1985.
Company Commander, by Charles B. MacDonald, Bantam, 1947.
Men Against Fire by S.L.A. Marshal, Combat Forces Press, 1947.
"Murder at Malmédy," by James P. Mattera and C.M. Stephan, Jr. *Army*, December, 1981.
War as I Knew It by Gen. George S. Patton, Jr., Houghton Mifflin, 1947.
Lines of Battle, ed. by Annette Tapert, Times Books, 1987.
The Bulge Bugle, various issues, published by Veterans of the Battle of the Bulge.
Manhay: The Ardennes, Christmas, 1944, by George Winter, J.J. Fedorowicz, 1990.

In addition, brief portions of this volume have previously been published in two periodicals, *Strategy & Tactics* and *World War II*, and are reproduced with permission.

Half-title page: *The Sturmgewehr 44 assault rifle. It was the most common German infantry weapon used in the Ardennes. It could fire either in semi-automatic or fully automatic mode; maximum firing rate was 500 rounds per minute. Effectively range varied between 300 and 600 meters depending on firing rate.*

Title page: *Panther of the 2nd Kompanie, 2nd SS Panzer Division, in action near Manhay, December, 1944.*

CONTENTS

Acknowledgments

Many have contributed to this volume: the late Charles B. MacDonald suggested that I go ahead and write the book. Before his passing, Charles graciously provided a much needed review of the manuscript. Other critique has been provided by Jean Paul Pallud, a remarkable French scholar on the Ardennes Campaign. William C. Cavanaugh, Ralph G. Hill, Jr., and Randy Heller have provided additional comment and correction. Particularly useful review has been provided from two historical societies. These are CRIBA, the *Centre des Recherches et d'Information la Bataille des Ardennes* in Belgium and CEBA, the *Cercle d'Etudes sur la Bataille des Ardennes* in Luxembourg. Three gentlemen from these societies, Pierre Gosset and Lucien Calloux of CRIBA and Jean Milmeister of CEBA, have provided invaluable assistance. My sincere thanks to both of these wonderful organizations and the much appreciated hospitality of the people of Luxembourg and Belgium.

In the U.S., Jim Bowman assisted with translation of German documents and Christopher Ruppert provided a much needed check on German syntax. Shelby Stanton, Forrest Opper, Matt Caffrey, James L. Picken and Richard Gutenkunst have provided additional research support. Ron Mazurkiewicz helped to procure period maps of the Ardennes region. At the National Archives, George Wagner helped me to locate dusty old documents. Similar assistance was provided at the U.S. Army Center for Military History by Dr. Richard Sommers and by Hannah Zeidlik at the Office of the Chief of Military History. Thanks also to the staff of the Bundesarchiv in Freiburg for their very efficient service in locating documents in the German archives.

In England, Michael Cox assisted with information on the British pictures of the battle. Personal photo collections have been made available by Pierre Gosset and Raphaël d'Amico-Gerard of Belgium. Many veterans have provided invaluable accounts and reminiscences of the battle; I mention the *Veterans of the Battle of the Bulge* for their considerable assistance in spreading the word. To the many who have written and go unmentioned here, I offer my sincere appreciation.

Finally, very special recognition goes to my wife, Lisa, who has exhibited great patience and understanding with the project she calls "The Golden Guide to the Battle of the Bulge."

Abbreviation of Ranks

Rank	Abbreviation	Rank	Abbreviation
Generalfeldmarschall	Genfldm.	Brigadier	Brig.
Field Marshal	Fld.M.	Colonel	Col.
General	Gen.	SS-Standartenführer	SS-Standf.
der Panzertruppen	d. Pztrp	Oberst	Obst.
der Artillerie	d. Art.	Oberstleutnant	Obstlt.
der Infanterie	d. Inf.	SS-Obersturmbannführer	SS-Ostbf.
der Kavallerie	d. Kav.	Major	Maj.
SS-Obergruppenführer	SS-Obgrf.	SS-Sturmbannführer	SS-Stbf.
Generaloberst	Genobst.	Sergeant	Sgt.
SS-Oberstgruppenführer	SS-Obstgrf.	Captain	Capt.
Generalleutnant	Genlt.	Hauptmann	Hptm.
SS-Gruppenführer	SS-Gruf.	SS-Hauptsturmbannführer	SS-Hptsf.
Generalmajor	Genmaj.	Oberleutnant	Oblt.
SS-Brigadeführer	SS-Brigf.	SS-Obersturmführer	SS-Obsf.
SS-Oberführer	SS-Oberf.	Corporal	Corp.
Lieutenant, Leutnant	Lt.	Private	Pvt.
SS-Untersturmführer	SS-Ustf.		

Preface

The Battle of the Bulge was one of the most famous military engagements of recent history. And like much of the stuff of legend, many theories and suppositions have been advanced to explain why the Ardennes Campaign ended as it did. Historians still argue about how it could have gone differently under other circumstances.

Like all events that have captured the public imagination, the Battle of the Bulge has more than its share of popular myths, many of which have been compounded through the years. "The first casualty of war," the old adage goes, "is the truth." We shall see that unlike the cinematic version of the Battle of the Bulge, the Germans did not almost win the war when they missed the capture of American fuel. Similarly, no single man in the Allied camp knew for certain that Hitler was going to attack in the Ardennes. The truth of these stories is less colorful. The Germans hoped to capture fuel, but did not know where to find it. And although at least two American intelligence officers ventured the possibility of a German attack in the Ardennes, neither was sure enough to press the issue with his superiors as did Hollywood's Henry Fonda.

Other myths are not so easily dispelled. Both combatants in the conflict differ on emotionally charged topics. For instance, some retired German SS officers still subscribe to the rather fantastic alibi that no atrocities occurred at the Malmèdy crossroads; they claim the U.S. prisoners were shot when they tried to escape. But Americans may have a difficult time accepting the fact that GIs shot down German prisoners in cold blood near Chenogne, Belgium in early 1945.

Most of the many soldiers in the Ardennes possessed intense loyalty not only to their country, but foremost to their unit, which they quite naturally regarded as superior to all others. Thus, it is sometimes hard to accept a history which indicates one's unit or army was not always the best. Suffice to say, that as a humble non-veteran, I have the utmost respect for those who served in the Ardennes. On the other hand, after more than ten years of study, I have felt compelled to tell the story as objectively as I can recount it, even at risk of offending some who were there.

Understandably, the history of the Ardennes Campaign, like that of other great battles, reflects the bias of the tellers, who were often participants. Devotion to country, respect for the dead, unwillingness to offend the living and a desire to justify one's actions during battle, both honorable and dishonorable, are just a few reasons for these distortions of the truth. Some of these errors have been deliberate, but most were unintentional, born of narrow perception, and now after nearly half a century, the inevitable failings of memory. In many cases, we now must rely solely on the written record. Forty-five years after the event, the trail is growing cold for the contemporary World War II historian in search of witnesses. Many of the leading personalities are dead, and gone with them are the answers to baffling questions that still plague the campaign. In certain cases the truth of the matter remains unclear or controversial. In these cases, I have tried to present both sides of the issue. Where doubts remain, I have used the historian's traditional wisdom: one witness, no witness.

The organization and level of my treatment have been essentially dictated by the extent of this modest effort. The written word must necessarily omit many particulars. In the main, the description of the battle relies on a division level treatment with lower levels covered in the opening phase of the battle when American units were widely separated and there was little in the way of a homogenous front. The narrative is organized around two-day periods with detailed maps to help the reader follow the action that eddied through the tiny Ardennes villages. Those desiring a more tactical account of the operations described are referred to Dr. Cole's splendid U.S. Army official history.

Readers will note that the book features a detailed daily German view of the situation. This was deemed important to understanding of the early stages of the battle when the Germans controlled the initiative. I have also wanted to make available newly translated material describing the enemy side of the hill. Most of the previous English works on the campaign have understandably concentrated on the Allied view since much of the material in the German archives is not so readily accessible. The author was fortunate to work on a research project for the Joint Chiefs of Staff in 1987-1988 which brought to light a number of previously untranslated German sources. These included von Rundstedt's richly detailed war diary and recently declassified interceptions of German radio communications during the battle. Information from these valuable documents appear in this volume for the first time.

The Ardennes Campaign was an exceedingly complex affair and the military historian is hard pressed to neatly describe the root causes of the conflict's progress and outcome in the classical von Rankian sense. Due to the compartmentalized nature of the terrain, the campaign cannot be reckoned as anything less than many swirling individual engagements, often with little relationship to others going on simultaneously. It is perhaps best to imagine the scene: a million men locked in desperate combat over an six week period in a mountainous, frozen and heavily forested region of 500 square miles. The absolute truth of such a situation will always evade us; we can never "tell it just like it was." Wellington said of Waterloo that "It is as impossible to describe a battle as a ball." And yet it is the job of the historian to try. I hope readers will find my efforts sufficient to the task at hand. Any credit for this volume must be divided among the many people who helped make it possible. On the other hand, the author alone is responsible for interpretations made as well as any errors of fact or omission.

—DSP

Introduction

Throughout the bloody course of the Second World War, no single episode so desperately and tragically tested the mettle of the Americans and their Allies as did the Ardennes Campaign. Commonly known as the Battle of the Bulge, it was the largest pitched battle of the entire Western Front. Counting both sides, over a million soldiers fought in the wintry Ardennes forest from mid-December of 1944 through January of 1945. Moreover, this dramatic, month-long campaign represented one of the most astonishing episodes of the entire European conflict.

The Battle of the Bulge was perhaps the fiercest combat which Americans would have to face in Europe and quite likely the most controversial as well. For after Pearl Harbor, it stands as the greatest Allied intelligence failure of the War. Owing to serious miscalculations of German capabilities, the battle imposed monumental confusion within Allied ranks. This was also a time of deep national humiliation for American soldiers in Europe including, as it did, the largest mass surrender of U.S. forces since Bataan. And even more, the confrontation culminated in a grave command crisis for the Allies as bitter disagreements between British and American leaders over strategy sowed the seeds of discontent.

For Adolf Hitler, the Ardennes Offensive was absolutely the last chance for his Third Reich. That the Germans could recover from six years of devistating warfare and still respond with the greatest offensive in the West will always stand as an astonishing military accomplishment. The Ar-

A Panther advances through the snowy Ardennes, one of the crew cupping his ears to protect from the cold.

dennes in 1944 represented an awesome display of the same cunning and teutonic military might that had dominated the European continent a scant three years before. As Hitler's last desperate gamble for success in a war already lost, this final blitzkrieg was the battle in which, for all practical purposes, the German fighting spirit was at last broken.

For those who fought there, the winter campaign in the Ardennes represented a conflict of grim and desperate determination with monumental loss suffered by both sides. Twenty-thousand men would fall in the dark forest, and eight times that would be wounded or taken prisoner. Many more would suffer exposure and frost-bite in Europe's worst winter in 30 years. The sheer ferocity of the conflict, the desperate determination of the German attack and the courageous stand by the Allied defense, place the battle for the Ardennes firmly beside such infamous campaigns as Stalingrad, Kursk, North Africa and Normandy.

For many, the Ardennes Campaign will always represent a supreme evocation of the epic struggle between Allied and Nazi forces in World War II. At the very least, the Battle of the Bulge insured that the struggle for a handful of otherwise obscure and anonymous Ardennes villages with quaint names such as Bastogne, St. Vith, Celles and Clervaux will always be writ large in the annals of military history.

Tough SS Grenadier of the 1st SS Panzer Division *photographed near Poteau on December 18th. The SS private was an MG42 machine gunner with* Kampfgruppe Hansen.

Aging tank obstacles of the West Wall seen today east of Ouren.

THE SETTING

Near Rötgen, an infantryman of the U.S. 78th Division stands guard over a captured section of the German West Wall. November, 1944.

Today remnants of the "Dragon's Teeth" can still be seen in the vicinity.

The Situation

In September of 1944, the dictator, war lord and self-styled Führer of Nazi Germany, Adolf Hitler, was facing almost certain defeat. After six costly years of war, his beleaguered National Socialist state that he called the Third Reich was losing ground rapidly on all fronts. In the East, the Russian summer offensive had crossed half of Poland and smashed to the very borders of East Prussia. In scarcely two weeks 27 German divisions had been written off there and *Heeresgruppe Mitte, Army Group Center*, had been almost totally destroyed. It was a calamity of unprecedented proportions.

In the West, after a long and costly battle, the Allies broke out from their Normandy beachhead on July 31st. By the end of August their forces had liberated most of France in rapid armored pursuit. At summer's end the Allies were fast closing in on Germany's western frontier, close to the industrial heartland of the Ruhr region. Emergency efforts were made to improve the Westwall fortifications along the German border, but these were considered obsolete by Hitler's generals.[1] Hitler knew that he could not afford to lose the Ruhr region; without its mines, refineries and factories he could not hope to continue on with the war.

In Italy, the U.S. Fifth and the British Eighth Armies continued to hammer at the German forces in the northern part of that country. The Allies were fighting in the Apennines and close to breaking into the Po Valley not far from the southern frontier of the Reich. Only the difficult terrain there kept the German line from totally giving way.

Elsewhere, North Africa had been lost and Hitler had abandoned Greece. Over the homeland of the Reich vast Allied bomber fleets daily visited death and destruction on German cities, leaving them scarred and in ruins. By any accounting, the strategic initiative had been firmly grasped by the Allies.

Politically, except for Hungary and Japan, the Reich was friendless. Italy and Finland were out of the war and the Rumanians and the Bulgarians were now fighting on the side of the Soviets. Even worse were the horrendous losses sustained by Nazi Germany. Although Hitler still had ten million men under arms, his armies had sustained fantastic losses. In the five years of war Germany had suffered 4.5 million casualties; the summer of 1944 alone had seen the loss of nearly a million German soldiers.[2] Against this backdrop of unmitigated disaster even Imperial Japan began to politely suggest that Germany begin peace negotiations with

Adolf Hitler, the leader of Nazi Germany, and Generalfeldmarschall Gerd von Rundstedt in charge of German forces on the Western Front.

the Soviets. But Hitler strictly forbade any dickering with the *Untermenschen* (sub-humans) in Russia. Of his enemies, he despised them most of all.

Germany had also sustained a series of crippling economic blows. With the territorial losses went such irreplaceable resources as Rumanian oil and ores and a tremendous reduction in the civilian labor pool. Most crushing of all were shortages of petroleum products, made constantly worse by devastating Allied air raids on the few operating German oil refineries. Production of synthetic oil from coal also

1   Generalfeldmarschall Von Rundstedt, in charge of the German forces in the West, had infuriated Hitler that fall by denouncing the West Wall as "a mousetrap."

2   The *OKW* war diary for September 29th shows that 600,000 had been lost on the Western Front that summer. Estimated available strength there was only thirteen infantry, three panzer divisions and two armored brigades fit to fight. Total "on the road" tank strength was scarcely 100 vehicles in *Heeresgruppe B*.

An American GI surveys the West Wall along the German border. The "dragon's teeth" were designed as an anti-tank obstacle.

dropped precipitously from 150,000 tons in January 1944 to only 26,000 tons in December.

Yet there were some encouraging aspects to this grim scene. Reichsminister Albert Speer, in charge of the German armaments and war production, had been given two years to reorganize, disperse and increase the efficiency of German manufacture. So successful had been Speer's program that despite Allied air attacks, most aspects of German war manufacture (with the notable exception of oil) actually reached peak levels of production only in the fall of 1944.[3] Also, in the East and in the West, the great enemy summer offensives appeared to have finally come to a halt as the Allies and the Russians had to pause to regroup and resupply. Thus Hitler's armies on both fronts gained a much needed breathing spell.

An attempt on Hitler's life on July 20th, 1944, by a cabal of German officers had failed, but had nonetheless injured the German leader. His health suffered and there were periods in which he was bedridden.[4] Although Hitler had promised his people a "thousand year Reich" after eleven and a half years of Nazi rule, some of the people of Germany were beginning to wonder if the limit had not already been reached. Every other day the officially sanctioned paper *Das Reich* carried long lists of the young men of Germany who had "fallen for the Führer" and hardly a night passed without the Allied bombers returning to pound the ruins that had been cities. Strangely, however, the attempt of the army on

Hitler's life rallied the German people around their leader. Morale remained good on the home front and the Germans seemed willing to sacrifice anything for their beloved Führer.

On July 25th the German people were called to greater concessions when Hitler charged that "all aspects of public life must be adapted to the requirements of total war." In the following weeks his propaganda minister, Josef Goebbels, announced the closure of all theaters and cinemas, a ban on concerts and the institution of a 60-hour work week. Meanwhile, convalescing in his *Wolfschanze* headquarters in East Prussia, Hitler pondered the adversity that had befallen his Third Reich. For all the bad news, the *Feldherr* was not ready to give up. "I cannot yet tell how the dice will fall," he concluded.

Hitler was convinced that the Allied strategic control of the air was the root cause for his recent reverses. Allied air power had thoroughly wrecked his panzer divisions in France. However, German jet aircraft were just coming into production. The corpulent chief of the Luftwaffe, Reichsmarschall Hermann Göring, believed those planes held the promise of reversing the nemesis of Allied air superiority. Hitler opined that production could be greatly expanded to make 3,000 of these "blitz-bombers" available by late fall 1944.[5] Also the new electro-U-boat, the Mark XXI, would be available in numbers by winter. Admiral Karl Donitz, the head of the German Navy, the *Kriegsmarine*, said that these fast submarines would turn the tide of the

---

3   For example, German tank production peaked in December 1944, reaching a figure of 598 — more than five times the production figure of 1942.

4   Some speculated that some of Hitler's health troubles — stomach spasms, insomnia and nervous twitching — were arising from the almost daily series of pills and injections administered by his personal physician, Dr. Theodor Morell. Many of his colleagues questioned the pudgy doctor's methods. "He is," said one, "a quack."

5   A characteristically unrealistic estimate by Hitler. Although German aircraft factories were able to vastly expand production: 40,593 aircraft in 1944 — more than in 1942 and 43 combined, they did so by concentrating on existing aircraft types. Of these, only 1,041 were jet Messerschmitt 262s or Arado 234s. Front-line operational strength of these planes during the Ardennes Campaign was barely 60 aircraft.

battle against Allied shipping lanes. Also there were even more revolutionary secret weapons in development. The V-2 rocket was now bombarding London; a multi-stage "New York rocket" was on the drawing boards. Finally, nuclear physicists in Germany were approaching creation of a self-sustaining fission reactor. Perhaps, within a year or two, his scientists told him, an atomic bomb could be developed "capable of destroying a city in a single blast."[6]

6   That the Allies were aware of these threatening developments is underscored by a *New York Times* headline on October 22nd, 1944. The article announced that Hitler had ordered work on the V3 rocket, a missile capable of reaching the United States, and said to carry a "secret bomb" with four times the explosive power of a conventional warhead.

At left: *The V-2 rocket. Hitler placed great faith in the development of secret weapons in the last year of the war. In December of 1944 the Germans were firing an average of five V-2s per day at Allied targets such as London or Antwerp. German rocketry experts already had the A-10, a multi-stage missile, on the drawing boards. It was appropriately known as the "New York Rocket."*

Below: *The world's first jet powered fighter aircraft, the Me-262, which many aviation experts believed could have turned the tide of the war in the air for Hitler had he produced the plane soon enough and in sufficient quantity. This plane flew with Kampfgeschader 51 which could never muster more than 40 aircraft during the Ardennes operation.*

The Heinkel-162A "Salamander" was Hitler's answer to his desperate need in late 1944 for a massed produced jet fighter to counter Allied air superiority. The Volkjäger, or "People's Fighter" went from drawing board to test flight in just 37 days! Even though it had a maximum speed of 520 mph, its single top-mounted turbojet led to questionable air worthiness.

Hitler Plans His Last Gamble

SS Reichsführer Henrich Himmler. Head of Hitler's personal army, the Waffen SS, Himmler was charged with raising the armies to be used for the Ardennes offensive.

In early August, 1944, it was clear to the leader of Nazi Germany that he would need time to develop these "secret weapons," a fact of which he constantly reminded his subordinates. First on his list of priorities was to raise a new field army to bolster his defenses both in the East and the West. He appointed SS Reichsführer Heinrich Himmler, the vile leader of his private army, the Waffen SS, to raise a large replacement force of at least 25 "People's Infantry" or *Volksgrenadier* divisions. Himmler was ordered to ruthlessly comb-out able bodied men from the Navy and Luftwaffe and top heavy administrative staffs — what the Führer referred to as "rear area swine." Himmler knew his charge well: "A new army, fully ready to fight," he told the home-front area commanders assembled at Posen on August 31st, "will give the Führer the arguments and the triumphs which will allow him to dictate the peace."[7]

Yet Hitler knew that defense with this new "National Socialist People's Army" would not be enough. A fanatic believer in the Clauswitzian doctrine espousing the superiority of attack, he was determined to take the offensive to regain the initiative and buy time. In *On War* the great German military thinker had already prescribed the answer to the Führer's dilemma in his treatise to the *Kriegsakademie* a hundred years before:

> "When the disproportion of Power is so great that no limitation of our own object can ensure us safety from catastrophe...forces will, or should, be concentrated in one desperate blow."

Accordingly, the time of year and the urgency of the situation turned Hitler's thoughts to the "magnificent opportunity offered by the coming winter with its fog, long nights and snow." The real question was where to launch his great gamble.

Hitler saw that his last offensive must be a rapid campaign that would produce a decisive result. To survive he must gain a separate peace with one of his enemies that were squeezing the Reich from both East and West. To accomplish this he would need a crushing victory on the battlefield to bring at least one of them to the negotiating table. On August 31st he told his subordinates that,

> ...it is childish and naive to hope that at the time of severe military defeats a favorable political moment will arrive....The moment will arrive when disagreements between the Allies have become so great that a break will come....I intend to carry on the fight until there is a prospect of peace that is reasonable, of a peace tolerable for Germany which will safeguard its existence of this and future generations.

Hitler considered Russia as the location for his great offensive for a time but then dropped the idea of using his reserve on that front. So vast were the *Bolshevik* numbers

---

7   In fact Himmler was able to create 43 new or rehabilitated divisions. Eighteen were ready by September. Fifteen of these went to the East, one to Norway and the rest to the Western Front before November.

(now estimated at 555 divisions) that a German force of forty divisions destroying a like number of enemy formations would have little long term effect on the outcome there.[8] Then, too, the Soviets were politically monolithic and unavailing; a favorable political decision was unlikely. Italy was also considered and dropped; there was no decisive strategic objective within reach and as the Allies had discovered to their cost, that mountainous region was more suited to defense than attack.

The situation in the West looked more promising. After the breakout at St. Lô, it became obvious to the German High Command that the western front was now a major threat. Thanks to complete mastery of the air, the Allies had managed to break out from Normandy and liberate France and Belgium with surprisingly few divisions — less than forty were in the line by September. An attack by 30-40 German divisions that resulted in the destruction of a like number of Allied units would have a dramatic impact on the battle on that front. Even better, an attack in the West would protect the German industrial heartland in the Ruhr northeast of the German border city of Aachen. In this, the German leader agreed with Schlieffen's dictum from WW I that it was better to have an enemy in East Prussia than one on the Rhine.

8   Due to the Russian strength the preponderance of German military forces were in the East. Of 3,421,000 million men on the field army rosters on October 13, 1944, some 2,046,000 were on the Russian front.

Perhaps most importantly, Hitler believed that a successful offensive in the West might bring about a radical political change. Recognizing that a purely military result was now beyond his reach, he believed a great blow might disrupt the Anglo-American alliance — an alliance that Hitler believed was fragile and vulnerable to begin with. Furthermore, a great victory on the Western Front might lead to the possibility of a separate peace and one that Hitler believed would be on his own terms. The German leader had made this decision as early as August 19th when he commanded that his subordinates: "Prepare to take the offensive in November when the enemy air force cannot operate. Some 25 divisions must be moved to the Western Front over the next two months."

Examining the Westwall line in late August, Hitler noted that the site for the beginning of his invasion of France in 1940, the Ardennes region, was being lightly screened by the American forces. The idea for the Ardennes Offensive was born in Hitler's mind — likely based as much on a wish to turn back the clock to the glory days of 1940 as it was rational military judgment. From his bedside, Hitler discussed his brain-wave with his right-hand man and confidant, Generaloberst Alfred Jodl. Jodl was the taciturn head of the High Command of the Armed Forces, *Oberkommando der Wehrmacht (OKW)*. The *OKW* and the *Wehrmachtführungsstab*, the Armed Forces Operations Staff, comprised Hitler's household military command center; being absolutely dominated by the Führer, it was an uneasy mixture of obedient

Debacle in Normandy. Allied air power took the wheels out of the German blitzkrieg. A motorized column of the 9th SS Panzer Division is shown under air attack in France.

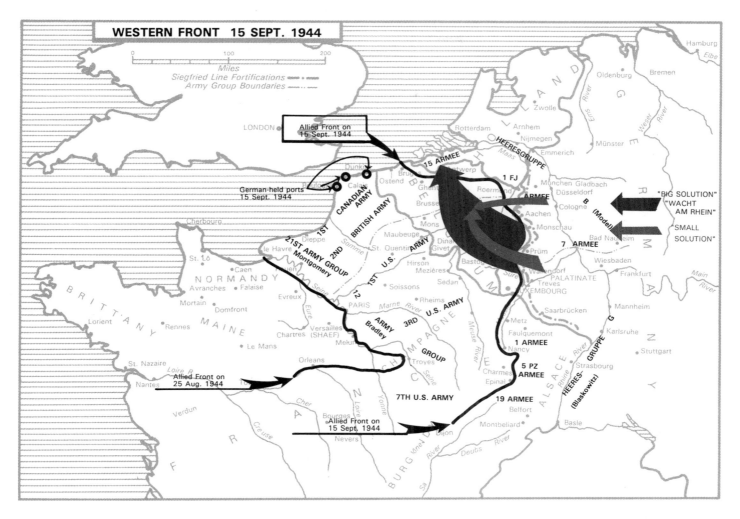

WESTERN FRONT 15 SEPT. 1944

military planners and sycophant yes-men.

In early September the U.S. V Corps reached Bastogne in the Belgian Ardennes and, although low on fuel and ammunition, pushed into the Westwall to cross into Germany. The 4th Infantry Division advanced on the Schnee Eifel, the 28th Division across the Our River towards Pronsfeld and the 5th Armored crossed near Wallendorf. Between September 12th and 15th they managed to push small forces through the German Westwall. Meanwhile, the Germans hastily gathered up scratch forces from the *2nd Panzer* and *2nd SS Panzer Divisions* and threw them against the two American infantry divisions at dawn on the 16th. The counterattacks were successful and drove the Americans back off German soil in some disorder. The event was fortuitous for the Nazi cause; later it was likened to a German version of the "miracle of the Marne" of the previous war.[9]

Later that day, on September 16th, Hitler attended his daily briefing at the *OKW* headquarters. From the Russian,

Balkan, Italian and Western Front, he heard of an unbroken stream of reverses and bad news. The only bright spot was the successful counterattacks delivered by the panzer troops in the Ardennes. At the word "Ardennes," Hitler leapt to his feet. "I have just made a momentous decision," he declared to those present. "I shall go over to the counterattack." He swept his hand across the situation map unrolled before him. "That is to say, here, out of the Ardennes, with the objective Antwerp." Antwerp, on the Belgian cost was the key for supply of most of the Allied forces in the West. It was also over a hundred miles from the front along the German border. Hitler's audience was stunned.

9   General Siegfried Westphal, von Rundstedt's chief of staff, said of the repulse of the enemy penetration across the West Wall: "If the enemy had thrown in more forces, he would not only have broken through the German line of defenses which were in the process of being built up along the Eifel, but in the absence of any appreciable reserves on the German side he must have effected the collapse of the whole west front within a short time."

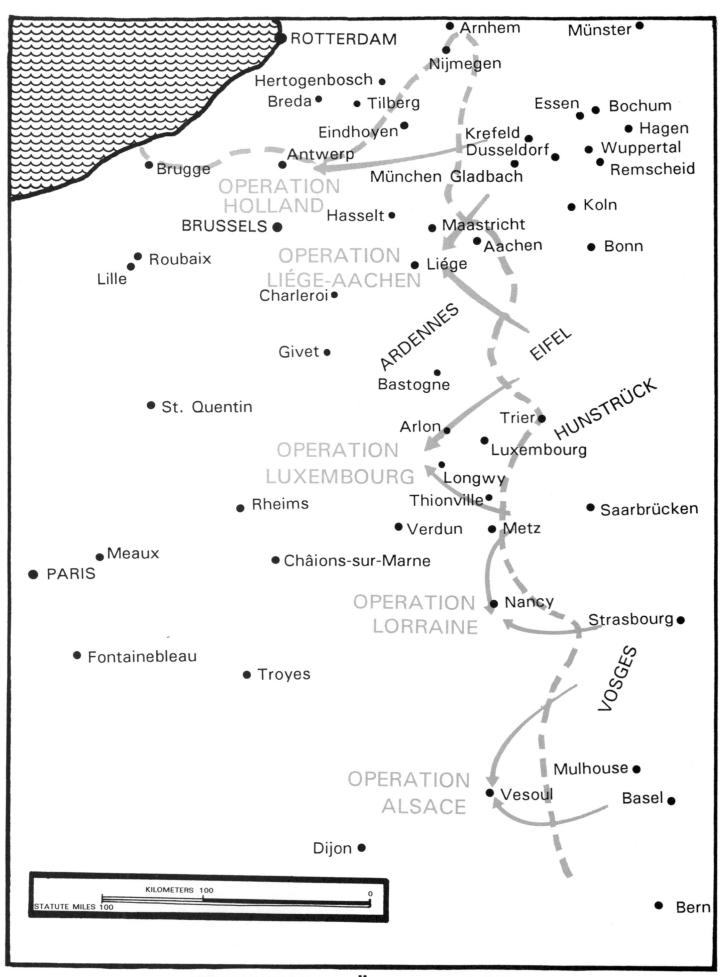

WEHRMACHTFÜHRUNGSSTAB:
FIVE ALTERNATIVE OFFENSIVE PLANS, October 9, 1944

Hitler Overides His Generals

In spite of his staff's disbelief, self-doubt seldom troubled Hitler. "The gods love and bless those who strive for the impossible," he once wrote. "That is a divinity in which I believe." Thus, the Führer characteristically ignored his incredulous assistants and bid them do his work. Over the next four weeks he directed Jodl and his inner circle to flesh out the stratagem. This they did, studying five possible courses of offensive action. These included:

1. Operation Holland: a single attack from the Venlo area with the objective the port of Antwerp.

2. Operation Liège-Aachen: a two pronged envelopment attack launched simultaneously from northern Luxembourg and northwest of Aachen that would come together at Liège trapping the U.S. First Army.

3. Operation Luxembourg: another envelopment attack with two pincers, one from central Luxembourg and the other from Metz converging on Longwy and trapping Patton's Third Army.

4. Operation Lorraine: a two pronged attack from Metz and Baccarat converging on Nancy.

5. Operation Alsace: a two pronged attack from Epinal and Montbéliard converging on Vesoul.

His staff recommended the first two operations as the most promising, but also the most risky. All this was merely a staff exercise, however, since the German leader had already decided by his "divine intuition" on an offensive in the Ardennes. Hitler asked that the first two ideas be combined — precisely the operation he had decided on in the first place and well beyond the scope of what the *OKW* planners believed militarily feasible.

But Hitler could not be dissuaded. The combined plan submitted to Hitler on October 11th was the same idea for an attack towards Antwerp through the Ardennes that he had proposed over a month earlier. Then, as a personal statement the Führer selected the offensive's code name from an old German nationalistic song: *Wacht am Rhein* ("Watch on the Rhine"). The operational plan was straightforward: The main attack would be lead by the newly raised *Sixth Panzer Armee* (five infantry and four SS panzer divisions) advancing from Monschau to Losheim following a massive artillery bombardment. The heavily armored wedge would then cut to the northwest, crossing the Meuse on both sides of Liège and then advance on Antwerp. To the south, the *Fifth Panzer Armee* (three panzer, one panzer grenadier and four infantry divisions) would thrust along the left flank of the *Sixth Panzer Armee* providing flank protection, ultimately joining

in the assault on Antwerp. From Echternach to Gemünd along the Our and Sauer Rivers, the *Seventh Armee* (consisting of a panzer grenadier and six infantry divisions) would advance to the west to the Meuse River dropping off troops to form a cordon of defense from Altrier to Givet.

Subsidiary operations were also included. To the north of the *Sixth Panzer Armee* several divisions of the *Fifteenth Armee* would attack to protect the main effort's rear once the German armor was nearing the Meuse River. This supporting attack was codenamed *Operation Spätlese* ("Late Harvest"). As the panzer divisions closed in on Antwerp, Hitler proposed that General Kurt Student's *Heeresgruppe H* attack southwest towards the port from the area of Venlo in Holland. This, Hitler opined, would help to seal his great victory.

Not only would such an offensive capture the most important port in Western Europe, but it would cut off an estimated thirty American, British and Canadian divisions

Gnfldm. Walter Model. In charge of Heeresgruppe B, *in the West, Model would be the overall commander for Hitler's* Wacht Am Rhein *offensive.*

from any sources of supply. With the annihilation of much of the British forces and the U.S. First Army, Hitler declared that it would be "a new Dunkirk!" With the tide turned in the West, Hitler believed that such a discouraging result might take the Americans out of the war and the prompt the British to sue for a separate peace. That accomplished, Hitler then could turn his full attention to the destruction of Soviet Russia and the *Untermenschen.*

The idea of such a far ranging offensive was met with little enthusiasm by Hitler's generals. Indeed, so secretive was the plan that the German war lord did not even bother to inform his key army field marshals until October 22nd, four weeks subsequent to the initial planning. After several years of reversals along all fronts, most of Hitler's more level-headed generals had become understandably skeptical of Germany's chances of winning the war. Noble old Generalfeldmarschall Gerd von Rundstedt, in charge of German forces in the West (*Oberbefehlshaber West*), was particularly dubious, although admitting that in concept *Wacht am Rhein* was a stroke of genius:

> Absolutely all conditions necessary for success were lacking.... When I received the plan in early November I was staggered. It was obvious to me that the available forces were far too small for such an extremely ambitious plan. Model took the same view as I did. In fact, no soldier believed that the aim of reaching Antwerp was really practicable. But I knew by now it was useless to protest to Hitler about the possibility of anything.

Although an ardent Nazi, Genfldm. Walther Model, in charge of *Heeresgruppe B*, was similarly unimpressed. When briefed on the nuances of *Wacht am Rhein* by his chief of staff, the monocled field marshal was unable to hide his displeasure. "The plan doesn't have a damned leg to stand on!"

Fervent in their misgivings, von Rundstedt and Model began separately working on more realistic alternatives to the Hitlerian scheme according to the time-honored tradition of the German general staff. Von Rundstedt and *OB West* synthesized *Plan Martin*, a double envelopment attack of thirty divisions. A large diversionary attack would be mounted by the *Fifteenth Armee* to pin down U.S. forces while three panzer corps swept through the Ardennes on a narrow front. The jaws of the two pincers would come together in the vicinity of Liège, thereby effectively engulfing the First U.S. Army in the Aachen area to the north of the Ardennes.

Similar to von Rundstedt, Model and his *Heeresgruppe B* staff tailored their proposal to fit what they thought were the limited capabilities of the German army in the fall of 1944. *Herbstnebel* ("Autumn Fog") called for a single powerful armored wedge to drive over a forty-mile front between the Hürtgen Forest south of Aachen and the road center of St. Vith in the Ardennes. The effort would be carried by the *Fifth* and *Sixth Panzer Armies.* The *Seventh Armee,* made up of infantry formations, would not advance immediately, but would follow in the wake of the panzers to peel off and provide flank protection. Like von Rundstedt's plan, the fundamental objective was to encircle and destroy the troublesome U.S. First Army.

These plans, that the generals took to calling the "Small Solution," were submitted to Hitler on October 27th. He summarily rejected both proposals as "incapable of producing decisive results." The German leader knew that he needed a great victory to reverse the tide of the war at this point — even if it seemed beyond the abilities of the German army. But Jodl confided to Hitler that he should either adopt the Small Solution or else be willing to strip troops and replacements from other fronts and surrender ground in the East to accumulate the number of divisions necessary for some chance of success for the "Big Solution." That, the stubborn Führer was unwilling to do. The attack to Antwerp would be accomplished with the thirty-eight promised divisions.

Hitler's faith in potential success of *Wacht am Rhein* was partly based on his misguided faith in juggled equipment production and manpower numbers that his placating staff provided. But even more importantly, Hitler was convinced of his divine destiny in Germany's future. The Führer hastened to liken himself to Frederick the Great whose huge portrait hung in his study. Had not that great leader dispatched his enemies in the Seven Years' War by a great blow that split the coalition against him? As Hitler the mystic saw it, the Ardennes would be his Rossbach and Leuthen. "Our enemies are the greatest opposites which exist on earth," he told his generals. "Ultra-capitalist states on one side; ultra-Marxist states on the other; on one side a dying empire and on the other side a colony, the United States, waiting to claim its inheritance." A winter battle in this dark forest would be his chance to "deal a heavy blow and bring down this artifical coaltion with a mighty thunderclap."

The German leader was also mindful of how close Ludendorff had come to victory in his offensive towards Amiens in March 1918. This near turning point had come at a time in World War I when the conflict seemed totally lost for the Kaiser; the effect on flagging German morale had been extraordinary. In *Mein Kampf* Hitler wrote:

> It was my luck to be in the first two and last offensives [of 1918]. They made on me the most tremendous impressions of my whole life; tremendous because for the last time the struggle lost its defensive character and became an offensive as it was in 1914. In the German army's trenches men breathed anew when, after three years of hell, the day for squaring the account had at last arrived.

Hitler drew parallels in his predicament in late 1944. "...We are now carrying on the war from a situation which gives us every possibility of holding out and sticking it through, particularly if we can eliminate the danger here in the West." But those around Hitler were not entirely swayed by the Führer's self-delusory historical ramblings. Jodl nervously jotted in his diary: "given our desperate situation, we must not shrink from staking everything on one card."

Meanwhile, Model and von Rundstedt combined their plans and political clout, the final alternative closely resembling the *OB West* proposal. To help curry Hitler's favor, the field marshals enlisted the help of the generals that would lead the armies of the last offensive. However, even SS-Oberstgruppenführer Josef "Sepp" Dietrich, who was to lead the *Sixth Panzer Armee*, and Gen. d. Pztrp. Hasso von Manteuffel, the little Prussian general who was to command the *Fifth Panzer Armee*, could not change the Führer's mind. On November 26th, Hitler issued a final edict: "There will be absolutely no change in the present intentions."

On December 2nd, the generals made one final effort to convince Hitler of the futility of the plan. Conspicuous in his absence was von Rundstedt who was so disenchanted with the entire matter that as a slap to Hitler he sent only his

chief of staff, Gen. Siegfried Westphal. But the generals' efforts were in vain. *Wacht Am Rhein* was to be carried out to the letter. The Führer's generals received their orders stoically. "If it succeeds," Model confided to his chief of staff, "it will be a miracle."[10]

10 Already on November 27th Model had sounded a prophetic warning concerning the deficiency in military resources to carry out *Wacht Am Rhein*: "Should the attack be stopped at the Meuse due to lack of reserves, the only result will be a bulge in the line and not the destruction of sizeable military forces.... The widely stretched flanks, especially in the south, will only invite enemy counteractions."

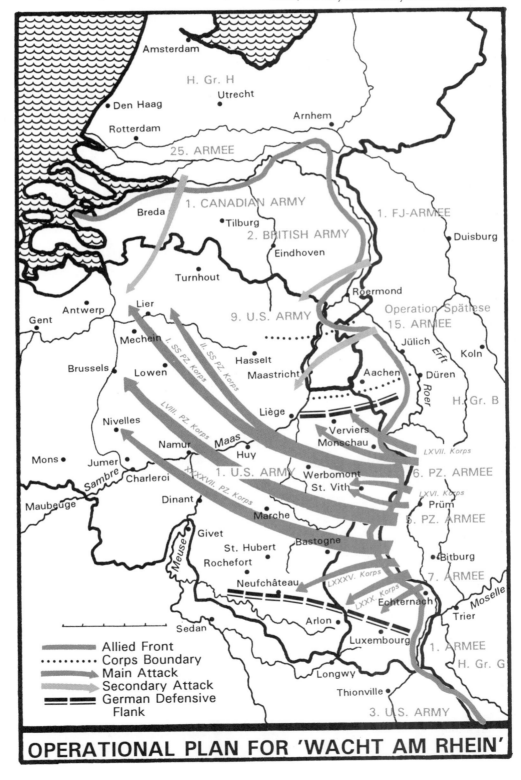

OPERATIONAL PLAN FOR 'WACHT AM RHEIN'

Grenadiers. German soldiers move forward to the front on December 16th.

The Final Days

Despite Hitler's resolve, the preparations for the offensive remained a particularly touchy matter. Although reduced in effectiveness by supply shortages, the Allies were by no means idle during the fall of 1944. In fact, German reserves slated for *Wacht am Rhein* were repeatedly embattled and burned out to prevent the German line from giving way. The battles of Arnhem, Aachen, Hürtgen Forest and Patton's offensive in the Lorraine were consuming German battalions at a rate faster than they could be replaced. Allied intelligence estimated 3,000 enemy casualties per day. Only Dietrich's favored SS divisions and the army's *2nd Panzer Division* were able to escape premature commitment during the battles raging in October and November.

The overall plan for the offensive was distilled from the outlines for the Ardennes break-through of 1940 and Ludendorff's offensive of 1918. Like those two previous German offensives in the West, several unique factors were important to the success of *Wacht am Rhein*. Of these, the most important was strategic surprise. Accordingly, security measures for *Wacht am Rhein* were ruthless. If word of the offensive leaked out, the offenders would be shot! Cover plans were also instituted and the number of individuals privy to the plan were kept to an absolute minimum. A bogus *Twenty-Fifth Armee* was even conjured up near Cologne to give the impression that von Rundstedt feared an Allied breakthrough between Bonn and Cologne and was assembling forces in the north for a defensive mission. The concentration of the *Sixth Panzer Armee* and the *Twenty-Fifth* near Cologne was to mask the last minute switch of Hitler's counterattack reserve to the Eifel.

Another consideration was weather. Although the May date of the 1940 offensive had been based on a forecast for good flying weather, the loss of air superiority over European skies had turned the tables. No longer trusting Göring's pledge of massive Luftwaffe support, Hitler knew that the Allied air forces could easily wreck his mechanized forces.[11] He also knew that overcast skies would be essential for the secret assembly of his panzer forces in the Eifel. The weather in the Ardennes region in late fall is dreary; typically rain or overcast with mists that do not lift before noon. Consequently, Hitler scheduled the attack date for the last days of November with the proviso that the offensive not begin without a six day forecast of bad weather. The mists of the Eifel would provide the cover the Luftwaffe could not.

On November 10th Hitler set the attack date, or *O-Tag*, for November 27th. However, as that date approached, Allied attacks in the Roer and Metz sectors had caused problems with the refurbishment of the panzer units for the attack. *OKW*'s 38 divisions for the attack was steadily whittled away to only 30, most of which had to be moved by rail. Accumulation of vital petrol and ammunition stocks was especially tardy.

There were other deficiencies too. "*Seventh Armee* is still short two bridging columns," worried General Jodl on December 12th. "We must provide an engineer battalion from the East and above all rubber boats." Such a string of delays saw the attack date slip to December 10th, then to the 12th, the 15th and finally to December 16th. A last minute request by von Rundstedt on the night before the offensive to await movement of tardy petrol supplies for one more day was denied.

Over the weeks, the secret strategic concentration proceeded. On December 8th *OKW* reported on the critical fuel inventory and the "Führer Reserve" of artillery shells: "7,150 cubic meters of fuel available, a further 6,000 on the way with 2,400 from the East. The remainder must come from production and must be moved up urgently....As for ammunition, out of 64 trains, some 55 have arrived."[12] By the eve of the offensive, Gen. Model's Chief of Staff was able to report that 10,887 cubic meters of fuel had been stockpiled for the attack force. To protect these vital stores from Allied air attack, most of the material was delivered to camouflaged supply dumps east of the Rhine. Although prudent, this decision was to have far reaching logistical implications for *Wacht Am Rhein*. So short were the fuel reserves immediately available to *ISS Panzerkorps* that on the night before the attack, most of the petrol allocation of the two reserve divisions of the *IISS Panzerkorps* were tranferred to the *1st* and *12th SS*. Even this extreme measure produced only 700 liters of fuel for each of the petrol-thirsty German tanks.

Over the first two weeks of December some 1,500 trains bearing troops, tanks and guns unloaded secretly in the marshalling yards east of the Ardennes at Gerolstein, Prüm and Trier. In the final three nights before the great attack some

---

11 Göring had assembled 2,360 aircraft under *Jagdkorps II,* mostly single engined fighters. He promised to use these to directly support the ground offensive while keeping Allied aircraft away from the battle zone. A major feature of the Luftwaffe plan was *Operation Bodenplatte.* This surprise raid was to strike Allied air fields on a fair weather morning to destroy Allied aircraft before they got off the ground.

12 As early as October 28th von Rundstedt had instigated rigorous conservation measures in the German army on the Western Front. According to his orders, units and individuals (including general officers) were prohibited from using motor transport if rails were available and horse drawn vehicles were to be used for everyday supply and administrative tasks. Diesel power vehicles were to be used whenever possible and 50% of passenger cars were to be taken out of circulation.

Mk V Panther of the 1st SS Panzer Division *pauses to take on supply.*

250,000 men, 717 tanks and assault guns and 2,623 pieces of heavy artillery moved stealthily into position less than four miles from the unsuspecting Americans opposite them.[13] Artillery pieces were laboriously hauled up to the front with the aid of horses. The movement of the less easily concealed panzers was rigidly staged over several nights to tread over roads covered with straw to deaden the sound while German planes buzzed over the Eifel to hide the noise.

Camouflage officers roamed the line, alert for soldiers not observing established procedures. For all the damp cold of mid-December in the Eifel, the German infantry were only allowed smoke-less charcoal fires. With all the secrecy, most of the German soldiers in the region were wary. "Everyone is on alert," a volksgrenadier penned in his diary. "Something big is in the making."

Since November 20th Hitler had planned *Wacht Am Rhein* from Berlin, but on December 10th, his personal train, the *Führersonderzug Brandenburg*, arrived in the Frankfurt area. That day he installed himself in his headquarters in the west, the *Adlerhorst* or Eagle's Nest. Near Bad Nauheim, it was from there that he intended to direct his last great offensive. Both von Rundstedt's and Model's headquarters were nearby and on December 11th and 12th, they and all the German divisional commanders were secretly bussed to *Adlerhorst's* collection of dreary concrete bunkers deep in the wooded Taunus hills. Security precau-

tions reflected the psychotic paranoia which now gripped Hitler's empire. Gen. Lt. Fritz Bayerlein, commander of the *Panzer Lehr Division*, recalled that, "We were all stripped of our weapons and briefcases and led between a double row of SS troops into a deep bunker." Then over the next two hours the Führer, looking sick and haggard, lectured them on the gravity of the occasion. Behind each man at the table stood armed SS guards who looked on so menacingly that Bayerlein was afraid to reach for his handkerchief. As always, Hitler implored them to great effort.

> If this offensive succeeds I will take a modest back seat and leave the laurels of victory to the generals. If it fails it will be my responsibility alone...For several months now the war industries have been working for nothing else other than this operation and the Eastern Front has gone short. But it will not be possible to concentrate so much equipment a second time. If we fail we face dark days...This battle will determine whether we live or die. I want all my soldiers to fight hard and without pity. The battle must be fought with brutality and all resistance must be broken by a wave of terror. The enemy must be broken — now or never! Thus lives our Germany!

Von Rundstedt, listening motionless for nearly two hours was painfully aware of Hitler's mistrust of his generals. In spite of von Rundstedt's coolness towards the Nazi cause, he and his generals were bound by the *Fahneneid*, the ancient oath of the Teutonic Knights. According to this solemn vow, they were obligated to loyally serve their leader to the death. At the end of Hitler's speech, the wrinkled old soldier finally spoke up to reassure his Führer. "We are staking

---

13 Combat ready armored strength of the entire *Heeresgruppe B* on December 15th was reported at 1,427 vehicles with 270 in short term repair.

Oberst Ludwig Heilmann, in charge of the 5th Fallschirmjäger Division, *briefs the men of his division.*

our last card," he told the audience. "We cannot fail."

Then, on the very eve of the offensive, Hitler gave his last instructions to Genfldm. Model of *Heeresgruppe B*: "The prerequisites for the success of the operation are all available. The size and extent to that success now depends on the leadership during the operation." The Führer then went on to warn Model not to allow Dietrich to become involved at Liège or to wheel north too early. The Small Solution, Hitler made clear, was still *verboten*. "If these principles are adhered to," the German leader concluded, "a very great victory is assured."[14]

Advancing to the front, the German soldiers plodded about through the mud and snow in obeyance to their orders, unaware of the intent of the strange maneuvers. Regimental commanders were informed of the *Wacht am Rhein* offensive only some three days before the attack; battalion leaders 48 hours before its launch; and the company commanders only the evening before. The average lowly Ger-

man rifleman was aware just before the great offensive was to begin, although already alerted by the large quantities of weapons and equipment nearby. Hitler's enthusiasm, although irrational, was infectious to many of the Germans learning of the plan, engendering some optimism even in some of the more hardened higher echelon commanders. To add to the emotion, there was even an enthusiastic evocation from old von Rundstedt himself:

Soldiers of the Western Front! Your great hour has arrived. Large attacking armies have started against the Anglo-Americans. I do not have to tell you more than that. You feel it yourself. WE GAMBLE EVERYTHING! You carry ... the holy obligation to give everything to achieve things beyond human possibilities for our Fatherland and our Führer!"

On hearing the stirring orders of the day, the morale and hope of many inexperienced German soldiers in the Eifel soared. Although these fighting men were of no comparison to Hitler's legions that had marched through the Ardennes in 1940, the drama gripped many of the German soldiers just the same. "There is a general feeling of elation," wrote one officer. "Everyone is cheerful."

14 Although Genfldm. Model hastened to assure Hitler of his obedience to the orders for *Wacht am Rhein*, he took the opportunity to point out that "a timely and sufficient delivery of fuel is decisive for the successful outcome of the operation." He closed with the observation that "at this time in spite of all efforts, supply is still insufficient."

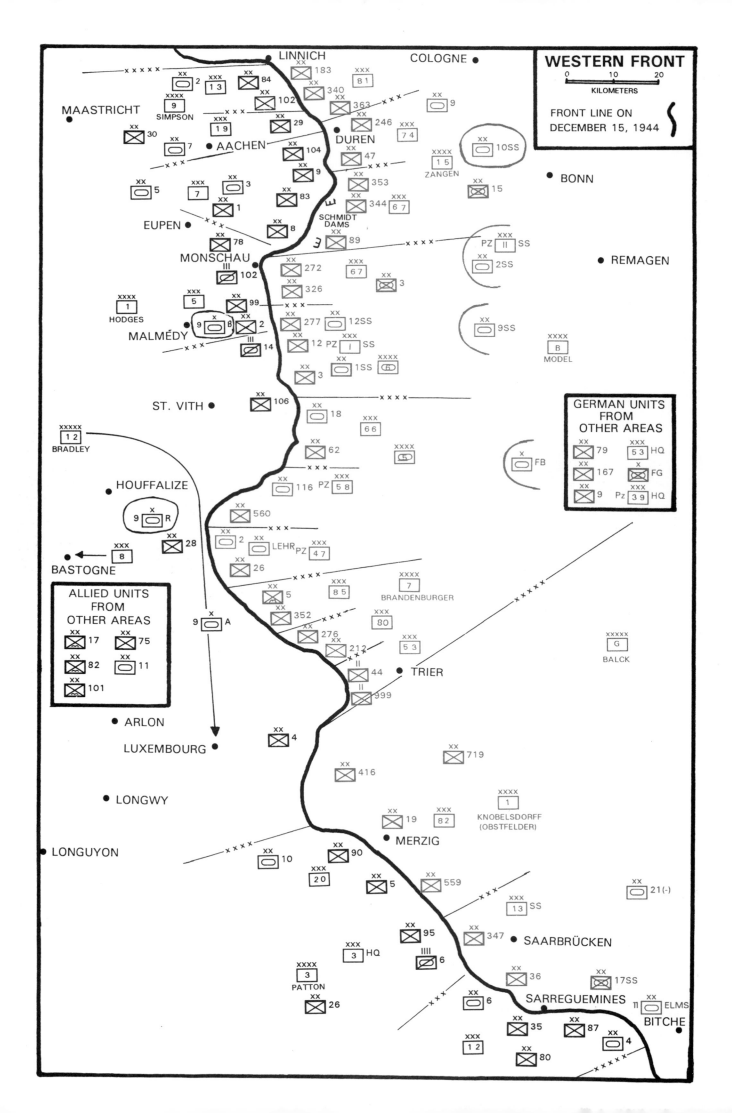

WESTERN FRONT

0   10   20
KILOMETERS

FRONT LINE ON
DECEMBER 15, 1944

LINNICH
COLOGNE

xx 2   xxx 13   xx 84   xx 183   xxx 81

xxxx 9 SIMPSON   xx 102   xx 340   xx 9

MAASTRICHT

xxx 19   xx 29   xx 363

xx 30   xx 7   ● AACHEN   xx 104   xx 246   xxx 74

DUREN   xx 47   xxxx 15 ZANGEN   xx 10SS ● BONN

xx 5   xxx 7   xx 3   xx 9   xx 353   xx 15

xx 1   xx 83   xx 344   xxx 67

EUPEN ●   xx 8   SCHMIDT DAMS

xx 78   xx 89   PZ xxx 11 SS

MONSCHAU   III 102   xx 272   xxx 67   xx 3   xx 2SS   ● REMAGEN

xxxx 1 HODGES   xxx 5   xx 99   xx 326

xx 9 x 8   xx 2   xx 277   xx 12SS   xx 9SS

MALMÉDY   III 14   12 PZ xxx 1 SS   xxxx B MODEL

xx 3   xx 1SS

ST. VITH ●   xx 106   xx 18   **GERMAN UNITS FROM OTHER AREAS**

xxxxx 12 BRADLEY   xxx 66   xx 79   xxx 53 HQ

xx 62   xxxx   xx 167   x FG

HOUFFALIZE ●   x FB   xx 9 Pz   xxx 39 HQ

9 x R   xx 116 PZ xxx 58

xx 560

xx 28   xx 2   xx LEHR PZ xxx 47

xxx 8   → BASTOGNE   xx 26   xxx 85   xxxx 7 BRANDENBURGER

ALLIED UNITS FROM OTHER AREAS   xx 5   xxx 80

xx 17   xx 75   xx 352   xxx 53

xx 82   xx 11   9 x A   xx 276   xx 212   xxxxx G BALCK

xx 101   II 44 ● TRIER

II 999

● ARLON   xx 4

LUXEMBOURG ●   xx 719

xx 416

● LONGWY   xxxx 1 KNOBELSDORFF (OBSTFELDER)

xx 19   xxx 82

● LONGUYON   xxxx MERZIG ●

xx 10   xx 90

xxx 20   xx 5   xx 559   xx 21(-)

xxx 13 SS

xx 95   xx 347 ● SAARBRÜCKEN

xxx 3 HQ   IIII 6

xxxx 3 PATTON   xx 36   xx 17SS

xx 26   xx 6   SARREGUEMINES   II xx ELMS

xx 35   xx 87   BITCHE

xxx 12   xx 80   xx 4

American GIs enjoy hot chow at a field kitchen at the front.

German Mk V "Panther" tanks, destined for the 9th SS Panzer Division, arrive by rail.

The Big Three. From left to right: Montgomery, Eisenhower and Bradley, the most senior Allied commanders on the Western Front in fall 1944.

The Allies

As 1944 came to a close, General Dwight D. Eisenhower, the Supreme Commander of both the American and British armies in Europe, found his Allied forces seven months ahead of his pre-invasion schedule.[15] At the end of the summer campaign, with the breathless Allied liberation of France, there had been hope of ending the war before 1945. Unfortunately, this hope was dashed by the logistical difficulty of supplying massive military forces over a make-shift supply line. As a consequence the Allied advance sputtered to a halt in September of 1944.[16]

In late summer Field Marshal Sir Bernard L. Montgomery, in charge of the British 21st Army Group, repeatedly implored Eisenhower to consider an alternative strategy to his "broad front" approach to the invasion of Germany. Montgomery advocated an attempt to quickly win the war based on a single powerful thrust into the heart of Germany in the north from Holland. Naturally, his British forces would lead this push.

Eisenhower gave the insistent Montgomery a chance to demonstrate his strategy in September. The British Field Marshal's plan, Operation Market Garden, was based on use of airborne troops to rapidly gain a bridge across the Lower Rhine at Arnhem that would be used by armored forces to push rapidly into the heart of Germany. The operation jumped off on September 17th. The two U.S. parachute divisions (the U.S. 82nd and 101st Airborne) landed in good shape. Unknown to the Allied planners, however, the drop zone of the British 1st Airborne was nearby the reforming *IISS Panzerkorps (9th SS and 10th SS Panzer Divisions)*. Ten days of savage fighting ensued in which the Rhine bridge could not be captured and the British 1st Airborne was nearly destroyed. Eisenhower, who advocated a broad front advance all along, was now convinced of the wisdom of this approach. The setback at Arnhem provided "ample evidence that much bitter campaigning was to come." Late September found Eisenhower's forces roughly on the German border with three army groups. Montgomery's 21st Army Group to the north, composed mainly of British and Canadian forces, was now under orders to clear the captured port of Antwerp which was urgently needed to relieve the supply situation. In the center was the heavy hitter — Gen.

Omar N. Bradley's 12th Army Group which included the U.S. First and Third Armies. Recently joined up from the south of France was the 6th Army Group under Lt. Gen. Jacob L. Devers extending all the way to the Swiss border at Basel. Although the Allied armies seemed in a good position to push into Germany, a number of factors conspired to slow any future plans of a major advance.

The cost of the battle in Normandy and the pursuit across France had been substantial. Allied losses totalled over 160,000 casualties, 500 tanks and 100 artillery pieces. Meantime, supplies were being used at a rate that was difficult to maintain. The American system of war required twelve communications zone personnel and thirty pounds of supply every day to support each front line fighting man. In September, the Allies were using 20,000 tons of provisions, six million gallons of gasoline and 2,000 tons of artillery ammunition every 24 hours. All this had to be trucked over a 300-mile distance from Cherbourg and the Normandy invasion beaches all the way to the front. By fall the Allies were running on empty. Until the more proximate port of Antwerp was available, there was not the logistical capability of maintaining an advance all along the front. Some areas would have to remain static if the Allies were to advance in the important sectors. Also, with only 38 Allied divisions facing a like number of German divisions, Eisenhower knew he would have to concentrate his forces in order to hope to achieve local military superiority.[17]

Then came the terrible autumn battles of Aachen, the Hürtgen Forest and the Lorraine. The German strength in the West steadily increased as the Allies sought more forces to throw into these attritional battles, so horrifyingly reminiscent of 1917 in World War I. The Allies suffered appalling losses in this static warfare on the German border. Between September and the first half of December 1944, the U.S. Ninth, First and Third Armies counted 134,182 casualties in the inconclusive fighting; non-battle losses from fatigue, exposure and disease nearly doubled this figure. Replacements arriving in Europe over the period made up for only half this loss. As a consequence, manpower became the overriding concern for Eisenhower and his military planners. The average effective strength of U.S. divisions in

---

15 On June 17th, after ten days of intense fighting in Normandy, SHAEF estimated that the Belgian frontier would not be reached before December 23rd and the German border north of Aachen before May 2nd, 1945. It was anticipated that the final battle would then be very rapid with the German surrender coming sometime around June 1st, 1945.

16 On September 11th, 1944 men of the U.S. 5th Armored Division, wading across the Our River near Wallendorf, Luxembourg, became the first U.S. troops to set foot on German soil.

17 These figures are for September 1st. However, the relative parity of force indicated was one that only existed on paper or in Hitler's mind. As of that date the Allies had brought 38 divisions and support troops onto the continent with roughly 2 million men. Against this force *OB West* could only muster 700,000 men in 41 divisions — a telling indicator of relative strength in the German army.

Conference. Maj. Gen. Troy Middleton (left), Lt. Gen Bradley (center) and Eisenhower meet to discuss coming plans in Wiltz, Belgium, November, 1944.

Europe in November dipped to only 78%. Pondering the problem, Eisenhower, in early December, warned his superiors in Washington that "our replacement situation is exceedingly dark."[18]

Strapped for soldiers with which to carry out his strategy, the supreme commander sought out less critical sectors where the enemy was weak so that he might gather forces for the really crucial sectors. In such less important places an Allied superiority of force could be maintained with a relatively thin line because the German forces opposing them were still weaker. This was what Gen. Bradley called the "calculated risk."

The Ardennes in Belgium and Luxembourg seemed the perfect location for such a venture. The German defense in this sector was thin. As Bradley and Eisenhower saw it, surely no German attack would come there. The terrain was totally unsuited for the employment of armor, particularly in winter. Besides, the Germans, they believed, simply lacked the resources with which to stage more than a local attack. So while Montgomery pushed for the industrial Ruhr in the north and Patton charged into the German's coal region in the Saar, the Ardennes was but lightly defended. GIs stationed in the Ardennes forests along the German border were thankful for its relatively quiet nature. The American soldiers there took to calling it the "ghost front."[19]

18 As of December 15th the shortage of riflemen, Military Occupation Specialty 745, was 17% in the U.S. First Army, 31% in Patton's Third and 25% in Simpson's Ninth Army.

19 Eisenhower's forces in the Ardennes were not intended solely for defense, however. In the upcoming battle for the Rhineland the supreme commander planned on using the divisions in the Ardennes to participate in the advance on the Rhine crossings to provide assistance on the flanks either of the First or Third Armies.

The Men at the Top

Napoleon once remarked that an army of rabbits led by a lion is far superior to an army of lions led by a rabbit. Throughout the war, German generalship was frequently more lion like than the Allied command. However, by late 1944, the American army in particular was becoming more aggressive. Meanwhile, German generalship was now tainted by the political SS institution while the troops to be commanded continued to decline in quality. Each army cultivated differing types of leaders that had much to do with their capabilities in command.

American leaders tended to have graduated from the approved academies and education was afforded a large weight in their advancement. Previous performance in combat was important, although many of the American leaders had never participated in war. American leadership, true to its democratic ideals, was often achieved by consensus. Frequently, leaders would consult those below them to develop agreement on aim and plan. American commanders, like the GI troops, were expected to have a human side other than just soldiering; any U.S. leader had to be a regular guy. This meant the ability to get the job done when need be, but then to "knock off" at the appropriate times, play poker and down a drink. Anything less was suspect.

The British did not lead by consensus. British officers were usually professionals and disagreement with orders from above was not generally tolerated. Qualification as a British leader was strongly based on social class and relationships between officers and the fighting men were taciturn and traditional. The British had a reputation for caution in battle. Part of this was the result of the British manpower situation which could not afford many casualties without a proportionate drop in combat effectives. In fall of 1944 British infantry replacements were simply not to be had.

The German system of command was rather simple. Advancement was based almost solely on performance. Although there was a large professional class of Prussian officers, anyone regardless of social standing or education that could win battles would be qualified to lead in combat. The German concept of leadership placed command in the hands of those who had the will and past performance to promise success. This system generally worked best since winning was all that was really important. The problems that showed within the system were usually associated with the Waffen SS, who by 1944, were being appointed based on their political, rather than military abilities.

General to the Army, Dwight D. Eisenhower
Supreme Headquarters Allied Expeditionary Forces (SHAEF)

After having commanded the Allied victories in Tunisia, Sicily and Italy, General Eisenhower was named the Supreme Commander, Allied Expeditionary Forces in 1943. Eisenhower was something of a late bloomer. He graduated 61st in the Westpoint Class of 1915. However, the Kansas native had assignments placing him with such inspirational generals as John J. Pershing and Douglas MacArthur. In 1924 he graduated in first place from the Army's senior tactical school, the Command and General Staff School at Ft. Leavenworth.

Many of his contemporaries considered Eisenhower to be more a political general than a field commander. Montgomery was convinced that Eisenhower was a mediocre leader, incessantly expressing criticism of the Supreme Commander's policy of a broad front advance. However, performance in the Bulge appeared to turn the tables on the assessment; if any great generalship was exhibited in the Ardennes, it must be ascribed to Eisenhower.

Many have criticized Eisenhower in the intervening years since the war for his decision on December 20th to place Montgomery in charge of the First Army in the Ardennes. However, examined in a factual light, this decision was a simple matter of expedience. Bradley, disadvantageously located in Luxembourg, was cut-off physically from the fighting in the north. A commander was necessary to coordinate the fight there and Montgomery was the logical choice. This decision had another important advantage: with Monty in charge of the north, the British XXX Corps were much more likely to take a hand in the fight at a time when the American troops in the Ardennes had been severely battered.

Others have criticized Eisenhower for his allowing the Ardennes to be defended lightly and of not having a strategic reserve with which to respond to the German offensive. During the fall Eisenhower had warned Bradley of the danger of a "nasty little Kasserine" in the Ardennes; if any fault can be leveled, it is that the Supreme Commander allowed Bradley to discount the threat between Monschau and Echternach. As for the lack of a strategic reserve, this mistake must ultimately rest with other critique of the broad-front advance. Eisenhower was a consensus leader. In the fall he worked with a number of difficult commanders, all waging an offensive on their front with an ever present need for more troops. SHAEF did not have a formal strategic reserve because in the super-confident days of early fall, all sectors of the Western front seemed safe from a German counteroffensive.

In December of 1944, Eisenhower had allowed himself to relax a bit more and enjoy life. Although there can be no doubt that the German offensive caught him by surprise, Ike displayed amazing aplomb in his handling of the attack. With the benefit of ULTRA, he immediately recognized the magnitude of the German offensive and in spite of protestations from his subordinates, he responded quickly to the situation in the Ardennes. Eisenhower did not hesitate to make sweeping changes to Allied plans, he immediately halted all offensives both to the north and south of the battle zone and rapidly shifted reserves into the threatened sector. His timely response in reinforcing the Ardennes was almost directly responsible for the ability of the Americans to hold St. Vith, Bastogne and the Elsenborn ridge.

The German dossier on Eisenhower said of him:

> ...He is noted for his great energy and his hatred of office work. He leaves the initiative to his subordinates, whom he manages to inspire to supreme efforts through kind understanding and easy discipline. His strongest point is said to be an ability to adjust personalities to one another and smooth over opposite viewpoints.

Generalfeldmarschall Karl Rudolf Gerd von Rundstedt
Oberbefehlshaber West

Scion of an old military Prussian family, von Rundstedt was to be the 68 year-old Commander in Chief in the West during the Ardennes Offensive. Von Rundstedt began a early military career, enlisting in the infantry in 1907 at age 17; by 1914 he was with the General Staff where he made a favorable impression during the Great War.

A general officer since the 1920s, von Rundstedt was called back to service after retirement between wars in 1938. His relationship with Hitler was stormy from the very time that the German leader took power. The old field marshal made no attempt to hide his disrespect for Hitler and National Socialism. Behind his back, von Rundstedt called Hitler "that Bohemian corporal," a scarcastic reference to the highest rank that the Führer achieved in the Great War. Yet von Rundstedt was an institution in the German Army and Hitler needed one of the Old Guard to imbue his soldiers with military confidence.

Hitler promoted him to field marshal in 1940, the same year that he commanded *Heeresgruppe A* in the victorious campaign in the West. Von Rundstedt and his chief of staff, Erich von Manstein, had convinced Hitler to make the major military effort through the Ardennes rather than Holland.

This caught the French by surprise and resulted in the crushing defeat of France and Great Britain in less than six weeks. But in late 1941, while commanding *Heeresgruppe Süd* in the Russian Campaign, the field marshal was dismissed for ordering his forces to retreat from Rostov during a major Soviet offensive.

A year later, Hitler recalled him again to command *OB West* to defend against the Allied invasion. However, von Rundstedt managed to get himself relieved of this command when during the Allied breakout at Normandy, he told Hitler and *OKW* to "Make peace you fools!"

Scarcely two months later, he was recalled for a third and final time to assist with holding the line in the west and to prepare for the Ardennes Offensive. Von Rundstedt made little effort to hide his displeasure over the Ardennes plan and chose to totally disassociate himself from it after it became clear that Hitler would not accept a more rational course of action. "It was a nonsensical operation," he scowled, "and the most stupid part of it was the setting of Antwerp as the target. If we had reached the Meuse we should have got down on our knees and thanked God —let alone tried to reach Antwerp."

More a figurehead than a commander during the battle, von Rundstedt sarcastically remarked that during the Ardennes Offensive, the only soldiers he commanded were the two guards outside his Ziegenberg headquarters. "They refused my advice," he said of Hitler and *OKW*, "so I let it become their offensive, their responsibility." For a time, the Battle of the Bulge was known to Europeans as the Rundstedt Offensive, because he had commanded the German forces in the West. This misnomer was one which the field marshal found especially repulsive:

> My entire staff training revolted against an operation of this sort. If old von Moltke thought I had planned this offensive he would turn in his grave.... Our forces were far too weak for such immense objectives.... With our Luftwaffe knocked out we could only move at night, whereas Patton could wind up his tanks and move day or night right

into our positions. Our manpower was shot too. All we had was rundown old men who could not fight and foreigners who kept deserting. And Hitler kept hollering, "Hold your ground!" as he did at Bastogne. It was absolute madness! And that was the man who wanted to be considered a great field general! He did not know the first thing about strategy!

On a personal level, von Rundstedt was quite capable, given his advanced age. He was the quintessential non-political general but was also fiercely loyal and patriotic. Von Rundstedt was a francophile, "extravagantly polite to women" and smoked too much. To those he disdained (and there were many) he was haughty, reserved and curt.

Field Marshal Sir Bernard Law Montgomery
21st Army Group

Without a doubt, Field Marshal Montgomery was one of the most controversial figures in the Ardennes Campaign. A graduate of the Royal Military Academy at Sandhurst, Montgomery served in France in World War I as a brigade major in the 35th British Division which provided him with his first wartime experience.

In 1935, his wife died, leaving him to care for their nine-year-old son. Montgomery never re-married, preferring instead to devote his energies to his army career. Montgomery was an ascetic; he did not drink or smoke, ate sparingly and did not seek the company of women. He was totally devoted to his work.

During the beginning of World War II, Montgomery commanded the 3rd Division, fighting at Dunkirk with the British Expeditionary Forces. Soon thereafter, he was given command of the British II Corps. Montgomery's later command of the Eighth Army in North Africa and his subsequent defeat of Rommel at El Alamein made his name a household word. Montgomery commanded the 21st Army Group when the Allies came upon the beaches at Normandy. In the fall of 1944, Montgomery proposed that he make the major single narrow thrust to reach Berlin before Christmas. His Arnhem parachute operation to capture a bridge across the Rhine River resulted in disaster in September.

Montgomery, like Patton, his American rival, was a glory hound. Historians have characterized him as arrogant, egotistical and abrasive. He also was also quite cautious in a tactical and operational sense, preferring meticulously planned set-piece battles where victory was not in doubt. During the Ardennes he offended many in the U.S. Army with his patronizing manner and caustic statements. On January 7th he enraged U.S. observers by relating the predominantly American fight in the Ardennes as "one of the most interesting and tricky battles I have handled." His needling of Eisenhower to be appointed as the overall ground commander at the end of the year resulted in unprecedented chaos in Allied command. This "difference of opinion" brought Bradley close to resignation and nearly cost Montgomery his job.

His German foes did not believe Montgomery to be exceptional. According to von Rundstedt's staff, "Montgomery was always extremely cautious and unwilling to take risks.... [He] was very systematic, which is all right if you have sufficient resources and sufficient time."

Lt. General Omar N. Bradley
12th Army Group

Bradley was known as the "infantry man's general." Hailing from modest means in Missouri, Bradley was an effective, if not pretentious commander. An exceptional graduate of the West Point Class of 1915, Bradley had been marked for a larger command early on. He missed combat experience in World War I although he served as the commandant of the Infantry School in Ft. Benning. He later commanded the 82nd and 28th Infantry Divisions. General Eisenhower sent Bradley to Tunisia to observe for him and he was soon made deputy commander of the II Corps under General George S. Patton, Jr.

Bradley lead a very successful campaign in Sicily which later earned him the title of Senior U.S. Ground Commander for the Normandy invasion — even overseeing his former boss, General Patton. In France, he was given command of the U.S. 12th Army Group, and made his headquarters in Luxembourg City in the fall of 1944. Patton thought well of his former student, even if he was not overly laudatory. "Bradley is okay," he wrote in his diary, "but he is not dashing."

The Ardennes would represent a time of immense strain for Bradley. It was Bradley, after all, who had convinced Eisenhower of the utility of the "calculated risk" of lightly defending the Ardennes in the fall of 1944. Bradley's headquarters, only a scant 25 miles from the fighting front, showed his attitude towards a German offensive threat in the Ardennes: as far as he and his G-2 were concerned it was non-existent. When the German offensive opened, Bradley was incredulous. Unlike Eisenhower, he believed the German moves only to be a spoiling attack. On the night of December 16th, he opposed the supreme commander's decision to move the U.S. 1st Infantry and 7th and 10th Armored Divisions into the Ardennes. Of course, the prompt movement of these reserves proved vital in stemming the German tide.

As the German offensive gained ground, Bradley's inopportune location quickly separated him from the north flank of the German bulge in the First Army, so that on December 20th, Eisenhower handed over the command of First Army to Montgomery. Bradley saw this change of command as an insult and threatened resignation early in the New Year if Hodges' army was not returned to him. This was done, although the feelings between Bradley and Montgomery remained anything but cordial for the remainder of the war.

On the positive side, Bradley was a much more decisive man than Montgomery. Already on December 26th he indicated the desire to immediately begin an attack from the shoulders of the Bulge to snip off the German salient. Of course, with the cautious Montgomery in charge, this did not happen (although later in January, Patton put this idea to work). The British commander delayed the Allied general offensive until January 3rd. Also, like Eisenhower, Bradley was a facilitator of men. He was able to extract cooperation and team work from the quarreling generals below him. Eisenhower rated Bradley second to none: "I consider him to be the greatest battle-line commander I have met in this war."

Generalfeldmarschall Walther Model
Heeresgruppe B

Entering the German Army in 1909 at the age of 18, Model remained on duty between the two world wars and commanded the *4th Korps*. In 1938 he was promoted to Brigadier General and his career moved rapidly as he was favored by Hitler. Model fought in the Polish and French campaigns as a staff officer (*Fourth Armeekorps* and *Sixteenth Armee*, respectively) until given command of the *3rd Panzer Division* for the invasion of Russia. As a division commander, Model displayed remarkable energy, and by fall of 1941 he was promoted to command of the *XLI Panzerkorps*. Scarcely six months later he was awarded the command of the *Ninth Armee*.

In Russia, he developed a reputation as a "lion of defense" and in 1943 he was promoted to field marshal. At age 53, he was then the youngest field marshal in the German Army. As Hitler's "fireman" he was sent to command *Heeresgruppe Süd* in Russia to hold the tide. Then during the summer of 1944, he took over command of *Heeresgruppe Center* in Russia when that front appeared near collapse. Through the use of a mobile defense with counterattacks to throw the enemy off balance (as well as blowing up the entire Polish town of Kovel) he kept the Soviets out of Warsaw. Later the same summer he took over *Heeresgruppe B* in August when the Allies had broken out of the Normandy beachhead. On Hitler's command, he ordered that Paris be burned to the ground, an order that his subordinate, Gen. Dietich von Choltitz, refused to obey. Choltitz was captured, but Model was furious and ordered him court-martialed in absentia. Later in September, Model was instrumental in foiling the Allied air drop at Arnhem with an improvised defense followed by counterattacks that defeated Montgomery's offensive.

Model had humble beginnings; he was born in 1891 in Magdelburg, the son of a school teacher. Regardless, he rose quickly in the German Army and with his stern manner, rigid discipline and monocle over his right eye, the field marshal looked the part of a Hollywood German general. There was a deep schism in his personality since he was both deeply religious and a fervent Nazi. He was a professional soldier who always rose at 5:00 A.M. to inspect his troops and, although he understood his soldiers, he often drove those under him like he drove himself —unmercifully. Model believed in personal command; he frequently visited the front where he directed operations and assessed the situation. An Allied intelligence assessment of him read: "He is known to be personally devoted to Hitler and likes nothing better than being asked to do the impossible."

The field marshal was not well liked by other generals because he had a quick temper and could be difficult both as a subordinate or a superior. A poor performance by an underling would get a tongue lashing at best, threats of court-martial at worst. Model's relationship with his immediate commander, von Rundstedt, was proper if not cordial (von Rundstedt had once disdainfully called him "a good regimental sergeant-major"). Of his subordinates, Model probably liked von Manteuffel, the commander of *Fifth Panzer Armee*, best. After a strained relationship in Russia, Model and the little Prussian general got along well in the Ardennes. Both attempted unsuccessfully to change the aim of Hitler's unrealistic plan to reach Antwerp. During the offensive the two would meet near Schönberg on December 17th while walking on foot to sort out the massive traffic jam near St. Vith. Later von Manteuffel said of his superior:

> Model was a very good tactician, and better in defense than attack. He had a knack of guaging what troops could do, and what they could not do. His manner was rough, and his methods were not always acceptable in the higher quarters of the German army, but they were to Hitler's liking. Model stood up to Hitler in a way that hardly anyone else dared...

By late 1944, Model had begun to drink, with the weight of the impending German defeat. Even before the Ardennes Offensive, Model was convinced of the hopelessness of the German cause. As a soldier, he was opposed to the grandiose objectives set by *Wacht Am Rhein* for his relatively small armies.

Model's career ended in tragedy. Surrounded in the Ruhr pocket and honest to his proclamation that "a field marshal does not become a prisoner" he took his own life on April 21st, 1945, near the industrial town of Duisburg.

Lt. General Courtney H. Hodges
U.S. First Army

Plain and methodical, Courtney Hodges lead the U.S. First Army in an effective if undramatic style. Although this Georgia native flunked out of West Point (failing geometry), he managed to overcome this difficulty by earning a competitive commission with the 17th Infantry Regiment. In 1916 Hodges accompanied John J. Pershing into Mexico on the punitive expedition against Pancho Villa. In France in the Great War, Hodges served with a machine gun company with the 6th Regiment of the U.S. 5th Infantry Division where he fought in the grim battles of the Meuse-Argonne Campaign. In action Hodges won the Distinguished Service Cross. Between wars, Hodges continued his military edification attending Field Artillery, General Staff and the Air Corps Tactical schools.

When the war broke out, Hodges was commandant at the Infantry School in Ft. Benning. In 1943, he was given command of the U.S. Third Army with the rank of Lt. General. In June 1944, Hodges went ashore at Normandy as deputy to Lt. Gen. Omar N. Bradley and then commanded the U.S. First Army in the rapid advance across France.

Unlike most other senior Allied commanders other than Patton, Hodges had considerable combat experience, and these lessons had made him appreciate the suffering of the common soldier. Hodges personally saw to it that rest centers were established away from the front lines where

men could eat, drink and cavort or "do whatever they wish within the limits of propriety." Both Eisenhower and Bradley thought highly of the taciturn Hodges. According to Eisenhower, his only fault was that "God gave him a face that always looked pessimistic." Of his abilities, on having them questioned by Field Marshal Montgomery, Eisenhower said that "Hodges is the quiet reticent type and does not appear as aggressive as he really is. Unless he becomes exhausted, he will always wage a good fight."

His mettle was sorely tested in the Ardennes. He saw his command come under a fierce German offensive, even collapsing in many places. He and his staff then had the disquieting experience of being forced out of their headquarters in Spa on December 18th as a German SS panzer column closed to within five miles of the Hôtel Britannique. Throughout, however, Hodges remained a trustworthy and steadfast leader.

SS-Obergruppenführer Josef "Sepp" Dietrich
Sixth Panzer Armee

Son of a Bavarian butcher, "Sepp" Dietrich was large, stocky and coarse in his mannerisms. He had been in the Regular Army between 1911 and 1918 and had finished out World War I as a non-commissioned officer. Dietrich

SS Oberstgruppenführer Josef "Sepp" Dietrich, the commander of the Sixth Panzer Armee during the Ardennes Offensive.

had early ties to Hitler during his street fighting days, as his chauffeur and bodyguard in 1928. Five years later he had command of Hitler's praetorian guard, the *Leibstandarte Adolf Hitler*, and became the chief executioner in the bloody purge of the Nazi ranks that came to be known as the "Night of the Long Knives."

In return for his loyalty, Sepp was given a military command, the *Leibstandarte* as a regiment in the French campaign, a brigade in the Balkans and a division in the war in Russia. In late 1943, Dietrich was proud to boast that only thirty men of the original 23,000 in his division were still alive and uncaptured. In the battles in Normandy, Dietrich commanded the *ISS Panzerkorps* which was nearly destroyed in the fighting there. Although his command had been less than brilliant, the loyal Dietrich was personally chosen by Hitler himself for command of the *Sixth Panzer Armee* in the Ardennes Offensive.

Like most of the SS, Dietrich had a sinister and unsavory side to his character. In Russia, when it was discovered that at Taganrog the Russians had butchered six of his men, Dietrich ordered that all Soviet prisoners captured for the next three days be put to death. This amounted to some 4,000 Russians shot in cold blood.

Hitler called him "a man who's simultaneously cunning, conscientious and brutal.... He is irreplaceable." While brave and loyal to the Führer, Dietrich was not much of a military commander. Regular army officers noted his rise within the Waffen SS with great skepticism. Von Rundstedt indicated that he is "decent but stupid" and Göring said he was "capable of commanding a division at most."

Dietrich ultimately had little to do either with the planning or execution of the Ardennes attack, since Hitler, knowing of his mental weakness, appointed a capable Wehrmacht officer to run the army for him — Genmaj. Fritz Krämer.

Of course, even Dietrich was smart enough to recognize the absurdity of Hitler's far flung objectives for *Wacht am Rhein*. After the war, he said of Hitler's plan:

All he wants me to do is cross a river,

capture Brussels, and then go and take Antwerp! And all this in the worst time of year through the Ardennes where the snow is waist deep and there isn't room to deploy four tanks abreast, let alone armored divisions! Where it doesn't get light until eight and it's dark again at four and with re-formed divisions made up chiefly of kids and sick old men — and all this at Christmas!

General der Panzertruppen Hasso Eccard von Manteuffel
Fifth Panzer Armee

Heir of an old Prussian military family, Manteuffel's rise in World War II was meteoric. Without a doubt, he was one of the finest operational German armor tacticians in the war. The small panzer general commanded the *Fifth Panzer Armee* in the Ardennes Offensive.

Training for the military at an early age, in 1916 von Manteuffel served with the infantry on the Western Front where he was wounded. Long an avid horseman, after the war von Manteuffel became captivated with the idea of armored warfare as espoused by Heinz Guderian. In 1934 he joined the Inspectorate General of the Armored Forces and trained armored troops for several years thereafter.

Anxious to get into the war, von Manteuffel served in Africa under General von Arnim until evacuated across the Mediterranean in May 1943. Von Manteuffel took a command in the *7th Panzer Division* in Russia and later the *Gross Deutschland Panzer Division* as a Generalmajor in February 1944. So successful were his exploits that year, that Hitler promoted the little panzer officer to a full general in the fall of 1944 completely bypassing the Corps echelon. Von Manteuffel was admired by Generalfeldmarschall Model, although there was uneasiness between the two due to a bitter dispute earlier in the war in Russia.

General von Manteuffel was one of the most highly decorated officers in the German army, holding the Iron Cross of the Knights Degree with Swords and Diamonds. His superior on the Eastern Front wrote of him: "in every facet an outstanding leadership personality."

Like other realistic generals, von

Manteuffel did not think highly of Hitler's grandiose Ardennes plan and tried unsuccessfully to get it changed to the Small Solution. Still, more than any other commander, the attack scheme for *Wacht am Rhein* bore von Manteuffel's personal imprint. "Keitel and Jodl had never been in the war," he explained, "At the same time their lack of fighting experience tended to make them underrate practical difficulties and encourage Hitler to believe that things could be done that were quite impossible. Hitler would listen to soldiers who had fighting experience and practical ideas."

Lt. General George S. Patton, Jr.
U.S. Third Army

Flamboyant, reckless, deeply religious and violently profane, the pistol-packing General "Blood and Guts" Patton was a living American legend by the fall of 1944. Descendant of an old Southern family, Patton was obsessed with the military profession from his early childhood. A graduate of the Class of 1909 from the U.S. Military Academy, Patton fought in World War I. He sailed to France as a member of Pershing's staff and was detailed to command the new tank corps. In 1917 he lead the 304th Light Tank Brigade in the St. Mihiel Offensive. The following year, he was wounded in September of 1918 in the Argonne Offensive. After the war, Patton's interest in the military and tanks continued. At the outbreak of World War II, Patton was in command of the U.S. 2nd Armored Division and later the I Armored Corps at Ft. Benning, Georgia.

In 1942, Patton commanded the U.S. II Corps in Operation Torch to eject Rommel from North Africa. The mission was highly successful and Patton went on to participate in the campaign in Sicily. There, however, he perpetrated the notorious soldier slapping incident which nearly cost him his field command and jeopardized Eisenhower's when Ike refused to reduce his rank. After further *faux pas* with the press (Patton had a gift for insult), he managed to obtain a field command in Normandy with his Third Army which made the critical Breakout at St. Lô.

Patton was an inspired and careful planner, with a strong temper and a fanatic belief in the importance of speed and constant attack. "In war, death is incidental," he once said, "but loss of time is criminal." Patton was also deeply religious and believed himself a reincarnated warrior. He once told a priest who recommended prayer that he already did so "every goddamned day." Big on pomp and circumstance, Patton's manner was calculated to win his troop's self-confidence. "My guns are ivory handled," he said of his .45 Caliber Colt revolvers. "Only a pimp in a New Orleans whorehouse or a thin horn gambler would carry a pearl-handled pistol. But I want the men of the Third Army to know where I am, and that I risk the same danger that they do."

Patton was adept at armored battle and greatly preferred a war of movement. At the same time, Patton understood the limitations of his command and emphasized mobility and firepower of his forces to make up for the lack of small unit tactics in the American forces. Regardless of his difficulty in swiftly breaking through to Bastogne, Patton wrote that it was "the most brilliant operation we have thus far performed, and it is in my opinion the outstanding achievement of this war. This *is my biggest battle.*"

The Germans were unanimous in their conviction that Patton was the best Allied commander. According to Gen. Siegfried Westphal, von Rundstedt's Chief of Staff, "He was by far the outstanding commander in the enemy camp. Patton was remarkable for his determined and bold actions." Gen. Blummentritt, Westphal's predecessor, said, "His operations impressed us enormously, probably because he came closest to our concept of the classical military commander." When asked who was the most dangerous Allied commander he faced, Gen. von Manteuffel, who fought the Third Army in the Bulge, was emphatic: "Patton! No

doubt about this. He was a brillant panzer army commander."

Gen. Bradley, who both served under Patton and then later commanded him, recalled: "An outstanding combat commander.... Of the ten general officers of his grade known to me, I would list him number one as a combat leader." Writing to his son, Patton explained that: "Leadership...is the one thing that wins battles. I have it — but I'll be damned if I can define it."

General der Panzertruppen Erich Brandenberger
Seventh Armee

At 50, bald and pudgy, Gen. Brandenberger looked to be the experienced and conservative soldier that he was. In 1942 Brandenberger had served with distinction as the commander of the *8th Panzer Division* in intense battles with *Heeresgruppe North* in Russia. In 1943 and 1944 he commanded the *XXIX Infanterie Korps* also in the East, proving himself valuable in heavy defensive fighting there.

In September 1944 Brandenberger was called to the Western Front to take over the German *Seventh Armee* in the Ardennes and hold the Westwall. Later he was called on to command that army in the Ardennes Offensive. Despite the poverty of forces allotted to Brandenberger, Hitler was always prepared to expect the impossible. In the planning for the offensive that followed in the fall of 1944, the strength of combat forces allotted to Brandenberger steadily diminished and Brandenberger was left out of several of the military briefings held by the commander of *Heeresgruppe B*, Genfldm. Model.

Model was not overly fond of Brandenberger who he called a "typical product of the General Staff" with the "features of a scientist." Brandenberger was too meticulous, and conservative for Model's tastes. The *Heeresgruppe B* commander was concerned that Brandenberger did not

possess the necessary drive and Nazi fanaticism to conduct a major counter-offensive. The bad feelings seem to have been mutual since on the day before the attack, Brandenberger lodged a note of protest via his chief of staff, Genmaj. von Gersdorff. The *Seventh Armee*, Brandenberger said, could not reach their objective without more support. Of course, this did not change Model or Hitler's mind one whit. The *Seventh Armee* would have to do with what it had.

In spite of Model's concerns, Brandenberger was a good commander — particularly for the type of operation with which he was involved. On the attack Brandenberger managed a good performance with the limited means available. On the defensive, Brandenberger and his staff showed their superior experience from the East, juggling meager reserves and artillery to frustrate the Allied counterattack. In spite of this, the feud between Model and Brandenberger was not over. In February 1945, the *Heeresgruppe B* commander complained that the Brandenberger surrendered ground in the Eifel too easily. In mid-month, under terrific pressure from Allied forces, Brandenberger lost a large section of Hitler's Westwall near Vianden. Model visited Brandenberger's headquarters on February 20th, gave the pauchy commander a tongue lashing in front of his staff and relieved him of command.

Regardless of whatever disgrace Brandenberger's dismissal might have caused him, Model's act probably saved his life. Moments after Model and Brandenberger's departure, a rain of bombs from American planes fell on the headquarters severely wounding or killing most of the staff. The new commander of the *Seventh Armee*, Gen. d. Inf. Hans Felber, on his way to say farewell to his *XIII Armeekorps*, was wounded in the bombing.

All Quiet in the Ardennes

The Ardennes "ghost front" scarcely moved after September. The American troops in the Ardennes were either veterans rotated there to recover from terrible losses on other fronts or new units introduced to this quiet sector to gather experience. The Germans manned the sector sparsely as well, so that the danger of a major offensive seemed exceedingly remote. In one part of the front, that of the U.S. VIII Corps, the defenses were particularly thin. A 75-mile line from Monschau to Echternach was covered by just four divisions. The defense in the Ardennes was almost casual, with the only excitement coming from the nightly patrols into no-man's land conducted by either side. Historically the region was a European resort area, replete with hot springs and quaint castled towns. And so it became for the fortunate American soldiers stationed there. "Lucky guys," a veteran 2nd Division man leaving the Ardennes chided a newcomer of the U.S. 106th Division, "you're coming into a rest camp!"

The German planners hoped to inspire the Americans in the Ardennes to even greater complacency. A well con-ceived deception plan was instituted to cover up the intent of the German troop build-up. The deception plan, slyly called *Abwehrschlacht im Westen* (the Defensive Battle in the West), was casually leaked onto German radio traffic. The plan indicated that the *Sixth Panzer Armee* would be used to counterattack the eventual Allied penetration towards the Rhine River. In the Ardennes, the German *Seventh Armee* continued to defend the area lightly. Status quo was the rule. Any mention of the real plan, or its code name, *Wacht am Rhein*, on the air waves was strictly forbidden by Hitler himself. All communication regarding the counteroffensive was accomplished in person or by courier.

Meanwhile, Allied intelligence services, heady from a string of unbroken victories, took the phoney bait as real. Since 1941, a team of British cryptographers had been breaking the code of German military radio transmissions,

Better times. Men of the U.S. 28th Infantry Division are given a festive welcome by the people of Bastogne after Allied liberation of the town in September of 1944.

Panther tanks of the 1st SS Panzer Division *refuel under the cover of the thick Ardennes wood near Schmidtheim.*

under the cover name of ULTRA. In the fall of 1944, the German deception plan was faithfully decoded by the Allied ULTRA team in England. ULTRA had never misled them before and they had no reason to doubt the authenticity of these communiques.

Blinded from aerial reconnaissance by the low clouds from late November on, and confident that ULTRA would tell of any major German moves, the intelligence officers could not see the great approaching blow in spite of accumulating conventional evidence. Part of this resulted from the unusual optimism that infected Allied intelligence in the fall of 1944. The Germans, they believed, were unequivocally beaten; some even went so far as to predict total collapse of the Western Front by New Year's. On December 12th, Edwin Sibert, Bradley's 12th Army Group G-2 predicted as much:

> The enemy divisions that have been in line since the beginning of our offensive have been cut by at least fifty percent...with continuing Allied pressure in the south and in the north, the (German) breaking point may develop suddenly and without warning.

Another problem was interpretation. Allied intelligence was expecting some response to their Roer River offensive and a general enemy counteroffensive as Eisenhower's forces approached the Rhine River. Regardless, as the G-2s saw

it, any enemy riposte was likely to appear up north, east of Aachen, not in the militarily unimportant Ardennes. And in concordance with Hitler's deception plan, most of the observed enemy movement in early December was in this area. It was only in the final days before the attack that enemy activity picked up in the Eifel.

Some of Allied intelligence did get notion of the trouble brewing. In his G-2 estimate No. 37, Colonel Benjamin "Monk" Dickson of the U.S. First Army ventured on December 10th that:

> The enemy ... has brought up and continues to bring up army and corps artillery formations and to build up his fighter and fighter bomber strength on the Western Front. It is plain that his strategy in defense of the Reich is based on the exhaustion of our offensive to be followed by an all out counterattack with armor between the Roer and Erft supported by every weapon he can bring to bear.... The use of secret weapons is to be expected.... It is apparent that von Rundstedt...is preparing for his part in the all-out application of every weapon at the focal point and the correct time to achieve defense of the Reich west of the Rhine by inflicting as great a defeat on the Allies as possible.... [The offensive] is to be expected when our major ground forces have crossed the Roer River.

But the Roer and Erft Rivers were north of the Ardennes, so Dickson cannot be credited with divining the German plan. In fact, Maj. Gen. Kenneth W. Strong, Eisenhower's personal G-2, was the only man in the senior intelligence community to predict and locate the enemy blow. In the first week of December he noted with apprehension that nine enemy panzer divisions had disappeared from the front and that significant enemy movement was in progress. The following week Strong circulated a top secret intelligence summary to the top Allied commanders. The summary was enciphered and all copies were read and then destroyed. In it Strong ventured that the German activity pointed at an enemy counterattack with one of two objectives — pinching off the Allied salient around Aachen or a winter offensive, possibly through the Ardennes. Eisenhower had worried all through the autumn about the possibility of "a nasty little Kasserine" through the forested region. Knowing of Strong's excellent track record in guessing enemy intentions, he dispatched him to Bradley in Luxembourg to warn him of the possibility of an enemy attack through the Ardennes. But Bradley was less than impressed by Strong's admonition because he was considered something of a worry wart. Mindful of his own G-2's prognostications of the hopelessness of the enemy situation and the power of his First Army, he brushed the warning aside. "Let them come," Bradley replied — a remark he would long regret.

On the other hand, Dickson, at the U.S. First Army headquarters, was getting more suspicious as well. He noted more news of increased enemy traffic in the Eifel and many POWs who now spoke of a coming big attack before Christmas. Pointing to a map on the night of December 14th, he suddenly exclaimed, "It's the Ardennes!" But Dickson was considered a pessimist and something of a doomsayer by his peers who tended to discount his pronouncement. Long due for a leave, Dickson left for leave to Paris on orders. His impetuous remark went no further than the circle of men who witnessed it.

Meanwhile in the Ardennes, the VIII Corps G-2 dismissed the reports in recent days of sounds of German motor traffic in the Eifel: "The enemy's present practice of introducing new divisions to this theater to receive front line experience and then relieve them for commitment elsewhere indicates his desire to have this sector of the front remain quiet and inactive." However, a final bit of disquieting news came on the night of December 15th. The U.S. 28th Division reported it had observed the enemy in great coats across the front before the Our River and that "the bearing of these Germans was much more soldierly than before...much saluting was observed." The report was correct; the Germans were from the elite *2nd Panzer Division*.

ULTRA: The Secret Battle

Hitler and His Deception Plan

Since the attempt on Hitler's life in July of 1944, the German leader had grown to trust no one. Somehow, he believed, the Allies were learning of his intentions in advance, a condition he attributed to leaks that had developed within the cabal of army officers that had attempted to kill him the previous summer. As with his *blitzkrieg* through the Ardennes in 1940, Hitler believed that he must achieve complete surprise to help his great offensive's chances. To prevent the Allies from getting wind of his last great gamble, he directed his chief of operations, General Alfred Jodl, to devise a deception plan. The offensive was to have the code name *Wacht am Rhein* ("Watch on the Rhine") which would seem to connote defense. The preparation plans were similarly misnamed *Abwehrschlacht im Westen* (the Defensive Battle in the West).

On November 5th, at Hitler's behest, Jodl provided "Orders for a Deception Plan and Maintenance of Secrecy." The basic tenet was this:

> the German High Command is expecting a heavy enemy attack against the line Cologne-Bonn this year. Two assault groups will be assembled to counterattack such a penetration on its southern and northern flanks — one group northwest of Cologne and the other in the Eifel.

To help sell the ruse, the Germans planned to conceal the true strength of their concentration in the Eifel while exaggerating their presence in the Cologne area. Accordingly, a bogus *Twenty-Fifth Armee* was conjured up and located in the Düsseldorf-Cologne area, where the *Sixth Panzer Armee* was training. There, military movements and radio traffic were carried out ostentatiously to persuade the Allies to believe what they already did — that Hitler was preparing to defend the last natural obstacle to Allied advance into the heart of Germany — the Rhine River.

Even more importantly, Hitler forbade any radio transmission remotely connected with *Wacht am Rhein*. The only radio signals allowed concerned the phoney *Abwehrschlacht im Westen*. The circle of individuals privy to the German Ardennes plan was deliberately kept small during the preparations in the fall of 1944. Even those admitted to the secret had to sign a sworn statement accepting the death penalty for any breach of security regarding the plan. All communications regarding *Wacht Am Rhein* were carried out by couriers who were closely tailed by Gestapo agents. Even German divisional commanders to be involved did not learn of the operation until only a few days before it was to begin. Hitler was determined that word of his coming counteroffensive would not leak out.

The ULTRA Secret

Heady from a long series of impressive victories, Allied intelligence in the fall of 1944 was completely ignorant of German intentions to launch the Ardennes Offensive. The total failure of Allied intelligence must be ranked as among the worst in history, nearly equal in embarrassment to the strategic oversight at Pearl Harbor. Unlike that *faux pas*, the lapse of battlefield intelligence that failed to see the coming Ardennes blow was aided by the ability to expeditiously break the codes of the German military radio transmissions. A closely guarded secret since 1940, this intelligence weapon was called ULTRA.

By 1943 the British ULTRA teams often knew German plans by the time they were received by the Wehrmacht commanders in the field. In his post war memoirs, Winston Churchill indirectly referred to the ULTRA mission as his "most secret sources." It had been a crucial Allied advantage in many battles fought against the Nazis: North Africa, Italy and Normandy. And just as astounding was the utter failure of this intelligence advantage to foresee the coming German Ardennes Offensive. How did all this come about?

The Enigma

The story of ULTRA began in the late 1920s when the German *Reichs-wehr* adopted a mechanical coding device called "the Enigma" for secret military radio transmissions. The Enigma resembled a primitive typewriter with one very important exception. When an operator hit an "A" key on the machine, an "A" was not typed, but some other key. This was accomplished by complex electrical wiring and a series of wheels whose settings could produce a great many unique codes. So many complex com-

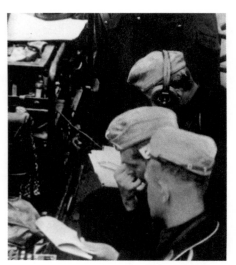

Rare photograph of the German Enigma coding machine in use. ULTRA decoded the German military radio traffic beginning in 1942 and allowed Allied intelligence officers to be forewarned of most major German operations. Unfortunately for the Allies, Hitler forbade all radio communication that had anything to do with his plan for an offensive in the Ardennes.

binations were possible that its Dutch inventor, Hugo Alexander Koch, was convinced that the code that it produced was absolutely unbreakable.

For a time it was. In an initial assessment, one British analyst estimated the possible settings at 6,000 trillion combinations. However, a brilliant and eccentric British mathematician, Alan M. Turing, pondered the possibility of computer machines and artifical intelligence before the war. This knowledge, he believed, could be used to decode Enigma's codes. In a bit of mathematical poetry he remarked that, "A sonnet written by a machine will be better appreciated by another machine."

This became the basic plan for breaking Enigma. The German codes produced by the machine could be most easily deciphered through the use of another machine of the same type. But this could only be accomplished by gaining clues from errors that the human operators made in making the Enigma communiques. Luckily for the Allies, although the machine's coding scheme was most vexing for crytologists, the German radio operators made enough slips to allow the codes to be broken. The problem was time. With the Germans prudently changing the codes daily, no one could afford to spend months accumulating evidence to break a single code.

In the 1930s the Poles managed some success by buying and stealing several Enigma machines and linking them together in an improvised machine called the "Bombe." This machine was like a primitive precursor to today's modern electronic computers. By 1937 the Poles with some French assistance were breaking some German codes with the Bombe, although the process was difficult and lengthy.

Work proceeded on assembling the Allied brain power to crack the Enigma in Britain. Turing was drafted from his studies at the Institute for Advanced Studies at Princeton University. He and his colleagues from Oxford Univerity were assembled and moved into a red brick mansion in a quiet neighborhood near Buckinghamshire called Bletchley Park. This unusual collection of mathematicians and cryptographers were called the British Code and Cipher School, although even this designation remained a secret. The men who worked there referred to themselves mockingly as the Golf Club and Chess Society. They worked under the command of Alexander Denniston, known even to his son as "the most secretive man I have ever known."

But where to get the Enigma machines? By July 1939 it seemed obvious to the British that war could breakout in Europe at anytime. In an act of daring espionage, Denniston arranged to have a machine smuggled from Poland. The machine was brought in on August 19, 1939, from Warsaw by an operative working under the cover name of Col. Sandwich. Colonel Sandwich was none other than Col. Stewart Menzies, the future head of the British Secret Intelligence Service. The procurement was timely, as by summer 1940 both countries had fallen under Hitler's conquest.

At Bletchley Park the team feverishly worked under the threat of Nazi invasion of their homeland. By mid-1940 the mathematicians and cryptographers had created a more efficient electro-mechanical computer. They affectionately called it the Mark I Heath Robinson after a popular British cartoonist. With the help of the British cryptographers, the new machine could expeditiously break the German codes when provided with the typical clues made available by careless German radio operators. The team at Bletchley had succeeded.

The "Secret Limeys"

Soon the deciphering of the German codes became an everyday event. It was obviously vital to get the content of the transmissions to Allied field commanders where they could use the information to their advantage. On the other hand, conspicuous use of the decrypted information might disclose the ULTRA secret. Group-Capt. Frederick W. Winterbotham, was brought in to deal with the vexing security dilemma. The great challenge was to use the enemy information without disclosing the Allied advance knowledge of the German intentions. Winterbotham created Special Liaison Units, or SLUs, of several hand picked men that attached themselves to headquarters to provide the secret communiques. Winterbotham personally selected the SLU personnel, binding each one to life long secrecy.

The SLUs were assigned to each army group, army, air force and tactical air command headquarters. The commanding U.S. generals in Europe were let in on the ULTRA secret, including Eisenhower, Bradley, Patton, Devers and Hodges. Still only a handful of men knew of the secret at any of the various headquarters. Each SLU consisted of a carefully chosen officer plus a small group of enlisted cipher and radio specialists.

The methods the British used were distinctly James Bond in character. Each group of deciphered German intercepts were re-encrypted at Bletchley into the Allied codes (oddly enough, using a machine very similar to the Enigma). These signals were then transmitted by radio. Upon their receipt, the text was decoded by the SLU and then read to the commanding officer, after which it was destroyed. In one case in France, when an ULTRA decoding machine was lost by a careless U.S. crew, Eisenhower ordered a fastidious search to find the truck in which it was loaded. Mysteriously, it was never located.

The extremely cautious nature of the entire process often meant that information received by the SLUs was often a day or more old. Even then, whether or not the commanders could act on the covertly gathered information was always uncertain. Allied intelligence knew that the Germans must not be allowed to come to the conclusion that the Allies possessed information that could have only come from decoding radio traffic. Thus, some information was withheld for a time or not even passed on.

The very presence of the SLU teams in France and Belgium in 1944 was enough to arouse suspicion in onlookers. Of course, the SLUs tried to be inconspicuous. Even so, a tent bristling with aerials right next to army headquarters and manned by British men in Royal Air Force blue along with U.S. men of mostly lower ranks was certainly out of the ordinary. Not only were these lowly officers afforded close proximity to the "big brass," but they also enjoyed unlimited access to these commanders. Military police soon discovered that these men were not to be questioned or detained. Sometimes the SLUs shared quarters with other high ranking staff members who were not privy to the secret; they carried on their conversations in whispers. So confounding were these men to the headquarter's clerks with the U.S. 12th Army Group, that they took to calling them the "Secret Limeys."

ULTRA served the Allies well in Normandy. Decoded messages in August alerted the U.S. First Army commander, General Hodges, to an imminent German armored counter-strike at Mortain aimed to "drive the Americans into the sea." Given this timely warning, Hodges was able to position the U.S. 30th Division to contain the German advance while pulverizing the enemy's armor with fighter bombers. The German counter was thwarted, beginning the rout of the Nazi Army in France.

Anytime the Germans transmitted by wireless they were unwittingly conveying their information into the hands of the Allied commanders. The Wehrmacht, of course, was not completely naive with regard to radio security and always preferred land-line telephone when it was available. As Hitler pulled his forces back into the Reich in September of 1944, however, the German lines became more widely useful and trustworthy. Even then, there were times when units in the field had to use radio. This was particularly true for the German Luftwaffe units which were unusually lax with respect to radio security. It was from the Luftwaffe transmissions that the ULTRA teams learned much of the German army's operations in the fall of 1944.

ULTRA Eavesdrops

Given the content of the ULTRA material in the fall of 1944, it seems extraordinary that Allied intelligence did not see that the Germans were preparing for a major offensive. Since early September, the British deciphering team at Bletchley Park had decoded an average of fifty messages per day. On October 20th they signaled Allied intelligence that the *Sixth Panzer Armee* and the *Panzer Lehr Division* were refitting at the direct order of Hitler himself. More importantly, on September 18th, the Allied cryptographers learned that Oberstgruppenführer Josef "Sepp" Dietrich, one of Hitler's old Nazi cronies, was to command the army which was to be lavishly equipped with first rate troops, tanks and guns. It would serve as the *OKW* reserve, a sign of the importance of this army, for *OKW* property was under the direct control of the Führer himself. Nor was this emergency refit confined to the elite SS Panzer Divi-

The "Phantom" headquarters of Montgomery's Twenty-First Army Group. Radio, operations and coding vehicles are parked together. The jeep is setting out to deliver messages and orders to Montgomery's patrol officers. "Phantom" was the British GHQ Signal's regiment.

sions. On November 11th, transmissions revealed that the *2nd, 9th, 11th, 21st* and *116th Panzer Divisions* had been placed on a priority "short term repair program."

A crop of de-coded German radio traffic showed evidence of massive German movements in late November and early December. On November 16th an especially provocative message was deciphered: The air liaison officer of the missing *Sixth Panzer Armee* referred to a *Jägeraufmarsch*, or concentration of fighter-planes, for "an imminent big operation." A communique on December 2nd showed that 200 trains had recently arrived in the Eifel, just east of the Ardennes, including cars off-loading Hitler's elite praetorian guard, the *Führer Begleit (Escort) Brigade*. What was this heavily armored panzer unit doing in the quiet zone of the Eifel? Days earlier, the staff of the mysterious *Sixth Panzer Armee* and its *12th SS Panzer Division* were known to have moved along amidst complaints that several divisions had fallen more than 12 hours behind schedule in their move. "No further delays will be tolerated." Why in early December would German operatives be so concerned for a movement time schedule?

An even more intriguing communi-

que decoded on November 24th requested top priority aerial reconnaissance of bridges across the Meuse River between Liège and Givet. The missions, "a matter of the greatest urgency," were entrusted to the Arado 234 jets of *Detachment Sperling* which were to take pictures on December 8th. Other sorties were to provide aerial reconnaissance of the Eupen-Malmédy, Liège and Prüm-Houffalize area, the pilots being briefed to look for Allied tanks concentrations and supply dumps. Why the sudden interest in Allied real estate 60 miles from the front lines? Finally, on December 10th came perhaps the most mysterious report of all; *Jagdkorps II*, the Luftwaffe unit in charge of the Western Front, reported that "all SS units are observing radio silence." Since the wireless came into common military use, such radio silence had become almost always a sign of secretive movement, often before a major attack.

"Nothing to report..."

Although pessimism comes almost naturally to most G-2 intelligence officers (their motto: "Regardless of what happens, there is always someone who said it would."), those in the Allied ranks seemed to be suffering from the same wave of optimism that was sweeping Allied ranks. Rumors among some young American soldiers in the summer of 1944 were of being home by Christmas — or at worst early in the new year.

In spite of the spirited enemy resistance in the fall, the German army, so Allied intelligence believed, was ready to quit. General Bradley's intelligence summary of December 12th reflected the prevailing sentiment:

> It is now certain that attrition is steadily sapping the strength of German forces on the Western front and that the crust of defense is thinner, more brittle and more vulnerable than it appears.... With continuing Allied pressure in the south and in the north, the breaking point may develop suddenly and without warning.

Montgomery's 21st Army Group intelligence was even more emphatic. "The German Army is in a bad way...and can no longer stage major offensive operations."

Interrogations of captured prisoners opposite the Ardennes in the fall of 1944 seemed to reinforce this view. German morale was low, training was poor and equipment was deficient. G-2s even began to see prisoners from convict formations, impressed Russian prisoners in *Ost* battalions and even conscripts with hearing disorders in *Ohren Abteilung*. Did not the commitment of these soldierly dregs indicate the desperate nature of the land battle in Hitler's Germany?

When General Bradley visited Maj. Gen. Troy H. Middleton at his headquarters in the Ardennes in Bastogne, the commander of the VIII Corps told Bradley that the line was too thinly defended. "Don't worry, Troy," his commander tried to assure him. "They won't come through here."

Then, just a few days before the German offensive was to begin, the Allied G-2s began to get wind of something big in the air. Aerial reconnaissance from the P-61 "Black Widows" of the 67th Tactical Reconnaissance Group noted a great increase in night-time vehicular traffic opposite the Eifel and long hospital trains west of the Rhine — always a tip-off for a coming offensive. Near

Gemünd, just east of the Ardennes, a convoy of over 120 vehicles were sighted! But these signs were summarily misread; the Germans, the Allies believed, were probably moving up units through the Ardennes to try to stop the advance around the Roer or Patton's Saar offensive to the south. One troubling note remained: prisoners recently taken from the *3rd Fallschirmjäger Division* on December 13th indicated that they were to be shortly relieved by the *1st SS Panzer Division*. This the interrogators simply refused to believe. What would an SS division be doing east of the Ardennes?

Inexperienced front-line U.S. troops from the U.S. 106th Division clearly heard the sound of motors on the night of December 14th and what they thought sounded like tanks near their front (This was, in fact, the German *2nd Panzer Division*). Reporting their experience to VIII Corps, a staff officer told them, "Don't be so jumpy. The Krauts are only playing phonograph records to scare you newcomers." Just the same, on December 15th two prisoners were interrogated from the *18th Volksgrenadier Division* opposite them (a note in the *Heeresgruppe B Kriegstagebuch* nervously notes three "deserters" from that division on the same day). The POWs reported they had heard of a great coming offensive, but discounted their own story; after all, they said, this rumor had circulated several times before!

There were other clues. A captured document told of formation of a commando unit of "English-speaking volunteers" under the infamous Nazi commando, SS Obersturmbannführer Otto Skorzeny, but not its mission. In the Allied order of battle, the German *Fifth Panzer Armee* seemed to have disappeared from the front: location unknown. Recently captured prisoners displayed surprisingly high morale and told of a great offensive to "recapture Aachen as a present for the Führer." But all these hints did not coherently assemble the puzzle to warn the Allied intelligence officers. It seemed too far fetched that the Germans had the resources to launch an offensive — especially in the "impassable Ardennes."

For all the accomplishments of ULTRA, its very success was perhaps the

major undoing for Allied intelligence. So reliable had it been in predicting German moves that Allied intelligence officers relied on it almost exclusively for a crystal ball on major German operations. The security measures for *Wacht am Rhein* were as draconian as Hitler's Gestapo could make them, and these provisions circumvented the ULTRA pipeline. Thus, while the anecdotal evidence from conventional sources continued to accumulate, the apostles of ULTRA were inclined to belittle its value. According to, Lt. Col. Adolf G. Rosengarten, the SLU officer for the U.S. First Army: "The Ardennes Offensive could have been foreseen.... Some clues came from open sources, but were not heeded as no clue came from ULTRA."

In spite of all this, one Allied intelligence officer did sense that something was up. Col. Benjamin "Monk" Dickson, who was head of First Army intelligence, concluded on December 10th that the Germans were preparing for an all-out offensive north in the Roer-Urft area (north of the Ardennes). This was not too alarming to the First Army, however; Dickson had developed a reputation as something of a doomsayer all through the Normandy Campaign. His peers regarded him as something less than an oracle. An anonymous member of the Washington D.C. based Office of Strategic Services (OSS) had penned a sarcastic comment under a picture of Hitler that hung in their 12th Army Group office: "He fools some of the people some of the time, but he fools Dickson all of the time."

However, on December 14th Dickson read a report from interrogation of a local Luxembourg woman who had observed, "many vehicles, pontoons and boats and other river crossing equipment coming from the direction of Bitburg." The area of which the woman was speaking was just east of the Ardennes opposite the U.S. 28th Infantry Division which had just recently reported sounds of motor traffic. That night on reading the report, Dickson told General Hodges that he knew where the all-out German attack would come: "It's the Ardennes!" he cried.

Hodges and his staff could hardly

take Dickson seriously, for while he cried "Wolf!" all the others were foretelling of the German Army's imminent collapse. Why, that very day, Maj. Gen. J.F.M. Whiteley, Eisenhower's Deputy Chief of Staff for Operations, had told a group of senior air officers that, "There is nothing to report on the Ardennes Front." Even if the Germans did decide to attack there, Hodges felt sure that his "secret limeys" would warn him in time. Fed up with the impetuous Dickson, Hodges ordered him to take a break. He was to go on leave to Paris. Further questioning of the woman from Luxembourg was desirable, however, and she was to be sent to the First U.S. Army headquarters the next day. But this was all too late; the next day was December 16th.

ULTRA and the Battle

Even the ULTRA staffs were caught off guard by the German attack. John Weston, attached to General Bradley's headquarters was unlucky enough to be visiting the front on December 15th: "I was in the little village of Echternach on the Luxembourg-German border. German spotter planes were in the air. That same night von Rundstedt attacked. To say that there was some confusion was to understate the situation. Due to the radio blackout ordered by Hitler...there was very little ULTRA."

However, once the Ardennes Offensive had begun, ULTRA was quick in giving early indications of the scope and aim of *Wacht am Rhein*. Although radio silence was observed all day on December 16th by the German Army, the Luftwaffe was still using the Enigma for its communications. That evening *Jagdkorps II* announced its intention to "support the attack of *5th* and *6th Armies* tomorrow morning." The signal was speedily deciphered and placed in the hands of the Allied commanders. Another transmission was decoded from von Rundstedt in which he exhorted the German troops to great efforts with the admonition that: "The hour of destiny has struck. Mighty offensive armies face the Allies. WE GAMBLE EVERYTHING!" Amid the flurry of desperate reports coming from the Ar-

dennes, these two messages were a telling disclosure of the German's hand; particularly since the reference to the *6th Army* was immediately recognized in the Allied camp as the previously missing German strategic reserve: Dietrich's *Sixth Panzer Armee*.

ULTRA interceptions on the following day told the Allies the order of battle for Dietrich's army as well as the locations of its various divisions. More importantly, the Allies deciphered the request to the Luftwaffe to provide photo reconnaissance of the Meuse bridges around Liège. Thus, when Eisenhower met with his subordinate commanders on December 19th at Verdun, he already had a good idea from ULTRA about the immediate German objective and how to stop it.

Signals decoded in the following days provided ample evidence of the German High Command's displeasure with the way *Wacht am Rhein* was unfolding. Transmissions revealed German trouble with bridges, shortages of heavy weapons and strong American resistance. The vitriol from Hitler's headquarters was especially caustic with reference to this lack of progress; a signal flashed on the 18th passed on Hitler's order that the *Führer Begleit Brigade* be used to take St. Vith at once. A transmission on December 20th detailed the developing lack of fuel in the *1st SS Panzer Division* against *OKW* orders for the *Sixth Panzer Armee* to "continue its thrust towards the Meuse." On December 21st the intercept of a report from *Heeresgruppe B* gave the total tank strength for Field Marshal Model's forces on that date.[20]

As the days wore on and Allied victory became more assured, ULTRA helped to provide confirmation for Allied perceptions in the field. German transmissions became ever more preoccupied with the tracing of fuel shipments and amounts on hand; ULTRA overheard Oberst Polack the *OKH*

20 The status of *Heeresgruppe B* on December 21st: 462 tanks (288 operational: 107 Mk IVs, 144 Mk Vs, 37 Mk VIs), with a further 146 assault guns and tank destroyers. A later report gave the ration strength of the army group at year's end: 882,560 men in four armies (*15th Armee*: 205,193; *6th Pz Armee*: 319,031; *5th Pz Armee*: 187,769; *7th Armee*: 170,567).

quartermaster indicate that petrol supplies had become so scarce that "it may become necessary to de-motorize the army, with panzer grenadiers moving by foot or on bicycle and only the panzer brigades remaining fully motorized."

With the clearing weather, ULTRA listened in on the Luftwaffe plans and was able to warn Allied tactical air commands to expect "air battles on a grand scale." So detailed were these intercepts that occasionally Allied sorties could be sent out against overheard German plans. For instance a Luftwaffe transmission on December 27th called for "formations of 30 aircraft flying at a height of 500 meters to make raids in the Dinant-Marche-Rochefort area at five minute intervals beginning at 0630."

The ULTRA signals also documented the destruction of German road and rail west of the Rhine. By January 4th the *Sixth Panzer Armee* indicated that its only two supply routes were now both blocked with shattered or out-of-fuel vehicles, while a report on the *Reichsbahn* told that "traffic is only possible on a small scale." ULTRA was unable to provide any warning of the Luftwaffe's disastrous New Year's Day raid on Allied air bases. Luftwaffe Reichmarschall Göring's command to "Execute HERMANN" was readily deciphered and passed on to the Allied commanders on December 31st, but there was no way of interpreting the codeword for the 800 plane raid. Regardless, after the operation ULTRA was able to report the Luftwaffe losses — 277 pilots did not come back. After this abortive foray the German air force was relegated to near impotence. An urgent request for air support during the German retreat from the Ardennes on January 14th produced a commitment of every remaining air worthy plane in *Jagdkorps II* — 216 aircraft.

The intercepts from the German ground commanders reflected growing frustration. In the early morning hours of December 27th the *Seventh Armee* lamented that the "enemy now has material superiority over the whole front" and that "the situation is critical on both flanks." At about the same time, a message decoded from Dietrich's headquarters called for the heaviest possible air strike on the enemy in the woods north of Bastogne. Hitler's great offensive to Antwerp had disolved into a bloody battle to capture this small town of 5,000.

ULTRA also was producing increasing evidence of a concentration of German troops opposite the Vosges Mountains south of the Ardennes. This time, however, the Allied intelligence officers were not to be caught napping. "Excellent agent sources (a.k.a. ULTRA)," related General Dever's G-2, "report enemy units building up in the Black Forest area for offensive." This concentration was for

Operation Nordwind, another of Hitler's last ditch offensives. When it jumped off on New Year's Eve, the American commanders in the U.S. Seventh Army were fully warned. Like the Ardennes, the battle there was bitter, however. Although ULTRA could provide fair warning, it could not fight the battle for the Allies.

By 8 January, Bletchley Park recorded transmissions evidencing the beginning of the end in the Ardennes; the *9th Panzer Division* reported its retreat from the tip of the Bulge while the *Seventh Armee* vowed to "defend what has hitherto been the sector of attack." Two weeks later ULTRA was

able to advise Eisenhower of the beginning German transfer of the *Sixth Panzer Armee* to what *OB West* referred to as the "serious crisis" in Russia. This was a great relief to the Supreme Commander, for he knew the terrible Ardennes battle was over. Although ULTRA had not been able to provide explicit warning of the German attack, once the enemy offensive had begun it proved a source of incalculable value in reading the German intentions. It had been, as one U.S. historian noted, "a pearl of great price."

Between Manhay and Malempré tanks of the 40th Battalion of the 7th Armored Division were shot up by the 2nd SS Panzer Division. They appeared as photographed in January, 1945 and later that same summer in "Grand Gotha" field.

Today the scene looks the same, but the Shermans are gone. Manhay is in the distance.

The Ardennes

"If you go into the death trap of the Ardennes," a French officer warned in 1914, "you will never come out." This view of the heavily wooded region had been the conventional wisdom for centuries. Caesar's legions described the *Arduenna Silva* as "a frightful place, full of terrors." Legend said that in its wooded depths the four sons of Duke Aymon had held out for eight winters against Charlemagne. In his time, Napoleon governed the remote region under the *"Départment des Forêts,"* but otherwise little happened there during his reign. Fld.M. Ferdinand Foch, of World War I fame, summed the military assessment of the region: "It is impenetrable."

In reality, although the Ardennes region contained some of the roughest terrain in Europe, its reputation as a vast contiguous forest was unfounded. The wooded areas occured in a patchwork pattern with cleared fields, although certain regions such as the Forêt d' Ardennes above Sedan were very heavily forested. The terrain is extremely varied. Ridges, plateaus and valleys, with forested steep ravines alternate with heath, bogs, narrow winding trails and trackless woodland. The area in which Hitler was to launch the offensive consists of two major regions, the Eifel and the Ardennes proper.

The Eifel consists of a complex of heavily wooded hills near the German border between the Rhine and Moselle Rivers. It was this extension of the German forests that gave the German troop concentrations shelter from Allied air reconnaissance. Thus, in a sense the dark forest with its lingering mists made the German surprise attack possible. East of St. Vith is a long fir covered ridge, the Schnee Eifel (Snow Mountains) which was crested by the German Westwall fortifications. During the fall advances the Americans seized much of this nearly self defensive position which they still possessed at the beginning of the German offensive. North of Malmédy is the Hohes Venn, a high plateau of lakes and marshes extending southwest from Monschau. Just as the Schnee Eifel forms a natural barrier to advance on St. Vith, the Hohes Venn poses a like obstacle to an advance on Liège. The Hohes Venn ends where the *Hürtgenwald* begins to the north. This piece of very heavily forested real estate had already developed a reputation in the autumn as an evil killing ground for those who fought there. It formed the boundary for the German advance to the north.

The Ardennes can generally be defined as a wedge circumscribed by the following lines: Aachen-Liège, Aachen-Arlon and Arlon-Sedan. The Ardennes include territory in three countries: Luxembourg, Belgium and Northern France. The entire area extends up to the Meuse River on the west. The region has three recognized sub-compartments: the High Ardennes to the south, the Famenne Depression in the middle and the Low Ardennes to the north.

The High Ardennes is not really mountainous; the most elevated point at the Baraque de Fraiture is less than 2,500 feet above sea level. It is heavily wooded, however, with rugged terrain features that tend to compartmentalize battle such that domination of one hill means little in terms of effective observation and domination of another. The more open northern portion around Bastogne and Neufchâteau is known from its marshy soil as Hautes Fagnes (High Heaths), while to the south extends the heavily forested country along the Semois River known as the *Forêt d' Ardennes*.

Further north is a thin section of the Ardennes known as the Famenne Depression. This long narrow nearly treeless plateau extends from the upper Ourthe River westward through Marche, reaching a good crossing site over the Meuse River between Dinant and Givet. The Low Ardennes is characterized by low rolling hills including two open elevated areas more suitable for advance — the Herve Plateau near Verviers and the Condroz Plateau between the lower Ourthe and the Meuse Rivers. However, as with the Famenne Depression, debouch into this march-through topography assumes that the invader had already achieved possession of the difficult terrain before it to the east.

Numerous streams and rivers tend to obstruct movement through the Ardennes. Other than the Meuse, most of the rivers are actually more like streams that might be easily fordable under the right conditions. However, the Ardennes streams have generally carved out deep gorges in the geologic past that make their approach difficult to achieve with any measure of surprise. Moreover, the time of year meant that wading the streams would be a numbing experience for soldiers who were unlucky enough to be called on to do so.

The Meuse itself is not easily forded although there are a good number of bridges. As with the smaller streams, its approach can be very difficult, the river having eroded precipitous cliffs to its edge up to 100 meters high in some areas. There is an area where the river is more easily approached near Dinant; it is not coincidence that the Germans had historically used this as a sally point for their periodic forays into France.

At the German border, the Our and Sauer Rivers provided immediate obstacles to the advance of the *Fifth Panzer* and *Seventh Armies*. To the north, the Amblève and Salm Rivers recommended careful consideration to any advance northwest through the Losheim Gap or from St. Vith. The

Ourthe River that originates west of Bastogne is perhaps the most difficult military obstacle east of the Meuse River. For much of its circuitous course to the Meuse, the river flows through deep canyons with very difficult approaches even along roads.

There are no cities in the Ardennes. Liège, Luxembourg City and Arlon lie on the region's periphery. In 1944 most of the towns were found at road intersections or along the numerous stream banks. In 1944 populations commonly ranged between two to four thousand. Even smaller hamlets of a few dozen to a few hundred inhabitants were often at intersections on the secondary roads. These old picturesque villages were serviced by narrow winding streets and stone bridges that showed little anticipation of the needs of motorized traffic; any such passage through these villages required a serpentine approach. Sturdy Belgian and Luxembourgish houses, often stone structures with basements, offered improvised cover from gunfire and artillery attack for soldiers who found themselves there. But somber towns in the northerneastern sector, like St. Vith and Malmédy, had belonged to Germany prior to the First World War and still had a decidedly teutonic complexion. To the American soldiers they seemed unfriendly.

The terrain along the American defensive line provided considerable influence on the coming German offensive. Generally, the terrain was difficult all along the front, although it was heavily forested and rugged in the *Sixth Panzer Armee* sector. The roads there were sparse and the soft ground made off-road movement nearly impossible. In the *Fifth Panzer Armee* sector, the Germans had to cross the Our River to get at the American outposts, although the going improved somewhat after this obstacle was negotiated. Generally, Manteuffel's panzer columns found the going easier to the north than in the densely forested area around Wiltz. The plateau between Clerf and Bastogne provided a particularly attractive, if somewhat obvious, approach to the west. The going in the *Seventh Armee* sector was difficult if terrain was an indication. The Sauer River was swift and difficult to cross in the area and the wooded ridges provided plenty of cover for a defensive infantry action. The network of hills, trees and deeply set stream beds did not really end until the area around Neufchâteau was reached — a long way from the starting line.

The ground offered the defender several natural defensive positions east of the Meuse River. However, none of these was really impervious to a determined and able aggressor.

The objective of the great German offensive, Antwerp, lay on a wide plain. All the land beyond the Meuse was relatively open, laced with roads and easily traveled. However, from the Meuse to the German border was quite another matter. The frequent gorges often run parallel with the road network and give small scope for lateral off-road movement. The road network itself is more extensive than the minor population of the area would seem to warrant. The reason is economic; after World War I the tourism potential of the area was developed through a road-paving program. However, the roads were generally narrow, following winding circuitous river valleys and, most importantly, many were unpaved. Generally, roads meander along a north-south axis because of the direction of flow of the rivers in the region. Consequently, a westerly advance would tend to run across the grain of the topography.

The rail network in the Eifel was also extensive; it was engineered prior to World War I to support the rapid deployment of the Kaiser's armies west of the Rhine. The main rails feed into the Eifel from Koblenz, Cologne and from along the Moselle Valley near the old Roman city of Trier. Although, the rail network coupled with the heavily wooded nature of the Eifel made it perhaps optimum for troop concentration, the course of the rails cross and recross the numerous rivers and ravines making them prone to interdiction from the air.

By World War II, the business of tourism had become important to the Ardennes. Quaint castled towns and villages were interspersed through the hilly forests. The region possessed a wonderful local flavor somewhat reminiscent to American visitors of upstate Vermont. And, of course, there were the mud baths and medicinal springs of Spa. Feather beds, movies, watered-down beer and U.S.O. shows were available. On December 16th, Marlene Dietrich, the shapely movie star, appeared at Diekirch. The quiet front of the Ardennes was considered something of a vacation spot for recuperating battle weary American soldiers in the fall of 1944. December 16th changed all that.

The Influence of Terrain

The battleground in the Ardennes offered the American defenders several natural defensive positions east of the Meuse River although none of these could be seen as really being impervious to a determined and able aggressor:

1) To the north, the initial American positions along the line from Monschau to Elsenborn offered strong positions to defend against armored assault; an advantage against infantry would exist only so long as a continuous line could be maintained as a cordon against enemy infiltration through the woods. Should this position fail the covering line of the Amblève River offered a difficult crossing for the German advance to the northwest. Should this be crossed or flanked as well, then the rugged Hohes Venn offered a back-stop position anchored on the dense Hürtgen Forest. The notable exception to this nearly self-defensible terrain was in the so-called Losheim Gap. This area is a relatively open depression south of the Elsenborn area and just north of the Schnee Eifel. It offered the best tank terrain along the entire U.S. line. The rolling hills had little cover and there were no rivers to be crossed prior to reaching the Amblève. It was here that the *Sixth Panzer Armee* committed its prime armored spearhead.

2) In the center of the battlefield, the Salm and Ourthe River lines offered similar obstacles to advance from the east although control existed only so long as the defender held the crossing sites. The terrain further west offered decidedly better going for the attacker. Even so, these crossing sites were distant from the German start line and demolition of these bridges caused extreme difficulty for the Germans. The Nazi engineers in late 1944 were short both bridges and the trained personnel with which to erect them.

3) In the south, no obvious line was present. The confluence of the Alzette and Clerf Rivers offered a natural defensive position although numerous crossings made it difficult to prevent enemy flanking thrusts. More difficult to negotiate, however, was the Sûre River over which Patton attempted his counterattack from the south. The area was very heavily forested with rather poor roads and few crossing sites able to carry tanks.

The roads tend to run along a north-south axis because of proximity to the Rhine River and international borders. Consequently, a westerly advance tends to run across the grain of the topography. Dr. Cole summarized the problem succinctly in the official U.S. History:

> The geography of the Ardennes leads inevitably to the channelization of large troop movements east to west, will tend to force larger units to pile up on each other, and restricts freedom of maneuver once the direction of attack and order of battle are fixed. To a marked degree the military problem posed by the terrain is that of movement control rather than maneuver in the classic sense. For the smaller tactical units, the chopped up nature of the ground plus the peculiar timber formations in which dense wood lots are interspersed with natural or man-made clearings, indicates the development of a series of small, semi-independent engagements once the larger battle is joined.

The terrain of the Ardennes is significant from an military point of view for two reasons. Firstly, the difficulty of off-road movement during the winter until the ground freezes tends to channelize an attack force along the roads, particularly when it is motorized. The most common type of enemy obstacle was a roadblock, often in positions that were extremely difficult to outflank. Small blocking forces could and did hold off attackers with great numerical superiority, at least until they could deploy and bring their strength to bear. If the attacking force was armored then this often proved impossible. Since holding a single road intersection could tie up a greater segment of the enemy mobility, battles for crossroads assumed a special importance in the Ardennes. Of course, the most famous of these was the struggle for Bastogne, although many others are suggested to casual inquiry — St. Vith, Clervaux, Marche, Manhay. In almost every engagement, however, the importance of roads was paramount.

This brings us to the second important point. The Ardennes Offensive was essentially a battle for roads on which to deploy the powerful motorized forces. The length and extent of the road network in an area directly determines the number of motorized troops that can be deployed for rapid attack. Unlike Eisenhower's strategic broad front advance so reminiscent of the Great War, Hitler could not afford such a deliberate pace.

To succeed, the German Army had to initiate a *blitzkrieg* and blast through the Allied line to the Meuse where the open terrain would allow their armor to be employed before Allied reinforcements and air power could be brought to bear. The general idea was to concentrate a powerful mobile attack force at a single enemy weak point and after overpowering the enemy line rapidly exploit the breakthrough. The motorized columns could then freely deploy on the road network with about 30 vehicles per kilometer and move at convoy speeds (up to a maximum of about 30 km/hr).

The measure of importance in terms of deployment of forces for such a rapid breakout scheme was the kilometers of road space available in the zone of the main effort. A German panzer division required 2,600 vehicles to get moving. A maximum of 125 vehicles per kilometer could be squeezed onto a road and still be able to move, albeit at a much reduced pace. Whether such a concentration of vehicles moved slowly or snarled in a huge traffic jam, depended on staff planning and road discipline as well as driver experience and radio communication. Of course, there were the additional considerations such as enemy opposition and road conditions. In December in the Ardennes, the Germans could count on adverse conditions in both regards.

All this meant that the German Army could only put so many trucks on the few hard-surfaced roads in the Ardennes. A panzer division would need at least 20 km of road space; even a volksgrenadier division with 1,100 horse drawn vehicles and 400 trucks would require 12 km at a minimum. To move at road march rates the road space requirements increased at least threefold.

Of course in a pinch, the German forces could attempt to deploy onto the more numerous unpaved roads. However, as the Germans soon learned, attempting to transverse the fire trails and wooded tracks in the conifer forests was something else again. After a few vehicles had traversed the ground, the claylike soils turned to quagmire after the fall rains, marooning 50-ton tanks in a sea of mud.

Obstacles to a man walking were fewer, however, and the tactical mobility of the infantry combat arm played a significant role in how battles were fought in the Ardennes. For this reason, as well as the limitations that weather brought to armor, the Ardennes Offensive was primarily resolved as an infantry battle.

Sepp Dietrich, the commander of the German *Sixth Panzer Armee*, blamed the poor roads as one of the prime reasons for failure of *Wacht am Rhein*. "Only four or five tanks can fight at one time," he observed after the war, "because there is no place to deploy. A big tank attack in this terrain is impossible."

Although the Ardennes area is dotted with castles and fortified churches, the area had seen little in the way of military action prior to the Great War. In 1914 as part of the famed Schlieffen Plan, the Kaiser's *Third, Fourth* and *Fifth Armies* advanced across the Ar-

dennes massif to protect the main effort further north from the inevitable French counterattack. Their march was largely unopposed as Richthofen's *I Korps* preceded the columns and the Belgian forces were retiring north to defend Liège and Brussels. The French reaction was slow and their advance into the Ardennes was cautious due to lack of intelligence regarding the German positions. The inevitable clash with the French ocurred in the south near Neufchâteau and Vitron on August 22nd leaving the French line in shambles. Further north the French Fifth Army was roughly treated at the confluence of the Meuse and Sambre Rivers. A few days later Joffre ordered a general retreat, setting the stage for the "miracle of the Marne." Since most of the German advance had been unopposed, the campaign shed little light on how the terrain might influence battle through the Ardennes. However, it had made a great impression on German military minds: it was possible to move major military forces through a region with terrain so difficult that was said to be "impassable."

In 1940 the Germans again invaded the Ardennes; the stately horses of Richthofen's cavalry giving way to the motorized din of Guderian's tanks. Based on a plan advanced by Erich von Manstein, the German attack plan was a marked departure from the Schlieffen scheme of the previous war. The main German effort came not in northern Belgium, but through the Ardennes itself under Rundstedt's *Heeresgruppe A*. On May 10th the offensive began with nearly 1,000 German tanks in *Panzergruppe Kleist* moving rapidly in an armored phalanx through the Ardennes. The French, expecting the main German assault up north, could do little with the second rate soldiers of Corap's 9th Army to stop the tanks. As in the earlier war, the *Chasseurs Ardennais* had moved north to leave the French to fend for themselves. Also, as before, the major engagements occurred not in the Eifel or low Ardennes but

near the Meuse River. Over a period of three days the powerful German armor coupled with complete mastery of the skies decimated the two French armies in the Ardennes beginning the rapid campaign that led to the fall of France. Thus the Wehrmacht in 1940 had proved that a heavily motorized force could rapidly advance through the Ardennes forest in good weather and under the cover of air superiority. The question that had not been answered, however, was whether a tank-heavy force could fight through the rough terrain of the Ardennes in inclement weather against a stubborn and resourceful enemy.

The Battle of the Bulge answered that question in detail. The lesson indicated that the Ardennes massif provided an imposing advantage to a determined defender. Small isolated U.S. detachments clung like beggar's lice to crossroads, villages and bridges to deny the Germans the free use of the road net. The difficulty of outflanking defensive positions recommended a methodical advance as a remedy for this problem (such as the Allies used to squeeze the Germans out of the Bulge). Unfortunately for Hitler, with only temporary tactical superiority, *Wacht am Rhein* could afford nothing less than a rapid and total breakout if it was to succeed.

In a real sense, the terrain of the Ardennes had made the offensive possible in the first place, while ensuring its ultimate failure. The heavily wooded Eifel had concealed the German intentions while the Allies had rightly depended on the terrain to bolster any necessary defense. On the other hand, the terrain robbed the Germans of any real chance for the breakout that Hitler needed for his desperate plan. It is perhaps then ironic that the month of December 1944 saw the Nazi *blitzkrieg* that had flowered in the Ardennes in May 1940 return to the dark forest for its final death dance.

Arms and Equipment

In many ways the weapons and equipment that men used in the Ardennes had a profound influence on the campaign. They prescribed how it was ultimately fought, how men experienced the battle and often whether they lived or died. Soldiers in the Battle of the Bulge lived on intimate terms with the tools of their trade or they perished at the hand of those of the enemy.

Small Arms

The basic weapon of the infantry on both sides was the rifle and in the case of the German volksgrenadiers, the machine pistol. The German rifles, the *Mauser Gewehr 98* and *Karabiner 98K*, were bolt action models virtually identical to that used by the Kaiser's soldiers in World War I. They could be very effective weapons when used by well trained soldiers. The Mauser

had a rather clumsy bolt-action, however, and when used by poorly trained conscripts its rate of fire and accuracy suffered when compared to the U.S. semi-automatic rifle, the Garand M-1. This excellent 9.5 lb weapon was accurate and reliable with a long effective range of over 500 meters.

General Patton called the M-1 "the greatest battlefield implement ever devised." A trained rifleman could fire off its eight-round .30 caliber clip in about twenty seconds. One minor defect of the Garand was the ejection of the eight-round clip when it was expended. Often the clip sailed through the air for several feet, striking frozen ground with a distinctive ringing sound. Alert German soldiers sometimes took advantage of such a moment to get in a free shot while the Garand owner struggled to get his new clip in place. The British rifle, the Lee-Enfield was similar to the German Mauser, although shorter and with a superior bolt action giving it a somewhat improved rate of fire, but lacking when compared with the American M-1.

The U.S. Army was a leading advocate of the semi-automatic rifle philosophy in WW II, pointing to the supply difficulties that fully automatic weapons might introduce. On the other hand, some, such as General William DePuy, were critical of this philosophy. General DePuy was a division commander in Vietnam who had previously led a battalion of the 90th Division in the Ardennes.

> The M-1 rifle was a precision weapon, but there were no precision targets. The rifle, coupled with the marksmanship program, worked to discourage active firing in combat by the average soldier. He was trained to shoot at and hit a target, but in combat, in the attack, he rarely ever saw a target. So, he was indisposed to shoot. The Germans, on the other hand, used machine pistols which were area weapons. They sprayed the area ahead of them and achieved fire superiority which we now call suppression.

The U.S. Garand M-1 semi-automatic rifle. A skilled GI could fire off 20 well aimed shots per minute to a range of about 600 meters.

The Germans had learned in Russia that most infantry fire fights were resolved at ranges of less than 300 meters under chaotic conditions. They also learned that the lethality of the battlefield in the 1940s had increased to the point that a rapid volume of fire counted for more than steady marksmanship — a careful rifleman might not live through the process of firing well aimed shots. This was a lesson that the Americans did not have the benefit of learning before 1943.

Because of this, the Germans in 1944 enjoyed a considerable superiority in automatic weapons. The *Sturmgewehr 44* assault rifle was an extremely significant development from this lesson. It had good accuracy and either semi-automatic or a high cyclic rate of fully automatic fire. The weapon fired special short 7.92mm rounds which reduced gun size and ammunition weight. It also resulted in less upward recoil when firing automatic bursts. It had an effective range of over 1,000 meters in semi-automatic fire. For the offensive, the *MP-44* was provided in large numbers and was the most common German infantry weapon in the Ardennes. Such firearms were more appropriate to the

German radio. Volksgrenadier operates a Berta two-part radio set.

skills of many of the inexperienced German troops in late 1944 than the old Mauser.

The German Luftwaffe paratroops fighting in the Ardennes possessed another advanced weapon of the same sort —the *Fallschirmjäger Gewehr 42* assault rifle. This light weapon (10 lbs) was a remarkably well designed weapon. It also fired the 7.92mm ammunition in either semi- or fully-automatic fire (600 rpm).

The American .30 caliber Browning Automatic Rifle (B.A.R.) was similar in capability to the German assault rifles. Although considerably heavier (17 lbs) than the German weapons, and possessing a violent recoil, it was still much coveted by the U.S. infantry who worked the war without an alternative light machine gun. It fired either in semi- or fully-automatic mode (550 rpm) with a 20-round magazine. Since there was no simple provision for changing barrels in the field, fully-automatic fire was out of the question.

Squad leaders in German formations were often supplied with the *MP-40* submachine gun. This weapon had an effective range of only about 100 meters and its recoil tended to scatter the shots from its 32-round magazine. Even so, the "Burp gun" was quite effective for in-close fighting. Like the *MP-44* assault rifle, such weapons tended to inspire confidence in their user since even erratic automatic fire from a single machine pistol could keep the heads down of an entire enemy squad in close contact. Accordingly, the machine gun became a primary German infantry weapon. The ratio of automatic *Sturmgewehr* and submachine guns to rifles in a German rifle company in 1940 was 1 to 11 while by 1944 it had increased to 1.3 to 1 in the German volksgrenadier company.

The U.S. sub-machine guns were somewhat inferior, partially stemming from the American aversion to these "gangland" weapons when the war opened. The M-3 "grease gun" was very inaccurate, tended to jam frequently and had a low cyclic rate of fire (400 rpm). Better was the U.S. Thompson "Tommy gun" sub-machine gun, which was more reliable

and better made with a rapid cyclic rate of fire of 650 rounds per minute. Both American weapons fired heavy .45 caliber slugs. Expensive to manufacture, the light 11-pound Thompson was often used by platoon leaders and always in demand. Although crude in appearance, the British Sten Mark 2 sub-machine gun was cheap, easy to make and acceptable in performance. It fired its 32-round magazine at a rate of up to 450 rounds per minute.

Both sides used semi-automatic pistols. Again the primary German models, the P-38 *Walther* and the *Luger*, had superior accuracy over the American Colt 45 caliber although the bullet from the U.S. weapon had twice the weight of the German 9mm rounds. The British wielded a sturdy and accurate .38 caliber Welby revolver as a side arm during the war.

Heavy Weapons

The heavy weapon category includes the infantry support weapons such as machine guns, mortars and rockets. They were typically an indigenous part of the typical infantry battalion and contained a large fraction of their firepower.

The Germans had a decided advantage in their machine guns. Not only were they lighter with a higher rate of fire, but the tactics developed for their use were superior to the way the Allies used them. The oft shown movie scene of desperate U.S. infantry grappling with a German machine gun nest is accurate. Infantry tactics on a small unit level in the German army were built around the machine gun as a base of firepower. The main German machine gun in 1944 was the 7.92mm *MG-42* which was light enough to be carried by a single grenadier. When crew served with a tripod and link belts, the Germans considered it a heavy machine gun and capable of indirect support fire. It was a very powerful weapon with a rate of fire of 1,200 rpm and an effective range of over 500 meters. The Germans often placed them in enfilade or flank positions and sited on reverse slopes even if it meant reducing the arc of fire — at 250 meters the Allied artillery could not be used against them without endangering their own troops.

The dreaded MG42 machine gun. The portability of this weapon is effectively demonstrated by the young SS machine gunner who is moving the gun forward with its bi-pod. Nicknamed "Hitler's Saw" by German troops, the gun featured an incredible 1,200 rpm rate of fire and possessed an effective range of between 600 and 3,500 meters, the greater range based on use of a tripod to steady the 26 pound gun.

The Allies used .30 caliber and .50 caliber machine guns (450 rpm) although both were much heavier and neither was so versatile as the German weapon. The .50 caliber M2 weapon did have one advantage; its huge bullets had a shattering impact. The British had a good light machine gun in their Bren Gun Mark 1. It fired .303 caliber ammunition at 500 rpm from a 30 cartridge clip. For heavy work, the tripod mounted Vickers Mk 1 water cooled model was available (40 lbs). With belt fed ammunition, this gun could fire 450 rpm continuously.

Both armies used a French made Brandt 81mm mortar to augment infantry firepower. Mortars may have been the deadliest weapon — they often fell with little warning. Casualty statistics from the European theater reveal that about 60% of all American casualties were caused by shell fragments, and mortar shell fragment wounds were consistently higher than those from artillery. The workhorse 81mm mortar had a range of 3,000 meters and were 50% lethal within 10 meters of impact. The Germans had an advantage in their large 120mm mortar with a maximum range of 5,000 meters which was seriously inaccurate after 3,000. Even so, it was greatly feared by those who had experienced its bombardment. Its 35 lb bomb was 50% lethal within 20 meters. The Americans also had a smaller portable Brandt 60mm mortar, although its lethality left something to be desired.

Artillery

The field artillery of both armies was quite similar. However, in its application, the Allied armies had a decided advantage in their better communications and fire control. The basic piece of both armies was the 105mm howitzer. Typically a 105mm

Correctly classified as a "heavy" weapon, U.S. Browning Automatic .50 calibre machine gun weighed in at 129 pounds. However, its 1,800 meter range and the shattering impact of its large slugs made it a deadly weapon.

American 81mm mortar position. Mortars provided much of the fire power for the infantry and were greatly feared by soldiers of both sides. A real difference between the U.S. and German mortarmen is illustrated here. The Americans were both well supplied with ammunition and an effective communications network with which to increase fire effectiveness.

artillery battalion (12 pieces) was married to the individual infantry regiments and formed the bulk of those units' firepower. The impact of such shells was 50% lethal within a range of twenty meters. The 105mm howitzer had a range of about 10 kilometers while the 150mm and 155mm pieces could hurl a shell about twice that far. In the American doctrine, the 150mm pieces were most often used as an offensive weapon, while the 105s were used both for barrage and defensive fire. The 90 lb shells of the 150mm guns were 50% lethal within 30 meters of impact although they took much longer to reload than the 105mm rounds.

Non-divisional artillery groups (*Volksartillerie Korps* in the case of the Germans) typically had the larger caliber tubes. Both sides used a 203mm (8 inch) gun which could fire a 250 pound shell a distance of 25 kilometers. The Germans tended to specialize in the larger weapons with 170mm and 210mm cannon that could fire a distance of 30 km.

The Germans also relied heavily on multiple tubed rocket launchers or *Nebelwerfer*. These had five or six tubes, weighed about 2,000 lbs and were easily towed behind other vehicles. There were three versions — 150mm, 210mm and 300mm, each with a short effective range of between 5,000 and 8,000 meters. The launchers were organized into *Werfer* brigades with 108 launchers of various calibers. The *werfers* had considerable firepower. When fully loaded a salvo of such a brigade could land 600 high explosive shells in the target area in a minute and a half! The suddenness of such a barrage (there typically was no registration) was deadly for anyone who happened to be walking about.

"Short Snort" was an American 105mm Howitzer. This trusty weapon provided fearsome firepower to the American ground forces in the Ardennes. Each U.S. infantry regiment had a battalion of 12 guns assigned to it to provide artillery shells on call.

On the debit side, the *wefers* were short ranged, took a long time to load, were very inaccurate and left a prominent back blast which invited prompt counter battery fire. However, when used for saturation fire prior to attack, they were probably more effective than anything else. Short on prime movers, the lighter werfers were a major factor in carrying German firepower along with the armored spearheads. This later point must be emphasized for all German artillery. The theoretical performance of the weapons was overshadowed by a lack of transport and fuel to move the guns in the wake of the offensive and the corresponding drought of ammunition supply resulting from the same problem.

Anti-Tank Weapons

The main weapon for both sides was the 75mm or 76mm gun in towed and self-propelled versions. The German weapon could knock out any of the Allied tanks, while the Allied weapon was good against all but the Panther or Tiger in frontal attack. The U.S. was stuck with an obsolete 57mm piece in the infantry divisions that was only good against German armor from the sides or flanks. The Germans had an excellent weapon in their 88mm gun. The towed version had an extremely high rate of fire and great accuracy. The Americans had a similar capability in their 90mm anti-aircraft gun which was successfully adapted to a Sherman chassis as the M-36 tank destroyer. It could take on even the heaviest of the German armor.

Both sides used towed versions of these guns and lost them in large numbers. On the other hand, the self-propelled anti-tank weapons fared much better in the Ardennes fighting. The two armies took different approaches on how the guns were mounted. The Germans opted for heavily armored hulls with no turret and limited gun transverse (*Hetzer, Sturmgeschütz, Jagdpanzer, Jagdpanther, Jagdtiger*). The Allies mounted their guns on a thinly armored turret that was open on the top. The U.S. TDs were the 76mm M-10 and M-18 and the 90mm M-36. The Germans went for the "ambush

"Screaming Meemie." Although inaccurate and short-ranged, the Germans relied on these rapid-firing six-barreled 150mm rocket launchers to provide them with firepower for their advancing mobile forces. The nickname came from the fearsome whistling sound the rockets made after being launched.

The famous German "88." This high velocity anti-aircraft gun proved a deadly adversary for allied armor throughout the war in Europe.

and slug it out" school of anti-tank tactics with heavy well sloped armor while the American TD philosophy can be best described as "hit and run." Generally, the German vehicles did better in a protracted armor versus armor battle, while the American TDs performed well in closed terrain where they could hide. In a pinch tank destroyers could be used offensively and the Germans had developed a fairly sophisticated doctrine for their use in this respect. The German vehicles did better in this role since the open topped U.S. TDs were susceptible to well placed grenades and artillery bursts. The German way of using these vehicles in attack made them surprisingly effective (in many instances, German *Sturmgeschütz* would be called

"Tigers" by frightened Allied soldiers). They moved offensively, but then fought defensively, often using a retreating reconnaissance team to lure the Allied tanks to the hidden guns.

Anti-Aircraft Weapons

Both armies had found in World War II that the anti-aircraft arm was not only good for shooting down planes; it could be quite powerful in a ground role — particularly in the defense. The Americans, with an unfortunate aversion to dual purpose weapons, had learned from experience that their smaller caliber anti-aircraft weapons made a deadly machine gun. The Germans took advantage of this too, but went a step further in that they also had a highly developed tactical doctrine for use of their larger 88mm weapons. This even included the use of the guns in a ground assault role using a leapfrog fire and maneuver tactic that is now called "overwatch" by modern day doctrine. The guns that found it possible to shoot down planes at a height of over 3,000 meters moving 400 mph, handily dealt with

American soldiers man-handle a towed 57mm anti-tank gun into position on a muddy Ardennes road. The 57mm proved virtually ineffective against German armor and was lost in large numbers.

German Sturmgeschütz III Ausf G at Kaiserbaracke crossroads. Note the MG 42 machine gun mounted on top and the Saukopf (sow's head) gun mantlet.

slower moving ground assaults of tanks and infantry at lesser distances.

The main German anti-aircraft or flak consisted of 20mm, 37mm and 88mm pieces. The 20mm pieces were sometimes mounted on a Mk IV tank chassis called a *Wirbelwind* that moved with the panzer divisions. The German flak was trained for use in a dual role, both against aircraft and ground targets. The flak arm was fully motorized and well supplied with ammunition. A rapid rate of fire (a well trained crew for an 88mm could fire 15 rounds per minute) and high quality optics made this a formidable ground weapon. However, during the latter part of December the German flak was usually quite busy dealing with Allied airplanes.

The American anti-aircraft battalions consisted mainly of 90mm guns, 40mm "Bofors" guns and .50 caliber machine guns. The rapid fire quadmount .50 caliber guns ("Meat Choppers") were mounted on halftracks and often used to protect the divisional artillery or assist the infantry in defence. The 40mm and 90mm guns were often used to guard supply depots, lines of communication and bridges from any German aircraft. Another problem for the anti-aircraft people was that their transportation (prime movers) were part of the corps pools and often were in use by engineers and artillery battalions towing ordnance around the Ardennes. However, in the first desperate days of the German assault, some of the guns were pressed into service against German armor near the U.S. First Army headquarters.

Tanks

Although the Ardennes offered poor terrain for their employment, both sides used tanks in the Ardennes in large numbers. The Germans knew this and were trying to get their armored spearheads out of the Eifel as quickly as possible and into more open Ardennes plateau to the west. When the German infantry was unable to overpower the Americans in the *Sixth Panzer Armee* sector, however, they committed their tanks to battle on the second day to try to decide the issue. To the south von Manteuffel decided to commit his tanks at the opening

A Flak Panzer IV "Wirbelwind" of the 1st SS Panzer Division in action in Honsfeld. The vehicle was armed with four 2 cm rapid fire anti-aircraft guns. The German tankers are firing with a Gewehr 98 rifle, a Walther pistol and an MP-40 sub-machine gun.

"Meatchoppers." Quad-mount .50 calibre machine guns of the 11th Armored Division in action near Neaufchâteau on New Year's Day, 1945.

gun. He reasoned that reducing the armored losses was less important than a rapid breakout. Although a compromise, this turned out to be the right decision.

The main U.S. armored vehicle was the 75mm M-4 Sherman. It had several undesirable characteristics. Its relatively low velocity gun was unable to deal with any of the heavier German tanks while its protective armor (combat weight was 30 tons) was pierced with ease by any of the German weapons. It also easily caught fire when hit, earning it the unflattering German nickname of the "Ronson." On the other hand, the Sherman was extremely reliable (nearly half the German tank losses were from mechanical breakdowns) and fast with a rapid turret transverse. Sherman's greatest advantage for the Allies however, was numbers. Each U.S. armored division on paper had 186 of them and even the U.S. infantry divisions had a battalion of 53. Further, their reliability meant

A M-4A1 Sherman tank of the 750th Tank Battalion leads a column of the 75th Infantry Division in the Bulge, January 10, 1945.

that often the divisions had 80-90% of their TO&E strength.

The M4A3 with a higher velocity 76mm gun was beginning to appear in greater numbers in the ETO, but the M4A1 was still the dominant type. There was also the British version of the Sherman, the "Firefly," which had mounted a high velocity 17 pounder gun that could knock out any of the German tanks. It was only available in relatively small quantities. Each armored division also had 70 light M-5 Stuart tanks. With a feeble 37mm gun as main armament and armor that could be endangered even by heavy infantry weapons, the M-5 could hardly be considered a tank as much as it was a light reconnaissance vehicle.

The Germans had three main battle tanks. The Mk IV, the workhorse of the entire war, was a good vehicle with a high velocity 75mm gun (considerably superior to the weapon on the Sherman). Its armor was not

Crew of an M5A1 "Stuart" light tank of the 759th Tank Battalion eat K-ratios around a fire on December 30th, 1944. The puny 37mm gun on the tank and its thin armor made them nearly worthless in armored engagements with German tanks. Note the crew's Thompson sub-machine guns standing ready against the tree.

heavy, however (25 tons), and poorly sloped. It was generally on equal footing with the U.S. M4.

The Mk V "Panther" was probably the best tank of the war. It was surprisingly nimble for a 45 ton tank, extremely well armored and mounted a high velocity 75mm gun. It was generally the German favorite for the Ardennes fighting and relatively immune to the Sherman in frontal attack.

The Mk VI Tiger had a fearsome reputation, mounting, as it did, the 88mm anti-aircraft gun and with extremely heavy armor. The Tiger I, of which only perhaps twenty fought in the Ardennes, weighed 60 tons with very heavy armor. The Tiger II or *Königstiger*, was the more numerous tank in the Ardennes (perhaps 50 Tiger IIs fought in the campaign). It featured still heavier, well sloped armor, although its weight (71 tons) made for trouble in finding suitable bridges. The Tigers were also slow and somewhat clumsy. Even so, they were more than a match for any Allied tank. Still prone to mechanical trouble after years of development, more Tigers broke down in the field than were destroyed in combat. Both the Panther and Tiger had a serious disadvantage for the German army in 1944. They were terrible gas hogs with their fuel efficiency measured in gallons per mile. Many of the German panzer losses in the battle occurred in its later phases when tanks were left by the roadside for lack of fuel.

Vehicles

The Allies were well equipped with the 1/4, 1/2, 1-1/2 and 2-1/2 ton trucks, jeeps and many other vehicles. The GMC 2.5 ton truck was especially numerous. As a result of a program of "efficiency through waste," they had few problems with transportation.

The Germans had three main models — the Opel, "Blitz" Damiler-Benz and French Ford models. However, a severe shortage of all types forced them to use Czech and Italian models for which few spare parts were available. Even with these measures, there were not enough to go around and a number of the panzer divisions were forced to put a battalion of their grenadiers on bicycles.

Signal Equipment

Both combatants emphasized the use of radio communications, although the Allied forces had far surpassed the Germans in this area by late 1944. The fact that both armies were almost always on the move in the Ardennes made the field telephone of limited use. Much of the existing American network was shot out on the morning of December 16th by the enemy artillery barrage. Even more problematic, the broken terrain and inclement weather served to reduce effective radio communications range by at least half. This often left forward military formations on their own.

With an enemy superiority in tank and automatic weapons, the American infantry relied on radio communications with friendly artillery to help establish U.S. fire superiority in battle. The importance of this ability to coordinate massed artillery fires as part of the success of American military doctrine cannot be overemphasized. Two FM radios produced in 1943 became the cornerstone of American communications. The SCR (Signal Corps Radio)-300 was a thirty-two pound piece that could be carried as a backpack by a single GI and could transmit five miles under optimum conditions. The other radio was a walkie-talkie, the SCR-536 which, as its name indicated, was a completely portable six pound hand set with a nominal range of one mile. Every U.S. rifle platoon had one of these sets. At the other end of the spectrum, an SCR-399 kept the divisional headquarters in touch with corps and army with a hundred mile range and a transmitter so large that it required a separate truck and accompanying generator. All the communications were tied in together to the artillery network fire direction center, or FDC, so that when necessary a single U.S. rifle platoon could enlist the help of all 48 guns in the division's rear if the fire mission was approved. The real problem in the Ardennes was that the Frequency Modulated (FM) signal of the smaller transmitters was "line of sight" which meant that the intended listener might not receive if the transmitter was in a defile or on the other side of a hill. Then too, German eavesdroppers often found that they

could make considerable use of the American habit of openly transmitting messages that belied their identity and future intentions. As always, U.S. artillery observers (FOs) were favorite German targets.

Theoretically, German equipment was of quality similar to the American issue although not nearly so lavishly supplied, even in the tables of organization. To make matters worse, the Germans were experiencing notable shortages in all signal equipment in late 1944. On paper the German maneuver units down to a company level were equipped with wireless sets such as the Dora (4 km range) and the two-part Berta (10 km range). The sets were similar to the Allied equipment although substantially less plentiful. Most of the German infantry divisions were woefully short of radios. According to the commander of the *9th Volksgrenadier Division*:

> Our poor radio equipment was of more decisive importance for the artillery duel than the supply of ammunition. The artillery was equipped with intricate short-wave radio sets which the signal men were not accustomed to using. These sets failed entirely in the mountainous and wooded areas....The functioning of the telephone net became of particular importance. Wire connections with the front were sometimes repaired ten times per day....It is certain that if this deficiency in radio equipment did not exist, the artillery duel in the sector of the division would have been very different.

Other German formations discovered the lack of communications resulted in loss of control of maneuver elements once combat was joined. As one young volksgrenadier said upon his capture, "No one knows where anybody else is."

Other Weapons

Other weapons included flamethrowers, rocket launchers and hand grenades. Flamethrowers had a limited range (less than 50 meters) but a large psychological effect. They were typically employed by engineer units. The Germans had two main anti-tank rockets, both which were superior to the American 2.36 inch bazooka. The *Panzerfaust* was a 150mm

A Mk V Panther tank of the 116th Pan-zer Division immobilized after it struck a mine near the village of Trinal.

American GIs fire a 2.36" anti-tank rocket, or "Bazooka" at German Panther tank near the village of Rochefort.

than 100 meters. In the case of the American weapon against the heavier German tanks, the charge would only work if it hit the target just right. The British had another hollow charge weapon, the PIAT (Projector, Infantry, Anti-Tank). It was a spigot launcher using a heavy steel rod to fire a hollow charge bomb about 100 yards. It was unpleasant to fire and users had to approach dangerously close to hit an enemy tank.

Hand grenades were a favorite infantry weapon but rarely hurled more than 40 meters. The U.S. Mills Bomb or "pineapple" grenade was designed to be easy and accurate to toss. The deeply grooved metal casing was designed to explode into lethal fragments. The German Model 24 "potato masher" stick grenade consisted of a hollow wood handle with a metal encapsulated explosive at the other end. Once the pin or ignitor was pulled, the owner had four to five seconds to get rid of the grenade before it exploded. The Germans were fond of keeping the stick grenades in the top of their jackboots; the Americans commonly hung the grenades on

single shot rocket on a stick supplied in large numbers to the volksgrenadier units. It came in versions with 30, 60 and 100 meter ranges. The *Panzerbüchse 38* was similar to the American weapon but of larger caliber (88mm). All these weapons were employed often in the Ardennes by unsupported infantry faced with enemy tanks. Their use was exceedingly dangerous with an effective range of no more

their person suspended by the handles. Although they could often decide small unit actions, grenades were not nearly so lethal as Hollywood leads one to believe, typically stunning or wounding victims. They were most effective when used against an enemy ensconced in a building or pillbox where the concussion would be amplified. The Americans had an M-79 grenade launcher while the Germans used a *Sturmpistole* for the same purpose although both sides found hand thrown grenades to be most effective. Rifle grenades had a range of reasonable accuracy up to 100 yards.

Mines were a defensive weapon mainly useful after long periods of position improvement. They were of two main types — anti-personnel and anti-tank. Anti-personnel mines typically consisted of fragmentation charges releasing steel balls. Anti-tank mines, such as the German Tellermine, were pressure activated with 11 lbs of TNT to tear the tracks off tanks. The main problem with mines was their weight (it takes at least a ton of mines to cover a frontage of 100 meters) and time to lay them. In the Ardennes ground was frozen making laying them difficult; snow made the fields ineffective. It took at least 10 hours to place a ton of mines and three times that long to dig them up if the enemy didn't fall for the trap. Often mine fields were covered by fields of fire from other infantry weapons to increase the chances that the enemy would stumble into them. U.S. engineer units specialized in mine laying operations in the Ardennes.

Panzerfaust. A German soldier takes aim with his anti-tank rocket during the Ardennes battle.

"Delousing." Engineers carefully search a snow covered road for mines some five miles southeast of Vielsalm.

THE FIRST DAY:
"We March!"

On the prowl. Panther of the 2nd Kompanie, 2nd SS Panzer Division, *in action near Manhay, December, 1944.*

Oberstgruppenführer Sepp Dietrich (right), who would be in charge of the Sixth Panzer Armee in Wacht Am Rhein, *greets Oberführer Wilhelm Mohnke. Mohnke, then a regimental commander with the* Hitler Jugend *Division, would later lead the 1st SS Panzer Division in the Ardennes.*

The Sixth Panzer Armee

In the cold, pre-dawn darkness of Saturday, December 16th, 1944, a young SS grenadier jotted a hurried note to his sister in Germany:

> I write during one of the great hours before we attack, full of expectation for what the next days will bring. Everyone who has been here for the last two days and nights, who has witnessed hour after hour the assembly of our crack divisions, who has heard the constant rattling of our panzers, knows that something is up. We attack and throw the enemy from our homeland. That is a holy task!

Scrawling on the back of the envelope he added a last minute postscript: "Ruth! Ruth! Ruth! WE MARCH!"

Wacht am Rhein called for the main offensive effort to be made by "Sepp" Dietrich's *Sixth Panzer Armee* between Monschau and St. Vith. As befitted the *Absoluter Schwerpunkt*, the *Sixth Panzer* was by far the strongest of the three German armies. It contained five infantry-type divisions and four of the elite SS panzer divisions. Including support elements, the army totalled over 140,000 men, 1,025 corps artillery guns and rocket launchers and some 642 tanks and assault guns. This powerful force planned to crush American resistance from Monschau to Krewinkel and then race across the Meuse on both sides of Liège, then turning north to capture Antwerp.

There seems to have been some hope in Hitler's headquarters that Dietrich might reach the Meuse River within 24 hours, perhaps based on the halcyon German experience in 1940.[1] According to the plan, an infantry corps would be used to secure the right flank near Monschau while the steel of SS Gruppenführer (SS-Gruf.) Hermann Priess's *ISS Panzerkorps* would ram-rod through the U.S. line of the 99th Division to the south. The two SS divisions were then to rapidly advance to the Meuse along five designated panzer *Rollbahnen*, or tank rolling roads, designated A-E to the Meuse. The two panzer divisions of the *IISS Panzerkorps* would follow immediately in the wake of the two lead divisions.

Well aware of "Sepp" Dietrich's limitations as an army commander, Hitler had personally seen to it that a capable officer was assigned to the *Sixth Panzer Armee* as chief of staff. That man was Genmaj. Fritz Krämer, now honorifically endowed with the rank of SS Brigadeführer. As such,

Obersturmbannführer Joachim Peiper, commander of the prime German SS panzer spearhead. The leader of Kampfgruppe Peiper was awarded the Oak Leaves and Swords to the Iron Cross for his exploits in the Ardennes.

Krämer was charged with actually directing the main offensive effort. He worried that Hitler's time schedule for reaching the Meuse was unrealistic. He drove to the SS bivouac area near Euskirchen to speak with Obersturmbannführer Joachim Peiper, who was in charge of the *1st SS Panzer Regiment*, about the possibility of a tank column advancing 80 kilometers in a single night. Not one to speculate, Peiper personally test drove a Panther that distance on the evening of December 11th. It could be done, he told Krämer, but whether an entire panzer column could maintain such progress in enemy territory and over poor roads was another question. Peiper suspected that an offensive operation was in the wings; on December 13th, SS Gruppenführer Hermann Priess of the *ISS Panzerkorps*, informed the SS colonel about the true nature of his unit's presence in the Eifel. *Kampfgruppe Peiper* was to be the main armored spearhead for the attack in the Losheim Gap — a historic point of entry for German armies invading Belgium in 1914 and 1940.

Handsome, well educated and a devout Nazi, Peiper had developed a reputation for ruthless and daring armored attack; at the youthful age of 29 he had received Germany's

---

1 Part of this naive optimism must be blamed on General Jodl, who in planning his first military operation, reckoned on the German armor being able to cover 125 miles in one day. This estimate conveniently ignored the experience in Russia which had shown that advance rates over poor icy roads could not be expected to average more than a quarter of that figure.

highest honor for bravery in battle, the Knight's Cross of the Iron Cross. In Russia the SS colonel's unit earned the epithet "blowtorch battalion" because his men burned the Soviet village of Pekartschina to the ground to forward their advance. Faintly surprised to still be alive in December 1944 (most of his comrades were long since dead or captured), Peiper found himself in charge of Hitler's name sake panzer regiment. Contemptuous of superiors who had not experienced the ferocity of modern tank battle, his command once claimed 2,500 killed with only three prisoners — a testament to the brutal savagery of battle on the Eastern Front. Already a legend in the German Army, Peiper demanded almost suicidal devotion from this soldiers; casualties in his command were always high.

In Ardennes, he was told, he would receive "the decisive role in the offensive." SS Obfh. Wilhelm Mohnke, Peiper's divisional commander, related that Hitler had expressed special confidence in "his Leibstandarte" in conference at Bad Nauheim on December 12th and expected it to "fight fanatically." Krämer with his eyes on the Meuse was more to the point. "Drive fast," he told the young SS colonel, "and hold the reins loose."[2]

In the murky pre-dawn fog of December 16th, commanders at all echelons read to their sleepy troops a personal message from their commander, Sepp Dietrich:

> Soldiers of the *Sixth Panzer Armee*! The moment of decision is upon us. The Führer has placed us at the vital point. It is for us to breach the enemy front and push beyond the Meuse. Surprise is half the battle. In spite of the terror bombings, the Home Front has supplied us with tanks, ammunition and weapons. We will not let them down.

The hundred huge panzers of *Kampfgruppe Peiper* stood waiting on the forest-lined Blankenheim road in a long serpentine column. The engines of the juggernauts coughed to life minutes before the beginning of the great attack. "Good-bye Lieutnant," said one German tank commander to another man standing in the turret of the big panzer behind him, "See you in America!"

A Flak 18 gun, firing as field artillery, shells the American front line, December 16th, 1944.

Precisely at 5:30 A.M. on that Saturday morning the Germans opened a tremendous artillery barrage along the length of the 85-mile "ghost front" and hammered American positions for thirty minutes.

> "The barrels of the artillery are pointed toward the cloud shrouded dark sky....Clutching their stopwatches the commanding officers in the firing positions follow the passing time. The front is yet quiet. The nocturnal silence is interrupted only by the occassional salvo of an enemy battery. Suddenly, all of the German barrels roar out in a raging fire, the sky vibrates with the glaring lights of the endless firing of flak, mortars, howitzers, guns and rockets. The crews release shell after shell from the gun barrels. The target areas are being pulverized by a hail of steel....Along the enemy front the clouds have turned red with the flames of burning farm buildings.

At 6:00 A.M. the cannonade ceased and squad after squad of gray-clad German infantry advanced out of the fog and mists of the Eifel. The American troops were completely taken by surprise. With communications disrupted by the artillery barrage and radios jammed by a tirade of German marches, most isolated U.S. units believed that they were experiencing strong enemy patrol actions on their front. They nervously huddled in their frozen foxholes or log huts while artillery shells whistled overhead exploding in a deafening roar. To add to the disquiet, German searchlights flicked on, bouncing their beams off the low hanging clouds to eerily change night to twilight. All the while, Hitler's robot V-1 "buzz bombs" roared overhead bound for Liège.

Nearby the quaint resort village of Monschau, some 20 miles southeast of Aachen, the Germans organized their northernmost attack in the *Sixth Panzer Armee*. Responsibility fell to the *LXVII Armeekorps* under the leadership of Gen. Lt. Otto Hitzfeld. Hitzfeld and his staff were informally known as *Korps Monschau* after the historic German town that was just to the other side of the line on their front.

The German plan called for an assault between Konzen and Kalterherberg by two volksgrenadier divisions. After breaching the American line they advanced northwest to the Vesdre River on the outskirts of Eupen. Along this natural barrier they built a fortified line to fend off U.S. counterattacks against the right flank of the *Sixth Panzer Armee*. Though not overly ambitious, the modest plan faced difficulty due to the chaotic conditions prevalent on the Western Front.

By December 13th, Hitzfeld's northernmost division, the *272nd Volksgrenadier Division*, was itself under attack by Maj. Gen. Edwin P. Parker's newly arrived U.S. 78th Division. The Americans were fighting to capture Kesternich some seven miles northeast of Monschau. The costly house-to-house combat for this gloomy little village surged back and forth inconclusively for days. As a consequence, other than a series of sporatic counterattacks against Kesternich on the 15th, Genlt. Eugen König's *272nd Volksgrenadiers* provided little in the way of assistance for the fight for the corner at Monschau. König, who had just taken over the *272nd*, had

---

2   Upon being assigned Rollbahn D, Peiper examined the narrow, at times unpaved, road on a map and sarcastically declared it "suitable not for tanks but for bicycles!"

Maj. Gen. Edwin P. Parker, addresses young soldiers of the U.S. 78th Infantry Division on German soil near Monschau in early December, 1944.

his hands full with the U.S. 78th Division.

Thus, the final plan for *Korps Monschau* devolved into an improvised assault by four infantry battalions of the *326th Volksgrenadier Division*. The other two battalions of Obst. Erwin Kaschner's division were unavailable, one having been sent to shore-up the nearly broken German line at Kesternich. The other had managed to get lost in the woods. Even the divisional replacement battalion was stuck defending Wahlerscheid crossroads to the south.

The situation with equipment was similar. Hitler had personally earmarked a group of monster 70-ton *Jagdtiger* tank destroyers equipped with 128mm guns to assist *LXVII Armeekorps* in blocking American reinforcements along the Monschau-Eupen road. However air attacks blocked rail transport of the *653rd Heavy Panzerjäger Battalion* and it did not arrive in time to assist Hitzfeld. There were not even any assault guns immediately available, although there was plenty in the way of army level artillery — a full artillery corps and a *Volkswerfer* (rocket launcher) brigade. Even then, Genfldm. Model forbade his guns to shell the quaint

German village of Monschau. With its ancient timbered buildings, the village was a favorite spot for young honeymooners and aspiring German artists. The artillery had to fire to the north and south of the town. Some said the orders came from Hitler himself.

In the sector between Monschau and Losheim, the U.S. 2nd Infantry Division had been attacking the *277th Volksgrenadier Division* nearby since December 13th.[3] This was part of a larger American plan to seize the Roer dams in the vicinity. By the eve of the German offensive, the American division had captured a crucial road juncture in the advance on the dams. "Heartbreak Crossroads" was taken in a bold night attack near the customs post at Wahlerscheid southeast of Monschau on December 15th. This offensive pressure was instrumental in thwarting the German assault plan at Monschau, drawing off for defense, troops which had been planned for the attack.

The German objectives in the northernmost sector were held by the 3rd Infantry Battalion of the U.S. 395th Infantry at Höfen and the 102nd Armored Cavalry Group in and north of Monschau. At 5:30 A.M. the American line was pounded by very heavy artillery fire. As ordered, Monschau escaped the *Feuerwalze*, but many buildings in Höfen were flattened and the town was set ablaze. The bombardment

3   On the last night before the attack, the *326th Volksgrenadier Division's* replacement battalion had taken over the unenviable duty of defending this sector.

Panzer IVs of the 12th SS Panzer Regiment *at inspection. The "Hitler Jugend" Division would prove to be fanatical opponent for U.S. soldiers in the Ardennes.*

blanketed the forward American positions with drum-fire and then maintained a harassing shellfire on the known locations of enemy batteries. However, the damage from the intense shelling was superficial due to the well improved nature of the American fox-hole line. Many shells fell on abandoned positions due to the unobserved nature of the German fire. "The day began with a vicious shelling of our command post area by the Krauts," remembered an engineer of the U.S. 2nd Division. "All took refuge in basements of houses on our hill as we were plastered by some big stuff. No casualties to us."

Then at daybreak, the inexperienced German grenadiers moved forward towards Höfen in a wave-like herd. The American infantry had been alerted by the heavy German artillery fusillade, however, and waited until the enemy was at a deadly close range. On signal the Americans unleashed a withering fire on the German infantry emerging from their sally point near Rohren. Most of the German grenadiers were cut-down in the first wave, some of the infantry toppling into the foxholes from whence they had been shot. German efforts to nurture the drive later that morning only increased Hitzfeld's casualties. By noon the Americans had driven the Germans back with heavy losses. The commander of the *326th* estimated his casualties at 20% of his rifle strength. Meantime, several miles back, the *3rd Panzer Grenadier Division* waited as a *Heeresgruppe B* reserve, their commitment to battle keyed to the German capture of the road leading through Monschau. But there was no armored exploitation this day; the German infantry of *Korps Monschau*

had been decisively repulsed.

To the south of Wahlerscheid crossroads near Losheimergraben were the *277th* and the *12th Volksgrenadier Divisions* which had been loaned to the *ISS Panzerkorps* for the initial breakthrough. These attacks represented the point of the main effort by the *Sixth Panzer Armee*. The two infantry divisions were to open the way to three of the five *Panzer Rollbahnen*. Over these march routes the plan called for the waiting *12th SS "Hitler Youth" Panzer Division* with its 136 tanks and assault guns to rapidly advance to the Meuse River. The *12th SS* was to advance in five columns: on *Rollbahn A*; a reinforced battalion of the *25th SS Panzer Grenadier Regiment*; on *B, Kampfgruppe Müller* comprising the rest of the *25th SS Regiment* and the divisional anti-tank battalion. *Rollbahn C* had the bulk of the division assigned to its hard-surfaced road. This included *Kampfgruppe Kühlmann*, the reinforced panzer regiment, *Kampfgruppe Bremer*, the reconnaissance battalion and *Kampfgruppe Krause* with the *26th SS Panzer Grenadier Regiment* and the divisional support and supply columns. Obst. Wilhelm Viebig's *277th Volksgrenadiers* were to open panzer *Rollbahnen A* and *B* which ran through the town of Krinkelt over the Elsenborn Ridge before heading to the Meuse River.

The terrain in this sector was extremely difficult. Even after breaching the American line along the international boundary, the Germans had to push over or around the south flank of the Elsenborn ridge. The ridge was a series of elevated hills in the vicinity of a Belgian military training center near the border town of Elsenborn. The roads in the area were poor and the dense forests and boggy ground made off-road deployment of panzer troops impossible. Dietrich had wanted to breakthrough with his tanks, but had been overruled by Hitler who believed the armor must be preserved for the dash beyond the Meuse. However, given the poor training of the volksgrenadier divisions that were scheduled to open the holes for the panzers, this decision would later be seen as an egregious miscalculation.

The German infantry thrusts at daybreak against the 393rd Infantry Regiment of the 99th Division yielded some minor gains in the densely wooded forests, but could not push the Americans aside. Although short on combat experience, the infantry of the 99th Division put up a fierce fight in the day's action, suffering heavy casualties while inflicting a like number on the German enemy. Yet, the *277th Volksgrenadiers* had more men and committed their reserve regiment later in the day. This added wave of German grenadiers threatened to cave in the teetering American line

in the woods. The situation for the Americans was so grim at twilight that the U.S. V Corps commander of the north sector in the Ardennes, Maj. Gen. Leonard T. Gerow, sent up the reserve 23rd Regiment of the U.S. 2nd Division to shore up the defense of 393rd Regiment.[4] But the German frustration was greater; at the end of the day the panzers were no closer to the Meuse. The *277th Volksgrenadiers* could only report "slow progress with bitter forest fighting."[5]

The story immediately to the south was similar. *Panzer Rollbahn C*, the paved International Highway, went through

---

4 Somehow, the intelligence officer for the *Sixth Panzer Armee* had inaccurately estimated the defense in the Elsenborn area to consist of only "a single inexperienced division," the 99th. Missing in his assessment was the veteran 2nd Infantry Division which proved pivotal in the fight there.
5 The contribution of the *277th Volksgrenadiers* over the following days was minimal. Checking his division that night, General Viebig found that of 12 assault companies used, nine had lost their officers; his formation was badly disorganized.

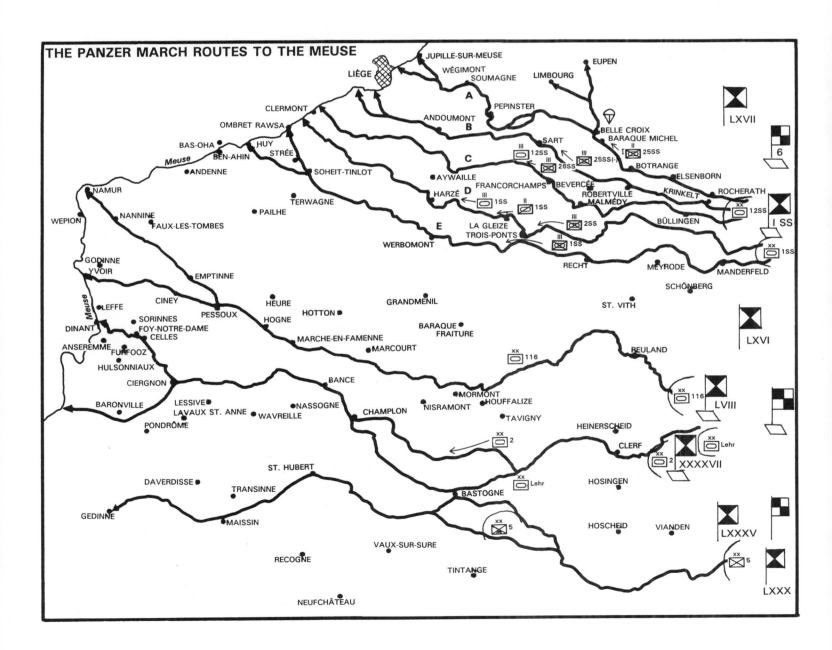

Honsfeld, Belgium, December 17th, 1944. The armored columns of Kampfgruppe Peiper *swiftly advance through the captured village.*

the village of Losheim to the border station at Losheimergraben and then on from Büllingen to Malmèdy and beyond to the Meuse. The entrance to this march route was to be opened by the *12th Volksgrenadier Division,* considered by the senior officers to be the best infantry formation in the *Sixth Panzer Armee.* The highway was to be the main advance route for the tanks of the *12th SS Panzer Division* and so was vitally important to the German effort.

Rapidly advancing in the wake of the pre-dawn artillery barrage, Genmaj. Gerhard Engel's *12th Volksgrenadiers* overwhelmed the U.S. outpost line and rushed into the town of Losheim by 9 A.M. However, efforts that afternoon to push along the highway to Losheimergraben and Buckholz degenerated into savage fighting in the dense Gerolstein forest. The U.S. 394th Infantry Regiment put up a valiant fight in the action; losses were severe on both sides. Most importantly, however, the German attacks did not break through to open the designated panzer march routes. As the dim light faded on the 16th, Maj. Gen. Walter E. Lauer's U.S. 99th Division was still in possession of every one of the *Panzer Rollbahnen.* Even worse for the Germans, the section of the highway that they did capture had a blown railway overpass that would have to be repaired before tanks could move.

Today the muddy firebreaks that cross the Krinkelter Wald evidence why the German armor had such trouble reaching the twin villages in strength along the Schwartzenbruch trail.

German SS panzer grenadiers of the "Hitler Jugend" division negotiate a boggy trail in the vicinity of Krinkelt.

German paratroopers of the 3rd Fallschirmjäger Division on march to the front.

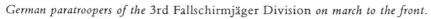

While the German infantry spent itself in the thick forests, the *12th SS Panzer Division* waited impatiently several miles back. "Sepp" Dietrich was visibly upset by the delay. At 12:45 P.M. he ordered that the SS troops were to move up, decide the fight and press on to the Meuse. Enough time had already been wasted; the German tanks were to blast through the American positions east of Krinkelt. "The *12th SS Panzer Division* with its advance units in Hollerath," went the confident noon report to Model's headquarters, "begins in half an hour to complete the breakthrough."

The Losheim Gap was along the south boundary of the *Sixth Panzer Armee.* More than anywhere else in the northern sector, the German forces heavily outnumbered the American forces here. The German soldiers that moved against the U.S. 14th Cavalry Group were from two regiments of the *3rd Fallschirmjäger Division.* The terrain was somewhat more favorable, being a sparsely wooded series of rolling hills several miles wide. But by daybreak Genmaj. Walther Wadehn's inexperienced German paratroopers were involved in a standoff with the American cavalrymen stubbornly fighting from halftracks, armored cars and dismounted machine guns. In a series of head-long attacks against the American strongholds at Afst, Krewinkel and Berterath, the German paratroopers suffered severe casualties and made little progress. Amid the bleak incoming reports, the chief of staff of *Heeresgruppe B* worried that "the *3rd Fallschirmjäger* does not seem too effective." The vitriol quickly moved down the chain of command from Model to Dietrich and finally to Hermann Priess. The orders were simple: Get the attack moving.

The commander of the *ISS Panzerkorps* wasted no time in following this edict. He promptly ordered the *1st SS "Leibstandarte Adolf Hitler* (Hitler's Own)" *Panzer Division* to march up. The two forward battlegroups of SS-Obf. Wilhelm Mohnke's division were to break through the American line quickly at any cost and thrust its 121 armored vehicles towards the Meuse.

Dietrich pinned high hopes on the heavily armored *Kampfgruppe Peiper.* During the morning the panzer spearhead was delayed by traffic jams, blown bridges and mines. But Peiper pushed his battle group forward ruthlessly, running other friendly troops that got in the way off the road. In the early morning hours of December 17th his SS soldiers broke free of the wild melee in the Losheim Gap near Lanzerath and bolted into the open behind American lines at Honsfeld. American resistance, Peiper radioed, had all but evaporated. He pointed his tanks west, and charged forward, oblivious to the melee he left in the village behind him.

Meanwhile, the other German SS attack force, a reinforced regiment of panzer grenadiers, *Kampfgruppe Hansen* (SS Standartenführer [SS-Standf.] Max Hansen), poured through the gap advancing to the south from Ormont to Manderfeld. Following in the wake of the SS columns, the *3rd Fallschirmjäger* advanced to Holzheim and Lanzerath the same night. The race to the Meuse was on.

Grim spoils of victory. German paratroopers of the 3rd Fallschirmjäger Division *advancing with Peiper, pause to remove the boots from dead U.S. soldiers killed in Honsfeld.*

The Fifth Panzer Armee

Of all the German generals that tried to change Hitler's plans for *Wacht am Rhein*, only the dimunitive panzer officer Gen. d. Pztrp. Hasso von Manteuffel was able to win any concessions about how the initial assault would be made. Von Manteuffel used the opportunity of the meeting with Hitler at the Reichschancellery in Berlin on December 2nd to discuss his concerns about the tactical plan. Most importantly, Von Manteuffel convinced Hitler that the extensive artillery preparation planned for the beginning of the attack would only serve to alert the enemy prematurely in his *Fifth Panzer Armee*. "Everybody knows that the American outpost guards sleep in the early morning hours," he told Hitler.

He also prevailed upon the German leader to allow him to commit two of his panzer divisions along the Our River from the starting gun. As von Manteuffel envisioned his attack scheme, he would send specially trained shock companies to infiltrate the enemy line in the pre-dawn mist "like rain-drops." The ground assault would be aided by artificial moonlight created by bouncing giant searchlights off the low-hanging clouds. When the German guns did bombard the American foxhole line at daylight, many of the American defenders would find that German grenadiers had already wormed in behind their positions.

Another advantage to von Manteuffel was the very thin American line in the *Fifth Panzer Armee* attack sector. In the wake of his assault would be the untested U.S. 106th Division which had been in the Ardennes for scarcely a week and two tired regiments of the Maj. Gen. Norman D. Cota's 28th Infantry Division, recovering from terrible losses in the Hürtgen forest.

Von Manteuffel knew he was playing second fiddle to Hitler's love of Dietrich's *Waffen SS* in the *Sixth Panzer Armee*. The diminuative panzer general preferred not to have SS divisions under his command, which he considered insubordinate. Still, he was less than pleased with the strength of his troops, which in his opinion, were far too weak to reach Antwerp. Even so, he would have four infantry, three panzer divisions and a panoply of support troops with some 90,000 men, 963 guns and rocket launchers and 396 tanks and assault guns. This substantial force was to face five U.S. infantry regiments with a smattering of support troops — an impressive superiority of strength by any accounting.

To the north, von Manteuffel planned an encirclement of the U.S. untried 106th Infantry Division with his *LXVI Armeekorps* under the command of Gen. d. Art. Walter Lucht. Lucht's forces were weak for a German corps, even in 1944. He had only two partly experienced volksgrenadier divisions (20,000 men), a meager allotment of corps artillery and 42 assault guns. To his advantage, Lucht, his staff and

Obst. Günther Hoffmann-Schönborn's *18th Volksgrenadier Division* were very familiar with the terrain, having occupied this part of the Eifel salient since late October. Lucht intended to use the open ground in the Losheim Gap with which to pass the two regiments of the *18th Volksgrenadier Division* and the self-propelled guns of the *244th Sturmgeschütz Brigade* right alongside the *3rd Fallschirmjäger* advance to the north. The left hook of the encirclement was to be carried out by the other regiment of the *18th*. With these forces he planned to surround the two regiments of the U.S. 106th Infantry Division that were defending just east of the Our River. After picking this plum, he would rapidly

General Hasso von Manteuffel, the commander of the Fifth Panzer Armee. *Von Manteuffel was an experienced leader who had serious doubts of Hitler's* Wacht Am Rhein *plan. The small panzer general had fought with Rommel in the desert and chalked up a dazzling record of accomplishments in the war in Russia.*

advance a few miles to the west to seize the road center of St. Vith before continuing northwest towards the Meuse.

The pincers attack proceeded according to plan that morning. One U.S. officer surveying the scene that afternoon reported the Losheim Gap was "crawling with Krauts." In spite of "bitter fighting" in the border villages of Roth, Kobscheid, Weckerath and Auw, the infantry assault broke the right flank resistance of the U.S. 14th Cavalry Group to the north. The infantry and assault guns pierced through to the hamlet of Andler on the Our River by the morning of the 17th. The other jaw of the pincers reported it had captured Oberlascheid, west of the U.S. troops in the Schnee Eifel, at 3:00 P.M. By nightfall of the first day the German infantry were already pushing to the rear of the 422nd and 423rd U.S. Infantry Regiments on the Schnee Eifel and routing the VIII Corps artillery that were emplaced behind them. However, another first day objective, the prize of St. Vith, eluded Lucht and von Manteuffel. Without armor, the *LXVI Armeekorps* had its hands full closing the trap on the U.S. 106th Division.

The other regiment of the 106th just to the south, the 424th, was more fortunate than its twins, not being located in such a dangerous salient. The 424th came under assault by Obst. Friedrich Kittel's green *62nd Volksgrenadier Division* and a panzer grenadier regiment of the *116th Panzer Division*. The attack erupted into an intense small arms duel in the darkness near Heckhuscheid-Berg along the German border. The volksgrenadiers took the high ground north of Eigelscheid and edged in close to Winterspelt, but could not reach Heckhuscheid. Moreover, the fighting went poorly

for the panzer grenadiers in front of Grosskampenberg. The first light of dawn revealed a shock company of the German infantry in front of the covered American positions. The grenadier assault company was shot to pieces and the 424th held its ground.

During the day, the commander of the 106th Division, Maj. Gen. Alan W. Jones took undue comfort in the fact that other than the Losheim Gap, the German advance in his sector had been repulsed or contained. Although possessing a distinguished life-time career with the army, Jones, like his division, had no combat experience. When the VIII Corps commander, Maj. Gen. Troy Middleton, told him that night to use his discretion in removing the two regiments from the Schnee Eifel, Jones elected to stay.[6] After all, he had been told that a full combat command of the 7th Armored Division (54 tanks) would be at his disposal the following day. But all this proved wishful thinking. The yawning jaws of the German pincers were closing on the Schnee Eifel and the frictions of war would not deliver the 7th Armored according to the schedule in the Leavenworth Army School march tables.

A few miles south of the 106th Division was the 112th Regiment of the 28th Division. It was defending in heavily wooded terrain along the German border just east of the Our

6 In fact, the telephone connection between Middleton and Jones was unintentionally disconnected during this fateful conversation so that Jones may never have heard his superior's permission to pull his regiments from the Schnee Eifel. To compound his problems, Jones was suffering from angina and his son, Alan W. Jones, Jr., was with the 423rd Regiment out on the Schnee Eifel.

A GI mans a cold and lonely post covering the front line with a .30 calibre machine gun.

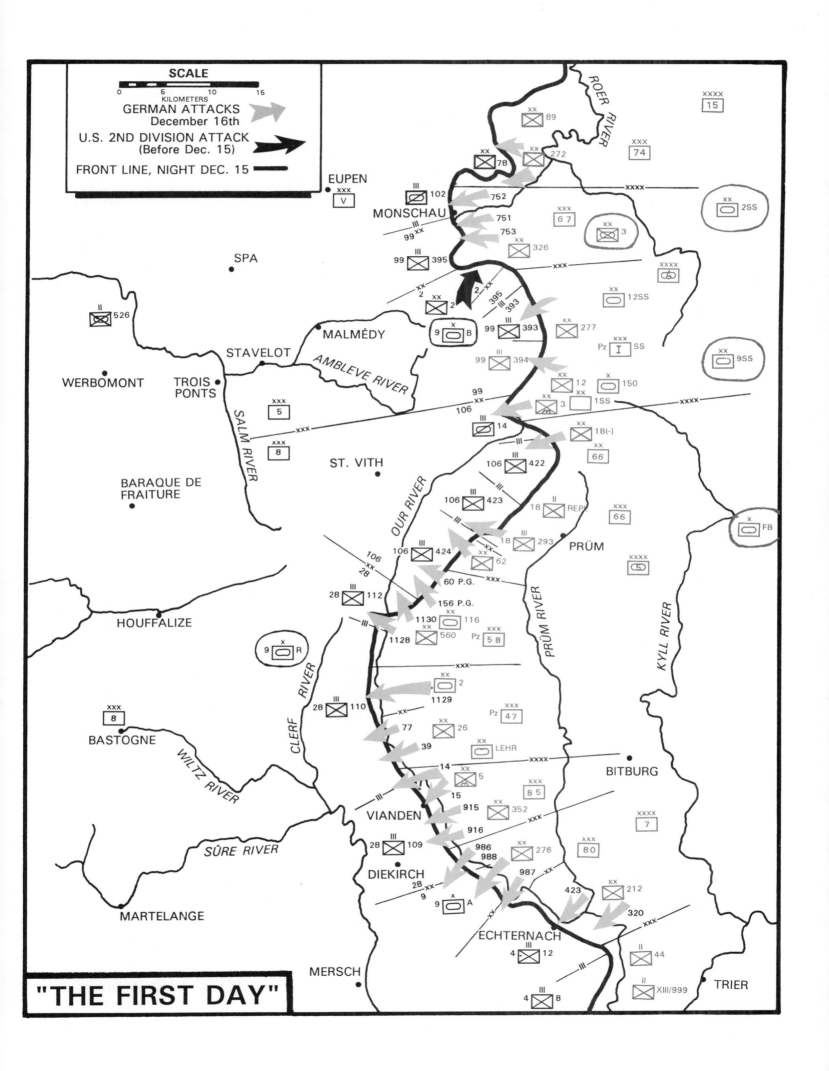

SCALE

0 5 10 15
KILOMETERS

GERMAN ATTACKS
December 16th

U.S. 2ND DIVISION ATTACK
(Before Dec. 15)

FRONT LINE, NIGHT DEC. 15

EUPEN

ROER RIVER

XXXX 15

XX 89

XXX 74

XX 78

272

V

III 102
MONSCHAU

752

751

753

XXX 67

XX 2SS

SPA

99 XX

99 III 395

753

XX 326

XX 3

2 XX 2

XX 2 2

395 III 393

XXX

XX 12SS

MALMÉDY

9 X B

99 III 393

XX 277

Pz I SS

XX 9SS

STAVELOT

AMBLEVE RIVER

99 III 394

WERBOMONT

TROIS PONTS

SALM RIVER

XXX 5

99 XX 106

XX 12

XX 150

XX 3 1SS

XXXX

XXX 8

III 14

XX 18(-)

XX 66

BARAQUE DE FRAITURE

ST. VITH

106 III 422

106 III 423

II 18 REP

XXX 66

OUR RIVER

106 III 424

18 III 293

PRÜM

X FB

XX 62

60 P.G.

XX 5

106 XX 28

156 P.G.

PRÜM RIVER

KYLL RIVER

HOUFFALIZE

28 III 112

1130 XX 116

9 X R

1128

XX 560

Pz 58

CLERF RIVER

28 III 110

X 2

1129

XX 77

XX 26

Pz XXX 47

XXX 8

BASTOGNE

39

XX LEHR

WILTZ RIVER

14

XX 5

BITBURG

15

XXX 85

VIANDEN

915

XX 352

XXX 7

SÛRE RIVER

916

28 III 109

986

988

XX 276

XXX 80

DIEKIRCH

987

423

XX 212

28 XX 9

9 X A

320

MARTELANGE

ECHTERNACH

4 III 12

II 44

MERSCH

4 III 8

II XIII/999

TRIER

"THE FIRST DAY"

River. This sole infantry regiment was the target of the German *LVIII Panzerkorps* under Gen. d. Pztrp. Walter Krüger. This was a panzer corps in name only, however. Krüger's forces amounted only to the inexperienced *560th Volksgrenadier Division* (Obst. Rudolf Langhaeuser) from garrison duty in Norway (of which one regiment was still in march on December 16th) and the understrength *116th Panzer Division* with only 83 operational tanks and assault guns. The usual corps artillery and volkswerfer brigade was available. Von Manteuffel pinned high hopes on Krüger's troops, however. Well aware of the good bridges to the rear of the U.S. troops east of the Our River, he believed that capture of these spans intact would give the panzer troops of Genmaj. Siegfried von Waldenburg's *116th Panzer Division* the fastest route to the Meuse River.

In the murky predawn the German assault began without an artillery preparation according to von Manteuffel's plan. The 112th was hit by both the *116th Panzer Division* and the *560th Volksgrenadier Division*. The attack by the corps from Heckhuscheid to Leidenborn was aimed at the bridges across the Our River at Reuland, Oberhausen and Ouren. The panzer regiment was to be thrown behind the first bridge captured.[7] The attack on the morning of the 16th faltered, mainly due to the captured German Westwall pillboxes that the Americans defenders occupied. The dragon's teeth there made it nearly impossible for the panzers to intervene. The single attempt to push tanks to the battle was stopped when flanking anti-tank fire from the 106th Division shot out five Mk IVs near Lützkampen. Without armored assistance, the panzer grenadiers took a beating near Welchenhausen and Harspelt along the east side of the Our River. At dark they were forced to pull back.

Just to the south of the *116th Panzer*, the righthand regiment of the *560th Volksgrenadier Division*, *Kampfgruppe Schumann*, was roughly handled in its first fight near Sevenig. After this rude indoctrination into battle, the green German infantry managed to seize the stone bridge over the Our River at Ouren, only to again lose it to a bold American counterattack. Meanwhile, a partially demolished bridge near Kalborn was seized by *Kampfgruppe Schmidt*, the other volksgrenadier regiment on the division's left. On closer inspection, however, it became obvious that it was too flimsy to support more than foot traffic. Losses in the German infantry ranks had been heavy; their commander estimated several hundred casualties in the first day's fighting.

Further south, the three divisions of Gen. d. Pztrp. Heinrich von Lüttwitz's *XLVII Panzerkorps* had to cross the Our River in order to get at the Americans. The U.S. positions were located on a highway ridgeline a couple of miles east of the river. The American soldiers, in deference to their fondness of driving, called the stretch "Skyline Drive." One German division, the *26th Volksgrenadier*, was determined to surprise the Americans, and forded across the Our River with two regiments in the pre-dawn hours of the 16th. They would be almost on top of the U.S. infantry at the starting gun. More than anywhere else in the Ardennes, the Germans here greatly outnumbered the American defenders.

7   The panzer rollbahn for the *LVIII Panzerkorps* was Reuland-Gouvy-Houffalize-La Roche-Marche and then to the Meuse at Yvoir, Namur or Andenne.

Private James Donnelly, Company K of the 424th Regiment, U.S. 106th Infantry Division keeps a watchful eye with his M1 rifle.

Young and old. German grenadiers of the 116th Panzer Division on the march in the Ardennes. They are armed with a variety of weapons, a bold-action Mauser rifle, a panzerfaust anti-tank rocket and an MG 42 machine gun.

Upper Right: *Organization of the XLVII Panzerkorps prior to the German attack on December 14th, 1944. Shown are the composition of the three divisions in the corps and the various support troops. Among other aspects the chart shows that half of the 304th Panzergrenadier Regiment (2nd Panzer Division) was forced to depend on bicycles for transportation!*

At Right: *A heavily camouflaged German truck column passes over a constructed J-type bridge guarded by a 20mm flak gun near Losheim. The Germans had a limited number of bridges capable of carrying their heavy tanks in the Ardennes and a shortage of trained engineers with which to construct them.*

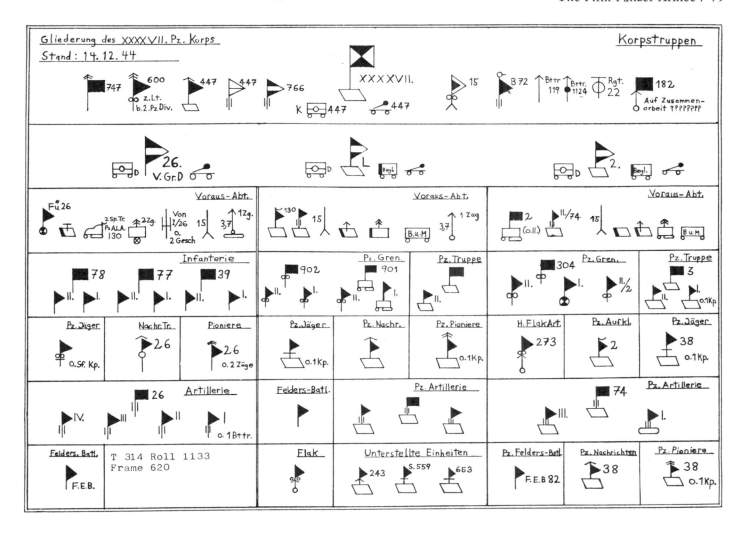

Three German divisions and corps artillery were pitted against a single U.S. infantry regiment, the 110th of the 28th Division.

The German objective in this sector, as with the rest of the *Fifth Panzer Armee*, was simple: Break the American resistance and drive for the Meuse.[8] A special problem for von Manteuffel's attack in the south was the paucity of roads in the advance zone. Even more problematic was the fact that most of the hard surfaced roads came together like a spiderweb at the market town of Bastogne. Early on during map exercises, the German planners had recognized the importance of seizing this crossroads, for without it the panzer division motor columns would not have room for maneuver or supply. The town lay some twenty miles beyond the German frontier and responsibility for its capture fell to von Lüttwitz's corps. Ideally, it was to be taken by a quick blow from the panzer spearheads. That failing, the armor was to skirt the town and drive for the Meuse River, leaving investment of the place to the infantry that followed.

Obst. Meinrad von Lauchert, in charge of the elite *2nd Panzer Division*, had just taken over command the day before on December 15th. His superiors had doubts about the aggressive spirit of the division's former leader, Genmaj. Schönfeld, and had made a last minute change. He had not even met some of his subordinate commanders when the

8   The *XLVII Panzerkorps Rollbahn* passed through Dasburg-Allerborn-Noville-Champlon-Hargimont-Rochefort and then onto the Meuse at Dinant or Givet.

panzer grenadiers of his division ferried across the Our River in assault boats. As it was, however, Lauchert with all the power of his 120 tanks and assault guns, spent a frustrating day waiting for inexperienced German engineers to complete a bridge across the Our River. Although the bridge was completed by 4:00 P.M., so tardy was its construction that it prompted a visit of reprimand from the Chief of Engineers of *Heeresgruppe B*. Meantime, the lightly armed panzer grenadiers advanced from the west bank of the Our River to stumble into a minefield. Beyond that they received an exceedingly warm reception from the American defenders in Marnach. German casualties were heavy, including even the commander of the grenadier regiment.

Similar to its sister division, Bayerlein's *Panzer Lehr Division* was snarled in a huge traffic jam leading down to that river, waiting for a bridge of its own a few miles south at Gemünd. Meanwhile, Obst. Heinz Kokott's *26th Volksgrenadier Division* engaged the U.S. troops of the 110th regiment of the 28th Division on the other side the river on the right flank of the corps. All through the day heavy fighting eddied back and forth for the control of tiny villages such as Hosingen, Holzthum and Wahlhausen. The "Old *26th*", however, bogged down in the face of the stubborn American riflemen. The defense at Marnach was not broken until late during the night when the tanks of *2nd Panzer Division* clanked forward to crush the remaining resistance and push ahead to the town of Clervaux.

The Seventh Armee

Gen. d. Pztrp. Erich Brandenberger and his *Seventh Armee* were like the "poor country cousin" to Hitler's *Wacht am Rhein* plan. Contrary to the title of its leader, the southernmost German army in *Wacht am Rhein* had no panzer divisions under its command. More than an army, it resembled a reinforced corps. Even worse, the striking power of the *Seventh Armee* consisted only of four poorly trained and mostly inexperienced infantry divisions. The *LXXXV Armeekorps* was on the north flank under Gen. d. Inf. Baptist Kneiss; the *LXXX* on the south came under Gen. d. Inf. Franz Beyer. Including support troops Brandenberger had about 60,000 men.

There were other deficiencies in the *Seventh Armee*. No tanks were available and only fifty assault guns could be promised. Although he had 629 artillery pieces and *nebelwerfers*, Brandenberger had little in the way of artillery prime movers or bridging equipment to move artillery corps and werfer brigades across the Our River. The army almost totally lacked motorization. Brandenberger's forces advanced at a walking pace with the big guns hauled forward by horse. If Hitler lacked the means, he never lacked ambition. All four divisions were to thrust westward almost to the Meuse River at Gedinne and then peel off to face south and so protect the flank of the German offensive. No one in the *Seventh Armee* staff really believed this possible.

The best thing Brandenberger had going for his army was the paltry strength of the American line in his path: an infantry regiment each of the 4th and 28th Infantry Divisions and an armored combat command of Maj. Gen. John W. Leonard's 9th Armored Division. Both U.S. infantry divisions had been severely mauled in the Hürtgen battles and were short of rifle strength; the combat command, although well trained, lacked combat experience. As elsewhere in the Ardennes when the Germans moved off at 6:00 A.M., they did so under a noisy curtain of shell fire, hopeful of success. Surprise was complete.

But even these advantages could not guarantee German progress. Almost from the start of the attack, the army plan went awry. Brandenberger's army moved down to the Our River in a vast infantry wave at first light. But crossing the Our and Sauer Rivers along the German border that marked the front line proved difficult. With the wet winter season the rivers were swollen and swift; the U.S. artillery cast a watchful eye over the few good bridging sites available. So difficult was the crossing in the German assault dinghies that the German artillery fire in the sector had long dwindled by the time the Germans collected sufficient numbers on the west bank to move on the American line. To their conster-

General Erich Brandenberger (left), the commander of the German Seventh Armee. *Brandenberger was dissatisfied with the strength of his forces which consisted only of four reinforced infantry divisions.*

nation they found American riflemen and gunnery observers alert and waiting.

The initial miscarry of the plan set the tone for the day. The *LXXXV Armeekorps* was faced with the U.S. 109th Infantry Regiment of the 28th Infantry Division just to the east of the Our River. Obst. Ludwig Heilmann's 15,000 man *5th Fallschirmjäger Division* managed to penetrate several miles establishing a bridgehead over the Our River at Vianden and capture the unoccupied village of Walsdorf. The furthest penetration lodged just east of Hoscheid, a few miles from the start line. In spite of this, a number of strongpoints such as the villages of Fouhren and Weiler remained in American hands, and they seemed determined not to give these up without a fight. Even worse, construction of a bridge at the village of Roth was delayed, first by a huge crater in the approach road to the site, and then by harassing fire from American artillery gunners. The German evening report aptly described the situation in this sector as "none too clear."

To the south, the *352nd Volksgrenadier Division* had better luck. Obst. Erich Schmidt's division thrust two miles beyond the German border to the villages of Longsdorf and Bastendorf in spite of a vigorous defense from the 109th Regiment. The nearby village of Tandel was taken by midday only to be lost again to a desperate American counterattack and the left hand infantry column was stopped short of Hoesdorf when pinned by accurate American artillery fire.

Still Brandenberger was pleased with the first day performance of these half trained grenadiers.

In the *LXXX Armeekorps*, the advance of the *276th Volksgrenadier Division* was at first aided by the thick fog, darkness and the wooded ravines on its front that allowed its grenadiers to infiltrate several kilometers through the American line. However, a broad front advance by the division was checked by the stubbornly held positions by of 60th Armored Infantry Battalion of the 9th Armored Division's Combat Command A near Wallendorf. All attempts at advance beyond the Our River past Dillingen and Bigelbach were checked by U.S. tanks. *Heeresgruppe B* declared the green division "kind of a loser" and "the problem child of the *Seventh Armee*;" they recommended that Brandenberger relieve its commander. Perhaps the reluctance of the division to fight had to do with its NCOs who were, in the main, previously wounded veterans returning to duty.

Whatever the reason, Brandenberger was thankful to have the *212th Volksgrenadier Division*, which he believed his army's best. The division, under the command of Genlt. Franz Senfuss, was located on the southernmost boundary of the attack just south of the Eifel near Bitburg. His volksgrenadiers were to penetrate southwest as far as Junglinster before assuming a defensive posture to protect the extreme southern flank of the German offensive.

The experienced German infantry penetrated the 12th Infantry Regiment of the 4th U.S. Division in the early morning hours on either side of Echternach. By noon they had reached the streets of the town and surrounded an American company in the Parc Hôtel in Berdorf, but could not overcome the stubborn companies of American infantry defiantly defending in either place. The trapped men in Echternach held out against overwhelming odds for five days. Undaunted, the German grenadiers bypassed the thorny American strongpoint and infiltrated west in the darkness, capturing the hill south of the town. Even so an advance German combat team reaching the village of Lauterborn "was forced to withdraw after a futile house to house battle with strong enemy forces." Other grenadier thrusts against Osweiler and Dickweiler were also thwarted. So repelled, the Germans planned a series of concentric attacks to capture the strong points once promised assault guns had shown up.

As the gloomy skies gave way to darkness, Brandenberger found himself quite displeased with his army's progress. Although some of his formations had penetrated a few miles beyond the Our River, no breakthrough was in progress anywhere in the *Seventh Armee*. Two problems were particularly vexing. No operable bridges were in place at the end of the day; his poorly trained volksgrenadiers were forced to fight without heavy weapons and even artillery until this was made good. Although some fifty assault guns had been assigned to his army, by the end of December 16th, only the *5th Fallschirmjäger Division* had received its shipment. Without these, how would his unseasoned riflemen subdue the U.S. armor that Brandenberger knew lay in their path?

Foot soldiers by another name. A group of German volksgrenadiers receive an inspection in the Ardennes in 1944. New German recruits in these divisions received an average of six weeks of training before they were sent to the front.

The View from OB West

Sixty miles east of the Rhine River at Ziegenberg Castle, haughty old Genfldm. von Rundstedt of *OB West* made no attempt to hide his misgivings about the first day of *Wacht am Rhein*. He observed that although complete surprise had been achieved, the tempo of the assault had been greatly slowed by "stubborn resistance in major enemy strongpoints three to five kilometers behind the front lines." He also warned that "as a result of the bad weather and bridging conditions, the anticipated rapid advance of the panzer formations had not yet taken place." On the other hand, he noted the penetrations in some sectors coupled with the low German losses "had created the essential prerequisites for the successful continuation of the operation." Orders to *Heeresgruppen G* and *H* gave them their assignments on either side of the offensive. To *Heeresgruppe H* in Holland, on whose front quiet prevailed, von Rundstedt ordered that "in the further course of the operation of *Heeresgruppe B* a drive by strong forces of the army group across the lower reaches of the Meuse in the direction of Antwerp would contribute significantly to success." Von Rundstedt instructed Gen. Student, in charge of the army group, to form strong mobile *Kampfgruppen* which could cross the lower Meuse at the appropriate time. *Heeresgruppe G*, south of the Ardennes, received the less ambitious mission of preventing an enemy breakthrough in the Palatinate and tying down enemy forces. Hitler himself commanded that "from now on do not give up one step's worth of ground."

Reports from Model's *Heeresgruppe B* at Münstereifel were more upbeat. As the attack opened at 6:00 A.M., his staff reported that, "Up to now everything is on schedule and the beginning is going according to plan everywhere." On a sour note, however, the war diary related that *Operation Stösser*, the German parachute operation, had not gotten off the ground due to lack of fuel. Later that morning Gen. d. Inf. Hans Krebs, Model's Chief of Staff, made an optimistic entry:

> ...tactical and operational surprise is apparently successful. Till now very little enemy counterattack and decidely little radio activity. Especially noticeable in all three attack armies is the very slight artillery fire. Due to weather conditions, air force action on both sides is not possible at this time.

But the atmosphere at *OB West* remained incredulous. At nightfall von Rundstedt vocalized his worries to *OKW* concerning the poor progress of the right wing of Dietrich's army. Perhaps to appease him, Hitler released the *3rd Panzer Grenadier Division*, waiting in *OKW Reserve* in the vicinity of Oberhausen east of Monschau.[9] The division was to be used to help set up the northern defensive flank from the northernmost German assault of *LXVII Armeekorps* to the town of Eupen.

If any of these cares unduly concerned Hitler, he did not show it. During the late night hours of December 16th-17th, the Führer excitedly telephoned Gen. d. Pztrp. Hermann Balck of *Heeresgruppe G*, to the south of the Ardennes. He told the experienced German general of the promising news from *Wacht am Rhein*. "Balck! Balck!" he cried. "Everything has changed in the West! Success — complete success — is now in our grasp!"

---

9   *OB West* had no military formations assigned at the beginning of the offensive. Even Model's *Heeresgruppe B* had only one infantry division under its direct control—an indication of the degree of autonomy which Hitler left to his senior commanders in late 1944.

Under fire, an American GI bolts for cover. A dead soldier lies at his feet.

The First Day: An Assessment

By dint of a tremendous effort, Hitler and his planners had managed to collect 13 infantry and 5 panzer divisions for the initial attack in the Ardennes. More German forces were waiting in the wings as second echelon reinforcements (two SS panzer divisions, one panzer grenadier division, one volksgrenadier division and two panzer brigades). With only six divisions on the Allied side, this appeared to give the German forces the traditional three to one advantage generally regarded as necessary for offensive success.

Of course, only two of the panzer divisions were used on the first day; the SS divisions and *Panzer Lehr* were not committed to the fighting until the 17th. A real problem, however, was the relative strength of the participating German divisions. Many of the German formations were weak, particularly in armor. The first assault wave and associated support troops consisted of about 250,000 men, some 382 panzers and 335 assault guns with 2,623 artillery pieces and rocket launchers. Another 55,000 men and 561 armored fighting vehicles were waiting to the east of the battle zone to reinforce the German attack (*2SS, 9SS, 3rd Panzer Grenadier Divisions* and the two *Führer* panzer brigades). In the path of the German assault, the Americans possessed an effective strength of 83,000 men, 242 medium tanks, 182 tank destroyers and 394 artillery pieces.

Overall the Germans achieved the traditionally assumed necessary 3 to 1 ratio in men. As for equipment, Hitler fell short with 1.7 to 1 in armor, but had a 7 to 1 advantage in artillery. Even the seeming German advantage in gunnery was largely negated by German shortages of ammunition, the lack of air observation, the paucity of communications equipment to direct the fire and the well entrenched American positions.

Another problem was the terrain. So forbidding was the forested Ardennes in winter, that a much more substantial superiority would appear necessary for a rapid breakout. The fuel situation was pathetic as well. When the offensive opened, with one and a half consumption units available at the forward dumps, the German tanks and trucks had barely enough to go 90 miles under optimal conditions. Antwerp was over 125 miles away and the initially available fuel would take a panzer no more than a third that distance on the winding and wintery Ardennes roads.

To be sure, there were a few bright spots for the German planners. Two regiments of the U.S. 106th Infantry Division appeared about to be trapped by the German advance. The American infantry were in an exposed salient in a section of the German Westwall positions that had been captured previously in the fall and was to be used as a jump-off position for future U.S. attacks towards the Rhine. Gen. von Manteuffel, commander of the *Fifth Panzer Armee*, had recognized the position as a good candidate for encirclement and proceeded to do so with a German infantry division.

On the other hand, the main effort, Dietrich's *Sixth Panzer Armee,* failed in its attempt to breakthrough the U.S. V Corps line from Monschau to Losheim. The Germans had been unable to over-match the American strength there. Perhaps more than any event, the riposte that the American soldier gave to Hitler in this sector served to endanger the *Wacht am Rhein* plan.

Taken as a whole, the German assault was a failure. On the evening of the 16th only one clear breakthrough had been attained — in the Losheim Gap. Another appeared to be developing in the thin sector held by the 28th Division. But more than this was required. *Heeresgruppe B's* timetable called for one day to break through the American line, another to cross the rugged Ardennes terrain with the Meuse being reached on the night of the third day. Gnfld. Model was obviously aware of these shortcomings with his general orders for conduct of the second day of battle along his front: "Quick exploitation of the successes of the first day of the attack will be decisive. The first objective is to achieve liberty of movement for the mobile units."

Model's operational plan, the *Aufmarschanweisung,* called for the German armor to be committed in mass on the morning of the second day of the attack to advance through the holes that the infantry had punched on *O-Tag*. The real problem, of course, was that except for one or two sectors in the line, the American defenders were still in place. The massive breakthrough required for the success of *Wacht am Rhein* had not materialized.

How the Battle Was Fought

The fundamental objective of modern battle is to destroy the enemy's military force. In fact, World War II combat in Europe, including the Battle of the Bulge, can be neatly described by referring to the infantry field manual in use by the combatants. The basic mission was to "close with, and destroy the enemy by fire and maneuver." The fire and maneuver tactic was fairly simple in application.

The heavy weapons (artillery and direct fire guns and heavy machine guns) would open up on the enemy while the infantry or infantry and tank force maneuvered and closed with the enemy. Hopefully, the fusillade of metal from the fire support force would keep the defender's head down or the maneuver force was likely to be shot to pieces. The attacking maneuver force would then take on the enemy force from his flank or rear while the covering heavy weapons engaged him from his front. In this way, the enemy was "captured or destroyed."

On a tactical level without long range weapon support, the small unit would split in half with one force providing the "fire" and the other the "maneuver." The small units would then advance in leap-frog fashion, alternately providing fire support for the other's advance. Even so, unless the friendly fire was enough to keep the enemy's head down he might subject such a force to return fire. Gen. William E. DePuy, during the Bulge a battalion commander with the U.S. 90th Division, clearly described this dilemma:

...the problem with infantry is that while you may get fire superiority through suppression, just at the time when you need it the most, during the assault, when the troops rise up out of their foxholes and move forward, you lose it. So, the enemy comes up out of his holes and starts to fire at you... So marching fire obviously was designed to overcome that problem and marching fire became the tactic through which you attacked (a Third Army tactic designed by Patton himself). We lined up two battalions with two companies up and they went across the line of departure, using marching fire. It might have worked if the enemy was not well dug in, not well camouflaged, and very weak; but, if the enemy was professional, as the Germans usually were, was well hidden and in very good positions, marching fire just wasn't sufficient. We marched into their killing zones.

One way to get around this predicament was to use armor in the assault. In such an attack the maneuver force combat team would typically consist of tanks and infantry — more infantry in the latter stages of the war as both sides came to understand the vulnerability of armor. Still the threat to the defender of these tactics was considerable.

On the attack a battalion would assume a narrow assault frontage often only 500 meters, half of the line assumed for a continuous defense. The attack would be opened with air support or artillery. Once the armor had pierced through the main line of defense and neutralized the artillery, the bulk of the enemy infantry firepower was gone. Bypassed and surrounded, isolated infantry was doomed to a fate of surrender within two to five days unless they could be resupplied. But just how had this effective tactic come about?

Historical Lessons

World War I had seen the dramatic increase in firepower resign the antagonists to a stalemated war of attrition on the western front from 1914 through 1916. The infantry, a necessity to claim territory in armed conflict, had not really changed in the last two centuries. It was true that advances in automatic weapons had resulted in a much higher rate of fire and killing range being available than in Napoleon's time. However, after a few blood baths in that war, commanders had learned to further disperse their men so that space itself brought the killing power of weapons back to a factor that could be reckoned with. The Great War had also taught that the power of such weapons — notably the machine gun — had enabled a numerically inferior group of defenders to literally slaughter a much larger mass of attacking soldiers advancing across the open. It seemed impossible for the offensive to run this gauntlet of fire and survived.

In 1917 the Germans developed a tactical solution to the problem of attacking in the face of overwhelming firepower. Since the defenders were widely spaced to avoid the massed fire-

Rare photograph of soldiers of the 87th Infantry Division advancing in an attack under fire. Gen. Patton advocated "marching fire" with the M-1 rifle to keep enemy heads down.

power of the enemy artillery, a series of assault groups (*Stosstruppen*) of highly trained and heavily armed soldiers would move forward and infiltrate the enemy line after a short but heavy artillery barrage hit the enemy artillery. Like runners in a football team, the *Stosstruppen* were trained to take advantage of their surprise and move quickly, avoiding any enemy resistance to infiltrate to the rear to get at the enemy artillery. This accomplished two things at once. It isolated and demoralized the enemy on the front who found themselves out of communication and stranded with enemy troops to their front and rear. It also promised to neutralize the enemy artillery that was the backbone of the entire army's firepower. In this way, the "Hutier tactics" gave a chance of decisive success as proved by the German offensives of 1917 and 1918.

The key to the success of these tactics lay with the high level of training and expertise achieved by relatively small assault forces. The antidote to the infiltration tactics was a defense in depth. Unfortunately this is a luxury which no army can afford everywhere on its front. Meanwhile, the Allied forces in World War I found a different and technical solution to the offensive problem — the tank. This development forever revolutionized the infantry battle. The armored vehicle allowed the offensive to breast the enemy artillery and machine gun fire behind steel plate. Coming late in the war, the unstoppable juggernauts had made an indelible impression on German military minds. What if *Stosstruppen* tactics for infantry were used with numbers of faster tanks like these?

The *Blitzkrieg*

Correctly diagnosing the required formula to revitalize the offensive, the Germans decided to incorporate both innovations as well as adding other elements — tactical use of air power and extensive use of radio communications for coordination of the attack. When the tank and air support was added to the infiltration tactics, it formed a volatile style of battle for the following war that emphasized firepower and maneuver over position. This type of warfare — the *blitzkrieg* — added a

German SS panzergrenadier signals his squad forward. The solder was a member of Kampfgruppe Hansen *in action on December 18th near the village of Poteau.*

new dimension to modern warfare. Clausewitz had identified this style of combat years before; battle could be won by indirectly disrupting and paralyzing the enemy's center of strength rather than a direct war of annihilation — "killing of the enemy's courage rather than of the enemy soldiers." The tactics revolved around a decisive rapid movement battle where the objective was to succeed in confusing and demoralizing the enemy to the point of its destruction.

This approach had a number of advantages. It did not necessarily require numerical superiority for success. Instead it could rely on surprise, local superiority of firepower and rapid maneuver. The primary ingredient in the recipe was well trained forces that understood proper application of all combat arms to achieve a decisive local success that would be exploited through rapid maneuver before the defender knew what had happened. In its ideal form, the *blitzkrieg* sought to maximize enemy demoralization to the point of surrender or retreat while minimizing friendly casualties and disorganization.

Central to application of the *blitzkrieg* was the idea of decisively massing firepower and maneuver (the *Schwerpunkt*) at an enemy weak point to ex-

ploit the position and destroy the enemy fire support to the rear (the enemy artillery). Firepower was maximized through the *Einheit* or unity principle which in modern armies is called combined arms. This meant forming operational battlegroups (*Kampfgruppen*) with a balanced number of tanks, infantry, artillery and air power so that they could flexibly deal with any battle development. To this was added extensive training on how each combat arm should work with each other. The *Kampfgruppe* was usually united under a highly motivated regimental or battalion commander since the mission for most of the German *kampfgruppen* in the opening attack was to breakthrough the enemy line. Penetration (*Einbruch*) and breakthrough (*Durchbruch*) was initiated by a concentration of firepower on a series of narrow fronts (frequently three kilometers or less) against enemy weak points by several divisions at once. This was precisely what von Manteuffel meant when he described the opening strategy of assaults in the *Fifth Panzer Armee* front in the Ardennes — if one knocked on many doors, surely one would find one open.

Secondary attacks in nearby sectors were often launched to draw away enemy attention to the area of main effort. The most common objective of such attack was encirclement, as this was considered the most decisive form of the offensive. The Germans considered the single envelopment and flank attack less desirable; the frontal attack was to be avoided if at all possible. Typically, armored divisions were used in the initial assault followed by motorized and infantry divisions.

Doctrine in the Ardennes

The increasing tank losses experienced in the later stages of the war had set the German military thinkers into a quandary by late 1944. Was it better to lead off the attack with infantry to clear the enemy front and reduce tank losses, or should the panzer column enjoin the assault? The difficult terrain of the Ardennes made the considerations even more important; the firepower and capability of tanks were severely limited until the panzer spearheads could reach the better terrain west of the Meuse River.

Hitler and *OKW* opted for an infantry led attack for the *Sixth Panzer Armee*. Von Mantueffel and the *Fifth Panzer Armee* stayed with the conventional wisdom — the panzer divisions lead his assault. Regardless of how the penetration was achieved, the Ardennes Offensive's need to rapidly reach the Meuse River reduced the German inclination for encirclement. Of course where an opportunity presented itself, the Germans did not fail to take notice. The Cannae that bagged the U.S. 106th Division in the Eifel was executed by a single volksgrenadier division!

Since the overriding concern was for the panzer forces to exploit rapidly west, the most common action likely with the enemy was a meeting engagement during the breakthrough. This occurred after the aggressor had broached the defender's front line positions as the defender moved up his mobile reserves to try and block the motorized exploitation. The German doctrine stressed the importance of avoiding such blocking forces if possible, and otherwise aggressive attempts to overrun them before they could be reinforced. Encirclements had to be realized quickly in battle; otherwise the enemy would evacuate threatened forces. Exploitation according to the German doctrine must avoid and bypass opposition at all costs. Where the breakthrough attempts did not succeed the German propensity was not to provide reserves. Experience had taught them the familiar lesson that one does not reinforce failure. Evidently, Hitler himself had not learned this lesson well enough in six years of war, for he kept insisting that the stalled *Sixth Panzer Armee* receive the available reserves during the Ardennes Offensive. It was another victory for politics over rationality.

In summary, the German doctrine always sought to turn the battle into a fluid and mobile engagement where their superior training and leadership

could be brought to focus. These concepts worked extremely well, but they required training, equipment and supply that was often not available in late 1944. Also, the Ardennes was hardly an ideal location for the mobile style of warfare the Germans envisioned. The terrain and winter conditions severely restricted the maneuver on which the *blitzkrieg* relied even had the Germans possessed the gasoline necessary to implement it.

Offensive American Style

The Americans had developed their own style of offensive warfare by late 1944. They also embraced the idea of combined arms, but generally went for a highly material sort of warfare dominated by the sheer volume of tanks, guns and shells. The Americans preferred the methodical steady advance with a well organized front and a minimum of confusion and fancy tactics. This contrasted sharply with the battle of maneuver that the Germans advocated. While the Germans preferred encirclement as the mode of enemy destruction, the Allies chose carefully orchestrated assaults dominated by intense use of indirect fire, air power and plenty of armor. Again, General DePuy:

> I honestly concluded at the end of World War II, when I soberly considered what I had accomplished, that I had moved the forward observers of the artillery across France and Germany. In other words, my battalion was the means by which

field artillery observers were moved to the next piece of high ground. Once you had a forward observer on a piece of ground, he could call up to ten battalions of artillery and that meant you had won the battle.

Although this was not as sophisticated as the German approach, it worked extremely well if you had an abundance of supply and munitions which, of course, the Americans did. The direct, no nonsense approach to battle that the Americans waged denied the Germans a chance to use their superior tactics for the most part. There were notable exceptions. Patton waged a freewheeling sort of extremely aggressive battle which was much admired from the German camp. The Allied forces had attempted enemy encirclement with limited success at Falaise in Normandy. Even so, as von Rundstedt noted, when the Americans were faced with an encirclement opportunity, they often opted for the "Small Solution."

The Americans could certainly not be faulted for a lack of courage. While not especially expert at drill routines like the Germans and British, the American soldiers were tenacious fighters. Of course, experiences such as those with the Japanese of WW II and the French in 1914 had shown that raw courage and reckless bravery were no substitute for ability. However, the American soldiers rapidly learned from their skilled adversary in Africa, Italy and the beaches of France. Rommel has said to have remarked that he

Combined Arms. U.S. GIs seek the cover of a ditch while a Sherman tank advances to eliminate enemy resistance ahead.

feared the Americans more than the British. According to the famous German general, while the British had to unlearn their bad habits, the Americans had only to survive their inexperience. "They are quick to learn," he said, "either by trial or error."

Still the Americans had some important advantages in their offensive capabilities. The Germans greatly feared their well coordinated artillery fire — especially the "time on target" or TOT fire. This radio arranged linkage would allow all the guns in an entire corps to suddenly fire on a single position at exactly the same time. The Americans often used this overwhelming concentration of fire for assaults on village or crossroad positions. As one might expect, this type of fire could have devastating results. Subsequent to the TOT, often only a collection of ruins and a few dazed German soldiers might remain. Also, the Allied airpower was used with considerable bravado. Although the *Jabos*, or fighter-bombers, were probably not responsible for most of the German casualties, they greatly injured their morale. The XIX Tactical Air Command bombed with white phosphorous based on the Third Army commander's conviction of its surrender inducing qualities.

Then too, the very style of American offense — well organized attacks with strong forward lines — denied the Germans the easy encirclements of exposed enemy forces in which they specialized. The Americans gave battle on their own terms and those terms were a punishing and attritional attack that sapped the Germans of men and supply to try and keep up.

The Defense

Clausewitz had correctly identified the fundamental paradox of the defense. It is, as he noted, "the stronger form of combat." However, even the most cautious had to admit that wars were never won by defense. The offensive was the combat of decision. While this might be true in a strategic sense, both sides would alternately find themselves on the defensive in the Ardennes. The defender in WW II still possessed this inherent advantage of getting to fire from carefully prepared cover. Even so, the combination of increased firepower and mobility in World War II had reasserted the power of the attack. Consequently, both sides clearly sought to retain the initiative and if they lost it, to regain its blessings. In terms of the fighting, if on the defensive, the maneuver force would remain stationary and help direct the fire support of the fire force to destroy the closing enemy.

The typical disposition of troops for both sides was based on the German concept of the mobile defense. Under this scheme, the line was primarily manned with infantry divisions (the shield) in order to fend off the assault. The armored formations were held in reserve (the sword) to parry any enemy breakthrough.

Both sides were fairly skilled at this style of defense although the Germans now had two years of experience with these tactics. In addition the Germans were undoubtedly the masters of the small scale counterattack that was invariably used to try and throw an enemy attack off balance. According to General DePuy, they were also expert in the ambush:

> I think the first thing that impressed everybody at the time was how a handful of Germans could hold up a regiment by sighting their weapons properly. If they had two assault guns and 25 men, they put one assault gun on one side of the road, perhaps on the reverse slope firing through a saddle, and put the other one behind a stone house, firing across the road. They protected them with some infantry and had a couple of guys with *Panzerfausts* up on the road itself, or behind houses. Now, here comes the point of an American unit roaring down the road, a couple of jeeps and maybe a tank, and bang!, you lost a tank....The company commander then decides to maneuver a platoon around and boom!, he loses another tank. So the commander decides to wait for the battalion commander to come up....Sometimes a unit would stay there and fight all day against 25 men and two assault guns. And, that happened all too often.

The Best Laid Plans . . .

Both sides, regardless of their offensive or defensive stance, were seeking to destroy the other. This meant that given two competent opponents, a large number of casualties were inevitable. When translated to the battlefield, the scenarios outlined above were seldom so neatly realized. As Clausewitz had pointed out long before, "war is the providence of uncertainty." Disparity in the confronting forces could often result in counterattacks where the fire force had its head down or terrain and weather resulted in poorly directed fire and the maneuver force was wiped out. On the other

A U.S. infantry squad rehearses their upcoming attack by sketching the plan out beforehand.

hand, a maneuver force with infantry and tanks confronting one without means of fighting the armor would likely see the defending infantry overrun. If the defender had anti-tank means then the advantage reverted back to that side. Worse still, the atrocious condition of the roads in the opening days of the Ardennes Offensive made the presence of tanks in the maneuver force an ever present question. Combat in Europe in WW II had a "rocks, scissors, paper" complexity to it for the various combat arms. If the aggressor had the right combination and numerical superiority or even parity then it would likely succeed; without these advantages excess losses or even a local retreat might result. Unfortunately, the fog of war was significantly dense in the Ardennes fighting that commanders rarely knew if they had the right composition for successful battle. They simply made accommodations and hoped for the best. As one armor commander put it:

> In my opinion, a battle never works; it never works according to plan....The plan is only a common base for changes. It is very important that everybody should know the plan, so you can change easily....

Von Moltke the Elder and a German champion of strategic planning, also recognized this dilemma. But he acknowledged that not only was uncertainty a curse, it could be an opportunity as well:

It is a delusion to imagine that a plan of campaign can be laid down far ahead and fulfilled with exactitude. The first collision with the enemy creates a new situation in accordance with the result. Some things intended will have become impracticable. Others which originally seemed impossible become feasible.

The Line of Defense

An infantry battalion could defend up to five kilometers of front. In the most extreme case the defensive position would be based on non-supporting strong points. A big disadvantage of this arrangement was the fact that the enemy could weasel around your strong point (particularly through woods or in the dark) and bring your position under flanking fire. If the frontage decreased to about half the maximum figure, the platoon and company-seized strong points would be within small arms range of each other and capable of support. With a frontage to defend to one kilometer or less, a continuous line was possible. This was desirable, but for the Americans in the opening days of the attack, it was almost impossible to provide. There were simply not enough soldiers to go around. The Germans relied heavily on their machine guns in the defense. Interlocking fields of fire from each strong point was often carefully plotted. In this way the Germans could use these guns to prevent enemy infiltration while not having to maintain a continuous line.

Armor and artillery were generally not appropriate for defense, being forces for attack and combat support respectively. In a pinch armor could defend, preferably against enemy armor in open terrain. Of course there was virtually nowhere in the Ardennes where conditions like this existed. When defending in a conventional engagement, armor needed infantry support if it were to survive. Artillery was simply too vulnerable to remain on the front — it had to be evacuated if the enemy broke through the lines. Engineers could be used when absolutely necessary and both sides in the Ardennes reluctantly committed these forces in such a fashion. However, their lack of combat support elements made them unable to hold a position long if confronted by a conventional enemy combat force.

The Rate of Advance

An important aspect in the German plans to reach the Meuse River was how rapidly they could advance against the Allied resistance. Generally, men can march unopposed on foot at a maximum rate of about 2 kilometers per hour. When mounted on tanks or halftracks, sustained rates of march of up to 30 kilometers per hour are possible (march rates at night are reduced by 50%). Given the weather and the state of the roads in the Ardennes, it seems that an optimal rate of unopposed advance would be less than half this figure. Even so, if an attack at this rate were possible, the panzer spearhead would reach the Meuse, a 150 kilometer distance within a single day. And although the timetable for the *Sixth Panzer Armee* called for the Meuse to be reached at the end of the third day, there seems to have been some hope in higher headquarters that vanguards of the *1st SS Panzer Division* and *2nd Panzer Division* in the south might reach that river within 24 hours. In 1940 Kleist's panzer divisions had reached the glittering Meuse within 48 hours. In the dead of

U.S. Engineers prepare a railway section near Vielsalm for demolition to prevent it from falling into enemy hands.

winter would it be possible with the heavier tanks of 1944 to better this performance? Not trusting the march tables Peiper had proved to his personal satisfaction on the evening of December 11th that a single Mk V tank could travel 80 km in one night. However, as Peiper told his superiors, whether an entire convoy of tanks and infantry could duplicate these results against stubborn enemy resistance was quite another matter. Upon hearing of this "wishful thinking," Dietrich remarked that *OKW*'s assessments were unrealistic since its officers lacked field experience. "Jodl waged war only on maps," the *Sixth Panzer Armee* commander observed. Generalfeldmarschall Model's timetable was perhaps the most realistic. He allotted one day for the infantry assault to penetrate the American lines; one day to exploit the breach in the lines and cross the rugged Hohes Venn — the Meuse to be reached on the fourth day of the offensive. At the very minimum, a 40 km per day advance rate had to be maintained to ensure attainment of this objective.

After the war, the U.S. Army produced a study which examined the historical rates of advance in WW II against enemy resistance. The study, known as FM 105-5 *Maneuver Control* presents this data as a series of tables useful for determining the average expected results. The tables show that the rate of advance depended primarily on the attacker's firepower ratio over that of the defender. Consistent with conventional wisdom, the data showed that generally, flank attacks treble the attacker's strength, while frontal assaults were less desirable. Also of little surprise was the finding that the tables show that the defender's defensive posture considerably affected the attacker's effective firepower ratio. The firepower ratio table is reproduced below.

The second table shows the average rate of advance for infantry and armored assault forces based on the type of terrain which the defenders occupy and the firepower ratio determined from the first table. Rates of advance for moving over constructed barriers are reduced by 10-25% over the values given.

The tables are interesting in several respects. Firstly, they show that at least a combat odds ratio of 1:1 is required for any advance (on the average). Also, the tables demonstrate how the rate of advance declines as the intensity of combat increases with decreasing firepower ratios. What the tables do not show is that elite forces (such as SS or airborne troops) could be expected to advance somewhat more rapidly than the rates indicated, and that weather, leadership and attack surprise can have other important effects.

The most important implication for the German attack force comes from the terrain effects. The closed and mixed terrain ubiquitously found in the Ardennes have an extremely retarding effect on the rate of armored advance. In heavily forested area (such as those found in the *Sixth Panzer Armee* area), the results indicate that foot infantry will advance about as well as armor — a fact echoed by von Rundstedt's order on the evening of December 17th that the armor must at least keep up with the infantry advance!

The attack strength firepower ratio in the Ardennes was on the order of the highest odds for Peiper's group and probably 3:1 for the *2nd Panzer Division*. Given the approximation of an equal parts of closed and mixed terrain, the tables indicate an advance rate of about 25 kilometers for the *Kampfgruppe Peiper* in a single day and half that figure for the *2nd Panzerkampfgruppe*. If we examine the progress of both attack forces for the period from midnight December 17th to midnight the following day we find that Peiper had moved about 35 kilometers from Lanzerath to a position just south of Stavelot. The *2nd Panzer* on the other hand had moved from Marnach just to the other side of the Our to Lullange west of Clervaux — a distance of nearly 12 kilometers. Given, the arbitrary nature of the maneuver control averages (and the wreckless determination of the Peiper group), these figures fit in nicely with the predictions.

Most importantly, however, the tables show that only over open terrain could the panzer spearheads have reached the Meuse on the timetable which the German generals had dictated. The three day trip to the Meuse would probably have been realized if the Americans had not been so prompt in throwing forces into Peiper's wake. However, that possibility was real only within Hitler's fantasy of the Ardennes Campaign. Unfortunately for the

Firepower Ratio: Attacker vs. Defender Effect of Combat Strength Ratio and Attack Direction Frontal Assault / Flank Assault					
Defense	1:1	2:1	3:1	4:1	5:1
Open Formation	2:1/3:1	3:1/6:1	4:1/9:1	5:1/12:1	6:1/15:1
Hasty Defense	1:1/3:1	2:1/6:1	3:1/9:1	4:1/12:1	5:1/15:1
Organized Defense	1:1/2:1	2:1/4:1	3:1/6:1	4:1/8:1	5:1/10:1

Rate of Advance Against Enemy Interaction of Firepower Ratio and Defensive Terrain (Armored/Infantry Advance Rate in km/hr)			
Firepower Ratio	Defender's Terrain		
	Open (Plain)	Mixed (Rolling, Light Woods)	Closed (Forest, Rough)
2:1	.60/.45	.40/.30	.25/.20
3:1	1.10/.55	.75/.40	.30/.25
4:1	2.20/.70	1.33/.50	.35/.30
5:1	3.30/1.10	1.50/.80	.50/.45

Death in Stavelot. This German grenadier of the 1st SS Panzer Division was killed in the village streets during the American recapture of the important bridge in the town on December 18th, 1944.

German leader, that fantasy was based on the events of 1940 and not 1944.

Attrition

Given the determination of both sides — the desperation of the German attack and the stubbornness of the American defense — heavy combat losses were certain. Furthermore studies made after the war of the nature of casualty rates in World War II suggest that the rate of losses in the Ardennes were apt to be very high. Experience has shown since 1940 that the minimum loss rate for a defending divisional force is about 1.5% per day; it is doubled if the force is on the offensive. These rates reflect the very lowest level of losses from combat, accidents, disease, capture and desertion. Even based on such a rate, one can see that in as little as a month of campaigning an average division could literally waste away, losing half its strength even when not in active combat! Various factors in terms of the formation's posture, the weather, time of day and intensity of effort will affect these average. The rates are important since they determine how long a unit can sustain combat before it "breaks." An attacking unit will likely break when it sustains more than 25% casualties in an action. This will make it unfit for further attack for a period of 48 hours. At a level of casualties of greater than 30% in a defending action, the formation will break and be unable to stop further enemy attacks for at least 24 hours. These limits were important since they were actually reached by some formations, both German and Allied, in the Ardennes.

In his book, *Numbers, Predictions & War*, Trevor Dupuy outlines a procedure adapted from FM 105-5 for estimating casualties in combat actions. The base loss rates are 1.5% per day for defense and 2.8% per day for the attacking force. Casualty rates are based on the firepower ratio, the formation size and posture and combat intensity. Based on these factors, an attacker's average losses can be anywhere from the base rate all the way to 14% losses in a single day; defending losses can be as great as 6% per day. Under these circumstances, a division could break in a period of as little as two days and be worthless to its owner for that much longer under average combat conditions. Dupuy also discovered that combat intensity could dramatically alter these casualty rates with the range varying by an order of magnitude! In the extreme case, this meant that an attacking division could lose more than 40% of the strength of its assault regiments in a single day of intense combat! This phenomenon helps explain how the 110th regiment of the 28th Infantry Division could lose 75% of its fighting strength in the first five days of the Ardennes Offensive.

A compilation of the average casualty rate in the U.S. Army in World War II showed the following loss rate for battalion sized units. These rates are 20% greater than the rate for regiments and 50% greater than those for divisions. The rates include a .6% non-combat loss rate and clearly shows that as the intensity of combat increases, the casualties do likewise, with the attacker generally taking the worst of it.

These tables are apt to underestimate the non-combat losses for the Ardennes fighting. Losses from exposure and trench foot alone resulted in over 9% of the Allied casualties suffered during the winter fighting. Many of these men were no longer able to return to active combat duty after hospitalization. The obvious solutions — better boots and warmer clothing were not immediately available, the quartermasters having been caught off guard by the severity of the problem. Eventually there were some 46,000 American trench foot cases on the Continent at a time when infantry replacements were simply not available.

The problem was at least as bad in the German camp. "I have my Christmas present," wrote home one German soldier grateful to be out of the Ardennes, "—two frozen feet."

U.S. Army Daily Casualty Rates in World War II		
Type of Action	Attacker Losses	Defender Losses
Inactive	2.6%	2.6%
Meeting Engagement	7.5%	4.9%
Prepared Attack	11.5%	6.1%
Attack Fortified Position	18.7%	9.8%
Pursuit	4.3%	3.2%

The Allied Reaction

Hitler knew that his superiority of force in the Ardennes would evaporate once the Allies moved reserves in to halt his advance. However, reflecting on the limitations of his own generals on D-Day in Normandy, he could not believe that the Allied field commanders could shift large numbers of troops without first consulting President Franklin D. Roosevelt at the White House and Prime Minister Winston Churchill on Downing Street. He reasoned that during the two or three days while Eisenhower and Montgomery dawdled about awaiting direction from their leaders, his panzers would smash resistance in the Ardennes and would be on their way to Antwerp.

The Führer also naively believed that the German divisions along the other parts of the Western Front would be able to pin down and prevent the Allied divisions facing them from being shifted to the battle zone. Unfortunately, Hitler again did not see what everyone else realized. Other than in the Ardennes, German divisions along the front were typically at half strength or less. As it turned out, the Allies were able to safely extend the lines of their troops elsewhere stripping away many divisions and moving them quickly to the zone under attack. Hitler's great assumption of disarray and confusion within the American and British ranks fell apart when faced by Allied pragmatism.

This, of course, is not to say that the American commanders were unshaken by the surprise German attack. Amid a blizzard of reports of enemy shelling and infantry assaults, Maj. Gen. Gerow of the U.S. V Corps reflected the thoughts of many American commanders. "What are those bastards of Huns up to?" he wondered aloud to an aide. As reports grew worse, he called Gen. Hodges to ask permission to call off his attack at Wahlerscheid crossroads. The 2nd Infantry Division was in danger of encirclement, he told the First Army commander.

But Hodges, and his U.S. First Army, were stationed at the Hôtel Britannique in Spa, from whence Hindenberg and Ludendorff had directed the German legions in the Great War. A fashionable military watering hole, Hodges' headquarters was further away from the action than Gerow in Eupen, although that night even he could hear the thunder of the German guns. With telephone lines to the front shot out, information on the German attack was slow in reaching his headquarters. He did agree that the situation in the 106th Division sector looked perilous; he released CCB of the 9th Armored Division to Gen. Middleton and his VIII Corps. But believing that these were merely local German counterattacks designed to call off his offensive towards the Roer dams, he told Gerow to keep up the pressure. "Pro-

Lt. Gen. Courtney H. Hodges, commander of the U.S. First Army during the Ardennes Campaign.

ceed with the offensive in the north," he told Gerow, "and hold where you are in the south." Concerned for his soldiers in the V Corps only a few miles away, Gen. Gerow could not sleep that night. In the early morning hours he received the disturbing news that German parachutists were landing barely five miles from his headquarters. And after that things just got worse.

Like Hodges, Middleton in Bastogne could hear the hollow booming of the German artillery twenty miles to the east. Ugly red flashes from the guns periodically lit up the distant eastern sky contrasted with the eery pencil-like beams of German searchlights used to illuminate the battlefield. Middleton, who had fought as a regimental commander on the French battlefield in WW I, knew trouble when he saw it. Justifiably worried about his men on the Schnee Eifel, he decided to provide the armor of Combat Command B, 9th Armored to Gen. Jones. Jones in St. Vith had the enemy almost on his door-step. He in turn ordered the combat command to proceed to St. Vith to assist his endangered 106th Division along its south flank. Even more foreboding was a copy of orders discovered on a fallen officer of the *116th Panzer Division* which featured an implorative from Genfldm. Model of *Heeresgruppe B*: "We will not disappoint the Führer and the Fatherland....Forward in the spirit of Leuthen!"

But in Bastogne itself, the war still seemed distant. The town market bustled as usual that Saturday and VIII Corps authorized its men to attend a ball that evening in a requisitioned French Franciscan monastery. The later event created quite a stir with the priest officiating at the monastery during high mass on Sunday. But this, too, was interrupted by a horde of refugees who began streaming through the town telling of the terrible fighting in Clervaux. Later in the day the town ominously lost electrical power and the sound of explosions grew nearer that evening as the mayor of the town imposed a curfew.

In the area directly threatened by the German offensive there was still an astonishing ignorance of the events transpiring just to the east. At Ligneuville, just 12 miles from the Losheim Gap where GIs were fighting hand to hand with German infantry, was the headquarters of the 49th Anti-Aircraft Artillery Brigade whose job it was to protect Liège from the V-1 buzz-bombs that regularly roared overhead. Brig. Gen. Edward W. Timberlake and his staff were comfortably stationed in the Hôtel du Moulin, long renowned for its *haute cuisine*. He and his brigade were enjoying a peaceful evening on December 16th. At the end of the day, many of the personnel had gone to the local cinema. During the picture an alert sounded, but it was soon called off. Word was only that German infantry had attacked somewhere towards Bütgenbach.

In reality, the German armored spearhead, *Kampfgruppe Peiper*, was pouring through a gap in the U.S. line at Honsfeld. But soon the all-clear was sounded and the men went unknowing back to their billets. The next day Timberlake and his men were so surprised by the speed of the German advance that Peiper and his men captured his abandoned headquarters at the hotel and dined on their still hot lunch. Several Americans captured there were brutally executed by Peiper's SS men.

Fifty miles to the south the Americans were equally naive about German intentions. In the town of Diekirch four miles from the German border, members of the 28th Infantry Division band were setting up in the town square to perform for the hotly anticipated arrival of Marlene Dietrich. But falling shells at 6 A.M. on December 16th sent band members running and worried civilians fleeing from the town. To everyone's dismay, Ms. Dietrich's appearance was cancelled.

December 16th at the Trianon Palace in Versailles, France, was a big day on the social calendar for the Supreme Commander of Allied Forces in Europe. Eisenhower was receiving a promotion to five star general — the U.S.

The Hotel du Moulin in Ligneuville as it appears today. On December 17th it was vacated by Brig. Gen. Edward Timberlake's 49th AAA Brigade and then occupied by the enemy only minutes later. Capturing the town, Obersturmbannführer Jochen Peiper and his panzer group killed seven U.S. prisoners behind the hotel in cold blood.

Actress Marlene Dietrich hands out 'lipstick autographs" to eager U.S. GIs during her U.S.O. tour of the Ardennes.

Army's highest rank. That morning began inauspiciously enough. He received a letter from Fld. M. Montgomery requesting leave for Christmas. Monty also reminded Eisenhower that a year before he had bet the Supreme Commander that the war would not be over by Christmas 1944. Ike owed him five pounds. "I'll pay," Eisenhower told his aide, "but not before Christmas. He can let me have these nine days." Later he attended the wedding of his personal aide, Sgt. Michael J. "Mickey" McKeogh. Everyone quaffed some spirits topped off by Ike's favorite meal — oysters. That evening Bradley and Eisenhower sat down to talk over the serious infantry replacement problem. After the discussion they toasted Ike's new star with some champagne.

But the festivities were soon interrupted by Maj. Gen. Strong, the SHAEF G-2, who had disturbing news. The Germans had strongly counterattacked in the Ardennes with infantry, he said, and had achieved penetrations in several places. The worst situation seemed to be along the seam of the V and VIII Corps in the Losheim Gap.

Although Bradley ventured that this was merely a spoiling attack, Ike had a hunch something larger was afoot. Since September the Supreme Commander had known from deciphered Japanese radio traffic of Hitler's offensive intentions in the West. The German leader had told the Emperor's ambassador of his plan to "open a large scale offensive in the west after the beginning of November." It was perhaps on this knowledge and the premonitions of Maj. Gen. Strong regarding the Ardennes that Eisenhower promptly ordered immediate reinforcement of the First Army sector. This sent the 7th Armored Division from the Ninth Army to St. Vith and the 10th Armored from Patton's Third Army to Luxembourg. Later the next day, Eisenhower ordered his only immediately available reserves, the 82nd and 101st Airborne to Werbomont and Bastogne, respectively.

Fld.M. Montgomery had been at Eindhoven playing golf with the Welsh professional Dai Rees when word came of a "hell of a row" in the U.S. First Army. Montgomery, too, reacted promptly to the German threat. By December 19th Montgomery ordered his XXX Corps to proceed to a backstop position west of the Meuse River in case the Germans were to break out of the Ardennes[10]

Whereas Hitler had expected the Allied command to dither and waste time, the actual Allied response was swift and to the point. The Allies moved quickly to counter the German offensive, the motorization of the American army making possible a rapid response to the German attack. The stubborn defense by the average American soldier in the Ardennes on the first day coupled with the massive supply of ammunition, tanks and guns that Eisenhower had punctually started moving to the threatened sector had already cast doubt on the viability of Hitler's plan to reach Antwerp.

10   Horrock's XXX Corps was composed of the 43rd, 51st and 53rd Infantry Divisions, the 6th Parachute Division, the Guards Armored Division, the 29th, 33rd, 34th and 6th Guards Armored Brigades and various corps artillery and support troops.

PROGRESS OF THE BATTLE

Soldiers of the 99th Infantry Division march in captivity towards Germany while a King Tiger tank of the 501st SS Heavy Panzer Battalion drives past them on the road to Lanzerath.

Breakthrough: December 17th - 18th

On the second day of *Wacht am Rhein*, Sunday, December 17th, the Germans resumed their attack, supported by extensive air activity. Dietrich's *Sixth Panzer Armee* put in a very heavy assault aimed to breach the American line at any cost. All along the front from Monschau to Losheimergraben the Germans pushed forward.

Again the right wing of the attack stalled. The lone fight of the *272nd Volksgrenadiers* at Kesternich continued, but reinforcements began to arrive on the American side. The tough 2nd Ranger Battalion was assigned to the 78th Infantry Division and CCR of the 5rd Armored Division moved up to Rötgen to serve as a back-stop for the untried U.S. division in case things got worse. The battle there had become a bloody stand-off.

To the south in the dense woods near Monschau, the *326th Volksgrenadiers* attempted to collapse the American line with a tide of infantry. The attack to the north of the town was designed to capture the high ground near Mützenich. The fight began before dawn at 4:00 A.M. with a heavy pounding by German guns and werfers. This fusillade was then followed by a battalion of grenadiers advancing in rushes. The Germans, aided by twenty strafing Luftwaffe planes, overran the thin armored cavalry screen north of Monschau and breached a 200 yard line in the American defense along Mützenich hill. The infantry onslaught was scattered by a deadly rain of U.S. artillery rounds, however, and the survivors were punished by 50 caliber machine gun fire. A counterattack in the afternoon by elements of the 146th Engineer Combat Battalion backed by tanks of Combat Command R of the 5th Armored Division (Maj. Gen. Lunsford E. Oliver) sealed off the penetration and reestablished the American lines. At day's end the American cavalry squadron counted 200 German dead in front of their position as reinforcements began to move up. The arrival of the 47th Regiment of Maj. Gen. Louis A. Craig's U.S. 9th Infantry Division in Mützenich effectively ended the German threat to the north of Monschau.

The assault of the *277th Volksgrenadiers* had failed in the center of the *Sixth Panzer Armee* line on the first day. As a result, *ISS Panzerkorps* raised the ante on the 17th by adding the *12th SS Panzer Division* to the fight. Before dawn SS-Stdf. Hugo Kraas launched his division into the attack. By late afternoon, for all their heroic stand on the 16th, the soldiers of the 99th Division were under such intense pressure from the SS panzergrenadiers and armor that they were forced to withdraw. Losses had been extremely heavy. The Germans might have broken through the Elsenborn ridge had not the American command moved quickly to thwart the enemy assault. A battalion of the 23rd Regiment of the 2nd Division was moved up from Camp Elsenborn to help support the American defense along with tanks attached to the division (745th Tank Battalion).

The gravity of the events transpiring in the Ardennes was not lost on the American commanders in the field. By morning of December 17th Gen. Hodges, in charge of the First Army, realized that his forces were in grave danger. As if to underscore the seriousness of the situation, a stray Luftwaffe bomb exploded a mile from his headquarters before dawn. The Luftwaffe had committed about fifty aging Ju-87 "Stuka" dive-bombers to hit Allied rear areas. Although largely ineffective, these raids became an almost nightly event. In Eupen, where V Corps held its headquarters, the German bombers struck under the cover of darkness as the 1st Division's 18th Regiment billeted down for the night. No one was hurt in this random flare and bomb dropping, but the effect was undeniable. What was the Luftwaffe doing carrying out nighttime raids against lonely American outposts in the Ardennes?

With enemy attacks both at Monschau and through the Losheim Gap, the danger of encirclement to the U.S. V Corps was an obvious threat. Apprised of the situation, Hodges quickly gave Gen. Gerow permission to fight the battle in V Corps as he saw fit and at midnight ordered the 1st Division to move south to defend the Elsenborn area. Soon Gerow flashed word to the U.S. 2nd Division to get out of the apparent trap developing at Heartbreak Crossroads. In a withdrawal that was fraught with peril, Maj. Gen. Walter M. Robertson's 2nd Infantry Division "skinned the cat," pulling out of the Wahlerscheid area to face the enemy before the villages of Rocherath-Krinkelt and Wirtzfeld. The maneuver was extremely complex: a nighttime withdrawal under fire to form a new line through which friendly soldiers could pull back. Probably few other than the veteran 2nd Division could have accomplished it.

But perhaps the greater credit lay with the 99th Division. New to battle, and badly damaged by the fury of the German assault, the American soldiers had thrown back superior German numbers for two days.[1] But, on hearing of *Kampfgruppe Peiper*'s advance through his supply line at Büllingen on the morning of the 17th, Gen. Robertson became gravely concerned with the situation in his rear. Since the 99th Division had been attached to his command, he ordered the remaining soldiers of the division to withdraw through the 2nd Infantry and relocate near Elsenborn to forestall any German attempt to turn that flank. Meanwhile, Robertson's crafty ploy placed his 2nd Division right smack on the road through which the Germans wanted to advance.

As a result of this maneuver, the lead *12th SS* panzer grenadier battlegroup, *Kampfgruppe Müller* (SS Stbf. Siegfried Müller), was soon entangled in a bitter house-to-house battle with the U.S. 2nd Division for possession of the twin villages of Rocherath-Krinkelt. The villages were important to the German scheme, since two of the three planned march routes of the SS division passed through them. But rather than racing to the Meuse, the Hitler Youth found themselves in a wildly confusing nighttime melee in the two drab hamlets only four miles from the German border. Admitting the lack of progress in their sector, the *ISS Panzerkorps* related to its superiors that "there is still bitter fighting against a tough enemy reinforced by strong artillery in Krinkelt." So intense was the combat in the villages that night that no one was really sure which side was in possession.

The third, and southernmost advance route of the *12th SS* was also still blocked. The hard surfaced *Rollbahn C* was the designated route for the armored battlegroup of the division, *Kampfgruppe Kühlmann*, (SS Stbf. Herbert Kühlmann). Stubborn infantry of the 394th Regiment of the

1   Losses for this valiant defense by the 99th Division were high. 393rd Regiment: 58 officers and 1299 men; 394th Regiment: 53 officers and 1,145 men; 395th Regiment: 26 officers and 396 men. The divisional engineer battalion lost over 100 men. The nominal strength of a U.S. infantry regiment was 114 officers and 3,049 men. The losses to the 393rd Regiment were particularly severe: the 1st Battalion came back with only 216 men and 14 officers—a casualty rate of 72%.

The 38th Regiment of the U.S. 2nd Infantry Division moves up to defend the line near Krinkelt on December 17th

SITUATION MAP
December 17th-18th

•LEUVEN

•ST. TRUI

•TIENEN

MEUSE RIVER

•ANDENNE

NAMUR

SAMBRE RIVER

•Ciney

•DINANT

LESSE RIVER

•PHILIPPEVILLE

•GIVET

RIVER

•COUVIN

FORÊT D'ARDENNES

SEMOIS

RIVER

BOU

CHARLEVILLE-
MEZIÈRES•

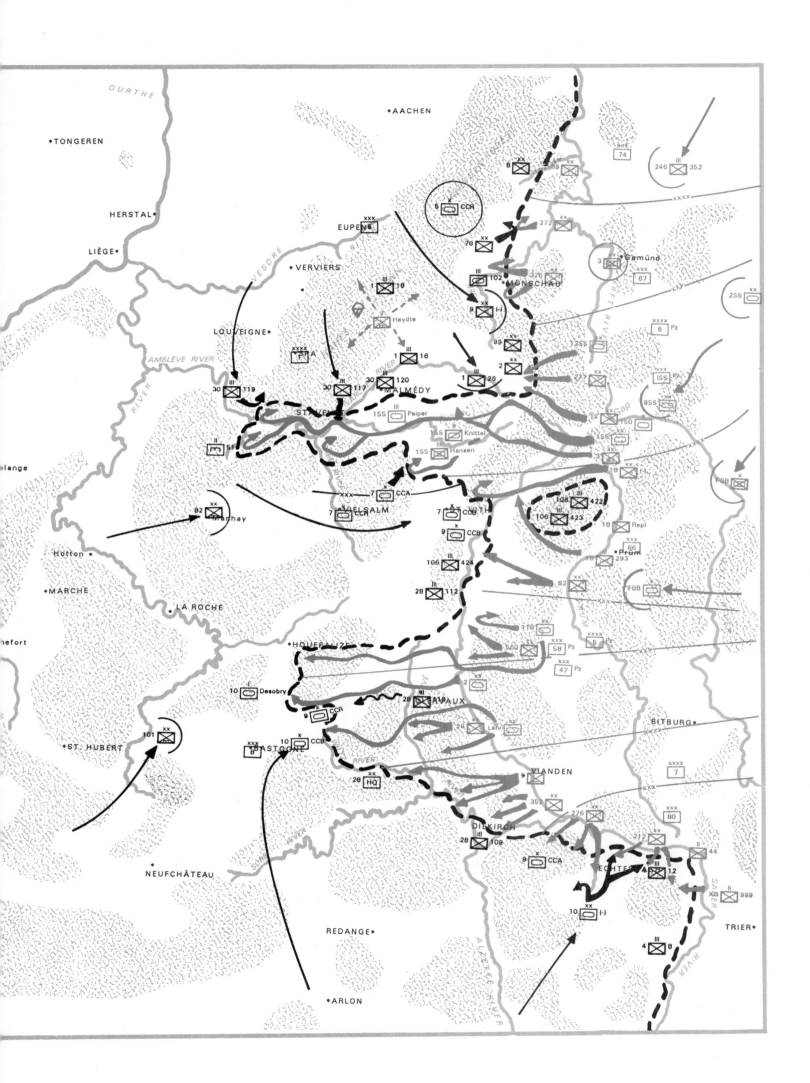

99th Division still held the crossroads at Losheimergraben. Only after "bitter battles lasting more than a day" was the *12th Volksgrenadiers* able to oust the Americans from the strategic crossroads. Even then, the road was found to be mined. With that the *ISS Panzerkorps* ordered Kühlmann's tanks to reinforce the fight at Rocherath-Krinkelt. At the end of 48 hours of intense fighting the *12th SS Panzer Division* had scarcely moved west.

To the south, however, Dietrich's left panzer spearhead had better luck. The heavily armored battlegroup of the *1st SS Panzer Division, Kampfgruppe Peiper,* had knifed through the Losheim Gap at Honsfeld and pressed on to Büllingen. There, in spite of American artillery fire and intervening fighter-bombers, the rampaging Germans seized 50,000 gallons of V Corps gasoline. After forcing captured American soldiers to refuel their panzers at gun point, Peiper's tank force thrust deep behind U.S. lines some 25 miles westward along *Rollbahn D.* The battlegroup ran afoul of some 9th Armored Division tanks in Ligneuville, losing several vehicles, but paused only briefly.[2] Peiper's men moved westward ruthlessly, spraying their path with gun fire and spreading terror as they went. Near the Belgian village of Malmédy members of the SS battle group killed 84 unarmed U.S. soldiers. Over the following days news of the event spread like wild fire through the U.S. ranks. But Peiper was moving too swiftly to know of the grim events transpiring towards the end of his fifteen mile column. That night, resting from two days of uninterrupted advance and waiting for German infantry to catch up, his tank force bivouaced just south of Stavelot. Peiper was confident that they would reach the Meuse River the following day.

Two other battle groups of the *1st SS Panzer Division* had also broken through in the Losheim Gap moving along *Roll-*

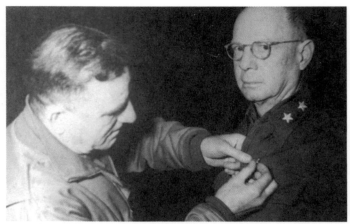

Maj. Gen. Leonard Gerow, commander of the U.S. V Corps, pins the Bronze star on Maj. Gen. William Robertson for his skillful handling of the U.S. 2nd Infantry Division on Elsenborn Ridge.

bahn E. Kampfgruppe Hansen, (the *1st SS Panzer Grenadier Regiment* reinforced by a battalion of self-propelled tank destroyers) followed by *Kampfgruppe Knittel* (the *1st SS Panzer Reconnaissance Battalion* under command of SS-Stbf. Gustav Knittel). Their long convoy drove from Ormont through the southern sector of the Gap to Andler and Heppenbach before pushing on to the village of Born by nightfall. This thrust placed these German forces only four miles north of the village of St. Vith, their move west only delayed by the

2   Peiper detoured from his assigned route in at least two instances: first to gain the fuel he knew to be in Büllingen and bypass the treacherous stretch of muddy trails near Schoppen and later to avoid similar quagmire near Thirimont. Contrary to what some historians have stated, the German march routes were not fixed in stone. According to Hermann Priess in charge of *ISS Panzerkorps:* "Each division had express permission to deviate from prescribed routes whenever the situation demanded...."

Ligneuville, 1945. Americans pose in front a knocked out Panther of Kampfgruppe Peiper shot down by a Sherman tank in the town in front of the Hotel des Ardennes on December 17th. The Panther belonged to SS Untersturmführer Arndt Fischer, a personal friend of Peiper's, who was badly burned in escaping the crippled tank.

The Horror. Men of the 99th Division shot down by their towed anti-tank gun in Honsfeld having fought an unequal battle with Kampfgruppe Peiper.

atrocious state of the muddy roads and a series of obstructions on their assigned route from Herresbach to Wereth.

The planned German parachute jump was finally made in the early hours of December 17th to a strategic road intersection at Belle-Croix crossroads nine miles southwest of Monschau. Widely scattered by windy conditions and inexperienced pilots, no more than 300 of the 870 parachutists floated to the right place. The rest of the German paratroopers landed pell mell from Verviers to Cologne surprising both Allied and German troops alike. With such a tiny force, no radio, few heavy weapons and almost no supplies, *Gruppe von der Heydte* had no real possibility of sealing off the Eupen-Malmèdy roadnet. In one sense the German mission was successful: hunting down the German parachutists occupied important American reinforcements for several days. Although urgently needed at the fighting front, the 18th Regiment of the 1st Division and later CCA of the 3rd Armored both remained in the Eupen vicinity until December 20th to protect V Corps against the airborne enemy threat. But six days later, the leader of the German parachute team, an experienced veteran from the German airborne operations at Crete, Obst. von der Heydte, surrendered to American forces near Monschau, clearly disgusted with the war.

Likewise, *Operation Greif*, the plan to use the *150th Panzer*

Oberst Frederich-August von der Heydte inspects German paratroopers. Baron von der Heydte would lead the final German parachute operation of the war in the Ardennes on December 17th. It was the only night time German parachute operation of the war.

Brigade with captured American equipment and Germans dressed as GIs to seize the Meuse bridgeheads, was not working out. Skorzeny's brigade had been stuck for the entire first day in monstrous traffic jams. The element of surprise gone, Skorzeny received permission to commit his "Trojan-Horse" panzer brigade as a regular combat unit.

SS Oberführer Wilhelm Mohnke of the 1st SS Panzer Divi-sion surveys the impossible traffic jam on Panzer Rollbahn E on the way to Ligneuville.

Continuing the battle on December 17th, von Manteuf-fel's *Fifth Panzer Armee* was joined by the tanks of the *2nd Panzer Division* which, after crushing American resistance in Marnach, were pushing on to wrest the town of Clervaux from the Americans who barred their way west. By now, the U.S. 110th Regiment had been repeatedly penetrated, was surrounded and under continuous assault. As darkness fell, German tanks thrust through the Americans in the an-cient castled town and seized a bridge across the Clerf River.

Just to the south, the *26th Volksgrenadier Division* was still waging a war of position against stubborn U.S. defenders just west of the Our River. Although the grenadiers could not force their way onto the road intersection at Hosingen, they did manage to seize a bridgehead across the Clerf River at Drauffelt. The stubborn American garrison did not give up until the following day. Amid a terrible traffic bottle-neck at the recently completed Gemünd bridge, the *Panzer Lehr Division* wormed across the river with its reconnaissance battalion.[3] On the other side *Kampfgruppe Kaufmann*, the combined elements of the lefthand regiment of the *26th* and the *Lehr* reconnaissance battalion, engaged the American company bravely defending the villages of Holzthum and Consthum. Ownership of the villages was vital to the Ger-

German faux pas. Shortly after crossing the constructed bridge over the Our River at Dasburg, Germans vehicles came upon three trunks that they themselves had cut down across the road when retreating the previous September. This obstacle slowed the German advance on Marnach and Clervaux

man cause, controlling, as they did, the roads leading into the Skyline Drive. By nightfall Consthum fell in bitter fighting to the overwhelming strength of the German infan-try and armor.

The right of the 110th Regiment was also under heavy

3   Paradoxically, the exit road from the Gemünd bridge was blocked by felled trees and shell craters the Germans themselves had left behind in their retreat in September.

Above: *Clervaux, 1945. The devastation after the battle.*

At left: *The picturesque village as it appears today.*

infantry assault and the Germans had taken the Clerf River crossing near Kautenbach. The foe here was the *5th Fallschirmjäger Division*. Although finally forced to withdraw, the 28th Division, the "Bloody Buckets," had held long enough to allow the commander of the U.S. VIII Corps, Lt. Gen. Troy Middleton time to assemble barrier lines on the road to the important road hub of Bastogne. Between Clervaux and that town he placed his meager reserves —a reserve combat command of the 9th Armored Division (which although well trained and led as yet had no combat experience) and some engineer battalions.

After 48 hours of hard fighting the Germans finally cleared Clervaux and the Skyline Drive. Furthermore, the *XLVII Panzerkorps* claimed 1,155 prisoners and 22 American tanks destroyed in the first two days of fighting. However, Gen. von Lüttwitz's divisions were more than a day behind schedule and still 15 miles from Bastogne. The cost to the Americans had been heavy, however; the 110th Regiment suffered 80% casualties in barely 72 hours of fighting.

To the north, the *116th Panzer Division* was once more frustrated in its efforts to force its way across the Our River

Personal Reconnaissance. Gnfldm. Walther Model (center) pays a visit to the 116th Panzer Division. Genmaj. Siegfried von Waldenburg, the divisional commander, stands on the right. Gen. Krebs, Model's chief of staff, flanks Model. The tank in the background is a Mk IV of the 5th Kompanie.

near the German border. Finally committing the panzer regiment of the division along with heavy corps artillery support, the Germans moved to evict the Americans from the Ouren area. Even though the 112th Regiment fought tenaciously with strong artillery and even air support, the German pressure was too much. By dark the U.S. infantry regiment was forced to pull back west of the river with German tanks just behind them. The Germans re-captured the span at Ouren, but alas, found it could not support their heavy Panthers. Disappointed, von Manteuffel ordered the division to cross over the *2nd Panzer Division's* bridge at Dasburg just to the south. The tenacity of the American defenders had cost him valuable time. So commanded, the division's panzer reconnaissance battalion, *Kampfgruppe Stephan* (Hauptmann Eberhard Stephan), moved across the Our at the light bridge near Heinerscheid. Almost as soon as they crossed they were engaged by the light tanks of the U.S. 707th Tank Battalion which they defeated in a one-sided battle.

Under orders from Gen. Jones, the 7th Armored had planned a rescue attack towards Schönberg on the 17th to reach the two surrounded regiments of his 106th Division. However, these hopes were dashed by the difficulty the division had reaching the town amid a terrible traffic snarl. All elements of the 7th Armored were not in hand until the early morning hours of December 18th. The command situation became a factor as well. Impressed by the gravity of events, Brig. Gen. Bruce Clarke, in charge of CCB of the 7th Ar-

mored, asked his division commander, Brig. Gen. Robert W. Hasbrouck, that the attack be cancelled on the morning of the 18th. Jones disagreed, but rather than insist that Clarke attack, Jones told him to take over command of the battle at St. Vith. The chain of Allied command over the battle at St. Vith was particularly confusing during the following days.[4] Clarke was well aware of the German threat to his supply line at Poteau. There also may have been some caution brought home by a brush the divisional columns had with the tail of *Kampfgruppe Peiper* between Pont and Stavelot on its way to St. Vith; the divisional chief of staff was killed in one of these encounters. However, it was the Germans who ended any plans for a relief operation.

Although short on armor and busy encircling the 106th Division in the Schnee Eifel, the *18th Volksgrenadier Division* was under direct orders from Gen. von Manteuffel to take St. Vith (both von Manteuffel of *Fifth Panzer Armee* and Model of *Heeresgruppe B* spent the afternoon of the 17th at the divisional command post prodding the corps into action and trying to sort out the monstrous traffic jam on the Schönberg road). Two simultaneous German thrusts towards the town north from Wallerode and Hünningen in the early morning were thrown back with some difficulty by CCB of both the 7th and 9th Armored Divisions. Even so,

4   Gen. Hodges later made Gen. Hasbrouck the overall commander for the forces in and around St. Vith. This included his own division as well as the 106th, CCB of the 9th Armored and later, the 112th Regiment of the 28th Division.

Traffic and mud. A stalled American motor column in the Ardennes.

these attempts coupled with other German attacks at Poteau to the north were enough to cancel the rescue attempt by the 7th Armored towards the two stranded regiments of the 106th Infantry Division.

The American armor missed a fleeting opportunity to reach the surrounded regiments, for only part of a German infantry regiment lay in the path to Schönberg. On the other hand, the fog of war was particularly obfuscating and the scene in St. Vith was one of wild confusion; no one was really sure what German forces lurked east of the Schnee Eifel. Some intelligence reports had mistakenly identified a full panzer regiment in the area. Regardless, the German attacks that had flared up around the edges of the defense perimeter had convinced Gen. Hasbrouck that his 7th Armored Division was itself in danger of encirclement.

The German story was this: on the morning of the 17th the *18th Volksgrenadiers* captured the bridges at Schönberg and Andler on the Our River while the left hand regiment fought its way past Bleialf and closed the jaws around the Americans in the Schnee Eifel. By noon a battalion-size group reinforced by assault guns even seized the villages of Setz and Heuem, only five miles due east of St. Vith. By dark small contingents of Germans were in contact with the defenses before St. Vith only two miles to the east of that town. But the reports of these accomplishments masked the German troubles in their effort. Artillery concentrations on Schönberg, an American air attack in the afternoon and the stand made by elements of the 14th Armored Cavalry at

Heum took much of the bite out of the German push. Part of the German advance circled around to Wallerode to attempt to seize the high ground there.

By dark on December 17th the Allied command had more information with which to judge the seriousness of the situation. With Eisenhower's approval, Gen. Hodges ordered the 1st and 30th Infantry Divisions to rush down from north of the Ardennes. The regiments of the 1st in their Herve and Eupen bivouacs were to move to the Elsenborn area where the 99th and 2nd Infantry Divisions were under vigorous attack. The 30th was to cast a net of road blocks before the dangerous armored penetration of *Kampfgruppe Peiper*. Meanwhile on the 17th, the 7th Armored Division moved south from the Ninth Army to the defense of St. Vith, bucking American traffic headed west.[5] At the same time, two U.S. airborne divisions were ordered to the Ardennes, the 82nd to Werbomont where it could block Peiper's anticipated move and the 101st to Bastogne to hold that key road center.

As a further reinforcement for the endangered northern flank, CCR of the 5th Armored Division was moved to the Eupen area to backup the American positions at Monschau. To bolster the weak defense in the Malmèdy area, the reserve of the Army Security Force, the 99th Infantry Battalion was dispatched to the town. To guard the critical fuel

5   This traffic included parts of the 14th Armored Cavalry Group and battalions of VIII Corps artillery which had been ordered to displace westward from their former positions before St. Vith.

Men of the 30th Infantry Division march to halt the German penetration near Malmédy.

Elated over the early German successes, a grenadier happily rides an assault gun in the advance east of St. Vith.

depot and the First Army Headquarters south of Spa, three separate battalions, the 526th Armored Infantry, the 823rd Tank Destroyer and the 110th AA Gun Battalion were deployed along the approaches from the Amblève River.

At the far southern end of the battlefield, Gen. Brandenberger's *Seventh Armee* was struggling to overcome the comparatively small American forces that lay in its path. The German bridge at Roth had not yet been completed so that some German assault guns of the *11th Sturmgeschütz Brigade* were ferried across the Our at Vianden. By late afternoon the *5th Fallschirmjäger Division* had taken Hoscheid at a cost of at least a hundred dead, while advance elements of the division pressed on towards the Wiltz River crossing at Kautenbach. Just to the south, the *352nd Volksgrenadiers* launched a concentric attack on the village of Fouhren seeking to erase the troublesome American company still holding out there.

In the *LXXX Armeekorps*, the *212th Volksgrenadiers* pressed home their attack. Maj. Gen. Raymond O. Barton, the commander of the 4th Infantry Division, had ordered "No retrograde movement." His men obeyed literally even though a coherent line was impossible; the southernmost sector was only held at the village of Lauterborn. This village was the subject to the attention of both combatants; five American tanks counterattacked the Germans headed for the hamlet who responded by swinging around the position to capture the village of Scheidgen in the American rear. At Berdorf, the American infantry company in the Parc Hôtel waited hopefully for tanks to break through the ring the Germans had drawn around them; the same was true of another company defending a hat factory in Echternach. Although Osweiler and Dickweiler still held out, the message from the defending companies was ominous: "Situation desperate." At Consdorf only an urgent and improvised defense composed of a single headquarters tank and "everyone that could shoot" kept the Germans at bay. And finally on the extreme left flank of the German offensive, a punishment formation, the *XIII/999 Festung Infantrerie Battalion*, crossed

the Sauer River and advanced on the village of Girst before being halted by small arms fire from the 4th Division.

Under prodding, the *276th Volksgrenadier Division* took the village of Beaufort and thrust through the Ernz Noire gorge to the outskirts of Breitweiler and Müllerthal. So surprising had been the German advance through the gorge that a hastily improvised American defense under a collection of troops fighting as Task Force Luckett (Col. James S. Luckett) was rushed to the area to prevent further German advance. But the Germans halted after taking Müllerthal, likely in response to their lack of heavy weapons and need for re-supply. Work on the volksgrenadiers' bridge at Wallendorf had been halted as equipment losses from the American shelling could not be made good; an alternative bridge at Bollendorf was not scheduled for completion for another four days! Gen. Brandenberger was clearly disappointed with the torpid advance of the half-trained division. He ordered its commander, Genmaj. Kurt Möhring, relieved of command.

Luckily for the hard pressed American infantry on the south flank, reinforcements had begun to arrive from Patton's Third Army. Combat Commands A and R of Maj. Gen. William H. Morris's 10th Armored Division were moving to assist in the defense of Luxembourg (CCB was sent to Bastogne). Not only was Luxembourg City the capital of that proud and tiny country, but the headquarters for Bradley's 12th Army Group and the Ninth Air Force as well. It was also less than 20 miles from the German front line. As Eisenhower saw it, the south flank, like the Elsenborn Ridge, must be held to thwart the enemy offensive.

The Allied Supreme Commander needn't have worried. So limited was the progress of the *Seventh Armee*, that on the 17th Hitler himself agreed to bringing up the *Führer Grenadier Brigade* to aid Brandenberger. Meantime, *OB West* pressed *Heeresgruppe G* for the rapid dispatch of the *11th Panzer Division* which was now urgently needed for the attack in this area. Gen. Balck, in charge of the army group was disingenuous. He had not really wanted to part with this capable panzer formation in the first place and tersely reported that damage to the rail system from air attack and inadequate fuel deliveries was making the scheduled transfer impossible.

The third day of the battle, the 18th, the fighting intensified once more. To the north, in the *Sixth Panzer Armee* the *326th Volksgrenadier Division*, now with assault gun support, made the final bid to take Höfen and Monschau. However, Allied artillery observers spied the German infantry and self-propelled guns gathering in Imgenbroich at daybreak and blasted the town with gunfire. Vectored American fighter bombers further pummeled the enemy assembly such that the final German effort was sporatic and uncoordinated. The 99th Infantry and recently arrived veteran soldiers of the 9th Infantry Division mopped up the enemy who managed to filter through friendly lines.

The final Allied touch was administered when Gen. Otto Hitzfeld's *LXVII Armeekorps* headquarters, east of Monschau in Dalbenden, was flattened by 30 American medium bombers. German command was paralyzed. As a temporary measure, SS Obergruppenführer (SS-Obgrf.) Wilhelm Bittrich of the *IISS Panzerkorps* took over. This change in command was of little consequence, however. The disasterous German effort to establish a defensive shoulder in the north for *Wacht am Rhein* was over. The cost had been heavy. Over the following days, Americans who had survived the onslaught counted 544 enemy dead before their lines.

While this transpired, savage fighting continued to the south as Dietrich attempted to gain the Elsenborn Ridge. In that vicinity the *12th Volksgrenadier Division* managed to shoot their way into the villages of Hünningen and Mürringen. However, after suffering very heavy casualties at the hands of the U.S. 99th Division, they could not proceed further.

To get things moving across the Elsenborn Ridge, the *12th SS Panzer Division,* with assistance from the *277th Volksgrenadiers,* launched a fierce attack paved by a powerful artillery preparation. This done, the assault again failed to

A dead soldier of the 277th Volksvolksgrenadier Division lies where he fell before two destroyed Panthers of the "Hitler Jugend" Panzer Division in Krinkelt.

break through the U.S. 2nd Infantry Division at Krinkelt. The German division had lost 67 armored vehicles and suffered "terrible infantry casualties" in the process. Word among young GIs that the SS were butchering surrendering American troops lent a special savagery to the battles for Elsenborn Ridge. Few prisoners were taken by either side.

On the right wing of Dietrich's army, the *1st SS Panzer Division* penetrated deep behind American lines. *Kampfgruppe Peiper* fought its way across the Amblève River at Stavelot, crushing the resistance of the hodge podge of engineers, anti-tank guns and members of the 526th Infantry Battalion who had barricaded the approaches to the bridge. Peiper's men did not even pause to secure the town and pressed on along the highway west to the next bridge at Trois Ponts. But as the first German tank lunged for that crossing, the waiting 51st Engineer Combat Battalion detonated charges which sent it crashing into the Salm River.

The favored avenue of approach denied, Peiper's tanks drove swiftly northwest along the Amblève River valley capturing La Gleize and then turned southwest to cross the river over the bridge at Cheneux. The battle group thrust towards Werbomont only to be delayed by roving American fighter-bombers as they crossed the stream at 1:30 P.M. Peiper lost three tanks and five halftracks to the strafing planes. But more serious than the loss of the heavy equipment, the narrowness of the road precluded passage down the thoroughfare until the wrecks had been laboriously pushed aside. Over two hours elapsed before Peiper could resume his march. Most important of all, the air attack had alerted the engineers of the 291st Engineer Combat Battalion. Again, as the German tanks approached the Neufmoulin bridge across Lienne Creek, the engineers dynamited the span in Peiper's face. "The damned engineers!" the SS commander swore.[6]

Peiper's armor prowled the eastern side the creek near the village of Chevron, but finding no span capable of passing his heavy tanks, the SS colonel had no choice but to turn back to La Gleize. His vehicles were now nearly out of gas. Although Peiper did not know it, his forces in La Gleize were only a few miles from a major American fuel dump with over two million gallons of petrol.[7]

Following in Peiper's wake, *Kampfgruppe Knittel,* along with Tiger tanks of the *501st SS Heavy Panzer Battalion,* crossed the Amblève at Stavelot and sped on to La Gleize to support the armored spearhead. However, Maj. Gen. Leland S. Hobbs's 30th Infantry Division had already moved to Malmédy and Stavelot to halt the German advance. They fought their way into Stavelot that afternoon, threatening to cut Peiper's supply. Significantly, both Knittel and the heavy panzer battalion did not act to secure the town before

6 After the war, Peiper lamented, "If only we had taken the bridge at Trois Ponts intact and had enough fuel, it would have been a simple matter to drive through to the Meuse River early that day."

7 The oft told story of Peiper's attempt to capture the fuel dumps is in error. Before the battle Peiper had been given a map showing the location of the dump he nearly captured at Büllingen and another somewhere near Spa. However, Peiper did not know of the precise locations and never made any attempt to capture them. When told after the war how close he had come to the gasoline depot he shrugged, "You would have no doubt destroyed them anyway."

At left: *Morning December 18th.* Kampgruppe Knittel, *the reconnaissance battalion of the* 1st SS Panzer Division *confidently advances past the Kaiserbaracke crossroads, northwest of St. Vith.*

Lower Left: *SS soldiers of* Kampfgruppe Hansen, *the* 1st SS Panzergrenadier Regiment *in action near the crossroads of Poteau on December 18th. The burning vehicles are from the U.S. 14th Armored Cavalry Group which lost possession of the battlefield that morning.*

Right: *A Jagdpanzer IV of the* 1st SS Panzer Division *in action near Poteau on December 18th.*

going to Peiper's aid. Only a small rearguard was left behind.

Meanwhile, to the south, the SS panzer grenadiers of *Kampfgruppe Hansen* reached Recht some five miles northwest of St. Vith, on the night of the 17th. There they ran into elements of Combat Command R of the 7th Armored Division which was assembling its forces in the area. A sharp nighttime firefight ensued in which the Americans finally ordered a withdrawal to Poteau, a few miles to the south.

The Germans continued to grow in strength in Recht while the remnants of the 14th Cavalry assembled as Task Force Mayes (Maj. J.L. Mayes) in an attempt to retake that town. An early morning thrust ran squarely into the Germans at Recht. The German pressure was too great and the cavalrymen were forced to withdraw leaving a great number of their vehicles that were tied up in a traffic jam on the road with the 7th Armored. The Germans pursued the cavalry, pressing on to take the crossroads at the village of Poteau. However, that key road intersection was vital to the 7th Armored Division's defense of St. Vith. On the orders "imperative you seize Poteau and hold it," Combat Command A struck towards the German held village that afternoon forcing its way into the town in fierce fighting. So bludgeoned, the panzer grenadiers pulled back to Recht.

Even so, the road to Vielsalm, and the 7th Armored's supply line, was endangered. An intrepid lieutenant from the 7th Armored's CCR had collected a miscellaneous panoply of stray tanks, straggling soldiers and some lost engineers to block the road at Petit Their. But luckily for Task Force Navaho (so named because its leader, 1st Lt. Joseph V. Whiteman had worked his way through college selling indian blankets) the German march route lay to the northwest and after their initial rebuff, Hansen's advance guard marched off towards Trois Ponts.

Meantime, the *150th Panzer Brigade* and *Kampfgruppe Sandig* (2nd SS Panzer Grenadier Regiment under command of SS-Ostbf. Rudolf Sandig) marched to Ligneuville and prepared to move to the Amblève River line to secure Stavelot. Supply problems began to surface as the *ISS Panzerkorps* had only one hard-surfaced road available both for troop movements and supply. This road was jammed with vehicles of three different German divisions.

Near St. Vith, the *LXVI Armeekorps* took up the fight east the town in earnest. Three separate attempts were made to rush the American line, now stiffened by the presence of the 7th Armored Division and the 168th Engineer Combat Battalion. All German advances were turned back with heavy

casualties.

Southeast of this action, the *62nd Volksgrenadier Division,* fighting the 106th Division's 424th Regiment, forced its way into Winterspelt in bitter fighting, but Heckuscheid could not be taken; possession of the village changed hands several times during the fighting that swirled through its streets. However, CCB of the 9th Armored Division had moved up behind the 424th to St. Vith. Pushing out to the east to meet the enemy on the Winterspelt road the armored infantry thrashed the Germans near Elcherath with a hail of artillery and tank fire. This effectively ended the German attempt to rush the Our River bridge at Steinbrück. Late that afternoon, however, word arrived from Gen. Jones, in charge of the 106th Division, that CCB and the 424th Regiment must pull back to the west bank of the Our River that night. This they did, with the finality of blasting the bridge at Steinbrück to deny it to the enemy. The volksgrenadiers moved up to the demolished span the following day.

Even with this successful defense of the area south of St. Vith, the other two regiments of the 106th Division were still locked in the jaws of the German pincers. The American infantry attempted to breakout through Schönberg to the west, but this attempt was repulsed by German flak guns. With supplies running low, U.S. air officers planned an air supply operation for the surrounded group. However, dense fog at the air bases in England grounded the transport aircraft. Still, the American-held town of St. Vith was a major obstruction to the German advance. After two appeals from von Rundstedt, Hitler consented to the use of the *Führer Begleit Brigade* to erase the stiffening American resistance there.[8]

On the 18th, von Manteuffel methodically set to work destroying Middleton's road blocks in front of Bastogne with his two panzer divisions. In night actions at the Féitsch crossroads and Allerborn, west of Clervaux, the tanks of *Kampfgruppe Guttmann* (Obst. Joachim Guttmann of the *2nd Panzer Division*) effectively annihilated Task Forces Rose

8   The *Führer Begleit Brigade* was an elite formation that had been recently created around Hitler's palace guard, now copiously equipped with heavy weapons, artillery and flak guns. Even the armored component (71 tanks and assault guns) was exceptional, being the elite second battalion (Mk IV-longs) from the panzer regiment of the *Grossdeutschland Panzer Division* of East Front fame. Hastily assembled, the major deficiency was the lack of training as a cohesive unit. Obst. Otto Remer was rewarded with the command for the decisive part he played in crushing the revolt against Hitler on July 20th.

U.S. gunners of the 7th Armored Division prepare a last ditch defense around a 3-inch anti-tank gun to hold the important bridge at Vielsalm.

and Harper of Combat Command R of the 9th Armored Division. Captain L.K. Rose was captured and Lt. Col. Ralph S. Harper was killed. Around midnight on the 18th, the *2nd Panzer Division* was about six miles northeast of Bastogne near Allerborn and bearing down on the nearby crossroads village of Noville.

Just to the south, *Kampfgruppe von Poschinger* (Oberstleutnant Joachim von Poschinger) of the *Panzer Lehr Division* had moved across the Clerf River at Drauffelt and advanced through Eschweiler at 3:00 P.M. Just to the south, *Kampfgruppe von Fallois* motored through Erpeldingen to join the other panzer column at Derenbach. There, they brushed aside Task Force Hayze of CCR of the 9th Armored Division. The Germans reached Niederwampach by dark, their advance slowed by VIII Corps engineers attempting to delay the enemy tanks and the gummy roads along their march route. But by midnight the German panzers, after grinding slowly forward on a muddy trail to Mageret, were only a scant three miles from the prize of Bastogne. There, however, Gen. Bayerlein, in charge of the German advance lost his nerve. He had become cautious from false reports of strong U.S. forces that lay ahead.[9]

Now across the Our at Dasburg, the *116th Panzer Division*, with the *560th Volksgrenadiers* marching in its wake, was moving via Heinerscheid and Trois Vierges into Houffalize in an unopposed advance. However, its rear elements were entangled as far back as the Our River with the supply columns of the *2nd Panzer Division*.

The fight in the *Seventh Armee* on the 18th continued to

Panzer leaders. From left to right: Genlt. Fritz Bayerlein, commander of Panzer Lehr Division, *Obst. Gerhardt, in charge of his panzer regiment and Gen. Walter Krüger commander of the* LVIII Panzerkorps.

9   The commander of the *Panzer Lehr Division*, Gen. Fritz Bayerlein, had been mislead by a Belgian civilian, Emile Frère, into believing the road was trafficable and made cautious by his report that a large American force lay ahead near the village of Neffe.

be an exercise in frustration for the German command. Although the north flank of the 109th Regiment had greatly delayed the German advance in this sector, the increasing enemy numbers, now with assault guns, caused them to pull back. The German paratroopers of the *5th Fallschirmjäger Division* followed their spore doggedly, crossing the Our at Bourscheid and then the Wiltz River at Kautenbach before sweeping toward the town of Wiltz with the left wing of von Manteuffel's army.

The *352nd Volksgrenadier Division*'s attack got moving on the morning of the 18th after passing its Czech assault guns over the Our River at a constructed bridge near Gentingen. The armor assisted assault carried the Germans through Longsdorf towards the village of Tandel; the surrounded U.S. garrison in Fouhren finally surrendered. By nightfall the division was closing in on the 1st Battalion of the 109th Regiment at Diekirch some six miles from the German start line.

The two left hand divisions of Brandenberger's army were nearly stalled, their engineers having great difficulty inserting bridges across the Sauer River while under shelling from American artillery. The *276th Volksgrenadiers* managed to wrest the village of Savelborn from CCA of the 9th Armored Division. After this they even turned back a counterattack by Task Forces Hall (Capt. John W. Hall) and Philbeck (Maj. Tommie M. Philbeck) which were ordered to "drive the enemy into the river." Instead, the abortive foray counted seven tanks lost to German *panzerfausts*. At dark on the 18th, the German infantry was infiltrating through the woods towards Haller. The U.S. 4th Infantry Division halted the *212th Volksgrenadier Division* south of Osweiler and Dickweiler, mopping up a number of German soldiers who had penetrated through the main line of resistance. Even so, U.S. units of the 4th Division were isolated at a number of points — particularly in the town of Echternach.

Meantime, the Americans moved up three task forces of Combat Command A of the 10th Armored to stop the German advance. Task Force Chamberlain moved into the Ernz Noire to stop the *276th Volksgrenadiers*, but came under such a hail of *panzerfaust* and small arms fire that they were forced to pull back. Task Force Standish pushed through to rescue the American garrison in Berdorf, only to be engaged in bitter house-to-house fighting in the town. Task Force Riley managed to reach the American defense in Echternach, but could not convince them to leave; Gen. Barton's "no retrograde movement" order was still in force. That afternoon the German artillery got to work pummeling the town with gun fire, and so harassed, the small tank force pulled back to the west. The Germans had deadlocked American efforts at relief with artillery interdiction fire. "Strong enemy pressure with tanks against the *212th Volksgrenadier Division*, went the evening report of *LXXX Armeekorps* to Model's headquarters, "There are counterattacks against the advance guard positions between Consdorf and Herborn. In the main, attacks are being repelled. "

Pouring over their carefully coded situation maps that night, the German high command was less than pleased with the progress of the German offensive in their evening report.

Although noting the breakout of Peiper's combat group, von Rundstedt recorded "no real progress by the panzer formations" and ordered the march westward to continue on through the night. On a larger level, von Rundstedt called for *Wacht am Rhein* to be discontinued; he was already convinced of its failure:

> We should abandon the offensive and prepare to defend the area we have gained. Sepp Dietrich's forces are held up between Monschau and Malmèdy. St. Vith has not been taken. We have only just reached Bastogne, which ought to have been taken on D plus 1. We have not made the most of our initial surprise. The offensive has never gathered speed due to the icy roads and the pockets of resistance which have forced us to lay in full scale attacks.

Genfldm. Model was having similar doubts. Although stating in his official report, "the third day of the attack is marked by the successful breakthrough on the broad front between Stavelot and Bastogne," he admitted serious qualms to those around him about the potential success of the offensive in light of recent events. Model was especially worried about the situation in the north. In his war diary he and his staff pondered whether their reserve, the *3rd Panzer Grenadier Division*, "should follow via Kalterherberg to assist *Operation Stösser*, or go to the *12thSS Panzer Division* should it begin to break through." However, the Nazi commander's worries were really much greater. His aide would later say that with the repulse of Dietrich's army to the north and the slow pace of Manteuffel's army to the south, "*Heeresgruppe B* came to the conclusion on the third day that the Big Solution had failed." Model himself telephoned both von Rundstedt as well as Gen. Jodl that evening to give the bad news.

Hitler's response was typical. He rebuked von Rundstedt and Model for their pessimism, ignored the grim tidings, and called for surgical removal of the enemy defense. The American troops fighting on both sides of the attack near Krinkelt and Echternach must be "cut-off from the rear," Hitler commanded, "so that they lose their supply and then will capitulate." On the other hand, the poor development of the attack thus far, in particular in the *Sixth Panzer Armee* sector, moved the German leader to cancel the planned offensive operation (*Operation Spätlese*) of the right wing of Ge. Gustav-Adolph von Zangen's *Fifteenth Armee*. Instead, he ordered that all forces earmarked for that attack (*9th Panzer* and *15th Panzer Grenadier* and *340th Volksgrenadier Divisions*) be hurried to the Ardennes to support the main assault of *Wacht am Rhein*. This move ended the threat that his generals might try to slip the "Small Solution" into the offensive plan. As Hitler had intended all along, Antwerp was now the only offensive goal.[10] In a gesture to reward success in the Ardennes, the German leader also ordered that the *9th SS "Hohenstaufen" Panzer Division* be committed to reinforce Peiper's advance in the northern sector.

However, Hitler's admonitions to greater effort could not

---

10 After the abandonment of *Operation Spätlese* von Rundstedt ordered Student to place great value on "accelerated completion of preparations pertaining to *Heeresgruppe H*'s assault across the Waal and Meuse Rivers towards Antwerp...the army group must be ready as of 22 December to attack without warning within 24 hours."

influence physical realities on the Ardennes battlefield. Scarcely 72 hours after the initial assault, ominous fuel shortages began to appear on the German attack front. The *Führer Begleit Brigade*, released by *OKW* the day before, was unable to move up for the attack on St. Vith because the allocation of gasoline was inadequate. Since front line *OKW* fuel reserves had been used up, Genfldm. Keitel was compelled to divert some 3,000 tons of petrol from other fronts and Reichminister Speer indicated his intention to deliver 4,500 tons from civilian stocks. Whether these fuel reserves could be transported to the front, however, was apocryphal. In December of 1944, truck transport in the Reich was in as short supply as the fuel it hauled.

The renewed bombing attack east of the Eifel on the 18th caused further difficulties to supply movement for *Heeresgruppe B*. Eight hundred medium bombers with 750 fighter escorts pulverized German transportation targets in the areas of Cologne, Koblenz, Kaiserslauten and Mayen in an attempt to choke off German fuel supplies. Meanwhile the Germans committed 650 fighters on the 17th and another 849 on the 18th to the Ardennes battle. As a consequence, many of the 1,300 Allied fighters had been unable to intervene in the battle. Even so, some American sorties did get through the German fighter screen and the soupy weather. U.S. fighters attacked the *116th Panzer Division* on December 17th, and the tanks of *Kampfgruppe Peiper* on the 18th. However, there were instances where German planes bombed and strafed American positions in the north — a rare experience for American troops.

The weather too was a problem. Although the cloudy skies continued to shield the German panzers from Allied fighter-bombers, the fog and mist of the 16th had begun to change to rain and sleet. The unpaved roads over which the heavy German tanks attempted to advance turned to quagmire. "Pulling up the werfers and artillery on the roads, which are often completely covered with mud, is very difficult," *Sixth Panzer Armee* reported.

The third day of the battle saw the tempo of American reinforcements increase. The 18th Regiment of the 1st Infantry Division was searching the woods south of Eupen for German paratroops while the 16th Regimental Combat Team organized the defense of Waimes, east of Malmédy. The 26th Regiment had already moved into place to defend a large Belgian farming estate, Dom Bütgenbach, south of the Elsenborn Ridge on the afternoon of the 17th. Combat Command A of Maj. Gen. Maurice Rose's 3rd Armored Division was currently assigned to guard the V Corps headquarters in Eupen based on fears of another German paratroop drop. Meanwhile, CCR of the division hastened to the Hotton-Baraque Fraiture area on the 19th where VIII

The 26th Infantry Regiment of the "Big Red One," the 1st Infantry Division, moves up to defend the critical are around Dom Bütgenbach.

Corps reports indicated a dangerous enemy penetration (*116th Panzer Division*). In the extreme south of the Ardennes, CCB of the 10th Armored Division was moving to the defense of the road hub at Bastogne amid an exceedingly uncertain situation.

In Bastogne the signs of local panic were increasing. At dawn Luxembourg refugees and routed remnants of the 28th Division streamed through the town, the former telling that the Germans were burning villages to the ground and the later swearing that the Nazi tanks were just behind them. But this was not completely rumor; the first German shell exploded in the streets of Bastogne that afternoon. Although the situation was threatening, Middleton remained calm. Reinforcements were on the way.

But Gen. Hodges, with one division surrounded and another being routed by a full panzer army, told Eisenhower he must have more to stem the German tide. With Bradley's blessing, Ike had sent his only strategic reserve: the two airborne divisions of the XVIII Airborne Corps. By midnight, December 17th, these elite divisions under the stalwart command of Maj. Gen. Matthew B. Ridgway were motoring east from France to defend the Ardennes. The ride was miserable — a hundred mile haul at night in freezing rain.

By monitoring Allied radio traffic, the Germans were privy to the American move. When XVIII Corps passed on orders for the movement of the two divisions on the 17th they did not reach the Americans alone; returning at dark to Daleiden to his command post of *XLVII Panzerkorps*, Gen. von Lüttwitz was given the same message translated into German. Ominously, Luftwaffe planes buzzed the American procession dropping flares in the night, sporadically lighting the convoy's path. But the 82nd and 101st Airborne Divisions kept with their schedule, moving across the mist-covered Meuse River the following afternoon into the uncertainty of the Ardennes. Gen. von Lüttwitz studied the American troop movements on his situation map. "They are moving towards the battlefield. They can have only one concentration area — Bastogne," he surmised. "We shall be there before them."

Trucks carrying the U.S. 82nd Airborne Division move up over the snow bound Ardennes roads near Werbomont.

Borrowed trucks. Members of the 101st Airborne Division depart Cape Mourmelon on the morning of December 18th in uncovered ten-ton trucks borrowed from supply duties. Their uncomfortable ride would end at the fateful location of Bastogne.

Operation Stösser: The Last German Parachute Operation

Adolf Hitler's parachute operation in the Battle of the Bulge was the last German airborne mission of the European war. In planning his last great offensive of the west, the German leader wanted to recreate the elements that had worked so skillfully for him in the conquest of France in 1940. Even though humbled by his pyrrhic victory at Crete, he still desired at least a token airborne operation for the Ardennes Offensive. For the German *Fallschirmjäger* troops in late 1944 the wheel came full circle on the High Ardennes plateau. They had been the artisans of some the Reich's most spectacular victories, opening the way for the early German conquests. Now they were to be sacrified in the darkness and snow in Hitler's last desperate gamble of the war.

The use of German paratroops in the great offensive had been suggested by Genfldm. Model of *Heeresgruppe B* on December 4th. Model suggested that "a local Luftwaffe land operation" be carried out in the Hohes Venn area "to hold open one or two important roads" for the *12th SS Panzer Division* using 20 troop carrying gliders and 160 paratroops. However, the following day, the Luftwaffe informed Model that such an operation could not be carried out by day due to enemy air superiority, nor by night due to insufficient training of the required crews.

Unfazed by this objection, Model ordered that the idea be pursued as a night parachute jump to "drop on *O-Tag* two hours after the initial assault with 300-400 paratroops to occupy the road center of Krinkelt." Hitler took to the idea right away, but changed the drop zone to the Mont Rigi crossroads on the highway from Eupen to Malmédy. Regardless of official sanction, however, the offensive was scarcely two weeks away. Could such an operation be organized and mounted in that time?

Code named *Operation Stösser* (Operation Auk) the last German para-

Oberst Frederich-August von der Heydte, a veteran of the German airborne conquest of Crete in 1941, inspects his troops. Baron von der Heydte would lead the last German parachute operation of the war.

troop operation of the war was organized in great haste in the second week of December. For his paratroop operation, Hitler enlisted the help of one of the most prestigious jump leaders, Baron Frederich August von der Heydte.

In fall 1944 Oberst von der Heydte was 37-years old. His family came from a long line of Bavarian aristocrats and was related to many of the great families in Europe. A noted scholar, von der Heydte was an Assistant Professor of Law in Berlin when Hitler took power. For several years he studied abroad under a Carnegie Foundation Scholarship. But in 1935, he returned to Germany and joined the 15th Cavalry Regiment in Paderborn. By the time the war broke out, von der Heydte was a regular officer and was detached as a captain in the airborne troops. He commanded a battalion in the Crete paratroop operation with exceptional bravery earning him the Knight's Cross. In 1943 he was the chief of staff to Ramcke's parachute division in Italy and later commanded a parachute regiment in the fighting in France in 1944. Like many others by

that time, the Bavarian officer was disillusioned with the war, but was not in a safe position to question Hitler's authority. He was already on the "suspicion list" since he was cousin of Oberst Claus von Stauffenberg who had tried to assassinate the German leader the previous summer. In fall 1944 Von der Heydte was the commandant of the Fallschirmjäger Battle Training School in Aalten where he had taught a privileged fraction of the German paratroops real jumping. He was determined to stay out of trouble and survive the war.

The Baron did not learn of his upcoming assignment until the great offensive was a little over a week away. On December 8th, he received orders to report at once to Genobst. Kurt Student, in charge of *Heeresgruppe H*. Student told von der Heydte that he was to organize an 800 man *Kampfgruppe* of parachutists for immediate employment. "The Führer has ordered a great offensive. Within the framework of the attack, there will be a parachute drop. You, my dear von der Heydte, are to form and command this force." Student could not tell him what the mission was or where it would be.

The Baron rightfully complained that such a battlegroup was not large enough for any combat mission and that besides, there was simply not enough time to properly organize such an undertaking. Of course, there could be no question, Student told him. It was Hitler's orders. Von der Heydte asked to use his own old regiment, the famous *6th Fallschirmjäger Regiment*, but this was turned down since movement of such a large combat formation might compromise the operation's security. Instead, Student ordered commanders of parachute regiments on the Western front to send their most experienced hundred men to Obst. von der Heydte that same night. Predictably, von der Heydte received the misfits and trouble makers that commanders most wanted to get rid of. "Never in my entire career," von der Heydte remembered, "had I been in command of a unit with less fighting spirit." The great majority of them had never even jumped before (there were, in fact, only 3,000 jump trained paratroops in the entire Luftwaffe!). Despite this inauspicious start, 150 veterans of the *6th Fallschirmjäger* deserted to join von der Heydte who prevailed on their commander to allow them to jump with him. The Baron returned 150 of the worst "dead weight" to their previous units and replaced them with his combat veterans.

On December 11th, von der Heydte received his tactical orders from the *Sixth Panzer Armee* commander in a particularly uncomfortable session, in which Dietrich was under the influence of alcohol. Krämer provided von der Heydte with the formal orders. They read:

> On the first day of the attack *Sixth Panzer Armee* will take possession of Liège or the bridges across the Meuse south of the city. At early dawn on the first day of the attack, *Kampfgruppe von der Heydte* will drop into the Baraque Michel mountain area, eleven kilometers north of Malmedy, and secure the multiple road junction at a Baraque Michel for use by the armored spearhead of the *Sixth Panzer Armee*, probably elements of the *12th SS Panzer Division*. If for technical reasons this mission is impracticable on the morning of the first day of the attack, *Kampfgruppe von der Heydte* will drop early on the following morning into the the Amblève river valley or Amay areas to secure the bridges there for the advance of *Sixth Panzer Armee*'s armored spearheads.

Dietrich made it no secret that he was opposed to the whole operation. "A parachute operation is the one certain way of alerting the Americans about our attack," Dietrich said with great disdain. Von der Heydte told him of the great deficiencies in the air crews that would fly him to the target. "I am not responsible for the deficiencies of the German Luftwaffe!" he snorted. Meantime, Krämer , his chief of staff, sat drumming his fingers on the table muttering at the madness of such improvisation, "It's crazy. What a lunatic operation!" Pointing to the crossroads at Mont Rigi on his opera-

tions map, Dietrich told von der Heydte, "You will go there and make great confusion." Krämer was quick to correct his superior's embarrassing mistake, "It's not von der Heydte's group that makes confusion," he told him. "You have it mixed up with Obersturmbannführer's *Operation Greif*. With this misunderstanding cleared von der Heydte asked Dietrich to assign an artillery observer to his paratroopers from one of the panzer divisions so that he could obtain long-range gun support. To this Dietrich agreed. But when asked about the locations of American reserves that his parachutists might run run into, Dietrich lost his patience. "I am not a prophet," the SS commander frowned. "You will learn earlier than I what forces the Americans will use against you. Besides, behind their lines there are only Jewish hoodlums and bank managers!" The conference was going from bad to worse. Von der Heydte meekly inquired if he might obtain some carrier pigeons for his operation. He feared that his radio might be broken in the air drop. "Pigeons!" Dietrich scowled. "I'm leading an entire army without pigeons. You should be able to lead a damn battlegroup without a zoo!" With that, the unpleasant meeting ended.

The Baron was disheartened by the improvised training and organization of his battalion as well as the fact that the jump was to be the first ever made at night in the German army. Then too, the area was heavily wooded and weather conditions in mid-December were apt to be unfavorable. With such inexperienced men, von der Heydte was nearly sure that these circumstances would doom the mission. However, nothing in the plan could be changed. Hitler's orders were "unalterable." Dietrich's assurances that he would only have to hold the crossroads for a few hours until the tanks of *12 SS Panzer Division* relieved him in the afternoon of the first day was of small comfort.[10]

By December 11th von der Hey-

dte's "improvisation" had taken the following aspect: Hasty training was undertaken in an improvised barracks in the Westphalian town of Oerlinghausen. There, he had about a thousand men, including support personnel of which only 200-300 had combat jump experience in the Crete operation. He organized his battalion force into four parachute companies, a company of heavy machine guns, a pioneer company, a signal platoon and a heavy weapons platoon with four 81mm mortars. Sidearms and parachutes were still in short supply. Yet the great offensive was but four days away!

On the 13th, von der Heydte and the chief of his air crew, Maj. Otto Baumann, met with Generalmajor Dietrich Peltz in charge of *II Jagdkorps*. They learned that the drop zone was to be marked with parachute flares and incendiaries. Luftwaffe searchlight batteries would be used to guide the planes from Paderborn past Bonn. From the front line, the hundred plane force of the old Junkers 52s would be guided by pathfinders of *Nachtschlachtgruppe 20* to the drop zone. The general was aware of the lack of training in the air crew for flying in formation, much less in doing so at night. Consequently, the final thirty miles would be flown with navigation lights on. To draw attention away from the main drop, Peltz told them, a fake drop using 300 dummies would be parachuted into the Elsenborn area. However, news of the preparations and mission did not change von der Heydte's mind about the advisability of the operation one whit.

Late on the evening of December 14th von der Heydte journeyed to the headquarters of *Heeresgruppe B* near Münstereifel to make his objections heard. Genfldm. Model was asleep so his monocled chief of staff Gen. Hans Krebs went over the tactical plan with the Baron. Von der Heydte complained that the resources were wholly inadequate, but Krebs could do nothing but roust his commanding general from his slumber to hear the complaints. Model was clearly fatigued, but patiently listened to von der Heydte's reservations. After hearing them out, Model asked von der Heydte bluntly, "Do you give the

---

10 Upon von der Heydte's capture, a U.S. interrogator asked the colonel what he thought about his SS commander Sepp Dietrich. "He," the Baron stated emphatically, "is a cur dog!"

parachute operation a ten percent chance of success?" "Yes," he responded. "Well, then it is necessary to make the attempt," Model continued, "since the entire offensive has no more than a 10% chance of success. It must be done since this offensive is the last chance to conclude the war favorably."

Although doubtful of the chances of *Operation Stösser* von der Heydte put all his energies into organizing the effort. Equipment and weapons were issued to his men along with rather rushed jump training — many had never attended jump school. Also, 112 aging Junkers 52 transports, "Auntie Jus," were gathered, with a frighteningly untrained group of pilots (half had never flown combat missions and most had never flown a Ju-52!). The tired old planes were from the old Stalingrad Squadron that had attempted the supply of Paulus' army in Russia — *Transportgeschwader 3*.

On the evening of December 15th, Oberst von der Heydte formed up his *Kampfgruppe* for transport to the waiting planes at Paderborn Airfield. He briefed his company and platoon leaders on the details of their mission. They were to make the parachute drop at 5:00 A.M. the following morning. However, due to the fuel shortage, half of the trucks necessary to transport the Baron's men never arrived and only a fraction of the battalion had arrived at the airfield by 4:00 A.M. At daybreak, von der Heydte cancelled the day's attempted jump and took the opportunity to take a nap. Maybe the nightmare was over.

Although the colonel had hoped the operation might be cancelled with this delay, a call from *ISS Panzerkorps* on the afternoon of the 16th changed that comforting thought. The progress of the *Sixth Panzer Armee* had been less than expected, he was told, and the mission of the paratroopers to delay American reinforcements was now more important than ever. "Hold on as long as possible," SS Brigf. Fritz Krämer told the Baron, "two days as a minimum, and do as much damage as you can to the American reinforcements." *Kampfgruppe von der Heydte* would jump at 0300 hours on December 17th. Operation Suicide was back on; by 11:00 P.M. all his troops were

in place at the airfield. In a thoughtful gesture, von der Heydte, a devout Catholic, made arrangements to have the planes and aircraft blessed by a priest at Paderborn before take off.

In the small hours of the morning on December 17th, von der Heydte and his group were packing themselves into the Ju-52s on Lippspringe field. By 2:30 A.M. the hundred plane force was buzzing through the windy night skies towards the *Baraque Michel* crossroads at the hamlet of Mont Rigi. To steel themselves against the growing probability of disaster, von der Heydte hoarsely led his men in a chorus of the paratrooper's song: *Rot Scheint Die Sonne* ("Red Shines the Sun"). The lyrics could hardly have been reassuring:

When Germany is in danger there is only one thing for us:
To fight, to conquer and assume we shall die.
From our aircraft, my friend, there is no return!

"It was a stormy night," von der Heydte remembered; there were exceptionally strong cross-winds, gusting up to 20 knots. Of the original 112 planes, perhaps only 15 reached the correct area with the commanders's lead plane. "It proved a really fatal mistake," von der Heydte judged, "that the troop carrier units were no longer accustomed to flying in regular formation." Many of the untrained pilots gave the order to jump based on dead reckoning, rather than by identifying the drop zone. With the high winds, the pilots' estimates of their airspeed was off considerably. The pathfinders of *Nachtschlachtgruppe 20*

returned at 3:30 A.M. after leading the first few planes to the drop zone. For the others, searchlights lit the way at first, but the last 35 miles of flying was made before the first incendiary marker was sighted. Many pilots lost their way. Of the 870 paratroopers who took off, fewer than 450 jumped into the Hohes Venn area, and only 100 were dropped more or less over the drop zone.

Even worse, once over the American line, the plane group with its navigation lights on proved good targets for the Allied anti-aircraft fire as they crossed the front line. The sky was full of flak and white and red tracer. Von der Heydte and his men saw machines near theirs go spiraling down with ugly orange flames. Von der Heydte's crew of ten were visibly shaken; other than the Baron only two of the group had ever jumped before! But at 3:15 A.M. their commander sighted the brilliantly burning incendiary cross that marked their drop zone. Fifteen minutes later von der Heydte and his troops jumped into the night. Willi Volberg vividly remembered that moment:

I repel myself vigorously outward before being pulled down by the weight of my body, weapons and equipment. When the parachute opens, I nearly go head over heels. Afterwards, swinging in the straps, I notice the noise of the engines becoming more and more gentle. We have dropped from a higher altitude than planned, because the pilot had tried to avoid being hit (by anti-aircraft fire). After bouncing against the ground I tumble down a small

Crash landed Junkers Ju-52s of Transportgeschwader 3, *similar to those used to drop von der Heydte's German paratroopers on the pre-dawn hours of December 17th.*

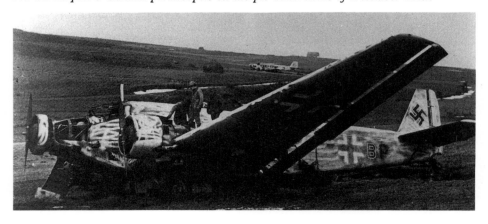

slope and then am pulled upwards again by the wind in my parachute. The forecasters had predicted a surface wind speed of 4-6 instead of the 12-15 meters per second conditions that we face. I think to myself, "This will cause a lot of casualties." My sliding ends when the parachute becomes entangled in a fir tree. I quickly loosen the straps and break out my automatic rifle so that I am ready to fight. Snowflakes are being blown by the wind. Nothing is to be seen of the parachute flares illuminating the drop zone. So, after several hours of daylight, only two sergeants, 13 privates and I have met each other.

Landing and taking stock of the situation von der Heydte was appalled:

I was the first to jump at precisely the correct place. However, only about ten other planes dropped their men into this same area. Even before I reached the assembly point, I realized that the formation had been scattered and that the drop had therefore failed. The operation as originally conceived had miscarried from the very start. . .It was snowing and very dark and it was very difficult to gather together my troops. Eventually after an hour I had only 35 men with me.

By 8:00 A.M. the number had only increased to 150. Worst of all, however, his heavy weapons and signals companies had disappeared to a man. Then, in the predawn mist, von der Heydte heard distant motors approaching. The Baron's hopes quickened. Could this be Dietrich's tanks approaching?

But this prospect was soon dashed, however, when the motors approached down the road from the north. It was the 26th Regiment of the dreaded 1st U.S. Infantry Division crammed in Ford trucks rolling down the tarmac in the morning half-light. "We had been lying in a ditch near the crossroads to hold it open for the SS tanks," von der Heydte recalled. "On this road an American unit came on trucks. Some of the American soldiers slept and others saw us and waved to us and we waved back." Recognizing the emblem of the "Big Red One" and realizing his good fortune in this first encounter, von der Heydte and his small band made no attempt to re-

sist and slipped quietly into the woods to hide. Besides, with most of the supply canisters missing, his troops only had enough ammunition for a single firefight.

However, within only a few hours, the 1st Division realized that those men in the ditches were not other American soldiers. The 18th Regiment of the division spent the entirety of the next three days searching for the parachutists. "So much for our rest period," complained a driver of the U.S. regiment. "And to think that in another hour I'd have been off to Paris....Now here we are hunting God-damned German paratroopers."

Things looked even worse for the commander of the Germans the driver had cursed.

With this pitifully small number of men, who had salvaged only a single medium caliber mortar, I had only the slightest chance of success. I decided to remain near the road junction until the sounds of battle approached; then to come forth from the forest to open up the road in the last few minutes before the arrival of the German tanks.

However, von der Heydte waited for two days before he gave up on this occurrence — the *12 SS Panzer Division* that he was waiting for was still stuck in fierce fighting in the Krinkelt area where Model had wanted him to land. Meantime the U.S. regiment that had slipped past von der Heydte later stopped the SS division in its attack to open Route C at Bütgenbach.

By sending out search parties, Obst. von der Heydte was able to gather up a force of another 150 men who had jumped too far to the north, but with this tiny force of only 300, it would still be impossible with so little in the way of weapons and ammunition to put up serious resistance.

I took up a narrow position of all around defense in the midst of the dense forest, after which I dispatched reconnaissance patrols of two or three men each to the roads leading to Eupen, Malmédy and Verviers. The patrols were to hide at the edge of the roads and avoid contact with the enemy except that they were to capture any enemy messengers traveling alone and bring them to me.

By late that afternoon the colonel

recalled that he had a "very accurate picture of the enemy." But without any radio he could not communicate this important information to his superiors. If only he had those carrier pigeons now!

Without radio communications, the long-range artillery battery was unable to communicate with its forward observer who had jumped with me (artillery officer, SS-Obstf. Harald Etterich, from the *12th SS Panzer Division*). Had this been possible, effective observed fire could most likely have been laid down on the spotted enemy gun positions and on the traffic between Eupen and Malmédy.

Meantime, as far as the German high command could tell, the German parachute operation had vanished without a trace. It would be December 19th before *OB West* had any news:

Two men have got through from *Gruppe Stösser* and report that 200 men are gathered under the command of Oberst von der Heydte in the woods five kilometers south of Eupen. They have cut the road at several places. There is no information regarding the rest of *Gruppe Stösser*.

What had happened to the several hundred men that had disappeared? Some of the German parachutists had died when their planes were shot down. However, the majority of those missing had landed pell-mell throughout the Ardennes and Aachen area. The signal platoon landed in front of surprised Germans near Monschau while a rifle company fell west of Bonn over forty miles east of the drop zone. Others fell nearly alone behind American lines. The lucky ones were made prisoner. Those who broke arms and legs in their first combat jump, often died of exposure in the snowy forests. As the snows melted in the spring, civilians in the Ardennes were still finding the pathetic corpses of those who had died in their first parachute jump. The December 22nd issue of the *Nachrichten Fur Die Truppe* (the German version of *Stars and Stripes*) bitterly referred to the mission as "Operation Mass Murder."

Never a defeatist, von der Heydte

American GIs of the 18th Regiment of the 1st Infantry Division searched the woods in the sector near Eupen for von der Heydte's paratroopers. Abandoned parachutes like this one were more than enough to arouse suspicion.

kept his small force moving, trying to give the impression that the air drop was much larger than it actually was. In a sense, this was the most successful part of his mission. Because of the scattering of his men and the ruse of the dummy parachutists, the Allies feared that another Crete-sized air drop was underway. On December 18th, the CCA of the U.S. 3rd Armored Division was sent on a three day goose chase to find the paratroopers. Behind every bush, soldiers were seeing English speaking German parachutists. Even though *Operation Stösser* had been an unqualified military failure, it had created such confusion and uncertainty that a U.S. infantry regiment of 3,000 and a armored combat command of over 100 tanks and several thousand men had to spend several critical days of the battle protecting the U.S. V Corps at Eupen and searching for the German parachutists.

During the first night von der Heydte had moved his force some three kilometers to the north away from the road intersection which would surely bring his small force into a disadvantageous battle with the Americans using the road. On the 18th his men had attacked single vehicles and captured thirty unsuspecting American soldiers.

But without supplies von der Heydte could not hope to carry on this guerrilla war for very long. Food was in very short supply and all of von der Heydte's men had long since consumed their "iron rations." A single nighttime parachute drop from a lone Junkers 88 on the 18th was a bitter disappointment. Most of the German planes had dropped their loads off target. The single *Essenbomben* retrieved did not contain food, but only some damp ersatz cigarettes and bottles of cheap cognac. Several of von der Heydte's men were injured from the jump and there was no medical care available. On the 19th, the paratroop commander became certain that Dietrich's tanks would not get through to him. The situation was hopeless.

> I realized that I could not hold the *Kampfgruppe* together for longer than one, or at most two days. I could only carry out a single engagement, after which ammunition for the machine guns would be exhausted. Originally I had intended to fight this single action to open the Eupen-Malmédy road just before the German armored point reached our hiding place. But within the *Sixth Panzer Armee* the offensive had apparently bogged down. I decided, therefore, to abandon my original

mission and break through to the German lines.

The single action possible was fought, not for the Eupen-Malmédy road, but for the road leading towards the east. At nightfall von der Heydte started his group for the German line thought to be in the Kalterherberg area. The exhausted men started moving eastwards fording the icy waist-high River Helle in the early morning hours of December 20th. This advance ran into a U.S. outpost line just east of the Eupen road and several of his men were wounded in the brief skirmish. Not wishing to "enter into an engagement at night in unknown wooded country against an enemy we could not even estimate" the Baron withdrew his men to the west bank of the River and organized a perimeter defense on Hill 584.

But at dawn on the 20th the American patrols began creeping in from the east with tanks of the 3rd Armored closing in on the west from the Malmédy-Eupen road. Consequently, at midday on December 20th, the Colonel decided to disband *Kampfgruppe von der Heydte* and ordered his men to try to infiltrate in small groups of two or three to make their way back to German lines in darkness. It was every man for himself. Several paratroopers were shot as they tried to find their way through the American patrols; others were captured.

In spite of the incredible hardship, about a hundred of his group did manage to find their way back. Von der Heydte, however, was suffering from an injured arm, frost bitten feet, incipient pneumonia and total exhaustion. Staggering into the resort village of Monschau (which he believed to be in German hands), von der Heydte knocked upon the timbered doors until he found someone home. A schoolteacher let in the ailing commander who promptly collapsed in the warm kitchen. Admiring von der Heydte's camouflage uniform, the owner's son proudly announced that he was a Hitler Youth. Unimpressed, von der Heydte requested pen and paper; the Baron was fed up with the war. "Take it to the Americans," he said handing the handwritten note to the child. "I'm surrendering." The next day,

December 22nd, he gave himself up to U.S. 47th Infantry Regiment of the 9th Division. The last German parachute operation of the war was over:

It was a few days before Christmas, when I saw that I couldn't fight anymore. We had no ammunition and no food. So I gave orders to my soldiers to form groups of two or three and try to reach the German line. So did I, and in the town of Monschau I tried to find a German house to have a rest. But in the morning I was so at the end of my resources, that I wrote a letter to the American commanding officer telling him that I surrender. And the funny thing was that he came with a lot of American soldiers to take me to their headquarters. There, an officer came and asked me if I wished to confess. And I thought, "My goodness, now at the end I shall be shot!" But, it was only an American chaplin and because it was Christmas night he asked me if I wished to confess to take the communion.

After his surrender to the U.S. 9th Infantry Division, Oberst von der Heydte is treated for exposure at Montjoie.

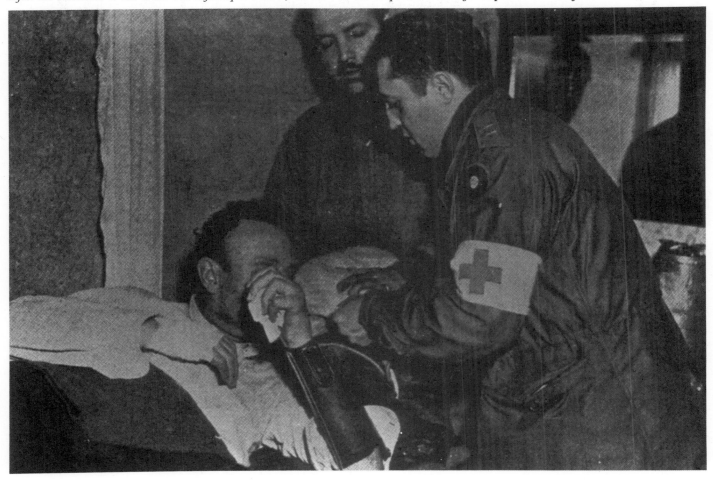

The Incident at Malmédy

No account of the Battle of the Bulge would really be complete without some description of the Malmédy Massacre. Like other Nazi atrocities, the incident at Malmédy helped to underscore for many Americans the reasons why they were fighting in the war in Europe.

Even today, the incident is still controversial and several conflicting versions of the massacre have been produced since the end of the war. As might be expected, the American and German versions of the story are at considerable odds with each other. As a result, it seems nearly impossible to reconstruct exactly what happened that gray Sunday, now over fifty years ago. The account that follows is based on corroborated fact:

On December 17th, the U.S. 7th Armored Division was in the process of moving from Heerlen, Holland, to St. Vith in the Ardennes to help rescue the encircled 106th Division. Battery B of the 285th Field Artillery Observation Battalion, about 140 men, was assigned to move south with Combat R of the division. At 11:45 A.M. the little convoy passed through the town of Malmédy, currently guarded by the 291st Combat Engineer Battalion. However, as the force passed through the Five Points intersection near the hamlet of Baugnez they were confronted with a long line of German tanks headed toward the crossroads. The tanks were the vanguard of *Kampfgruppe Peiper* of the *1st SS Leibstandarte Adolf Hitler Panzer Division* commanded by SS-Ostbf. Joachim Peiper. The Germans opened fire on the tiny convoy, which after a short and unequal fight, was forced to surrender. As the Americans crawled out from under their trucks with their hands held high, a German tank commander called out to them in formal accented English: "The *1st SS Panzer Division* welcomes you to Belgium, gentlemen." However, the American prisoners were not amused. The SS were not known for their compassion.

According to Dietrich, before the great offensive, the *Sixth Panzer Armee* had been supposedly enjoined by Hitler himself to conduct the offensive "with a wave of terror and fright" and "without regard to humane inhibitions" (although, not surprisingly, records of this order could never be found). Commanders were told that no time was to be wasted with prisoners. Although not specifically ordered to execute their captives, according to Peiper, "they were all experienced commanders to which this was obvious." Some of Peiper's men, however, were later to dispute this; they said they had direct orders. Unteroffizer Ernst Kohler testified that his platoon was specfically told to "avenge the lives of our women and children. Show no mercy to Belgian civilians. Take no prisoners." Many of the SS men of the division had recently come from the conflict in Russia where barbarity knew no bounds. On the Eastern Front it was not uncommon for sides to take no prisoners in battle. The stage was set for the events that followed.

The American captives were herded into an open field near the Café Bodarwe by the intersection. It was a cold, 12 degrees, and snowing lightly. Momentarily, the main part of the column approached. In a passing halftrack, Peiper called to the huddled Americans, "It's a long way to Tipperary boys!" As the German spearhead moved on toward Ligneuville, the Americans still hiding in the ditches were rounded up and put in with the rest under a light guard. Pvt. James P. Mattera of Marrietta, Pennsylvania, was one of these prisoners:

> The enemy milled all around us by now. Then a sight occurred which cancelled any thoughts of resistance. Over the crest of the ridge came row after row of infantrymen, from right to left as far as the eye could see.,... An SS soldier removed my Elgin watch. All the prisoners becames victims of widespread looting: watches, rings, buttons, pockets emptied, clothing and gloves. As we moved toward the Baugnez crossroad — hands up or be shot — one of our officers, a captain, objected to the confiscation of his watch: "You're violating the Geneva Convention." The SS trooper drew a P-38 and shot the officer in the forehead.

What happened next is disputed,

A U.S. soldier surveys the macabre scene at the Baugnez crossroads. Here dozens of U.S. GIs were gunned down in cold blood by soldiers of the 1st SS Panzer Division *on December 17th. The burned out building to the rear is the Café Bodarwé.*

and there are a number of conflicting theories. However, the stories of the Americans who survived the grisly events to follow are in general agreement. According to the official U.S. version, at sometime around 2:00 P.M. a gunner of Mk IV tank # 731, SS Sturmann Georg Fleps, fired a pistol into the American group, followed by more shots. Then Mattera distinctly heard the SS shout a fearful order: *"Macht alle kaputt!"* — "Kill them all!" Several machine guns from two tanks opened fire, the guns repeatedly transversing from right to left. With this hail of bullets, most of the prisoners were either killed outright or wounded. Several American soldiers screamed with pain. Amazingly one GI was left standing. Fleps promptly felled the man with two pistol shots. The moans of the severely wounded men lying on the ground filled the air "almost like a lowing." Mattera had dived for the ground. The man to his right, Charles Haines, sprawled on top of him. "Mattera," he groaned, "I'm hit bad, in the back." Within minutes he was dead, his warm blood saturating Mattera's uniform.

The events that followed were indisputably a war crime — a phenomenon known as a *Blutrausch*, or "killing frenzy." German SS men moved through the group of bodies lying in the snow, shooting those through the head who seemed still alive. However, a number of Americans were feigning death. One man raised his head from the ground and was heard to say, "By God, I am still alive." He should have remained silent. An SS pioneer shot the man through the temple with his Mauser rifle. A medical aid man crawled to another man and began to bandage his wounds. A German moved over the aid man telling him, *"Das ist sehr nett. Gut gemacht"* (That's very good. Good job). Raising his rifle, he pumped a bullet into each man's head. Sergeant Kenneth Ahrens was sprawled on the ground with a machine gun round in his back:

I could hear them walking down amongst the boys that were lying there...there was a lot of moaning....You would hear a stray shot here and a stray shot there; they were walking around making sure that no-

body was left. Each time they would hear somebody moan, they would shoot him; and there was one particular time when I could feel a foot step right alongside me, where one of the boys laid across the back of me and they shot him. But why they didn't shoot me I don't know....Every once in a while a tank or half-track would roll by and turn their guns on us, just for a good time. I mean they were laughing and having a good time.

The SS word for the grisly killing spree was *rabatz* — to have fun in killing everything in sight. Amazingly, although most were badly wounded, some twenty soldiers were still alive and conscious. After an indeterminable period, someone whispered, "Is anyone alive?" A few other faint whispers answered. Waiting until the Germans seemed inattentive, James Mattera knew they could not lie there long. Finally, he called, "Let's go!" and the wounded men leapt to their feet and made a break for freedom. Mattera stumbled over the bodies to run across the fields to the woods in the distance. The Germans reacted quickly: *"Halt Amerikaner!"* The ground around the staggering men was alive with bullets. Several were felled by machine gun fire before they could reach the nearby woods. Others ran to take refuge in the Café Bodarwe.

The German response to the escapees in the cafe was brutal and effective. They set the cafe on fire and then shot down the Americans as they emerged from the flames. The group running across the field had better luck. As a German machine gun kicked up the ground around him, Mattera fell to the snow and feigned death again. After the gun-fire moved away, he rose and dashed for the woods. Amazingly several men actually escaped their would be executors by reaching this haven.

Between 3:30 P.M. and midnight of December 17th, 17 survivors reached the friendly American lines of the 291st Combat Engineer Battalion. Some had crawled for hours in the snow, too badly wounded to walk. Another, T/5 Warren Schmitt had hidden in an icy stream for hours to avoid detection. Most were near death from exposure and shock. In all

about 80 men had been killed at the crossroads. More had been killed in the initial skirmish. Sobbed one American survivor, "We didn't have a chance...."

News of the incident reached Hodges at the U.S. First Army headquarters at 4:30 P.M. The next day, news of the massacre was flashed to Eisenhower's headquarters. An immediate decision was made to give news of the incident the widest publicity. In view of the emotional turmoil of December 18th, by nightfall that Monday, many front-line American soldiers knew of the reported massacre of American soldiers by SS men.

At about the same time, Joachim Peiper, who was in the middle of a losing battle in the Amblève River valley, received mention of a "mix-up" to his rear. Stbf. Gustav Knittel, in charge of the arriving *1st SS Panzer Reconnaissance Battalion*, clarified: *"Die haben 'ne ganze Menge auf der Kreuzung umgelegt"* (They've killed a good few at the crossroads). It was the first time Peiper heard of the incident that was to follow him for the rest of his life.

Certainly news of the incident steeled the will of Americans to fight, and obviously made it more difficult for SS men to surrender. A regiment of the U.S. 26th Division issued an order on December 21st which read: "No SS troops or paratroopers will be taken prisoner, but will be shot on sight." Although the order was later rescinded, the fact that the Allies shot prisoners as well seems nearly certain. As example, on New Year's Day, members of the inexperienced 11th Armored Division shot down 21 German prisoners in cold blood near the village of Chenogne. However, these incidents must be understood in perspective. While, execution of prisoners in the heat of battle is a seldom mentioned, but undeniable aspect of war, the SS units were notorious in this respect. Such wanton ill-regard for human life was further evidence of the Nazi criminal element that infused the *Waffen SS* organization.

After the war 74 defendants were tried for the massacre at Dachau, the scene of one of the notorious concentration camps. Among these were Dietrich, the head of *Sixth Panzer Ar-*

mee, and Peiper himself. The verdicts for 43 (including Dietrich and Peiper) was for death by hanging, life imprisonment for 22 and varying terms for another eight. Most of the sentences were commuted, largely due to the efforts of the American defense attorney Col. Willis M. Everett, Jr. He convinced the jury that coerced confessions from the defendants did not make for a fair trial. Furthermore, the evidence showed that Peiper was not even at the massacre scene but further up with his column. Peiper claimed not to have approved of executing prisoners, although circumstances may indicate otherwise.

After the battle, SS-Obf. Wilhelm Mohnke, the commander of the *1st SS Panzer Division*, submitted a written summary of Peiper's exploits during *Wacht am Rhein*, recommending him for the Swords to the Knight's Cross. Significantly, among other military accomplishments, the commendation referred poignantly to the battlegroup's *Vernichtung* or annihilation of an enemy motorized column at Baugnez. It is likely that the description of the battlegroup's actions was drawn directly from Peiper's personal after-action report to Mohnke; there can be little doubt that the event alluded to was the Malmédy Massacre. Given the ruthless ethos of Himmler's SS, it seems likely that both Peiper and Mohnke understood *Vernichtung* to include killing prisoners of war.

No proof was available that Dietrich even knew that the incident had happened, much less approved. Dietrich died in retirement in 1968. Peiper, however, was haunted by his past in the post war years and was forced to move often. In spite of this, in 1976 he was killed when French assassins fire-bombed his home in Traves, France.

The Malmédy incident was by no means the only atrocity committed by the Germans in the Ardennes. Indisputable evidence shows that *Kampfgruppe Peiper* killed another eight prisoners at Ligneuville a further three miles down the road, 12 GIs and three civilians at La Vaux Richard, several U.S. soldiers at Honsfeld and dozens of civilians in the town of Stavelot. In the tiny villages of Steyr, Parfondruy and Renardmont, the U.S. 3rd Armored Division found bodies of 117 local civilians. Some of these appeared to have been killed by American shelling, but many had been brutally murdered by the SS. Nor were such atrocities necessarily confined to the *1st SS Division*. Evidence suggests some shooting of prisoners by the *12th SS Hitler Jugend Panzer Division* in the twin villages of Rocherath-Krinkelt. Elsewhere, at Bande, between Bastogne and Marche, the nefarious SS police, the *Sicherheitsdienst* or SD, shot down 32 civilians who they claimed were Belgian terrorists.

In terms of casualties, the Malmédy Massacre was a minor incident in the Ardennes Campaign. However, it did give the American GI a taste of the mentality that had produced the *Sonderkommandos* of the Eastern Front, Oradour-sur-Glan in France and the diabolical concentration camps within Germany. If the typical American soldier in fall of 1944 wondered why he was fighting, incidents like that at Malmédy provided some good reasons.

Twenty-three innocent civilians of Stavelot were brutally murdered by soldiers of the 1st SS Panzer Division. *The SS soldiers accused the townspeople of having opened fire on them.*

Heros of the Elsenborn Ridge: 644 TD Bn

One lesson that the Ardennes battle taught the U.S. Army was the need for self-propelled anti-tank weapons. Faced by German armor, the towed 57mm and 76mm pieces were lost in great numbers. Many had to be abandoned due to the difficulty of limbering the guns under hostile fire.

On the other hand, as the official U.S. history notes: "the mobile, tactically agile tank destroyers are clearly traceable in the Ardennes fighting as over and over influencing the course of battle." This is a short story of one of these battalions that had a pivotal part in stopping the main German attack of the *Sixth Panzer Armee*.

The tactics for the use of U.S. tank destroyers were perhaps less developed than any U.S. ground combat arm during the war (with the possible exception of mechanized cavalry). The primary mission, as described in Army doctrine, was defensive and revolved around the concept of the ambush. However, the thin armor on the tank destroyers and their open top made prolonged engagements with enemy armor and infantry exceedingly dangerous. The primary tactic was therefore "shoot and scoot" —ambush enemy tanks with fire and then commence moving to a new position of concealment. In an assault role, the TDs often accompanied the infantry in attack to reduce enemy fortifications and strongpoints. However, experience in the Hürtgen Forest fighting showed that the lack of cover on the top of the TDs could make artillery tree bursts deadly for crews operating in closed terrain.

By December of 1944, the 644th Tank Destroyer (TD) Battalion was amply experienced from its fighting across France from Normandy to the Ardennes. The crews of the lightly armored M-10 tank destroyers thought highly of their mounts and their 3 inch guns if not always the leadership that determined their fate. The organiza-

tion of the 644th was standard: 671 men and officers with 36 M-10 TDs in three companies of twelve each. Each company in turn had three platoons of four 76.2mm SP guns.

It is not commonly understood that only a very small fraction of the millions of officers and men who served in Europe ever saw any combat at all. In general, those who did were in the front line infantry, tank, anti-tank and combat engineer units. It was perhaps natural that some of the front-line units had contempt for the rear-area artillery, command post and communications zone types. The front-line soldiers took for granted that without these services, they would have been reduced to ineffectiveness without ammunition, fuel or food. It took at least ten men in the rear to keep one fighting. During the Bulge fighting these unsung soldiers "worked their tails off 24 hours a day" so that the front-line man could win.

Lt. Col. Ephraim F. Graham experienced a relatively frustrating time

with his command in Europe. A brave and capable commander, he quite naturally wanted to lead his battalion into action. However, the fact that the three TD companies were typically parceled out to different infantry regiments meant that he effectively had few troops under his direct command. But Graham did the best he could to stay with his troops. He located his forward CP in Krinkelt to guide the actions of his TDs.

In December of 1944, the 644th did not fight as a battalion. On December 17th, the dispositions of the companies were as follows: Co. A was 3 km north of Rocherath; Company B was detached from the battalion and left behind in the Hürtgen Forest with the 8th Infantry Division; and C and the Recon. Co. were both at Krinkelt.

The day before the big German attack, Capt. Harlow F. Lenon, the commander of Company C was meeting with Col. Graham in Elsenborn. Lenon, a modest and thoughtful man, now found himself in the midst of the

A M-10 advances along a muddy road through dense forest terrain. The open top of the U.S. tank destroyers made artillery tree bursts exceedingly dangerous for TD crews.

great war in Europe. It was a long way from the law practice he planned for himself in Portland, Oregon. Lenon returned to Sourbrodt to do maintenance of some of the M-10s that afternoon. Ordinary stuff. That night he listened to a local German girl squeezing music out of an old accordion. It was almost civilized. Only the noise of German buzz bombs passing overhead reminded him that the war was still on.

The next day that all changed. There were sounds of artillery fire to the east and rumors that the 99th Division was under a big attack. By noon increasing numbers of U.S. infantry stragglers were seen moving on foot through Krinkelt. Amid these ominous developments Lenon brought up his C.P. to Krinkelt, putting it in a house in the west part of the village. Meanwhile the U.S. attack at the Wahlerscheid crossroads continued, but clearly something bigger was brewing.

On the morning of December 17th all hell broke loose. *Kampfgruppe Peiper* of the *1st SS Panzer Division* launched an armored attack southeast of Büllingen aimed at reconnoitering the path north of that village to Wirtzfeld. One platoon of 1st Lt. Harold L. Hoffer's Recon. Co. was sent out to maintain contact with the enemy. "I sent a section led by S/Sgt. Edward Patterson toward Büllingen to determine the make-up of the column, report the information by radio and return to Krinkelt." This tiny group ran into more than they bargined for.

Sgt. Patterson led his eight men in an M-8 armored car and two jeeps to the outskirts of Büllingen. As they approached the town at 10:00 A.M. they drew heavy fire and all three vehicles were destroyed. Two of the men were slightly wounded and all of them scattered into the surrounding streets. Patterson removed one jeep's radio and with his men sneaked into the town on foot. Entering the basement of the Hotel Rauw, Patterson peeked out a small basement window to ascertain the composition of the westward bound German column of tanks, trucks and infantry. Hourly Patterson reported his counts until he and his men were forced to evacuate the

building by a German group moving into their building. Although, they tried to escape, Patterson and his men were captured in the late evening of December 18th. The SS men of *Leibstandarte Adolf Hitler* were in a foul mood and threatened to execute the men. Luckily, intervention from an SS major stopped the proceedings. Only one man escaped; the other seven spent the rest of the war in a POW stalag in Hammelburg, Germany.

Lt. Owen McDermott was a big strapping man from Mud Butte, South Dakota. His friends knew him to be quiet and shy, but according to Harlow Lenon he was without fear and the "best soldier I saw in the Army." On the morning of December 17th, McDermott needed all the courage he could muster. His 1st platoon of Company C moved to the vicinity of Wirtzfeld to meet *Kampfgruppe Peiper's* big tanks attacking to the north. The lead German vehicle edged over the ridge about 1,000 yards south of the village. McDermott gave the signal to let them have it just as they crossed into the TD gun sights. Soon all the German tanks had been halted, smoking from their wounds. The Ameri-

cans had been damaged too; the commander of C-11, Sgt. Emory Ellis was hit in the exchange of fire. Sgt. Tom Myer's C-12 had blasted two Mk IVs (although Myers was wounded in the action) while Sgt. George Holiday's C-9 holed two Mk V Panthers and a half track.

The Germans were discouraged by these results, and Peiper gave up on any northern foray towards Wirtzfeld, choosing instead to stick to his orders to head for the Meuse. This action was pivotal, however, and ended the most dangerous German threat to the Elsenborn position from the south during the Ardennes battle. For his part in this decisive encounter, Owen McDermott received the Silver Star.

That same morning, another two M-10s of C Company were providing anti-tank defense for the 23rd Regiment of the 2nd Infantry Division in the forest trails east of Rocherath-Krinkelt. Fighting against German tank destroyers of the *12th SS Panzer Division,* Sgt. Marlan Sammon's C-23 destroyed at least one of the German armored beasts peering out of the woods before being pulled back to Krinkelt in response to mounting German pressure.

Members of the 644th Tank Destroyer Battalion. From left to right Harlow Lenon, Charlie Coats and Bob Grant. The Ardennes, December, 1944.

One of two Panzer IVs of Kampfgruppe Peiper *put out of action by Sgt. Tom Myers of the 644th on the morning of December 17th just south of Wirtzfeld.*

Co. A was ordered to move to Wirtzfeld and arrived just as the morning's actions were ending. However, its commander, Capt. James C. Williams, was wounded by shellfire. 1st Lt. Clarence Steves assumed acting command of the company and then relieved the first platoon of the defense of the 2nd Division CP in Wirtzfeld. The task force also included towed guns of the 612th and 801st TD battalion which were attached to defend General Robertson's headquarters. These twenty-odd anti-tank guns remained there throughout until Wirtzfeld was evacuated at midnight on December 19th. They never saw any German armor or fired a single round at anything!

Meantime, the commander of Co. C, Capt. Lenon, was ordered to provide anti-tank defense of the twin villages of Rocherath-Krinkelt without delay. Simultaneously, Graham's forward CP was ordered to move to Wirtzfeld, coming under the command of the cool commander of the 38th Infantry Regiment, Col. Francis Boos. Boos also had other anti-tank capability in the fifty odd tanks of Lt. Col. Robert N. Skagg's 741st Tank Battalion. Unlike the headquarters task force, Co. C and Skaggs' battalion found plenty of action.

The shuffling about for the organization of defense was made very diffi-cult by the heavy German artillery fire, the poor road conditions and the fact that the 99th Infantry Division was attempting to move through the 2nd Infantry to an new assembly point at Elsenborn. Frank Arieta, the Charlie Company radio operator, dutifully noted these difficulties in his log:

> At 12:30 A.M. [18 December] the C.P. starts moving out. The roads are bad, impassive with mud and abandoned vehicles. It is the first time we have ever made any with-drawal; we are attempting to get to Wirtzfeld which is only about 2 and 1/2 miles away. It takes us 13 hours to do so. At one part of the road we have to go across country....

At about 8:30 P.M on December 17th, elements of the *12th SS Panzer Division's Kampfgruppe Müller* (the *25SS Panzergrenadier Regiment* and the *12SS Panzerjäger Battalion*) attacked the town of Rocherath Krinkelt with infantry and assault guns. The Germans succeeded in breaching the line of the 38th Infantry and entered the village, stopping by the church only 100 yards from where Hoffer's Recon Co. CP was located. Sgt. Tony J. Diagiacoma remembered that, "Although several of our men jumped into our M20s and attempted to fire their 50 caliber machine guns at the Panthers [these were Jagdpanzer IVs], I ordered them out of the vehicles just before the 75s destroyed the vehicles."

That same evening, Capt. Lenon and his runner, Sgt. Losgar, set off to look for the tanks of the 2nd Platoon which were supposed to be guarding the northern entrance into the twin villages. Moving down the crossroad north of the town, the two men could hear the terrific noise of gunfire to the east. Now on foot, they passed a crossroads where an American infantryman was posted. Poking their heads over the ridge to look east they could see the blinding muzzle flashes of the German tanks grinding their way. The air was filled with fog and smoke; the acrid smell of cordite hung heavy in the air. Heading back to the C.P. of the 38th Infantry, they again came across the rifleman at the crossroads. They were horrified to find that his body had been cut in half by a German anti-tank round.

Back at their C.P. conditions were chaotic. There they learned to their dismay that there were now "kraut tanks in the churchyard." The sky was filled with tracers; the noise of artillery shells and small arms fire was deafening. Lenon's C.P. was illuminated by burning buildings. This wartime depiction of hell reminded Harlow Lenon of *All Quiet on the Western Front.* He and Sgt. James Tatum sized up their situation while watching the dark shadows of German panzergrenadiers occasionally darting down the streets. Both men agreed that they were unlikely to survive the evening.

The hair-raising night was no better at Harold Hoffer's Recon. CP. On orders of Lt. Col. Graham, Hoffer's group had concealed themselves. Graham assured Hoffer that his Recon. Co. was very much alone in Krinkelt. Harold remembered that night vividly:

> No one slept. I spent most of the night on the 2nd floor of the command post with Cpl. Monroe S. Block as my runner. Several German soldiers entered the house across the street where half of our company was located, but our troops remained concealed and the Germans shortly came back into the street. Sometime during the night, a Panther tank (at this time it would have been a Jagdpanzer IV of *Kampfgruppe Zeiner*) shot the corner off the room in which I was standing. I was

hit in the mouth with a piece of brick or stone, but no one was otherwise injured. At about 5:00 A.M., the Germans noisily prepared and ate their breakfast seemingly confident that no American GIs were anywhere near. They then climbed into their tanks and moved back east.

Hoffer's Recon. Co. had lost two M-20 armored cars and one jeep but suffered few personnel casualties of its own. However, the fun was far from over. At first light on the following morning, Hoffer and his men were just sitting down to a breakfast of flapjacks when:

I heard a rumbling and looked through the lace curtains of the living room window and saw at least six Panther tanks moving to and past the church from the east. All bedlam broke out, and I remember yelling, "Here they come — let's get them." Everyone was in motion as trained, including the cooks, grabbing bazookas and ammunition, grenades and rifles. I grabbed a bazooka and shouted to a cook to grab ammunition and load for me as I scrambled out the back door. Just outside sat a rumbling Panther not more than ten feet from the door. It was so close that I was apprehensive that firing the bazooka this close might injure our troops so I moved some twenty feet away at an angle facing the side of the Panther. Our first shot glanced off the area between the tracks, the most vulnerable spot. From a slightly different angle, the second projectile too glanced off the Panther. The Panther then spun completely around and came rumbling directly for the cook and myself. We were near a rectangular building and sprinted for its protection. On it came, firing. We ran around the opposite end and stopped. We heard the motors again rev up and seek us out. We completed circling the building with the German tank following on our heels in hot pursuit. We spied a stone wall across a small road where we could find shelter. However, we could hear that the tank had other problems. We heard exploding bazooka shells and saw that the Panther was knocked out. Then I heard other firing and explosions and sought our company executive, Lt. Robert Parker. I found him hunting more bazooka ammunition, blood streaming down his face and neck.

For this particularly heroic action on December 18th, Lt. Robert A. Parker of the Recon. Co. received the Distinguished Service Cross from General Hodges, the commander of the First Army. At 7:30 A.M. on December 18th Parker climbed to the top of the church in Krinkelt where with field glasses he spied a serpentine column of German tanks crawling forward from the East. Wasting no time, Parker ran back to the Recon Company CP and borrowed a bazooka and the services of Pfc. John Cullinane. He and Cullinane then made their way along the fire-swept streets to a ruined barn where Parker scored a direct hit on the lead vehicle. He advanced further towards the group of tanks dodging enemy bullet fire. Approaching within 40 yards of the group of German armor, Parker loosed a rocket, setting one of the tanks ablaze and immobilizing another. Drawing fire from the crippled German vehicles, Parker still managed to damage three more tanks before being wounded by machine gun fire.

The battle in Rocherath at dawn continued unabated as the Germans committed more of the Panthers of the *12th SS Panzer Regiment* to the battle. The 2nd and 3rd platoon of Company C was now in place to wait for the Germans. Sgt. Stashio "Stash" Kempinski's M-10, C-22, accounted for two of the armored beasts that morning and Sgt. Elias Belles' C-18 KOed another pair before being disabled by return fire. Sgt. John Hartzog in C-2 put away another two German tanks. Tragedy struck A-17 that afternoon, however. Sgt. Peter DiStefano was felled by a sniper's bullet, although his TD managed to destroy a German vehicle at 1 P.M.

In Rocherath, the gun of TD C-15 was facing the wrong way. It was impossible to transverse the gun to shoot the German tanks that were milling about only yards away. In frustration T/4 Jim Murphy gunned the engine of C-15 and charged a parked Panther. In the 75 ton crash of steel, the 30 ton M-10 was disabled, but the shaken Panther managed to hobble away. In the confusion, the crew of C-15 also managed to bale out and join the men in C-16. Standing in the crowded turret of C-16, Sgt. John Olivetti was wounded in a case of mistaken identity. An infantry sergeant of the 2nd Division thought the low slung M-10 silhouette of C-16 was a German Tiger (in fact almost every German armored vehicle with tracks was called a Tiger in the infantry after action reports). The sergeant blasted Olivetti's machine with a bazooka, leaving Olivetti badly wounded. While "Ollie" waited for stretcher evacuation, the sergeant apologized to him about "how sorry" he was about his mistake.

Meantime, the fighting continued around the twin-villages on the 19th of December. The German assault was taken over by the *103rd Panzer Battalion* of the *3rd Panzer Grenadier Division*. The stars on this day were the TDs of Company A under 2nd Lt. Philip Di-Carlo. Further assistance was provided by the 1st and 2nd platoons of C under Lt. Owen McDermott and Lt. Ray Kilgallen. In all, these men accounted for another 11 German tanks and assault guns. M-10 A-16 under Sgt. Mel Mounts was the ace, accounting for five German vehicles that day; C-17 under Sgt Cles Chester chalked up another three. Losses were also heavy, however. The M-10 of Sgt. Bill Hughes was hit that afternoon. The TD caught fire, and the ammunition on the interior began to explode. The incident killed Hughes and Pvt. Joe Garpetti and wounded the rest of the crew. Heavy artillery fire fell throughout the 2nd Infantry Division sector.

On the 19th, Lt. Col. Graham was advised of the plan to finally withdraw from the twin villages that day along with the 2nd Infantry. Lt. Charlie Coats had just arrived from three days leave in Verviers and was in a "Class A dress uniform, all hung over and red-eyed." When Coats showed up, Lenon gave him and his 3rd platoon, the unenvious rear-guard detail. Luckily, the withdrawal to a new line some three miles to the west was accomplished without difficulty. Lenon and his men were dead tired and "relieved to leave Krinkelt."

On the morning of December 20th, Lenon and his executive officer Lt. Paul Stevenson took two jeeps west towards Bütgenbach-Waimes to find the missing M-10s of Coats and DiCarlo. Stevenson remembered the curious episode that followed:

> We looked in Berg and Bütgenbach, and saw no M-10s. We asked many GIs along the way if they had seen our strays, but none had. At speed, we tore west out of Bütgenbach, having discovered to our surprise the presence of the "Big Red One" (1st Infantry Division). As Lenon's jeep slowed slightly for a sharp curve to the left, two GIs jumped from a ditch alongside the deserted road, waving frantically at my jeep to stop. My driver hit the brakes and they ran over to us. By then Lenon's jeep had disappeared around the curve which rounded the small hill on the left. The two guys wearing the 1st Division patch told us that this was their point....They said there were enemy parachutists ahead of them beyond that curve (the *3rd Fallschirmjäger Division*). As they spoke, we heard bursts of machine gun fire, and then saw Lenon's

driver backing down the curve heading towards us in reverse. Lenon told us of his narrow escape. As he rounded the turn, he saw what he thought were two GIs kneeling by the side of the road. He told his driver to pull up so he could ask if they had seen any M-10s. As they drew closer he noticed they wore "funny helmets" and that one was raising a machine pistol on a sling. He realized they were krauts and hollered for his driver to reverse and hit the accelerator. The Germans fired at the zig-zagging jeep causing minor damage but not hitting its two passengers.

After their close call, Stevenson and Lenon headed back to the east. On a tip from one of the waving GIs, they were told to look in the woods nearby where they had seen some tanks hidden in the trees. Sure enough, about 10 A.M. they found Coats and his TDs. He and his crew were snoozing soundly inside their TDs in a peaceful orchard south of Bütgenbach.

A few days after Christmas, Maj. General Walter Robertson, the commander of the 2nd Infantry Division and Col. Boos, the intrepid commander of the 38th Infantry Regiment, paid a social call to Lt. Col. Graham at his Elsenborn CP. The jaded infantry commanders had nothing but praise for the "personal bravery and leadership" of Lenon and his Company C of the 644th. According to Boos, Lenon was "most talked about commander at Krinkelt." Lenon was a modest man, however. The others, he said, were the real heros of Rocherath-Krinkelt.

The total action in the twin villages and Wirtzfeld had resulted in the official confirmed destruction of 19 German tanks and assault guns and another two damaged (more refined estimates show a count as high as 27). The 644th lost two M-10 TDs damaged beyond recovery along with two M-20 armored cars and a jeep. In addition, the battalion suffered 30 casualties

Tank Destroyer C9 of C Company, 644th TD Battalion. This particular M-10 was commanded by Sgt. George Holiday. On top are Pvt. John Grimaldi, Corp. Henry McVeigh, Sgt Holiday and with the 3 inch shell, Corp. Ed Kummer. Standing to the side are Pvt. Bragg and Lt. Owen Mc Dermott, the platoon commander.

with three men killed.

Most importantly, however, due to the action of brave men like Harlow Lenon, Harold Hoffer, Owen McDermott, Philip DiCarlo and Bob Parker the Germans had been stymied at Wirtzfeld and Rocherath-Krinkelt. The German march route had been blocked and the Nazi panzers of the *12SS Hitler Jugend Panzer Division* lay broken and smoldering in the ruins of the twin villages. Hitler's advance timetable for the *Sixth Panzer Armee* had been thoroughly wrecked.

Epilogue

After the war the U.S. Army disbanded the tank destroyer battalions after a reassessment of their combat performance. The U.S. First Army After Action Report provided the following testimony:

> The TD mission, as originally conceived, has been superseded... TDs should be replaced by a tank which can equal or outgun enemy tanks and which has sufficient armor to protect itself from normal anti-tank and tank weapons. In other words, make killer tanks, not tank killers.

Panzer killing ground. Two knocked out Panthers and a jagdpanzer IV of the 12th SS Panzer Division *bear mute testimony to the magnitude of the German defeat in Krinkelt.*

The Allied Crisis and the German Advance: December 19th - 20th

December 19th, 1944, was one of the most dismal days of the last year of the war in Europe. Word from the Ardennes was of a frightful rate of German advance. The headline in the Parisian paper *Le Monde* nervously told that the enemy was on the move over a front of fifty miles. The weather continued to be abysmal. Low clouds and mist clung to the wintry Ardennes hills; intervention by the Allied air force was still impossible. And on the home front in the U.S. and Britain, the press worried about the ominous developments. During the first few days of the German offensive, Eisenhower had ordered a complete black-out of news from the Ardennes, infuriating journalists there. The first stories coming out the battle were bad enough — *The New York Times* headline for December 18th read in large print "NAZI OFFENSIVE PIERCES ARMY LINES." But meanwhile, uncertainty of the enemy's intent in the offensive coupled with knowledge of the V-2 rockets bombarding England led to a near hysterical speculation in the Allied press. Some went so far as to wonder if Hitler might be trying to buy time to use some secret weapon of diabolical power.[12]

By any accounting, however, it was clear to the Allied High Command that they were dealing with a major German offensive. Amid the gloom and loneliness of that gray day, Eisenhower journeyed to Verdun to meet with his top generals. He, Bradley, Devers and Patton and their staffs sat in a damp squad room around a glowing pot-bellied stove. Gen. Hodges absence was conspicuous; he and his staff were in the process of evacuating their headquarters from Spa, where they had been nearly ambushed by *Kampfgruppe Peiper*.[13] Eisenhower told his commanders that he had decided to go over to the defensive on the entire front in order to acquire strength with which to attack the southern flank of the German penetration. "The present situation," Ike told his somber audience, "is to be regarded as one of opportunity for us and not of disaster. There will be only cheerful faces at this table."

Eisenhower's plan for dealing with the German offensive was the classic response developed in the Great War. First the ruptured flanks or "shoulders" of the ruptured line were reinforced so that the zone of the enemy advance was constricted. Meanwhile, key towns and road intersections in the path of the German thrust were held to delay the enemy and deny the attack a depth that threatened supply heads near Namur and Liège. This done, the Allies accumulated a

The overwhelming strength of the German attack and the thinness of the initial American defense often meant that lonely and desperate defensive positions, like this U.S. bazooka team, were set up to cover the roads over which the panzers were likely to advance.

---

12 *The Daily Mail* featured a headline on the 19th which read "Secret Weapon, Background to Nazi Push," and later on January 3rd, "U.S. told: V-Bombs in 30 Days. New York and Washington D.C. Probable Targets." In reality, the secret Allied ALSOS mission had determined in late 1943 that the Germans would not have a nuclear weapon for at least two years. However, the deperation of Hitler's attack led some nervous members of the Allied intelligencecommunity to worry that they might have been misled.

13 Hodges and his staff moved fifteen miles northwest to the relative safety of the Hôtel des Bains in Chaudfontaine near Liége.

counterattack reserve to lop off the German spearhead.

The Supreme Commander would also seek to acquire more forces for the battle. The 75th Infantry, 17th Airborne and 11th Armored Divisions, green and just arriving in England, were promptly moved to the salient. Both the Ninth and Third Armies moved available reserves to the Ardennes. The Commander would also authorize the use of artillery rounds using the super-secret proximity (VT) fuse.[14] As for the current situation, he sought immediately available troops to defend the Meuse River line, its bridges now in great danger of capture by the German advance. Six general service engineer regiments and several battered field artillery groups were rushed to the river as provisional combat teams.

Brig. Gen. Charles O. Thrasher, of the Oise Intermediate Section of COMZ, the Communications Zone, had two locally available engineer regiments which he organized as Task Force Thrasher. With hastily assembled crews, some 257 bridges across the Meuse River were prepared for demolition with orders to blow them sky-high should the Germans approach. Each span was to be guarded by a detachment with searchlights and machine guns with the bridge pylons surrounded by barbed wire to keep off German frogmen.[15] The southern sector of the Allied line in the western Ardennes was particularly weak. Remnants of the 28th Infantry Division's 110th Regiment and the divisional headquarters set up a road block near the French border at Neufchâteau along the highway that lead from Bastogne. Engineers were to lay minefields and construct pillboxes at strategic road intersections; by the end of the battle the First Army alone had laid some 335,000 mines in the battle zone.

Even given the severity of these measures, Gen. Patton was characteristically optimistic. "Hell, let's have the guts to let the sons of bitches go all the way to Paris. Then we'll really cut them off and chew 'em up!" But he said no, mindful of the location of Allied supply depots. "The enemy must not be allowed across the Meuse."

But Eisenhower agreed that Patton should attack to relieve the pressure at Bastogne. He turned to the Third Army commander with a serious question: "When can you start?"

"As soon as you are through with me," Patton told him.

But Ike wanted a more specific answer. "The morning of December 21st," Patton replied, "with three divisions."

Eisenhower was worried that Patton might weaken the attack by moving too soon with too little. "Don't be fatuous, George," he told his subordinate. "You will start on the 22nd and I want your initial blow to be a strong one! I'd even settle for the 23rd if it takes that long to get three full divisions."

14 VT or POZIT rounds were conventional artillery shells with radio controlled proximity fuses. So designed, they exploded over the heads of enemy soldiers with a rain of deadly shrapnel. At the time the weapon was a tightly guarded American secret, although circumstances caused them to be used against the Germans on the very first day of the battle at Monschau.

15 The Germans had used frogmen to attempt to blow bridges at Nijmegen in the Arnhem battle and would later try the same tactic to demolish the Rhine bridge at Remagen. In fact Dietrich's *Sixth Panzer Armee* did have a detachment of Navy divers assigned to assist in procuring the Meuse bridges.

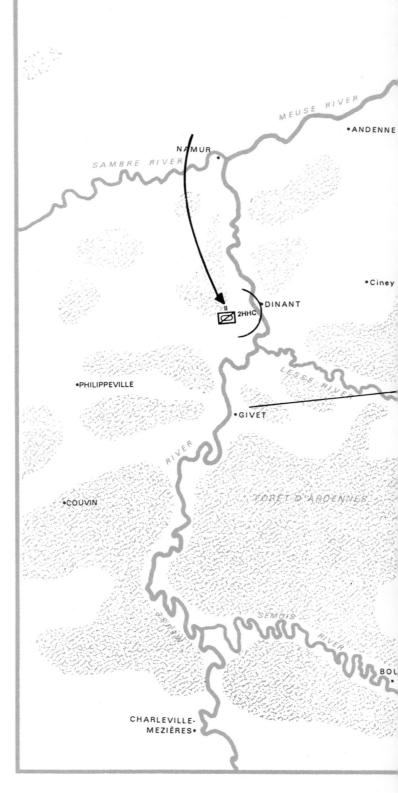

SITUATION MAP December 19th-20th

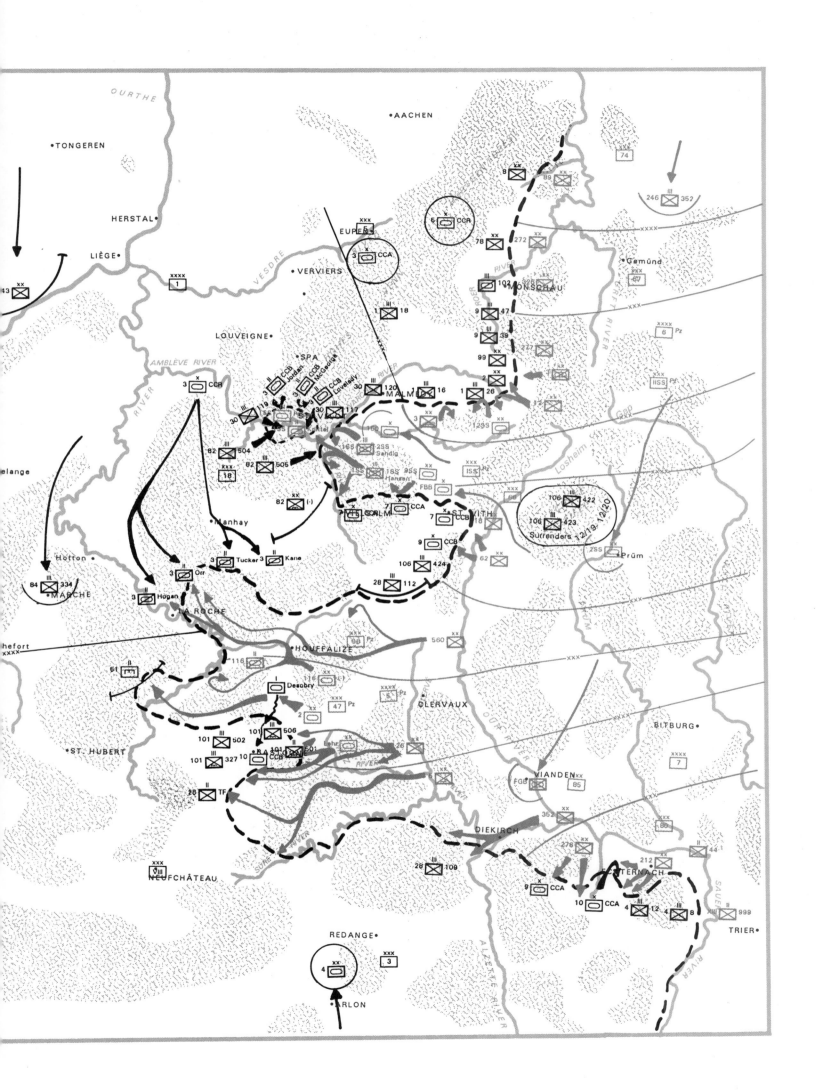

German Sturmgeschütz. The 3rd Panzer Grenadier Division moves up to the fighting front near Rocherath.

At first the audience was skeptical of even this timeline, but Patton assured them that his Third Army would make the schedule. This put in motion, south of the battle area the 4th Armored, 26th Infantry and 80th Infantry Divisions assembled for his counterattack scheduled to begin on the 22nd near Arlon, some twenty miles south of Bastogne. Patton was to attack to the north moving through Bastogne in conjunction with a push by First Army from the North. The two pincers would meet somewhere around Houffalize. Gen. Devers' 6th Army Group, already stretched thin to the Swiss border, would stretch even further to take over the defense of the Saar region from Patton's Army moving to the Ardennes. This, too, worried Eisenhower, for now the Al-

sace would be as scantily defended as had been the Monschau - Echternach front.

But the far away ruminations of their commanders meant little to the men desperately fighting for their lives in the Ardennes. In the northern sector of the battlefield, the German attack was again turned back on Tuesday, December 19th. Dietrich's army continued to try to crack the American line, now reinforced by divisions Eisenhower had ordered to deploy there. The *12th SS Panzer Division* sideslipped a few miles to the south to attempt to unhinge the flank of the newly arrived American 1st Division at Bütgenbach. Taking this key position the Germans planned to advance to Malmédy and then onto the riverfront village of Engis on the Meuse. This was the wide hard-surfaced road the Germans designated as *Panzer Rollbahn C*. Fierce attacks launched on both the 19th and 20th by the division were foiled by potent American artillery fire and "strong enemy resistance." Half hearted jabs by the *3rd Fallschirmjäger Division* to take Waimes just to the west were also easily repelled by the U.S. 1st Division.

Up until the 19th, *Heeresgruppe B* could only wonder at what had become of their parachute operation. Since their pre-dawn jump on December 17th, there had been no word of the status of von der Heydte and *Gruppe Stösser*. However, two men from the operation found their way through to German lines on Tuesday with a shocking report. Only 200 of the parachutists had assembled at the crossroads south of Eupen with Obst. von der Heydte. Most of the heavy equipment, including all the radios, were lost. Although the two men enthusiastically reported that the *Stösser* group had "broken through the road south of Eupen," they knew nothing of the whereabouts of the other 600 parachutists. The truth was far less inspiring. Von der Heydte and his men

Below: *99th Infantry Division, December 19th, 1944. The 372nd FA Battalion of the infantry Division pulls back through the village of Wirtzfeld towards Elsenborn Ridge. A TD of the 644th Tank Destroyer Battalion looks on. (U.S. Army)*
Below right: *The 99th Division lives! A WWII vintage jeep, painstakingly restored by Belgian enthusiasts, is pictured on the road leading to Krinkelt, Belgium. The jeep bears the markings of the 394th Regiment.*

were hiding in the woods from the Americans searching for them.

Elsewhere in the *Sixth Panzer Armee*, Genmaj. Walter Denkert's *3rd Panzer Grenadier Division*, delayed by muddy roads, arrived in front of Rocherath- Krinkelt to take up where the *12th SS* had left off. Just after midnight on December 19th the U.S. 2nd Infantry Division began a carefully staged withdrawal from the twin villages to the Elsenborn Ridge, joining the reorganizing 99th Division, a regiment of the 9th Division and a massive assembly of U.S. Corps artillery. On December 20th, the panzer grenadiers finally entered the blasted ruins of the twin villages. The *ISS Panzerkorps* ruefully reported: "Krinkelt captured in bitter fighting against an enemy supported by strong artillery and tanks. Each individual house had to be fought for causing considerable German losses." Attempts to push further forward were met with a hail of gunfire from the hills to the west. One grenadier described the macabre scene in his diary, "Spent the night in a house in Rocherath. There are dead bodies everywhere."

As with the *Stösser* battlegroup, headquarters worried about their loss of contact with *Kampfgruppe Peiper*. At midday, Genfldm. Model called for "air reconnaissance to determine the location of the advance guard." Out of radio contact, and under orders to thrust rapidly "without concern for your flanks" Peiper had managed to get his battle group

Spoils of War. Elated SS men of Kampfgruppe Peiper *help themselves to local beer and American cigarettes in Stoumont having captured the village earlier from the 30th Infantry Division.*

trapped in the Amblève River valley. Attacking west from La Gleize to cross the river near Lorcé, the heavily armored force managed to take Stoumont three miles to the northwest, but an attempt to penetrate further to Targnon was checked by determined resistance from the U.S. 30th Infantry Division, dwindling fuel supplies and anti-tank fire (the hastily assembled 740th Tank and 110th AA Gun Battal-

Ruins of Stavelot. The village as it appeared after the battle. The highly contested bridge is in the center of the scene. Off to the left is a knocked out Königstiger *tank. The town has been shattered by American artillery fire.*

ions). Unknown to Peiper, newly arriving American forces were closing in on his battlegroup. Ridgway's XVIII Airborne Corps took over responsibility for the region south of the Amblève bringing with him the 82nd Airborne Division. Soon CCB and CCR of the 3rd Armored Division were attached and moved down from Verviers to deal with the German tanks. As planned, three task forces of the 3rd Armored were to attack Peiper from the north while the 82nd Airborne assaulted the German bridgehead at Cheneux.[16]

The 117th Regiment of the 30th Division had recaptured Stavelot, so that Peiper's logistical lifeline was now severed.[17] The Germans, however, were determined to support this key advance. Priess's ISS Panzerkorps was told in no uncertain terms to reopen the way to their spearhead. The mandate moved swiftly down the chain of command; the rest of the 1st SS Panzer Division had their orders: recapture Stavelot and set the situation right. Kampfgruppe Knittel was to turn back and attempt to recapture the town from the West. At the same time, the panzer grenadiers of Kampfgruppe Sandig attempted to storm the town from the south bank of the Amblève using Tiger tanks aimed at the bridge and amphibious Schimmwagens to cross the water. But these efforts were turned back by intense artillery and small arms fire; all the grenadiers not killed in the water were shot down upon reaching the other side. Worse still, the Tigers were turned back by anti-tank fire before they could reach the bridge. The 30th Division could look back on their victory that day in Stavelot with only one major regret. In weeding out the Germans, the 743rd Tank Battalion took to blasting buildings suspected of harboring the enemy. Sadly, one of these was later found to have been filled with champagne and cognac.

The other battlegroup of the 1st SS Panzer Division, Kampfgruppe Hansen, held onto the town of Recht while CCR of the 7th Armored continued to clear out Germans attempting to infiltrate into Poteau to the south. In the meantime Hansen received orders to continue on his assigned Rollbahn E to Trois Ponts. Accordingly, he reorganized his regiment, handed over the fight for Poteau to the advance guard of the 9th SS Panzer Division and set off that night over the abysmal roads leading to the village of Wanne.

The IISS Panzerkorps had begun to arrive on the field with the 9th SS and 2nd SS Panzer Divisions although greatly delayed by flagging fuel deliveries and the heavy traffic on the poor Ardennes roads. So insidious were these troubles that the grenadiers of SS-Obf. Sylverser Stadler's 9th SS Panzer Division marched on foot to take over the battle at Recht. Although the 9th SS managed to infiltrate into the woods around the crossroads, they could not take Poteau with the small number of troops so far available.

The delays before Elsenborn Ridge forced a change of plans. SS-Brigf. Heinz Lammerding's 2nd SS "Das Reich"

Happy tanker. An elated Obersturmführer Alfred Hargesheimer of the 2nd SS Panzer Division *moves up towards the Ardennes just prior to the offensive. The 26-year old panzer leader of the* 2nd Kompanie *has amassed 19 tank victories on the Eastern Front.*

Panzer Division that had been assigned to follow behind the stalled 12th SS Panzer was now shunted south. There it was to operate with von Manteuffel's Fifth Panzer Armee where it might find free road space to drive west.

Near St. Vith, the two surrounded 422nd and 423rd Regiments of the 106th Infantry Division surrendered. Including attached units the loss totalled over 7,000 men.[18] Attempts by the encircled men to escape via attacks to the west were all repulsed by the Germans ringing the Schnee Eifel. Meanwhile, the 7th Armored Division in St. Vith received a breathing spell since the 18th Volksgrenadier Division had its hands full keeping up the pressure on the beleaguered 106th Division. But Gen. Hasbrouck was very concerned with his vulnerable southern flank. He organized Task Force Jones (Lt. Col. Robert B. Jones) around a portion of the 814th Tank Destroyer Battalion to guard the southern approaches to St. Vith from Gouvy to Chérain.

To the left, the 62nd Volksgrenadiers rebuilt the Our River bridge at Steinbrück and took the village of Lommersweiler. Concerned lest the need for a withdrawal would find too little room in the narrow streets of St. Vith, Combat Command B of the 9th Armored Division was pulled back to a new line along the hills just south of the town. As this was being done on the night of the 19th, the 62nd Volksgrenadiers struck on the right flank, although the Germans were driven off by mortars and tank fire. To the east, the powerful Führer Begleit Brigade was toiling towards the town although delayed by the impossible road congestion and tardy fuel deliveries. Its advance column reached Schönberg and turned north to Wallerode to encircle St. Vith from the north.

---

16 The tank combat teams were, Task Force McGeorge (Maj. K.T. McGeorge), TF Lovelady (Lt. Col. William B. Lovelady) and TF Jordan (Capt. John W. Jordan). Each was approximately of battalion strength.
17 Peiper had left a small rear guard in Stavelot on the mistaken belief that the 3rd Fallschirmjäger Division was close behind his column. Unknown to Peiper, the sluggish infantry columns had gotten no further than Schoppen in their march on the 19th.

18 The VIII Corps air liaison officer was bitter about the lack of air resupply to the 106th Division: "Somebody in the First Army should be court-martialed for the delay involved." Given the previous day's sorties, one would have thought that improvised drops by IX TAC fighter-bombers could have been flown.

Dejected prisoners of the U.S. 106th Division surrender to the Germans, December 19th.

Gen. Lucht, in charge of *LXVI Armeekorps*, personally took over directing traffic before St. Vith; the *9th SS Panzer Division* had taken the liberty of moving through roads in his corp's sector and was tangled with columns of the *Führer Begleit Brigade* and the horse drawn artillery of the volks-grenadier divisions. But for all his efforts, the infantry commander could do little to improve the traffic jam; Lucht found the SS troops surly and uncooperative.

So desperate now was the German threat at Bastogne, that upon arrival, CCB of the 10th Armored was divided into small tank combat teams. Team O'Hara (Lt.Col. James O'Hara) was sent east of the town to the village of Wardin where the *Panzer Lehr Division* was advancing. The panzer troops pushed through the towns of Neffe, Mageret and Wardin, just two miles east of the road hub. But Gen. Bayerlein had been made cautious by misinformation from civilians. He did not push aggressively towards Bastogne.

However, disaster loomed for the American armor just arriving before the town. Teams Cherry (Lt. Col. Henry T. Cherry) Hyduke (Lt. Edward P. Hyduke) and Ryerson (Capt. William F. Ryerson) of CCB of the 10th Armored division were hit very hard by Bayerlein's *Panzer Lehr*. In a sharp battle that afternoon between Longvilly and Magaret the American combat teams lost nearly two hundred trucks, tanks, and half-tracks. A good part of CCB of the 10th Armored was utterly smashed.

The story of the northernmost detachment of 9th Armored's CCR, Task Force Booth (Lt. Col. Robert M. Booth), was tragically similar. Located north of Allerborn, the tank force was encircled by nightfall on December 18th by advance of the *2nd Panzer* and *116th Panzer Divisions*. Attempting to make a break to the northeast the following morning, the task force was ambushed near Hardigny. All their tanks were lost and some 600 men were killed or captured.

Just north of Bastogne, the advancing *2nd Panzer* locked horns with the 10th Armored Division's Team Desobry (Maj. William R. Desobry) at Noville. Desobry's force was small — 19 tanks and tank destroyers along with the 1st Battalion from the 506th Airborne Regiment under Lt. Col. James L. LaPrade, which had rushed up after unloading from their trucks in Bastogne. La Prade's men fought a confused battle in the fog which continued all through the day. In the end the Germans were turned back in three separate attempts, unable to properly deploy their arriving tanks on the muddy ground. Despite their rebuke, the guns of the *2nd Panzer* maintained a constant rain of artillery fire on the Americans in the village. That night after repulsing still another enemy attempt to coup the crossroads, LaPrade was killed when a salvo of German shells blew the American command post apart. Desobry was severely wounded. Throughout the night the panzers prowled the edge of the

Forty-four ton Panthers of the 116th Panzer Division advance through the Ardennes.

village while grenadiers stalked the perimeter to find a weak point in the American foxhole line. Team Desobry could not hold out much longer.

That day, the *XLVII Panzerkorps* reported 30 American tanks destroyed; another ten captured. The sacrifice bought the Americans time, however. Clearly, the Germans had lost the race to reach the town before the Americans. The first regiment of the 101st Airborne Division reached Bastogne by the first hours of December 19th. By nightfall that same day the entire division with all four regiments had unloaded from their borrowed trucks and deployed for defense in and around the town. Many were soon fighting to hold onto the strategic crossroads.

In conformity with Hitler's orders, the two panzer divisions began to skirt the strategic road hub to continue the advance on the Meuse and leave the town's capture to the infantry division. As a minor compromise, *Panzer Lehr* did leave behind its *901st Panzergrenadier Regiment* and a handful of tanks to aid the German infantry. Meantime, the rest of the *26th Volksgrenadier Division* commenced a forced march to Bastogne to speed its capture. Advance elements of the division reached the village of Bizory by nightfall.

To the north the German panzer spearhead advanced against spotty resistance. The reconnaissance battalion of the *116th Panzer Division*, *Kampfgruppe Stephan*, rapidly drove to the Ourthe River at Bertogne, but here their luck soured. As the lead armored car approached the crossing, the bridge was blown to bits by U.S. engineers Middleton had sent to deny these river crossings. Disappointed, the commander of the panzer division decided that driving across the Ourthe at Hotton, some fifteen miles to the northwest, offered the best chance of a bold thrust to the Meuse River. Wheeling north, the *116th Panzer* took the town of Houffalize without a fight and motored up the winding Ourthe valley. However, this reversal and counter march was later seen as critical by German commanders; the lead panzer division had lost precious hours. Meantime, the sole infantry division of the *LVIII Panzerkorps*, the *560th*, commenced a rapid march from the Our River near Ouren to Nadrin north of Houffalize. While on the move, the division fought a series of sharp skirmishes with Task Force Jones near the village and railroad station of Gouvy.

On the extreme south end of the battlefield, the 19th saw the *212th Volksgrenadier Division* under counterattack by U.S. tanks of the 10th Armored that recaptured Berdorf and the high ground overlooking Müllerthal. Even worse for the Germans, the stubborn American infantry company was still holding out in a hat factory in Echternach. Elsewhere, the German corps did manage some advance. The village of Christnach, a few miles south of the Sauer River, fell to the

Troops of the 101st Airborne Division move up east of Bastogne on December 19th.

276th Volksgrenadier Division and Task Force Chamberlain of the 10th Armored was so battered from the close-in fighting that they retired to Consdorf. But this success was marred by news that the division commander, Genmaj. Kurt Möhring, had been machine gunned to death while driving from the front in his staff car between Beaufort and Müllerthal. Ironically, he was returning to headquarters after having been relieved of command.

In anticipation of Patton's future counterattack from the south, Brandenberger began to prepare to go over to the defensive. German radio intercepts had already determined American intentions in this regard due to the somewhat careless American communications protocol. Two combat commands of the 10th Armored Division had arrived to stabilize the Allied position southeast of Ettelbruck and Maj. Gen. Manton S. Eddy's XII Corps prepared to come to the aid of the U.S. 4th Division on the extreme southern flank. The left wing of the German offensive was jammed.

The right wing of Brandenberger's army gave a better showing. Contrary to orders, the *5th Fallschirmjäger Division* invested the town of Wiltz, looking for warm accommodations for the night. At the same time the *26th Volksgrenadiers* attacked the town from the north — desperate fighting raging through the day at Erpeldange and along the perimeter of the town itself. But by morning the Germans were in control; this action nearly captured the headquarters of the 28th Division and netted six Sherman tanks and 520 prisoners. Another regiment of the parachute division marched west reaching Harlange close to the Bastogne-Arlon road. At the same time, the *352nd Volksgrenadiers* reported the capture of Bettendorf, just east of Diekirch, which the 109th Infantry Regiment had held for three days. Bitter fighting took place in Diekirch itself. The German divisional commander, Obst. Erich Schmidt, was seriously wounded while personally leading an assault. But the 28th Division had been dealt a serious blow. Cota's Division had orders to withdraw from Diekirch and the Wiltz Valley and infiltrate

Survivors. GIs of the band and quartermaster company of the U.S. 28th Division who escaped the debacle at Wiltz. The men are pictured in Bastogne.

as best they could back to VIII Corps headquarters west of Bastogne.[19]

The night of December 19th von Rundstedt submitted a report summarizing the results of the first four days of the attack. He counted 8,000 American prisoners taken, claims of 100 enemy tanks destroyed, 13 captured and 102 enemy planes shot down. More to the point, however, the old field marshal observed that the situation in the *Sixth Panzer Armee* was "totally unsatisfactory." Presently, staff officers including Hitler's personal adjutant Maj. Johannmeier, arrived to peer over the shoulders of Dietrich's failed SS leaders. Johannmeier reported that "the bad road conditions, from the prevailing wet weather, especially in the area of Krinkelt and St. Vith, is delaying the complete development of a breakthrough."

Von Rundstedt agreed. The abysmal state of the roads had left "insufficient room for deployment of the army." He therefore, proposed that *IISS Panzerkorps* should command further attempts to win over the Elsenborn area, which in his opinion could be achieved "with appropriate leadership." "Appropriate leadership" meant SS-Obgrf. "Willi"

19 Casualties to the 109th Infantry were heavy; 500 men had been killed, wounded or captured and most of the regimental heavy weapons had been lost.

Bittrich, a tough tank leader who had recently demonstrated his fighting skills and command obduracy in key battles at Arnhem in September.

Meanwhile, along the Western Front on either side of the Ardennes region, German commanders indicated diminishing enemy pressure. However, reports also told of American units being withdrawn from these fronts probably to be committed against the German penetration. Radio messages from *Luftwaffen Kommando West* indicated that three armored divisions had been withdrawn from the Aachen area (3rd, 7th and 5th Armored) and two armored and one infantry division (4th and 10th Armored and 80th Infantry Divisions) from the Third Army front. Four of the divisions had already appeared in the Ardennes; the others would soon make their presence felt.

The Germans, too, were bringing up more forces. The tardy *246th Volksgrenadier Division*, planned for the initial attack, was finally moving into the northern sector of the *Sixth Panzer Armee*. Also, SS Brigf. Heinz Harmel's *10th SS Frundsberg Panzer Division*, although still in reserve, was marching into the area of Euskirchen-Münstereifel, ready to be fed in as a reinforcement should Dietrich's stalled army shake loose and get moving. The weather was also still favorable for the German attack. Cloudy skies, fog and poor visibility permitted little intervention by the air forces of

Boggy roads. The Germans use manpower to haul a captured U.S. jeep out of the mud between Manderfeld and Büllingen.

either side. However, the Allied bombers continued to pound German rear-area communications. As a result, the transportation situation was degenerating: *OB West* reported that the movement of the *9th Panzer* and *15th Panzer Grenadier Divisions* would be delayed by two days because road obstructions "do not permit the rapid transit of these divisions into the attack area." The *Führer Grenadier Brigade,* urgently needed by the *Seventh Armee,* was slowly straggling on the field around Vianden, a victim of delayed fuel delivery and roads made treacherous from freezing rain.

December 20th witnessed some of the largest German advances of the battle, particularly in the *Fifth Panzer Armee* sector. By evening of that day, the Germans had surrounded the defenders in Bastogne and prepared to charge to the west.[20] A request for permission to invest the town of Bastogne by the *2nd Panzer Division* was met with disdain by the *XLVII Panzerkorps* commander, Gen. Heinrich von Lüttwitz: "Forget Bastogne," he snapped, "Head for the Meuse!"

In spite of von Manteuffel's improving fortune in the south, the 20th brought no discernable improvement of the German situation in the *Sixth Panzer Armee* sector. An attack was launched by the *12th SS Panzer Division,* in conjunction with *Kampfgruppe Holz* of the *12th Volksgrenadier Division* against the village of Bütgenbach. The Germans made only small gains in the territory of the U.S. 1st Division before being forced to retreat in the face of massive U.S. artillery fire. A desultory attack directed at the U.S. 1st Division near Waimes by the *3rd Fallschirmjäger Division* also came to naught.

The only real estate gained by the Germans in the Elsenborn area was ground the Americans had vacated: the *12th Volksgrenadier Division* took over the village of Wirtzfeld while the *326th* satisfied itself in re-occupying the road near Wahlerscheid. To the north, the lone battle of the U.S. 78th Division and the *272nd Volksgrenadiers* for the possession of Kesternich continued to drag on inconclusively as it would for the next several weeks. The grave threat of the preceding days appeared to have subsided, however, and CCR of the U.S. 5th Armored Division moved into V Corps reserve in case the situation worsened in the Elsenborn area.

But perhaps most significantly for Dietrich's army, attempts failed to reopen the lines of communication to *Kampfgruppe Peiper.* A desperate night assault by *Kampfgruppe Sandig* to recapture Stavelot was turned back, as was the smaller blow of *Kampfgruppe Knittel* to retake the town from the west. Even so, *Heeresgruppe B* somehow got the erroneous report that the Germans had recaptured Stavelot. The truth was that the American engineers from the 30th Infantry Division had blasted the bridge across the Ambléve River on the south end of the town after shooting down the Germans attempting to wade the icy waters.

Knittel's battlegroup had been pocketed between Stavelot and Trois Ponts on the north bank of the Ambleve as Task

Stoumont, December 19th, 1944. The lead German Panther of Kampfgruppe Peiper *goes up in flames as it approaches the village —only one man in the panzer survives. The following tank cautiously move up to destroy the U.S. anti-tank gun fielded by the U.S. 30th Division.*

Force Lovelady interdicted the winding road to La Gleize from the north. The umbilical cord to the German spearhead was completely severed. Even so, under cover of darkness, Sandig did manage to send part of a battalion across a foot bridge at Petit Spai west of Stavelot. These were the last German troops to reach Peiper's isolated group.

The other large force of the *1st SS, Kampfgruppe Hansen,* was collecting its troops in the village of Wanne just southeast of Trois Ponts with the objective of striking across the Salm River to take *Rollbahn E* to the Meuse. The road from Recht, hardly more than a forest track, had greatly delayed the assembly of Hansen's regiment. What few panzergrenadiers he did have on hand, he sent to reconnoiter crossing sites along the river.

Now almost totally out of gasoline, Peiper radioed for a Luftwaffe drop of fuel, not knowing how close he was to American petrol. At 4:15 P.M. on the 19th, one of his reconnaissance parties almost overran an American fuel depot north of La Gleize near Borgoumont, only to be turned back in a firefight with a hastily organized task force consisting of the "palace guard" for the U.S. First Army. No fuel was lost and the Germans remained in ignorance of the stores there.

Meanwhile, the U.S. 30th Division and part of the 3rd Armored had launched a concentric assault on Peiper's vanguard in Stoumont. The 119th Regiment was reinforced by artillery and the 740th Tank Battalion, a screwball outfit with a motley collection of armor: "They're bastard tanks, but we're fightin' fools!" Designated Task Force Harrison (Brig. Gen. William K. Harrison, Jr.), this provisional combat team fought its way to St. Edouard's Sanatorium inside the village during the afternoon. However, just before midnight, the Germans with heavy tank support descended from the hills ringing the town shouting "Heil Hitler!" and firing wildly. The American tanks were promptly shot up and savage fighting eddied back and forth through the village all night with the sanatorium repeatedly changing hands. A savage room-to-room brawl ensued, reminiscent, on a scale, of the battle for Stalingrad.

South of this grim episode, the *9th SS Panzer Division*

---

20 The U.S. forces in Bastogne included the 101st Airborne Division, 10 Armored's Combat Command B, 705th Tank Destroyer Battalion, attached corps artillery and Team SNAFU (Army vernacular for "Situation Normal, All Fucked Up"), a group of stragglers from the 110th Regiment of the 28th Division.

Desperate battle in Stoumont: SS Sturmbannführer Werner Pötschke, the commander of the 1st Battalion, 1st SS Panzer Regiment, *turns to retrieve an abandoned panzerfaust while a knot of German paratroops open fire with a MG 42 machine gun at the American resistance along the road.*

continued to collect forces at Recht. There, the panzer grenadiers attempted to overpower the American defense at Poteau and then move via Vielsalm towards the Meuse. However, the SS division's effort was severely handicapped; there was only enough fuel for the divisional reconnaissance battalion. The grenadiers had been forced to march on foot leaving the tanks and artillery of the panzer division strewn along the road from Stadtkyll. Then, too, most of the division's advance force had been ordered to the northeast to cross the Salm River at Grand Halleux and bring the *Sixth Panzer Armee*'s left flank abreast of Peiper's position. All German attempts to infiltrate the woods to seize Poteau were foiled. To the south, the *2nd SS Panzer Division* straggled onto the field near Prüm, also with no fuel for its vehicles; its 134 tanks and assault guns remained behind awaiting petrol delivery.

The appearance of the *2nd SS* and *9th SS Panzer Divisions* to the north and south of St. Vith's "fortified goose egg" threatened the town with total encirclement. "Along about December 20th, I was beginning to feel very lonely," Gen. Robert Hasbrouck of the 7th Armored remembered. "Looking out, there were Germans to the east of me, Germans to the north of me and Germans to the south." Fortunately for Hasbrouck, the Germans were short of fuel and obedient to their orders which called for a westerly advance. Most threatening was the *Führer Begleit Brigade* which had finally appropriated enough gas to launch a hasty attack against St. Vith from Ober-Emmels. But this foray was abandoned when U.S. tank destroyers blasted four of the brigade's tanks as they formed for the assault.

Meanwhile, the situation in St. Vith was surprisingly quiet with the *18th Volksgrenadier Division* reorganizing its fragmented command for a major effort the following day. Regardless, Gen. Hasbrouck, was concerned for his weak

southern flank and hurriedly dispatched a scratch combat team, Task Force Jones (Lt. Col. Robert B. Jones) composed of some tank destroyers and remnants of the 14th Cavalry Group to protect this sector.

On the left of the *LXVI Armeekorps* the *62nd Volksgrenadiers* launched an attack designed to encircle the town by an advance to the south. The Germans captured the villages of Maspelt and Breitfeld but were halted by severe losses from American shelling and tank fire in the woods east of Grüfflingen. Although St. Vith had not yet been taken, the *LXVI Armeekorps* reported that American resistance seemed to be weakening.

The *116th Panzer Division* marched from Houffalize to Samrée, fencing with the battalion-sized Task Forces Kane, Tucker and Orr (Lt. Col. Matthew W. Kane, Lt. Col. William R. Orr and Maj. John Tucker) of CCR of the 3rd Armored Division. At Samrée, the division seized a fuel dump of the 7th Armored, completely filling the nearly empty tanks of the division's panzers. Although the captured American supply personnel told their captors that the petrol was now tainted with sugar, the enemy tank commanders assured them that it suited German motors very well! Nearby, the *560th Volksgrenadier Division* managed remarkable march performance, advancing through Dochamps to Devantave north of La Roche. At the time, this foot march placed the division further west than any German unit in the Ardennes.

To the south, the *2nd Panzer Division* finally seized the village of Noville from Team Desobry of the 10th Armored Division. This proved a costly encounter however; at least a score of German tanks were left smoldering and broken before Noville and a panzer grenadier battalion took heavy losses. On orders the U.S. combat team attempted to withdraw south from Noville to reach friendly lines at Bastogne.

Near Noville. A Panther left by the German invader as photographed by a local villager in July, 1945. Its front mantlet shows how difficult American tanks found German armor to destroy in a frontal engagement. No less than six shots have ricocheted off the tank before it was destroyed.

The Germans were ready for this move, however, and Desobry lost 400 men and 16 tanks and tank destroyers, running a gauntlet of fire through the village of Foy.

After this serious delay, the *2nd Panzer Division* finally dashed westward capturing a bridge intact across the Ourthe River at Ortheuville. But there additional adversity struck when the division's panzers sputtered out of gas. Although any advance on the Meuse from this point would be almost unopposed, this fleeting opportunity was already vanishing as the 334th regiment of the 84th Division hastily trucked its riflemen to the Marche area. Equally frustrating to von

Lüttwitz, an attack on Bastogne by elements of the *Panzer Lehr Division* had made little headway at Marvie. *Kampfgruppe von Fallois*, (Maj. Gerd von Fallois) the reconnaissance battalion of the panzer division and the *füsilier* battalion of the *26th Volksgrenadier Division* (*Kampfgruppe Kunkel*) bypassed Bastogne to the south and cut the Bastogne–Arlon road at Remoifosse. The rest of the *26th* was in the process of marching up to assemble for an assault on the town.

South of Bastogne, near Arlon, Maj. Gen. Hugh J. Gaffey's 4th Armored Division and the rest of Patton's forces had begun to assemble. Eisenhower was still nervous that Patton's impetuosity would lead him to piecemeal commitment of his forces on the south flank. "Be methodical and sure," Ike reminded him. Under a watchful eye from the Supreme Commander and virtually ignorant of the enemy order of battle facing him, Patton ordered that his attack was not to begin until he had all three of his divisions in line. This lead to a strange episode on the 20th when Task Force Ezell (Capt. Bert Ezell) of the 4th Armored drove north to Bastogne with a company each of tanks and armored infantry. The combat team found the way into the town open only to be ordered back to the 4th Armored in interest of keeping the division together. A unique opportunity to hold the way open to the 101st Airborne was lost, for the town would soon be encircled.[21]

While the Third Army assembled for commitment, the

21 On the night of the 20th, the Allied commanders in the south were dubious of their ability to hold Bastogne. General Middleton, the VIII Corps commander in Neufchâteau was skeptical, since the Bastogne was under attack by three German divisions. Also, it is a little known fact that even Patton himself had ordered him the previous night to prepare to evacuate the town.

A Sherman tank of the 3rd Armored Division carefully negotiates the icy road between Dochamps and Samree.

German *Seventh* struggled to reach its objectives. The *5th Fallschirmjäger Division* pushed on to the west across the Bastogne-Arlon road with its motorized reconnaissance in an unopposed march while the mass of the division concentrated in the area southwest of Wiltz. By dark, the *5th* had taken Martelange, on the main highway south of Bastogne as well as the nearby villages of Hompré and Hollange. Likewise, the attack of the *352nd Volksgrenadier Division* picked up speed after its artillery had been brought across the Our River. The division pushed back the tiring U.S. 109th Infantry, entered Diekirch and drove west four miles to prepare a concentric assault on the town of Ettelbruck. Only a blown bridge at the later town stopped further German progress.

Anticipating a full scale American counteroffensive on the southern flank, the attack of the *LXXX Armeekorps* on the 20th was designed to dislodge the American footholds in Echternach and Berdorf. The German plan was to capture ground more favorable for the coming defense. That day, the meager allocation of assault guns and some rockets and artillery finally reached the headquarters of the hard-luck *276th Volksgrenadier Division*. So nourished, the attack through Müllerthal ousted the elements of the 10th Armored Division defending Waldbillig. With this modest accomplishment, an advance of only six miles, the *276th* went over to the defensive.

Further south, savage fighting erupted in the 4th Infantry Division sector. Determined soldiers of the *212th Volksgrenadier Division* finally blasted the American infantry company and Task Force Standish from Berdorf in bitter fighting. But that was not all. In Echternach, the German fusilier battalion, supported by some self-propelled guns and personally led by the division commander, Gen. Lt. Franz Senfuss, finally compelled the 116 surrounded Americans in the town to surrender.

At the top, the German high command was heartened by the "spirited drive" of von Manteuffel's army. Genfldm. Model of *Heeresgruppe B* declared that the breakthrough the American line of the U.S. First Army had succeeded. The prospects for "striking a shattering blow before the establishment of a new defensive line east of the Meuse is very great." On the other hand, Model eyed the poor progress of the *Sixth Panzer Armee* and the flagging fuel deliveries with particular concern. Sensing the need to reinforce von Manteuffel's success in the center of the attack, he called for a free hand with *OKW* reserves.

Von Rundstedt was equally certain of the need to strike while the iron was hot. He insisted that the main weight of the offensive be immediately shifted to *Fifth Panzer Armee* since Dietrich's command was obviously stalled. "A rapid forcing of the Meuse at Liège is no longer likely," he concluded. But, with Hitler's consent, von Rundstedt ordered the *9th Panzer*, *15th Panzer Grenadier* and *2nd SS Panzer Divisions* to move up to reinforce von Manteuffel's thrust to

German artillery prepares to shell an American position. German gunners often found shells in short supply.

Cheerful German soldiers. Volksgrenadiers shoulder their panzerfaust anti-tank rockets. In the initial stages of the Ardennes battle, German morale soared with the early victories.

the Meuse. To control these new divisions, he ordered a new headquarters, *XXXIX Panzerkorps*, under Gen. Lt. Karl Decker from the Eastern Front to the Ardennes.

In light of recent events Von Rundstedt also altered his position regarding the envisioned attack by *Heeresgruppe H* towards Antwerp. He approved the army group's plan, submitted the day before, of first establishing a bridgehead over the Meuse with the *346th, 711th* and *712th Infanterie* and the *6th Fallschirmjäger Divisions* and then subsequently advancing on Antwerp. However, von Rundstedt prudently pointed out that such a venture could not count on any reinforcement and that fuel could be provided "only to the most limited degree."

With the continued murky weather, both air forces were almost totally grounded. However, with Liège no longer a nearby German target, the *5th Flak Korps* received permission to resume the V-1 flying-bomb terror-assault both on that industrial city as well as Antwerp. On the same day, SS Reichsführer Heinrich Himmler demonstrated his unscrupulous reputation once more in volunteering the *27th* and *28th SS Grenadier Divisions* composed of Belgian Flemings and Walloons for police and security duties in the Ardennes.[22] They were required "to establish order in the rear of the fighting troops and to neutralize the Bolshevik forces which have become widespread in Belgium." Luckily for

the people of the region, these fascist anti-partisans were never unleashed on the countryside, since the battle was nearly over by the time the legions had been formed.

On the ground, the average German soldier was elated. Most could not have imagined that the German high command already considered *Wacht am Rhein* a failure. For, after a terrible summer and autumn, Germany was again on the offensive and spirits soared. "What glorious hours and days we are experiencing," a German volksgrenadier wrote home, "always advancing and smashing everything. Victory was never so close as it is now."

In Gen. Bradley's U.S. 12th Army Group at the Hotel Alpha in Luxembourg City, the mood was anything but cheerful. The general had not been sleeping well and at his morning briefings, his folksy smile was conspicuously absent. His staff was still cool and assured, with the notable exception of his intelligence officer, Edwin Sibert. Sibert looked haggard, faced as he was "by a situation he did not believe possible." But everyone knew that 12th Army Group had been cut in two by the great German offensive. On the evening of December 17th, Bradley acknowledged

22 An indication of Himmler's character is illustrated by his disappointment upon being informed in summer 1944 that only 6,000,000 Jews had so far been put to death in "the final solution" at Nazi concentration camps. He had hoped for many more.

his misjudgment of German intentions, "This is Rundstedt's all out attack," he conceded looking at a map covered with angry red arrows and German division symbols, "but where in the hell has this son of a bitch gotten all this strength?"

Physical contact with the forces in the north was impossible for Bradley over the following days. The three radio relay stations at Jemelle, Ettelbruck and Aubange were captured by the Germans; even buried telephone lines had been cut. Radio communication, with on-going German interference, was unreliable and enemy agents were certain to be eavesdropping. Less than 24 hours after the German offensive had begun, Eisenhower had urged Bradley to move his command west of the Meuse to Verdun to maintain unilateral control of the front. But the 12th Army Group commander and his staff were gravely concerned that such a move might panic the civilian population of Luxembourg and even the troops on the front. When Bradley elected to stay put, he could not know that this action would ensure his loss of command of the First Army.

In a controversial decision, Eisenhower ordered that on the 20th at 1:30 P.M. British Fld.M. Montgomery take charge of all the American forces on the north side of the penetration. Bradley would retain command of Patton's forces in the south including the U.S. VIII Corps. Eisenhower saw a great advantage in this course of action. Giving Montgomery command of the northern forces assured the use of British reserves at a time when commitment of these troops could be pivotal to the outcome of the battle. Bradley, of course, was bitter. Patton, his underling, agreed; he thought Eisenhower's decision was a sop to British interests, born out of political weakness. There was no love lost between Montgomery and Patton.

The change in command in First Army was less than smooth. On December 20th, Montgomery of El Alamein, cocky and chipper, strode into Hodges' new headquarters "like Christ come to cleanse the temple." Rudely declining an offer for lunch with Hodges and his staff and ignoring their operations map in favor of one provided by his own liaison officers, the imperious Britisher managed to affront almost everyone present. On a military level, he was only slightly less discourteous. That evening he telegraphed back to his staff a message that was certain to inflame growing American distrust. Speaking of the situation at Hodges' headquarters, he relayed that, "There is a definite lack of grip and control; no one seems to have a clear picture as to the situation...."

Montgomery saw his first task to build a defensive line between Monschau and Malmédy and the Meuse River from Dinant to Namur. He ordered the British XXX Corps, under the steady command of Lt. Gen. Brian G. Horrocks, with four divisions to move between Namur and Brussels as a backstop in case the Germans forced the Meuse. He further commanded the 29th Armored Brigade to the Namur-Dinant area to establish patrols and guard the bridges across the Meuse.

Captain of controversy. Field Marshal Montgomery in the Ardennes.

At first Montgomery wanted to pull the U.S. 1st Division from the Elsenborn Ridge which it and the 99th and 2nd Infantry Divisions had so far successfully defended. This, he said, would "tidy up the line." Only after a tirade of acrimonious protests from Hodges and his staff did he allow himself to be dissuaded from this strategy. Still, he indicated that he wanted to pull the American forces out of St. Vith. This would be difficult, however, since Hodges believed the German offensive was trained on Liège and wanted to hold the salient between Monschau and Malmédy with an iron hand. As a bit of extra insurance, Hodges had just given over command of the St. Vith salient to Gen. Ridgway — a stodgy general known for his distaste of surrendering any ground.

In any case, although Montgomery believed a general retreat to the Meuse River might eventually be necessary, he could not persuade Hodges or the other dissenting U.S. generals of the utility of any withdrawal. On the evening of the 20th his resolve gave way. "I see no reason for the moment to give up an inch of the territory we have won at the price of severe fighting in recent days," he told Eisenhower. That was that.

Materialschlacht: The War of Supply

By December of 1944 the German Wehrmacht was reduced to fighting a poor man's war. Sufficient allocation of ammunition, and fuel in particular, were becoming progressively more limited in the Third Reich. Five years of savage combat and an intense Allied strategic bombing campaign steadily sapped the flow of supply to the German forces in the field. Meanwhile, catching their breath after the summer advance across France and the logistical restraint of the fall campaigns, the Allies were accumulating a significant supply reserve. The way the German soldiers saw it, the American Army was inferior to the German one in a qualitative sense. However, the *Amis* had more fuel, ammunition tanks and planes than the war weary German Army of 1944. The Germans called this Allied logistical superiority *materialschlacht* and regardless of how they accepted it philosophically, it was winning the war in Europe.

German loss of the Rumanian oil fields in August of 1944 and destruction by air of the synthetic oil plants in the Reich promised even greater difficulties for the liquid fuel supply. The loss of the oil fields had reduced the general fuel supply by 25% and Allied air raids by the end of November had left only about 30 of 91 facilities with any production at all! German fuel

supply at the end of the month stood at only 400,000 tons — less than a third of the supply they possessed before the concentrated air attacks had begun.

Regardless of the overall situation, through considerable hoarding, Hitler and his staff had managed to accumulate a sizable reserve of ammunition and fuel for the last great offensive of the war. On November 3rd, Obst. Friedrich John, the *OB West* quartermaster, reported that 10 million of the 17 million liters of fuel were now in place at the depots and that the forty train load reserve of ammunition would be in place by the 25th of the month. The final figure of fuel allocated by Genfldm. Keitel to *Heeresgruppe B* on the eve of *Wacht am Rhein* totalled some four million gallons (17,000 cubic meters). However, this figure was exceedingly deceptive in that very little of this fuel supply had

Heeresgruppe B, Genfldm. Model, had requested 5 *VS*, for his panzer forces for the attack. It is important to remember that a consumption unit only could take the vehicles of a formation 100 km under optimal conditions. Negotiating the difficult roads of the Ardennes under combat conditions could be expected to reduce the mileage by half. Then too, the amount of fuel for 1 *VS* varied greatly depending on the formation type. A panzer battalion would require twice the fuel to keep moving that a trucked panzer grenadier battalion would consume. When the logistical shoe pinched, the panzer commander would often be forced to leave the heavy tanks behind! The reason becomes obvious when examining the fuel consumption characteristics of German tanks used in the Ardennes. It was possible to move nearly two Mk IV tanks the same distance that a single fuel thirsty Tiger

Tank Fuel Economy			
Tank Type	Level Ground, Good Roads miles/gallon	Ardennes Terrain, Bad Roads miles/gallon	Bn Use*
Mk IV	.78	.39	6,154
Mk V "Panther"	.64	.32	7,500
Mk VI "Tiger"	.44	.22	10,909
M4A1 "Sherman"	.70	.35	6,857

*Gallons to move a battalion of 48 tanks 50 miles in Ardennes terrain. This is somewhat unrealistic since each armored battalion required roughly 100 trucks and other vehicles to move. This would serve to increase the estimated amounts by 2- 3,00 gallons of fuel.

appeared at the forward corps dumps by December 16th. The fuel dumps were located east of the Rhine River, safe from any anticipated Allied offensive, but rather distant from the Eifel.

The German Army measured their operational fuel reserves in consumption units or *Verbrauchssatze* (*VS*) — the amount of fuel necessary to take the vehicles of a formation a distance of 100 kilometers. The commander of

Material war. Stockpiled U.S. supplies, like the one seen here, ensured that GIs on the front line were well equipped for battle. The Americans had large supply depots in the Namur and Liège areas.

could go.

On December 15th the *ISS Panzerkorps* could count only a half *VS* in the corps depots for its *1st SS* and *12th SS Panzer Divisions*. An urgent dispatch to *Heeresgruppe B* that afternoon produced further fuel, but by dark the two SS divisions would only show 1.3 *VS* available. Even worse, the fuel had been pirated from *IISS Panzerkorps*, the second wave assault force for *Sixth Panzer Armee*, based on the rationale that they would not be needing it immediately. As we shall see, this would have dire consequences for the advance of the *2nd SS* and *9th SS Panzer Divisions* into the battle. In the *Fifth*

Lack of transport in the German attack force is convincingly shown here by the heavy ridership of a Steyr truck carrying soldiers of the 1st SS Panzer Division towards the village of Recht. One man is even clinging to the right front fender!

Blitzkrieg on bicycles. Severe shortages of motorized transport lead the German Ardennes planners to often outfit a battalion of the panzer divisions on bicycles

Panzer Armee the situation was slightly better with 1.5 *VS* available. Based on this situation, von Mantueffel the commander of the army noted:

> This lead to unexpected and very serious difficulties. As a result, we could move forward only half of our artillery and nebelwerfers. All our attacks on Bastogne were made by small groups because of this fuel shortage.

Meanwhile, at the strategic reserve dumps east of the Rhine, there were perhaps ten consumption units for all of *Heeresgruppe B*, but no trucks to transport it. According to Mantueffel:

> The location of the fuel east of the Rhine led to some confusion at higher headquarters because the Oberquartiermeister stated that the fuel was available, but was not received by the tanks doing the fighting. Thus, when I would say we were unable to move because of lack of fuel, the higher commanders would always tell me that we had a sufficient supply.

In planning the last great German offensive of the First World War in 1918, Ludendorff noted the most difficult planning element to overcome was the shortage of horses to move supply. The mechanized mode of warfare that the Germans had brought to the world in 1939 had seen the truck replace the horse to keep up with

a motorized advance. A severe oversight on the part of Hitler's planners was not foreseeing the limitations on moving the fuel and munitions reserves from the dumps east of the Rhine to the assault forces in the field. As it was, with the poor roads and weather conditions, it often took the German trucks two days to make the trip to and from the Rhine dumps to the battle front. Later when Allied air power was out in force, the truck columns could only move under the veil of darkness.

The German Army in the fall of 1944 was desperately short of motorized transport. The thin skinned trucks had proved remarkably vulnerable to Allied air power in Europe. *OKW* reported the loss of 109,113 trucks from January through August 1944 — equal to the entire production in 1943 and representing a reduction of the military rolling stock of 39%. These losses were enormous and not immediately replaceable by an already overtaxed German manufacturing system.

In October alone strategic air raids brought 3,548 tons of bombs on German truck manufacturing plants and another 2,165 tons on the ordnance depots that supported them. Since August, even with Speer's magic hand, production of trucks had begun to wane. From August to November the

Opel, French Ford and Daimler-Benz factories recorded the loss of 11,592 vehicles due to Allied air raids.

Many of the vehicles now available in the field were either aging models or foreign ones which proved nearly impossible to procure parts for repair. Then too, the icy precipitous roads in the Ardennes considerably reduced the speed of divisional supply trains and rated road capacities by nearly half. Later, clear skies left the long columns naked before the Allied airpower.

In describing the mobility of the German Army, it must be remembered that even in the fall of 1944, many of the German divisions in the Ardennes were supplied and transported by horses. The German volksgrenadier divisions were almost entirely dependent on horse transport. There is ample evidence that the German military in the Ardennes found it easier to fuel their horses than the tanks of their heavy panzer battalions. Hay and forage were plentiful in the agricultural land spread throughout the Ardennes. Coupled with the difficulty that the terrain and icy roads presented to armor, this explains the fact that often German infantry units were ahead of the fuel-starved panzer forces.

Both sides generally had sufficient food for their troops in the Ardennes. Livestock, potatoes and spirits were appropriated in mass by both armies in the region. However, the German

A camouflaged grenadier munches on chocolate. Germans in the Ardennes were particularly fond of captured American rations and cigarettes.

transport failure did result in inadequate rations of flour for the field bakery units. Furthermore, as the battle wore on and forage was depleted, the German foodstuffs became more scarce. As early as Christmas Eve, Patton, the commander of the U.S. Third Army, noted that the German prisoners were increasingly "cold and hungry." The American fighting man was well fed as usual, although the exigencies of combat created a large demand for combat convenience food — such as the K-ration and the assault ration,

D-bar. The later concoction of ersatz chocolate was affectionately known to GIs as "Hitler's Secret Weapon."

Medical care was of a high standard on both sides considering the fluid nature of the battle. However, the German transport problem caused grave difficulties. At the end of December the *Fifth Panzer Armee* had to convey its casualties all the way back to the Rhine at the expense of those wounded on the front. Here again, the Allied logistical expertise paid off. On January 1st, 1945, in spite of losing

numerous field hospitals to advancing German spearheads, the First and Third Armies had a total of 9,000 vacant beds available.

Contrary to the German experience, the U.S. formations that the Germans faced had ample fuel and transportation. Although the American Army was not fully motorized in an organic fashion, large truck pools ensured that no one had to walk to the battlefield. The First Army alone possessed 37 truck companies at the time of the offensive with another eight borrowed from the Ninth Army and the Communications Zone. The mobility of this logistical tail was staggering. Over the period 17-26 December, 197 convoys with 48,711 vehicles moved an estimated 248,000 personnel to the Ardennes from the north. On the 17th alone, some 60,000 men were set in motion on 11,000 vehicles. The offensive movement of the Third Army in a strike north to the Ardennes was even more impressive. From December 17th - 23rd, 133,178 vehicles including 37 truck companies moved six infantry, three armored divisions, 26 field artillery battalions and nearly 42,000 tons of supply. And this was done over a hundred miles on icy roads while moving into the wake of a powerful German offensive. Furthermore, there are no indications of any Allied difficulty with procurement of sufficient fuel. Third Army stocks stood at 2.8 million gallons at the end of the month after nearly 1.5 million miles of vehicular travel in the previous two weeks.

There had been some hope on the part of the German field commanders that their attack force might advance off fuel supplies captured from the Allies. In actuality, this source failed to materialize. Peiper captured some 50,000 gallons near Büllingen from the 2nd Infantry Division stores and later narrowly missed capture of almost a million gallons near Stavelot (Peiper did not know of its existence). The *116th Panzer Division* captured some 20,000 gallons from a 7th Armored supply train near Samrée (enough to fuel all its vehicles). Another 4,000 gallons intended for surrounded Task Force Hogan of the 3rd Armored Division also parachuted into German

American GIs line up for hot chow at a field kitchen at the front.

Fresh meat. Enterprising young GIs of the 4th Infantry Division augment their diet with Ardennes game.

hands on December 23rd near Marcouray. However, these relatively minor finds were of only tactical importance.

Although it is known that Peiper's supply officer had a map indicating Allied petrol installations, this information did the division little good. Some three million gallons of fuel were evacuated by rail between December 17th and 19th from First Army depots 2 and 3 in the Stavelot-Spa area to Liège using some 3,000 trains. On December 18th, 124,000 gallons of fuel was burned from Depot 3 near Francorchamps to create a flaming roadblock and prevent German capture of the dump, but the prize remained out of German reach. Indeed, the Germans did not even make an attempt to capture the dump.

Peiper also missed a chance at a fuel depot north of La Gleize. Around noon on December 19th, in desperate need of gasoline, Peiper sent a small patrol of grenadier laden half-tracks north of Cour. Peiper's men had confirmed the existence of a huge American fuel dump with local villagers. Moving north, the small *Kampfgruppe* met the guarding troops of the dump and after a sharp skirmish withdrew south. The guarding force had only been a hundred men, a few half-tracks and some 90mm anti-aircraft guns, although Peiper's patrol was even smaller. Inexplicably, Peiper made no further attempt to capture the fuel which was evacuated to Liège over the next two days.

Overall, the largest loss of Allied fuel resulted when a V-1 buzz-bomb attack on Liège on December 17th detonated

400,000 gallons. Still, any fantasy the Germans entertained about capturing enough fuel to carry *Wacht am Rhein* to the Meuse proved to be just that.

Just as in the great 1918 offensive of the First World War, the attack tended to force the Allies back upon their logistical base, while further extending the increasingly tenuous logistical tether of the German army. Of course, the hazard existed that nearby U.S. supply depots might be captured or destroyed in contact with the enemy. The Advanced Security Zone supply dumps were disposed in mass in the Namur-Liège areas. On three separate occasions Brigadier General Robert M. Littlejohn was ordered to evacuate the enormous dumps at Liège. But rather than evacuate these depots, the U.S. quartermasters merely stepped up the flow of supply.

However, had the German advance reached the Liège-Namur area, severe disruption of the flow of U.S. supply to the First Army would have resulted.

Over two million gallons of gasoline in two U.S. fuel depots were located in the Stavelot-Francorchamps area lined along the roads. Threatened by the German advance, it was evacuated to locations west of the Meuse River beginning December 19th.

Foxhole cuisine. A GI dines on K-rations for Christmas dinner at the front line.

Unlike the Hollywood version of the Battle of the Bulge, the Germans in the real battle never came close to capturing the American stocks, nor did they even know of their location! In the single instance where the Germans approached the fuel, Belgian guards created a flaming roadblock with some 124,000 gallons of fuel even though the German tanks turned the other way before reaching the vicinity.

Moreover, the magnitude of the Allied supply in this area and the fact that it had been stockpiled by rail over a period of weeks made total evacuation impossible. Thus, the advance of the German forces to the Meuse River line in the north posed grave danger to the Allied forces. Although it would have been possible to commit the British forces to defend these precious resources, introduction of XXX Corps supply lines across those of the First Army would have lead to considerable confusion and "would have seriously disrupted all U.S. supply operations north of the Ardennes and jeopardized supply and support of the U.S. First and Ninth Armies to an extent which, if continued, would have seriously affected their combat effectiveness."

The Germans also experienced difficulty with ammunition supplies in the battle, although most of these problems stemmed from the failure of the German transport system. The total stock of artillery ammunition available to the Germans at the opening of the offensive was roughly half that available when the war began in Sep-

tember 1939. A special *Führer Reserve* of ammunition expressly designated for *Wacht am Rhein* had been created, consisting of some 40 ammunition trains dispersed in 100 small depots for protection against air attack. The supply on hand and in shipment to the three armies just prior to the offensive consisted of some 9,746 tons.

Before the Allied counterattack on January 3rd, supply officers at *OKW* ventured that no shortage of ammunition existed. However, this statement did not reflect the reality of the situation in the field where the shortage of transport led to artillery rationing in the German attack on Bastogne as early as December 21st. By December 28th the commander of *Panzer Lehr Division* grimly noted that not only was he out of fuel, but was short on ammunition as well. Meanwhile the German army in the Ardennes consumed ammunition at a rate of 1,200 tons per day — a rate considerably greater than Hitler's planners had anticipated but still less than the tactical needs of German artillery officers in the field.

On the other side of the fence, no such shortage existed for the Allied artillerymen. During the same period, the Third Army alone fired off 3,500 tons per day with the First Army dropping another 3,000 tons per day on German heads. In terms of units of fire, the Allied gunners enjoyed a 5 to 1 superiority over their enemy.

There were two distinct phases of the German fuel supply failure in the Ardennes. The first period began with the opening of the offensive when traffic jams, bad roads and poor logistical planning and the paucity of transport led to local shortages. As early as 18 December, the *Führer Begleit Brigade,* which had been committed to the battle at St. Vith, could not move into the battle zone for lack of fuel. Meantime, in order to make the fuel supply more secure, Generalfeldmarschall Model requested that six fuel trains be delivered on a daily basis. The quartermaster's report replied that "in the best case situation we can only deliver up to four trains daily."

Since *OKW* fuel reserves had been consumed, Keitel was compelled to divert 3,000 tons of petrol from allocation to other fronts. In addition, Reichsminister Speer declared the intention to deliver another 4,500 tons from civilian stocks. The key question was whether the transport of these amounts to the front could be accomplished. Fuel trucks were in short supply. The intentions had no immediate effect, for on the following day, the 19th, the *XLVII Panzerkorps* reported a severely strained fuel situation.

The situation on December 20th was extremely serious for the *1st SS Panzer Division* with its panzer regiment's tanks dry near La Gleize. SS Gruppenführer Priess ruefully noted:

> The Peiper kampfgruppe reported that they had no further supplies of fuel and only slight quantities of ammunition.

Circumstances were even worse for the *IISS Panzerkorps*. On the 21st of December the *2SS Panzer Division* reported:

> Due to the lack of fuel, the units of the Kampfgruppe "Der Führer" are not able to leave their current assembly area. The entire division is having the same difficulty....For the time being, part of the panzer regiment, the artillery regiment and the flak battalion have to stay behind due to lack of fuel.

A reports from its sister division, the *9th SS Panzer* for that day told a similar tale of woe:

> The fuel supply is sufficient only to keep the panzer reconnaissance battalion mobile. The artillery and panzer regiments are still waiting on gasoline... On the 21st enough fuel was acquired to mobilize the II battalion of the panzer regiment (Mk IVs), the Panther battalion would not arrive in the Poteau area until the 24th.

The fuel supply situation for the three panzer divisions in the *Fifth Panzer Armee* the situation was also deteriorating:

> *2nd Panzer:* "During the night of the 21st, the first elements of the panzer grenadier regiments arrived at the Tenneville bridgehead. The tanks were yet unable to follow as they were still without gasoline."

> *116th Panzer:* " The division's gas supply on the 20th was very critical. The reconnaissance battalion, artillery and panzer grenadier regiment 156 had run out of fuel..."

> *Panzer Lehr:* "On the 22nd refueling the forces caused a lot of trouble. West of Moircy, for the first time, tanks had to be refueled from cans which the panzer grenadiers had available on their Steyr transport vehicles. The formations had expected to capture fuel stores in the St. Hubert area, but only empty cans were found."

> *Führer Begleit Brigade:* "The brigade had been scattered in the detour

German gunners carefully load ammunition packed in their wicker containers from a forward supply dump. Shortages of shells severely plagued German artillery operations during the battle.

around St. Vith and we were short many of our tanks due to the gasoline shortages."

The second phase of the German supply failure began on December 23rd and was characterized by the systematic attack of the Allied air forces on the German supply lines, the road network and the rail transport system. Fighter-bombers strafed and bombed the road bound convoys while snow drifts in the Eifel further reduced rated road capacities.

By December 26th the supply trucks could only move by night to escape the Allied Jabos. So desperate was the need for transport capacity, that panzer divisions fighting on the Eastern Front were ordered to use horse drawn transport. The fuel shortages in the Ardennes reached drastic proportions with a round trip for the divisional trains extended from 12 hours to four days in some cases. During the period December 23 to 25th the motorized divisions under the *Sixth Panzer Armee* were finding it difficult to keep their motorized elements in battle. *12th SS Panzer Division* was moving to the Manhay area in starts and stops and attempts at resupplying *Kampfgruppe Peiper* by air had proved a dismal failure — Peiper broke out without his tanks on Christmas eve to evade his would-be captors. The problems in *IISS Panzerkorps* continued in a like fashion. In the case of both its divisions, the Panther battalions were intentionally left back as a reserve due to their fuel thirsty appetite for Treibstoff (they got a less than half a mile to the gallon!).

The circumstances in *Fifth Panzer Armee* were even more desperate being further from the Rhine dumps. Upon being informed by *Heeresgruppe B* of the lack of fuel in *XLVII Panzerkorps*, *OB West* ordered that the advance toward the Meuse would "proceed on foot." Only *116th Panzer Division* which had managed to capture fuel on the 20th was immune to the severe shortages. Thus the *2nd Panzer* advance to the Meuse was carried out by the still fueled reconnaissance battalion and lightly armed grenadiers. Unaware of the presence of the U.S. 2nd Armored Division, the division was caught flat footed near Celles and

German grenadiers scrounge for fuel picking up a few jerricans left behind by fleeing Americans near the village of Honsfeld. Supplies of petrol were an ever present problem for the German panzers in the Ardennes. Contrary to the hope of some of Hitler's planners, only relatively small amounts of Allied fuel were captured.

nearly destroyed in a two day battle.

> December 25th found the *2nd Panzer Division* in a very difficult position. Lack of fuel hindered considerable elements of division on their way to the front line battle groups. Only weak forces managed to go forward. The reconnaissance battalion, fighting heroically was now overwhelmed by superior enemy forces.

The period that followed brought the return of poor weather, again grounding Allied air power; blizzards and icy conditions further hampered supply. By New Years, three of the five panzer divisions of *XLVII Panzerkorps* were nearly immobile due to lack of fuel while *10th SS Panzer Division* remained in reserve near Bonn with 8 consumption units in its trains. Obviously, the greatest problem was one of transport rather than availability of fuel. The *116th Panzer Division's* combat diary for December 27th is illustrative of the fate that had beset the German formations:

> The supplies can no longer be counted on. The roads are partially blocked or impassable. At the front, all essential war means are lacking....The daily concern for the scarcity of fuel is always greater and pressing and only by the strictest of measures is this difficulty overcome. The division has barely enough fuel

due to the precautionary measures of the Führer HQ in locating supply far away over long ice-covered and bombed supply routes. The ever growing enemy air activity in the rear is bringing nightmarish dangers to our supply troops. The total supply situation is dreary.

In the final analysis it is apparent that the last great German offensive of World War II was launched on a logistical shoestring. Actual shortages due to the transport failure were further compounded by the inadequacy of German logical planning for the attack. Wishful thinking about capture of Allied supplies did not substitute for rigorous logistical planning — further evidence of the decline in the quality in German staff work in 1944. According to von Rundstedt: "There were no adequate reinforcements, no supplies of ammunition, and although the number of armored divisions was high, their strength in tanks was low —was largely paper strength." Von Manteuffel pointed to the lack of realistic experience in the *OKW* planning staffs:

> Jodl had assured us there would be sufficient petrol to develop our full strength and carry our drive through. This assurance proved completely mistaken. Part of the

trouble was that *OKW* worked on a mathematical and stereotyped calculation of the amount of petrol required to move a division a hundred kilometers. My experience in Russia had taught me that double this scale was really needed under battlefield conditions. Jodl didn't understand this. Taking account of the extra difficulties likely to be met in a winter battle in such difficult country as the Ardennes, I told Hitler personally that five times the standard scale of petrol supply ought to be provided. Actually, when the offensive was launched, only one and a half times the standard scale was available. Worse still, much of it was kept too far back, in large truck columns on the east bank of the Rhine. Once the foggy weather cleared, the Allied air forces came into action, its forwarding was badly interrupted.

To balance this criticism, it should be noted that many of the preparations for *Wacht am Rhein* were seriously compromised in interest of maintaining concealment from air observation. For reasons of camouflage the fuel dumps had been located far too distant from the battlefield. In light of the limitations of the German transport system, it would have seemed a much better system to have located numerous dispersed depots in the areas around Trier and Euskirchen. However, this would have been a risky strategy indeed, as the fuel had been accumulated since late October and locations of the dumps east of the Rhine ensured that no Allied offensive in November would reach them. Then too, the German quartermasters knew nothing of the German intentions for an offensive in the Ardennes; they were told the reserves were being accumulated for *Abwehrschlacht im Westen* — the Defensive Battle in the West. In this case, the German coverup backfired on the planners themselves.

The supply failure ranks as one of the major factors, if not *the* decisive cause, of the German failure to reach the Meuse River. According to official U.S. history, a primary reason for the failure of *Wacht am Rhein* was that "tactical support and logistic transport had not kept pace with the advance of the combat formations."

Put more directly, by Christmas Day 1944, the German blitzkrieg in the Ardennes had simply run out of gas. The month long battle that followed was predominantly an infantry fight under atrocious weather conditions. Sapped of petrol — its very lifeblood, the German panzer arm that had once terrorized Europe was reduced to only a tactical threat. On the other hand, being a German tank man with one of the heavy panzer battalions with the second wave reinforcements was one of the safer, if somewhat frustrating combat duties during the Ardennes Offensive. Such an assignment meant long periods of bivouac in rear areas waiting for gas while the infantry fought up front without you.

The Shoulders Hold, The Center Collapses: December 21st - 22nd

Thursday, December 21st, witnessed a great increase in German logistical troubles. Both the *2nd Panzer* and *2nd SS Panzer Divisions* remained idle most of the day waiting for their supply trains. Had not the Germans been slowed by this lack of fuel, the Meuse might well have been reached. On the other side, Allied reinforcements, arriving on the field in increasing numbers, enjoyed the improved ground conditions brought on by a developing ground freeze. Observation on both sides was hampered during the day by falling snow. However, on the 22nd and the days that followed the blanket of fresh snow starkly outlined the troops, tanks, and guns of both sides as they moved over the battlefield.

The *12th SS Panzer Division* with assistance from the *12th Volksgrenadiers* again launched a very heavy blow at the town of Bütgenbach. The Germans bombarded the 26th Regiment of the U.S. 1st Division for three hours with concentrated artillery and rocket fire before committing every available tank of *Kampfgruppe Kühlmann* to break the American line. Although a number of panzers penetrated the American infantry positions, the accompanying grenadiers were driven off by a hail of U.S. artillery fire and the resolute defense of the U.S. 1st Division. Unable to consolidate their victory, the unsupported German tanks were forced to retire at dark with heavy losses. Similarly, an attempt by the *3rd Panzer Grenadier Division* to advance west towards Elsenborn was stopped cold by the 99th Division with more artillery shelling. Further north, the Monschau front was quiet, strongly reinforced by the 39th and 47th Infantry regiments of the U.S. 9th Division.

To the west, Skorzeny's conventionally employed *150th Panzer Brigade* launched a fierce attack to capture the town of Malmédy and cross the Warche River. In particularly savage fighting, the Germans dressed as Americans, were thrown back by the 120th Regiment of the 30th Division and the 99th Infantry Battalion. Powerful American artillery fire rained on the retreating Germans, even wounding Skorzeny himself.[23] The only result of these actions was the

23 In the defense against this German attack, the new proximity fused "POZIT" artillery rounds were employed with devastating effect. German prisoners later told their captors that the "tree-smasher shells" caused momentary panic amongst Skorzeny's troops.

Aftermath at Dom Bütgenbach. A destroyed Jagdpanther of the 560th Heavy Panzerjäger Battalion lies abandoned by the road from Büllingen. The 46-ton beast fought with the 12th SS Panzer Division. *The Germans were soundly defeated in the four day battle there. .*

Phoney tank. This was one of Skorzeny's Panthers crudely disguised to be an M-10 tank destroyer and painted American olive drab. Skorzeny himself was under no illusion about the subterfuge: "They might fool very young American soldiers, very far away and at night." This one was knocked out near the bridge in Malmédy. All of its American dressed crew were killed as they tried to escape.

Ready to blow it sky-high. Engineers guard a dynamited span of the bridge across the Warche River in Malmédy. The white tape attached to the stone walls was a standard warning. The charge: 850 pounds of TNT.

developing Allied impression that the German offensive was directed at Liège.

Out of gasoline with its supply line cut at Stavelot, *Kampfgruppe Peiper* in Stoumont and La Gleize repulsed attacks from all sides by the 30th Infantry and 3rd Armored Division. At mid-day Peiper held a conference with his battalion commanders in the chateau of *Froide Cour* just east of Stoumont to discuss their increasingly desperate situation. It was decided that the village must be surrendered in order to hope to successfully defend against future attacks. By evening his troops and the battlegroup command post had been moved back to La Gleize where the situation remained grim as well; the tiny 50-house village was being swept by gusts of artillery fire.

In spite of radio delivered assurances from SS-Obf. Mohnke at divisional headquarters that help was on the way, Peiper could see his grip was slipping. During the day the 508th and 325th Regiments of the 82nd Airborne deployed along the Salm River to bar any German advance there. In bloody fighting the 504th Parachute Infantry regiment captured Peiper's bridgehead across the Amblève River at Cheneux. The airborne troops suffered 225 casualties in close combat with SS troops fighting from mounts on self-propelled flak guns, but wrecked the better part of a German battalion. The noose was fast tightening on *Kampfgruppe Peiper.*

Just to the east, *Kampfgruppe Hansen* struck from Wanne to force a crossing at Trois Ponts and open *Rollbahn E.* However, the first German assault gun that attempted to cross the fragile span at Petit Spai brought down the bridge so that the SS infantry on the other side had to fight without armor. Soon a hot fight developed between the 505th Para-

The trouble with bridges. On December 21st the 1st SS Panzer Division attempted to put its battalion of self-propelled anti-tank guns across the frail bridge at Petit Spai. The first 25-ton Jagdpanzer IV attempting to cross, that of Obersturmführer Otto Holst, collapsed the structure with panzer and bridge dropping into the Amblève River.

Too few. German engineers of the 1st SS Panzer Division *put in a small foot bridge at Petit Spai after the main bridge had been put out of action.*

chute Infantry Regiment and the SS panzer grenadiers. The Germans got across the bridge at Trois Ponts, only to be forced back in a counterattack and then have U.S. engineers blow the span. Another attempt by a small detachment of assault guns from the panzer division failed to take the Salm bridge at La Neuville. There was no getting past Gavin's paratroopers.

Meanwhile, the *9th SS Panzer Division* was toiling into the area north of St. Vith, frustrated with its meager allocation of fuel and "the miserable roads." The developing circumstances in Stoumont-La Gleize had altered the *Sixth Panzer Armee* orders to the division. Whatever elements that had already walked or motored to the front were to go immediately to the aid of *Kampfgruppe Peiper.* So countermanded, the division marched off towards the Salm River. At that stream, *Kampfgruppe Altrogge,* a reinforced panzer grenadier detachment of the division, attempted to force a night crossing at Grand Halleux. However, this move too was blunted by the 82nd Airborne Division. Meanwhile, back at Poteau, the *9th SS* put in a strong bid to take the troublesome crossroads. Enough *Treibstoff* had been scrounged to get its Mk IV and reconnaissance battalions (*Kampfgruppe Recke*) to Recht so that some of the tank strength of the division (130 armored vehicles) could at last be employed. However, the attack on Poteau at 1 P.M. was turned back by artillery and anti-tank fire from Combat Command A of the 7th Armored Division.

The American forces in front of St. Vith were overwhelmed on the night of the 21st. Montgomery, who had taken charge of the Allied forces in the northern part of the salient, wanted to pull the American forces out of the fortified goose egg. On the other hand, Hodges, who had his sights set on a future Allied attack to close the gap between Malmèdy and St. Vith, and Ridgway, who was now in charge of the defense there, wanted to hold onto the town. Even so, Hodges left the decision up to the commander on the ground — the 7th Armored's Gen. Hasbrouck. To Hasbrouck the situation seemed too dangerous to hold onto St. Vith. His commander there, Gen. Clarke, had already stated his preference: "This terrain is not worth a nickel an acre to me." Hasbrouck decided to reform a new line west of the town.

The 7th Armored Division, and parts of the 9th Armored and 28th Division were under concentric attack. The *62nd Volksgrenadier Division,* although severely chopped up by American tank counterattacks near Volmersberg, took Grüflingen in an advance from the south. Meanwhile, following extremely heavy artillery and violent fire, the *18th Volksgrenadiers* drove straight for the town with tank support from Wallerode forcing its way into St. Vith. Even worse for the American defenders, the *Führer Begleit Brigade,* now driving from the north in the vicinity of Rodt, cut the one good road leading west from the town. By midnight the *18th Volksgrenadier Division* reported itself to be firmly in control of St. Vith.

Although, having pulled out of the town, Hasbrouck's division was still faced with encirclement from the German forces closing in on all sides. Had not the *2nd SS Panzer*

Vanquished German armor. On a road near St. Vith, German assault guns lie scattered. They were knocked out by the 7th Armored Division and then unceremoniously pushed aside on January 23rd, 1945.

Division been out of fuel northeast of Houffalize on the 21st (the fuel thirsty panzer regiment was just now crossing the Our at Dasburg), and on orders to proceed to the Meuse, the American forces in St. Vith would have likely been surrounded. Even though they were forced to abandon St. Vith, the 7th Armored did manage to repel other German punches leveled at Poteau and Vielsalm by the *9th SS. Kampfgruppe Telkamp* lost five tanks in the gun duel including the Panther of the panzer regiment leader, SS-Stbf. Eberhard Telkamp.

The German delay at St. Vith had been fundamental to the dwindling German prospects for an early strike at the Meuse. Von Manteuffel later said, "I was very astonished to find the 7th Armored Division in St. Vith. The town had to be taken for the attack to succeed in the shortest possible time. The delay imposed there put the entire German offensive plan three days behind schedule. I didn't count on such stubbornness."

Nearby, the *116th Panzer Division* continued its rapid march to the northwest via Beffe, charging for the Ourthe River bridge at Hotton, east of Marche. The Germans had lost the element of surprise prior to this abortive foray, however, and were stopped just short of the bridge by a "hailstorm of fire" from the 51st Combat Engineer Battalion and elements of CCR of the 3rd Armored Division. Meanwhile, in the panzer division's wake, the *560th Volksgrenadier Division* fanned out to the north pushing elements towards Gouvy, Les Tailles and north of Samrée.

The battle astride the Ourthe River was particularly confused. One battalion of the 3rd Armored Division, Task Force Hogan (Lt. Col. Samuel M. Hogan), had become surrounded in the *116th Panzer's* rear near Marcouray. Even so, resistance before the Germans was increasing and losses coupled with fatigue were beginning to tell. "The troops slowly began to sense that the great plan had failed," recalled the commander of the *116th Panzer Division*. "Morale and performance began to suffer."

On the northern front the balance of force was tending to the Allied favor. Combat Command A of the 3rd Armored

SITUATION MAP
December 21st-22nd

LEUVEN

TIENEN

ST. TRU

MEUSE RIVER

ANDENNE

NAMUR

SAMBRE RIVER

Ciney

DINANT

PHILIPPEVILLE

GIVET

COUVIN

FORÊT D'ARDENNE

CHARLEVILLE-
MEZIÈRES

BOUI

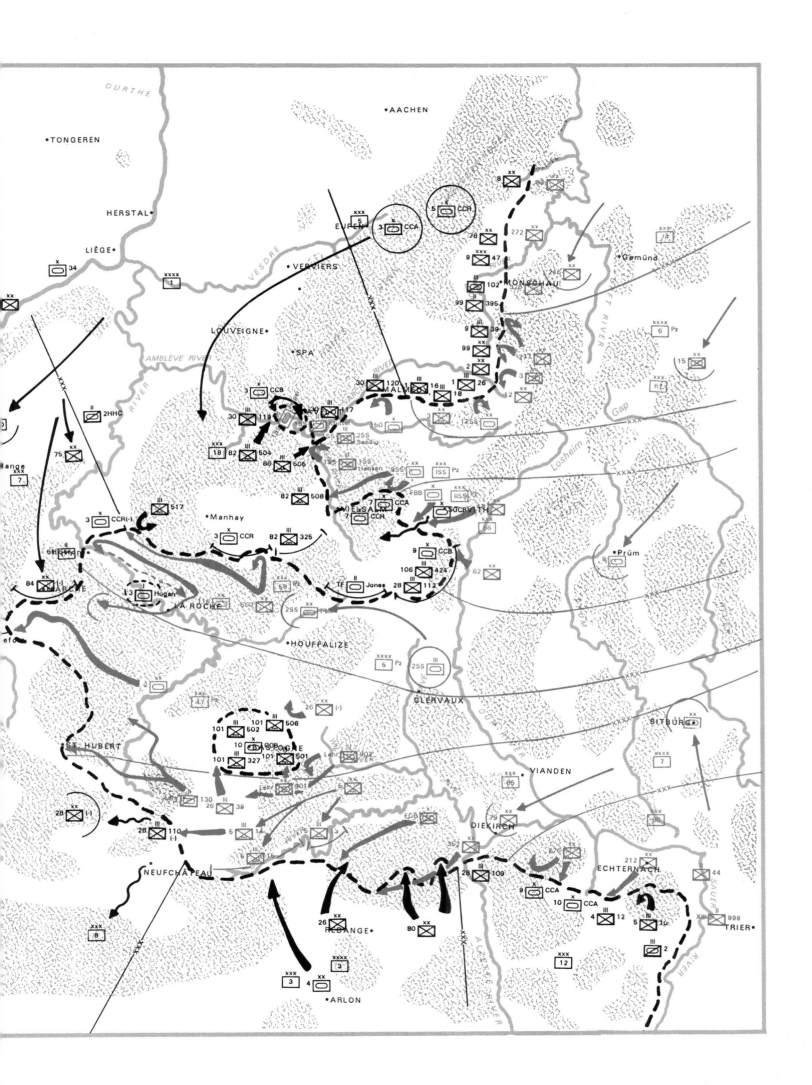

was arriving in the Werbomont area after having been released from hunting German paratroopers near Eupen. Independent parachute units were also being moved to the battlefield; the 517th Parachute Infantry Regiment and the 509th Parachute Infantry Battalion were assembling north of Soy. The 551st Parachute Infantry battalion was moving up to assist in throwing the *1st SS Panzer Division* out of the Ambléve River valley.

Near Bastogne, the *2nd Panzer Division* and *Panzer Lehr Division* skirted the town and moved west, delayed by spotty American resistance and flagging fuel deliveries. Throughout the entirety of the 21st, the *2nd Panzer Division* had to be content with expanding its bridgehead at Tenneville and tangling with troublesome American engineers on the Champlon highway (the ubiquitous 51st Combat Engineers had felled trees with dynamite across the highway). Although little enemy resistance blocked its projected path, the division was totally without gasoline. The panzer troops were also fatigued. "The relentless employment of the *116th Panzer Division* and the *2nd Panzer Division*," the *Heeresgruppe B* daily report observed, "has caused their fighting power to greatly decline."

To the south, the *Panzer Lehr Division* continued its drive around Bastogne. The final efforts of the *902nd Panzer Grenadier Regiment* against the village of Neffe, just east of Bastogne, were repulsed by the 101st Airborne in "vicious close in fighting" so that the battlegroup was ordered to circle around the stubborn defenders and continue west to the Meuse. The division was forced to leave one of its panzer grenadier regiments behind. *Kampfgruppe von Hauser* was to assist with the reduction of Bastogne. But meanwhile, *Kampfgruppe von Fallois*, the heavily reinforced reconnaissance battalion, was moving rapidly now prodded along by von Manteuffel himself who was unimpressed by Bayerlein's display of initiative over the preceeding days. By nightfall it had over-run an American artillery battalion, blown through the villages of Tillet and Amberloup and snatched a bridge across the Ourthe River at Moircy. The battlegroup had even bagged the entirety of a U.S. truck column in the process. With this sweep, the U.S. defenders in Bastogne were totally encircled. On the following day the German division's advance took them to Pironpré and St. Hubert.

On orders, the *26th Volksgrenadier Division* turned up the pressure at Bastogne. Two regiments launched a night attack northeast of Bastogne at Bourcy, aimed at infiltrating through the American paratroopers before advancing into the town. It was late afternoon before the 501st and 506th Parachute Infantry Regiments had thrown back the enemy and restored their lines. On the other side of the encirclement, *Kampfgruppe Kunkel*, the reinforced fusilier battalion under the energetic leadership of Maj. Rolf Kunkel struck from the south. At Sibret, the German battle group met with Task Force Caraway, an ad hoc formation of remnants of the 110th Infantry Regiment organized by Gen. Cota to hold open the vital Bastogne- Neufchâteau road. But by 9:00 A.M. the German pressure had increased to the point

Gen. Manton Eddy of the U.S. XII Corps runs for cover during a German artillery barrage in the town of Echternach. The photograph was taken as the Americans recaptured the devastated village on February 9th, 1945.

Foot soldiers. Men of the U.S. 5th Infantry Division march into the Ardennes to set the situation right along the extreme southern flank of the offensive.

where the defending Americans were forced to relinquish the town. Kunkel pressed on to the north capturing an artillery battalion intact as he advanced on Senonchamps. Here Lt. Col. Barry D. Browne had hastily organized a combat team under his namesake. Task Force Browne was built around his 420th Armored Field Artillery battalion with some stray tanks and infantry to ward off the German threat from the south.

The offensive in the German *Seventh Armee* reached its high water mark on the 21st when advancing units were prudently called back in response to the threat from Patton's Third Army to the south. Ordered to create a hard southern defensive cordon, Brandenberger urgently requested a panzer formation and another infantry division to help man his perilously over-extended line. The answer to these pleas was already moving onto the field: the *Führer Grenadier Brigade* was advancing its 92 armored vehicles and infantry battalions in dribs and drabs towards Heiderscheid. At the same time the *79th Volksgrenadier Division* began to march into its assembly area around Diekirch.

The German *LXXXV Armeekorps* consolidated their defensive positions between the Alzette River and the Bastogne-Arlon highway. The *5th Fallschirmjäger Division*, on the highway to Bastogne, blew the bridge at Martelange and moving west, shared in the capture of Sibret with *Kampfgruppe Kunkel*. The *352nd Volksgrenadier Division* made pro-

gress as well, seizing the town of Ettelbruck from the exhausted 109th Regiment of the 28th Division. The Germans then boldly advanced, capturing Niederfeulen, Bettborn, Bissen and Pratz by the following day. After that the division would be forced over to the defensive.

Events further south on the *LXXX Armeekorps* front took a decidedly unfavorable turn. In its furthest penetration, the *276th Volksgrenadier Division* nearly reached the village of Savelborn, but was there stopped by "entrenched enemy tanks." A powerful bid by the 10th Armored Division and CCA of the 9th to take Waldbillig was stopped with great difficulty. The American armor took over a hundred German prisoners.

At the southernmost point of the German offensive, the *212th Volksgrenadiers* — yelling "kill the sons of bitches" in broken English — advanced in mass along the main Echternach-Luxembourg highway. The German assault carried through Lauterborn, and then continued south. However, the U.S. 4th Division and Combat Command A of the 10th Armored rallied to repulse German infantry essayed towards Consdorf and Osweiler, parrying these attacks with counter blows of their own. Ominously, however, the division still had no word from the company sized garrison of Americans trapped in Echternach (they had, in fact, surrendered on December 20th). Help was on the way: the forward command post of Maj. Gen. Manton S. Eddy's XII Corps had opened

XXX Corps. Tankers of the British 29th Armored Brigade patrol the Meuse River at Namur. The tank is a Sherman "Firefly" mounting the more powerful British 17-pounder gun.

in Luxembourg City and the 10th Regiment of Maj. Gen. Leroy Irwin's 5th Infantry Division was sent marching to the aid of the endangered south flank.

The night of the 21st found von Rundstedt still fretting over the trouble with the main effort of the offensive. He decreed that it was of "decisive importance that the right wing of the *Sixth Panzer Armee* quickly regain its freedom of movement" which required the "most rapid possible resolution of the situation in the Elsenborn area." The other edicts of *OB West* were: "capture of St. Vith" and for von Manteuffel's two panzer corps to hasten towards "accelerated establishment of bridgeheads over the Meuse between Huy and Givet."[24] The issue of reserves came up as well. The *10th SS Panzer* had arrived in mass in Münstereifel, part of the *9th Panzer Division* was assembling in the area around Prüm and a single grenadier regiment of Genlt. Wend von Wietersheim's tardy *11th Panzer* had shown up at Kyllburg (albeit without its 114 tanks or half-tracks and other heavy weapons). However, all these formations had strings attached; they could not be committed without Hitler's express approval.

The situation in the Allied high command reflected the confusion and crisis of the battle. Aware of the German threat to the Meuse crossings, the Allies set to hurriedly assembling forces to block the German path to the west. To deny German use of the highway to Namur, Brig. Gen. Alexander R. Bolling's U.S. 84th Infantry Division moved di-

rectly from road march from the Ninth Army to a perimeter defense in and around the town of Marche. The immediate line covered by his limited rifle strength extended to the villages of Jamodenne, Marloie, Baillonville and Hampteau. To further bar German access over the Meuse River, the British XXX Corps began to arrive on the west bank of that river with the 29th Armored Brigade, the 2nd Household Cavalry Regiment and the 53rd "Welsh" Infantry Division (Maj. Gen. R. K. Ross). The 43rd "Wessex" Division was held in reserve, north of the Meuse, near Hasselt, Belgium, to counter the Germans should they force their way across the river.

Confounding Allied plans was a lack of knowledge of German intentions coupled with the extremely fluid situation at the front. Hodges worried that the Germans might suddenly pivot north to capture Liège, its precious supply depots and trap the First Army (the Small Solution). On the other hand, both Patton and Middleton were afraid that the Germans might suddenly turn to the south towards Sedan in a replay of 1940.[25] The American line in this sector was

24 The town of St. Vith fell at 9:30 P.M. on the night of the 21st when German tanks breached the American defenses along the Prümmerberg road that lead into the town from the east.
25 The Allied French General Staff had made much the same assessment. On December 22nd Bulletin No. 9 asked the rhetorical question: "Antwerp or Verdun?" the reply being that after the Meuse is reached, "the latter appears more probable since it would open up the rear areas of Patton's army."

especially weak. Remembering 1914 and 1940, Parisians had the jitters and the *gendarmes* there were enforcing an all night curfew. Even the British stationed guards to man roadblocks near Brussels.

December 22nd marked the beginning of the climax of the Battle of the Bulge. Eisenhower issued a rare Order of the Day admonishing the Allies fighting in the Ardennes to "rise to new heights of courage, of resolution and of effort....By rushing out from his fixed defense the enemy may give us the chance to turn his great gamble into his worst defeat."

The fighting now was particularly desperate. With Luxembourg City threatened, Bradley ordered his 12th Army Group's battalion-sized Special Troops under Brig. Gen. Charles R. Doan to prepare defenses in Verdun and along the west bank of the Meuse to Commercy should the German advance go unchecked. It was their only tactical assignment in the entire war. And as if to underscore the urgency, that same day Patton began his offensive from the south in the midst of a swirling snow storm.

The pistol-packing general's objectives were ambitious: halt any further advance of the German *Seventh Armee*, rescue the encircled paratroopers in Bastogne and cut through to Houffalize and cut off the German spearhead. Despite Patton's affinity for armor, his staff and his corps commanders were infantrymen, including Eddy, an old-timer with the Third Army and Middleton whose command was now split up. Only his chief of staff, Maj. Gen. Hobart R. Gay, and Maj. Gen. John Millikin, the new-comer in III Corps had been comissioned as cavalrymen. The Third Army began the attack with three divisions in the van: the 26th and 80th Infantry Divisions and Patton's favorite, the 4th Armored Division.

But the rush to Arlon had its cost; one battalion of the 4th Armored lost 33 tanks in its long push to the north. Although Patton told the commander of III Corps, Maj. Gen. Millikin, to "drive like hell," his troops almost immediately ran into tough resistance from the determined defense of the *5th Fallschirmjäger Division* and its attached *11th Sturmgeschütz Brigade*. That day Patton's forces only reached as far as Martelange, still twelve miles south of Bastogne. Regardless, the outspoken commander intended to make good on his promise to Brig. Gen. Anthony C. McAuliffe in charge of the garrison in Bastogne: he would be there by Christmas.

The U.S. 26th Division (Maj. Gen. Willard S. Paul) marched 16 miles before making contact with the Germans in the Rambrouch-Grosbous area, ten miles south of Wiltz. A scrambling night melèe developed between the Americans pushing north and the slowly arriving *Führer Grenadier Brigade*. Near Arsdorf the German brigade commander, Obst. Hans-Joachim Kahler, was severely wounded, throwing the formation into confusion. Meantime, Maj. Gen. Horace L. McBride's 80th Division advanced unopposed five miles before running into stiff resistance from the *352nd Volksgrenadiers* at Mertzig and nearby Ettelbruck. East of this action, the U.S. 10th Armored continued to hold its positions along the south flank. However, Patton was so encouraged by the progress on the right on the first day that he ordered Millikin's III Corps to continue the advance through the night.

To the east, Gen. Eddy's newly arrived XII Corps, with parts of the 5th Infantry, arrived to reinforce the overtaxed 4th Infantry Division that had been forced to give up ground

The Queen of Battle. Infantry of Patton's Third Army move up to the front in the Ardennes.

south of Echternach the previous day. The German divisions of the *LXXX Armeekorps* had fought themselves out in recent days with some infantry companies reporting an available strength of only 30 to 40 men. Even so, the entirety of the 5th Infantry Division was not available until December 24th when a concerted attack on the Germans west of the Sauer was planned. The single regiment on hand, the 10th Infantry, planned for a counterattack on the enemy around Michelshof. As fate would have it, this enterprise ran head on into a final German attempt by the *212th Volksgrenadiers* to win Scheidgen. Both opponents had their plans thwarted in a bloody encounter.

The situation on the right wing of the German *Seventh Armee* was degenerating as well. Genmaj. Ludwig Heilmann's *5th Fallschirmjäger Division* routed the headquarters of the U.S. 28th Division from its post near Vaux-les-Rosières. The beleaguered remnants of the U.S. division and various support troops pulled back to Neufchâteau. But this was the last offensive motion for the German corps. At daybreak the 4th Armored Division appeared on Heilmann's south flank at Martelange. Even worse, the Navy sailors-turned-soldiers of the *352nd Volksgrenadier Division* were totally surprised by the rapid advance of the U.S. 80th Division. A good part its *915th Regiment* was encircled near Grosbous and the rest of the division was thrown back to Ettelbruck.

In the *Sixth Panzer Armee* sector, the *12th SS Panzer Division*'s final all-out attempt to break through the U.S. 1st Division at Bütgenbach on the 22nd was again turned back by American artillery and anti-tank fire. *Heeresgruppe B* tersely reported that the "attack for the purposes of opening the Bütgenbach-Waimes road had to be stopped because of the high number of German casualties." At the close of the four-day showdown the division limped away from the battlefield leaving behind the wrecks of 44 tanks and assault guns. The human losses were still greater; American observers reported enemy dead "as common as grass" and one patrol counted 300 dead Germans in the woods south of Bütgenbach alone.

To the north of this macabre scene, the *277th Volksgrenadier Division* launched a surprise night attack against the boundary of the 99th and 9th Infantry Divisions between Monschau and Elsenborn. The thrust nearly reached Kalterherberg before it was halted by the recently arrived 39th Regiment of the 9th Infantry Division and a rain of artillery shells. A counterattack by the 9th Infantry the following day restored the American line and forced the German infantry back to the east. The finality of the German failure even had command repercussions. Having failed to carry the American line, the *LXVII Armeekorps* from Monschau to Elsenborn was returned to the command of the *Fifteenth Armee*.

On the 22nd von Manteuffel launched the attack that he hoped would finally take his *Fifth Panzer Armee* to the Meuse River. After the capture of St. Vith, the *LXVI Armeekorps* (*62, 18th Volksgrenadier Divisions* and the *Führer Begleit Brigade*) began attacking to the west towards Vielsalm and the Salm River, although taking considerable time to disentangle the traffic snarl in and around the town. The panzer brigade took the village of Rodt while the *62nd Volksgrenadiers* fought a see-saw battle for Neundorf and Grüfflingen. Still pushing hard against the 7th Armored, the *18th Volks-*

Far from sea. This bedraggled looking member of the 352nd Volksgrenadier Division was captured by the U.S. 26th Infantry Division. He had been a regular sailor in the Kriegsmarine since 1938 until Hitler's pre-Ardennes manpower comb-out made him a foot soldier.

Upper right: *Grizzly Bear. A Brummbär armored assault howitzer of the 217th Sturmpanzer Battalion in action near Dom Bütgenbach on December 22nd, 1944.*

Lower right: *Conference in a snow-storm. German SS commanders meet before the attack on Bütgenbach, December 22nd, 1944.*

grenadier Division took Crombach.

The situation for the Americans in the "fortified goose egg" near St. Vith was looking desperate. Montgomery recommended to Hodges that the defense there be abandoned. Hodges reluctantly agreed and sent out the appropriate orders to Gen. Ridgway. Ridgway and Maj. Gen. James W. Gavin, in charge of the 82nd Airborne Division, found the prospect disgusting. "The division had never withdrawn throughout all its battles," Gavin later related. And although Ridgway wanted to hold the salient the commanders of the 7th Armored were dubious. But personally inspecting the situation around the perimeter, even Ridgway became convinced of the wisdom of evacuating the pocket. The real problem would be physically extricating the 20,000 men and their vehicles over the muddy roads across the vulnerable

Airborne Commanders. Maj. Gen. Matthew Ridgeway, XVIII Airborne Corps, meets with Maj. Gen. James Gavin, 82nd Airborne Division at Remonchamps near the end of the Ardennes battle. The dangling hand grenades were Ridgeway's trademark.

American hero. Brig. Gen. "Tony" McAuliffe, of "Nuts" fame, is decorated with the Distinguished Service Cross by "Old Blood and Guts" Gen. George S. Patton. The occasion took place in Bastogne on December 28th, 1944.

bridge on the Salm River near Vielsalm. The withdrawal began that night.

To the west of St. Vith, the Germans continued their advance. The *116th Panzer Division* still had orders to cross the Ourthe and push on the Meuse. Gaining bridges had proved problematic for the *Windhund Division*, however. The assault on Hotton the day before had not taken the town and its bridge and the panzer division had sustained heavy losses. The decision was made to reverse direction once again, moving back south to cross the Ourthe at La Roche which the panzer division had taken without a fight the day before. Changing horses in mid-stream was no simple matter; the division spent most of the day sorting out traffic, fueling its vehicles and repulsing attempts by the 517th Parachute Infantry Regiment and the 3rd Armored Division to clear the Soy-Hotton road. By nightfall the division was in the process of giving over its positions to the *560th Volksgrenadier Division*. To further complicate the switch, the German infantry of the later division were engaged in a hard fight with Task Force Orr of the 3rd Armored Division for possession of the village of Amonines. Meanwhile, a bold thrust by a company of the volksgrenadiers from the division's *Kampfgruppe Schumann* to take the strategic crossroads at Baraque Fraiture was shot to pieces by the small force of American defenders gathering there.

The stalled *2nd Panzer Division*, received a visit by Gen. von Lüttwitz who tongue-lashed and then relieved the battalion commander of the advance guard for his lack of initiative. So implored, the group advanced on Marche before running into resistance there from the 84th Division. Rather than be delayed, however, the division bypassed the town to the south and drove west reaching the village of Hargimont by nightfall. Garnering additional reinforcements the 84th Division had placed outposts in the road intersection villages of Wanlin, Rochefort and Beauraing to block the German way west.

Back at Bastogne, there had been "no change in the siege and encirclement front." Mindful of the mass capitulation of the American pocket in the Schnee Eifel, the commander of the XLVII *Panzerkorps*, Gen. von Lüttwitz, took it upon himself to make a surrender request of the American bastion at Bastogne. "Along about December 22nd I was having my greatest doubts," Gen. McAuliffe remembered. "Many were wounded and supplies were short. Some guns were down to ten rounds each." Regardless of any personal misgivings, McAuliffe was not about to give up. His defiant reply that day to the German surrender request of his 101st Airborne — "Nuts!" — would be forever etched into the annals of American military history.

While this went on to the south, the situation for *Kampfgruppe Peiper* on the 22nd had become desperate. Out of fuel, surrounded by two American divisions and under constant shelling, Peiper had abandoned Stoumont and moved two miles east to hold out in the "La Gleize cauldron." A Luftwaffe attempt on the night of the 22nd to parachute 1.5 tons of fuel to the kampfgruppe proved a miserable failure. Believing the Germans to be in possession of Stoumont, most of the fuel drums were parachuted into the hands of the U.S. 30th Division which now held that town.

While the *ISS Panzerkorps* had instructed that "all means must be employed" to liberate Peiper, all the attacks to open

Kampfgruppe Hansen. SS Grenadiers of the 1st SS Panzer Division *on the advance in the Ardennes.*

a way to the beleaguered German group through Stavelot had failed with high losses. The only success came early on December 22nd from German panzer grenadiers of *Kampfgruppe Hansen* who crossed over the Amblève River near Petit Spai, a continuing sally point for German efforts to reach Peiper. Hansen's grenadiers captured the tiny villages of Ster, Parfondruy and Renardmont, surprising Task Force Lovelady of the 3rd Armored Division. The *ISS Panzerkorps* requested permission for *Kampfgruppe Peiper* to breakout, but knowing of Hitler's view on retrograde movement, this was rejected by Dietrich's staff.

By nightfall the lead troops of the *9th SS Panzer Division* had by-passed the 7th Armored at Poteau and struck out towards Vielsalm with light elements taking the village of Grand Halleux on the Salm River from the 82nd Airborne Division. According to plan, the division would capture Vielsalm, and then in concert with the *2nd SS Panzer* advance to Mormont-Erezée and push beyond to the northwest to cross the Ourthe at Durbuy.

In order to reinforce the success of von Manteuffel's army, von Rundstedt ordered that the *9th* and *167th Volksgrenadier Divisions* be made ready to support the attack. He also issued a new order concerning the future conduct of the offensive. Any idea of the drive on Antwerp or the attack in concert by *Heeresgruppe H* vanished from von Rundstedt's pragmatic entries in his war diary. He stressed as the objec-

tive "a wheeling movement to the north from the area around Marche to push the enemy away from the river on this side of the Meuse and destroy him." Here again, was the idea of the Small Solution, which now under the pressure of failure, Hitler was hard pressed to reject.

Among the panzer divisions, the shortage of spare parts began to surface as an important problem. As example, the *116th Panzer Division* was forced to cannibalize a number of newly delivered tanks on the rail unloading platform to patch up tanks in need of repair on the front.[26] Of even greater concern was the fuel shortages. On the evening of December 21st the *116th* reported only 0.7 fuel consumption units on hand.[27] As a result, repaired tanks could no longer be driven forward; 23 Mk V Panthers of the division were currently stranded on roads in the rear although urgently needed for combat at the front. Similarly, German prisoners interrogated by the U.S. First Army were beginning to complain of the lack of food and many told stories

26 Many German divisions reported tank breakdowns. A mechanic with the *2nd Panzer Division* reported "considerable mechanical difficulties and frequent breakdowns" due to "faulty workmanship or sabotage rather than poor materials." A captured tank commander of the *9th SS* reported his Mk V failed on 19 December, and due to the shortage of gas it was 12 January, 1945 before his Panther was back in action.
27 The German fuel consumption unit (VS) was enough to take a motorized unit about 30 miles in the Ardennes terrain. A Panther held 700 liters (185 gallons) of gasoline to give it a 2 VS range.

of long marches with their heavy equipment left behind for lack of transportation.

However, the greatest concern on the German side was the weather. Although, it had continued to be overcast and favorable for the German attack on the 21st and 22nd with little effective Allied air activity, the German weather service reported a rapid build-up of high pressure approaching from the East. According to the forecasts, a sustained period of improved weather could be expected in one or two days. Genfldm. Model took the opportunity to recommend elimination of road congestion along with dispersal of motorized troops under wooded cover before this good flying weather broke. Von Rundstedt warned that the Luftwaffe was "despite the heaviest commitment, not in a position to adequately shield its own troops."

Skorzeny's Commandos

From the beginning of the war, Hitler had showed remarkable faith in commando operations and fifth columnists. For Hitler's last great offensive of the war, the German leader pulled out all the stops. Soon after he conceived the idea of the Ardennes attack in the fall of 1944, Hitler decided that a commando operation to seize the Meuse bridges for the panzer divisions could be of deciding influence. He believed that such an operation would be most effective if it consisted of a German formation disguised as an American one to bluff their way through the Allied line. Hitler was also convinced that such an operation of English speaking German commandos would exact tremendous confusion within the American ranks which could be of decisive importance to the success of the German attack towards Antwerp.

For this operation Hitler enlisted the help of the one of the most famous German operatives of World War II — SS Ostbf. Otto Skorzeny. Long known to British intelligence as "the most dangerous man in Europe," Skorzeny had snatched Mussolini from his Allied captors in 1943, and in October with *Operation Panzerfaust* had kidnapped the son of Admiral Horthy, the regent of Hungary to prevent that country's defection from the German side. A year earlier, the six-foot Austrian had appeared on English newsreels towering over a dejected Mussolini. He appeared the perfect Nazi, enormous in stature with closely cropped hair, an iron cross dangling from his neck and a scar that stretched from his left ear to his mouth (the result of a duel in Vienna with another student over the affections of a female ballet dancer). The "Liberator of Mussolini" was one of Hitler's favorites.

On October 22nd, Hitler warmly welcomed Skorzeny at his Rastenburg headquarters in East Prussia. "Well done, Skorzeny!" Hitler said promoting the Austrian to SS Obersturmbannführer for his latest coup. However, Hitler had another assignment for him. "I am going to charge you with a new mission, perhaps the most important in your life." Hitler then told him of *Wacht am Rhein*. "In December, Germany will start a great offensive," he said. "It may decide her fate." The Führer informed Skorzeny that he was to organize a special "deception" panzer brigade under the title of *Operation Greif* that could be of decisive importance to the success of the great attack. All organization of the brigade and preparations for the attack must be carried out in less than five weeks. "I know the time given you is very short," Hitler conceded, "but I can count on you do do the impossible!"

The commando unit, with the rather innocuous title of *Panzer Brigade 150*, consisted of English speaking German soldiers wearing American uniforms. They were to travel in captured Allied tanks, trucks and jeeps to infiltrate through the American line and proceed ahead of the German armored advance to seize the all-important bridges across the Meuse River from Namur to Liège. Special commando units traveling in jeeps and posing as American officers would run about the Allied rear area creating as much confusion as possible by issuing false orders, cutting communication lines and spreading wild rumors.

Hitler gave Skorzeny sweeping powers to requisition what he needed for *Operation Greif*. However, a few days later, on October 26th, Skorzeny received a printed notice that was being distributed all over the Western front. At the top was printed "Secret Commando Operations." The opening read: "The Führer has ordered the formation of a special unit of approximately two battalion strength for use on the Western Front in special operations....The body of the notice went on to ask for all English speaking officers and men from all three services to volunteer to serve in a special operation under *Dienststelle* Skorzeny. They were to report for duty at the training center at Friedenthal by November 10th. The tall Austrian was rightfully shocked by this idiotic notice, which he believed, surely would reach Allied intelligence. In fact the notice did reach Allied intelligence by

Hitler receives Otto Skorzeny. Skorzeny was known to Allied intelligence as "the most dangerous man in Europe" after his successful rescue of Mussolini from his Allied captors in 1943.

early November, but was discounted as a propaganda plant since surely no covert German operation involving the infamous Skorzeny would be broadcast in such an ostentatious fashion! Moreover, that such a notice, signed by Keitel, could be so widely distributed given the magnitude of the security precautions for *Wacht am Rhein* seemed absolutely preposterous.

Skorzeny contacted Hitler and told him that *Operation Greif* must be abandoned since the element of surprise had already been lost. Although Hitler agreed that this leak was unfortunate, he persuaded Skorzeny to carry through with plans for the operation. On a personal level, Skorzeny was worried about the fate of his men should they be captured in enemy uniform. An expert in international law assured that his commandos would be all right if they removed the uniforms covering their German ones before opening fire. To Skorzeny, however, it seemed all together unlikely that this could be accommodated in the heat of battle. Generaloberst Jodl responded by saying that, "All the men selected are volunteers. They are quite aware of the possibility that they may be treated as partisans. This they have accepted; no-one has forced them into it." In spite of increasing personal doubt, Skorzeny set about to accommodate the Führer's wishes.

At the commando training camps at Grafenwöhr and Friedenthal, the security for "American School" was ruthless. Volunteers were completely cut-off from the outside world; the camp was closely guarded and one volunteer was shot for sending home a letter describing their activities. Upon seeing the first batch of "English speaking volunteers" Skorzeny indicated that he "struck a new low in despondency. I wanted to consign the whole thing to the devil." Only ten men could speak the language perfectly with a working knowledge of slang (most were sailors from the *Kriegsmarine*). Thirty five more could speak well, but knew no slang (and a troubling number of these had heavy accents). Another 300 might get by if they weren't required to say too much and the overwhelming majority could say "yes" or "no." Skorzeny remem-

bered that most of the German commandos "could certainly never dupe an American — even a deaf one!"

To improve this poor state of affairs, the members of the brigade were subjected to intensive language training; how to chew gum, to cuss and use American gestures and slang. Those whose English was poor or stilted were taught the appropriate irreverent American responses. A come back to "Who goes there?" was "It's okay, Joe, don't mind me." A request for a password was the reply, "Aw, go lay an egg" or "So is your old man, buddy." If these didn't work, the commandos were to use choice swear words and pretend to be in a hurry and losing patience.

After a few weeks of preparation, the physical readiness of the panzer brigade was indeed disappointing. Skorzeny had a mixed batch of summer American uniforms, many that were very fine, except for brightly colored POW patches on the backs. The brigade was still short the necessary 1,500 U.S. steel helmets that had been requisitioned; only half of the necessary U.S. rifles were available and little ammunition for the foreign weapons. Only radio equipment and aggressive troop morale seemed in good supply.

The planned organization of *Panzer Brigade 150* envisioned a 3,300 man force well equipped with captured Allied equipment; 15 Sherman tanks, 32 armored cars, 198 trucks and 147 jeeps had been requisitioned from *OB West*. However, by November 27th, Skorzeny reported he had but two American M-4 Shermans (one of which broke down before the attack with transmission trouble), six armored cars (only two American ones), 6 German half-tracks, 57 jeeps and 74 trucks (only 15 of which were U.S. Ford models). The only uniform appearance that this rag-tag assembly of equipment could boast was a fresh coat of olive green paint prominently flagged with white five-pointed Allied stars. Five Panthers and five assault guns were crudely disguised with sheet metal to resemble M-10 tank destroyers to supplant the armored deficiency. These Trojan Horse tanks, Skorzeny said after the war, were only likely to fool "very young American

recruits — and then only very far away and at night."

Furthermore, Skorzeny barely had more than 1,000 men now under his command and demanded some regular army units for stiffening. He received two parachute infantry battalions from *Kampfgeschwader 200*, the *7th Panzer Grenadier Company* and a mortar and signals company. To this he added his own specially trained commando unit of battalion strength (*SS Jagdverbande Mitte* and *SS Fallschirmjäger Battalion 600*). All vehicles were given fictitious markings of the U.S. 5th Armored Division.

A company of "special" jeep teams were organized under SS Hauptsturmführer Steilau. These 150 men included the men who spoke English best and were completely outfitted with American uniforms and equipment. They were to sow confusion in the American rear and were organized into nine, four-man *Einheit Steilau* commando parties. Three basic missions were outlined for the commandos:

1) Demolition squads of five to six men who were to sabotage bridges and U.S. supply dumps.

2) Reconnaissance parties of three to four men who were to reconnoiter the Meuse crossings and report on Allied troop movements in the rear areas.

3) Lead commando teams in three to four man groups who were to proceed directly in the path of the German advance to issue false orders, prevent bridge demolition vital to the German advance, create fake minefield markings to halt the enemy advance, switch road signs and cut telephone communications.

The shortage of jeeps, however, was to prove the undoing of some of these commandos. Unfathomable as it was to the German organizers of the subterfuge, U.S. transport was so plentiful that seldom did more than two men ride in a jeep. The three and four-man *Einheit Steilau* proved recognizable from this organizational habit once Allied knowledge of the operation became widespread.

By the time preparations were completed, *Panzer Brigade 150* numbered about 2,500 men and a dozen tanks and assault guns. Skorzeny organized

The lead Panther "M-10" of Skorzeny's battlegroup hit a mine just outside Malmedy in fierce combat on December 21st. Two GIs reveal the phoney tank's American star.

the brigade into three *Kampfgruppen*, unimaginatively designated *Kampfgruppe X, Y* and *Z*. One each would be assigned to either SS panzer division in the breakthrough with the other assigned to the *12th Volksgrenadier Division*. Tank crews were provided by the *Panzerjäger Battalion 655* and the *6th Panzer Division*.

After the war Skorzeny described the objectives of his combat force: "The mission of the brigade was to seize at least two Meuse bridges from among the following possibilities: Amay, Huy, Andenne." The brigade was to advance into the fray when the *Sixth Panzer Armee* reached the Hohes Venn area near Spa. Following in the wake of the SS panzer divisions at night they expected to reach the Meuse bridges in six hours. Elaborate recognition signals using flashlights were worked out to prevent confusion within their own ranks. On the night of December 14th, Skorzeny moved his brigade to Münstereifel to brief SS-Gruf. Hermann Priess of the *ISS Panzerkorps* about their mission in the coming offensive.

Regardless of his careful prepara-

tion, on the afternoon of December 16th, SS Ostbf. Skorzeny did not find himself and his brigade racing to the Meuse. Instead, he and his brigade, like thousands of other Germans in the Schmidtheim area, were tied up in a frustrating and massive traffic jam along with the rest of the *1st SS Panzer Division*. By nightfall there was still no breakthrough in progress from either of the SS panzer divisions. Even worse, the experienced commander of *Kampfgruppe X*, SS Oberstleutnant Willi Hardieck had been killed when his command vehicle had crossed over a mine. Disappointed, Skorzeny glumly decided to rest his brigade and await developments. Regardless, he did dispatch his nine commando teams to wreak havoc behind the American line. Eight of Steilau's jeep teams easily penetrated the American security and on the night of December 16th were moving freely behind enemy lines.

Although the strong armored *Kampfgruppe* of the *1st SS Panzer Division* had peirced the American lines at Honsfeld, the traffic log-jam continued in the Losheim area. By the eve-

ning of the second day of the attack, it seemed apparent to Skorzeny that no decisive breakthrough was going to manifest in the *Sixth Panzer Armee*. He therefore asked its commander, SS Obgrf. Sepp Dietrich, to commit his brigade as a regular combat unit. To this, Dietrich reluctantly agreed.

By December 20th, the brigade had reorganized as a cohesive unit and concentrated in the area around Ligneuville. On December 21st the brigade attacked the 120th Regiment of the U.S. 30th Division at Malmédy and the 99th Infantry Battalion atop the railway embankment between the Pont de Warche and the town. The desperate fight eddied back and forth before the bridge across the Warche River in Malmédy. However, by the end of the day the German brigade was forced to retreat by a punishing U.S. artillery fire (which was using the super secret proximity fused rounds). Skorzeny himself was wounded by shrapnel and nearly lost an eye.

On the morning of December 22nd still another effort was made although meeting the same result as the day before. After only two days in battle, Skorzeny's brigade had lost at least 15% of its strength. With the failure of the brigade at Malmédy, it was considered for a time to re-employ the brigade in the *Fifth Panzer Armee* where the German attack was achieving greater success. However, this idea was ultimately dropped since the element of surprise had been lost. On December 28th the brigade left the Ardennes for Grafenwöhr.

SS Hptsf. Steilau's jeep teams had been more successful than the combat operation. His 44 men were organized into four reconnaissance teams, two demolition groups and six lead commando teams (one each with *12th SS, 1st SS, 12th Volksgrenadiers* and three with *Panzer Brigade 150*). Behind Allied lines, they cut communications, misdirected traffic and doled out terrifying tales of Nazi successes. At least one team actually reached the Meuse on December 17th. Another team at the Mont Rigi crossroads north of Malmédy moved a signpost sending the entire 16th Infantry Regiment in the wrong direction. There is even evidence that a special team prevented the destruction of the bridge over the Amblève at Stavelot on December 18th.

However, the largest success of these teams was the confusion created by the mere fact of their presence. In General Bradley's words, "Half a million G.I.s were forced to play cat and mouse with each other each time they met on the road." The now famous spot checks proved embarrassing, both for those unfamiliar with baseball, comic books or the current husband of Betty Grable.

Near St. Vith on December 21st, Gen. Bruce Clarke was arrested. "I'm General Bruce Clarke of CCB," the commander insisted. "Like, hell," the MP said, locking up Clarke, "I was told to watch out for a kraut posing as a one-star general." The general then ensured his incarceration by placing the Chicago Cubs in the American League. "Only a kraut," the MP assured him, "would make a mistake like that." It was half an hour before an enraged Clarke would escape his shackles. The following day, Bradley was questioned by a recalcitrant MP who did not believe Springfield was

Above and right: *"Half a million GIs played cat and mouse with each other each time they met on the road,"* remembered General Bradley. *Almost no GI or civilian was above suspicion after U.S. MPs found that Skorzeny's American impersonators were operating behind their lines.*

the capital of Illinois.

The problems were further complicated by American soldiers of German descent and the habit of American soldiers in collecting captured German equipment such as jackboots and MP-44 machine guns (which some soldiers felt superior to their own weapon).

In spite of the monumental confusion, a number of Steilau's jeep teams were killed or captured. On December 18th a suspicious looking group of American soldiers appeared out of the woods near Poteau on self-propelled guns abandoned earlier by the 14th Cavalry Group. Challenged by the American sentry of the 7th Armored Division, the Germans approaching in the distance replied in stilted English that, "We are E Company!" Unknown to the impostors, however, the tank destroyers of a cavalry group are known as a "troop" rather than a company. Recognizing the ruse, the American security force opened fire on the Germans, killing them all.

So great was the Skorzeny commando paranoia, that tragic instances of mistaken identity were common. All over the Ardennes American soldiers nervously attempted to persuade trigger happy American security patrols that they were genuine govern-

ment issue. Tragically, on December 20th two American soldiers were killed by a jittery U.S. military policeman. The confusion that Steilau's group created was not exclusively American either. Special recognition signals were used to help identify the "special guides" as Germans, although these signals did not thoroughly make the rounds in the German army. Such shortcomings made mixing with friendly and enemy troops hazardous alike for the commandos. In at least one verified instance, on being challenged at a road intersection by a U.S. MP, a German commando meekly surrendered. Making no effort to conceal his identity, he told his captor of his subterfuge. "I'm sorry." The masquerading U.S. policeman replied, "but, I am from Steilau's company too!"

A German team was apprehended at Aywaille on December 17th, just 12 miles from the Meuse bridge at Engis when they failed to produce the password. The three men were arrested and on them were found German military pay-books, $900 U.S. dollars and sundry weaponry of U.S., British and German origin. As Skorzeny had feared, the men, masquerading as three U.S. privates were tried as spies on De-

Oberfahnrich Günter Billing, one of Skorzeny's jeep mounted commandos, was apprehended with two other compatriots on December 17th near Aywaille. Convicted as spies, Billing and his men were put before a firing squad at Henri-Chapelle on December 23rd.

cember 22nd and sentenced to death. The next day, Gunther Billing, Manfred Pernass and Wilhelm Schmidt were shot by firing squad at the tiny village of Henri-Chapelle. Two more captured German "spies" were shot on the 26th and seven more impostors taken at Malmédy were executed on December 30th.

In all, 18 of Steilau's commandos were shot by their captors at Huy or Henri-Chapelle during the Ardennes battle. Only three of the jeep teams returned intact. One had reached Huy on the Meuse and another reached Amay on that river. However, with no duty since the German panzer spearheads were so far away, they and the third team which had reconnoitered the Salm area, returned to German lines. Three other teams managed to return after having one or more of their members wounded in encounters with the now wise American sentries. Eventually 16 survivors of Steilau's company regrouped at the village of Wallerode, northeast of St. Vith, on January 10th. In spite of their losses, *Operation Greif* had been a wild success, creating great confusion within the Allied ranks all out of keeping with the size of the tiny German force.

Probably the most outrageous rumor concerning *Operation Greif* came from the confession of Wilhelm Schmidt from the group captured at Aywaille. Prior to his execution he told his interrogators that the real mission of Greif was to assassinate Eisenhower in Paris. A group of professional German killers from the brigade would rendezvous at the *Café de Paris* and then stalk the headquarters of SHAEF! Given the fantastic nature of Skorzeny's previous exploits, Allied security was certainly not willing to discount

this possibility. The commander-in-chief was promptly quarantined in his Versailles headquarters while a double, Lt. Col. Baldwin B. Smith of Chicago, was driven in an staff car about Paris to try to lure out Skorzeny and his crew. Then on December 19th, when Eisenhower prepared to go to the war conference at Verdun, his security colonel insisted that the general take a bullet proof vehicle. "I have positive knowledge," the officer told Ike, "that Otto Skorzeny has sent special teams of American dressed commandos to assassinate you." Of course the whole story was a hoax. The rumor had started among one of the younger commandos of *Panzer Brigade 150*, and Skorzeny, knowing the value of wild rumors, made no attempt to suppress it once it started.

Caught! A German from Skorzeny's brigade is helped out of his American uniform by U.S. soldiers of the 30th Infantry Division.

Twelve rifles fire in unison at the three condemned German commandos, the bullets raising clouds of dust behind each man. Moments before the firing squad executed them, Billing called out shrilly in German, "long live our Führer!" At least six other commandos of Skorzeny's unit were subsequently executed at Henri-Chapelle.

Nuts to Nuts!

When Brig. Gen. Anthony McAuliffe off-handedly dismissed a German surrender request in Bastogne three days before Christmas in 1944, he could not know that his frustrated utterance would soon become a thing of military legend. His defiant reply, along with the tale of his intrepid troops, the "Screaming Eagles" of the 101st Airborne, and of Bastogne itself sailed straight away into the history books.

The stage was set on December 22nd. The Germans had surrounded the 101st Airborne Division two days earlier in their final great offensive. On December 19th a pocket of over 7,000 Americans had capitulated to the Germans in the Eifel. Gen. d. Pztrp. Heinrich Freiherr von Lüttwitz, who was in charge of the force responsible for the capture of Bastogne, hoped that such a negotiated surrender might help to avoid a costly battle to pry the stubborn American troops out of the town. The fighting there had already cost the Baron many casualties. So without seeking the blessing of his superior, Gen. von Mantueffel, Lüttwitz set about composing a surrender request for the American garrison.

At about 11:30 am that day, soldiers of the 327th Glider Infantry Regiment spied four Germans approaching American lines under a large white flag along the Arlon road near Remoifosse. The Germans paused in front of the American foxhole line amid steadily falling snow. Presently they were approached by two sergeants, Oswald Y. Butler and Carl E. Dickenson, and a medical aid man, Pfc. Ernest D. Permetz, who spoke German.

The emissaries included two enlisted men, Maj. Wagner from the *XLVII Panzerkorps* and Lt. Helmuth Henke from the operations section of the *Panzer Lehr Division*. Henke, who had been in the import business before the war, spoke passable English. "We are parliamentaries," he said producing a copy of the ultimatum. "We want to talk to your commanding general." Soon, the two officers were blindfolded and driven by jeep to Marvie.

Their message was quickly relayed from Company F of the 327th to Gen. McAuliffe's headquarters in a damp cellar under the Heintz military barracks in Bastogne. But within minutes, a rumor spread like wildfire among many American soldiers: the Germans wanted to surrender! Nothing was further from the truth, although many paratroopers made use of the sudden calm to shave or crawl out of their frozen holes to go to the latrine. McAuliffe, himself, was on the run congratulating the Americans in the front lines who had recently repulsed the enemy. But presently Col. Joseph H. Harper, the commander of the 327th and Col. Ned D. Moore, his acting chief of staff, caught up with him. They informed him that the Germans had sent emissaries. "What did they want?" McAuliffe asked, looking a bit impatient. "They want us to surrender," Moore told him handing over the papers. "Aw, nuts," McAuliffe chortled. The demand was absurd. He quickly read the note:

To the U.S.A. Commander in the Encircled Town of Bastogne:

The fortune of war is changing. This time the U.S.A. forces in and near Bastogne have been encircled by strong German armored units. More German armored units have crossed the river Ourthe near Ortheville, have taken Marche and reached St. Hubert by passing through Hompré-Sibret-Tillet. Libramont is in German hands.

There is only one possibility to save the encircled U.S.A. troops from total annihilation: that is the honorable surrender of the encircled town. In order to think it over, a term of two hours will be granted beginning with the presentation of this note.

If this proposal should be rejected one German artillery corps and six heavy A.A. battalions are ready to annihilate the U.S.A. troops in and near Bastogne. The order for firing will be given immediately after the two hours' term.

All the serious civilian losses caused by this artillery fire would not correspond with the well-known American humanity.

McAuliffe gagged on the last item. Any German appeal to American humanity was ludicrous, he thought, for it was his enemy, after all, who had started the fighting here in the first place. The Germans had allowed only two hours for an American response before they would resume their shelling and attacks. But when it came time to draft a reply, McAuliffe was at a loss for words.

"That first remark of yours would be hard to beat," Lt. Col. Harry W.O. Kinnard, his G-3, told him.

"What was that?" McAuliffe asked.

"You said 'nuts,'" Kinnard told him. The general's staff voiced their approval.

"That's it!" McAuliffe beamed. The irreverence of the response was perfect. It was so typically American, so oddball, so go-to-hell GI. Reaching for a pen, he quickly scrawled onto the page:

22 December 1944

To the German Commander:

NUTS!
The American Commander

McAuliffe handed the note to Harper, "See that this is forwarded to the Germans."

"I'll hand it over myself," Harper replied, "It will be a lot of fun."

Soon Harper reached the still blindfolded German emissaries who were under close guard near Marvie. When the surrender request was read to Lt. Henke, whose English was quite good, he was unable to translate the phase. *Nüsse* were things you cracked. All this made little sense under the circumstances.

"Is the reply affirmative or negative?" Henke wanted to know. He offered to negotiate further, but Harper was tiring of the German's patronizing manner.

"It is decidedly not affirmative," Harper told him with a rising voice,"If you continue this foolish attack your losses will be tremendous." The Germans were driven back towards Kessler farm where their two compatriots were still waiting with the white flag. As the blindfolds were removed and the Germans were escorted to the main road, Harper spoke up once more. He wanted to make sure they understood the nature of the reply.

"If you don't understand what NUTS means," he continued, "in plain English it is the same as 'Go to Hell.' And I will tell you something else: if you continue to attack, we will kill every goddamned German who tries to break into this city."

The Germans saluted stiffly. "We will kill many Americans," Henke tersely concluded. "This is war."

"On your way, Bud, " Harper pointed to the German lines. And then he thoughtlessly added, "and good luck to you." Harper bit his tongue; he would long wonder why he said that.

By 3 P.M. the Germans, strolling along the road, reached their lines in the midst of lightly falling snow. The message was soon delivered to Baron von Lüttwitz at his new headquarters in the Chateau Roumont. "Nuts!" If the response was unorthodox, the meaning was unequivocal: The Americans in Bastogne would not surrender and the history of the Battle of the Bulge would never be the same.

The Germans Approach the Meuse: December 23rd-24th

The advance warning of the German meteorologists had been correct; on Saturday, December 23rd the weather made a dramatic change. The sun rose to reveal a bright frosty landscape under a clear blue sky. Within two hours, the air over the Ardennes was filled with swarms of Allied planes. For the first time in a week Allied air power was able to intervene in the German counteroffensive. Hitler's luck had finally run out.

Over 3,100 Allied planes flung themselves at the German salient. "In the entire army area," reported *Heeresgruppe B*, "there was heavy enemy flying activity with fighter bomber attacks on German spearheads as well as bomb drops from four-engined bombers on roads and traffic targets in the attack zone." Even though the Luftwaffe tagged 800 sorties for the Ardennes, many were engaged far to the east of the battlefield. Over the combat area Allied air superiority was undeniable.[28] The previously isolated 101st Airborne Divi-

28 'There were the usual tragic mistakes of identity of friend and foe in the air war. Perhaps the worst was the mistaken bombing of the town of Malmédy, erroneously taken to be St. Vith or "an alternate target." Once set aflame it continued to attract U.S. bombers, being hit on three successive days from December 23rd to 25th. Some 125 civilians were killed along with 37 U.S. soldiers of the U.S. 30th Division.

Dogfight. Third Army anti-aircraft gunners watch swirling aerial combat between U.S. Air Force and Luftwaffe planes over the Ardennes.

sion was resupplied from the air by 241 C-47 transport aircraft; over 144 tons of supplies were dropped including much needed food, ammunition and medical supplies. Meanwhile, escorting fighter-bombers blasted and strafed the German forces surrounding the pocket. Until nightfall many German soldiers cowered in foxholes and cellars; tanks and artillery pieces hid in the woods. The effect of 1,200 Allied bombers on the German rail system was devastating, halting much of the rail traffic west of the Rhine.

The situation in the *Sixth Panzer Armee* sector saw no improvement for its exasperated commanders. *Kampfgruppe Peiper* was still encircled and throwing back the unremitting attacks of the 30th and 3rd Armored Divisions; "for breakfast on December 23rd," remembered one of the German battlegroup, "we got a double helping of artillery and mortar fire." Part of *Kampfgruppe Hansen* managed to slip across the Amblève River at Petit Spai and had come to Peiper's aid. Still, the situation for the German panzer group was hopeless. Around noon, Peiper received a radio message from Mohnke informing him that the relief column was "stuck" and ordering him to attempt to break out to the east. But accomplishing this feat with almost no gasoline would be something else again.

Meanwhile the battle between the 3rd Armored and Hansen's grenadiers trying to extend their bridgehead at Trois Ponts raged all day. By dark American armor had regained the three villages the Germans had captured the day before.

Having failed miserably in its attempt to breach the U.S. line at Bütgenbach, the *12th SS Panzer Division* limped off to the Born-Moderscheid vicinity to reorganize before going to the aid of the *Fifth Panzer Armee*. The *9th SS Panzer Division* was advancing near Vielsalm, attempting to slip past the withdrawing American divisions and open a way west to the Meuse. But, the 82nd Airborne there stubbornly defended their ground, inflicting many enemy casualties and

The Iron Cross. SS-Sturmbannführer Ernest Krag receives the coveted Ritterkreuz from his commander, Brigadeführer Heinz Lammerding of the 2nd SS Panzer Division. *Krag energetically commanded a battlegroup in the Ardennes.*

turning back the German bid.

However, just to the west the American line was weak and the *2nd SS Panzer Division* had managed to finally scavenge enough fuel to put a panzer grenadier regiment and a company of Mk IV panzers in motion along the highway from Houffalize. All afternoon the Baraque de Frature crossroads and its ring of defenders was swept by gusts of German artillery fire. By 4:00 P.M. the American *Jabos* had gone home for the day, signaling the Germans to begin their armored assault. The blow was too much; within a hour the hodge-podge of American detachments defending there under Maj. Arthur C. Parker III were consumed when German tanks blasted the perimeter as panzergrenadiers rushed the position from three sides.[29] Obstf. Horst Gresiak, commander of *II Battalion* of the *2nd SS Panzer Regiment*, which

Baraque Fraiture. A German assault gun left behind from the fierce battle for the strategic crossroads.

overan the American defense there was a veteran of many savage battles on the Eastern Front. "Although brief," he recalled, "it was the most violent and the toughest battle that I experienced during the war."

In the XVIII Airborne Corps, the 7th Armored pulled back from the St. Vith area. The ground freeze had opened a way for the tanks through a muddy trail from Hinderhausen, Crombach and Commanster to the bridge across the Salm at Vielsalm. While this was happening, *Kampfgruppe Krag*, the *2nd SS Panzer Reconnaissance Battalion* under Iron Cross holder SS-Stbf. Ernest Krag, struck in two assault prongs at Joubiéval and Salmchâteau. Although turned back by devastating American artillery fire along the Ottre-Joubiéval road, Krag's move toward Salmchâteau momentarily endangered the withdrawal of the U.S. forces. The move was further complicated enemy attacks by the *9th SS Panzer* at Poteau and a hot pursuit of the 7th Armored columns by the *Führer Begleit Brigade* advancing from Rodt. Meanwhile, just to the south the 112th and 424th Infantry Regiments and CCB of the 9th Armored ran a gauntlet of fire from the *62nd Volksgrenadier Division* via a route running through the villages of Maldingen, Beho, Rogery and Cierreux to the bridge at Salmchâteau across the Salm River. Although the withdrawing group narrowly averted total disaster, elements of the 112th Infantry Regiment were trapped against the river and forced to surrender.

The bulk of CCB of the 7th Armored Division represented by Task Force Lohse (Maj. Leslie A. Lohse) commenced to withdraw from the salient at daybreak on a muddy forest track from Hinderhausen to Commanster. In spite of its condition the tanks were across the Salm River at Vielsalm by noon. The exit was timely, since the next day the Germans took possession of the bridge there. Though forced to pull back, the American defenders at St. Vith had put up a stout defense. Even Montgomery provided a stirring complement to the heroic defenders of St. Vith. The Americans withdrew "with all honor....They put up a wonderful show."[30]

Further south, the *LXVI Armeekorps* with its two infantry divisions and the *Führer Begleit Brigade* advanced west, sweeping through the hamlets of Gomels, Burtonville and Maldingen while nipping at the heels of the retreating U.S. 7th Armored Division. Since the right wing of the *Sixth Panzer Armee* was hopelessly stuck, Genfldm. Model shifted the main weight of the attack to the north wing of von Manteuffel's *Fifth Panzer*. His aim there a breakthrough to the northwest along the Bastogne-Liège highway.

In the early morning, the *116th Panzer Division* was in the process of pulling back across the Ourthe River at La Roche. Their orders were to achieve a breakthrough just east of Marche along the west bank of the river around

New wheels in Vielsalm. Elated German soldiers of the 62nd Volksgrenadier Division *sport about in their newly captured U.S. jeep from the booty at St. Vith. Note that one of their comrades to the rear is still getting about on a bicycle.*

Marenne. The assault was intended to evict the American 84th Division posted near Marche and then approach the Meuse near Namur. For this task, the *2nd SS* and *9th SS Panzer Divisions* and the *Führer Begleit Brigade* would be attached — an optimistic order of battle that was never realized. By nightfall the *116th's* panzer reconnaissance battalion had reached Grimbiemont, southeast of Marche, although the bulk of the division was strung out along roads for miles and would not reach this point until the next day. The division's former sector north and east of the Ourthe was taken over by the *560th Volksgrenadier Division*. Their relief mission was not simple, however; the U.S. 3rd Armored was attacking to recover Dochamps on Christmas Eve. Only in hard fighting near the village of Soy, did the volksgrenadiers avert a complete breakout by the American armor.

In the mean time, the *2nd Panzer Division* received enough fuel to continue operations. The division boldly marched from Hargimont all the way to the village of Conneux only a few miles from the Meuse River. Von Rundstedt cheered the division's effort: "Well done to Conneux!" he told them in a radio transmission that afternoon "Keep it up!" More to the point, von Rundstedt promised additional forces. The *9th Panzer Division*, which was now moving over the Our River at Dasburg, would provide fresh troops to von Lüttwitz's corps to widen the blow at the Meuse.

Regardless of von Rundstedt's enthusiasm, *Kampfgruppe von Böhm*, comprising the *2nd Panzer's* reconnaissance battalion, saw grave trouble ahead. At 9:25 A.M. the German vanguard ran afoul of British tanks of the 29th Armored Brigade patrolling the approaches to the Meuse around Dinant; the *2nd Panzer* quickly lost three Panthers in the clash. The tiny battlegroup called for additional support and radioed that they were out of gas; fuel was urgently needed. Just to the south, the *Panzer Lehr Division* moved from St. Hubert via Forrières, fighting its way into the town of Rochefort by midnight. The intent was to cover the left flank of the German thrust to the Meuse River.

The Germans around Bastogne were still frustrated. In spite of fierce fighting *Kampfgruppe Kunkel* could not wrest

29 These included a few stray howitzers from the 589th Field Artillery battalion, some half-tracks from the 203rd Anti-aircraft Artillery battalion, 11 tanks and a reconnaissance platoon from Task Force Kane, a platoon of tank destroyers (643rd TD Bn) and a tank and infantry platoon from Task Force Richardson (Lt. Col. Walter B. Richardson) of the 3rd Armored Division.

30 Including the 14th Cavalry Group, loss estimates for the St. Vith garrison show 3,397 casualties with losses of 39 medium and 29 light tanks, 25 armored cars, and hundreds of other vehicles.

Senonchamps from Team Browne. And lacking the forces for a full-blooded concentric attack, the *26th Volksgrenadiers* elected to hit Bastogne from the northwest. Artillery and *werfer* fire commenced before daybreak as the grenadiers wormed in close to the paratrooper foxhole line. The initial rush took the Germans into the village of Flamierge, but a hard fought counterattack managed to push them back out.

On the other side of the salient, the attack by the *Panzer Lehr Division* to capture Marvie could not get underway untill nightfall after the American Jabos buzzing through the Ardennes sky had gone home for the day. In spite of of the strenuous efforts of the *901st Panzer Grenadier Regiment* the attack see-sawed through Marvie with each side in partial control of the village. Tanks and tank destroyers of the 10th Armored gunned down each German tank that attempted to push beyond to Bastogne. To finish off the American bastion, the Germans obviously would need more resources than the reinforced infantry division could provide. Von Lüttwitz had been promised Obst. Hans-Joachim Deckert's *15th Panzer Grenadier Division*, but its two regiments and 72 tanks and assault guns had been delayed. The division was making its way from the north in stops and starts plagued by short fuel deliveries and Allied fighter-bombers. "Movements possible only after twilight," the German commander reported.

Christmas Eve 1944. The Germans, elated by their dash to the Meuse, did not know of the calamity about to befall them. Maj. Gen. Lawton "Lightning Joe" Collins, one of the most capable American battlefield commanders, and his intrepid VII Corps had begun to secretly arrive on the field. From the north he moved the 2nd Armored Division along with the new 75th Infantry Division (Maj. Gen. Fay B. Prickett). Just a few miles north of the Germans in Conneux, the U.S. 2nd Armored Division with the attached troops began secretly assembling in the town of Ciney to lop

German spearhead to the Meuse. Kampfgruppe von Böhm, 2nd Panzer Division on the road near Hargimont.

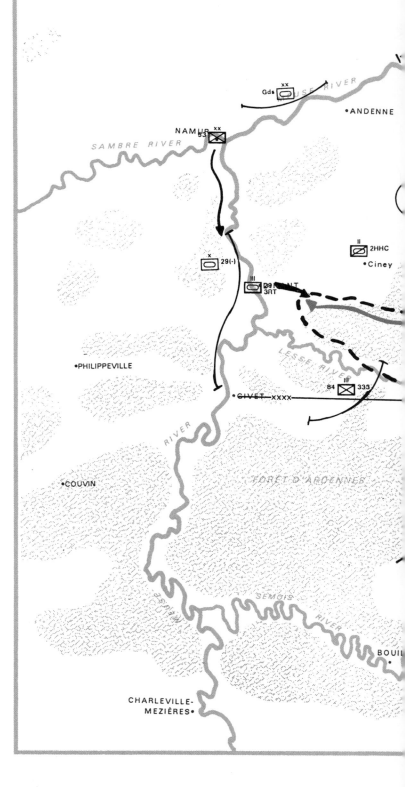

SITUATION MAP
December 23rd-24th

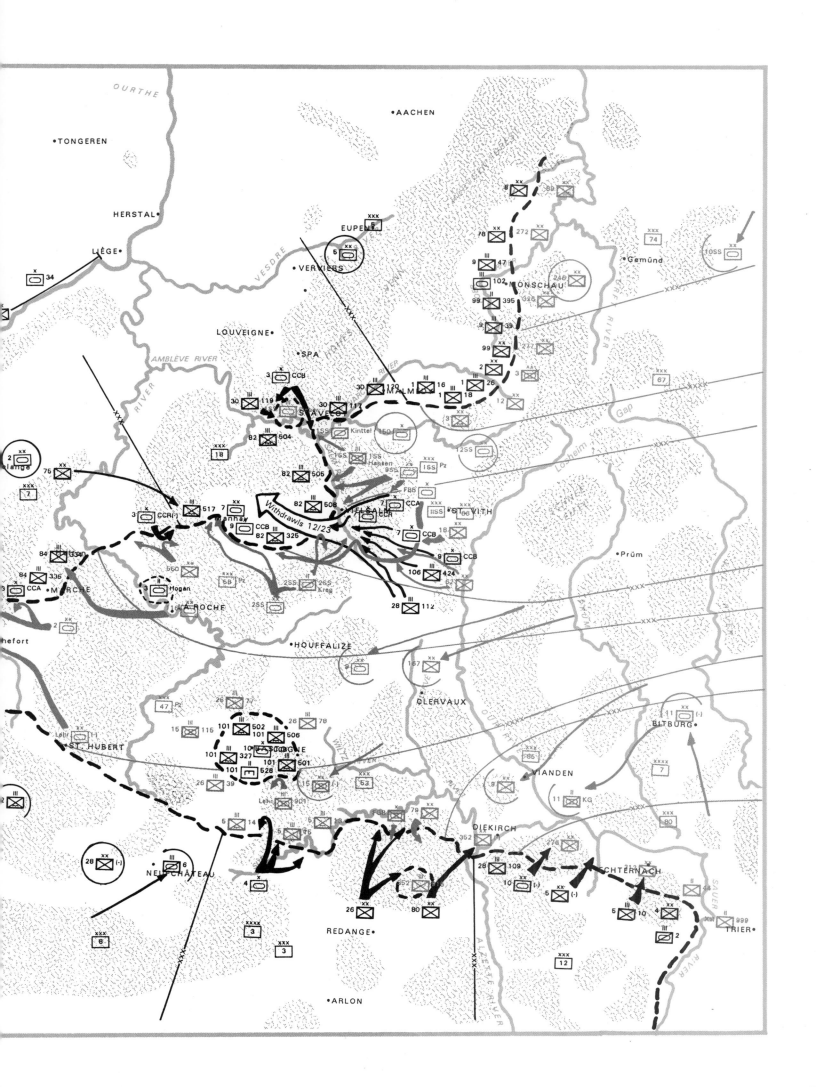

Assault gun. A Jagdpanzer 38t "Hetzer" of the 26th Volksgrenadier Division *left behind in the village of Sibret by* Kampf-gruppe Kunkel.

off the German penetration[31]. The untried 75th Infantry Division was to move up from reserve along the Ourthe River to provide infantry strength to the 3rd Armored Division in the Hotton area.

On both sides of the Bastogne perimeter the combatants spent the 24th regrouping, although the German efforts were severely hampered by the ever present American fighter-bombers. In addition another 160 transport planes dropped 100 tons of supplies to the surrounded U.S. garrison. Fighter-bombers again pounded the German positions; such air power was particularly heartening to the American defenders. All through the evening the defenders observed fires of burning German vehicles blazing around the salient. In retaliation, twice during the night the German Luftwaffe responded with lethal bombing strikes of their own. So, while the Americans tightened their lines and enjoyed the second day of air re-supply, the Germans brought up reinforcements to add credence to their threats. Half of the *15th Panzer Grenadier Division* under the command of Obst. Wolfgang Maucke showed up before dark with less than festive orders for Christmas Day: "Displacement of enemy at

Unlikely trio. Genmaj. J. Lawton Collins (left) in charge of VII Corps, Genmaj. Matthew B. Ridgway (right) in charge of XIII Airborne Corps and their boss, Field Marshal Sir Bernard L. Montgomery, during the height of the crisis in the Ardennes.

Bastogne."

In the south, Patton's troops continued to slug it out with the delaying forces of the *5th Fallschirmjager Division*, but even a relentless attack could not produce a rapid breakthrough to carry them to the beleaguered 101st Airborne in Bastogne. The 4th Armored cleared Martelange, although

31 The attached troops included the 4th Armored Cavalry Group, the 60th Infantry Regiment of the 9th Division and the 87th Armored Field Artillery and 957th Field Artillery Battalions.

Manna from Heaven. C-47 Transports of the IX Troop Carrier Command parachute supplies to the surrounded garrison of the 101st Airborne in Bastogne.

CCB was repulsed from Chaumont. At this village a determined German counterattack of German paratroopers, self-propelled guns and 88mm anti-tank fire cost the Americans 11 M-4 tanks and 65 casualties in fierce fighting. The Third Army commander was impatient. "There is too much piddling around," Patton told Millikin, the commander of III Corps. "Bypass these towns and clear them up later. Tanks can operate on this ground now."

The advance rate on the Third Army right was slowing as well. The U.S. 26th Infantry captured Grosbous and Wahl, while the 80th Division seized Heiderscheid, a strategic bridge crossing along the Sûre River just six miles south of Wiltz. But German resistance in this sector was stiffening. After bitter fighting for their objective, the 80th had to hold

the village against repeated counterattacks by the *Führer Grenadier Brigade* and the recently arrived *79th Volksgrenadier Division.*

To the south, Brandenberger's army suffered a series of crushing reverses: the *5th Fallschirmjäger Division* lost Martelange and was forced north by the powerful attack of the U.S. 4th Armored Division. Its defensive sector — nearly 24 miles long — was far too wide for its available strength. Although the surrounded battlegroup of the *352nd Division* managed to escape encirclement, the German soldiers lost nearly all their heavy weapons and equipment. The division struggled to hold onto Ettelbruck under the pressure of the U.S. 80th Division. Only through the resourcefulness of the new commander of the *LIII Armeekorps*, Gen. d. Kav. Frie-

The 4th Armored Division passes dispirited German prisoners south of Bastogne.

Patton's favorite. The U.S. 4th Armored Division moves up the road to relieve the garrison at Bastogne.

drich-Wilhelm von Rothkirch, were the Germans able to prevent an American breakthrough to Wiltz.

The situation with the *276th* and *212th Volksgrenadier Divisions* was ominous as well. For three days, the staff on the American side, the U.S. XII Corps, under Gen. Eddy, had laboriously planned their counterattack to sweep the Germans from the west bank of the Sauer River. On the 23rd, the attack of the lone regiment of the 5th Division around Michelshof had yielded poor results. However, beginning on Christmas Eve, the increasing gun tubes of the XII Corps artillery pounded the German line, 21,173 shells falling on the heads of the German infantry during the day. At 11:00 A.M. the attack began, the American infantry moving forward across the snowy fields clad in bed-sheets. A breakthrough by the U.S. 5th Division materialized near Schleidgen when the German defenders in Savelborn were overpowered by the 10th Armored Division which fought to the outskirts of Eppeldorf. Task Force Rudder (Lt. Col James E. Rudder) lead two understrength battalions of the 109th Infantry Regiment in a seek-and-destroy mission against the Germans along the boundary of the *LXXX* and *LXXXV Armeekorps*. This foray took the avenging Americans through Gilsdorf, south east of Diekirch, almost to the Sauer River at Moestroff.

Overhead, Beyer's staff of *LXXX Armeekorps* reported "brisk enemy fighter bomber employment." But despite their grim circumstance, the volksgrenadiers continued to succeed with counterattacks in sealing off major American penetrations of the fragile line. Attacks by the 5th Division through the Schwarz Erntz gorge near Müllerthal and at Haller and Waldbillig were turned back by the Germans who knew the lay of the terrain and made liberal use of available artillery and rocket fire.

In the pre-dawn darkness on December 24th, Christmas Eve, Peiper and his battlegroup were in the process of escaping from the "cauldron" in La Gleize. Hopelessly surrounded and under continuous attack from all sides, Peiper and 800 men managed to slip out of their encirclement in the dark. The heavily armored battlegroup had been practically destroyed, being forced to leave behind countless dead, 400 wounded and almost all of the division's panzer regiment.[32] The situation in the *Sixth Panzer Armee* was static. The northern wing of Dietrich's SS panzer army had been fought to a standstill.

While Peiper's men made their getaway, a group of 400 American tankers were also in the process of escaping encirclement. Task Force Hogan of the 3rd Armored had been surrounded since December 22nd in the village of Marcouray south of Hotton. Their situation hopeless, they too sabotaged their tanks on Christmas Eve and slipped away from the would be captors of the *LVIII Panzerkorps*. Within 24 hours most of Hogan's men had reached the American line to the north.

Close by the scene of Hogan's escape, the *560th Volksgrenadier Division* made a final all-out effort to crack the American 3rd Armored defenses between Soy and Odeigne. On the right, *Kampfgruppe Happich*, the just arrived missing regiment of the division, flung itself at the hamlet of Freyneux only to enter the place and then be cut to pieces before being cast out by Task Force Kane. Another German jab, backed by armor, at Lamorménil was similarly broken. The *560th*'s battle to the west by *Kampfgruppe Schmidt* was even more desperate. Attacking Task Force Orr on Christmas

---

32 The armored litter of *Kampfgruppe Peiper* in the La Gleize area alone amounted to 31 tanks and self-propelled guns and 47 halftracks.

Junk of War. Two abandoned German halftracks (Sd Kfz 251) (facing page), a Mk IV Panzer (above) and a "Wirbelwind" flak-tank (below). These were all part of the wreckage left behind in La Gleize by Kampfgruppe Peiper. The rear halftrack mounts a 7.5 cm gun with a limited traverse mount.

Eve night in twelve separate assaults, the battle for Amonines was a close run fight. "If they had three more riflemen they'd probably have overrun our positions," related Lt. Col. Orr, whose tankers stood their ground.

Just to the east, the *IISS Panzerkorps* continued its determined attack from the Salm towards the Ourthe River. Lammerding's *2nd SS Division*, astride the Bastogne Liège highway N15, plowed into the American line to the north-west gaining Odeigne by dark. Even worse, with an all-out night tank assault the Germans encircled Task Force Brewster (Maj. Olin Brewster) of CCB of the 9th Armored Division who were blocking access to Manhay on the Bastogne-Liège highway. Further up the road the German Panthers, advancing through the darkness, were mistaken for Shermans, and the SS division punched through the hasty defense of the 7th Armored Division before the surprised tankers could react. Amid the ensuing confusion in Manhay the German armor prevailed. Finding the enemy waiting along the sole open road to Malempré, Brewster's men realized they were now surrounded; he ordered his men to abandon their tanks to escape into the night.

The loss of the Baraque Fraiture crossroads along with Manhay so threatened the 82nd Airborne Division with encirclement that Montgomery ordered the paratroopers to withdraw to a shortened line from Trois Ponts to Vaux Chavanne. Amid protests from Gen. Ridgway, the adjustment took place on Christmas Eve. Taking advantage of the American withdrawal, the *9th SS Panzer* crossed the Salm at Vielsalm and probed west as far as Arbrefontaine. However, much of the mass of the division, including the divisional command post, was thrown into confusion when a devastating napalm attack by the British 2nd Tactical Air Force hit Recht that afternoon. At least 40 German vehicles went up in flames along with a score of grenadiers who were killed or wounded.

The *LXVI Armeekorps* following the Americans pulling out of the St. Vith salient, reached the Vielsalm-Salmchâteau

Belgian refugees flee across the bridge at Dinant as word spreads that the Germans are approaching the river, Christmas Day, 1944.

area. Meanwhile, the *Führer Begleit Brigade* took the nearby villages of Regné and Fraiture from the 82nd Airborne before being ordered to the support of the *LVIII Panzerkorps* near Marche. The *116th Panzer Division*, after back-tracking across the Ourthe at La Roche, was attempted to breakthrough the American 84th Division between Marche and Hotton. In bloody fighting, the village of Verdenne was captured, but the sought after breakthrough to Bourdon and the main Hotton-Marche highway could not be reached.

At midnight on Christmas Eve, as German tankers listened over their radios to the yuletide bells tolling in the great cathedral in Cologne, the *2nd Panzer Division* was reaching their farthest advance. *Kampfgruppe von Böhm* motored through Humain, Buissonville and Conjoux and into the hamlet of Foy Notre-Dame scarcely three miles from the Meuse River. However, most of the mass of the panzer division, particularly the heavy equipment, was strung out for miles all the way to Hargimont due to the continuing fuel shortage. So chronic was the problem, that upon receiving the message that the division was out of gas, von Rundstedt ordered the grenadiers "sent off to the Meuse on foot."

The *9th Panzer Division* with 85 tanks and assault guns (including attached Tigers from the *301st FKL Heavy Panzer Battalion*) was slowly grinding towards the salient. That evening Genmaj. Harald von Elverfeldt, the *9th Panzer* division commander, strode into the headquarters of the *2nd Panzer* with the unwelcome news that his forces would not be there in time to prop up the division's flanks. Fuel was low, he told Lauchert, and with the Allied fighter bombers roving the battlefield, a daylight march around Bastogne was out of the question. The *Panzer Lehr Division* on the *2nd Panzer's* left had been held up in "difficult house-to-house fighting" in Rochefort and was only now pushing toward the Meuse by way of Ciergnon. The situation at Bastogne was unchanged, although the *15th Panzer Grenadier Division* was now closing in to put in an assault on that town.

Christmas Eve brought little in the way of holiday cheer to the *Seventh Armee*. The best that Brandenberger could report was that "in bitter fighting the enemy breakthrough into Bastogne and into the bridgehead south of the Sauer was frustrated." The *5th Fallschirmjäger* was under a punishing assault from Patton's 4th Armored Division at Chaumont. Even worse, a breakthrough by the American forces at Warnach was reported at dark and Bigonville was lost to the Third Army. But Patton was furious with everyone, particularly with Millikin, whom he told to get up to the front where he could "hear" the battle and lead the III Corps from there. "This has been a very bad Christmas Eve," he confided in his diary. "All along our line we have received violent counterattacks, which forced...the 4th Armored back some miles with the loss of ten tanks."

To the east, the *352nd Volksgrenadiers* were compelled to relinquish Ettelbruck to the 80th Division, and east of Diekirch, the Americans reached the south bank of the Sauer River. German counterattacks to clear up the American penetration near the Sûre River at Heiderscheid produced little except heavy casualties for the *Führer Grenadier Brigade* and *79th Volksgrenadier Division*. Even so, an American attempt to coup bridges near the hamlets of Kaundorf and

Christmas at War. A chaplin conducts Mass out of the back of a jeep for American soldiers.

Tadler saw both spans go up with a blast before GIs could get across.

Having cleared the confluence of the Sûre and Sauer Rivers of the German foe, Christmas passed quietly for the 10th Armored Division between Ettelbruck and Eppeldorf. The 5th Division had no yuletide celebration, however. In bitter fighting the division captured Haller and Waldbillig by nightfall. Seeing the futility of this struggle, the Germans began a staged withdrawal from its advanced positions west of the Sauer.

Meanwhile, *OB West* moved up reserves to deal with the dangerous situation developing east of Bastogne. The *167th Volksgrenadier Division* advanced by forced marches to the area north of Clervaux while the *9 Volksgrenadier Division* moved into reserve near Wiltz. Furthermore, a battlegroup of the *11th Panzer Division* was held in reserve near Wallendorf as a backstop. The Germans were understandably worried that Patton might advance into Germany by crossing the Sauer River. The rest of the division, including its panzer regiment and heavy weapons, was now in the process of detraining — a process that would take some time given Allied fighter-bomber activity.

In his daily report, von Rundstedt expressed the opinion that the German offensive had passed its zenith, although he still saw some promise for "further progress" by the *Fifth Panzer Armee*. But the ominous situation of the *Seventh Armee* compelled the field marshal to observe that circumstances "pointed to a decision based on the counterattack against the southern flank of the salient."

On the Allied side, circumstances were none too encouraging either. Although the enemy advance had been contained in the V Corps sector and in the extreme south, the center was still spottily defended and under severe pressure from recently committed German divisions. To correct this situation, Eisenhower had the brand-new 17th Airborne Division hurriedly flown from England and moved up the green 11th Armored Division to reserve positions along the Meuse south of Givet. Additionally, Patton had ordered the tired 35th Division from Metz to the Ardennes to add mettle to his attack.

Meanwhile, the 112th Infantry and Combat Command B of the 9th Armored Division, which had been severely battered from the early fighting, were ordered in corps reserve for the U.S. First Army near Aywaille. So assembled, they were to regroup along with the surviving 424th Regiment of the 106th Division. Little did the exhausted troops know that enemy actions along the VII Corps front would soon end their brief respite.

The Allied air forces were committed to the Ardennes fighting in mass on Christmas Eve with over 5,000 sorties aimed at choking off *Heeresgruppe B's* supplies and smashing the panzer spearheads. In fact, the 24th featured the greatest concentrated confrontation of air forces during the entire European war. Although the Luftwaffe managed 1,088 sorties, their largest air effort since D-Day, this "could not produce the required relief." That day, the *Seventh Armee* bitterly reported not sighting a single German plane.[33] Allied fighter-bombers buzzed over the battle area almost incessantly while bombers continued to pound railways and supply columns in the rear areas. Later the same evening, Genmaj. Ludwig Heilmann, in charge of the *5th Fallschirmjäger Division*, reported that: "At night, one could see from Bastogne back to the West wall, a single torchlight procession of burning vehicles."

33 The situation was little better in the favored *Sixth Panzer Armee*. Sepp Dietrich later said of Allied air power: "And the worst of it is that those damned Jabos don't distinguish between generals and anyone else— it was terrible!"

Hitler's Weather

One immutable factor with which both combatants had to contend in the Ardennes was the winter weather. Inclement weather had the potential for being an extremely important factor in the Ardennes battle. This was because it could affect the ability of the Allies to bring their air power to bear. On the other hand, poor winter weather could also affect the off road mobility of Hitler's tank forces as they attempted to negotiate the marshy Ardennes plateaus. For these reasons, the weather had differing impacts on the two antagonists. It denied the Allies their punishing firepower and reconnaissance from the air while at the same time reducing the mobility of the German panzer attack force.

Unlike 1940 when the attack through the Ardennes had been predicated on a long term forecast of good flying weather, Hitler and his staff had chosen the target date in December precisely because that time of year in the Ardennes promised overcast, sullen skies. This would give cover from the Jabos both for the troop concentration and the blitzkrieg that was to follow. As early as September Dr. Percy Schramm, the *Wehrmachtführungsstab* War Diary keeper recorded that Hitler and Jodl believed this factor to be fundamental:

The attack can only be carried out at a time when the prevailing weather conditions will be a considerable handicap for the enemy air forces.

Unfortunately for the meteorologists that would try to read the skies before and during the offensive, prediction of the weather patterns in the Ardennes is difficult if not inscrutable since the area lies on the boundary between the northwestern and central European climatic regions. The Ardennes weather features great rainfall in autumn, deep snows in winter and cold stiff winds that blow across the plateaus. At Bastogne freezing weather prevails on the average of 145 days a year and snowfall can accumu-

Ground crew personnel sweep off snow from the wing of a P-47 "Thunderbolt" of the Ninth Air Force. Bad weather grounded the Allied air forces for the first week of the German counteroffensive.

Even outfitted with chains, this U.S. 2 1/2 ton truck is marooned in a sea of mud. Snow and rain in the Ardennes turned the macadam roads into gummy trails unfit for motorized travel.

late up to 12 inches in a single day. Typically, however, the colder weather and the deeper snows come later in January.

Actually, the German general staff had preferred to launch the attack in November when overcast weather is most common, but were slowed by delays in troop arrivals and transportation difficulties. As the date was pushed back into December, the lack of a forecast of long term poor weather and the continuing difficulty in the strategic concentration resulted in a series of *O-Tag* date changes and further anxiety. Hitler could not afford to wait much longer. Troubled that the high pressure systems that seemed about to move in, Dr. Schuster, the Director of the Luftwaffe Weather Service and Hitler's personal meteorologist, was relieved to be able to make a favorable forecast on December 13th. Dr. Werner Schwerdtfeger, one of the most brilliant of the young German meteorologists in charge of the forecasting section at the weather center in Berlin went further in his gaze into the crystal ball. He predicted that the "Allies cannot bomb visually or use air support for seven days in the West." Hitler indicated that he preferred not

to depend on what he considered an inexact science (although the Führer, himself, had an interest in astrology). Even so, Schwerdtfeger had a most impressive forecast track record over the past few years. Made more confident by the second opinion, Hitler affixed the final date of December 16th at Ziegenberg the following day. In fact, Schwerdtfeger was right. The poor weather continued for nine days. In his speech to his generals on December 28th, Hitler described his delight with the forecast:

> The best omen (for the offensive) was the weather development which had been forecast by a young weather forecaster who actually proved to be right. The weather situation enabled us to camouflage the final build up so that the enemy failed to recognize it.

The hanging mists and ground fog that are so common in the Ardennes in December gave another advantage; a natural veil to cloak and deny the enemy long distance observation of the German assault forces. This was the gloomy and inclement weather, "Hitler's Weather" that prevailed when the offensive was launched on December 16th. On the morning of

O-Tag the thermometer at the U.S. V Corps in Eupen stood at 28 degrees (F), reaching a high of 38 degrees that day — decidedly chilly. In the VIII Corps weather report from Bastogne the G-2 noted "Cloudy conditions with snow beginning around 1300." American forces on the ground noted that deep snow still remained on the ground and that the ground was frozen in patches. Even though it greatly reduced their effectiveness, the overcast and mists that clung to the Ardennes was not completely sufficient to still the air forces. On December 17th the American air forces managed over 1,000 sorties and the Germans some 650. Many of these did not reach the battlefield, however, but were locked in aerial combat further east. German planes on the scene dropped flares over U.S. forces and made blind strafing runs. Often air crews of both sides had to report "unobserved results."

On the 18th an Atlantic high pressure system momentarily worked against the German attack. A large scale thaw set in that made off road movement even more difficult and the heavy ground fog began to suddenly lift stripping the German attack of its veil. By December 20th the thaw had melted practically all the snow contributing to the mud that was evident nearly everywhere. The ground fog was extremely heavy in the mornings and visibility in some cases was less than 1,000 yards. Coupled with the terrain this had the effect of considerably reducing the effectiveness of armor. The potential of artillery was similarly reduced; often the observers could not see their targets. Meanwhile as the German advance gained momentum the anxiety of the Allied air commanders grew daily. On the 20th only two night fighter missions over the Ardennes were possible; the next day, 100 sorties, but none was able to penetrate the murky fog over the battlefield. Allied forecasters could offer little hope. Their reading on the morning of December 22nd indicated a continuing pall over the Western Front. St. Vith had fallen and Bastogne was surrounded and under assault. The situation was discouraging:

At the afternoon target conference in the Ninth Air Force Advanced

Headquarters war room at Luxembourg City, Major Stuart J. Fuller's forecast of the weather was one of unrelieved gloom. No break could be expected before 26 December. A front had settled east of Luxembourg in the Rhine valley and seemed disposed to stay there....The entire session was pervaded by a feeling of frustration — a feeling that deepened with the rumble from outside the windows as the armor of the Third Army rolled through the city on its way north. General Vandenberg listened to the briefing and then returned to his office with Major Fuller to mull over even the most remote possibility of a break. One of the mightiest striking forces in Europe was impotent and at a time when its strength was sorely needed by the hard pressed ground forces.

On December 21st and 22nd the high ground began to freeze, although still leaving many of the roads slippery and treacherous. On the 22nd a confused weather pattern brought a dismal mixture of snow, rain and fog. Both

air forces were almost entirely grounded. In the Low Ardennes, the *Sixth Panzer Armee* was beset by a morass of mud; swirling snow and dense fog hampered the *Fifth Panzer Armee* in its swing around Bastogne. Meantime, a heavy curtain of snow fell on the German supply columns in the Eifel. Atmospheric conditions were probably worse in this period than anytime in the entire Ardennes Offensive. The despair at 12th Army Group headquarters continued. According to Bradley:

Each morning our gloom had deepened as the Ninth Air Force's youthful meteorologist opened the daily briefing with his dismally repetitious report. And each morning Vandenberg, in a chair next to mine pulled his head a little tighter into his leather flying jacket. On more than 100 socked in airfields from Scotland to Brussels, an Allied Air Force of more than 4,000 planes waited for the end of von Rundstedt's conspiracy with the weather.

Yet on the afternoon of December

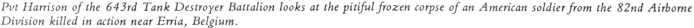

Pvt Harrison of the 643rd Tank Destroyer Battalion looks at the pitiful frozen corpse of an American soldier from the 82nd Airborne Division killed in action near Erria, Belgium.

Tankers of the U.S. 3rd Armored Division huddle around a fire to keep warm. January, 1945 brought sub-zero temperatures to the Ardennes.

22nd, while the Allied commanders groaned their disapproval and the forecasters continued to sing the low pressure blues, far to the east in Russia, a break was in the making. German meteologists on the Eastern Front noted a forming high pressure system and dutifully reported the information to Generalfeldmarschall Model of *Heeresgruppe B* in charge of the battle in the Ardennes. On the Allied side it was first noticed by the 21st Weather Squadron attached to the Ninth Air Force who saw lower moisture and temperature readings from the east along with a rising barometer. Very early on the morning of December 23rd, Fuller rushed into the 12th Army Group TAC war room with astonishing news. His forecast identi-fied an eastern high pressure cell known as a "Russian High" that would result in good weather all along the front. Hitler's luck had finally run out.

The high pressure brought a sudden and dramatic change to the battle. The cold dry winds cleared the skies and ground fog by noon leaving the German forces naked before a waiting Allied air force. In Luxembourg City the streets swelled with people craning their necks to watch the B-26s and P-47s of the Ninth Air Force roar off in attack. Further east in the Eifel, the winds caused the snow to drift blocking roads and obstructing the desperately needed supply traffic from the Rhine. Snow plows were scarce and by afternoon American fighter-bomb-ers were blasting every German vehicle that moved in daylight. With the high pressure cell and clear night skies, the thermometer plummeted. The Americans with fuel for their tanks and mastery of the skies benefited to a much larger extent than their disadvantaged adversary. This clear weather continued unabated through the 27th giving the Allied air force a field day to destroy German ground transport, wreck their roads and bridges and harass ground forces on the front. U.S. artillery observation planes buzzed about, promising prompt artillery fire for any German forces in range and not under cover.

The next day the weather again soured. Clouds and overcast were followed on the 29th by arctic winds, blizzards and extremely cold temperatures. Traffic was reduced to a standstill and what snow fences could be erected were cannibalized by cold soldiers on both sides looking for wood for fires. Cross country movement for tanks was nearly impossible and even infantry had to wade through snow drifts.

The wounded would surely die if left in the snow for more than half an hour. As the British entered the fight at the tip of the Bulge, they remarked that "We are fighting the weather as much as we are the Germans." The tactical fighting took on a new and desperate character called the "battle for the billets" as both sides fought for village shelter to escape their frozen foxholes.

On New Year's Day it was 5° below

zero at St. Vith, a steady zero at Bastogne and a bone chilling -7°F at Wiltz. The Third Army commander, Patton, ruefully noted that trench foot casualties were now exceeding those from combat. It was a sort of 20th Century "Valley Forge in Europe." Heavy ground fog covered the frozen Ardennes while sleet and rain added misery to the somber scene. Such were the conditions when the Allied forces went over to the counterattack to erase the Bulge on January 3rd.

The German architects of *Wacht am Rhein* considered the success of the operation to depend in a large measure upon the prevalence of poor flying weather to ground the Allied air forces. As fate would have it, this desire was realized for the first week of the offensive. What the German plan-

ners did not foresee, however, was that the winter conditions would also serve to limit their own mobility in obtaining the rapid breakout that was so important to success of the offensive.

A study by T.N. Dupuy in his book *Numbers, Predictions and War* has shown that poor weather tends to reduce the effectiveness of offensive armored formations more than it reduces the relative defending power of a like force in the hands of the defender. Cold weather resulted in combat actions that were slowly fought due to the inhibiting effect on the comfort of troops and the effect of freezing on transport and ordnance. Representing the Luftwaffe, Reichsmarschall Hermann Göring reflected on this fact in a 1945 interview:

Daily Temperature During the Ardennes Campaign

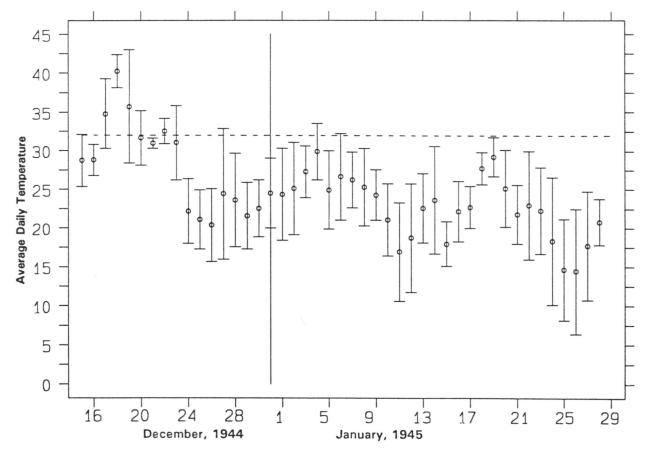

I thought the idea of bad weather as an advantage (for the Ardennes Offensive) was over emphasized. In the end, bad weather stalled us more than it helped us. It is also of my opinion that bad weather alone cannot entirely stop a modern air force.

Göring was not alone in this assessment. The German generals were unanimous in naming the weather and road conditions as important factors in the German defeat. Generaloberst Jodl provided a very explicit argument:

On the basis of past experience the worst flying weather is always in November. From December on, conditions gradually improve for flying. But this exercised no decisive influence on the success or failure of this operation. The decisive factor was that we had expected hard, frosty ground, not mud. With solid enough ground, we would have expected to push through with our tanks in a single day (the 17th).

Weather was not really decisive in this offensive. Of course we would not have attacked in perfectly clear weather, but we did not have to be assured of particularly bad weather. We could not have waited much longer, anyway.

Summary of Daily Weather during the Ardennes Camapign

Date (December)	Temperature	Skies	Visibility
16th	Cold	Overcast	Fair
17th	Cool	Overcast	Good
18th	Cool	Overcast	Poor
19th	Cool	Overcast	Poor
20th	Cool	Overcast	Poor
21st	Cool	Overcast	Very Poor
22nd	Cooler	Overcast	Poor
23rd	Cold	Partly Cloudy	Good
24th	Cold	Clear	Good
25th	Cold	Clear	Good
26th	Cold	Clear	Good
27th	Cold	Clear	Good
28th	Cold	Snow	Fair
29th	Cold	Overcast	Poor
30th	Cold	Overcast	Fair
31st	Cold	Snow	Poor

Patton's Prayer

On December 23rd Patton made his famous prayer for fair weather in the ancient chapel of the Pescatore Foundation in Luxembourg City:

"Sir, this is Patton talking. The last fourteen days have been straight hell. Rain, snow, more rain, more snow — and I'm beginning to wonder what's going on in your headquarters. Whose side are You on anyway?

"For three years my chaplains have been explaining that this is a religious war. This, they tell me, is the Crusades all over again, except that we're riding tanks instead of chargers. They insist we are here to annihilate the German Army and the godless Hitler so that religious freedom may return to Europe. Up until now I have gone along with them, for You have given us Your unreserved cooperation. Clear skies and a calm sea in Africa made the landings highly successful and helped us to eliminate Rommel. Sicily was comparatively easy and You supplied excellent weather for our armored dash across France, the greatest military victory that You have thus far allowed me. You have often given me excellent guidance in difficult command decisions and You have led German units into traps that made their elimination fairly simple.

"But now, You've changed horses in midstream. You seem to have given von Rundstedt every break in the book and frankly, he's been beating the hell out of us. My army is neither trained nor equipped for winter warfare. And as You know this weather is more suitable for Eskimos than for southern cavalrymen.

"But now, Sir, I can't help but feel that I have offended You in some way. That suddenly You have lost all sympathy for our cause. That You are throwing in with von Rundstedt and his paper-hanging-god. You know without me telling You that our situation is desperate. Sure, I can tell my staff that everything is going according to plan, but there's no use telling You that my 101st Airborne is holding against tremendous odds in Bastogne, and that this continual storm is making it impossible to supply them even from the air. I've sent Hugh Gaffey, one of my ablest generals, with his 4th Armored Division, north toward that all-important road center to relieve the encircled garrison and he's finding Your weather more difficult than he is the Krauts.

"I don't like to complain unreasonably, but my soldiers from the Meuse to Echternach are suffering tortures of the damned. Today I visited several hospitals, all full of frostbite cases, and the wounded dying in the fields be-

Lt. Gen. George S. Patton Jr.

cause they cannot be brought back for medical care.

"But this isn't the worst of the situation. Lack of visibility, continued rains have completely grounded my air force. My technique of battle calls for close-in fighter-bomber support, and if my planes can't fly, how can I use them as aerial artillery? Not only is this a deplorable situation, but, worse yet, my reconnaissance planes haven't been in the air for fourteen days and I haven't the faintest idea of what's going on behind the German lines.

"Damn it, Sir, I can't fight a shadow. Without Your cooperation from a weather standpoint I am deprived of accurate disposition of the German armies and how in hell can I be intelligent in my attack? All of this probably sounds unreasonable to You, but I have lost all patience with Your chaplains who insist that this is a typical Ardennes winter, and that I must have faith.

"Faith and patience be damned! You have just got to make up Your mind whose side You're on. You must come to my assistance, so that I many dispatch the entire German Army as a birthday present to Your prince of Peace.

"Sir, I have never been an unreasonable man, I am not going to ask you for the impossible. I do not even insist upon a miracle, for all I request is four days of clear weather.

"Give me four clear days so that my planes can fly, so that my fighter-bombers can bomb and strafe, so that my reconnaissance may pick out targets for my magnificent artillery. Give me four days of sunshine to dry this blasted mud, so that my tanks roll, so that ammunition and rations may be taken to my hungry, ill-equipped infantry. I need these four days to send von Rundstedt and his godless army to their Valhalla. I am sick of this unnecessary butchery of American youth, and in exchange for four days of fighting weather, I will deliver You enough Krauts to keep Your bookkeepers months behind in their work. Amen."

The Turning Point: December 25th - 26th

Christmas Day 1944 marked a decisive turning point in the Ardennes battle. The weather was again favorable for Allied air power: "Christmas dawned clear and cold," Patton, the commander of the U.S. Third Army remembered. "Lovely weather for killing Germans." Early that Monday morning, without permission from Montgomery, "Lightning Joe" Collins committed the powerful 2nd Armored Division on its German counterpart, the *2nd Panzer Division* near the Meuse[34]. The experienced commander of the 2nd Armored, Maj. Gen. Ernest N. Harmon, knew the time was ripe, "The bastards are in the bag!" he told Collins. The Germans in and around Celles were out of gas and

under fierce air attack when the American armor of Combat Command B of the 2nd Armored Division and British tanks of the 29th Armored Brigade closed in for the kill. The U.S. First Army reported discovery of "significant" evidence of the enemy straits: the capture of 13 self-propelled guns near Celles apparently abandoned for want of fuel.

Paced by a devastating artillery barrage, the 400 tanks of

34 Both the 2nd and 3rd Armored Division retained the 1942 tables of organization which allotted them 232 medium tanks and some 14,500 men as opposed to 186 tanks and 10,000 men in the other U.S. armored divisions.

First in Bastogne! "Cobra king" of the 37th Tank Battalion of the 4th Armored Division and its proud crew after pushing through the Germans to the 101st Airborne on December 26th. The tank commander was Lt. Charles P. Boggess. (Courtesy of Bastogne Historical Center)

Harmon's "Hell on Wheels" blasted through the thin German northern flank. The northern Task Force A fanned out through the villages of Celles, Boisselles and Conjoux while the southern Task Force B hove in on Humain, Havrenne and Buissonville. These two moves threatened to close a steel trap on the Germans near the Meuse. *Kampfgruppe von Böhm* was quickly surrounded near Foy Notre Dame as well as *Kampfgruppe von Cochenhausen* near Conneux (the major portion of the *304th Panzer Grenadier Regiment* under Maj. Ernest von Cochenhausen). In response, the *Panzer Lehr Division* launched a hasty armored attack to the northwest to reach the encircled German spearhead. The phalanx of German Panthers re-captured Humain, but could not reach Buissonville, halted as it was by heavy losses from rocket firing British Typhoon fighter-bombers and devastating American artillery fire. Meantime, the vanguard of the *9th Panzer Division* had finally arrived near Hargimont relieving part of the *2nd Panzer* for employment to reach the German pocket. During the night the German force was organized under the command of Haupt. Fredrich Holtmeyer. His *Kampfgruppe* made a bold relief attempt at dawn on the 26th.

In the rest of the *Fifth Panzer Armee*, the situation rapidly deteriorated. The *560th Volksgrenadier Division* was violently assailed by elements of CCA, 3rd Armored and the untested and newly arrived 75th Infantry Division. This action east of Soy effectively ended German plans for an advance in this area although causing terrible casualties among the inexperienced riflemen of the 75th. To check the American penetration, the *Führer Begleit Brigade* was being brought up to "advance in the general direction of Amonines."

The *116th Panzer Division* was now desperately fighting to relieve the tanks of *Kampfgruppe Bayer* (Obst. Johannes

The end of the road. Two Panthers of the 2nd Panzer Division *knocked out in the climatic battle that raged at the very tip of the Bulge on Christmas Day near the village of Foy-Notre Dame.*

Bayer) that were trapped by the 84th Division in a pocket near Verdenne. Promised support of the *9th Panzer* was no longer available since that division had its hands full trying to hold open a retreat route for the remnants of the *2nd Panzer Division* near Celles.

As ordered, *Kampfgruppe Maucke* of the *15th Panzer Grenadier Division* put in an assault on Bastogne as soon as its troops had been hastily assembled. The reckless armored attack that followed drove right through the rifle line of the 327th Glider Infantry Regiment and advanced nearly a mile towards the town. But, near the hamlet of Hemroulle the German assault was halted when the German column was shot to pieces in a prepared ambush. None of the 200 German troops and 18 tanks that pierced the American line were

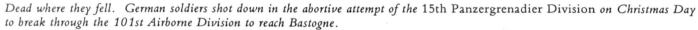

Dead where they fell. German soldiers shot down in the abortive attempt of the 15th Panzergrenadier Division *on Christmas Day to break through the 101st Airborne Division to reach Bastogne.*

Bob Lott and Jack Greoh of the 401st Glider Infantry Regiment stalk a German tank with a bazooka on Christmas Day. Although the German attack was repulsed, Greoh was killed three days later.

able to escape; all were killed or captured. Even with this victory, however, the 101st Airborne was in a critical situation. Ammunition was low and the defenders were not sure they could contain another enemy blow of similar magnitude. Even worse, no air supply drop could be made on this day due to weather conditions in England. On the other hand, the situation was also grave for Obst. Heinz Kokott's *26th Volksgrenadiers*. That night Kokott telephoned Gen. von Manteuffel and warned him that, "I could not watch two fronts and that the southern situation was most dangerous." He said that he expected the 4th Armored to breakthrough to Bastogne at any moment.

Patton was well aware of the American predicament in the isolated market town, but the Germans in the path of his 4th Armored Division were putting up a brave if hopeless fight. After clearing Warnach, CCA was held up at Tintage and Hollange while CCB finally wrested Chaumont from Germans. It would took all night and part of the next morning to cast the stubborn *5th Fallschirmjäger* out of the hamlet of Remichampagne. As a tanker of the 4th later recalled, "In their own way, these panzer-trained German paratroopers were saying 'nuts!' to us." Frustrated in his direct approach from the south, Patton ordered CCR of the division to try an end-run along the road from Neufchâteau. By dark the advance re-took Vaux-les-Rosières and was involved in a scrambling fight for Remoiville. The Third Army commander ordered the attack to be continued on through the night.

In light of the continuing failure, the costly German attacks of the *LXVII Armeekorps* against the Elsenborn area were now suspended. The *3rd Panzer Grenadier Division* west of Rocherath was relieved by the newly arrived *246th Volksgrenadier Division* (Obst. Peter Körte) so that the former unit could be fed into the offensive drive to the west. Most of the German formations left were drastically understrength. "There are only a few men left in the battalion," wrote a *Landser* of the *277th Volksgrenadier Division* in his diary on the yuletide. "A sad Christmas and still no food. The only water we have is from a foxhole."

On the morning of December 25th, 770 absolutely exhausted men of *Kampfgruppe Peiper* reached German lines along the Salm River near Rochelinval after suffering some casualties from repeated brushes with the 82nd Airborne Division. With the capitulation of *Kampfgruppe Peiper*, the Germans along the Amblève River were forced over to its south bank. *Kampfgruppen Hansen* and *Knittel* crossed over to the south side of the river at Petit Spai. The attack of the *ISS Panzerkorps* towards the Meuse was over.

The *IISS Panzerkorps* had mixed fortune on the battlefield. The *9th SS Panzer Division* took the villages of Arbrefontaine, Goronne and Lierneux just west of the Salm River. But this was a relatively simple task since the U.S. 82nd Airborne was withdrawing to a new line between Manhay and Trois Ponts. But the Germans of the *19th SS Grenadier Regiment* were of stern stuff; an attempt at dark to penetrate the lines of the 508th Regiment north of Odrimont was only turned back in a three hour firefight. Nearby, a regiment of the *62nd Volksgrenadiers* attacked Bra at 3:30 P.M. and although the infantry advance was broken, the enemy still succeeded in driving the American line back half a mile north of the town.

The *2nd SS Panzer Division* attacked west to gain the road fork at Grandménil. From there they advanced through Erezée in order to reach a crossing of the Ourthe River at Durbuy. The Panther tanks of the division took Grandménil at 7 A.M., but got no further. The German armor was halted by a withering fire from American artillery and chased into the woods by roving Allied fighter-bombers. The U.S. troops in the vicinity, the exhausted 7th Armored and 424th Regiment of the 106th Division, even vainly attempted to recapture Manhay. The later regiment managed to get within 50 yards of the village, although losing nearly 35% of its rifle strength of one battalion in severe fighting with SS grenadiers heavily armed with automatic weapons. But if the Americans had been "cut to ribbons," the Germans suffered terribly too, and the resistance of the *"Das Reich" Panzer Division* slackened noticeably over the next days.

Now partly reorganized, the *12th SS Panzer Division*, hobbled up to join Bittrich's corps reaching the vicinity of Bovigny. But due to the shortage of fuel and the difficulties attendent to movement under Allied air power, the division had not been available to aid Bittrich's strike towards the Ourthe. Rather than a concerted blow, the German attacks on the north flank had dissolved into a series of haphazard improvised assaults.

Elsewhere in the *Sixth Panzer Armee*, the *62nd* and *18th Volksgrenadier Divisions* moved north to relieve the *1st SS*

Panzer Division south of Trois Ponts-Stavelot along the Amblève River. The German infantry was harrased as they went by Allied fighter-bombers. *"Jabos* hung in the air like a swarm of wasps," a POW from the *18th Volksgrenadiers* reported to his interrogators.

After failing to carry the attack at Malmédy, the *150th Panzer Brigade* was transported back to Grafenwöhr in Germany. Further use of Skorzeny's commando brigade in the *Fifth Panzer Armee* had been considered for a time, but was rejected since the element of surprise had been lost. Elsewhere, from Monschau to Bütgenbach relative calm prevailed. The U.S. V Corps, with the 5th Armored Division in reserve, reported only light patrol activity. Meanwhile, the British 51st Division passed to First Army control and began to assemble in Liège ending much of the threat to the Meuse River crossing nearby.

In an effort to shorten the American lines and halt the German advance between the Salm and the Ourthe Rivers, the XVIII Corps pulled back the 82nd Airborne Division from Vielsalm to a line extending to the southwest between Trois Ponts and Manhay. Subsequent to Peiper's departure, the 30th Division entered La Gleize and began to mop up German pockets of resistance on the north bank of the Amblève River. The withdrawal was made on the orders of Fld.M. Montgomery. But the American commanders were quickly tiring of his cautious and pedantic command.

That evening Bradley and Patton shared a quiet Christmas dinner. Patton related to his superior the pessimistic assessment Montgomery had given him that day. The field marshal told him that "First army could not attack for three months and that the only attacks that could be made would be made by me, but I was too weak. Hence we would have to fall back to the Saar-Vosges line and even to the Moselle to gain enough divisions for me to counterattack." Both commanders were furious. Bradley called up Beedle Smith and asked that his command be immediately returned so that they could get on with a counter to the German offensive. He was ready to move his headquarters to Namur and with three of the arriving new divisions he and Patton would encircle the German penetration by pushing north towards Bonn from Echternach. But Eisenhower was not ready for this move; he would give Monty a final chance to give a good accounting of himself in a general counterattack from the north.

Opposite the disgruntled Allied commanders in Luxembourg, Gen. Brandenberger's *Seventh Armee* continued to experience the most trying circumstances. His doubts were increasing as to whether he could hold the line against the vigorous attack from Patton's Third Army. Although the 4th Armored Division did not crack the defenses of the stubborn *5th Fallschirmjäger Division*, the commander of the German paratroopers warned that the situation was critical and a "breakthrough of the enemy is imminent." Meantime, southwest of Wiltz, Maj. Gen. Willard S. Paul's 26th Division took Arsdorf and gained a toehold in Eschdorf after hard fighting with the *Führer Grenadier Brigade*. Nearby, the 80th Division contained German counterattacks along the Sauer while pushing almost to Kehmen near the confluence of the Sûre and Clerf Rivers. A lively exchange of fire between

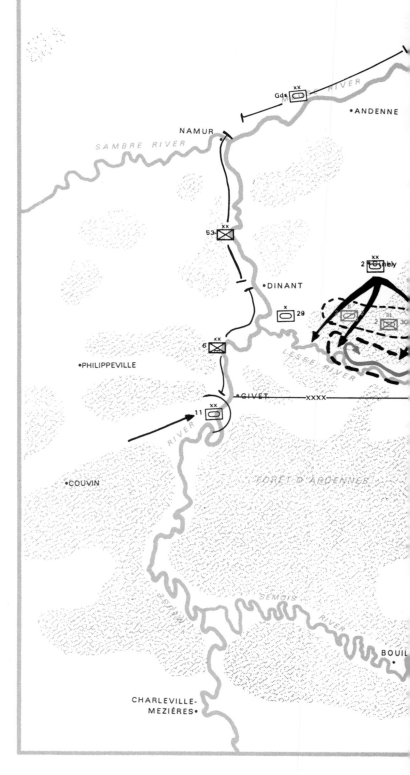

SITUATION MAP
December 25th-26th

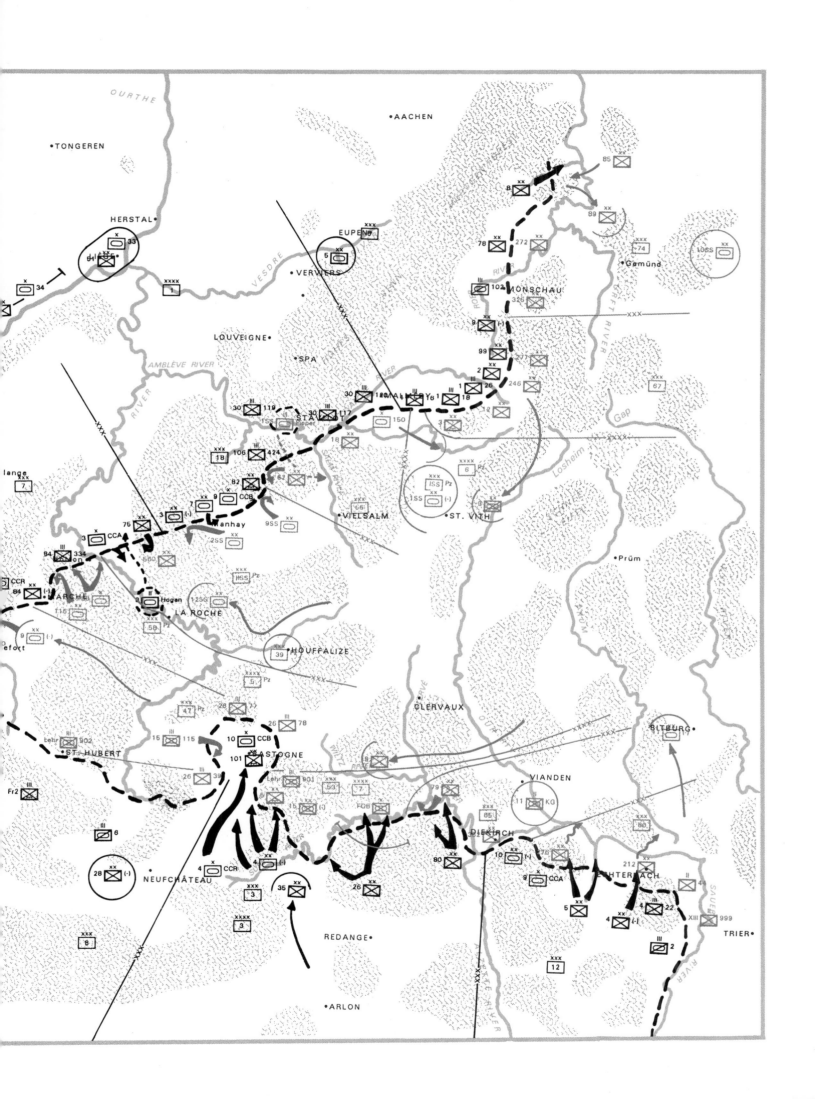

Turning point. Wrecked and captured vehicles left behind by the 2nd Panzer Division in its defeat near the village of Celles.

the U.S. 80th Division and the *352nd Volksgrenadier Division* saw the German commander, Obst. Erich Schmidt, severely wounded and evacuated. To the extreme south, assaults by the 5th Division took the villages of Waldbillig and Haller along the Sauer River in "heavy localized fighting." So vanquished, the Germans in the *LXXX Armeekorps* were forced to cross to the German side of the river at the bridges at Dillingen and Bollendorf.[35]

With the clear, cold weather, the Allied air forces were again aloft. The Ardennes battlefront and the rear areas of

Heeresgruppe B were repeatedly hit by 1,700 fighter bombers and 820 medium and heavy bombers. "The enemy carried on with its heavy air attacks on the same focal points...because of bomb attacks on St. Vith, traffic through the town is not possible," Model's staff reported, "However, the employment of the Luftwaffe has prevented them from repeated precision bombing of our spearheads." Even so, by this time Luftwaffe casualties had been so great over the preceding days that their participation in the battle commenced to wane; only about 600 sorties were flown on Christmas Day.

The predicament in the Ardennes was exactly as Genfldm. Model had forseen it in the planning process for *Wacht am Rhein* a month before: the Germans had been stopped short of the Meuse and no sizable Allied forces had been destroyed. The front resembled a big "Bulge" in the line. For Hitler, however, the Nazi officer struggled to conjure some sense of optimism out of the grim circumstances. In his daily communique to *OKW*, Model expressed his belief that there was still a possibility of annihilating the American forces east of the Meuse River, but he emphasized that this would only be possible if adequate supplies of fuel could be made available and with "a weather situation which precludes unhindered enemy aerial commitment."

At his *OB West* headquarters, von Rundstedt was even less sanguine in his Christmas Day assessment. He informed Hitler in a sharply worded message that now it was neither possible to attain Antwerp or the *Kleine Lösung* (Small Solu-

---

35 Other volksgrenadiers were not so lucky and on Christmas night had to swim across the icy Sauer to escape the U.S. 5th Division.

"So narrow you could spit across it;" An appraisal by a tanker of the 4th Armored Division of the slim U.S. corridor leading into Bastogne from the south. Here a 30 calibre machine gun and a Sherman tank guard the fragile lifeline near Assenois on January 3rd.

tion) of destroying the enemy due to the supply situation. He recommended that the offensive be called off immediately and German troops pulled back to the West wall before the Allies attempted to cut off the German salient from the north and south. Needless to say, this depressing note had little effect on Hitler's resolve to continue the bloody battle.

On December 26th, the right flank of the *Sixth Panzer Armee* was on the defensive from Monschau to Trois Ponts. The *LXVI Armeekorps*, moved up to relieve the *1st SS Panzer Division* which moved south to Emmels near St. Vith. There, SS ordnance mechanics began to work to wring a single operational panzer battalion from the armored wreckage of the *1st SS Panzer Regiment*. Between the Salm and the Ourthe River, the *IISS Panzerkorps* received its share of reverses in a series of bitter tank battles against the 3rd and 7th Armored Divisions. The *2nd SS Panzer Division* was thrown back from its push west of Grandménil with large tank losses by elements of the 3rd Armored and 75th Infantry Divisions. That same day the *9th SS Panzer* drove the 82nd Airborne out of Erria and Villettes, but could push no further, pummeled, as it was, by a deadly concentration of artillery. And there was other bad news: the movement of the *12th SS Panzer Division* to the left of the corps had been greatly delayed by Allied air attacks.

In the *Fifth Panzer Armee* the *560th Volksgrenadier Division* beat off attacks by the U.S. 75th Division east of Amonines. The 84th Division, with a battalion attached from the arriving 83rd, inflicted heavy casualties in throwing back the tank lead jabs by the *116th Panzer Division* at Ménil and the *Führer Begleit Brigade* at Hampteau between Marche and the Ourthe River. Hardly had Remer's panzer brigade attacked, than its troops were ordered to pull out of the battle and march to Bastogne. The gravity of the events near that town was already leading to a great shift in plans. Emaciated from eleven days of continuous combat, the *116th Panzer Division* went over to the defensive. With hard fighting the division saved most of its encircled armored regiment, *Kampfgruppe Bayer*, which managed a night escape from the Verdenne pocket east of Marche. Even so, the U.S. First Army reported 320 German prisoners taken from the panzer division in the fighting in and around Marenne.

At the tip of the Bulge, a bid by the *9th Panzer Division* and the *Panzer Lehr Division* to take Ciergnon and Buissonville faltered on the defenses of the rampaging 2nd Armored Division in the process of crushing all remaining resistance from the Germans surrounded near Celles. Likewise, an assault by the main body of the *2nd Panzer, Kampfgruppe Holtmeyer*, debouching from Hargimont, found itself caught by Allied guns and planes in a "hellish fire" near Custinne. So punished, the battlegroup was then nearly ripped apart by tank thrusts from the 2nd Armored. The relief attempt faltered and Holtmeyer was killed. With this reversal, the *2nd Panzer Division* was in danger of total destruction.

The breakout of the Germans from the *Kessel* was finally authorized by Hitler himself. But even this was too late. Many of the *2nd Panzer* could not escape and the entirety of the reconnaissance battalion, the *304 Panzer Grenadier Regiment* and half of the panzer regiment were smashed. In all, 600 Germans managed to flee on foot. But most important

of all, only three miles from the Meuse River and some 60 miles from the starting line, the German spearhead of Hitler's last great offensive lay shattered and broken in the snow. The Germans would get no further.

Back at Bastogne, the battle reached its climax. Another air drop was made over the town, although the response of German flak guns was telling. On the 26th and 27th 962 transports and 61 gliders dropped a massive 850 tons of supplies, with were shot down and 261 damaged from gunfire. On the ground in the early morning, the *26th Volksgrenadier Division* made a "last desperate effort" to capture the town. On the west side of the perimeter the Germans launched the attack with assault gun support from near Senonchamps. However, American artillery was ready for this move and shelled the German grenadiers into head-long retreat.

Then that afternoon the situation took a decisive turn in the Allied favor. At 4:45 P.M. a U.S. engineer on the south of the American perimeter near Assenois excitedly reported the approach of "three light tanks, believed friendly." Although down to only 20 Shermans, U.S. tankers of Combat Command R of the 4th Armored Division broke through the German ring of the battered *26th Volksgrenadier Division* to reach the paratroopers of the 101st Airborne. "Gee, I'm mighty glad to see you," exclaimed McAuliffe. The four day siege of Bastogne was over.

Still the "Bastogne corridor" was narrow and treacherous and unarmored vehicles could not risk the trip. On Patton's orders, two American divisions, the 6th Armored and the 35th Infantry began moving from the south to Bastogne to secure the highway from the town to Arlon. *Heeresgruppe B* was quick to recognize this move and its danger: "There is a gap between St. Hubert and Bastogne in which the enemy can insert troops at any time. Staff fears that the 35th American Division will be sent up against this area which is only sparsely defended."

In the *Seventh Armee* sector the German infantry had been resolutely driven back to the river line between Diekirch and Echternach under strenuous attack from the 5th, 26th

Disaster at Heiderscheid. Soldiers of Hitler's personal guard, The Führer Grenadier Brigade, *lie dead near the shattered armor.*

and 80th Infantry Divisions. The *5th Fallschirmjäger Division* was nearly at the end of its resources. The 4th Armored Division had pierced its defense at Clochimont and Assenois just south of Bastogne; attempts to re-close the opened breaches had failed and 500 German prisoners were taken. The American 26th Division established a bridgehead on the north bank of the Sauer five miles south of Wiltz — such a dangerous penetration that elements of the *Führer Grenadier Brigade* were moved up to counterattack. The U.S. 80th Division managed to clear the village of Scheidel, but was halted in heavy fighting at nearby Kehmen. Meantime, the U.S. XII Corp's 5th Division took Echternach and Berdorf after having forcing the *276th* and *212th Volksgrenadier Divisions* back to the north bank of the Sauer in fierce attacks. Only two small bridgeheads at Hamm and Dillingen — both north of Echternach — were retained. The later span was under American artillery and machine gun fire.

With continued favorable flying weather, the Allied air forces once again decisively intervened in the ground battle. A nearly ceaseless Allied air attack from the sky strafed troops and machine gunned supply trucks and chased German panzers into the woods. One German prisoner described the conflagation at St. Vith: "Where once houses were one can see nothing but big craters. Only a very few people are still here trying to rescue some of their belongings. The cattle are howling, the ammunition is exploding...."

In all, a total of 3,500 Allied machines operated over the battle area and the rear of *Heeresgruppe B*. This completely dwarfed the Luftwaffe effort: a total of 404 planes. The situation had deteriorated to the point that Genfldm. Model of the army group was forced to forbid German daylight movement. "On the entire front there was the heaviest enemy low flying attacks, with a focus on the *Fifth Panzer Armee*, which made movement and supply on the battlefield nearly impossible during the entire day...the Luftwaffe could only offer localized and temporary relief in the face of massive employment of enemy aircraft over the battle zone." Von Rundstedt agreed, noting that "all movement forward of troops and supplies is as good as ruled out, as the Luftwaffe, in spite of the heaviest commitment, can not adequately get through against the enemy air superiority." He bluntly informed Reichminister Speer that "Heavy damage is accumulating and the transport situation is becoming extremely grave."

With the bad news coming in from all directions to Hitler's headquarters, the usual air of fantasy had begun to creep into the assessment at the *Wehrmachtführungsstab*. "The envisioned thrust across the Meuse to the northwest still appears possible," *OKW* opined, "but is contingent on the re-establishment of a balance on the Sauer River and the destruction of the forces located between the Ourthe and the Meuse." Amid this quixotic assessment, Gen. Guderian appeared at *Adlerhorst* to plead for Hitler's help for *Heeresgruppe*

Süd in Russia. He described the grave situation there and warned that without assistance "a total Russian breakthrough in the vicinity of Budapest" could not be averted. Although less than he had asked for, he did secure the use the *711th Infanterie Division* from the *25th Armee* north of the Ardennes.

Von Rundstedt believed the reason for the *Fifth Panzer Armee's* recent reverses was a lack of depth in the assault. He judged that fresh divisions were essential to the chance of any further success. Therefore, he ordered the *340th Volksgrenadier Division* and the *89th Infantrerie Division* to be moved immediately to the Ardennes with the *9th* and *167th Volksgrenadier Divisions* attached to the *Seventh Armee* to deal with the crisis there. *SS Grenadier Divisions 27 "Langemarck"* and *28 "Wallonien"* were transferred to Düren for garrison duty. Von Rundstedt did not directly comment on Model's requirements regarding the supply of fuel and the neutralization of the Allied air force as requisites for a chance of continued success. However, the old Field Marshal did warn that "All planning is rendered null and void," if there was no success "in rapidly removing the damage caused to *Reichsbahn* and traffic facilities." He further lamented the damage to the rail system since the meager fuel supply could not withstand the "double consumption" from trucked supply to the forward combat forces.

On the Allied side, great efforts were under way to ensure that the Germans did not regain the initiative that they had so recently lost. More divisions had been wrung out of Patton's Army, including the 35th and 87th Infantry and 6th Armored Divisions which were on their way north; the 90th Infantry was to be added later. Maj. Gen. Robert C. Macon's 83rd Infantry Division was sent from the Ninth Army to Hodges' First. In addition, two brand new divisions were moving up to the fight around Bastogne: the 11th Armored, the 17th Airborne Division.

The British were ready to lend a hand as well. Lt. Gen. Brian G. Horrocks' British XXX Corps was moving up to ensure that the Germans would find it difficult to cross the Meuse should they reach the river. The 29th Armored Brigade operated east of the Meuse while the 53rd Division took over defense from Namur to Dinant. The Guards Armored Division assembled with the 34th Tank Brigade from Namur to Visé along the north bank of the Meuse River. The next day Maj. Gen. Eric L. Bols' 6th Airborne Division arrived west of the Meuse in the Givet area south of Dinant while the British 43rd Wessex Division (Maj. Gen. G.I. Thomas) guarded the north bank of the Meuse between Huy and Liége. As the threat to that sector subsided the 43rd would move into reserve near Maastricht on the 27th. The other British reserve division, the 51st "Highland" (Maj. Gen. T.G. Rennie) with the attached 33rd Armored Brigade gathered as a U.S. First Army reserve near Liége on Christmas Day. The German chance for an uncontested capture of the Meuse crossings had all but vanished.

The War Correspondents

Covering a war has always been something of a opportunity for career-minded journalists. The Battle of the Bulge was no exception. However, unlike the "fun war" of the previous summer in France, the Ardennes in December 1944 proved to be a much more dangerous place to get a story. Most sensible correspondents had fled to Maastrict or Paris where they tried to file stories composed of "sheer hysteria." This group, writing of events second hand provided ample work for the U.S. Army field press censors. The other group of correspondents were more dogged; they were determined to cover the big German offensive first hand.

On December 27th, just a few miles south of the hotly contested village of Bastogne, near the hamlet of Assenois, just such a group of four noted correspondents pondered their fate. It was a case of story versus longevity. Walter Cronkite sat in a blasted Belgian farmhouse shivering over a fire, huddled together with his three other scruffy looking friends. They were John Driscoll of the *New York Daily Tribune*, Norman Clark of the London *News Chronicle* and Cornelius Ryan of London *Daily Telegraph*. All four newsmen knew that the *real* story was in Bastogne. But all their efforts to follow up the tanks of the 4th Armored Division had met with German bullets

Fred MacKenzie, of the Buffalo Evening News, was the only reporter in the besieged town of Bastogne. MacKenzie is pictured recuperating after a brush with death when a German artillery shell scored a direct hit on his sleeping quarters. Four GIs in the room were killed instantly.

The treacherous road to Bastogne near Assenois as it appeared on December 27th. Army ambulances brave enemy fire to evacuate U.S. wounded.

and mortar and "88" fire along that single road. It wasn't healthy.

Besides, they all knew that Fred MacKenzie of the *Buffalo Evening News* had the real scoop, being the only journalist trapped in the Bastogne pocket. He had narrowly escaped death during the seige when he decided to stay up late to type up his notes in a room across from his sleeping quarters. While he was working, a German artillery shell suddenly exploded, scoring a direct hit on his vacant bunk and killing the other four soldiers sleeping in the room.

Bill Davidson of *Yank* had been caught up in the very midst of the big German attack. Rather than filing a lead story he had ended up spending several days hiding from Germans in the *Fôret de Freyr* protecting two Jewish children from capture by the dreaded Nazi secret police, the *SD* or *Sicherheitsdienst*. By the time he arrived at the Paris bureau, his presence was greeted with less than enthusiasm: "It's about time I heard from you," Merle Miller, his bureau chief harangued. "New York needs copy about the big German offensive." Davidson rattled off about his weeklong ordeal in the cold. "What kind of story is that?" Miller scowled. "Go back to Luxembourg and get us some real combat stuff about the war!"

Then too, the famous Ernest Hemingway had come down from Paris for the story for *Colliers* with other assorted misanthropes. But the Nobel Prize winner was too sick (or drunk) to cover much of the action in the 4th Division sector. On top of that he was being hounded by his estranged wife.

Cronkite and his friends didn't feel especially privileged at their location near the "real combat stuff." The group had taken refuge in the bombed-out house for the same reason that many others in the Ardennes had sought shelter that day — to keep warm. Occasionally an enemy artillery shell exploded outside their hovel just to keep everyone awake. Presently, they were joined by a few officers from the 4th Armored Division.

After a harrowing ride Maj. Gen. Maxwell Taylor greets Brig. Gen. Anthony McAuliffe in the besieged town of Bastogne on December 27th.

One of the group was posted to watch the road outside. All suspected that Germans might appear at any time. After all, the front line was only about half a mile away in either direction.

Soon a vehicle appeared in the distance, speeding down the road. To everyone's relief, it sounded like an American jeep. As the vehicle approached the shell pocked road, the German firing increased. The reporters were amazed by the fool-hardiness of its driver. "Look at that nut!," Driscoll exclaimed. "When are they going to learn?" All the men had witnessed numerous GIs killed by taking chances like this jeep's driver. Regardless, the men made the best of it in true GI fashion. They took bets on whether he would make it to the farmhouse.

The odds were running one in three when General Maxwell D. Taylor, the commander of the 101st Airborne Division, screeched to a halt outside their ruin. With him was his driver, Sgt. Charlie Kartus, a native of North Carolina. Taylor was decked out in a dress uniform a steel helmet and combat boots. Seemingly oblivious to the German small arms fire, the general sauntered over to their dilapidated accommodations. Kartus ducked and sprinted for the farmhouse. General Taylor was fearless.

The general told the small group that he was determined to get into Bastogne by nightfall. Taylor was a dedicated professional soldier and preferred

to be at the head of his troops in combat. He had missed out on the opening battle by being back in Washington when the German offensive broke. His artillery officer, General McAuliffe, in charge of the garrison in the small crossroads town, had already entered the 101st into the history books with his defiant reply of "Nuts!" to a German request for surrender.

On arrival in England Taylor had asked to parachute into the Bastogne, but this had been over-ruled by Eisenhower's chief of staff, General Bedell Smith. In his anxiety to get to his troops, Taylor had not even taken time to get into warmer clothing when his plane had landed in Luxembourg. "I have to get in tonight," Taylor told the small group of correspondents. Such a drive, an officer of the 4th Armored assured him, would be very dangerous. "The corridor is so narrow you can spit across it. The Jerries have this road zeroed in for now." But, try as they might, the men could not convince Taylor to wait to ride into town in a tank or armored car. He would get there tonight.

As there was space in his jeep, General Taylor magnanimously offered it to any of the four who wanted to go along. Cronkite had jumped with the 101st Airborne at Arnhem, but this foray up the road seemed a bit too risky. Cornelius Ryan politely declined for the group. As the General rode off the German firing picked up once more. All agreed with their previous odds on the General's chances. None of them expected to see him again.

Luck was on the General's side, however. After a hair raising twilight ride, Taylor was soon enjoying an evening cognac in Bastogne with McAuliffe. A few miles down the road, Cronkite and his crew spent an uncomfortable night in their ruined farmhouse. It was several days before it was safe to travel to Bastogne for soldiers and correspondents alike.

Hitler's Last Christmas

The holiday season in Germany is traditionally celebrated on three days — Christmas Eve, Christmas Day and December 26th. Christmas 1944 was the sixth Christmas that Hitler had spent in the toils of the titanic struggle that he had unleashed on Europe, already widely known as the Second World War.

In 1939 Hitler had been able to celebrate his lightning victory over Poland; at Yuletide 1940 he and his generals toasted the utter conquest of France and Western Europe. However, by December 1941, although his panzer armies were nearly to the gates of Moscow they were under heavy counterattack from the *Bolshevik* forces. The following year, 1942, found even less holiday cheer. He had lost the entire *Sixth Armee* in the winter debacle at Stalingrad, and North Africa had been re-conquered by the British and Americans. Christmas tide 1943 was still worse. Hitler had lost his last great offensive in the East at Kursk, the Allies had landed in Italy, and the Reich was under increasing air attack.

The year 1944 had seen the rot really set in. In June the Allies landed at Normandy and liberated France; the great Russian offensive that summer had swallowed an entire army group. Vast bomber fleets roamed freely over Nazi air space pulverizing German cities and factories. In July a group of German officers even attempted Hitler's assassination. But strangely, this only served to increase the Führer's resolve, "Who says I am not under the protection of God!" he proclaimed after surviving the attempt. "I'm immortal!" But even a fanatical belief in his divine destiny could not reverse the tide of the losses in the field.

Christmas 1944 saw the German leader in the midst of his last great gamble — the Ardennes Offensive in the West. Near Ziegenberg, Germany, Adolf Hitler commanded the great offensive from his *Adlerhorst* headquarters — the "Eagle's Nest."

Photograph of Hitler taken only a short time after the failed assassination attempt on July 20th, 1944. Hitler is obviously still shaken; Jodl's head is bandaged from the injury he received in the bomb blast.

Certainly, the headquarter's evocative title was more attractive than its reality. *Adlerhorst* was a collection of drab concrete bunkers in the wooded Taunus hills. Deep within its catacombs the self-proclaimed leader of the Third Reich carried on the battle that was to "decide the destiny of the Reich." Even here, many miles from the battlefield, the hollow thunder of artillery fire in the Ardennes was plainly audible.

At the beginning of the Ardennes Offensive Hitler was euphoric. Upon visiting Hitler at 12:30 P.M., Dr. Theodor Morell noted that his patient was "alert and lively, but got no sleep because of the coming offensive. . . permanent tremor in his left hand." Never one to hold back on the medication, Hitler's personal physician injected the German leader with glucose, iron and vitamin complex. "Great emotional crisis because of the offensive," he jotted on the medication data card. At the war room in Hitler's headquarters, the official record keeper, Karl Thöt, described the scene on the morning of December 16th when *Wacht am Rhein* was launched:

When [Stenographer Ewald] Reynitz and I went over to the war conference at 3 P.M., an impressive number of German fighter planes passed overhead and Maj. Büchs, evidently recovering at this instant from the perpetual inferiority of our Luftwaffe, turned to everybody present and declaimed with a glance skyward, "Now let me hear one of you say anything against the German air force!' As we approached the conference room we saw that the Führer was already present, contrary to his custom. We could read only too clearly in his expression how engrossed he was in the first favorable news about our offensive.

It was 4 A.M. on December 17th before Hitler finished tea and settled into bed, satisfied that "the offensive is making slow but sure headway."

However, in spite of its auspicious beginning, the results of the first week of the attack had been mixed. Taken completely by surprise, the German forces had knifed through the thin U.S. defense and seemed to be within reach of the Meuse River on their way to Antwerp. On the other hand, the *schwerpunkt* of the attack, the *Sixth Panzer Armee*, had bogged down amid stubborn U.S. resistance. Perhaps worse, the American airborne troops in Bastogne were still holding out and fuel deliveries to the panzer spearheads were flagging. The commander of *Heeresgruppe B*, Generalfeldmarschal Model, had already told Hitler that the offensive had failed and could not reach Antwerp.

That the war had taken its toll on the German leader was obvious to those who had not seen him in some time. Hitler's appearance in December of 1944 was shocking. Although only 55, Hitler was an old man; his back was bent, his famous moustache was now ashen-white and his skin was pale. His left arm twitched continuously and could only be restrained by holding it with his right. Since the explosion he was hard of hearing and occasionally he appeared to daydream. Other times he rambled on in monotonous monologues about the Roman Empire, Frederick the Great (a favorite historical theme) and even dog breeding. "The longer I study men," he was fond of saying, "the more I like dogs."

The German leader loved to discuss the advantages of a "natural existence," although his schedule and accommodations were far from such an ideal. Hitler did not get up before 11 A.M. and then held a briefing conference in mid-afternoon. The only time he ventured outside his gloomy concrete accommodations was to briefly walk his German Sheperd, Blondi. At 5 P.M. Hitler took a nap and then began the evening briefing session that consisted of interminable conversations and tea drinking. These meetings seldom ended before the small hours of the morning, leaving Hitler's entourage absolutely exhausted. "You realize this war is no fun for me," he told those around him. "I've been cut off from the world for five years. I've not been to a theatre, a concert or a film. I devote my life to the single task of running the war, because I know if there's not an iron will behind it the battle cannot be won."

Christmas eve, *der Heilige Abend*, was something less than a "holy evening" in the Führer bunker. On one hand, word arrived at *Adlerhorst* that the reconnaissance battalion of the *2nd Panzer Division* was only three miles from the Meuse River! Regardless of the tone of this message, word that the commander of the tiny German force was without gasoline, and hiding from Allied aircraft must have cooled the ardor of the German field commanders.

In the afternoon Hitler stood outside the *Adlerhorst* bunker and watched with his staff as over a thousand enemy bombers glittered in the winter sky, swarming eastward to the heart of Germany. Over his vegetarian lunch, his secretary Christa Schroeder worried at this sight: "Mein Führer, we have lost the war — haven't we." Hitler calmly assured her that they had not.

Late that night, General von Manteuffel, in command of the spearhead *Fifth Panzer Armee*, rang up the *OKW* headquarters to reach Hitler's right hand man, Alfred Jodl. He tersely informed Jodl that, as ordered, he would assault Bastogne again in just a few hours, although he did not believe that he could both take that town and continue his advance of the Meuse River. The time had come, he informed Jodl, for the plan to be altered; the objective of Antwerp was clearly unattainable. Jodl told von Manteuffel that he did not believe that Hitler would abandon the Antwerp objective, although knowing the little Prussian general was right, he agreed to pass along the word. As if to compound this impression, Generalfeldmarschall von Rundstedt in charge of *OB West* again

stopped by to petition Hitler to halt the offensive since now even a "limited solution" appeared possible. But Hitler was unimpressed with their stance. "When all goes well people are on top of the world," he cried, "but when everything starts to go wrong they just fold up and give in." It was near four in the morning when *Feldherr* finally retired.

At noon, Hitler finally awoke. Late in the day he joined the rest of his household staff to celebrate the yuletide. Surely the atmosphere there must have been one of enforced festivity. To those around him in the shabby war room the Führer appeared to be cheerful although feeble. They remembered that "his face was haggard and his voice wavered...his hand shake was weak and soft; all his movements were those of a senile man; only his eyes retained their flickering gleam and penetrating look." According to Baron von Steengracht he "still put on a brave face, but he was frail and his hand trembled." Such was true. Since early December Hitler required a trusted servant to forge his very signature onto official documents.[36]

But Hitler was in a surprisingly good humor. To everyone's surprise, the Führer drank a glass of wine which he distinctly seemed to relish. In a brief ceremony all present awkwardly toasted Hitler and the Third Reich. An SS adjunct who was there recalled:

> After a short break, we worked on during the night. Supper last night was quite good. Field Marshal Keitel made a speech, short and sweet, then we all sat around a candlelit Christmas tree for a while before going back to work. This morning I ran into the Führer. He shook my hand, asked about my family, and even remembered that we

The irony of time. Hitler parades through the town of Bastogne on May 17th, 1940 to visit Genfldm. von Rundstedt's victorious armies in France. Hitler could hardly suspect that four years later he would be waging an desperate offensive in this region to save a war already lost. His great gamble would fitfully end with his panzers deadlocked in battle to win this small market town.

have two children....I could do and sacrifice anything for this man.

It was late in the wee hours of the morning after the lights of the *Weihnachts* had dimmed and the goose and *Lebkuchen* been eaten, when Hitler finally retired from the war room to his dreary quarters.

By noon December 26th on St. Stephen's Day, or the *Zweite Weihnachtstag*, Hitler awoke to see the worries of Christmas Day translated into a series of crushing reverses for his final great gamble. The German *Seventh Armee* had nearly been forced back to the Sauer River it had crossed ten days before while under punishing attack by Patton's Third Army. Worse still, the 4th Armored Division, under that swashbuckling general had broken the German siege of Bastogne piercing the ring of Germans surrounding the town and relieving the U.S. airborne garrison there. Finally, although the *2nd Panzer* near the Meuse had finally received permission to try and break out of its pocket near Celles, it was out of fuel and under a devastating attack from the U.S. 2nd Armored Division. Jodl now confronted Hitler with the truth: "Mein Führer," he exclaimed, "we must face the facts. We cannot force the Meuse!" Even an eternal optimist such as Hitler had to now admit that the great offensive was not going according to plan. But in spite of these disasters, Hitler was unwilling to concede defeat:

We have had unexpected setbacks — because my plan was not followed to the letter, but all is not lost. The war cannot last as long again as it has already lasted. Nobody could stand it, neither we nor the others. The question is, which side will crack first? I say that the side that lasts longer will do so only if it stands to lose everything. We stand to lose everything. If the other side announces one day, 'We've had enough!' no harm will come to them. If America says, "Cut! Stop! No more American boys to Europe!" it won't hurt them. New York remains New York....Nothing changes. But if we say "We've had enough, we're packing up" — then Germany will cease to exist."

It was with this logic and a monumental capacity for self-delusion that Hitler was determined to carry on the war at any cost. However, others less sanguine in the German Army saw a more horrible truth. Even with the German people prepared to lose everything, the Allied forces were simply too powerful to be defeated. At 7:15 P.M. in the *Heeresgruppe B* headquarters, the Chief of Staff, General Krebs examined the situation in the Ardennes and made a telling appraisal: "Today a certain culminating point has been reached." The initiative of the attack had slipped from Hitler's hand into those of the Allied enemy. That the 26th had been the day of decision was tacitly conceded even by the Nazi propagandists. Near the close of the day Reichsmarschall Hermann Göring, the Luftwaffe commander in chief, became involved in a bitter quarrel with Hitler. The two men argued at length over the severity of the battle being waged on the two fronts. Finally, Göring lost his patience. "The war is lost," he declared. The head of the Luftwaffe then meekly suggested to the Führer that the Third Reich seek a truce. Hitler was livid. "I forbid you to take any step in this matter," he warned. "If you go against my orders I will have you shot!"

On the following day German radio abandoned the glory of the Ardennes battle to feature mundane coverage of activities in Greece and Budapest. Meanwhile, the war-weary grenadiers of Hitler's *Wehrmacht* read *Nachrichten Fur Die Truppe*, the Nazi version of "Stars and Stripes," which bitterly featured the story of a Christmas gift for the rotund Göring —a Reichsmarschal-sized portion of caviar from Spain. Rather than "a present of Antwerp for the Führer" from the *Wehrmacht*, Hitler now was willing to settle for post holiday revenge at Bastogne.

With the end of December 26th, Christmas 1944 was over. The sixth Christmas of World War II would be Hitler's last.

"We Must Have Bastogne": December 27th - 28th

By Wednesday, December 27th, the initiative in the great Ardennes battle was slowly slipping into Allied hands. Eleven days after the start of *Wacht am Rhein*, the large volume of American and British infantry, tanks, artillery and planes had tilted the scales decidedly in the Allied favor. However, Eisenhower's generals were unsure of how to apply their advantage. Some, like Generals Bradley, Ridgway and Patton, proposed to immediately attack from the shoulders of the Bulge to pocket the entire German salient.

But Montgomery and Hodges believed this strategy too risky; roads in the sector along the German border were sparse and narrow and jumpy Allied G-2s were seeing a new panzer division behind every bush. Consequently, Eisenhower opted to attack further to the west — a cautious strategy Genfldm. von Rundstedt would note with irony in his war diary as the Allied version of the "the Small Solution." Others on the Allied side of the fence would have agreed with the German field marshal's assessment: "We would have been able to launch the counterattack on Christmas," Brig. Gen. Clift Andrus, the commander of the U.S. 1st Infantry Division wrote after the war. "We are convinced that we could have crushed all resistance and contributed by a decisive effort to an immediate victory." Most of the 1st Division, part of the 9th and the 5th Armored Division would have been available for such an attack from Elsenborn Ridge. But it was not to happen.

However, German plans were about to change as well. The Allied relief of Bastogne on the 26th enraged Hitler. He saw the American stand at the town as a fundamental cause for the failure of *Wacht am Rhein* to gain the Meuse. Thus, on this date Hitler issued an unalterable decree that "Bastogne be cleared" — a euphemism for the destruction of the American forces in and around the town. The SS panzer divisions (or what was left of them) were to be immediately pulled out of the line along with the *Führer Begleit Brigade* and the *3rd Panzer Grenadier Division*. These formations were to then be expeditiously moved to the Bastogne salient where they were to "lance this boil."

The situation on the front of the *Sixth Panzer Armee* offered little hope for renewed German success. The *LXVII Armeekorps*, fought out from Monschau to Malmédy, was returned to the *Fifteenth Armee*. A local attack by the *62nd Volksgrenadier Division* against the village of Basse-Bodeux, just east of Trois Ponts, came to nothing, being easily re-

pulsed by the 82nd Airborne Division. Similarly, raids by the U.S. 99th Infantry Battalion against the *18th Volksgrenadiers* south of Malmédy were turned back. To the east, the shattered *1st SS Panzer Division* remained in the St. Vith area to reorganize.

To the west, the *IISS Panzerkorps* continued its futile attack to rupture the American front between the Salm and the Ourthe Rivers. Although there were minor successes, with the *12th SS Panzer Division* capturing Freyneux, Lamormenil and La Fosse, the overall result was not promising. In the *2nd SS Panzer* sector the Germans captured Grandménil only to lose it to an American counterattack by Task Force McGeorge of the 3rd Armored Division. American artillery so blasted the Germans in Manhay that a bold assault by the 517th Parachute Infantry Regiment knifed through enemy resistance to recapture the town astride the Bastogne-Liège road. Similarly, the *9th SS Panzer* was forced to give up the villages of Erria and Villettes west of the Salm River to a determined counterattack by the 82nd Airborne Division. The Germans left over a hundred dead at the two crossroads villages and reported one of their grenadier regiments "cut to pieces." The German corps commander, SS-Obgrf. Bittrich threw in the towel. He realized that his divisions were too weakened to continue.

Von Manteuffel's *Fifth Panzer Armee* was also forced to the defensive, fending off continuing attacks from Collin's

The reality of foxhole life in the Ardennes is graphically portrayed in this winter scene of 84th Infantry Division positions on the north flank of the Bulge.

VII Corps. The *116th Panzer Division* which was holding the line southeast of Hotton was greatly depleted from the severe fighting of the past week — the rifle strength of its grenadier battalions had dipped to only 150 men and armored strength consisted of only about 15 panzers and 40 armored cars along with a few tank destroyers. Transport was especially in short supply — many vehicles had been lost in the preceding days.

The mission for the *XLVII Panzerkorps* became defensive. The *9th Panzer Division* at Hargimont, near the tip of the Bulge, and the *2nd Panzer Division* had pulled back to Rochefort abandoning much of its equipment in the "Conneux pocket." The *Panzer Lehr Division* repulsed enemy probes along its south flank. Meantime, the U.S. 2nd Armored Division cleared the stubborn resistance from Humain, east of Marche. As this transpired, the 83rd Infantry Division arrived in the area of Havelange, northwest of Marche, to begin relief of the armored division so it could be employed further east along the line. The Allied counterattack on the German spearhead had been a resounding success. An inventory of the battlefield litter left by the three panzer divisions fighting west of Rochefort counted 88 tanks and assault guns, 74 artillery and flak pieces and 405 wrecked trucks and halftracks.

The focal point of the battle in the *Fifth Panzer Armee* lay in the Bastogne area. To widen the Bastogne corridor, CCA of the 9th Armored Division had been brought up from the Echternach area, inserted on the VIII Corps right wing and sent off in two task forces to open the Neufchâteau-Bastogne road. In intense house-to-house fighting Task Force Collins took Sibret from the *26th Volksgrenadiers*. The next morning Task Force Karsteter took the villages of Villeroux and Vaux-les-Rosières with heavy fighter-bomber support. Meanwhile, the *Führer Begleit Brigade*, which was intended to re-encircle the 101st Airborne, did not arrive in *Kampfraum Bastogne* until late evening, unable to march in daylight due to the air situation. However, upon arrival it immediately launched a hastily contrived night assault with the few elements on hand to sever the American held corridor to the south along the Arlon-Bastogne highway. The poorly coordinated venture quickly faltered on the American defenses and the Germans quit for the day. Repercussions from Hitler were quick in coming: a new attack was to be readied immediately with new leadership. The *XXXIX Panzerkorps* under Gen. Lt. Karl Decker, an old hand at armored battle from the Eastern Front, assumed command of the fight there. Decker was told, in no uncertain terms, that he was to use the armored brigade and the arriving *3rd Panzer Grenadier* and *167th Volksgrenadier Divisions* to take Bastogne at any cost.

But the Germans were not the only ones increasing their strength in the Bastogne sector. Combat Command A of the U.S. 9th Armored Division had been called up from near Echternach and the veteran 35th Infantry Division (Maj. Gen. Paul W. Baade) from Patton's army was inserted between the 4th Armored and 26th Infantry Divisions. In its first commitment in the Ardennes, the 35th captured the towns of Boulaide and Surré, deep in the dense forests southeast of Bastogne. The powerful 6th Armored Division, with 185 M-4 tanks (only one less than its table of

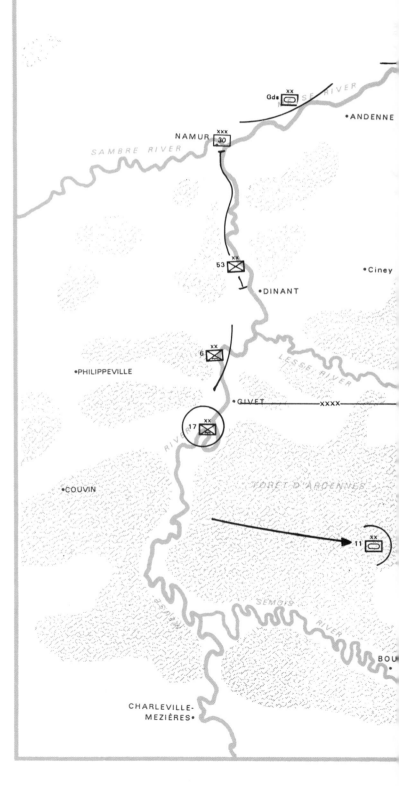

SITUATION MAP
December 27th-28th

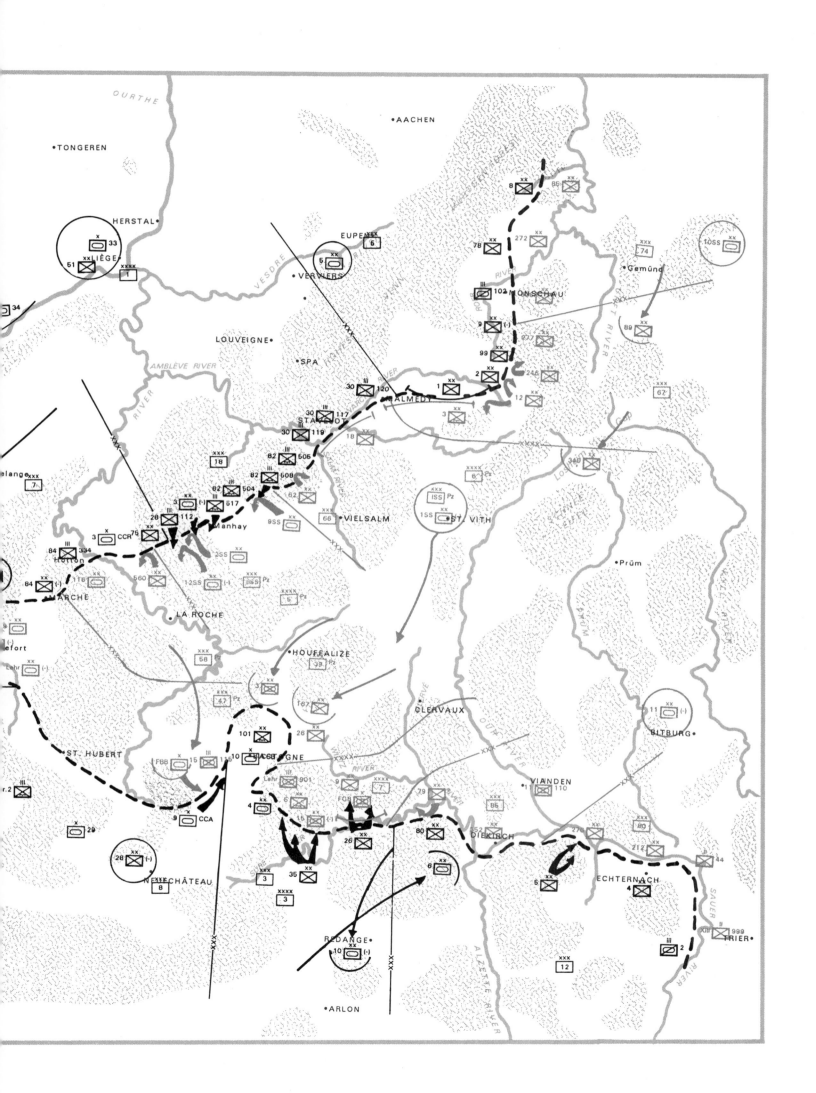

organization) was also on the way and planning to add metal to the American offensive to the north, scheduled for December 31st.

By now, the Bastogne corridor was broad enough that American ambulances were able to enter the town to evacuate the many wounded, although not without risk from enemy fire. Meanwhile, Maj. Gen. William M. Miley's untried 17th Airborne Division moved up from SHAEF reserve to a back-stop position along the Meuse River south of Givet after coming straight from training in England. Switching places with the 17th, the 11th Armored moved off to Bastogne 24 hours later "on a clear, cold night under an unimaginably bright moon."

To the south, the *Seventh Armee* was under increasing pressure from Patton's forces; the German mission was to simply hold onto what had been won. A deep penetration was achieved in the *LIII Armeekorps* just east of Bastogne by the U.S. 26th Division which had crossed the Sûre River at Bonnel, captured Kaundorf and threatened to take Nothum just south of Wiltz. Further American progress might encircle the weakened *5th Fallschirmjäger Division*. As a consequence of this dangerous development, the few elements of the *9th Volksgrenadiers* that had arrived along with a few troops from the *Führer Grenadier Brigade* were hastily thrown against the Americans in Kaundorf. The piecemeal counterattack broke down with heavy losses — the 26th Division was barely contained on a line stretching southeast of Bastogne from Harlange to Buderscheid. Meanwhile, the 80th Division at Ringel, south of Wiltz, continued to repel the almost daily attacks by Obst. Alois Weber's *79th Volksgrenadier Division* to capture the high ground there. The battle degenerated into a rifleman's standoff.

Relative calm continued to prevail on the German line of the *LXXXV Armeekorps*, although the extreme left wing of the *Seventh Armee* was again attacked by the U.S. 5th Division. The towns of Beaufort and Bigelbach were recaptured with the German infantry forced back across to the North bank of the Sauer. Both divisions of the corps had sustained debilitating reverses; Echternach and all nearby bridgeheads

Tintage, December 27th, 1944. The U.S. 35th Infantry Division on the move in Patton's Third Army.

Hit! Fighter Bombers of the Ninth U.S. Air Force attack a German command post near Houffalize during the Ardennes Campaign

had been lost and the *276th* and *212th* reported casualties amounting to over 30% of their divisional strength. However, losses in the 5th Division had been heavy as well, totalling to over 800 killed and wounded.

Allied air power continued its ruinous assault from the sky. Some 2,770 Allied planes operated over the Western Front against the mere 415 the Luftwaffe was able to muster. On the 27th, the *Sixth Panzer Armee* complained of "heavy enemy air activity while the German air force has not put in an appearance." The Allied air attack had taken a fearful toll on German truck transport capacity. Later that evening von Rundstedt ordered an emergency requisition for 1,000 tons of truck capacity whereupon his quartermaster had to respond that he "did not have any material resources upon which to draw."

The 28th, however, brought a respite for the beleaguered German forces when a blinding snow storm ended the Allied air attack. Even so, Allied air forces had operated on a massive scale on the preceding four days flying nearly 10,000 sorties and claiming 2,323 trucks, 207 tanks, 45 trains and seven bridges.[37] This pummeling was taxing the already

37 Subsequent investigation of air force claims to actual kills by inspection of the U.S. Ordnance Evacuation Companies in the Ardennes showed that claims outnumbered the actual tally by at least ten to one for armor and perhaps two to one for other vehicles.

Improvised German armor. One of six U.S. Sherman tanks captured in Wiltz and them pressed into service in Brandenberger's tankless Seventh Armee. *This one was abandoned in the village of Esch-sur-Súre twelve miles south of its point of capture.*

strained German logistical system. "The progressive destruction of railway lines and train stations as well as road junctions in the Eifel made the supply of goods very difficult," *Heeresgruppe B* reported. "Therefore, certain trains had to be unloaded along the Rhine which were intended for the *Seventh Armee.* Because of the distances, the troops cannot be adequately supplied."

On the 28th a belated attempt by the *246th* and the *12th Volksgrenadier Divisions* to take the Elsenborn Ridge was blown apart by American artillery fire. The divisional commander of the later, Genmaj. Engel, was wounded in the gunfire leading to command changes on the German side. Obst. Langhanghaeser took over the *12th* while command of the *560th Volksgrenadier Division* was transferred to Genmaj. Rudolf Bader, who had just returned from hospitalization.

Further west, the *62nd Volksgrenadiers* at Basse Bodeux turned back an attack by elements of the 82nd Airborne Division. Meantime, the tired *IISS-Panzerkorps* renewed its attack towards Erezée-Mormont led by *Kampfgruppe Krag* and part of the *12th SS Panzer Division.* This final lunge was thrown back by a counterattack by the U.S. 112th Infantry Regiment (28th Division) and the 509th Parachute Infantry Battalion at Briscol-Sadzot. Over a hundred German prisoners were taken. Further north, the *1st SS Panzer Division* had received orders to proceed immediately to the Bastogne area.

The *Fifth Panzer Armee* continued to beat off attacks against the salient around Rochefort. The 83rd Infantry Division had taken over the fight from the regrouping 2nd Armored in the Buissonville sector and was involved in stiff fighting to find a way into Rochefort. Meantime, a final westward German riposte by the *560th Volksgrenadier Division* near Amonines came to nothing; the infantry division was almost totally spent. At Bastogne, the promised *167th Volksgrenadier* and *3rd Panzer Grenadier Division* with its 45 assault guns had still not arrived. Even so, the *Führer Begleit Brigade* and part of the *15th Panzer Grenadier Division* launched another piecemeal attack to sever the 4th Armored corridor which was again turned back.

In the *Seventh Armee*, the attacks on the *5th Fallschirmjäger*

Division diminished although the violence of the attacks on the *Führer Grenadier Brigade* by the 26th Infantry Division greatly increased. The Americans liberated the villages of Nothum, Kaundorf and Bavigne. Only with added rifle strength from Obst. Werner Kolb's *9th Volksgrenadier Division*, did the corps succeed in "preventing threatened enemy penetrations."

In the rest of the *LXXXV* and *LXXX Armeekorps*, the fighting had died down although brisk American artillery fire pummeled the German positions. By the 28th, both the *276th* and *212th Volksgrenadier Divsisions* had withdrawn back across the Sauer River before blowing the Dillingen bridge. Further west, the U.S. III Corps reported slight progress against delaying opposition between the Sauer and Wiltz Rivers. The 35th Division continued its drive on the south flank of the enemy salient near Bastogne in spite of "very heavy fire" near Villers-la-Bonne-Eau. Clearly, the offensive battle for the *Seventh Armee* was over.

Looking over these calamities Genfldm. Model reported to his superiors on December 28th that, "the first phase of the winter battle in the West had ended." Conceding their frustrated plans and recent failure, the commander went on to describe how the Germans might regain the initiative through substitution of the Small Solution": the destruction of the Allied armies east of the Meuse. "For now," Model concluded, "the old objective of Antwerp must be shelved." Von Rundstedt was even more emphatic. "It has become obvious that the long range objective of the plan cannot be reached with the forces at hand." Reading Allied intentions von Rundstedt foresaw that the Americans might thrust "pincers to meet at Houffalize to cut off the entire western portion of the attack salient."

In fact, Eisenhower had expounded precisely this course of action at his meeting that day with Montgomery in Hasselt, Belgium. The Supreme Commander and Gen. Bradley urged the field marshal to turn the U.S. First Army quickly over to the offensive now that the Germans had been turned back. Montgomery protested such a hasty move, however. He told Ike that he anticipated a final desperate German effort on his front. In light of recent events, such a perception could not be completely discounted. However, there was an urgent need to call off the German dogs at Bastogne. Both men agreed that if no major enemy attack in the north had come by the turn of the year, a general First Army offensive was to begin on January 3rd.

On the other side of the fence, December 28th saw even Hitler admit that his offensive had failed. "We have had remarkably bad luck," he told Genmaj. Wolfgang Thomale, his Inspector of Motor Transport.

> Although, unfortunately, the offensive has not resulted in the decisive success which might have been expected, there has been a tremendous easing of the situation. The enemy has had to abandon all his plans for attack. He has been obliged to regroup his forces. He has had to throw in again units which were fatigued. He is severely criticized at home. Already he has had to admit that there is no chance of the war being decided before August. This means a transformation in the situation such as nobody would have believed a fortnight ago.

Hitler proceeded to enunciate the problems which had arisen in the Ardennes Offensive. Of primary importance, he claimed, were "the horrendously bad roads." He blamed the failure of the offensive to unfold on traffic congestion; "a great part of our panzer divisions have not even been committed."

> Only the first wave of the *12th SS Panzer Division's* tanks were in action, whilst behind them there was an enormous convoy jammed solid, so that they could go neither forward or back. Finally, not even petrol could get through. Everything was stationary, and the tanks' engines were merely idling. To keep the men warm the engines were run all night. This created enormous petrol requirements. The roads were bad. They could only use first gear....There was no end to it.

Hitler blamed the traffic congestion partly on his assertion that the panzer divisions were "over-endowed with vehicles." He even claimed that it might be best to de-motorize all infantry.[38] "In this connection," he surmised, "we might learn from the Russians." But other than traffic woes, there was the obvious stubbornness of the Americans defending the Ardennes. He looked at the stand of the 101st Airborne with particular disdain. "Above all," he told his generals pointing to the tiny market town, "we must have Bastogne!"

Moving away from the dreary prospects in the Ardennes, Hitler spoke confidently of his next offensive, code named *Operation 'Nordwind'*, that was to begin to the south of the Ardennes west of Strasbourg on New Year's Day. This blow, Hitler claimed, would encircle Patton's entire army to the south of the Ardennes. "Then," he glowered, "we will see what happens."[39]

38 Hitler was referring to the fact that some of the panzer divisions had more than their establishment of automobiles. However, there existed a severe shortage of the really vital transport vehicles and prime movers: Even before the offensive *9th Panzer* was missing 526 trucks, *2nd Panzer* 333, *116th Panzer* 432 and *10th SS Panzer* 294.

39 Hitler even told his surprised audience on December 28th of a "further blow" after the completion of *Nordwind*. Code-named *Operation 'Zahnarzt'*, the objective of the proposed attack was to be the city of Metz in the Lorraine. Needless to say, *'Zahnarzt'* never got beyond the planning maps.

Forgotten Legions

The U.S. Black Combat Battalions

By the fall of 1944, the manpower cupboard of the American army was almost totally bare. The U.S. Army had been reduced to "stripping" existing U.S. divisions awaiting shipment to Europe in order to obtain rifle replacements. At the same time that the Supreme Commander desperately needed combat infantrymen, Eisenhower was unable to tap the large reserve of "colored" servicemen. The U.S. Army of 1944 was still strapped with a policy of racial segregation. Ike weighed a proposal to offer blacks, serving in segregated service battalions, the opportunity to volunteer for front line combat duty, a course which he approved. However, both Maj. Gen. Bedell Smith, Eisenhower's chief of staff, and Maj. Gen. John C. H. Lee in charge of supply and the communications zone, disapproved of such a radical plan. Faced with a potential flap, their boss acquiesced. To prevent further embarrassment Eisenhower decreed that all available black volunteers continue to go to the existing black combat battalions. Several

Above and below: *German photographers had a field day comparing the features of Black GIs of the 333rd Field Artillery Battalion captured in the Schnee Eifel with the Aryan features of German grenadiers.*

of these "Negro battalions" fought in the Ardennes Campaign.

VIII Corps Artillery

Three black field artillery (FA) battalions were present in the Ardennes on December 16th when the German offensive began. The 333rd Field Artillery Group contained the 333rd Negro FA Battalion (along with the white 587th FA Bn). The 402nd FA Group contained the 578th FA Battalion which was also black. Both battalions were east of the St. Vith area; the 333rd's location proved indeed unfortunate. Headquarters was in Atzerath with its 155mm guns in firing positions just north of Schönberg. As such, the battalion was directly in the wake of the *Fifth Panzer Armee's* planned encirclement of the U.S. 106th Division.

Similarly, the 578th and 969th FA Battalions were billeted in the Burg

Reuland area. This was in the path of the projected advance of the *116th Panzer Division*, but still several miles behind the front line. The men of these battalions had it better than their cohorts since the local Army Rec center was located there. The fall featured miserable damp and freezing weather: "When the wind blew," recalled one gunner, "it made you think you'd forgotten your drawers." Still, life on the Ardennes front line was better than most. There were USO shows, a beer hall, Red Cross girls with coffee and doughnuts and a camp bowling alley to add a bit of civilization to the otherwise spartan accommodations. All the personnel were billeted in abandoned houses or winterized huts. The snowy Ardennes in December of 1944 was "tranquil to a point of almost approaching garrison conditions." A good part of the battalion was even rehearsing for a choral play for the Christmas season.

The quiet Ardennes existence of these men was rudely interrupted on the morning of December 16th by a sharp pre-dawn enemy artillery barrage — a decidedly unusual event. By 11:00 A.M. some forward observers were already under small arms fire. Near the village of Heckuscheid, the commander of the 578th FA Battalion, Lt. Col. Thomas C. Buckley, and several other men fought off German infantry in a sharp gunfight killing at least a dozen of the enemy. Meantime, Buckley's black artillerymen fired 774 rounds that first day against the swarming enemy.

The next day began badly for the 333rd Battalion. At 8:15 A.M. the battalion commander, Lt. Col. Harmon S. Kelsey, headquartered at Schönberg, was shocked to see his emplaced battalion under ground attack by a contingent of the *18th Volksgrenadier Division*. Three of his big howitzers became stuck in the mud. Kelsey quickly ordered the guns abandoned and the men of Battery C and the Service Battery jumped in trucks to cross the Our River at Schönberg. As they approached that town, however, they found themselves faced with German infantry and assault guns. Most of Kelsey's men were captured; only about forty of Battery C and the Serv-

Black artillerymen. The 969th Field Artillery Battalion in action.

Negro troops of the 969st Field Artillery Battalion photographed moving westward out of Bastogne. The battalion received the Distinguished Unit Citation from Patton for its unflinching performance in the battle to hold Bastogne.

ice Battery managed to escape. The 333rd lost seven of its guns that day.

Meantime, the German *SS Kriegsberichter* had a field day with the captured black American POWs. The Nazis had long considered blacks to be physically inferior. The German cameras went to considerable lengths to compare the victorious Aryan German physique with the dejected blacks of the 333rd.

On orders, the rest of the VIII Corps artillery made a dash for the rear to get out of the path of the powerful German attack. On December 18th, the black 969th FA Battalion was assigned to the 333rd FA Group as it motored into Vecmont. At the same time, the 578th FA Battalion ran a gauntlet of German fire from Cherain to Houffalize to reach friendly lines. Then, on December 19th, the 333rd Group was attached to the 101st Airborne Division whose mission it was to defend the crossroads town of Bastogne. By 5:30 P.M. that day, the 333rd arrived at Mande St. Etienne, just west of Bastogne. In tow was the remainder of the 333rd Battalion and the 155mm howitzers of the 969th and the 771st FA Battalions.

That night was one of wild confusion as the Germans cut the main Bastogne-Marche highway. All three battalions began receiving counter-battery and small arms fire; their commander ordered them to displace to safety at St. Hubert. Several guns were abandoned which had become stuck in the mud. However, this action did not suit General McAuliffe of the 101st Airborne. He relieved the commander of the 333rd FA Group for moving the guns without first consulting a superior. Lt. Col. Hubert D. Barnes took over this command and advanced back to former positions by 8:00 P.M. on December 20th to recover the lost guns. As this transpired the Germans continued to tighten the noose on Bastogne.

In action south of the crossroads at Villeroux and Sibret, the three battalions came under intense German attack on December 21st by the *Kampfgruppe Kunkel* of the *26th Volksgrenadier Division*. The white 771st FA Battalion broke and ran in the ensuing battle, losing all its guns in the process and not stopping until it reached Matton, France. In contrast, the two Negro battalions remained in place fencing with the enemy and firing their guns at minimum elevation. The 333rd Battalion lost three howitzers to German tank fire while the 969th lost its motor officer and several enlisted men. On orders from the 101st Airborne, the guns displaced to a position half a mile west of Bastogne. The 333rd now only had three serviceable guns left.

Soon thereafter, the German encirclement was complete and the two black battalions were locked in with the rest of the "battered bastards of Bastogne." Throughout the coming days, both battalions operated as one providing important artillery support for the surrounded garrison. On Christmas Eve, the 333rd suffered another calamity when Luftwaffe bombs struck killing two battery officers and three enlisted men. Then on December 26th when Patton's 4th Armored Division relieved Bastogne, the ambulances of the black 590th Ambulance Company were among the first to reach the wounded in the town. On December 28th, the 333rd Battalion was ordered out of the seige to Matton, France, where most of the remaining VIII Corps artillery was assembling as a reserve. The battalion had lost six officers, 222 men, 9 guns and 34 trucks in the Ardennes fighting. With the scarcity of black replacements, it was April, 1945, before the unit could be built back to strength.

The 969th remained in the Bastogne area until January 12th lending yeoman assistance in the heavy fighting there. The battalion received a citation from Gen. Maxwell D. Taylor of the 101st Airborne Division as well as a Distinguished Unit Citation from Patton himself on February 7, 1945.

The 578th FA Battalion had narrowly missed disaster in its escape from Burg Reuland on December 18th. On December 20th the unit, along with the 402nd FA Group, closed on Mierchamps west of Bastogne eventually reaching the *Forêt du Luchy* near Flohimont. From there, the battalion was to provide support for the 101st Division in the event that the paratroopers were forced to evacuate the town. On December 22nd the battalion was attached to Patton's III Corps reaching firing positions at Nagem north of Arlon. From there, the 12 guns of the battalion provided fire support for the Third Army until December 26th. On Christmas Eve three volleys left the German-held town of Bigonville in ruins; 52 rounds on Christmas Day left German traffic in Boulaide wrecked and burning. On December 29th the

Proud tanker. Sgt. Harold Gray of the all-black 761st Tank Battalion poses with his M3 "Grease gun" machine pistol.

battalion moved to Neunhausen firing both for the 193rd and 203rd FA Groups until January 16th.

The 761st Tank Battalion

The 761st Tank Battalion ended the war with an enviable service record. The only all-black tank battalion, it moved to France on October 16th and was assigned to Patton's Third Army. Patton showed that not only the Germans were racially prejudiced when he complained of the assignment of this "Negro" unit to his command. Patton went so far as to air his racist opinion in his postwar memoirs. Discussing the 761st Tank Battalion he said:

Individually, they were good soldiers, but I expressed my belief at the time (when the battalion joined the Third Army), and have never found the necessity of changing it, that a colored soldier cannot think fast enough to fight in armor.

Regardless of Patton's personal views, he nevertheless challenged the battalion to great effort in combat. On November 2nd the pistol-packing general addressed the black soldiers from atop a half-track near St. Nicolas, France:

Men you are the first Negro tankers to ever fight in the American army. I would never had asked for you if you weren't good. I have nothing but the best in my army. I don't care what color you are as long as you go up there and kill those Kraut sonsabitches. Everyone has their eyes on you and expects great things from you. Most of all your race is looking forward to you. Don't let them down, and damn you, don't let me down!

From the time the battalion was committed to combat on November 7th, the black tankers were in almost constant fighting for a period of 183 days. Its men were determined to set a good performance record, fighting with nearly reckless abandon. In its first action November 7th, its commander Lt. Col. Paul L. Bates was severely wounded. In combat on the next day both the acting commander of the battalion as well as his replacement were both wounded in the fighting.

The 761st experienced very heavy combat throughout November in the Saar region while attached to the 26th Infantry Division. Losses were also heavy; 24 men were killed, and another 81 wounded. Due to the shortage of black replacements, the battalion had to train their new men on the job. Losses in tanks were also very heavy; 14 Shermans were shot out from under the black tankers in November alone. Mechanical failure and enemy action resulted in dwindling strength such that by the time the battalion rolled into Saar Union for maintenance on 15 December, only three of its machines were operational.

The tank battalion moved into the Ardennes beginning on December 24th under the command of Maj. John F. George. Christmas dinner was eaten on the move in Wuisse, France. In transfer the battalion lost ten tanks in the long road march from Saare to Neaufchâteau. One man, Sgt. Robert A. Johnson, was even killed when his tank slipped off the icy roads. Regardless of these travils, by December 31st the battalion reached the south flank of the Bulge and was attached to the relatively inexperienced 87th Infantry Division.

The 761st then fought a series of bitter battles alongside the 345th Infantry Regiment. In terrible weather the black tankers assisted in the recapture of the villages of Rondu and Nimbermont on December 31st. Later, the battalion supported the 347th Regiment in its futile attempt to cut the Bastogne-St. Hubert Road. Heavy German artillery and anti-tank fire stopped the effort on New Year's Day. A similar attempt the following day saw the American infantry repulsed once more leaving four Shermans of the 761st smoking and broken near the *Haies de Tillet* woods. Over the next days, the battalion assisted the 87th Division in taking the towns of Remagne, Bonnerue and Pironpre only to repeatedly lose the later two villages to desperate German counterattacks.

On January 4th, the battalion began five days of fierce combat to capture the approach to the village of Tillet, Belgium and end the see-saw battle to win the St. Hubert road. "I shall never forget Tillet," tanker Eddie MacDonald remembered, "It took us one week to drive the Germans out of that town. They were really dug in. After an hour of fighting we knew we were fighting SS troops." In fact the 761st was facing the elite *Führer Begleit Brigade* — Hitler's fanatically dedicated palace guard. This tough enemy tank brigade waged a grudging defense there in dense pine woods south and east of the town. The Germans had fortified the area, turning the real estate before Tillet into a killing ground. Enemy positions were carefully planned and backed by numerous machine gun nests covered by self-propelled guns and tanks. Two men of the 761st died the first day of the fighting. Another assault on the following day was repulsed with infantry of the 87th Division dying "by the score." The weather was so bad that the battalion trucks could not negociate the sheet ice on the roads; the light tanks of D company moved fuel and ammunition to the medium tanks at the front.

The continuing fight for Tillet reached a climax on January 9th. On this day Capt. Charlie A. Gates launched ten tanks against the German hilltop position after a personal reconnaissance under fire. Then with great personal bravery Gates lead the assault on foot. After five hours of fierce combat, only two tanks and a remnant of the American infantry were still left when they reached their objective. However, a Mk IV tank, a 75mm German assault gun and an 88mm anti-tank gun had been wiped out along with a large number of the enemy killed or captured. Capt. Gates recieved the Silver Star for his gallantry in the action.

But by no means was Gates the only example of bravery that day. Lt. Moses E. Dade had the top of his turret shot off, but still kept fighting. Sgt. Frank C. Cochran's Sherman was hit repeatedly by German anti-tank fire. Asked about his condition he radioed, "They've hit me three times, but I'm still giving them hell." Sgt. "Teddy" Windsor of C Company had his tank shot out from under him killing his driver. But Windsor managed to escape to another tank with William H. McBurney and Leonard J. Smith. However, in the action that followed this Sherman was hit as well, and the men were forced to abandon the tank. Under enemy fire, the three men crawled through the snow for nearly three miles until they safely reached friendly lines.

After this brutal fighting, the Germans finally pulled back to Roumont. The 761st remained with the 87th Division through January 15th of 1945 providing much needed tank support in other successful actions. Later the battalion fought with the 17th Airborne Division in the reconquest of the Bulge at Gouvy, Hautbillain and Wattermal. The tank strength of the battalion plummeted once more both due to enemy action as well as mechanical failure from the hilly terrain, sheet ice and the boggy Ardennes ground. Luckily, the battalion mascot, a rooster named "Cool Stud," came out of the Ardennes no worse for the wear.

The performance of the 761st tank battalion in the ETO was exemplary. By war's end the battalion had won 11 Silver Stars and 69 Bronze Stars, four of the later with clusters and nearly all for deeds of heroism under fire. Finally, in 1978 the 761st received long overdue recognition when it was awarded the Distinguised Presidential Unit Citation by Jimmy Carter.

The Separate Infantry Regiments

Unknown to most of the public, the U.S. forces in summer of 1944 had a terrible problem with "bandits" skimming from their supply columns as they motored across France. These pirates were some 20,000 AWOL American soldiers engaged in a lucrative black market business selling rations, cigarettes, gasoline and even vehicles! Just before the German attack an average of 70 Allied vehicles were being reported as stolen each day! One apprehended soldier had recently shipped home some $36,000 from his criminal exploits. The rear area supply services to the French ports were known as the Communications Zone. Two U.S. separate infantry regiments —the 29th and the 118th had orders in the fall of 1944 to nab this band of entrepreneurial moochers.

By December 17th, knowing that the Meuse crossings might be endan-

gered, Gen. Eisenhower charged the commander of the Communications Zone with the improvised defense of the Meuse River. Of particular concern was the possibility that the Germans might suddenly turn their attack to the scantily defended southern flank of the salient in a repeat of the German attack in 1940 at Sedan. Maj. Gen. John C. Lee assembled a rag-tag force of the separate infantry regiments, some French police units and U.S. engineer general service regiments to check any such move.

The 29th Infantry Regiment

For guarding the particularly critical bridges, Lee ordered the 29th Separate Infantry Regiment to take over the defense. The regiment had long provided demonstration troops for the Infantry School at Ft. Benning, Georgia; recently the regiment had been pursuing GIs turned black marketeers in the Allied rear in France. General Lee ordered the regiment on December 21st to cover all the bridges in Belgium from Namur to Verdun. This, of course, was practically impossible for a single regiment, although platoon and company-sized forces were ordered the same day to the bridges. A small troop was also posted at Jemelle, near Marche, to guard the important radio repeater station there against German

paratroopers and saboteurs. This mission was accomplished and the small contingents of the regiment waited quietly for the appearance of the enemy. The 1st battalion defended the area from Namur to Vireux, the 2nd battalion from Fumay to Sedan and the 3rd battalion from Liège to Huy.

By December 22nd, the German *XLVII Panzerkorps* was threatening Jemelle and the Meuse River line near Dinant. The platoon destroyed the radio equipment as ordered and joined the defense of the village of Rochefort. There they participated in the defense of that town on the night of December 23rd. The German *Panzer Lehr Division* broke their defense, however, and the platoon retired to Givet to join the other forces of the 29th Infantry. As of New Year's Day, the regiment was still defending the Meuse River line from Selessen to Herstal.

The 118th Infantry Regiment

Another separate infantry regiment, the 118th, was partly committed to the Meuse River Defense. The 2nd battalion of the regiment arrived to defend the Meuse River bridge at Givet at 10:30 A.M. on December 24th. Although it was never forced to fight, its participation in the Bulge has never received even the slightest acknow-

On the move. An M4 Sherman of the 761st Tank Battalion in action.

ledgment by military historians.

The Belgian 5th Fusilier Battalion

The Belgian 5th Fusilier Battalion was the first unit of the Belgian army to be formed after the country's liberation in September of 1944. The men of the battalion were a hard nosed lot, mainly former members of the underground resistance who had risked their lives for four years to help topple their Nazi oppressors. The men were equipped with British uniforms and equipment and were attached to the First U.S. Army for special assignments. General Hodges saw to it that the Belgians defended his important forward supply dumps. The 3rd Company of Capt. Jean Burniat drew the assignment to defend a million-gallon stockyard of 5-gallon jerricans in the woods just north of Stavelot along the road to the village Franchorchamps.

On the morning of December 18th it looked as if *Kampfgruppe Peiper*, which was in the process of storming Stavelot, would soon capture the fuel on the ridgeline above the town. To insure this did not take place, the Belgians placed jerricans along a deep cut in the road and set them ablaze. The Belgians then fed the blaze periodically to create a flaming roadblock. Although Peiper and his German panzer group would later be in desperate need of fuel, he had no knowledge of the location of the depot. The conflagation proved unnecessary, however, since Peiper with his eye on the Meuse to the west, had not even sent a light reconnaissance to the north. The story of the flaming roadblock blocking Peiper's capture of the petrol in the cinematic version of *The Battle of the Bulge* was pure fiction. It never took place.

When U.S. reinforcements from the U.S. 30th Infantry Division approached the roadblock from the north, Lt. Col. Robert Frankland, in charge of the 117th Regiment, ordered that the burning cease, since he needed the road himself to attempt to capture Stavelot back from the Germans. The Belgians had burned some 145,000 gallons of petrol. Later that same night, the American infantry was battling in Stavelot to wrest the town

from the Germans; the danger to the fuel depot was averted. The remaining 800,000 gallons were evacuated in the succeeding days by truck from Stavelot.

The French in the Ardennes

Two hundred French paratroopers fought under George Patton's Third Army during the Ardennes Campaign. The French soldiers were from the 16th and 30th Chasseurs Battalions from the 2nd French Parachute Regiment under the command of Maj. Puech-Samson. The unit reported directly to the British Special Air Service. It had carried out duties in central France and for the eight weeks previous to the German attack had been in reserve in Champagne. On December 21st these French soldiers were ordered to "fill the gap" west of Bastogne — an area where almost no Allied units defended against any German attempt to wheel the direction of the offensive to the southwest. The French moved first to Bertrix and then to Libin and Raumont to maintain the link between the arriving U.S. 87th Infantry Division and the British 6th Airborne. On January 10th two of its patrols entered the town of St. Hubert in a surprise raid just as the *Panzer Lehr Division* was moving out.

Other French units were posted along the Meuse River to guard against German access to that river. On December 21st, Brig. Gen. Charles O. Thrasher, commanding the Oise Intermediate Section of the Communications Zone, asked General Preaud, who was in charge of the Saint-Quentin military district, to man the approaches to the Meuse from Givet to Verdun. The French commander immediately moved three provisional. battalions (from Mézières, Beauvais and Chauny) to the Meuse between Givet and Mouzon. These troops came under the command of General Middleton's VIII Corps on Christmas Day. Later, the military govenor of Metz, Gen. Dody, was charged with "setting up between the Sambre and Meuse along the Meuse from·Givet to Commercy, a security screen to guard against enemy thrusts and infiltrations." An additional three battalions were provided.

This motley security force could hardly be considered a military formation. Not only were they missing 40% of their allotted personnel (5 companies per battalion), but had virtually no heavy weapons and inferior side arms — mainly pistols and rifles. Most did not even have uniforms. Gen. Dody remarked that some were "still in civilian clothes, and merely had sky-blue overcoats unrecognized by the Allies." They were suitable only "for traffic control," he concluded, "and were unfit to fight."

The U.S. Parachute Infantry Battalions

The story of the two separate U.S. parachute infantry battalions that fought in the Ardennes is tragic. Not only did these two battalions take horrendous casualties in the fighting in the Bulge, but they were disbanded at its conclusion. With the few survivors parceled out to the 82nd Airborne Division, these two battalions have nearly vanished from history books.

The 509th Parachute Infantry Battalion

The 509th was an elite veteran parachute infantry battalion. It participated in far reaching campaigns in the European Theater from North Africa to Italy and then Southern France. It had been the first U.S. airborne unit to fight in Europe, dropped in the attack on Rommel in North Africa in November 1942. Under the capable command of Maj. Edmund J. Tomasik, the small force of 800 men had been called "the finest parachute unit in the U.S. Army." The paratroopers of the 509th called themselves "gingerbread men" because of the likeness of the emblem on their arm patch.

Orders to move from Epernay, France, to the Ardennes battleground were greeted by something less than enthusiasm from the paratroopers. Since early December the battalion had been enjoying a more civilized existence. Epernay had real feather beds, hot meals, booze (a lucky portion of the troops were billeted near a champagne factory) and a local population which included attractive French "dames." But, on December 21st the orders came. The 509th was to move

Troops of the 509th Parachute Infantry Battalion, supported by an M5A1 light tank of the 7th Armored Division push towards German positions near St. Vith, January 24th, 1945. The proud battalion was disbanded at the end of the Ardennes Campaign. Of the 745 man who had left France for the Ardennes, there were but 54 men left when this photograph was taken.

to Belgium and report to General Ridgway with the XVIII Corps. Destination: Manhay. The drive was foreboding if uneventful. The scuttlebut said that the "krauts" had launched a major attack; they were going to help stop it.

The rumor was true. By December 22nd the 509th Parachute Infantry Battalion along with the 1st Battalion of the 517th Regiment was defending the seven mile area between Soy and Hotton on the north flank of the Bulge. There the battalion beat off repeated attacks by the *2nd SS Panzer Division* which was attempting to push to the north. With little more than side arms and bazookas, the battalion held off the SS tankers. Casualties were heavy.

Later the battalion fought bitter actions at Sadzot, Belgium on December 27 - 28th and participated in the final re-capture of the town of St. Vith from January 13th to the 23rd, 1945. How-

ever, the cost of these engagements was frightful. Only seven officers and 48 men emerged from the Ardennes Campaign of the 745 men that had entered the battle. So heavy were the battalion's losses that it was deactivated on March 1, 1945.

Maj. Tomasik went to the 13th Airborne Division. His handful of survivors were turned over to the 82nd Airborne Division. With this administrative action, the gallant battalion ceased to exist. For its troubles, the battalion was awarded its Second Presidential Citation. However, for the men of the battalion, such an honor did little to assuage the heartbreak of losing the identity of their proud unit.

The 551st Parachute Infantry Battalion

Having successfully participated in the invasion of Southern France in August of 1944, Col. Wood G. Joerg's

551st Parachute Infantry Battalion was a veteran airborne unit by fall of 1944. The men of the battalion considered themselves elite. Their distinctive patch, sporting the acronymn "GOYA" for "Get Off Your Ass," reflected their independent and somewhat irreverent attitude. In mid-December, with the great need for Allied forces to stem the German onslaught, the battalion, like the 509th, found itself earmarked as a reinforcement to Ridgway's XVIII Corps in the Ardennes.

The 551st moved from Laon, France, to Werbomont in the Ardennes by the afternoon of December 21st. It was first attached to the 30th Infantry Division. Initially, the battalion was essayed to help finish off the stubborn *1st SS Panzer Division* in and around Stavelot. However, this mission was cancelled when the German force abandoned its positions north of the Amblève River. On Christmas

Eve, the XVIII Corps reported that the 551st was at hand for its use in the Ardennes battle. Paratrooper Don Garrigues of the 551st remembered their first days in the Bulge as a montage of misery —"no sleep, frozen feet, trench foot, knee deep snow, cold food and hallucinations." His memories of Christmas Eve were equally vivid:

> The attack had been cancelled and we were to move back to an area near Ster. Along with my buddies, I went into one of the houses. Some troopers from another outfit had managed to get some "C" rations and had built a fire under a tub of water in the fireplace of one of the buildings. They offered to share with us so I picked one of the cans out of the hot water. Eating the warm food by the fire and thinking of the mission that had been cancelled, I felt that I had been given one of the best Christmas presents ever.

The next day the battalion reported to the 508th Parachute Infantry Regiment of the 82nd Airborne Division near Basse Bodeux. On December 27th the battalion carried out a night raid against the Oberst Friederich Kittel's *62nd Volksgrenadier Division* taking 18 casualties in the process of securing the tiny hamlet of Noirefontaine. Later, on January 3rd, the battalion participated in the First Army offensive beside the 517th Parachute Infantry Regiment near Basse Bodeaux. The enemy were again the stubborn grenadiers of Kittel's division along with the less than enthusiastic impressed Russians of the *669th Ost Battalion*. Casualties in several days of fighting within the dense forests were heavy. Even so, the battalion captured the villages of St. Jacques and Dairomont from the Germans by January 6th.

On January 7th tragedy struck. The battalion, now down to only 250 men, was to take the village of Rochelinval, Belgium, along the Salm River. The defending enemy was the *183rd Volksgrenadier Regiment* backed up by a flak regiment of 88mm guns and a battalion of 105mm howitzers. The ground was covered with over a foot of snow as Col. Joerg waited for a planned artillery preparation before launching his infantry assault. However, at dawn he learned that the artillery preparation could not be carried out. With this Joerg asked his superiors to delay the attack. It was now daylight and his un-camouflaged men would have to cover half a mile of open ground with little chance of surprise. Their only cover would be their 81mm mortars. However, Joerg's efforts were to no avail and he was forced to order his men into what he called a "suicide attack." Don Garrigues remembers:

> The riflemen charged out of the woods, down the sloping area and across the cleared field. The Germans were fully awake by that time and had taken positions behind a rock fence. They seemed to have a sizeable force, including several machine guns and automatic weapons. Several of our riflemen fell from the hail of enemy bullets. I was firing point blank at a German machine gun and our tracers were crossing. Pascal from Company A was lying beside me feeding the ammunition belt into the machine gun. Soon a burst of bullets tore into his arm and shoulder. He yelled, "I'm hit!" and managed to crawl toward a depressed area behind us while I kept firing. A short time later I felt a jolt like getting hit on the shoulder with a ball bat. At first I though that was it and then I felt the burning pain and blood. I instinctively yelled "Medic!" and began crawling and pulling myself toward the depression or ditch behind me. It wasn't long before a medic came to where I was lying and gave me a shot of morphine.

Although Rochelinval was seized along with 400 German prisoners (200 more were killed or wounded), the cost had been devastating. Of the 840 men of the battalion that entered the Ardennes, scarcely 114 men were left at the end of that day. Tragically, Col. Joerg was killed when an enemy shell exploded in the dense pine trees over his command post early that morning.

On January 8th Maj. W.N. Holm replaced Col. Joerg as commander and the few men of the battalion screened the Salm River crossing at Rochelinval, repulsing a small counterattack by the *18th Volksgrenadiers*. The next day the 98 exhausted survivors of the battalion were relieved of their combat duty, pulling back to Juslenville to regroup.

However, the final blow came not from the Germans, but from the U.S. Army. On February 10th, a directive effectively disbanded the gallant battalion. The remaining few of the proud unit were unceremoniously turned over to the 82nd Airborne Division. With combat records lost and the unit deactivated, the brave 551st has nearly been forgotten in the history of the Ardennes Campaign.

Stalemate: December 29th - 30th

On Friday, December 29th, quiet reigned on the northern Ardennes front in the *LXVII Armeekorps* of the *Fifteenth Armee* and the *LXVI Armeekorps* of the *Sixth Panzer Armee*. The *II SS Panzerkorps* once again attempted to recklessly break through with the *12th SS Panzer Division* at Erezée and the *2nd SS Panzer* at Mormont. But by afternoon the *Hitler Jugend* sent back word that it was "stuck fast south of Erezée in heavy artillery fire." The *2nd SS* and *9th SS Panzer Divisions* were repulsed as well, reporting they "did not penetrate against a tenaciously fighting enemy with strong artillery support." With this, the sector went over to the defensive while the *1st SS Panzer Division* pulled out of the line and marched off to Bastogne.

The *Fifth Panzer Armee* stood on the defensive east of Marche with the *9th Panzer* and *116th Panzer Divisions*. An attack by the U.S. 83rd Infantry Division into Rochefort was thrown back with the greatest difficulty by the *2nd Panzer Division*. So precarious was the German position in the salient that by nightfall the town was ordered to be evacuated.

The British continued to expand their role in denying the Meuse crossings to the Germans by moving up formations. The 53rd and 6th Airborne Divisions crossed the Meuse between Givet and Dinant and in concert with the U.S. 83rd Division relieved the 2nd Armored Division for employment to the east. At the same time, the British 29th Armored Brigade continued patroling the southern German flank along the line between St. Hubert and Rochefort. On the north bank of the Meuse River the 51st "Highland" division maintained battalion strength back-stop defenses between Huy and Liège in case the German attack suddenly regain momentum.

The main focus of the *Fifth Panzer Armee* now reflected Hitler's belated desire to erase the American presence at Bastogne. But continuing transportation problems and Allied air power plagued the German assembly of a sufficient attack force. Genfldm. Model could already see the slip from cup to lip on the 29th when he ordered the operation postponed since the *167th Volksgrenadier* and *1st SS Panzer Divisions* were not yet fully assembled. The field marshal did decide to alter the command structure to get things moving, however. The *XXXIX Panzerkorps* was subordinated to Heinrich von Lüttwitz of *XLVII Panzerkorps*. Lüttwitz had developed something of a reputation for getting things done on the Ardennes battlefield. For his efforts, the monocled panzer leader received temporary command of an ad hoc force elevated to the lofty status of *Armeegruppe von Lüttwitz*.

While the Germans schemed, Patton forged ahead with his own offensive plans. Maj. Gen. Charles S. Kilburn's 11th Armored Division launched an attack on Chenogne, southwest of Bastogne, but was eventually forced back. To the east of the hotly contested town, the 35th Infantry Division captured Villers-la-Bonne-Eau. However, the German defense by troops from the *5th Fallschirmjäger* was resolute; they stood their ground on the line Lutrebois-Bavigne with bitter fighting in the vicinity of Harlange. The rest of the sector to Echternach was quiet. To the east, the *Führer Grenadier Brigade* was in the process of being relieved by the *9th Volksgrenadier Division*. The 26th Infantry Division, was still attacking north for Wiltz, but finding the German resistance more difficult as the assault progressed. A counterattack at dark by the German infantry recaptured Nothum and Roullingen throwing the American assault into confusion.

As the German armored forces shifted southward, they found their movement hampered by fuel shortages, deep snow and sub-zero weather. With the return of clear, sunny weather in the afternoon the Allied air forces were again out in strength. A total of 2,600 aircraft were aloft. Against this

Pass the ammunition. Panther of the 2nd SS Panzer Division, *taking on armor-piercing rounds, December, 1944.*

Traffic desert. The village of St. Vith looks more like a lunar landscape than a Belgian town after a nearly constant bombardment by the U.S. and British air forces. The aerial photograph was snapped on January 24th.

imposing total, the Luftwaffe was able to muster only 130 fighters. Noting the extensive damage to the rail resupply stations at Euskirchen, Düsseldorf, Koblenz and Remagen, *OB West*, reported a "further battering of all rearward communications" and "the attempt by the enemy to create a 'traffic desert' in the entire rear area behind *Heeresgruppe B* and *G*." Even nighttime was not safe: on the previous evening 380 Allied medium bombers attacked road centers in the Ardennes under cover of darkness. Only 35 German night-fighters had been scrambled to oppose them. On the 29th *OB West* gloomily recorded "a substantial strain on supply" adding that the "severity of the effects of the enemy air force could now definitely be compared with that of Normandy."[40]

Later that evening Gen. Heinz Guderian, in charge of the Eastern Front, called on Hitler and warned him that the Russian winter offensive was drawing near. In view of the state of the German forces there — he described them as "a house of cards" — he argued vehemently that the Ardennes offensive be broken off at once so that "everything could be thrown to the East." However, he could not convince Hitler who persisted in discounting the Russian threat. Re-

40 Remarkably, the *OB West* diary for December 29th records that despite the existing Allied air activity 2,622 military trains had operated in the *Heeresgruppe B* combat zone during the month.

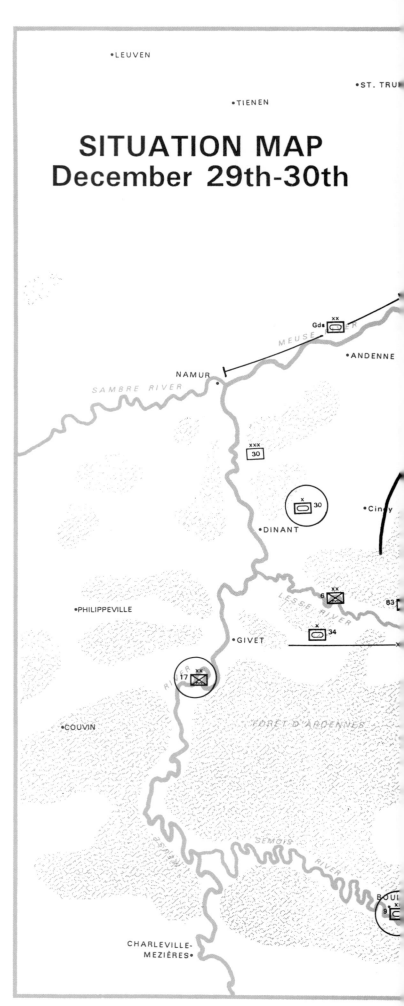

SITUATION MAP
December 29th-30th

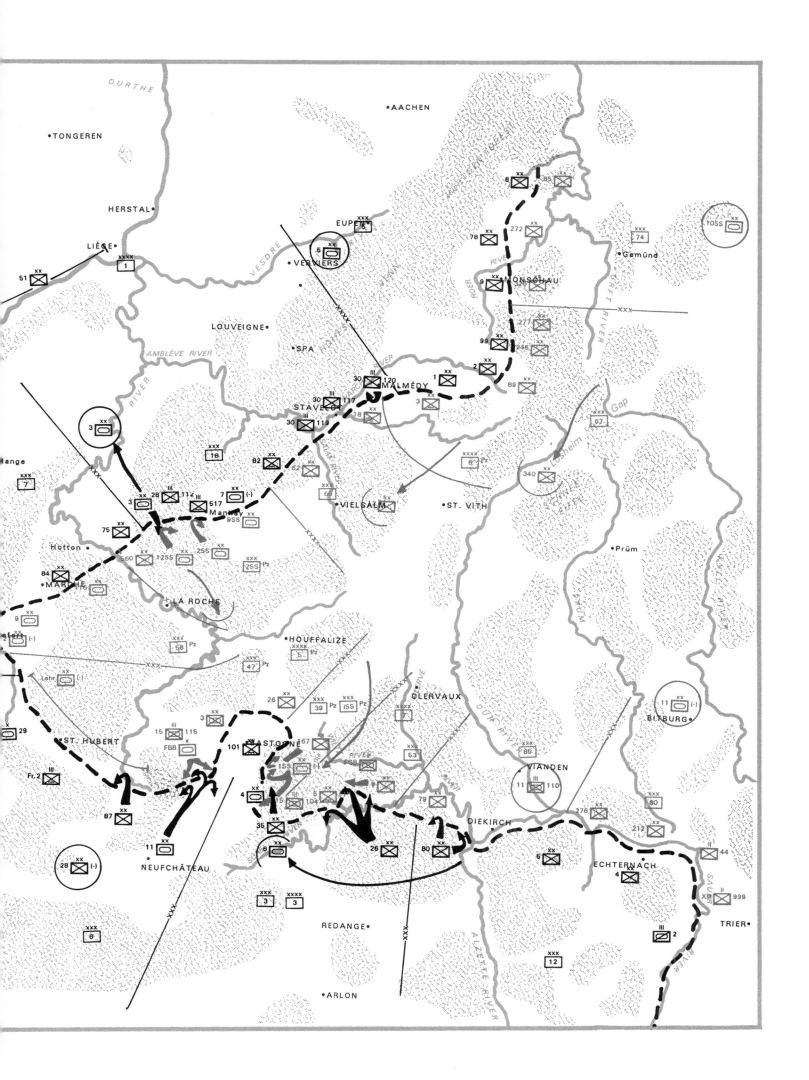

membering his soldiering days, Hitler, who was obsessed with the notion of history repeating itself, compared the relative inaction there to the situation in World War I following the treaty of Brest-Litovsk which had left Hindenberg and Ludendorff free to turn their attention to France in 1918. Hitler brushed aside Guderian's facts and figures; *Wacht am Rhein* was to continue.

Scavenging for forces with which to carry out his master's "clear Bastogne" directive, von Rundstedt again appealed for a free hand with two available mobile formations in reserve: the *11th* and *10th SS Panzer Divisions*. This Hitler refused once more, stating that they were "planned for other tasks." He and Model would have to make do with the tired troops they already possessed.

December 30th brought on isolated American attacks on the northern flank of the Ardennes front. The *18th Volksgrenadier Division* which had recently taken over the positions of the *1st SS Panzer* along the Amblève repulsed another two raids by the 99th Infantry Battalion near Malmédy. In the *LXVII Armeekorps*, the *12th Volksgrenadier Division* was relieved by a new arrival, Genmaj. Walter Bruns's *89th Infanterie Division*. This two-regiment formation was so fought out, however, that it was only capable of defense. In the switch-off the *12th Volksgrenadier* was to be used to relieve the *9th SS* and *12th SS Panzer Divisions* so

Gen. d. Pztrp Heinrich von Lüttwitz. The monocled German leader controlled the XLVIII Panzerkorps and his own ad hoc provisional field army in the Ardennes.

Tired grenadiers. German soldiers of the Panzer Lehr Division fighting to hold onto the tip of the Bulge near Rochefort.

that they could be moved to the developing battle at Bastogne. Similarly, the *2nd SS Panzer Division* relieved the *560th Volksgrenadiers* so that the later could be sent to the endangered German sector along the Salm River.

Meantime, at the tip of the Bulge, the U.S. 83rd Infantry Division attacked the *9th Panzer Division* with a vengeance, forcing the German troops back to the L'Homme River at Jemeppe. Nearby, *Panzer Lehr* was finally forced to relinquish the town of Rochefort.[41]

But the decisive action of the day for both opponents was waged at Bastogne. Before that town, *Armeegruppe von Lüttwitz* punctually opened the German attack at 6:25 A.M. with a sharp artillery barrage from 321 guns and 306 *werfers*. Ushered in by this introduction, the tanks and half-tracks of the *Führer Begleit Brigade* and the *3rd and 15th Panzer Grenadier Divisions* clanked west towards Sibret while Genlt. Hans-Kurt Höcker's *167th Volksgrenadiers* and the *1st SS Panzer Division* cut from the East towards the Bastogne-Arlon road.[42] According to the German stratagem, the pincers would come together south of the town. By 2:10 P.M. Genfldm. Model was able to report that ground had been gained, but that the western attack was not progressing according to plan.

During the night of December 29-30th what serviceable armor the *1st SS Panzer* still possessed had clanked up the Tarchamps- Lutremange road to deliver the eastern German assault. At dawn half the panzers turned south, piercing Villers-la-Bonne-Eau and surrounding two companies of the 35th Infantry Division. Isolated the Americans there would eventually be forced to surrender. The other group of German tanks thrust northwest and near Lutrebois became inextricably drawn into a scrambling melee with U.S. infantry, tanks, tank destroyers and Allied fighter bombers. Although the German panzers were able to reach Losange, within a few hundred yards of the critical Bastogne-Arlon

41 Reported operational armored strength for the German panzer formations at the tip of the Bulge on December 30th: *116th Panzer* 28, *9th Panzer* 75, *2nd Panzer* 63 and *Panzer Lehr* 100.
42 The armored strengths of the German formations involved on December 30th were: *Führer Begleit Brigade* 51, *3rd Panzer Grenadier Division* 41, *15th Panzer Grenadier Division* 48, *1st SS Panzer Division* 58.

road, they could get no further and took heavy losses. Another German effort by the *167th Volksgrenadiers* just to the north was actually able to reach the highway before being "cut to pieces" and forced back by half-tracks from the 4th Armored Division.

Meanwhile, southwest of Bastogne, the new U.S. 11th Armored went directly from a road march into its first battle at 7:30 A.M. pushing northeast with the 87th Division on its left. The assault of Task Force Poker ran head on into the more experienced *Führer Begleit Brigade*. Cloaked in mist, the opposing armored columns stumbled onto each other in an extremely confused meeting engagement in the vicinity of Lavaselle. Task Force Pat was ambushed by Remer's tanks, losing seven Shermans before withdrawing.

The American attack had gone nowhere and resulted in many casualties among the green GI tankers (the 11th Armored lost over 600 men and 54 tanks in four days of fighting). Regardless, this monkey wrench threw off German plans as well. By nightfall, the western German attack group had been forced to halt their advance towards Sibret to face the approaching 11th Armored Division between Morhet and Hatrival. Fearing disaster, the commander of the German armored brigade radioed for help from the neighboring *3rd Panzer Grenadier Division*. Patton believed this meeting engagement was fortuitous: "...had we not hit the flank of the Germans they might have again closed the corridor into Bastogne."

To the west, the other part of the planned American attack, Maj. Gen. Frank Culin's U.S. 87th Infantry advanced into battle after a rapid march to their assemby points between Bertrix and Libramont. A portion of the 11th Armored was assigned to add mettle to the infantry attack. The division captured the villages of Moricy and Remagne between Bastogne and St. Hubert only to be forced back out by a determined counterattack by the *Panzer Lehr Division*. The Germans claimed ten U.S. tanks destroyed from Task Force White of CCA of the 11th Armored. A similar attempt to take Morhet by another combat team of the 11th was repelled in "bitter fighting" by a battlegroup of the *15th Panzer Grenadier Division* near Rechrival. Casualties were heavy.

Air attack. This Panzer IV of the 7th Kompanie *of the* 1st SS Panzer Division *was caught in the open near Lutrebois by American fighter-bombers on December 30th.*

December 31, 1944. Halftracks of the 11th Armored Division mass on the outskirts of Bastogne.

Meanwhile, the German *LIII Armeekorps* was involved in heavy defensive fighting against attacks by the 26th Infantry Division which had orders to take Wiltz. Fierce fighting was reported south of the village of Harlange and a tank led thrust from Nothum was only stopped by a desperate counterattack from the *9th Volksgrenadiers*. Just to the south the tired divisions of the *LXXXV Korps* fought off attempts by the U.S. 80th Division to gain a bridgehead at Ettelbruck. In this sector, both sides had literally fought each other to a standstill.

At the same time, the American commanders still worried about the threat of a German turn south toward Sedan as they had done in 1940. The southern part of the Ardennes salient was very lightly defended. In deference to this concern, the battered 9th Armored Division was ordered back to the Meuse River to reorganize and function as SHAEF reserve to be available in this area.

With "misty and gloomy" weather, the Allied air forces were less active over the battle front, although the bomber sorties continued to operate in strength against the German lines of communication to the rear, particularly south of the Ardennes. *OB West* surmised that "relief of the transportation and supply situation cannot be expected in the near future." Meanwhile, however, the Luftwaffe struck back. In all, 147 German planes were essayed to intervene in the Ardennes battle, including 32 jet aircraft. As with many of these Luftwaffe sorties before, most German flights were intercepted long before they crossed the Rhine. However, on the night of December 30-31st, the Germans struck Bas-

Scene of destruction. Blankets cover bodies of U.S. soldiers killed in Bastogne during one of the nightly Luftwaffe bombing raids on the town, December 29th, 1944.

togne in a 73-plane bombing attack on the town, designed to pave the way for a coming ground assault. A smaller raid hit Neufchâteau. Describing the mission over Bastogne, *Jagdkorps II* reported "good aiming of bombs at the middle of the target — entire town covered." The claim was accurate; the air raid killed many civilians. In the town of Bastogne, fires raged out of control throughout the night.

Offensives Collide:
December 31st - January 1, 1945

As 1945 arrived German and American attacks crashed into each other with great violence around Bastogne. The plan for the U.S. III Corps seemed simple enough: Maj. Gen. Robert W. Grow's 6th Armored Division would move through Gaffey's tired 4th Armored (now down to only 42 tanks) and drive northeast out of the Bastogne corridor with the 35th and 26th Infantry Divisions joining the armor on the right. Naturally, Patton was unwilling to let the German attack the previous day stop his party. Task Force Brown (Lt. Col. Charles E. Brown) of Combat Command A of the 6th Armored, drove to the town of Neffe, east of Bastogne, while another column punched through towards Wardin although slowed by snow squalls, treacherous roads and increasing enemy fire.

On the German side of the fence, the battle was no longer a great offensive pointed at the port of Antwerp; it had dissolved into Hitler's personal vendetta against the small market town of Bastogne. *Heeresgruppe B* in its end of the year assessment noted the swing in the balance of military force. The Allies had brought up 25 new divisions at this point with 38 divisions now in the Ardennes. Model characterized the German situation as a "transition to the defensive on the whole Ardennes front." The prospect of future offensive operations, Model and von Rundstedt agreed, rested with the outcome of the conflict of *Kampfraum Bastogne*.

The fighting around the contested road nexus continued unabated. Once again on the night of December 30-31, the eastern German attack group with the *1st SS Panzer Division* and the *167th Volksgrenadier Division* launched a strong assault against the "neck" of the American salient at Bastogne. By noon of the following day, *Heeresgruppe B* had received the unwelcome news that although the attack had recaptured Villers-la-Bonne-Eau, it had otherwise "been able to gain very little ground." Von Rundstedt ventured that the German forces were inadequate in light of the difficult objectives noting "bitter enemy resistance" and "continual counterattacks." To make up this deficiency the German force essayed to coup Bastogne was to be reinforced by the *340th Volksgrenadier, 9th SS* and *12th SS Panzer Divisions*.

West of Bastogne, elements of the U.S. 87th Infantry Division seized Remagne and closed on the hamlet of Moircy. The newly arrived 11th Armored Division experienced a terrible baptism of fire in its advance on Pinsamont and Chenogne. It was a dark day for Gen. Kilburn's 11th Armored; more men were lost on the 31st than on any single

A rare photograph of Hitler taken during the Ardennes Campaign on January 1st, 1945. The German leader is intently studying a map discussing the plan for Operation Bodenplatte *the German attack on Allied airfields. Reichsmarschall Göring if on his right; Gen. Guderian on the left.*

day of the war. By January 3rd the division's casualties reflected a bitter accounting: 661 men killed, wounded or missing and 53 tanks shot up and broken.

Southeast of Bastogne, the U.S. 35th Infantry Division was unable to relieve their isolated forces in Villers-la-Bonne-Eau and they were given up as lost. Nearby, between Buderscheid and Bavigne, the 26th Infantry helped to repel a counterattack of the *9th Volksgrenadier Division* while the III Corps artillery placed Time on Target (TOT) barrages on the German held town of Wiltz.

On the north side of the Bulge in Collin's VII Corps, the 3rd Armored Division shuffled east to assemble for the planned counterattack towards Houffalize along the Bastogne-Liège highway. The British 53rd "Welsh" Division

Snow capes. Sporting winter camouflage, member of the U.S. 5th Infantry Division in action near Haller on January 1st, 1945

now held the front between Aye and Hotton; the 6th Airborne on the right from Dinant to Aye. The 51st "Highland" and Maj. Gen. A.H.S. Adair's Guards Armored Division were maintained in XXX Corps reserve.

The U.S. First Army made strenuous efforts to bring its units back up to strength. Artillery losses incurred up to the end of the month were hastily replaced with weapons in transit. Armored units had lost more than 230 tanks during the initial blow of the enemy counteroffensive. All tank deficiencies were repaired or replaced by extraordinary effort on the part of the U.S. ordnance service — in a single day one heavy maintenance company had repaired and delivered 48 tanks to front line fighting units. Meanwhile, scarce manpower replacements were fed into the understrength U.S. infantry regiment over the following week.

Overhead, the weather was clear and sunny again bringing back the contest for the airspace above the Ardennes. The Allies dominated with 3,550 aircraft aloft; some 1,200 of these were fighter bomber sorties over the battlefield and west of the Rhine. Against these numbers the Luftwaffe could only provide a mere 550 planes. Göring ordered that planes and fuel be conserved for the "Big Blow" he was about to unleash. It was the largest and costliest single Luftwaffe operation of the entire war.

And as if to underscore the desperation of the Nazi situation, at precisely midnight as 1945 began, Adolf Hitler went on the air to address the German people. Despite a long absence from public oratory, the Führer's dark New Year's Day message was heard clearly over the airwaves throughout Europe:

> Our people are resolved to fight the war to victory under any and all circumstances....We are going to destroy anyone who does not take part in the common effort for the country or makes himself a tool for the enemy....The world must know that this State will, therefore, never capitulate....Germany will rise like a phoenix from its ruined cities and will go down in history as the miracle of the 20th Century! I want,

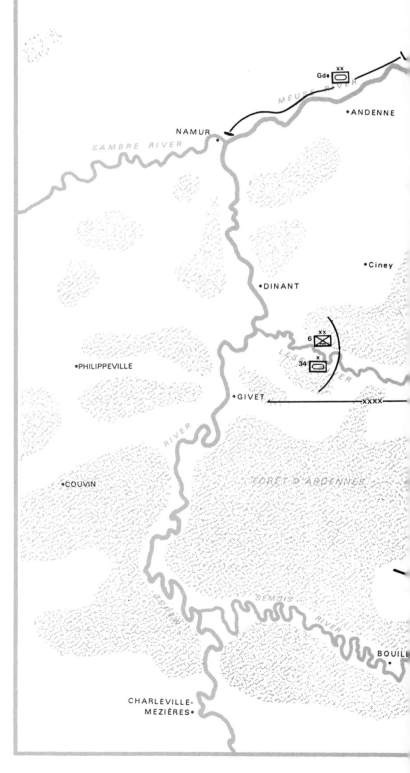

SITUATION MAP
December 31st-January 1s

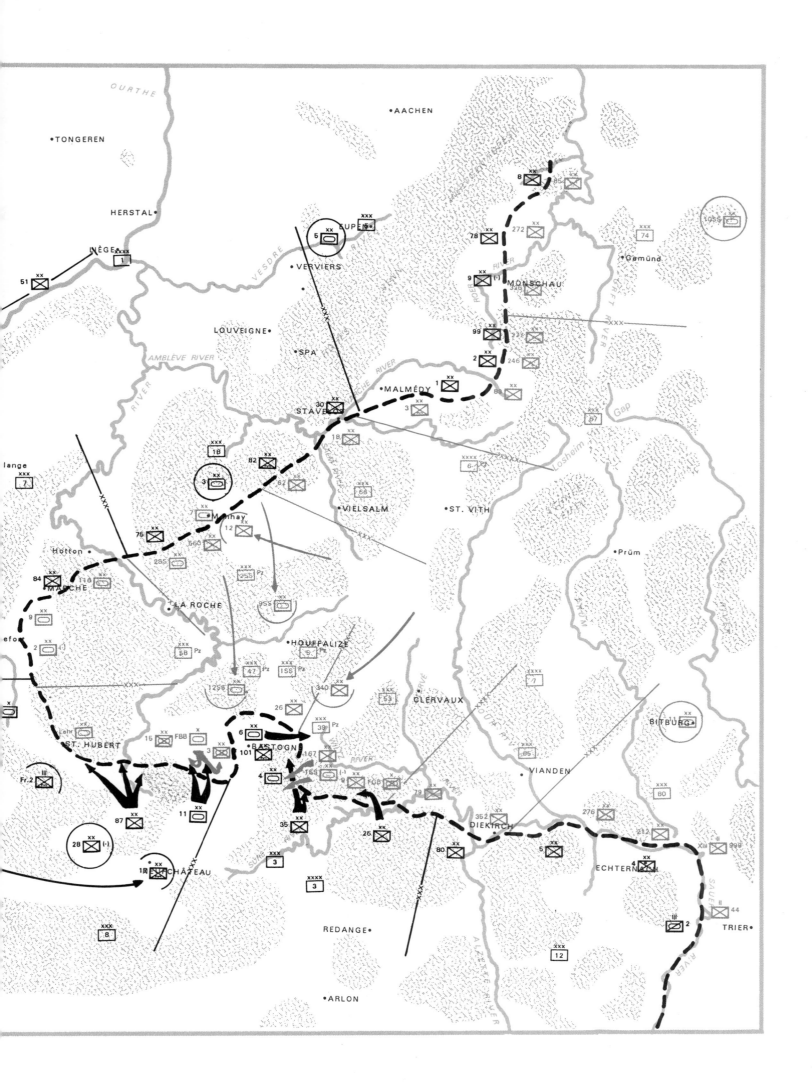

therefore, in this hour, as spokesman of Greater Germany, to promise solemnly to the Almighty that we shall fulfill our duty faithfully and unshakably in the New Year, in the firm belief that the hour will strike when victory will ultimately come to him who is most worthy of it, the Greater German Reich.

But Monday, January 1st, saw little change on the relatively inactive northern Ardennes front of *Heeresgruppe B*. American attacks against the southern flank of the German salient only compelled the *3rd Panzer Grenadier* and *26th Volksgrenadier Division* to make minor territorial concessions between Pironpré and Chenogne. Undaunted by the previous failure, Model readied a new German attack at Bastogne. The *ISS Panzerkorps* headquarters had arrived, but the *12th SS Panzer* and *340th Volksgrenadier Divisions* were still in transit.

To herald in New Year's Day, Patton ordered rapid fire at midnight for twenty minutes from every gun in the Third Army on the enemy positions. At the end of the barrage the forward observers reported they could hear the Germans screaming in the woods. Later that day, the U.S. 6th Armored captured the long-contested town of Magaret only to lose it once more to a German counterattack. Nowhere else in III Corps could Patton find events to cheer him. Attempting to recapture the area around Marvie and Villers-la-Bonne Eau, the 35th Division engaged in a ferocious battle with the *1st SS Panzer Division* that dragged on inconclusively for days.

The 4th Armored Division continued to defend the Bastogne corridor against unremitting German assaults. Similarly, the 26th Infantry, with a mission to clear the Wiltz-Bastogne highway, found the fresh *9th Volksgrenadier Division* an able and deadly opponent. West of Bastogne, the small gains of the 87th Infantry to the village of Jenneville had to be measured against the heavy casualties suffered by the division. Similarly, the 11th Armored slugged it out with the Germans in Chenogne in terrible fighting to capture the ruins of that village. Near Neufchâteau, the newly arrived 17th Airborne Division assembled to support the Bastogne battle.

To the south of the Ardennes, *Operation Nordwind* opened with several German division-sized attacks in the Alsace. Although much smaller than *Wacht am Rhein*, this new German offensive compounded Eisenhower's manpower problem in the Ardennes, endangering the city of Strasbourg and nearly lead to the French leaving the Allied fold.

However, undoubtedly, the big German event on New Year's Day was the final major Luftwaffe effort of the war — *Operation Bodenplatte* (Ground Slam). In the early morning hours of the new year, *Jagdkorps II* began a carefully prepared attack on Allied airfields in Southern Holland and Belgium. The idea was that such an attack would destroy many Allied aircraft and secure some relief for the ground troops by means of at least a temporary reduction of the Allied aircraft availability.

All told, 1,035 German planes flew in the operation divided evenly between Messerschmitt 109s and Focke Wulf 190s. In what became known as the "hang-over raid," the Germans destroyed around 280 Allied aircraft on the ground damaging another 100 and shot down 80 enemy machines in aerial combat. Even Montgomery's personal C-47 Dakota was destroyed on the Brussels-Melsbroek airfield. German Luftwaffe losses were very heavy, however. Three hundred machines were lost including 170 pilots killed and another 67 taken prisoner. The operation was so costly that there could be no question of a repetition. Even worse, the long-term weakening of the Allied air forces was not achieved.

The British and Americans could make good their plane losses in a matter of weeks; the German machines destroyed and the fuel they burned was irreplaceable. Worst of all, the Germans lost more of their trained aircrew than did their enemy. Gen. Lt. Adolf Galland, the inspector of the Fighter Forces summarized the operation: "In this total effort, we sacrificed our last substance."

Upper right: *German fighters. Me-109Gs of* Jagdgeschwader 27 *scramble into the air.*

Upper left: *Aftermath. The results of* Operation Bodenplatte *at Eindhoven air field. British planes of the 2nd Tactical Air Force burn after being bombed and strafed on the ground.*

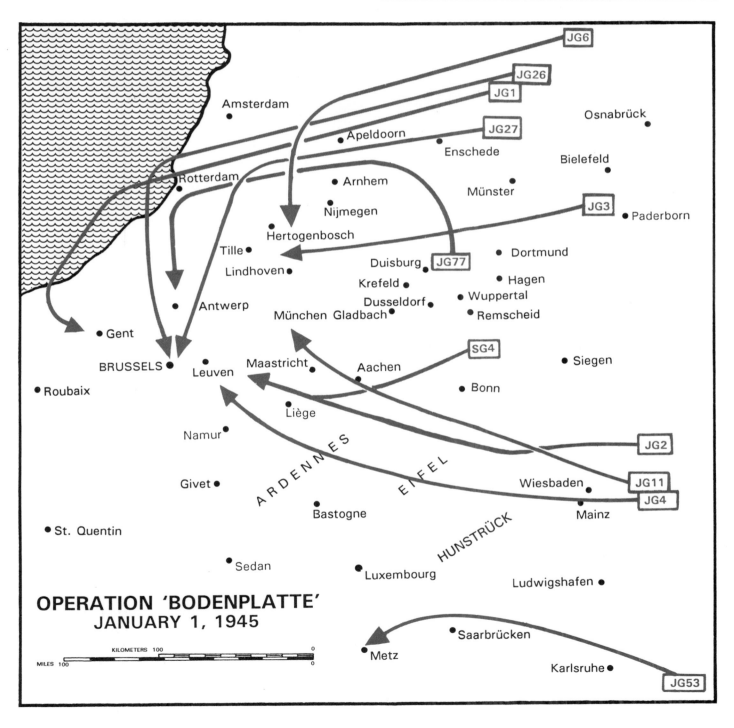

OPERATION 'BODENPLATTE'
JANUARY 1, 1945

The Tigers of Winter

Reports from most American units during the turbulent days of December 1944 told of "Tiger tanks" in almost every sector of the Ardennes battlefield. A casual reading of American accounts indicated that at least half of the German tanks employed in the Ardennes were the feared Tigers. Even the U.S. official history estimated that no fewer than 250 Tigers were employed in the German offensive.

Such estimates grossly overestimate the number of Tigers that the Germans were actually able to employ in the battle. A careful tally shows that no more than 136 of these beasts were ever committed to *Wacht am Rhein*. The operational number actually reaching the battlefield was still less: only 87 armored vehicles. So why the great disparity between the U.S. estimates and the actual numbers of Tigers employed?

American soldiers were generally unfamiliar with German tanks in the fall of 1944. Any armored vehicle with tracks and a long gun was a Tiger to most GIs. This was true even of American tankers and tank destroyers! This state of affairs came about for a number of reasons. Most American soldiers had never confronted Nazi tanks, and when faced by a 50-ton killing machine, most were not too concerned with proper model identification. Too, the Germans used a plethora of different types of tanks, assault guns and tank destroyers, increasing the confusion. Anything that was larger than a U.S. M-4 Sherman was called a Tiger. But research has documented that even smaller German assault guns (Jagdpanzer IV, Sturmgeschütz and Jagdpanzer 38t) were often called Tigers in American after action-reports. The heavier Panthers and Jagdpanthers were almost always called Tigers.

Of course, there was some basis for this Tiger-phobia. The German Tiger tank was certainly one of the more respected weapons of the war. At over 55 tons and four inches of frontal armor in the Ausf E (and 70 tons and six

Armored beasts. A white-washed M4A1 Sherman tank stands beside one of Peiper's Königstiger Mk VIb panzers in Spa, 1945.

inches of armor in the *Königstiger*), it was the most heavily protected tank in the entire war. Its 88mm cannon had already developed a infamous reputation with Rommel in North Africa. It could engage and knock out Allied tanks at a distance of almost two miles. With its 700 horsepower Maybach engine, such a heavy beast could move at an impressive rate of 24 mph and its wide tracks made the Tiger more maneuverable than one might expect.

However, the German attitude towards the Tigers was generally less complimentary than the Allied opinion. Of course, Hitler had once remarked that "each battalion is worth an entire panzer division." But, his conviction can readily be discounted in light of that of experienced panzer leaders.

Although it had been conceived as a breakthrough tank, the Tiger was never able to live up to that role. It was not suited to the rapid mechanized battle that was envisioned by the German planners for the Ardennes Offensive. The Tiger fought best when on a defensive footing or in attack on static enemy positions. Then too, the blocked nature of the terrain in the heavily wooded Ardennes made long-range engagements unlikely where the

88mm gun could be used to best advantage. Most tank-to-tank engagements in the Bulge were rather like High Noon gun fights at close range. The faster traverse of the turret made the American Sherman more likely to get in the first shot. Even here, however, in a frontal engagement, the Sherman stood little chance. Only a flank shot of the Sherman's poor gun could penetrate the armor of a Mk VI. In one verified case, fourteen direct hits from a Sherman bounced harmlessly off a Tiger. An improvised Allied solution was to plaster the behemoths with artillery. This often was enough to send them running or else cripple them so that a Sherman or tank destroyer could maneuver around them to hole them from the side. However, unless the turret of such a Tiger was immobilized, this tactic might cost a Sherman or two.

The 70 ton weight of the Tiger II was also a distinct disadvantage in the Ardennes. Rivers and creeks were common in the dark forest and the frail bridges over them would often not carry the great weight of a Tiger or Panther. The certainty with which U.S. engineers blew the few good bridges and the paucity of German heavy bridging equipment made this even more a problem. Their somewhat slower speed and short range made it difficult to keep the tanks in the fighting. The Tiger II was especially fuel thirsty; the tank got only half a mile to a gallon of gasoline (the light U.S. Sherman tank got twice the mileage). This resulted in a range of only 90 miles on the best roads in good weather. The muddy tracks and hilly terrain in the Ardennes served to cut this figure by half.

Then too, in spite of Henschel's engineering efforts, certain faults in the machine itself remained. There were many field breakdowns of the Tigers (it had over 26,000 parts) and easily mired in the soft Ardennes soil. The great weight of the monsters made them notoriously difficult to retrieve. As example, on 10 December, the *501st SS Heavy Panzer Battalion* had all 15 of its machines down for maintenance; on December 17th only 8 out of 30 of the Tigers in the *506th Heavy Panzer Battalion* were combat ready. Part of this problem was arising from internal sabotage at the production facilities. Many Tigers had "installed defects," an implicit danger resulting from the use of impressed foreign labor in the tank factories.

Beyond its troublesome maintenance, the Tiger itself was a fickle machine. In the hands of an experienced crew, it was deadly armored vehicle — more than a match for any other. However, many of the Tiger veterans, such as Michael Wittmann, were dead or captured (Wittmann had destroyed 119 tanks in Russia and two dozen in Normandy). Replacements were hand picked from volunteers. There was always a large number of these, since service with the Tigers was something of an honor in the German Army. However, the high esprit d' corps of these new members could not make up for their lesser experience; performance in the Ardennes was uneven.

Regardless of these problems, one advantage did help to outweigh the others. The typical American soldier greatly feared the Tiger. This was particularly true for the U.S. tankers. An anonymous gunner for the 2nd Armored Division told a reporter that: "The Sherman gun is ineffective. The crews know it, and it affects their morale." In one case an American tank

German King Tiger tanks of a Heavy Panzer Battalion lined up for review, 1944.

commander refused to order his Shermans to take on advancing Tigers for fear that he would be disobeyed. The individual American rifleman knew that a bazooka had to hit a Mk IV or Panther "just right" to knock them out. Of course, the Tigers presented an even greater problem. A flank shot at close range was the only sure course and this could be exceedingly dangerous since other tanks or German panzer grenadiers were likely to be lurking about. In general, all American soldiers had a similar way of coping with the German Tigers: avoid them.

501st SS s. Panzer Battalion

The *501st SS Heavy Panzer Battalion* under SS Obersturmbannführer Heinz von Westerhagen was the most famous of the German Tiger units in the Bulge. Perhaps the most famous Bulge photo is that of Tiger '222,' photographed at the Kaiserbaracke crossroads on December 18th while moving with the *1SS Panzer Division*. The allotment of the panzer battalion showed an assigned strength of 45 Königstigers, although only 30 were on hand on December 17th.

Half a dozen accompanied *Kampfgruppe Peiper* in his thrust to La Gleize. In the movie, *The Battle of the Bulge*, the German panzer spearhead commander, Colonel Hessler, was de-

lighted by the assignment of Tigers to his command. The real-life Hessler, SS Ostbf. Joachim Peiper, was less than enamored with the heavy tanks. He considered them "too slow" and too heavy for the lightning advance he had planned. Peiper placed them to the rear of his column. According to the commander of the *3rd Kompanie*, SS Hptsf. Heinz Birschein, "the battalion had the mission to drive behind the first battalion [*Kampfgruppe Peiper*], and after we came out of the hilly terrain, we were to drive ahead to the Meuse River."

The three companies of Tigers followed in the wake of *Kampfgruppe Peiper*. Most of the thirty Tigers moved directly behind Peiper from Honsfeld to Ligneuville and Stavelot. However, a number of tanks had just been repaired, and those leaving the workshop managed to take a wrong turn lumbering through Heppenbach and then Born. These tanks moved with *Kampfgruppe Hansen* where they were photographed at the Kaiserbaracke crossroads north of St. Vith.

On December 18th the ten Tigers of Hptsf. Rolf Möbious' *2nd Kompanie* crossed the Amblève River with the intention of joining the lead battlegroup. Several were subjected to strafing attack from Allied aircraft. The heavy panzers were undamaged although a number of the German paratroopers who were clinging to their decks were wounded. However, the following *1st Kompanie* found their passage through Stavelot blocked by the riflemen of of the U.S. 30th Infantry Division.

Tiger 105 the mount of the commander of the *1st Kompanie*, Jürgen Wessel, was hit by an American rifle grenade on the gun mantlet as it moved through the village of Stavelot. Ordered to pull back along the steep and narrow street, the driver, who had no field of vision, sent the vehicle crashing into a house where it was buried by the wreckage. Wessel was one of the more experienced Tiger crewmen, having served with Michael Wittmann both in Russia and Normandy. Not to be put out of the battle, Wessel joined the panzer of SS Oberscharführer Jürgen Brand, staying in Stavelot for the night.

The following morning, Brand in Tiger 131 followed by Tiger 133 moved to the west to join *Kampfgruppe Knittel* and the *1st SS Panzer Reconnaissance Battalion* although the battle with the Americans in the village continued unabated. Later that day, Knittel became concerned that the Americans were trying to recapture Stavelot and ordered Brand and his two Tigers to check out the situation there. Pushing east, Brand was stopped by a daisy-chain of mines across the road leading to Stavelot. Returning to Knittel's command post, he was forced to report that the Americans were indeed back in possession of the town. The Germans of *Kampfgruppe Peiper* and *Kampfgruppe Knittel* were trapped.

Blocked from entry to Stavelot, the two Tigers moved back to Trois Ponts to provide covering fire for Knittel's forces in the area. On December 22nd Tiger 133 was disabled by an American anti-tank shell in another failed attack by *Kampfgruppe Knittel* to retake Stavelot. Its huge hulk effectively blocked the narrow valley road. A final desperate attack to take the town from the east on Christmas Eve saw Brand killed by an American artillery shell while outside his panzer.

The six heavy Tiger tanks which got to *Kampfgruppe Peiper* gave the U.S. 3rd Armored Division a tough time in their attempts to recapture La Gleize and eliminate the German positions north of the Amblève River. Blocking roads leading into the German salient, several Shermans were knocked out. However, the fuel thirsty tanks were out of gas and most had to be abandoned when Peiper made his escape from the pocket on Christmas Eve. Several were stopped by mines and one by anti-tank fire. A few tanks were able to ford the Amblève River and escape towards Wanne. Said one German Tiger commander upon his breakout, "We are far too few, I am young and have only one

Impervious to bazookas. Paratroopers of the 82nd Airborne Division examine the results of their handiwork from firing their anti-tank rockets at a German Tiger abandoned by Kampfgruppe Peiper *in La Gleize.*

Königstiger "222" of the 501SS Heavy Panzer Battalion passes the kaiserbaracke crossroads loaded with German paratroopers. The date is December 18th, 1944. The tank, commanded by SS Unterscharführer Kurt Sova, would late be knocked out in its vain attempt to recapture the bridge at Stavelot from the U.S. 30th Infantry Division.

centimeter of armor over my head!"

Another portion of the panzer battalion participated in the attack on December 19th to re-open the bridge captured by the Americans at Stavelot by attacking from the south. SS Obstlt. Heinz Buchner was present at the battle:

> We came down the road from Lodomez to Stavelot and stopped there because we were short on fuel and were being fired on by an anti-tank gun. Towards the evening of the 19th, my Tiger and several Mk IVs attacked the bridge and the entrance to the town of Stavelot. The attack was broken and our tanks retired in the direction of Wanne. The bridge was blown an hour later.

Tiger 222, extensively photographed by the SS *Kriegsberichter*, was knocked out in this assault just south of the contested span. By the end of December the *501 SS* had lost 13 of its Tigers — over half of these being abandoned with the armored wreckage of *Kampfgruppe Peiper.*

Many of the heavy tanks had had mechanical troubles in the first days of the battle. According to Edmund Zeger, a mechanic with the battalion, only two Mk VIs from his company managed to link up with Peiper. The other 12 developed mechanical troubles along the way. He repaired these and the company reformed in Ligneuville on December 20th. Tiger "222,"

Decapitated Tiger II of the 506th Heavy Panzer Battalion. The huge panzer, commanded by Lt. Jürgen Tegethoff, was knocked out by the 6th Armored Division on January 13th near the village of Moinet northeast of Bastogne. The blizzard of shells necessary to immobilize the beast is evidenced by the numerous richocet marks on the front mantlet.

Huge 77 ton Jagdtiger. The huge panzer was armed with a 128mm gun and carried a crew of six. This abandoned monster is being inspected by the members of the U.S. 740th Tank Battalion.

pictured at the Kaiserbaracke crossroads, was one of these repaired machines.

As 1944 drew to a close, Hitler's "clear Bastogne" order took effect and the *1st SS Panzer Division* was among the chosen. By the time the division reached the Bastogne vicinity, the *501st SS* had 13 operational vehicles with another 14 still in repair. Over the following days, another dozen Mk VIs were lost. When the battalion was transferred to the Russian front on January 27th, it only had 13 Tigers left.

506 s. Panzer Battalion

The *506th Heavy Panzer Battalion* was assigned to the *Sixth Panzer Armee* for the Ardennes battle. Under the command of Maj. Gerhard Lange, the battalion had an notorious history, being the German Tiger unit that smashed the attack of the U.S. 2nd Armored Division on November 17, 1944, at Puffendorf, Belgium. In the

engagement, the U.S. armored division lost 57 tanks in a single day! One gunner from "Hell on Wheels" described the effect of the Sherman gun on the Tigers as "like hitting them with a pea shooter."

When the offensive began, however, the battalion of 30 *Königstigers* was still with the German *LXXIV Armeekorps* near Düren. The tanks began their rail transport to the front on the night of December 17th. By December 21st, *OB West* recorded that four of eight trains had unloaded (another two unloaded in the next day) and the advance party of the battalion had arrived at the front. Even so, we do not know the precise time of the arrival and commitment of the battalion in the Ardennes. Its march route was Euskirchen-Hellenthal-Losheim-St. Vith-Bastogne, which would indicate that it did not arrive earlier than December 20th and possibly later towards the end of the year. Only eight

of the panzers were operational on December 17th, the rest being down for repair or in shipment.

However, the battalion concentrated in the area around Wardin, north of Bastogne, on New Year's Day with 13 operational Tiger IIs. In the following days, the battalion fought a tough engagement with the U.S. 6th Armored Division. On January 2nd, the 68th Tank Battalion moved on Arloncourt only to lose all but one Sherman in Company B to "terrific nebelwerfer concentrations and two camouflaged Tigers." Over the next days, the 15th Tank Battalion attempted to lure the heavy German tanks into the open, but most of their efforts were fruitless since the 75mm AP shot "bounced off the Tigers like marbles off a brick."

On January 13th, the 5 Königstigers of the *1st Kompanie* under Oblt. Paul clashed in the woods with the M4 Shermans of the 15th Tank Battalion near the village of Moinet. Two other Tigers under Leutnant Jürgen Tegethoff moved up to assist in the heavy fighting. Tegethoff's panzer was struck by eight 75mm rounds which benignly bounced off the glacis plate. Finally, a Sherman got a flank shot which set the panzer ablaze. Incredibly, Tegethoff and his crew were able to escape from the burning tank just before it exploded. Others were not so lucky; casualties for the German tank crews had been heavy as well. Maj. Lange complained to his superiors about the piecemeal commitment of his battalion. For this he was relieved of command.

301 FKL s. Panzer Battalion

The *301st Funklenk Heavy Panzer Battalion* was originally assigned to the *Sixth Panzer Armee* for the Ardennes Offensive along with the *319th Panzer Kompanie*. This was the radio or *Funklenk* (FKL) Tiger unit that had hit the U.S. 29th Infantry Division on the Roer plain on November 26th. It was the only German panzer unit with Tiger Is in the Ardennes fighting. The attached *319th Panzer Kompanie* consisted of remote control B-IV demolition tanks (3.5 ton low-profile tracked bombs powered by a 49 hp motor) and

a few *Sturmgeschütz*. The theory was that the Tigers would control and provide protection for the demolition tanks so that they might advance to the obstacle and blast a hole through the enemy line with their 450 kilogram charges. The robot tanks could also be used to establish a path through enemy minefields. The Tigers would then exploit the breach in the line: a nice idea that usually didn't work. Generally, the Tigers were employed as regular panzer units.

The *301st* theoretically contained 31 Tiger I/E command tanks and 59 B-IVs in the *319th Panzer Kompanie*. As of 16 December, the battalion reported its strength at 27 Tiger I tanks of which only 14 were combat ready with the rest in repair. The assault panzer company had 36 B-IVs with five *Sturmgeschütz* in long term repair. The battalion was still with the *LXXXI Armeekorps* to the north on O-Tag. Hptm. Krämer's Tigers were subsequently detached from the corps on December 20th and assigned to the *9th Panzer Division*, which it accompanied into the Bulge fighting. The Tigers appear on *OB West* maps at the end of the year, defending the tip of the salient with 20 operational Tiger Is. In the withdrawal from the Ardennes,

one of the tanks was destroyed near Oberwampach where it was photographed by members of the U.S. 90th Infantry Division.

The overall usefulness of the panzer *Funklenk* concept was questioned in the after-action report submitted by Hptm. Krämer in early 1945 to the General Inspector of Panzer Troops:

> During the entire employment of the battalion since November 16th, due to both tactical and technical reasons, it was not possible to utilize this unit as a panzer funklenk battalion. The battalion was employed exactly as a normal panzer battalion as part of a panzer division to attack enemy tanks or employed in tank pack of 5 Tigers for mobile defense and counter attacks. The operations in which the BIVs were employed, in all cases, resulted in complete failure or at best a partial success. Due to the small number of 'Lenk-panzer' (Tigers with control sets) only a few BIVs could be employed. These were, for the most part, destroyed by heavy enemy fire before reaching their objective. The employment of this expensive equipment is by no means justified by the end result.

s. Panzerjäger Battalion 653

This was the first German panzer

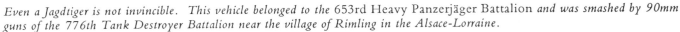

Even a Jagdtiger is not invincible. This vehicle belonged to the 653rd Heavy Panzerjäger Battalion and was smashed by 90mm guns of the 776th Tank Destroyer Battalion near the village of Rimling in the Alsace-Lorraine.

formation with the huge 128mm Jagdtiger tank destroyers. The gun was exceedingly powerful and at 77 tons, the armor was extremely thick. Hitler expected these behemoths to be invulnerable. Under command of Maj. Gillenberger, the formation had nine of the juggernauts on December 17th and was in the process of expansion as production of tank hunters rolled off the assembly line at Nibelungenwerke. The battalion was first assigned to the *LVIII Panzerkorps* on December 7th, then to the *Panzer Lehr Division* by December 14th. For the planned employment, the *LVIII Panzerkorps* had been given a section of special bridging equipment to pass the monsters over the Our River.

However, Hitler had one of his last minute brainwaves and asked that the Jagdtigers go to the *Sixth Panzer Armee* to block American reinforcements from moving south along the Eupen - Monschau road. In this way, he believed that the huge tank destroyers might be pivotal in stopping the expected American reaction from the north. However, the spreading chaos of the *Reichsbahn* foiled everyone's plans. When the offensive opened, the *Jagdtigers* were still in rail transport to Blankenheim.

Days after the offensive began, the American reinforcements were streaming into the German attack zone from the north. Hitler insisted on finding out what had become of *s. Panzerjäger Battalion 653*. "What about the Jagdtigers?" he demanded. General Herbert Büchs, a staff officer at *OKW*, had bad news for the Führer. "A check has been made," he began, "and the trains bringing the battalion forward have been blocked by air attack on the rail lines." The battalion had never even crossed the Rhine! Hitler was outraged. "They must be mad!" he cried. "If the enemy attacks our defense with ten or twelve heavy tanks, there's enough screaming to bring the house down; but when we have 24 of the heaviest tanks in the world, they aren't even used!"

A message to *OB West* on December 29th shows that two of the tank destroyers had unloaded and were now headed to the *Sixth Panzer Armee* front. One of these appears to have been knocked out west of St. Vith in Maldingen and then sketched by a teenage Belgian civilian in 1945. The rest of the battalion, now up to a strength of 26, had new marching orders and had been shunted south to *Operation Nordwind*. Even the movement to Piramasens had been disrupted, however. "In view of the circumstances," *OB West* concluded, "a better march performance cannot be expected."

A week later, however, the Jagdtigers rumbled into battle on a plain near Rimling, France. In the action that followed, the monsters were repulsed by the 90mm guns of the U.S. 776th Tank Destroyer Battalion. At least one was destroyed, giving lie to Hitler's myth of their invincibility.

1000 and 1001 Sturmmörser Companies

By any accounting, the most peculiar of Tiger units in the plans for the Ardennes Offensive were the *1000* and *1001 Sturmmörser Kompanies*. These were a limited-edition vehicle with a huge 380mm *Rakentenwerfer* rocket mounted on an old Tiger I chassis. The vehicle had been designed in response to Hitler's demand for an assault panzer sufficient to destroy an entire block in city fighting. Both companies totalled only seven of these vehicles — the majority of German production of this curiosity during the war.

According to an *OB West* communique on December 15th, the two assault panzer companies along with two heavy batteries of *Karl* guns were earmarked for the reduction of Liége after the *Sixth Panzer Armee* had by-passed that city in the advance on Antwerp. At the beginning of the Ardennes fighting, the two companies were in the Elsdorf-Gemünd area in the *LXVII Armeekorps* on the right-wing of the *Sixth Panzer Armee*. The numbers of the available assault tanks were too small to have any appreciable effect on the fighting. In any event, the German attack in the Simmerath-Monschau area was totally halted by December 18th and with this reversal went any plan to use these armored siege mortars.

Myth and Mystery

It is perhaps useful to lay to rest some of the popular myths in the historical literature concerning German Tigers in the Ardennes battle.

* There were no Tigers in the battle at Krinkelt. The only armored vehicles used there were Jagdpanzer IVs, Panthers and assault guns from the *12SS Panzer* and *3rd Panzer Grenadier Divisions*.

* There were no Tigers with the *2nd Panzer Division* at the fight north of Bastogne at Noville. These were a combination of assault guns and Panthers.

* The *506th Heavy Panzer Battalion* did not fight at Andler on the morning of December 17th. These were likely assault guns from the *244th Sturmgeschütz Brigade* attached to the *18th Volksgrenadier Division*.

* We do not know if the tanks described as breaking the defense at St. Vith were Tigers from the *506th Panzer Battalion*. However, it is possible since the advance party of the battalion was reported to *IISS Panzerkorps* as reaching the front on December 17th.

* It is likely that the Tigers described by Kokott of the *26th Volksgrenadier Division* south of Bastogne on December 24th were *Jagdpanthers* from the *Heavy Panzerjäger Battalion 559* attached to the *Panzer Lehr Division*.

The Final German Throw: January 2nd - 4th

On Tuesday, January 2nd the situation on the front of the *Sixth Panzer Armee* was quiescent; both sides were too fought out to provoke the other. Meanwhile, the U.S. forces continued their shift along the VII Corps line to the east in order to concentrate for their coming offensive south towards Houffalize. For this move, the British continued to extend their lines to relieve U.S. units for the operation. The British 53rd Division took over the front from Marche to Hotton from the U.S. 84th Division which moved off to assemble for the coming attack.

In contrast to the dormant conflict in the north, vicious fighting continued in the Bastogne area, now the clear focus of the battle. On the German side of the fence, Genfldm. Model, himself, paid a visit to the headquarters of the *ISS Panzerkorps* to make sure that the planned German attack to capture the town would go ahead without delay. Ominously for the German plan, the U.S. III Corps attacked with the "heaviest artillery support" under an umbrella of strafing planes. Indeed, between January 1st and 8th one of the great artillery battles of the war was fought near Bastogne. In an unusual show of gunnery strength, the Germans had managed to bring up two *Volksartillerie Korps*, the *766th* and the *401st*, along with the *15th Volkswerfer Brigade* into firing position on both sides of the Bastogne corridor. This artillery *Schwerpunkt* was designed to steel the German effort to cut the Bastogne- Martelange road. But the Americans more than countered this with the four battalions of the 193rd Field Artillery Group, local divisional artillery, air observation and a massive supply of ammunition. During the first week of 1945 the U.S. artillery group fired a total of 53,054 rounds.

Southwest of Bastogne, Gerimont and Bonnerue fell to the 87th Infantry Division while Mande St. Etienne was taken by the 11th Armored. Losses in the 11th were high, however, moving the usually ebullient Third Army commander to report that the new armored division had lost a third of its tanks and was "badly disorganized."

But in the same vicinity west of Bastogne, Senonchamps was captured by Combat Command B of the 10th Armored and CCA of the 9th Armored. Pushed back by these tank columns, Genfldm. Model reported that the projected attack to re-encircle the troublesome town could not be carried out as foreseen due to the loss of the assembly areas from which it was to be launched. As approved by Hitler, he recommended that the new attacks be launched by the *9th SS* and *12th SS Panzer Divisions* and the *Führer Begleit Brigade* from the northeast where the ground promised better tank going.

Gen. von Manteuffel, on the other hand, had lost patience with the continuing bloodshed. He wanted no new

Jagdpanther of the 559th Heavy Panzerjäger Battalion that fought with the Panzer Lehr Division before it was lost in the village of Rochefort near the tip of the Bulge. Large German tank destroyers such as these were understandably taken by American troops to be "Tigers."

Rare Sturmtiger captured in the village of Elsdorf on February 28, 1945 by the 30th Infantry Division. Armed with a huge 380mm mortar, only eight of these monsters were built. They were designed to give close support to infantry when assaulting built up areas.

Slick Roads. An American M5 "Stuart" tank passes an M4 Sherman which has slid into the ditch.

attacks anywhere and pleaded with Model to allow him to pull his *Fifth Panzer Armee* from the Ardennes while there was still time to escape the Allied trap. Model told him no; although he professionally agreed with the assessment, he also knew that such a course would run afoul of Hitler's long professed decree of no retreat. And after being chastised repeatly before and during the Ardennes Offensive, Model had ceased attempting to alter Hitler's interpretation of withdrawl as defeatism or even treason.

But in the field, a new German crisis arose in the *Seventh Armee* east of Bastogne when the American 6th Armored again attacked and achieved a deep penetration to the village of Wardin. This exacted great pressure on the *9th Volksgrenadiers* and threatened to cut-off the *5th Fallschirmjäger Division*. The U.S. armor was only stopped when tanks of the arriving *12th SS Panzer Division* were committed to the battle. These shot up 15 Shermans in the abortive encounter that forced them out of Michamps. Meanwhile, brutal, inconclusive fighting continued to rage in Lutrebois between the 35th Infantry and *1st SS Panzer Division*.

With permission to retreat denied by Hitler, the *Seventh Armee* ordered the *276th Volksgrenadier Division* (with the strength now of a single regiment) to be pulled out of the *LXXX Armeekorps* and committed alongside the *5th Fallschirmjäger*. Meantime, the army's quartermaster reported grave ammunition shortages brought on by the breakdown of the transportation system. Luckily for the Germans, quiet prevailed in the *LXXX* and *LXXXV Armeekorps* to the east.

Montgomery's expected "final German blow" on his front had failed to materialize, primarily due to the greater German attention given to Bastogne. With this, he could delay his promised offensive no longer. Finally, on the morning of January 3rd Montgomery ordered the advance to begin. Eisenhower, who had become irritated with the British Field Marshal's haughtiness and cautious attitude, was relieved. "Praise God from whom all blessings flow!" he exclaimed.[47]

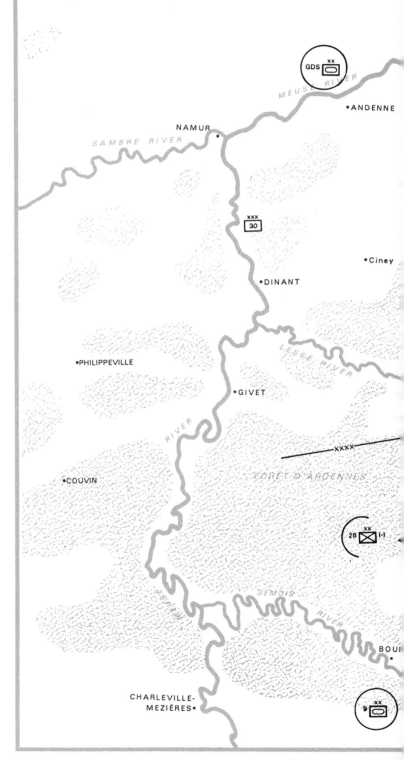

SITUATION MAP
January 2nd-4th

"The Führer gives us orders, we will obey!" SS graffiti left behind in Moinet by the zealous Hitler youth of the 12th SS Panzer Division.

In the offensive plan, the First U.S. Army attacked on the north flank while the British XXX Corps took on the Germans in the tip of the Bulge with the 53rd and 6th Airborne Divisions. Collins' Corps would link up with Patton's Third Army attacking from Bastogne near Houffalize trapping a major portion of the *Fifth Panzer Armee*.

Three German divisions of Bittrich's *II SS Panzer Korps* drew the defensive assignment in Collin's projected line of advance. The *12th Volksgrenadiers* defended the line on the U.S. left flank, the *560th Volksgrenadiers* held the center and the *2nd SS Panzer* posted the right flank. All were fought out; the *560th* was down to scarcely 2,500 grenadiers. But the weather promised anything but campaigning conditions: bitter cold, icy roads, deep snow and low-hanging fog and mist. Air support would be impossible and the U.S. artillery was hamstrung by lack of air observation coupled with the dense woods and broken terrain.

In spite these circumstances, the American forces struck from the north on a 25 mile front with two armored divisions and a regiment of foot soldiers riding on the tanks of each, planning to pierce through to Houffalize.[48] The attack advanced only a few miles, constrained mainly by the weather: waist-deep snow, sub-zero temperatures and minefields. At first German resistance was light, but this changed as the Allied intent to pinch off the Bulge became evident.

The conditions encountered on January 3rd set the pace for what was to come for the remaining campaign. The two

armored divisions were used in hopes of a rapid penetration of the German northern front. According to the plan, the role of the two infantry divisions was to mop up the by-passed points of resistance. However, as the Germans had discovered before, the effectiveness of armor in the Ardennes was considerably less than ideal.

Whenever tanks found fairly open ground they could move cross-country over the frozen terrain, but this was the exception. More often than not hilly terrain and dense woods confined the armor to the slick and icy roads where they could be almost certain that the Germans were waiting. When the shock of the armor failed to produce a breakthrough the role of the infantry became more fundamental. Enemy roadblocks with felled trees, mines and concealed anti-tank guns could only be broached by eliminating them with dismounted infantry. The American riflemen had to slog through the deep snow to flank the enemy positions — moves that the Germans usually anticipated and took under

47 Montgomery continued to pester Eisenhower to make him the overall ground commander of the Allied forces, a move that Eisenhower was clearly not going to make. Both Bradley and Patton had already informed Ike that they would both resign under such an arrangement. The row reached such a point that Eisenhower was forced to tell him that, "It is you or it is me. If one of us has to give up his job, I do not think that it will be me." So threatened, Montgomery dropped the matter.
48 Collins' order of battle for the attack on January 3rd comprised the 2nd Armored and 84th Infantry Division on the right with the 3rd Armored and 83rd Infantry on the left. The relatively inexperienced 75th Infantry Division was held in reserve.

Armored might. The 6th Armored Division outside Bastogne, January, 1945.

fire. If the German position was breached then the Americans could be almost certain that a enemy riposte was soon to follow, typically preceded by a sharp artillery barrage and paced by a handful of tanks or assault guns. Of course, such counterattacks would have to be thrown back before the advance could continue. And so the battle continued in a monotonously grim series of winter battles, horrifingly remininscent of a World War I version of Valley Forge. Casualties were high and advances were deliberate and painfully slow. Before the close of operations in the Ardennes the casualties in the two infantry divisions were much

A white-washed M4 tank of the 7th Armored Division threads down a snowy lane near Manhay.

greater than two armored divisions who nominally made the main effort.

Consequently, on the first day the 2nd Armored with the 84th Division on its right did well to slog their way to Beffe, Trinal and Magoster. At the same time the 3rd Armored with the 83rd Division managed to seize Malempré. On the left, the XVIII Airborne corps moved off at 8:30 A.M., and took Trois Ponts before running into serious resistance from the *62nd Volksgrenadier Division* west of the Salm River around Dairomont.

The British attack against the tip of the Bulge at Wavreille and Bure began that morning in the midst of a blinding snowstorm. The bitter "confused fighting" continued on for days. The next morning, the *9th and 116th Panzer Divisions* would be compelled to pull back their front. But the greatest enemy was the weather. On the 4th a brigade commander with the "Welsh" Division was killed when his scout car skidded on sheet ice and overturned. Winter played no favorites. American tanks attempting to climb a steep icy road slid backwards into each other blocking the approach for hours and two Ford trucks pulling 105mm howitzers plunged off a cliff.

The other side of the fence saw Hitler finally aknowledging that the German offensive had hopelessly bogged down and the original objectives "no longer offered prospect of success." Along with further blows from *Operation Nordwind* he saw the mission of *Heeresgruppe B* to tie down as many strong enemy forces as possible. The army group now had the new assignment of holding the territory gained and clearing up of the situation at Bastogne. According to Hitler, Bastogne with its nexus of roads, was vital to anchor the German defense in the Bulge.

Although mindful to keep personal doubts about the upcoming operation to themselves, Hitler's generals did propose a change in the approach to capturing the Bastogne. So far the German attacks had aimed at re-enveloping the thorny position by thrusts from the east and west. However, Genfldm. Model pointed out that the Americans had become strongly reinforced to the southeast of Bastogne and the German saliant there was now so constricted that the impoverished road net would not allow additional troops to be inserted. As an alternative, Model suggested that the assault be made from the north and northeast where the American defenses were yet untried and the terrain better suited for employment of the tanks of the *ISS Panzerkorps*. This request, Hitler approved.

According to his wishes, preparations for the decisive German attack on Bastogne continued throughout the night of January 3rd as the SS divisions arrived and organized for the final blow. The strength of the German formations reflected the punishment they had taken in the preceding weeks. The *9th SS Panzer* had only 30 tanks and assault guns with six under strength infantry battalions averaging only 160 men each. The *12th SS Panzer* was in like shape with 26 armored vehicles and infantry battalions averaging only 120 men. The riflemen in Obst. Theodor Tolsdorf's *340th Volksgrenadier Division* were under strength as well.

But if tired, the SS divisions were made of stern stuff. The *12th SS Panzer Division* launched a bold attack northwest of Bastogne aimed at Bizory steeled by the arrival of Tiger tanks from the *506th Heavy Panzer Battalion*. The panzers, Hitler Youth and a detachment of the *340th Volksgrenadiers* burst through the American lines of the 6th Armored Division to re-take Michamps and Oubourcy. The Americans responded with heavy artillery fire on the German held villages of Arloncourt, Michamps and Bourcy. That same afternoon the *9th SS Panzer* threw itself at Longchamps only to be repulsed, but then returned later to penetrate into the village in a nighttime raid. However, the American resistance of the 101st Airborne, now back under the command of Maj. Gen. Maxwell D. Taylor, was fierce. Thrown back, the thwarted SS vanguard described their enemy as "very good troops who fought hard and tenaciously." And observing the savage German attacks that day, Patton grudgingly admited, "they are colder, hungrier and weaker than we, to be sure. But they are still doing a great piece of fighting."

The battles to the south in the *Seventh Armee* had slackened although the Germans there continued to suffer from the unremitting U.S. artillery fire. As a result, General Brandenberger took the opportunity to move the *276th Volksgrenadier Division* out of the line so it could function as an emergency reserve. However, in Millikin's III Corps, the fierce battle around Bastogne continued unabated. Both sides suffered greatly from the horrible weather unable to even dig foxholes in the frozen ground. The fighting had degraded into what one American soldier grimly called the "battle for the billets." In the VIII Corps, the 87th Division experienced a very trying day, elements becoming temporarily surrounded by the *Panzer Lehr Division* in the woods around St. Hubert. The badly battered U.S. 28th Division began to reorganize its shattered command while defending a back-stop position at the Meuse River from Givet to Verdun. Meanwhile, Gen. Baade's 35th Infantry Division persisted in its costly battle east of Bastogne with the *1st SS Panzer Division* near Lutrebois. At the same time the 26th Infantry continued its fight against the *9th Volksgrenadier Division* in the Buderscheid area to further expand its bridgehead across the Sûre River.

On January 4th the weather became impossible. Montgomery's attack against the German northern flank came to a halt in the face of a blinding snow storm. The 2nd Armored with the 84th Division took the village of Lamorménil, but was then forced to shake off a violent counterattack by a half dozen tanks and a group of infantry from the *2nd SS Panzer Division* near Beffe and Freineux. Meanwhile, the 3rd Armored poked its way through dangerous enemy mine fields to clear Jevigne and Lansival from the *12th Volksgrenadier Division*. Likewise, the 82nd Airborne Division plodded slowly in its advance through the snowy forests of the *Ranal Bois*, being forced to repulse strong en-

Engineers vs. Winter. A snowplow of the 202nd Combat Engineers in action southwest of Bastogne.

Dead Man's Ridge. Soldiers of the 17th Airborne Division trudge into the front line along the frigid hills southwest of Bastogne. Many would not return.

emy counterattacks near Arbrefontaine by elements of the *62nd Volksgrenadier Division.* By nightfall the paratroopers had taken the hamlet of Odrimont.

West of Bastogne, the newly arrived 17th Airborne Division moved off in near zero visibility into a disastrous attack against the *Führer Begleit Brigade.* Some battalions of the division lost 40% of their strength in the violent German counterattack which swirled through the villages of Pinsamont, Rechrival and Hubermont. "God, how green we are," reflected one regimental commander, "but we are learning fast and next time we will beat them." So grim was the bitter combat that even the usually confident Patton was affected. "We can still lose this war," he wrote in his diary.

Meanwhile, in Hitler's headquarters, unrestrained optimism was an increasing popular theme. In spite of the many reverses of the past week, Obst. Wilhelm Meyer-Detring, who was section chief in the operations department of the the *Wehrmachtführungsstab,* ventured a rosy description of the situation in the west. "The basic objective remains," he told Hitler and his small audience on the afternoon of January 4th, "the piecemeal destruction of the enemy whenever and wherever an opportunity is afforded." And if this bromide was not enough, the young officer went on to describe a future obviously tailored for his master. Looking to *Operation 'Nordwind'* he spoke hopefully of "the reestablishment of a strong position in the Vosges" for the purpose of "cutting off those elements of the enemy which still remain in the northern Alsace. This will give us a base for new operations."

But far away from the rarified atmosphere in Hitler's *Adlerhorst,* the last desperate German attempt to maintain the iniative was about to be played out in the Ardennes. Northeast of Bastogne the final big attack by *ISS Panzerkorps* moved off in a blizzard. A dense concentration of artillery and *nebelwerfer* fire bracketed the American foxhole line northeast of Bastogne. As it lifted the German panzergrenadiers and tanks rushed forward. Almost at once the fighting degenerated into a desperate back and forth blood bath. In fierce battle, the U.S. 6th Armored division was forced out of Magaret and Wardin. It was the first time since Normandy that they had given up ground and the worst day of the war for the division — sixty men were killed in action that day. But as the *Hitler Jugend* tanks and grenadiers thrust

The pathetic result of battle. The body of a German machine gunner who will fight no more.

beyond the villages they were plastered by American artillery fire and themselves forced into headlong retreat. Nearby, the attack by the *15th Panzer Grenadier Division* was repulsed by the 101st Airborne Division in Champs. Similar to the experience of the 6th Armored, the fighting was the bloodiest the Screaming Eagles experienced in the Ardennes; men on both sides fell by the score.

Southeast of Bastogne, the 35th Division reported that it had finally cleared the long-contested village of Lutrebois from the *1st SS Panzer Division,* but was unable to reach Harlange. Advances of Gen. Paul's 26th Division near Roullingen were measured in yards, while the 87th Division was completely stymied at Pironpré by the *Panzer Lehr Division's* fortified position there.

The danger of the American moves to the north now loomed large to the German field commanders. Von Rundstedt and Model both pleaded with Hitler to begin evacuation of the salient before it was too late. Their supplications had some effect, for the next day the Führer ordered the *9th SS Panzer* from Bastogne to the threatened north flank. The Hitler Youth of the *12th SS Panzer Division* also threw in the towel and began withdrawl on January 6th. The last German offensive actions of *Wacht am Rhein* had failed miserably.

The Guns of December

"Although I feel the American Air Force did not substantially affect the breakdown of the offensive, the Allied artillery was very unpleasant as usual." — General Fritz Bayerlein, Commander, *Panzer Lehr Division*.

The German Artillery Preparation

In planning the Ardennes Offensive during the fall of 1944, Hitler repeatedly looked back at his last successful blitzkrieg there in 1940 for inspiration and guidance. The Führer could no longer count on the Luftwaffe; even he no longer put any credence in Göring's empty promises in the fifth year of war. Regardless, the firepower of the Stuka dive bombers seemed to have been of significant importance in deciding that campaign particularly in the breakout across the Meuse around Sedan. To supplant what could no longer be made available, Hitler looked back further to the nearly decisive German offensive in the West of 1918. In that great battle, Ludendorff had come close to victory in that campaign in spite of not having air power or armor available. What did stand out, however, was the massive concentration of artillery — the "hurricane bombardment" with which the Kaiser's paladins had opened their assault. Accordingly, it seemed advisable to lavish all the artillery support that could be mustered with which to launch *Wacht am Rhein*. What was missing in 1944, however, were captive observation balloons and aircraft with which to direct the fire. Still worse, there were simply not nearly as many gun tubes or ammunition rounds as had been available to German planners in 1918; massive use of artillery fire or intense counter-battery missions were not possible.

On the opening day of the assault, the artillery available to *Heeresgruppe B* was significantly less than the Kaiser had been able to count on in 1918. For that offensive, Ludendorff was able to amass 6,600 heavy guns and 3,500 mortars over a 69 kilometer front — a

truly massive concentration of artillery averaging nearly 150 tubes per kilometer. Meanwhile, Model in 1944 had been able to only concentrate 1,660 heavy guns, 957 werfers (rocket launchers) and 188 heavy flak guns over the meandering 83 kilometer line from which the Ardennes Offensive was to be unleashed. Although this included all divisional and non-divisional guns that could be scraped together, this came to just over 32 tubes per kilometer — less than 25% of the concentration in 1918 that the *OKW* staff was seeking to replicate.

Furthermore, for the Kaiser's offensive, a tremendous stockpile of 1.6 million shells had been amassed for a five hour bombardment. Not ignorant of these requirements, Hitler had made special efforts to provide artillery ammunition to nourish the counteroffensive; he allocated one hundred trains of ammunition to a special "Führer Reserve." But the magnitude of this stockpile was not in keeping with its grandiose designation. On December 13th, Oberquartermeister Alfred Toppe reported only 15,099 tons of ammunition available for all of *Heeresgruppe B*. And of this, over 5,000 tons of this figure was allotted to von Zangen's *Fifteenth Armee* which would not join in the initial assault. The German logistical planners had reckoned on a need for 1,200 tons of ammunition per day — a figure that proved less than adequate for the actual tactical demand for artillery rounds during the battle. The Luftwaffe's *III Flak Korps* with 47 heavy and 51 medium and light batteries in the Ardennes that were to assist in the initial bombardment were better off than the artillery quartermasters in the German Army; they had seven basic loads of ammunition on December 16th.

Although in the early war years, the Germans typically maintained six basic loads of ammunition for a major offensive, Toppe was more realistic; he counted on four basic units of ammunition with which to support the attack. A basic unit of ammunition was

100 rounds of ordnance for each artillery piece. By the second week of December, two units had been delivered to the *Heeresgruppe B* dumps although non-sanctioned dipping into the reserve to cope with the Allied attacks during the early month had whittled the available figure down to only one and a half. Although there were prospects for another two units, the ubiquitous transport problem plagued its arrival to the fighting front. Toppe expected to use one unit for the initial artillery barrage, another half for the breakthrough of the American main line of resistance and another 1.5 units to keep the rolling assault sustained with artillery fire.

Others did not agree with the OKW calculations, however. General Staudinger, in charge of *Sixth Panzer Armee* artillery operations, deemed no less than twelve units of fire sufficient for the first ten days of the attack. General Thoholte, in charge of *Heeresgruppe B* artillery was in fundamental agreement; four units of artillery ammunition was not sufficient for the task at hand. Thoholte believed that five to six issues of ammunition would have been necessary "to furnish adequate artillery support and to open a rolling barrage at the spots where such was required." *Wacht am Rhein* was launched with less than the number of rounds of ammunition available for the entire offensive that Ludendorff in 1918 had allotted for his initial bombardment!

Hitler, the World War I rifleman, wanted a long protracted three hour bombardment in the style of the Great War. However, von Manteuffel advised him that this would simply alert the enemy of the coming ground assault. What the little general had not mentioned was the fact that there was simply not enough ammunition for such an extravaganza even had it been a good idea. In the end he agreed with von Manteuffel's assessment — a short half-hour, intense pre-dawn barrage.

The form of the artillery fires took a different course in each of the three armies. Under the guidance of General-leutnant Walter Staudinger, the fusillade in the *Sixth Panzer Armee* began promptly at 5:25 A.M., starting with a hail of howitzer and werfer fire against the American main line of resistance. The artillery composition of this army included the largest collection of guns available. The resulting bombardment was very heavy; in some sectors buildings burned to the ground and American forward communications were knocked out. After a twenty minute period of punishing fire for the forward lines, the fire plan moved to the big guns. Large caliber 22, 24, 30.5 and 35cm guns opened up on targets deep behind the American lines. Huge destructive 24cm shells fell on Malmédy from a K-3 rail battery east of Monschau.

Infantrymen of the *12th Volksgrenadier* were awed by the shelling. Said one,

> ...the earth seemed to break open. A hurricane of iron and fire went down on the enemy positions with a deafening noise. We old soldiers had seen many a heavy barrage, but never anything like this....

On the recieving end, American soldiers were understandably startled by the enemy fire. Many heard the distant booming as friendly fire only to dive for cover as the German rounds commenced to drop around them. In the V Corps area, the G-2 intelligence officer had estimated the enemy artillery facing the American line as two horse drawn pieces. Cowering in a foxhole under an intense barrage of exploding shells an American soldier sarcastically remarked to another that, "They sure are working those two poor horses to death!"

In spite of the impressive pyrotechnics, in many cases the fire did not have the desired effect of destroying the American resistance. One lesson the First World War had taught artillerymen of both sides was that regardless of the severity of artillery preparation, a complete neutralization of the forward enemy line could not be expected, even when the bombardment went on for days. In this case, however, the casualties to the American defenders were remarkably light,

ORGANIZATION OF GERMAN NON-DIVISIONAL ARTILLERY IN THE ARDENNES
December 15, 1944

HERRESGRUPPE B (1,537 pieces in the Ardennes)
Eisenbahn Art Bn 725 (2 24cm Kan., 1 27.4cm Kan., 1 28cm K-5 Kan., 2 K.5 gl. 30/12)

Sixth Panzer Armee (584 pieces)
Hvy Art Btry 1100 (3 30.5cm Mörser)
Hvy Art Btry 1098 (3 35.5cm Mörser)
Hvy Art Btry 1120 (3 22cm Mörser)
Hvy Art Btry 428 (2 54cm Mörser)
Festung Art Btry 1123 (2 K-3 24cm)
LXVII Armeekorps
Volksartillerie Korps 405 (18 FK 40, 18 IFH 18/40, 12sFH 396, 12 KH 433, 12 10cm K)
Volkswerfer Brig. 17 (72 15cm, 18 21cm, 18 30cm)
ISS Panzerkorps
Volksartillerie Korps 388 (18 FK40, 18 8.8cmFlak, 18 IFH 18/40, 12 sFH 396, 12 sFH 18, 3 17cm Kan., 6 21cm Mörser
Volksartillerie Korps 402 (18 FK40, 18 IFH 18/40, 12 sFH 396, 12 KH 433, 12 10cm Kan.)
Volkswerfer Brig. 4 (72 15cm, 36 21cm)
Volkswerfer Brig. 9 (70 15cm, 54 21cm)

Fifth Panzer Armee (527 pieces)
H. Art. Btry 1094 (6 12.8cm Kan.)
H. Art. Btry 1095 (6 12.8cm Kan.)
H Art. Btry 1119 (3 30.5cm Morser)
H. Art. Btry 1099 (3 35.5cm Morser)
H. Art. Btry 1121 (3 22cm Morser)
Festung Art Btry 25/975 (4 15.5cm 425)
LXVI Armeekorps
460 H. Art Bn. (9 sFH 18)
10SS Panzer Division Artillery Regt. (on loan)
Volkswerfer Brig. 16 (72 15cm, 18 21cm, 18 30cm)
LVIII Panzerkorps
Volksartillerie Korps 401 (18 FK40, 18 IFH 18/40, 12 sFH 396, 12 KH 433, 12 10cm Kan.)
Volkswerfer Brig. 7 (88 15cm, 18 21cm, 18 30cm)
XLVII Panzerkorps
Volksartillerie Korps 766 (18 FK40, 18 IFH 18/40, 36 sFH 18, 3 17cm Kan, 6 21cm Mörser)
Volkswerfer Brig 15 (72 15cm, 18 21cm, 18 30cm)

Seventh Armee (420 pieces)
H. Art Btry 1092 (6 12.8cm Kan.)
H. Art Btry 1093 (6 12.8cm Kan.)
H. Art Btry 1124 (6 12.8cm Kan.)
H. Art Btry 1125 (6 12.8cm Kan.)
H. Art Btry 1122 (1 28cm Mörser, 1 22cm Mörser)
H. Art Btry 660 (2 21cm Kan.)
LXXXV Armeekorps
Volksartillerie Korps 406 (18 FK40, 18 IFH 18/40, 12 sFH 396, 12 KH 433, 12 10cm Kan.)
Volkswerfer Brig. 18 (70 15cm, 18 21cm, 36 30cm)
LXXX Armeekorps
Volksartillerie Korps 408 (18 FK 40, 18 IFH 18/40, 12sFH 396, 12 KH 433, 12 10cm Kan.)
Volkswerfer Brig. 8 (70 15cm, 18 21cm, 36 30cm)

mainly because of the habit of infantry of occupying log-covered foxholes and winterized huts in widely spaced strong-points rather than a continuous line. Then too almost all of the fire was unobserved, much of it falling on unoccupied crossroads, villages and woods. Staudinger in particular disowned the fire plan as defective and too dispersed. "I did not think very much of this artillery preparation," he said after the war.

The barrage in the *Fifth Panzer Armee* was not to precede the ground assault for Manteuffel believed that this would belie the surprise element which he felt was a large advantage. At 6 A.M. after the shock troops were beginning to infiltrate the American positions, the barrage in that army began; the guns and rocket launchers fired forty rounds for each piece in the first twenty minutes against pre-determined targets followed by a *Feuerwalze,* or rolling barrage, with sixty rounds fired for each gun. In some cases there were differences; the *26th Volksgrenadier Division* assault waves moved before a salvo of artillery fire from the *766th Volksartillerie Korps* fired at American targets along the Skyline Drive illuminated by searchlights.

In the *Seventh Armee,* the fewer number of available pieces meant that the fire had to be concentrated against a few promising targets. The American artillery groupment south of Echternach attracted long range German fire which had been carefully reconnoitered prior to the attack. In the *LXXXV Armeekorps,* the *408 Volksartillerie Korps* fired ninety rounds from 72 guns as rapidly as the gunners could load and shoot. However, in the *Seventh Armee* as elsewhere, the bombardment dwindled quickly as the ammunition was used up.

The German Artillery Does Not Advance

In the immediate battle to rupture the American lines the German artillery was instrumental in the Nazi advance. However, as the battle progressed both the supply for the artillery as well as its transport to the fighting front became problematic. Road conditions and fuel shortages

German assault artillery "Brummbär" of the 217th Sturmpanzer Battalion opens fire on U.S. positions near Bütgenbach. The battle took place amid a snowstorm on December 22nd.

made it extremely difficult to move the artillery forward; the situation was further aggravated by the lack of prime movers. According to the artillery commander for *Heeresgruppe B,* "There was a shortage of towing mediums and transport space was lacking for ammunition and motor fuel. We did not see far enough ahead to contemplate the difficulties which would later ensue owing to the roads and terrain." There were no tractors for the heavy army batteries of 22-35cm and even a chronic shortage of movers for the lighter guns.

For instance, in the case of the *XLVII Panzerkorps,* both the *766th Volkartillerie Korps* and the *15th Volkswerfer Brigade* were without any prime movers, having "loaned" them to the *Panzer Lehr Division* which had arrived in the Waxweiler area with no organic transport for its divisional tubes. The web of problems that beset the artillery, particularly the shortage of ammunition and fuel, led to an early decision to leave half of the weapons behind — there clearly was no reason to haul around guns for which there was no ammunition. Even when an effort was made to move the guns, the time required to change position could often try the patience of the German commanders on the field. For instance, an effort to move the *388th Volksartillerie Korps* from the *LXVII Armeekorps* to the *IISS Panzerkorps* on December 19th took four days to

move the guns only twenty kilometers over the crowded roads. Walter Staudinger, the *Sixth Panzer Armee* artillery commander described the problems:

In my opinion, reports on the number of guns available for the effort was misleading in terms of our own artillery strength. I informed Field Marshall Model telling him that the description of our own artillery situation would only be clear if the numbers of guns available were given with the quantities of ammunition that were available for the pieces....The Corps artillery was to fire from its original positions as long as it could. As many of the larger caliber guns required special emplacements, Army artillery was not to displace until the Meuse was reached. Most of the volksartillerie battalions didn't move forward because of the lack of fuel and the clogged roads. Even if displacements of artillery units only amounted to a few kilometers, the change of position of a VAK with its five battalions needed at least ten cubic meters of fuel. Generalfeldmarshal Model found two or three of these battalions in their original positions and ordered me to court martial their commanders. When I told him it was because of fuel shortages and road conditions that they hadn't moved, he rescinded his order.

The situation had a mirror image in the *Fifth Panzer Armee.* The traffic bottlenecks at the Our River had hampered the displacement of the artillery over that river; *LVIII Panzerkorps* artillery did not cross until the fourth day of the offensive. Later, as Christmas approached and the danger from the Bastogne salient increased, Manteuffel looked to the artillery to assist in the capture of that troublesome town. However, his artillery commander, Generalleutnant Richard Metz, was forced to persuade his commander to take a different course:

On the 24th of December, the situation caused the senior artillery commander to dissuade the commander of the *Fifth Panzer Armee* from bringing up the artillery which were still left at the line of departure to be committed before Bastogne. Considering the fuel scarcity which had already seriously handicapped the supply of ammunition, we were forced to propose that this idea be dropped for the present in order to supply the artillery and nebelwerfers already committed...

In general, only about half of the German corps artillery was able to follow in the wake of the offensive and the German infantry was forced to rely on their divisional guns, mortars or assault gun fire. Most of the corps artillery that did manage to move along with the assault consisted of the lighter 150mm werfers that could be towed behind other vehicles. The "screaming meemies," as the Americans called them, were much feared by U.S. soldiers in the Ardennes. Concentrated defensive fire barrages on the U.S. 4th Division were reported as the "heaviest enemy fire encountered in the war in Europe." The real problem was the usual shortage of rocket ammunition.

The organization of the *Volksartillerie Korps* presented a glaring problem that grew more serious as the offensive

progressed: each corps consisted of no less than five differing types of guns each requiring different ammunition. The Russian 12.2 cm guns, pressed into service for the Reich, had only the ammunition with which they had been captured; no more was to be expected. Even given these drawbacks, occasionally, through great effort, the Germans were able to form a fire direction battery which was used to concentrate corps artillery as "centers of gravity" as they were used on the Eastern Front.

This was done by the artillery commander in the *Seventh Armee* on December 19th to get the left flank moving again. Later towards the close of December, Model had another concentration formed that was used to add punch to the counterattack to close the Bastogne corridor. Even so, the transport problems and the difficulty of obtaining sufficient ammunition constrained the usefulness of these im-

provisations. As one German commander observed, "the shoe pinched everywhere."

American Artillery Responds

During the first hours of the German offensive, the American artillery was caught temporarily unaware. The German barrage cut communications to the corps artillery up and down the front; some battalions were hit by gusts of counterbattery fire from German guns which knew the American gunners' location. The ground assault deprived the American artillery of their eyes as sound ranging equipment was lost and the forward OPs were overrun and killed or captured.

Eight of the nine VIII Corps battalions were positioned just west of the Schnee Eifel to support the untried U.S. 106th Division. The German ground assault quickly surrounded the American division and the corps artillery found themselves under small

German troops load 15cm rockets into a six-tubed nebelwerfer in the Ardennes. These "Screaming Meemies" had a short-range (less than three miles), were inaccurate and produced a prominent back-blast that invited prompt Allied counterbattery fire. In spite of these limitations, their fantastic rate of fire and great mobility (they could be manhandled into position) played a large part in carrying German firepower forward.

arms fire as early as the evening of the first day of the attack; the 275th Armored Field Artillery battalion was temporarily surrounded near Auw. The guns and their crews proved very vulnerable to the German armored ground assault in the following days.

On December 17th the corps battalions were forced to withdraw in mass —losing a number of guns and much vital equipment in the process. A number of guns were lost and some panic ensued in the scramble to move the batteries out of harms way past St. Vith. Records show only 2,500 rounds of artillery fired on the 16th by VIII Corps. Even so, the 422nd FA Group to the south regained its balance in the afternoon long enough to give the Germans advancing into Echternach a welcome of exploding shells.

Further north the American 406th Artillery Group and the 62nd AFA battalion northwest of Monschau came to life on the afternoon of December

ORGANIZATION OF NON-DIVISONAL ARTILLERY IN THE ARDENNES - FIRST U.S. ARMY
December 15, 1944

First U.S. Army (348 pieces)
  32 FA Brigade/ 79 FA Grp
    18 FA Bn [4.5-inch Rockets]
    Prov.FA Bn [Captured German 105H]
    551 FA Bn [240H]
    552 FA Bn [240H]
    268 FA Bn [8G]

V Corps
  406 FA Grp
    BtryC 272 FA Bn [240H]
    186 FA Bn [155H]
    955 FA Bn [155H]
    941 FA Bn [4.5-inch G]
    200 FA Bn [155G] (-BtryB)
  Other:
    16 AFA Bn (CCB,9 Arm)
    62 AFA Bn (102 Cav)
    Btry C 987 FA Bn [155G SP] (2nd Inf)
    196 FA Bn [105H] (2nd Inf)
    7 FA Bn [105H] (78th Inf)
    987 FA Bn [155G SP] (78 Inf)
    Btry B 200 FA Bn [155G] (99 Inf)
    776 FA Bn [155H] (99 Inf)

VIII Corps
  174 FA Grp
    965 FA Bn [155H]
    969 FA Bn [155H]
    770 FA Bn [4.5-inch G]
  333 FA Grp
    333 FA Bn [155H]
    771 FA Bn [4.5-inch G]
  402 FA Grp
    559 FA Bn [155G] (-BtryC)
    561 FA Bn [155G]
    578 FA Bn [8H]
    740 FA Bn [8H]
  422 FA Grp
    Btry C 559 FA Bn [155G]
    81 FA Bn [155H]
    174 FA Bn [155G]
  Other:
    687 FA Bn [105H] (28 Inf)
    275 AFA Bn (14th Cav)

Mainstay of American firepower. Howitzers of the 969th Field Artillery Battalion attached to the 101st Airborne Division dig in within the surrounded perimeter of Bastogne.

The big gun. A 155mm howitzer in Patton's Third Army opens fire on distant German positions. The gun was primarily used to support U.S. offensive operations and could hurl its shell a maximum range of about twelve miles.

16th firing the then super secret proximity fuse at the waves of German volksgrenadiers who were attacking. This fire was probably the dominant reason for the failure of the German plans in this sector.

Here, Hitler had forbade artillery fire on the picturesque town of Monschau and, according to General Hitzfeld, the few assault guns that the *326th Volksgrenadiers* had possessed were taken away. The result was that the Germans were completely outgunned in this sector. On the morning of December 17th when the Germans readied for a new bid for the sector, the 32nd FA Brigade and the 406th FA Group chimed in with a two hour counterpreparation on the hapless grenadiers cowering in the wooded draws around Monschau. However, as it became clear that things were going wrong in *Korps Monschau*, the restriction on fire on the town was rescinded and the *902nd Sturmgeschütz Brigade* assigned. By then, however, it was too late. The ground battle had already been decided on the very first two days. The support merely reinforced a deepening failure. A final bid for the sector on December 18th was greeted with a salvo of over 1,000 rockets from the 18th FA Battalion near Kalterherberg. In Rohrern, where the Germans had

concentrated, this blast left the town in flames.

As the Americans lines stabilized on the northern and southern shoulders of the offensive, the American superiority in the artillery arm became paramount to the success of the U.S. defense. During the night of December 17th, a single battalion of the 99th Infantry Division was covered by defensive fire comprising 11,500 rounds. Lt. Robert D. Bass with the 99th's 324 Combat Engineer Battalion wrote of this shelling in a letter home in January:

> ...Sure enough, we had only been in these positions a day and then came the German tanks followed by their infantry. Their main thrust was in our own sector. Our own small arms fire stopped the infantry, but those tanks kept coming. There was an artillery forward observer with us and he was trying to adjust his fire on those tanks. I don't imagine a bunch of engineers ever said quite so many prayers as we did in those few minutes, when the German tanks were almost upon us before the artillery observer could get his fire on them. The tanks were less than 200 yards from us when our artillery finally began hitting all around them. Dad, remember about the terrific barrage that I told you about when I was at O.C.S. at Fort Sill, layed down by 109 artillery pieces? Well, that bar-

rage was child's play compared to the barrage the good old American artillery put on those attacking German Tiger tanks. I can't tell you how many tanks or Germans were knocked out in front of our positions that night, but they were really stacked up. What few German tanks that weren't knocked out, turned tail and fled. All night we could hear the wounded Germans out in front of us hollering "Surrender."

Later German sorties to approach the Elsenborn Ridge positions after December 19th were met each time by a wall of shell bursts from the guns ensconced there. German troop concentrations south of Bütgenbach on December 20th (*12th SS Panzer Division*) and in Rocherath-Krinkelt on December 24th (*3rd Panzer Grenadier Division*) were hit each time before the grenadiers had fully formed for the assault.

To the south, the gunners of the 402nd Field Artillery Group gave the German engineers of the *Seventh Armee* a perilous job. On December 18th, the Americans shot out the precious German pontoon bridge at Echternach and accurate observation and heavy artillery fire dropped on the approach when the engineers dared approach. Brandenberger was faced with a classic paradox. The infantry assault must get under way at once to dislodge the American observers so that he could bring heavy weapons across the river, but without his meager allotment of assault guns in the first place, it was hard to get his men moving. It took four days to get a serviceable bridge in place. By then, as on the north shoulder, the fate of the *Seventh Armee* offensive was already decided.

By December 24th when more corps artillery was available and American spotter planes took to the air (always a popular target for the German flak gunners), the German panzer spearheads could be almost certain of powerful disruptions to their attack plans by the American fire. Within two days, this problem coupled with the strafing Allied planes led to a German emphasis on night attacks to avoid observation. Even so, the record of events evidences numerous instances where the American artillery decided the issue. On Christmas Day the *2nd*

Panzer Division near the Meuse was pummeled continuously by American fire; attempts by the *Panzer Lehr Division* to aid its sister formation were met by a curtain of shells. On the Bastogne-Liege highway, the *2nd SS Panzer Division* was turned back in its attempt to move beyond Manhay by accurate concentrations of American artillery. Peiper's surrounded *Kampfgruppe* had been forced to evacuate La Gleize after two days of bombardment from V Corps artillery. Attempts by the *150th Panzer Brigade* to rush Malmédy were met by a deadly fusillade of the POZIT proximity fused rounds. These stories of frustrated German attacks being pounded by U.S. artillery continued to increase in the coming days.

Towards the end of the month as the grim fighting developed around the Bastogne corridor, both sides sought to increase their artillery firepower to decide the battle. This resulted in a rare counterbattery duel between the German guns (*388th and 401st Volksartillerie Korps and 15 Volkswerfer Brigade*) versus the 193rd FA Corps Artillery Group of Patton's Third Army. Just as in the ground battle, the American gunners eventually prevailed firing off 11,000 rounds in a single day in support of a single U.S. division. It was a weight of metal that the German gunners could not hope to match. Hitler's last offensive was

American mobility. Artillery was all armored and self-propelled in the U.S. Armored Divisions. Each division had 36 M7B1 105mm howitzers like these. This photograph shows a gun of the 212th AFA providing fire support for its parent 6th Armored Division near Bastogne on January 8th, 1945. This particular battalion established a firing record averaging over 1,000 rounds per day—double the average firing rate of such units in heavy action.

over.

Considering the great similarities between the U.S. and German artillery, it is understandable to pose the question as to why the U.S. gunners were so much more effective? There are several answers to this question. Among the most important reasons are:

1) Artillery ammunition was in such short supply that the most rigid rationing methods had to be applied to the German fire plan. Even the greatest economy on other fronts had been able to create more than 2.5 basic loads of ammunition for the Ardennes attack; even then the preparation had to be of limited duration and concentrations of artillery later was the exception rather than the rule. The difficulty of procuring the right type of ammunition plagued the *Volksartillerie Korps* which had a large number of captured Russian guns as their heavy tubes. Nebelwerfer ammunition was also in very short supply.

2) The general shortage of fuel aggravated the German ammunition supply problem and made it nearly impossible to move the German artillery in the wake of the offensive. Typically only the lighter werfers were brought forward in mass and movement of the *Volksartillerie Korps* was only accomplished through the dent of great effort. Much of the German equipment was horse drawn while all the American guns were fully motorized — the U.S. armored field artillery battalions were decidedly superior to anything the Germans fielded in non-

Prime Movers. An American 8-inch howitzer is pulled along the Manhay road by an Allis-Chambers 18-ton M4 Tractor, December 31st, 1944.

Young artillery observers of the 1st SS Panzer Division adjust fire for their self-propelled 15cm "Bison" infantry guns near the village of Poteau. This well equipped unit was the exception, however. Lack of sufficient radio gear dogged German efforts to judiciously use their artillery in the Ardennes.

divisional guns.

3) The loss of air superiority made air observation impossible. The German artillery was at a constant disadvantage in being unable to direct their fire other than by ground observation. American fighter planes harrassed the German artillery when the weather cleared making it dangerous for them to fire in daylight.

4) Material losses during the last year of the war, particulary in the withdrawl from France had been severe and much of the available equipment was not in good condition. Prime movers were in exceedingly short supply and replacement parts for the captured equipment were virtually non-existent.

5) Communications equipment was inferior to the Allied gear. Shortages of radios and wire further aggravated the problem such that available ground observation from combat formations could not be reported to the guns in the rear.

Thus the German artillery, despite its sound doctrine and good organization, could only function at a much reduced level compared to its scale of operation earlier in the war. To be sure, German artillery officers were critical of the American artillery fire as being wasteful, predictable and subject to exploitation.

Experienced German officers often took advantage of the fact that fire was virtually non-existent on the American divisional and corps boundaries and used this knowledge to safely infiltrate the U.S. positions. It is also probably true, as the German artillery officers allege, that a very heavy weight of fire was expended by the

German guns were usually towed, even in the better equipped SS divisions.

American gunners for each German killed. During the Ardennes fighting, the Americans brought 4,155 artillery pieces onto action on the battlefield and fired off 1,255,000 rounds of ammunition by the end of December.

These guns were decisive. Although it cannot be said that the American artillery single handedly won the Battle of the Bulge, it often was the critical difference for the U.S. between battles won and lost. Gen. William E. DePuy, then a battalion commander in the U.S. 90th Infantry Division perhaps puts it best:

I really believe, based upon my experience [in WWII], that the combat power provided by the artillery, I'm sorry to say, probably represented 90% or more of the combat power actually applied against the enemy. That's why I say that getting a forward observer to a high piece of ground was the most important function that infantry performed in that war. That is not to degrade the infantry, it's just an objective analysis.

Shellpower. A firing position of the 489th Field Artillery, U.S. 7th Armored Division shows an important American advantage—a plentiful supply of 105mm artillery rounds.

The Allies Attack: January 5th - 11th

The Allied offensive that had begun on Wednesday, January 3rd, made slow progress in the Ardennes. Although the Germans had been turned back in their bid for Antwerp, the Battle of the Bulge was far from over. As much an enemy as the Germans was the dreadful weather. Sub-zero temperatures were the norm; Allied soldiers wallowed in waist-deep snow drifts unable to see through the haze and ice fog. Tanks and trucks spun crazily on the roads covered with sheet ice and dense fog and mist often prevented the Allied air forces from operating at all. Over the next two weeks on only three days could they provide support to the Allied ground forces that needed their help so badly.

Although beaten and far under strength, the German soldiers in the *2nd SS Panzer* and the *12th* and *560th Volksgrenadier Divisions* continued to resist stubbornly in the path of Montgomery's offensive from the north. The American as-

Cold war. Engineers, prepared to fight as infantry, return from the front line near Wiltx.

Sub-zero. GIs of the 82nd Airborne Division trudge through knee deep snow in the Ardennes.

sault forces comprised the 83rd and 84th Infantry Divisions and the 2nd and 3rd Armored of Collin's VII Corps. On the left, Ridgway's XVIII Airborne Corps advanced towards the Salm River with the Gavin's 82nd Airborne and Hobb's 30th Infantry Division facing the tired *18th* and *62nd Volksgrenadiers*. Meanwhile, Gerow's V Corps held in place, ready to advance towards St. Vith after sufficient progress had been made on the right.

January 5th was one of the few clear days which allowed air support, but so bad were the roads that armored advance nearly ground to a halt. The 2nd Armored managed to wrest part of the village of Odeigne from the Germans, but made little progress in its push towards Consy. Meanwhile the 3rd took La Vaux from the *12th Volksgrenadiers* in "violent house to house fighting," while the 82nd Airborne secured Arbrefontaine from the enemy for good. But all these advances were less than a mile and enemy resistance was dogged. Reinforcements were arriving to prop up the faltering German line as well: the *326th Volksgrenadier Division* was marching into the sector from its former post near

Monschau. But even worse for Allied aims, that night, the weather closed in once more. So dismal were the conditions that Patton's normally aggressive army was forced to the defensive. The attacks that day by his 35th and 87th Divisions made only neglibible gains save the usual violent reactions from their enemy.

Given the weather, it would be January 6th before Gen. Rose and his U.S. 3rd Armored Division took the Baraque de Fraiture crossroads on the Bastogne-Liège highway from the reconnaissance battalion of *Kampfgruppe Krag*, now on loan to the *560th Volksgrenadier Division*. With its flank thus turned, the nearby *12th Volksgrenadiers* were forced to abandon the nearby village of Lierneux. The crossroads had been an early objective for Gen. Collins. On the following day, in the midst of bitter cold and a snow storm, Ridgway's XVIII Corps launched a determined attack against stubborn German resistance from *Korps Felber* (Gen. Hans-Gustav Felber). Felber, who had recently come down from the *Fifteenth Armee* and taken over the sector along the west bank of the Salm River from the *LXVI Armeekorps*, had seen fit to prop up his sagging infantry line with locally available heavy corps artillery; he also brought down some other infantry reinforcements.

As a result of the enemy preparations, casualties were extremely heavy in the subsequent fighting. An American advance of a mile a day was a major achievement. At Rochelinval, on January 7th, the 551st Parachute Infantry Battalion was all but wiped out in a violent encounter with the *62nd Volksgrenadiers*. On that same day the men of the U.S. 30th Division, with the attached 112th Infantry Regiment slogged forward through the snow to surprise the enemy between the Salm and Amblève Rivers. They went on to seize the hamlets of Wanne and Spineux deep within the frozen Grand Bois. "We are fighting the weather," observed Gen. Leland Hobbs, the commander of the division, "and losing about one hundred a day. . . It's a hell of a country."

On the American nothern right flank, the attack picked up steam. The 2nd Armored seized the villages of Dochamps and Marcouray from the *560th Volksgrenadier Division* while the 3rd Armored and 83rd Division took Regne,

Even though winter conditions were hardly inviting, American soldiers did have the decided advantage of motorized transport of their infantry. Here GIs of the 30th Infantry Division move cautiously along the icy roads. The windshield of the lead vehicle, sporting a bullet hole, shows the dangers of ambush to motorized columns.

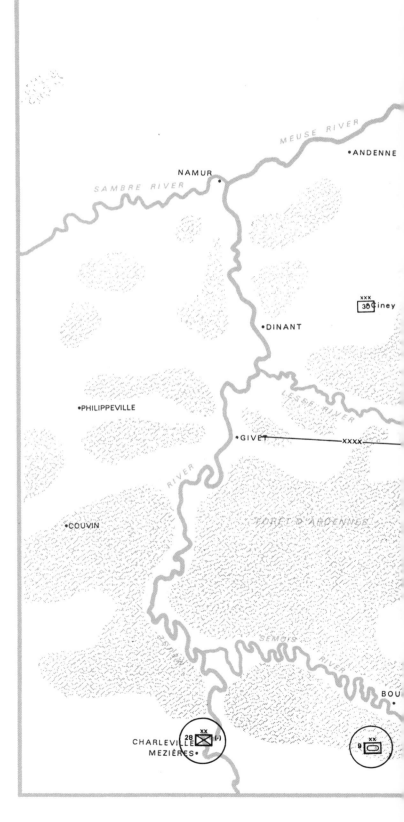

SITUATION MAP
January 5th-11th

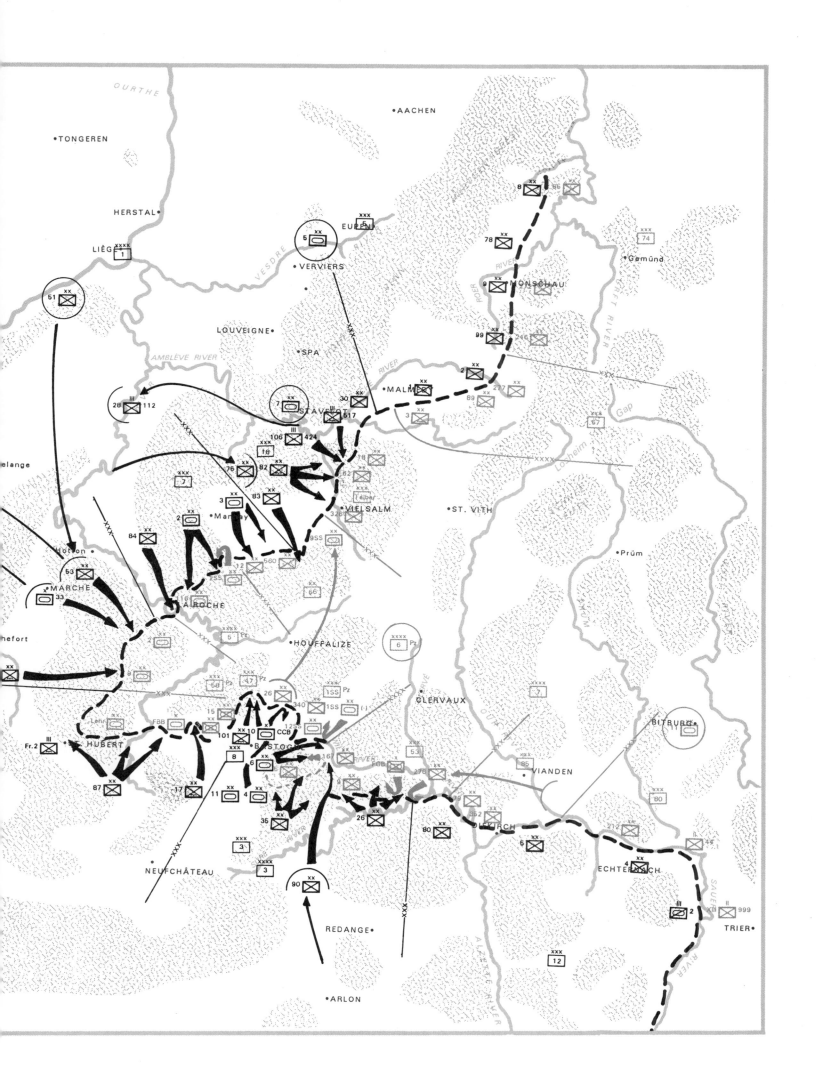

Verleumont and Sart in sharp fighting with the *2nd SS Panzer.* Meanwhile on the left, the intrepid 82nd Airborne Division pushed over two miles to capture Goronne, Farniers and Mont from the *62nd Volksgrenadiers.*

In Patton's Army, the 87th Division continued its assault southwest of Bastogne, still frustrated by fanatic resistance from the *Führer Begleit Brigade* before the village of Tillet. Nearby the "gung-ho" paratroopers of the Miley's 17th Airborne rushed Rechrival and Flamierge in spite of withering enemy fire from the *3rd Panzer Grenadier Division.* German artillery claimed many of the young men of the division; over a hundred were killed that day. Even so, the American assault had nearly reached the German divisional headquarters of Gen. Denkert in the tiny hamlet of Tronle. Impressed by the demeanor of the first paratrooper prisoners taken in, the German leader took prompt action to defend his position. Fierce fighting raged all day in Flamierge, but at dark the Americans retired from the battlefield. A subordinated tank battlegroup had just arrived from the *9th Panzer Division* at Denkert's command post. Sensing the importance of the crossroads of the Marche-Bastogne highway, the German general immediately ordered them to counterattack.

Just east of Bastogne, the 6th Armored beat off German assaults in the Neffe-Wardin area. The enemy tangling with Grow's armor was *167th Volksgrenadiers* backed by Tiger tanks of the *506th Heavy Panzer Battalion.* The battered 6th Armored relied heavily on the artillery to repulse the Germans; supporting guns fired 11,655 rounds on the 5th. Even as this transpired, the division commander received orders to go over to the offensive. Gen. Grow was dubious, "This is a poor plan by Army," the general noted for the record, "who does not appreciate the situation where we are being attacked daily and strength is way down." But Patton was not to be denied. The orders stood.

Meanwhile, southeast of Bastogne, the 35th Division pushed for Lutremange-Lutrebois road, but was stopped short of its objective by the usual fanatic resistance from the *1st SS Panzer Division.*

But if bloody and miserable, the Americans' unrelinquishing battle was weaking the enemy resolve in the Ardennes. Even Hitler himself could recognize another Normandy-like "Falaise Pocket" in the making. On January 8th he consented to pull the endangered *Fifth Panzer Armee* back from the tip of the Bulge, not all the way back to Houffalize as Gen. von Manteuffel had urged, but at least to a line between Dochamps and Longchamps extending northwest from Bastogne. Even as the Führer gave this order, German units at the tip of the saliant were prudently retreating under Allied pressure. The 84th Division took Consy and then marched on into Cielle, just north of La Roche. Their opponent was Gen. Waldenburg's over-leveraged *116th Panzer.* At the same time the 3rd Armored fanned out, clanking through the streets of Joubieval, Provedroux and Hebronval against scant resistance. The 82nd Airborne consolidated its positions along the Salm River clearing the Germans from the villages of Grand Sart and Comté.

The day before, the British 51st Division, which had taken over the assault role around Hotton from the departing

53rd, noted diminished resistance from the *116th Panzer Division.* Moreover, Hitler also began reallocating the priority for replacements and equipment to other fronts. During the day the Führer ordered two *Volksartillerie Korps* to be transported elsewhere, a sure sign that *Wacht am Rhein* had fallen out of his favor.

But the exodus of the SS armor and the other German support troops was not in evidence in the battle on either side of Bastogne. Here, the Germans continued their grudging defense, making frequent use of their penchant for counterattack whenever a position became impossible. To the south, the Americans found their old adversary, the *Führer Begleit Brigade* a formidable opponent; the 87th Division suffered continuing setbacks in its fight to take Tillet and Bonnerue. Just to the east, the 17th Airborne was forced to relinquish Flamierge once more from the *3rd Panzer Grenadier Division* after severe tank-lead counterattacks. The only good news was from the 6th Armored, which had recovered the ground lost the previous day from the *12th SS Panzer.*

On January 9th, as the Germans commenced to move out of the western edge of the salient, Patton launched his counterstroke northward from Bastogne with eight divisions including the secretly assembled 90th Infantry (Maj. Gen.

Death in Nothum. The body of Lt. Col. George B. Randolf lies where he was killed by a German artillery shell on January 9th, 1945. Randolf was the commander of the 712th tank battalion fighting with the U.S. 90th Infantry Division.

James A. van Fleet). It was bitter cold; snow was nearly two feet deep and the thermometer stood at -6F. Casualties were very heavy. The enemy opposite the 90th Division, however, was taken by surprise. Van Fleet's men thrust rapidly to the village of Berle on the first day — an advance of over a mile. On its flank the 26th Division pushed north of Bavigne. With these moves the right flank of the *9th Volksgrenadier Division* was under such severe pressure that it was forced to yield ground.

Near Bastogne, the 6th Armored went over to the attack near Wardin as the 35th Division took on the Germans near Lutremange. By the following day, both Villers-la-Bonne-Eau and Harlange were retaken as the *1st SS Panzer Division* received orders to pull out and assemble in the St. Vith area.

A large German saliant southeast of Bastogne now jutted out into the American line. As seen by Gen. Rothkirch of the *LIII Armeekorps*, the entire *5th Fallschirmjäger Division* was threatened with encirclement. A desperate German counterattack by hastily assembled elements of the *9th* and *276th Volksgrenadiers* and the *Führer Grenadier Brigade* was launched against the 26th Infantry Division. The stroke faltered near Dahl with heavy casualties. The situation looked equally bleak for the Germans elsewhere in the south. The hard fight of the 87th Division near Tillet which had run on for days was nearing a climax. By January 10th the village

was finally cleared of Germans. And out of the Bastogne salient, the 101st Airborne, with support from the 10th Armored advanced towards Noville running head on into the last ditch defense of the *26th Volksgrenadier Division*. The most encouraging American progress appeared about to develop east of the main Houffalize-Bastogne highway near Bourcy where a combat command of the 4th Armored Division had been thrown in. But no sooner than had the armor begun to advance than Patton abruptly called a halt.

An explanation for this uncharacteristic act is not hard to find. Having failed to divine the enemy's intent to launch the Ardennes counteroffensive and now in the midst of another enemy blow in the Alsace, the intelligence staffs at SHAEF and the 12th Army Group were "seeing burglars under every bed." Some now worried lest the wily Germans spoil the Allied offensive in the Ardennes with another surprise operation emanating from the south of Trier designed to capture Luxembourg City. As a result, Gen. Bradley ordered Patton to pull out an armored division to maintain a reserve. Seeing no threat himself ("I think the Hun has shot his wad!") Patton chose the 4th Armored since it needed rest and reorganization anyway. The next day Bradley would allow Patton to resume the attack, but the 4th Armored was now out of the fight. "This is the second time I have been stopped in a successful attack due to the fact that the Ger-

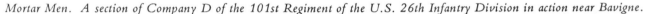

Mortar Men. A section of Company D of the 101st Regiment of the U.S. 26th Infantry Division in action near Bavigne.

The Hun vanquished. A 90mm M-36 of the 703rd Tank Destroyer Battalion passes by a knocked out Mk IV of the 15th Panzer Grenadier Division *near Langlir, Belgium.*

The 87th Infantry Division photographed liberating the village of St. Hubert from the Germans on January 11th.

mans have more nerve than we have," the Third Army commander lamented.

Opposite Patton, Gen. Collins continued his squeeze on the Bulge from the north. On January 9th the 83rd Division, passing through the 3rd Armored, assumed the assault role in VII Corps. Gen. Macon's men were drawn into fierce fighting with the *560th Volksgrenadiers* for the villages of Bihain and Petit Langlir. On the VII Corps right flank, the 84th Division and 2nd Armored blasted the *116th Panzer* out of Samrée after a preparatory bombardment of 12,514 artillery rounds.

On both sides exhausted troops were moved into reserve. The First Army took the tired 82nd Airborne out of the line along with the 28th Division and what was left of the 106th. Similarly on the other side, the Germans moved the *12th SS Panzer* into reserve near Bleialf and also shifted the exhausted *62nd Volksgrenadier Division* out of fighting. The next day the *1st SS Panzer* was alerted to prepare to move into reserve as well. The German offensive at Bastogne now over, the German field command was streamlined for defensive action. Decker's *XXXIX Panzerkorps* was ordered to the Alsace and the *LXXXV Armeekorps* left the front immediately, its responsibilities to be assumed by the *LIII* and *LXXX Armeekorps*.

By January 11th the Third Army attack had begun to pay dividends. After a frustrating week, the 87th Division's hard fight with the Germans on the south flank finally led to a two day advance as the enemy pulled back. Gen. Culin's division seized the villages of Bonnerue, Pironpré, St. Hubert, Amberloup and Sprimont. Nearby the 17th Airborne made similar progress, taking Mande St. Etienne and Flamizoulle. However, the *15th Panzergrenadier Division*, which vacated the area, left it covered with dangerous stretches of mined roads. The 6th Armored took over the positions of the departing 4th Armored Division along the Bastogne corridor. Even though Gen. Grow worried that his division's combat effectiveness was only about 50%, his frost-bitten tankers went over the attack. The "Super Sixth" took the long-contested village of Wardin the following day.

But the most important development on January 11th in Patton's Army was in the sector of the intrepid 90th Division. Van Fleet's infantry took Doncols and Bras east of Bastogne and closed the net on a pocket containing a thousand German prisoners from the *5th Fallschirmjäger Division*. In desperation the German field commanders hastily recommit-

ted the *1st SS Panzer* to slice open a way to the trapped division via Oberwampach. This was not to succeed; the German parachute division was almost totally destroyed. Even so, violent tank battles arising from the German rescue attempt raged about Oberwampach for days.

To the north, Gen. Bolling's 84th Division cleared the town of La Roche of the last vestige of the *116th Panzer Division* while the 75th Infantry relieved the tired paratroopers of the 82nd Airborne Division along the Salm River. The 83rd Division secured the village of Langlir and beat off the inevitable enemy counterattacks. The next day the 2nd and 3rd Armored took Chabrehez and cleared the Bois de Cendrogne of the *560th Volksgrenadier Division*.

In the north there was a symbolic development in the campaign. The battered 424th Regiment of the 106th Division established a bridgehead across the Amblève at Stavelot in front of the *18th Volksgrenadier Division*. It was here that *Kampfgruppe Peiper* had boldly advanced at the height of the German offensive nearly a month earlier. Now the crossing was in American hands once more.

The Civilians

The citizens of the Ardennes awoke on December 16th, 1944, to find that the war had returned. For over six weeks the countryside would see two large armies fight a terrible battle over some 2,000 square miles of the Ardennes. A few of the villages and hamlets of the quaint resort region would see their ownership change as many as four times in the course of the campaign.

The experience of total war in their backyard was all too familiar to the citizens of Belgium and Luxembourg. People there had the disquieting experience of being the only Europeans to be liberated and then be re-conquered by the Nazis. The Germans were greatly feared and hated by many of the people in the Ardennes — particularly the fanatical soldiers from the dreaded Waffen SS. The Kaiser's legions had goose-stepped through the region in 1914 and Hitler's panzers had motored through the countryside in May 1940. Relief had come in September, 1944, when the U.S. First Army had liberated the region. Now, in December 1944, the Germans were back again.

Mr. Walthere Jamar, of Chevron, Belgium was in the path of the advance of *Kampfgruppe Peiper* of the *1SS Panzer Division*. He wrote in his diary on December 18th:

> From my window, I look towards Stavelot and I see streams of refugees as far as I can see. Again there is panic!...We go to bed, fully dressed and of course worried, without closing an eye; any moment the Germans can charge into our home. Around 11 P.M. while in bed I hear the sound of vehicles, undoubtedly driving along the route to Stavelot. The Germans are bringing in their tanks at great speed....Again invaded by these Nazi criminals. What sad days still lie ahead of us?

Knowing the dangers of war, many citizens left their villages at the first sounds of gun-fire, snatching what meager possessions they could carry and stampeding to the safer regions to the West. Remembering the terror of the previous four years, some 200,000 Belgian and Luxembourg citizens spontaneously took to the road upon hearing of the German advance. Cold, hungry and destitute, many wandered about helplessly for weeks. Such

Citizens of Bastogne flee the town as the Germans near the vicinity.

hordes of refugees proved to be a major headache for U.S. Military Police trying to direct American traffic while watching for Nazi saboteurs dressed as Belgian peasants.

A good example of this was the situation in the town of Diekirch in Luxembourg. On December 19th, 3,000 civilians streamed from the village in freezing weather, fearful of reprisals from the Germans now closing in. The townfolk were particularly worried because members of the local *gendarmerie* had fought alongside the Americans in September. Twenty German prisoners from this episode were still housed in the local jail. The resulting stampede upset American plans to reinforce the area. Even with this mass exodus, however, some 400 villagers stayed behind out of concern for their aged relatives or for their property and possessions.

Those who stayed often hide in cold, damp cellars for as long as four weeks, not venturing forth until sounds of the guns and bombs had ceased. A family hiding in Chenogne remembers the frightful time when their cellars had been turned into a German Red Cross station:

> ...The third night in the cellars is haunted by the groans of the dying. By the sound of the machine gun crackle, it would seem that a hand to hand struggle is going on in the village. The injured are quickly treated and then return to the fight. A shell has just burst two meters off the western door to the cellar. The plaster falls from the ceiling and a thick cloud of dust obscures the exit. Over and above the crackling of the machine guns, the earth trembles; bombs explode and shake the houses. The wounded flow in again. To the prayers of our people, mingle the desperate cries of dying soldiers. We have to abandon one of the cellars and turn it into a morgue.

Less fortunate citizens sought refuge in less secure stables and barns or even camped in the countryside. Many suffered terribly from the cold and lack of food. Madame de Coune of Assenois remembers Christmas Eve in refuge in a nearby woods:

> The menu of dinner is fresh bread and frozen snow. The whole night shells whistle overhead. It is clear and cold. In spite of the din we are able to sleep from time to time. There were four heavy pieces of German artillery very close to our woods. The gunshots resounded loudly and the smell of gunpowder was acrid.

In spite of their efforts, however, many of those living in the Ardennes did not escape the carnage of battle. Many villages that came under guns or bombs were be reduced to pitiful rubble heaps. Many lost nearly all of their worldly possessions. But they were the lucky ones. Over 2,500 innocent Belgians and Luxembourgers perished

Leaving home before Christmas. Civilians flee the village of Manhay on foot and bicycle as German SS combat teams approach from the south on December 23rd, 1944.

during the Ardennes Campaign — some at the hands of SS criminals, but more under the rain of indiscriminate bombs and shells from both sides. Over 500 died in the Bastogne area alone. Part of the civilian population of that town, terrified by the return of the Nazis, had streamed off along the roads to Neauchâteau, St. Hubert and Marche with no clear idea of their destination. But those that remained, however, seemed absolutely impervious to fear, remaining active in their daily affairs in town almost heedless of the artillery fire dropping into the town. But soon this ended. General McAuliffe, the commander of the garrison, was so afraid that German saboteurs dressed as civilians might infiltrate his defenses that he forbade civilians out of their cellars except between midday and 2 P.M. to gather food. Over the next week the citizens of Bastogne lived underground, noting

each day the arrival of 6 P.M. when the German heavy gun in the entrance to Kautenbach tunnel sent six shells crashing into the town. Later the awful Luftwaffe vengeance bombing came each night slowly turning the market square into a pile of ruins. "We lived as if in a dream," M. Leon Jacqmin, the mayor of the town, recalled. But hardships for civilians on the outside of town were even worse. Many were mistakenly identifed as the enemy. This tragedy was all too common.

At the tiny hamlet of Houmont, southwest of Bastogne, the Americans launched an assault on December 30th to recapture the village. The evening before Mr. Chalon had fled his blasted out village of Chenogne, now totally destroyed and on fire. He and his family and his son-in-law, Rene Roland, his wife and their children sought refuge in a stable in Houmont. Then on

December 30th, an artillery shell set the farm on fire as well as the stable. Their shelter ablaze, Mr. Chalon and his family fled the barn setting off across the fields in the midst of shells and bullets crashing into the village. As soon as they emerged from the smoke from the barn, however, a machine gun opened fire on them. It was an American gunner, who had mistaken the group for fleeing Germans. Mrs. Roland was the first to fall, scarcely thirty yards from the barn. Her husband stopped to help her, but he was wounded as well and could see that she was dead. As Mr. Roland crawled along the ground he was horrified to see the other six members of his family drop to the ground as they were chopped down by the machine gun. Somehow, Rene dragged himself to the farmhouse where he was found Mr. Zabus the owner. "They are all dead," he wept. This, then, was the

The same location near Manhay shows destruction after the battle. A smashed Panther of the 2nd SS Panzer Division stands watch over the forlorn ruins of the crossroads.

great tragedy of war.

Many civilians risked their lives to hide wounded or entrapped U.S. soldiers behind German lines. Housewives provided white linens and Belgian lace tablecloths — many of them priceless family heirlooms — to the GIs who needed the material for snow camouflage. The Americans did what they could in return to try and reduce the suffering of the local populace, sharing their food and medical supplies when possible. Most were deeply moved by the civilian plight. Recalling travel posters he had seen of France before he enlisted, an American colonel wrote his wife:

> ...the beautiful girls of the travel posters have gone, or are not beautiful any longer. The healthy, happy people of the posters are hungry, thin, and have fear and bewilderment instead of smiles on their faces. You can't expect them to smile when their sons, brothers, and husbands are in labor camps, or are no more. We wouldn't smile either if our friends and neighbors were crowding the roads to get away from

Bedsheets donated by local Belgian women were used to camouflage American vehicles from German observation.

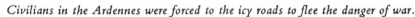

Civilians in the Ardennes were forced to the icy roads to flee the danger of war.

the war. They load what few possessions they have left, or can push, into carts, baby buggies, wheelbarrows, or any transportation they have. Tiny babies are sometimes strapped like papooses on the back of luggage carriers, or bicycles. We can't do anything about it. When we see old women or mothers with small children plodding along the edge of the roads, splashing in the snow and slush with their wooden shoes, trying to avoid being hit by trucks, and getting splashed by them...they seem to walk all night. I hope they find a place to rest and get warm....

The citizens of the Ardennes often aided the Americans during the battle. Over the month long campaign, they helped to provide the Germans with "disinformation" directing panzer columns down bad roads, overestimating U.S. strength just over the hill, while warning the Americans of German moves. Some citizens even went so far as to fire guns from village windows at the German intruders. Such acts of patriotism had terrible consequences, however. At the villages of Stavelot, Ster, Parfondruy and Renardmont soldiers from the *1st SS Panzer Division* killed over a hundred Belgians supposedly in retribution for their having fired on German soldiers nearby. At the village of Bande, the dreaded *SD* killed 32 Belgian youths in cold blood as a vendetta against the local resistance movement that had been active there the previous summer. On December 20th, a task force of the 3rd Armored Division came upon this "revolting scene" of murdered civilians in the tiny villages:

Ten or twelve completely burned bodies, charred black, were seen where a small shed had once stood...in the adjacent house, there was the body of a middle-aged woman who had been stabbed with a knife and then shot. Bodies of two boys between the ages of six and ten were seen with bullet holes in their foreheads...One old woman had been killed by a smash over the head, probably with a rifle butt....Near a foxhole were bodies of a 13 year old boy and a fifteen year old girl who had been shot, apparently, as they tried to escape.

Nor was such harsh behavior con-

fined to the *1st SS Division*. Other hungry soldiers of the *2nd SS "Das Reich" Panzer Division* threatened civilians in the Manhay area with death if they did not provide the impatient soldiers with hidden food stocks. These were men from the same division that had murdered an entire French village in Oradour-sur-Glane the previous summer. The terrorized civilians had no choice but to comply.

Contrasted with the Waffen SS, the average German soldier of late 1944 acted as properly towards the local populace as modern warfare might allow. The nefarious acts of massacre and retribution were perpetrated mostly by the SS and SD. But so heinous were the actions of the SS men that even today many older Belgians around Stavelot still deeply hate the Germans.

Although they did not commit monstrous atrocities like those of the SS, at least an equal number of deaths for the citizens of the Ardennes must be ascribed to the Allied forces. This is true if only because of the effusive use of American artillery fire and bombs on villages suspected of harboring Germans.

Many citizens were buried by the resulting devastation. A total of 2,179

civilians were killed in Belgium alone and many others wounded. Entire villages were leveled; over 11,000 residential buildings were devastated. Dead livestock, and the accompanying stench, littered the Ardennes countryside after the battle. Over 26,000 animals had been killed.

In St. Vith Allied bombing to deny the road center to the Germans killed 250 civilians and destroyed almost every house there. Similar bombing of Houffalize and La Roche left 306 innocent civilians dead. In some cases, mistakes were made, so that bombs fell of towns such as Malmédy, that were not even occupied by the enemy. At least 125 villagers and 37 U.S. soldiers were killed there by the errant bombing.

Of course, the American GIs were no angels either. In spite of strict rules forbidding such behavior, some American soldiers broke into houses and plundered. Other GIs were rude and threatening to the local women. According to Belgian civilians, the U.S. airborne men were perhaps worst in this regard. Gen. Bruce Clark, the U.S. defender of St. Vith, was only half joking when he characterized American soldiery as "two shooting and one looting." But all armies in

Citizens of Malmédy survey its smoking ruins. The town was mistakenly bombed three times by the U.S. Air Force. Many of the towns people were killed and the village was "reduced to a burned out pile of cinders and rubble."

Armored Relic. This Jagdpanzer IV/70 ended its hull-down in weeds near the village of Magaret. After the battle, the Ardennes area was littered with weapons of all types.

history have harbored such behavior; it goes with the territory of modern warfare. Most of all civilians in the Ardennes dreaded the saturation artillery fire the Americans lobbed on German occupied towns. Even so, one Belgian man explained that, "We can stand the bombs. But the Germans — we can't stand the Germans here again."

They would not have to put up with the Germans again. For by the end of January, when the German armies were finally forced out of the Ardennes, they were vanquished for good, never to return. Even then, the personal tragedy continued for the inhabitants of the Ardennes. Many returned to find all their possessions gone, their homes devastated and their land littered with the dead and their wrecked machines. Joss Heinz has described the picture faced by occupants

of the tiny village of Marvie when its inhabitants returned in 1945. The Marenwez woods nearby had been the scene of intense fighting to control the Bastogne area:

> Late in March 1945, three months after the battle, those who occasionally dared venture forth in those woods dotted with mines were still able to discover dozens of corpses frozen stiff, faces swollen and blue....Countless numbers of dead horses littered this vast wooded expanse of the Belgian- Luxembourg border. Burnt out caterpillars, panzers torn apart, and wrecked carts completed the scene of German collapse.

The houses were re-built, the corpses were buried and the broken tank wrecks were sold for scrap metal. However, death continued to linger

over the region. The very ground in the Ardennes was deadly, being sown with over hundreds of thousands of mines and countless unexploded bombs, shells and grenades. These were slowly excised from the countryside over several years, killing 14 bomb experts and wounding another 48. In all, 114,000 mines and 5,800 tons of munitions were deactivated.

However, for a time in 1945, deaths from this cause became so frequent that they dominated local obituary columns. Over half were children playing in the fields and woods of the region. Of course, even the massive mine-clearing operation could not find all the dangerous ordnance. Ten years after the battle, citizens of the Ardennes were still dying from this tragic legacy.

Hemingway in the Battle of the Bulge

The only people who ever loved war for long were profiteers, generals, staff officers and whores. They all had the best and finest times of their lives. — Ernest Hemingway

Ernest Hemingway, the well known author and Nobel Prize winner had what he called "a good war." Now a war correspondent for *Colliers*, as well as a legend in his own time, Hemingway was free to do pretty much whatever he pleased in Europe. Ernest relished his job, covering a macabre human activity he once called "man's favorite outdoor sport."

That summer in France Ernest was almost killed by German machine gunners while on a personal devil-may-care motorcycle reconnaissance in Normandy with Bob Capa of *Life*. In August, he participated in a drunken liberation of Paris, which he enjoyed immensely:

Retaking France and especially Paris made me feel the best I have ever felt....I had been in retreats, holding attack, victories with no reserves to follow them up etc., and I had never known how winning can make you feel.

But Hemingway was disappointed by the liberation of the gay city, which he admitted was more of an emotional, rather than a military operation. He wanted to get into "some of the real fighting."

Hemingway tended this desire by attaching himself to the 22nd Regiment of the 4th Infantry Division throughout the summer and fall of 1944. He developed a strong friendship with its commander, Col. Charles T. "Buck" Lanham. Hemingway accompanied Lanham's regiment in the Allied liberation of the Ardennes in September. Just west of the Schnee Eifel the author had quarters in an old Ardennes farmhouse in Buchert, Germany which Ernest nicknamed "Schloss Hemingstein." Amid this improbable background, the famous writer carried on with his wild and raucous version of the war, surrounded

Ernest Hemingway pictured at the 4th Infantry Division command post in Junglinster on December 20th, 1944. On his right is the divisional commander, Maj. Gen. Raymond Barton; on the left is Col. Robert Chance in charge of the 12th Infantry Regiment.

by AWOL soldiers of literary persuasion that called themselves "Hemingway's Irregulars." Everyone there worshiped the man; they called him "Colonel Hemingway."

In November, Ernest finally got a chance to see front line action with Lanham's regiment in the Hurtgen Forest. He had already been in trouble over carrying sidearms (strictly taboo for a war correspondent). However, he probably saved Lanham's life on November 22nd during a German infantry attack on his headquarters. Lanham's headquarters commandant, Capt. Mitchell, was killed instantly by the hail of bullet fire. Showing his characteristic lack of personal fear, Hemingway charged into the melee, killing several Germans with bursts from a Thompson sub-machine gun and breaking up the attack.

However, after 18 grueling days in the Hürtgen Forest, the author had had enough of the war. "He stayed with me for several days," recalled battalion commander Swede Henley, "in the rain, sleet and snow. He was always

right in the thick of the heaviest part of the fighting, looking for something to write about. He carried two canteens — one of schnapps, the German equivalent of southern corn whisky, and the other of cognac. He always offered you a drink and he never turned one down."

The wet and cold weather of November had given the 45-year-old writer a severe head and chest cold and he returned to the Ritz Hotel in Paris in early December looking forward to flying stateside for a rest in Cuba. However, on December 16th, Hemingway somehow learned of the great German attack under way. He managed to contact General Raymond Barton's 4th Infantry Division headquarters. He explained to Barton that he was sick and on his way home, "But he wanted to know if there was a show going on that would be worth his while to come up for...for security reasons I could not give him the facts over the telephone...so I told him in substance that it was a pretty hot show and to come on up."

Liberation of Belgium, Then and Now. The 746th Tank Battalion emancipates the town of Harze, September, 1944. The same view as it appears today.

Hemingway conned a jeep and a driver from General Red O'Hare and roared off on the morning of December 17th although he was still running a fever. By the time he reached Luxembourg on the 19th, the worst of the German attack had been contained. At divisional headquarters, Barton explained to Hemingway that "Bob Chance was carrying the ball for the 4th Division." However, Ernest was still much too sick for covering the battle just yet and accepted Buck Lanham's invitation to move to his command post near Rodenbourg. There, the regimental doctor of the 22nd Regiment heavily dosed Hemingway with sulfa drugs and ordered him to stay quiet and out of trouble.

The command post was set up in an abandoned priest's house who was said to have collaborated with the "krauts." Ernest rummaged through its contents and was delighted to discover a store of sacramental wine that he took great pleasure in labeling "*Schloss Hemingstein, 1944.*" After quaffing the contents, he irreverently used the bottles in lieu of a chamber pot.

On December 22nd Hemingway was back in circulation and accompanied Col. Jim Luckett to observe the routing of Germans on a snowy forested hillside near Breitweiler. For the next two days Hemingway gathered material that was used by *Life* on the battle. Christmas Eve Ernest attended a holiday party thrown by General Barton at his mess in a Luxembourg schoolhouse. Turkey, mashed potatoes and cranberries were washed down with Scotch, gin and local brandy. The wee hours of Christmas morning were spent at a champagne party with the 70th Tank Battalion.

On Christmas Day, Ernest and his current and estranged wife, Martha Gellhorn, made an uneasy holiday tour of Lanham's battalion command posts. Hemingway's nagging wife in the rear seat of the jeep did little for the author's macho image among their 4th Infantry tour guides. Travel was made dangerous by the Allied fighters indifferently strafing friend or foe on the Luxembourg roads and their trip was cut short. They did see one fantastic sight, however — a thin, white vapor trail rapidly etched on the clear blue sky. This, Lanham explained, was a German V-2 rocket headed for England at supersonic speed.

The following days were difficult as it became apparent to everyone that Hemingway's current marriage had reached a parlous state and was near dissolution. In early January, Ernest returned back to the Ritz in Paris. Other than further conflict with Martha and his future wife, Mary Welsh, the Bulge was the last battle of the war in which Hemingway was to participate.

Hemingway told the following anecdote at a dinner with fellow correspondents while the Allied forces were busy pushing the Germans out of Belgium and Luxembourg:

The Honorable Mr. Moyne
By Ernest Hemingway

The firing stopped. A dog barked, some chickens scrambled across the yard of a farmhouse by a narrow, willow-embedded brook. The smoke from the self-propelled guns cleared. Tri-color flags fluttered at the windows.

Children came running, yelling and laughing toward our half-tracks. The major jumped from his jeep and walked ahead of his task force into the village we had just liberated.

Those kids shouted even louder now. A few broad-hipped, large-bosomed women wearing strange sun hats like nuns' bonnets joined them. Someone handed the first trooper a bottle of red-plum brandy which went down the line, by quick swigs of two, until the last man at the bottom of the line had gulped the last drop. On the steps of the town hall, two men stood waiting. The major went up to them. He was careful to take short, casual steps. From looking at his backside, you could see what he was thinking: No strutting, mind. This is liberated country, not kraut territory. Just amble, easy.

The major came to a halt, saluted. Not too smartly, but jauntily, his right hand almost touching his right eyebrow, then jerking forward and doing a quarter turn to the left, until the palm was turned inward. "A good day to you, Gentlemen," he said, "May I know who is your Burgomaster?"

The two Luxembourgers looked at each other, then at the major. They took off their caps, beamed and said: "Moyne."

I'm sorry to say, Gentlemen, that Burgomaster never turned up. There was none in that village. It took us just about two days to find out that "Moyne" is to Luxembourgers what "Hi there" is to you.

(Reprinted by permission from *Letzebuerger Land*, December 1, 1972)

The Bulge Is Erased:
January 12th - 28th:

News of the great Soviet winter offensive on January 12th finally caused Hitler to see red.[49] He immediately ordered the *Sixth Panzer Armee* pulled out of the line for emergency replenishment. He also authorized a further withdrawal along the Salm River to Houffalize. In particular, the *2nd Panzer*, *9th Panzer* and *Panzer Lehr* divisions were ordered to assemble to the east to prevent encirclement near the tip of the Bulge. The *116th Panzer Division* on the northern flank was left the unenviable job of holding the roads open over which its sister units were to pull back. Ostensibly the German leader maintained that withdrawl of the SS units made available a reserve in case the base of the

Bulge gave way to American pressure. But in reality, the German leader's attention had already turned to Russia and its developing horrors. And to top it off, he himself headed East on January 15th, departing *Adlerhorst* for Berlin on his personal train, the *Führersonderzug 'Brandenburg.'* He never returned to the Western front.

On January 13th Gen. Ridgway began an attack from the north that was designed to capture the defile near Ondenval for the employment of the 7th Armored Division in the Amblève area. According to the plan, the second phase of the attack would capture St. Vith and bag the two volksgrenadier divisions of Gen. der Inf. Hans Felber's *XIII*

Death for a German anti-tank crew of this 75 cm Pak 40 gun near the village of Malbompré. They knocked out two American tanks before they too were silenced.

Armeekorps.[50] Two American divisions, the 30th and the 75th Infantry, formed the jaws of the pincer along with 424th Regiment of the ill-fated 106th Division, now under the command of Brig. Gen. Herbert T. Perrin. The 30th Infantry made good progress on the 13th and 14th in spite of heavy fighting in the villages of Henumont and Thirimont with the *3rd Fallschirmjäger Division.*

By the night of the 14th, the 30th had established bridgeheads over the Amblève River at Ligneuville. But the rate of progress was not sufficient for the impatient Ridgway who let Hobbs, its division commander, know that no further delay would be tolerated. However, the advance of the 75th Division, new to combat, was also slow and deliberate. By the time the 75th and 30th Division's pincers came together the Germans of the XIII *Armeekorps* had escaped the trap without much difficulty. Gen. Ridgway was a tough and determined commander and had little tolerance for what he saw as the mishandling of an infantry division. He dismissed the commander of the 75th, Maj. Gen. Fay B. Prickett, who was then replaced by Maj. Gen. Ray E. Porter.

However, as night fell on January 13th there was a new development that could serve to cheer the gloomy circumstance in the U.S. First Army. Men of the U.S. VII Corps, looking to the south, could see lightning-like flashes of the big guns supporting Patton's Third Army. Over the next days the divisions eagerly put out strong patrols, seeking to end the nearly month long separation imposed by the enemy counteroffensive. But getting this far had been costly. The VII Corps alone had suffered 5,000 casualties and the battle was far from over. German losses were at least as bad; several hundred more than that figure had passed through the First Army prisoner of war cages alone.

Meanwhile, on January 13th, Patton's forces continued their push from the south, although still experiencing intense enemy resistance. After withdrawing under orders for the two previous days, the German foe now stood his ground; the Americans found them full of fight. The 87th Division was halted on the 16th by the *2nd Panzer* which was holding a roadblock north of Bonnerue. Nearby, the 11th Armored Division enveloped Bertogne and cut the Houffalize-St. Hubert highway on the 15th. However, advancing further beyond Compogne they found themselves suddenly facing intense automatic fire and set upon by a dozen tanks from the *116th Panzer Division.* The 11th Armored prudently withdrew under a reprisal from a covey of friendly fighter aircraft; the next day they returned to take Compogne for good.

North of Bastogne, the 101st Airborne boldly advanced to seize the village of Foy, but it too was forced to relinquish the village when the *340th Volksgrenadier Division* counterattacked. At the same time, the 6th Armored fought a sharp battle for Magaret, the enemy "fighting with the desperation." Alongside, the 90th and 26th Infantry Divisions continued to slug it out with the enemy in the Doncols-Bras area. Resistance in the Gen. Van Fleet's sector was exceed-

ingly tough, requiring a systematic advance to oust the enemy out of the maze of Wiltz Valley railroad tunnels.

By the 15th, the 101st Division was back in possession of Bertogne and Noville after bitter fighting. At the same time, the 6th Armored and 35th Infantry conducted a house-to-house fight with SS rearguards in Benonchamps, Oubourcy, Arloncourt and Longvilly. The hopelessness of the German position was aptly reflected in von Rundstedt's report from *OB West* on the evening of the 13th:

> Heavy enemy attacks in the area east of Stavelot and northeast of La Roche and in the Bastogne area continue with undiminished intensity. With high losses on both sides, the enemy was able to achieve a few deep penetrations. Fierce fighting is in progress to seal off the enemy salients.

Meanwhile, the modest British part in the Ardennes fighting was coming to a close. On January 14th the British XXX Corps commenced to move out of the Ardennes on Montgomery's orders. The divisions had just cleared the villages of Ortho, Mierchamps and Hives east of La Roche from the clutches of the *2nd Panzer Division.* Now they were to pull back and move into reserve with the 21st Army Group.

To the north in the Ourthe Valley, the German rearguard, the *116th Panzer Division*, was being assailed from all sides. The 84th Division cleared the village of Nadrin on the 13th and 14th while the 2nd Armored fought a tough tank battle for Wibrin before advancing on to Wilogne. The next day the 84th Division took the village of Berismenil crossing over the Ourthe River while the 3rd Armored pushed onto the crossroads at Baclain.

On the 15th the 83rd Division attacked Bovigny, but was unable to force the stubborn troops of the *9th SS Panzer Division* aside. Balanced against this setback, however, was the success of the 2nd Armored. Harmon's tanks pushed for Houffalize against evaporating enemy resistance clanking through the hamlets of Achouffe and Tavernaux and nearly capturing the fleeing headquarters of the *116th Panzer Division.* At dawn the 75th Division crossed the Salm River and recaptured Salmchâteau in particularly costly fighting (the division reported 55 men killed in action, the bloodiest day of the war for the division). The advance ended when the reconnaissance battalion of the *2nd SS Panzer Division* launched the customary German counterattack halting further progress. On the right, the 30th Division cleared the village of Pont and continued its grim fight with the *3rd Fallschirmjäger* for the possession of Thirimont. Casualties were alarmingly high.

As the V Corps began its drive from the north on the 15th, a new commander took over. Brig. Gen. Ralph C.

---

50 The *OKW* bulletin for January 13th reported that: "the winter battle in the West has risen to a new intensity. Our panzer and infantry formations were engaged the entire day in severe fighting with American divisions attacking along the entire salient. Enemy attacks south of Malmédy failed...the enemy gained only insignificant ground."

Above, right: *The 75th Infantry Division passes through the village of Beffe on the march towards the front.*

Right: *The "Battered Bastards of Bastogne." Soldiers of the victorious 101st Airborne Division march past a bullet-riddled sign at the outskirts of town.*

Forest foxhole. The 35th Infantry Division near Wiltz on January 11, 1945

Huebner, who had led the veteran U.S. 1st Division since Sicily assumed leadership of V Corps. The former commander, Gen. Gerow, had drawn the assignment to lead the new U.S. Fifteenth Army. Under Huebner's guidance, the corps joined in the assault from the north with the 7th Armored and the 1st and 2nd Infantry Divisions. The attack captured Steinbach and part of Faymonville from the *3rd Fallschirmjäger Division*, but was held up south of Butgenbach by heavy artillery fire.

Then, on January 16th, elements of the American 84th Division from the north and Task Force Greene from the 11th Armored Division from the south finally linked up at Houffalize and the American pincers finally came together. The U.S. First and Third Armies were rejoined. But for the most part, it was a hollow victory; so much had the Germans and the weather delayed the measured Allied advance that most of the enemy forces to the west had escaped the developing Allied trap. Regardless, Eisenhower used the occasion to reunite these powerful commands under the steady leadership of Omar Bradley. Montgomery, who had caused such bitter consternation in the Allied command, retained command of his British forces and Gen. William H. Simpson's Ninth Army to the north.

On the battlefield, the 3rd Armored Division fought the *9th SS Panzer* for the villages of Sterpigny and Cherain, but was turned back in a bid for Brisy. The 83rd Division worked to reorganize its tired troops while the 75th continued its plodding attack. Meantime, the 30th finally cleared the enemy from Thirimont and trudged south towards the important road junction at Recht. In the V Corps, the 1st Division captured Ondenval and mopped up elements of the overtaxed *3rd Fallschirmjäger* in Faymonville.

To the south, the attack of the 101st Airborne was again halted by the *340th Volksgrenadiers* near Bourcy while the 35th Division retook Michamps and Longvilly from the *9th Panzer Division*. The 90th Infantry was still caught up in violent fighting with the *1st SS Panzer Division* over control of Oberwampach and the road intersection at Derenbach. Attack followed counterattack and the possession of the villages changed hands back and forth over the 16th and 17th. On the later date the 101st, north of Bastogne, finally couped Bourcy and Hardigny before the Corps went over to the defensive. Nearby, the 6th Armored shook off German counterattacks in the Longvilly vicinity.

SITUATION MAP
January 12th-28th

LEUVEN

ST. TRUI

TIENEN

MEUSE RIVER

ANDENNE

NAMUR

SAMBRE RIVER

XXX
30
Ciney

DINANT

LESSE RIVER

PHILIPPEVILLE

GIVET

RIVER

COUVIN

FORET D'ARDENNES

SEMOIS

MEUSE

RIVER

BOUI

CHARLEVILLE-
MEZIÈRES

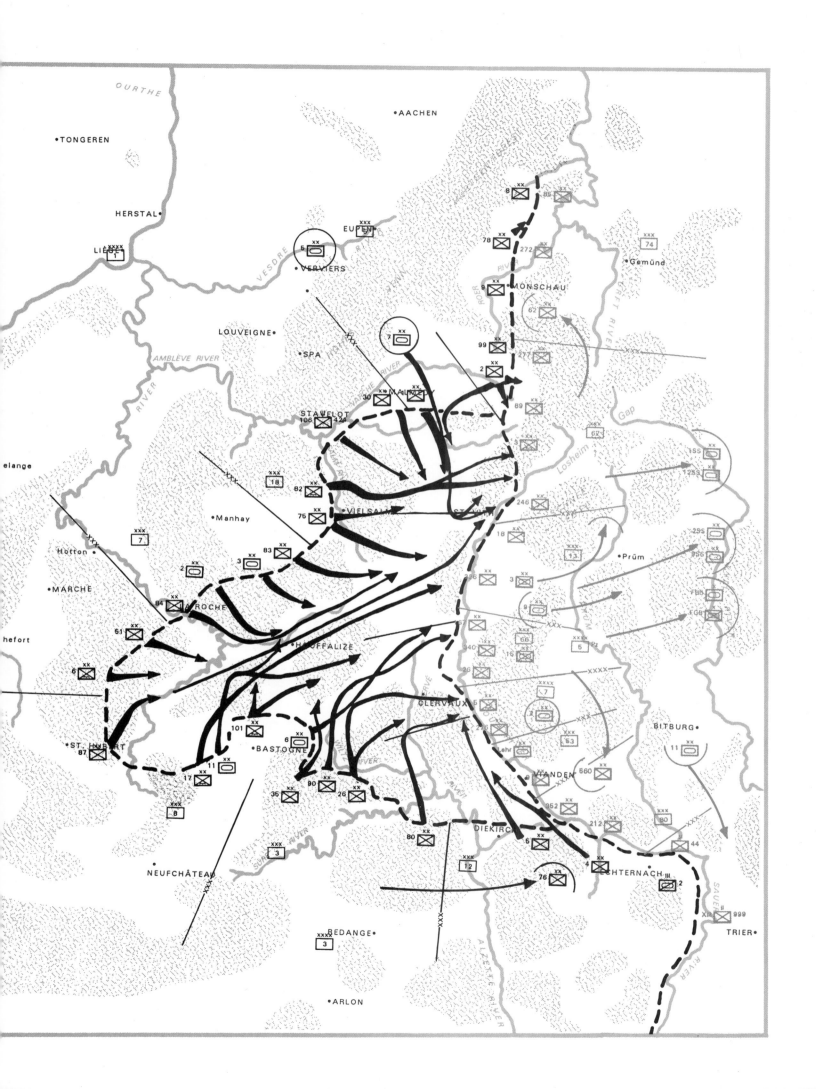

The juncture made at Houffalize gave Patton an opportunity to return to his original concept to reduce the enemy penetration. He, like Gen. Ridgway, believed it essential to attack the base of the Bulge. This, he was convinced, was the only way to snare the Germans in the Ardennes. Accordingly, he ordered preparations for an attack by the XII Corps across the Sûre River. Culin's 87th Infantry took over the 4th Division zone from the Sauer to Echternach while the 4th took over a portion of the 5th Division sector. So freed, the 5th Infantry concentrated in secrecy to surprise the Germans defending the area around Diekirch.

In the north, on January 17th and 18th, the 3rd Armored consolidated its gains near Cherain while the 83rd Division systematically cleared the *9th SS Panzer* from Courtil. The V Corps continued its effort to clear a channel through the Ondenval defile by advancing on Amblève and repulsing an armor supported counterattack in the dense forests along the route of its advance. The German commander reported the *3rd Fallschirmjäger* "badly mauled." By the close of the 18th the debouch was firmly in the hands of the Americans. Just to the south, in XVIII Corps, the 75th Division took Petit Thier, Vielsalm and Burtonville, the later village falling only after a particularly heavy fight. On the right flank, the 30th Division was unable to clear enemy nests of resistance in Recht and Poteau. Their adversary was familiar. The *18th Volksgrenadier Division* had drawn the unenviable defensive task in this sector where only a month before its soldiers had wondered in their diaries if they might now be in Paris. Genfldm. Model sensed the American threat to St. Vith. To facilitate the defense, he unified command by moving Gen. Hitzfeld and his *LXVII Armeekorps* under Dietrich's *Sixth Panzer Armee* and then coaxing the support of the SS commander's collection of heavy artillery to help shore up the faltering line. Model saw the defense of the village of Deidenberg as critical to the German cause since its control gave access to the two big highways between St. Vith and Büllingen and St. Vith and Ondenval.

On the southern front, Patton now feared a total German escape from the Ardennes. On the 18th he ordered an attack to begin without delay from the base of the Bulge with Eddy's XII Corps. In the pre-dawn darkness the the 4th and 5th Divisions silently crossed the icy Sauer River between Reisdorf and Ettelbruck in assault boats. Elements were across the river before a shot was fired, the falling snow perhaps reducing the enemy's observation. By the end of the day the Americans occupied Erpeldange, had thrust beyond Bettendorf and by-passed Diekirch. Their old enemies, the *212th* and *352nd Volksgrenadiers* were totally taken by surprise. All three villages were be secured from the enemy over the next two days.

To add weight to the assault, Gen. McBride's 80th Division joined in the attack on the left. With the punch of that unit, the village of Nocher was back in American hands by nightfall. The German *9th* and *276th Volksgrenadiers* had opposed this move stoutly. Genmaj. Dempwolf, in charge of the hard luck *276th*, was wounded in the fighting; two days later he was replaced by Obst. Werner Wagner. The American moves in the south placed Rothkirch's *LIII Armeekorps* in grave danger of encirclement. Although it did not make rapid enough progress to entrap them, Patton's attack did lead to a near panic of German forces as they streamed across the Clerf and Our Rivers to reach the security of their border.

So obviously endangered, the Germans struggled to move back from the Ardennes to the Westwall, fighting both the Americans and the weather. Von Rundstedt's report on the 19th painted a dreary picture indeed:

> In snowstorms and snow drifts, the defensive fighting at crucial points along the front between the Meuse and the Moselle continued with undiminished intensity. For friendly movements, the major problem at this time is the road situation in the Eifel. In an instant, movements come to a standstill. Urgently needed fuel columns cannot keep moving because of the deep snowdrifts. Snow plows are too few in number and have no fuel.

But the American drive from the north gave the enemy little rest. On January 19th the 3rd Armored pushed forward in a blizzard to reach its final objectives, clearing Rettigny and Renglez and the rest of the northern zone as far as the Ourthe River. Meanwhile, the 75th Division continued to thread its way through the *Grand Bois* and the 30th Division evicted the *18th Volksgrenadiers* from the crossroads at Recht. To the right, the Big Red One finished clearing the path through the Ondenval defile and the 7th Armored concentrated in secrecy just to the north in Waimes. Gen. Hasbrouck was hopeful for a rapid advance on St. Vith.

Despite the snowstorm on the 19th, the armored division reached Schoppen and Eibertingen prompting the emergency commitment of elements of the *12th SS Panzer Division*. The next day the 7th Armored drove several miles to reach the contested village of Deidenberg. Beyond this position, however, they were held up by the usual troubles: mines and knee-deep snow just north of Born. The 30th Division encountered even worse circumstances: a battalion sized enemy counterattack by the *246th Volksgrenadiers* from the woods near Nieder Emmels supported by artillery and hastily patched up tanks of the recuperating SS armored wreckage of *Kampfgruppe Peiper*. Similarly, a battlegroup of the *2nd SS Panzer* struck the 75th Division near Burtonville. It took nearly two days to turn the Germans back. Again, on the 21st, a heavy snow fell over the northern Ardennes; the Germans there were spent.

In the Third Army sector on January 20th, the 11th Armored advanced two miles towards Bourcy while Miley's 17th Airborne marched east of Tavigny. Both divisions encountered little opposition. In the III Corps, the 6th Armored finally ousted the Germans from Moinet and swept

Upper left: *North meets South. GIs of the 84th Infantry Division shake hands with T/5 Angel Casey of the 11th Armored Division from Patton's Army. The meeting took place near Houffalize on January 15th. The armored car is an M-8 "Greyhound" reconnaissance vehicle.*

Left: *Solidarity in war. American GIs move a badly wounded German soldier on a stretcher made of straw.*

through the villages of Lullange and Hachiville the following day. East of Bastogne, the 90th Division continued its hard fight in the vicinity of Allerborn and Derenbach. The later village fell on the 20th. At the same time, the 26th Division established a bridgehead north of the Wiltz River near Oberwampach; within 24 hours Paul's division were fighting in the streets of Wiltz.

The XII Corps continued its attack at the base of the Bulge on January 20th. The 4th Division, now under Brig. Gen. Harold W. Blakeley (Barton had taken ill), enveloped the village of Longsdorf and recaptured Tandel. On its side, the 5th Division took Brandenburg and the 80th secured Burden. However, even more than St. Vith, it was imperative for the Germans that they maintain their possession of the Skyline Drive which ran west of the Our River. Without this commanding highway and the bridges over the Clerf and Our, the withdrawing forces in the entire southern saliant would be endangered.

Genfldm. Model lost no time in moving up reserves to seal off the penetration north of the Sauer. On his orders the *XLVII Panzerkorps* (*2nd Panzer*, *Panzer Lehr* and *9th Volksgrenadier Divisions*) transferred to Brandenberger's *Seventh Armee* where they along with the *352nd Volksgrenadiers* immediately took over the former sector of the *LXXX Armeekorps*.[51] The newly constituted force had clear orders: hold fast against the Americans advancing from the south. To bolster to these admonitions, three heavy anti-tank battalions (the *519th*, *668th* and *741st Panzerjäger*) were added to the local order of battle. With the snow bound roads, Allied air power and the usual dearth of gasoline, the mandate would take some time to translate to German strength on the battlefield.

Even so, on the 21st, the 4th Division evoked a violent enemy reaction when it attempted to secure the village of Fouhren. In spite of this setback, Irwin's 5th on the right managed to wrest possession of Lipperscheid. On the left, the 80th Division captured Bourscheid and Kehmen in heavy fighting with the *79th Volksgrenadiers*, now under the command of Obst. Kurt Hummel. The Americans were obviously headed to Hoscheid, a village on a commanding hill astride the Skyline Drive. Loss of this position would severely endanger the withdrawl of the entire *Seventh Armee*. Consequently, Brandenberger rushed what meager reserves he had to block the Americans: some 88mm guns of the *668th Panzerjäger Battalion* and *Kampfgruppe Poschinger* of the *Panzer Lehr Division*. It was enough; the progress of the American advance ground to a halt.

By January 22nd Hitler ordered Dietrich's SS army as well as the *Führer Begleit* and *Führer Grenadier Brigades* to entrain for transfer to the Eastern Front. This was slowly accomplished over the following days, engendering great bitterness in the German regular army soldiers who were left behind to deal with the overwhelming Allied strength. As a parting gesture, Hitler finally approved a withdrawal to the Westwall, but there they were to stand.

Unfortunately, due to the skillful German withdrawal, most their army had managed to slip out of the Allied trap. Still, *Heeresgruppe B* lost many vehicles and much heavy

---

51 There were many order of battle changes during this period due to the departure of the *Sixth Panzer Armee*: *LXXX Armeekorps* would retain control only of the *212th Volksgrenadier Division*. The composition of the *LIII Armeekorps* southeast of Bastogne would remain the same with the *276th* and *79th Volksgrenadier Divisions* and *Kampfgruppe Poschinger* of *Panzer Lehr*. On the 22nd the *LVIII Panzerkorps* with the *340th* and *5th Fallschirmjäger Divisions* would transfer to *Seventh Armee* as well. The *167th Volksgrenadiers* were placed in army reserve.

For them the war is over. German prisoners are escorted to the rear, by members of the 7th Armored Division: Nieder Emmels, Belgium, January 23rd, 1945. Assault gun "332" probably belonged to the Führer Begleit Brigade.

equipment in the Ardennes. Without fuel and spare parts for repair, German commanders were forced to abandon their precious remaining vehicles by the snow-bound roads and flee on foot.

Then, on January 22nd, the clouds again cleared and 627 Allied air sorties flattened stalled bumper-to-bumper German motor columns attempting to escape across the Our River to the Westwall. The German retreat from the Ardennes salient had degenerated into a disorganized rout. Columns of foot soldiers, trucks, tanks and horse drawn artillery, piled up at the Our River, scurrying for cover each time the *Jabos* swooped down to bomb and straff. The headquarters of the *LIII Armeekorps* took a direct hit, wounding almost everyone on its staff; another American bomb found its way to a large fuel train near Kochen where 800 barrels of the precious stuff went up in flames. "For the first time," recorded Gen. Brandenberger, "the situation in the air was similar to that which prevailed in Normandy." Artillery observers were equally wild-eyed at the rich variety of gunnery targets. "Let her go boys," one observer radioed. "You can't miss a Jerry wherever you land them."

Taking advantage of the situation in the north, the 84th Division captured Gouvy and Beho while the 75th took Commanster and the 30th secured Hinderhausen and Nieder Emmels. Driving straight for St. Vith the 7th Armored was stopped short of the town by hastily assembled enemy roadblocks, but nonetheless cleared Hünningen. And as if to signal ultimate Allied victory, on January 23rd Brig. Gen. Bruce Clarke led the 7th Armored Division back into the blasted ruins of St. Vith, crushing the remaining resistance of the *18th Volksgrenadiers* who had ejected Clarke and his men from that crossroads a month earlier. To seal the coup the other divisions in the XVIII Corps swept up the territory near St. Vith. The 30th seized Crombach and Neundorf from the *3rd Fallschirmjäger* while the 75th Infantry secured Maldingen, Aldringen and Braunlauf in a series of sharp engagements with the *326th Volksgrenadier Division*.

Patton's Third Army was now rapidly clearing the territory east of the Our River of the enemy. The 11th Armored and 17th Airborne Divisions struck out east against little opposition. Gen. Grow's 6th Armored motored through Basbellain, Asselborn and Weiler while Van Fleet's 90th Division took Donnage, Boxhorn and Stockem. The 26th Division mopped up the enemy in Wiltz and Eschweiler. The following day the 90th Division took Binsfield and reached the outskirts of Hupperdingen. Resistance stiffened, however, as the Americans caged their enemy up against the Our River. On 23rd the *15th Panzer Grenadiers* in Trois Vierges elected to fight it out, requiring a full battalion of tanks from the 6th Armored to vanquish the invaders. It took nearly two days to oust the Germans from the crossroads at Weisswampach only five miles to the east.

On the 21st, Gen. Brandenberger became gravely worried that the Americans at Bourscheid might capture one of his two remaining tank bridges across the Our at Gemünd. In spite of buzzing American fighterbombers, the general paid a special visit to Rothkirch's *LIII Armeekorps* to make sure that resistance along the Skyline Drive was resolute. The 80th Division crossed the Wiltz River without much

encounter with the enemy — the German had pulled back — but the situation to the northeast was something else again. There, the 4th and 5th Divisions gained ground along the west bank of the Our River in violent fighting, taking the villages of Walsdorf and Gralingen. *Kampfgruppe Poschinger* put up fierce resistance at Hosheid, however, and it was still in German hands at the end of the day. Similarly, a battle group of the *2nd Panzer Division* fought the Americans before Fouhren to a standstill. They would not finally clear the town until late on the 23rd after savage fighting in which the crossroads changed hands repeatedly. Eddy's men were successful on the extreme southern flank, however. Attacking across the Sauer, the 87th Division secured the village of Wasserbillig. But no sooner had this been accomplished than the division received orders to transfer to the fighting front just south of St. Vith.

That the Germans were quitting the Ardennes was becoming ever more apparent. A new edict from Hitler on the future conduct of German operations on the entire Western Front became effective on January 23rd. As von Rundstedt spelled it out to his subordinates, necessary measures were to begin immediately to withdraw to the Westwall, although the usual stubborn delaying action was to be executed. German divisions in the Ardennes were to begin moving their heavy equipment back across the Our River immediately and to plan the most suitable defensive lines. To cap this off, on the 24th, the last elements of the German SS divisions pulled out of the line to prepare to move off towards Hungary. Despite tremendous hardships, the Germans were, for the most part, successful in their move back to the West wall.[52]

Meanwhile, on the battlefront in the north, the U.S. 1st Division renewed its attack, first pulverizing the positions of the *89th Infanterie Division* with artillery, and then seizing Moderscheid, Büllingen and the highway south to Amblève. The next day the 7th Armored Division captured Wallerode in its push to the east from St. Vith.

In the south the Americans continued their relentless advance, pausing only to repulse a German counterattack against the 90th Division near Binsfeld. The 80th Division overran the enemy in Kautenbach and the 5th finally seized Hoscheid along the Skyline Drive in a fierce back and forth battle with the *79th Volksgrenadier Division*.

On January 25th the American advance gathered momentum. The 6th Armored regained positions along the St. Vith-Clerf road at Weiswampach while the 90th Division seized Heinerscheid and Grindhausen. In XII Corps, the 80th Division cleared Wilwerwiltz from the *276th Volksgrenadier Division* and the 5th Division took Merscheid from the *9th*. But perhaps most heady, the 26th Infantry Division cleared the enemy from the town of Clervaux only a few miles from the German starting point at Dasburg. As the invaders fled, American soldiers, hidden and sustained at great risk for more than a month by Luxembourg citizens, emerged from the devastated ruins.

On January 26th the Allied liberation of Luxembourg and

---

52 For instance, *LVIII Panzerkorps* reported by month's end that 68 of its 70 remaining tanks had successfully crossed over the Our River.

Belgium villages continued. To the north the 1st Division and the 82nd Airborne resumed their attack; over the next two days they gained Heppenbach, Herresbach and Hepscheid. In the extreme south, in Patton's Army the tired 4th Division was finally withdrawn from the fighting. The newly arrived U.S. 76th Division (Maj. Gen. William R. Schmidt) took over the former positions of the 87th Division which, in turn, relieved the departing 17th Airborne Division.

While these changes were in progress, the villages of Weiler, Wahlhausen and Holzthum fell to the American forces along the Our River in spite of fierce house-to-house fighting before Putscheid. Nearby, the villages of Drauffelt, Hosingen and Pintsch were finally wrested from the *276th Volksgrenadier Division* by the U.S. 26th and 80th Divisions. Most of these tiny places had changed hands several times in severe combat. So bitter was the parting German battle that Hosingen would not be finally secured until January 27th and violent fighting re-erupted near Putscheid that was not be quelled until the end of the month. All the while, the battered rabble of the *Seventh Armee* streamed over crossing

sites at Dasburg, Gemünd and Eisenbach. The remaining German resistance was like a laundry list of Nazi soldiery; in the final actions west of the Our River, the 6th Armored alone took prisoners from ten enemy divisions.

To the north the Germans were forced back as well. Along the Our on the 29th severe fighting flared up with the *326th Volksgrenadier Division* near Burg Reuland. Even so, by month's end the Americans were back in the villages which had been the scene of such bitter combat in the early days of the German counteroffensive.

The 87th Division took Andler and Schönberg while the 82nd Airborne cleaned out the enemy from the dense forests near Holzheim, Losheim and Lanzerath. There were other signs of victory in the V Corps. The 2nd Division retook Wirtzfeld and Rocherath-Krinkelt and the 99th Division, after a month of recuperating, went over to the attack to expel the enemy from Rohren. Equally inspiring for the U.S. 78th Division was their capture of Kesternich on the last day of January. The 90th Division and 6th Armored even crossed the Our River into Germany to strike at Welchenhausen and Kalborn. By February all these villages

There is perhaps no more telling picture of the danger of the fighting in the Ardennes than this one. Taken on January 25th, the scene shows soldiers of the 7th Armored Division pushing east near Wallerode. Seconds after this photograph was taken, T/5 Hugh F. McHugh of the 165th Signal Photo Company was killed by enemy fire. His assistant was wounded, but recovered the camera and with it, the last photograph taken by McHugh.

were free once more and the enemy had been pushed back to the frontier.

So, in the last days of January 1945, the Allies advanced slowly but inexorably, mopping up the last pockets of enemy resistance west of the German border. By January 28th, the American soldiers, for the most part, stood again on the lines they had occupied on December 16th. The way back had been a long, grim and costly struggle, but the Ardennes Campaign was over.

Dejected prisoners of the 12th Volksgrenadier Division surrender to the 82nd Airborne Division between Manhay and Vielsalm.

LOOKING BACK

Aftermath

The objective of Hitler's last desperate gamble to win the war was Antwerp. This Belgian coastal city was the largest port in Europe and Eisenhower planned on using this facility to supply his final offensive into Germany. Hitler was certainly correct in judging that its capture would be a devastating blow to the Allied forces. Unfortunately for the German leader, his assessment of the military situation and how his army would capture the great port was based on a generous amount of wishful thinking.

The Germans failed to reach Antwerp or even get a single tank across the Meuse River. No large pockets of Allied units were encircled and destroyed, so even the aims of the Small Solution could not be met. Strategically, the offensive had been an utter failure.

Not only did the Germans fall short of reaching any meaningful strategic aims, but they lost the tactical battle as well. The disunity of German command as well as the im-poverished training of the volksgrenadier infantry combined to leave the Nazi soldiery handicapped in the face of a very proficient enemy.

In almost every respect, the *Wacht am Rhein* Ardennes Offensive stands out as another example of Hitler's shortcomings as a military leader. As he had done repeatedly in the war, Hitler severely underestimated the abilities of his enemy while greatly overestimating his own means. With his resolute determination to stay with the Big Solution of an offensive to Antwerp, Hitler showed that he had little notion of the relationship between force and objective. Almost every German general involved with the Ardennes operation mentioned the relative weakness and inadequacy of the attack force as a fundamental reason for the offensive's failure. As always, however, Hitler's generals found the Führer ready to expect the impossible.

The Big Three. The battle won, Bradley, Eisenhower and Patton meet on Bastogne's wrecked main street in early January.

Airpower. U.S. cargo planes escorted by P-47 fighters fly over Bastogne. The might of the Allied air forces effectively sealed the German fate in the Ardennes once the weather cleared.

Reasons for German Failure

Perhaps the largest lesson of Hitler's debacle in the Ardennes was that an offensive of modern mechanized armies which lacks air cover is doomed to failure. The effort of the German Luftwaffe proved completely inadequate when clear skies appeared over the Ardennes. The Allied air force quickly established indisputable air superiority; such air supremacy ushered the total collapse of the German supply system in the Ardennes. Every move of German forces in daylight was made under the scornful eyes of the Allied air forces. This severely restricted the mobility of the German attack force, its armor being forced to hide in the woods, move at night or risk destruction while running the gauntlet of fighter-bomber fire on the Ardennes roads.

Post-war assessments have found a number of reasons for the German failure. Most find considerable common ground. Von Manteuffel, the commander of the *Fifth Panzer Armee*, believed that the major reasons for failure were: not enough troops, the unexpected quick reaction of the Allied forces, the failure of supply and the improper allocation of reserves. "It was a brilliant plan," the small panzer general later admitted, "but it depended on a number of conditions for it to succeed. The German forces depended on a strict time table, unbroken sources of supply and complete surprise." Carl Wagener, von Manteuffel's chief of staff, ascribed the responsibility for failure in the *Sixth Panzer Armee* to the lack of professionalism in the SS Army:

> The insufficient training condition of the SS organizations especially among their commanders and subordinate commanders was also to blame for the failure. Its motorized units, having no driving technique and no road discipline, were soon standing hopelessly wedged into four columns beside each other on those roads selected for advance, but still blocked by the enemy. It did not help them any to force their way into the sector of the *Fifth Panzer Armee* and thus clog the northern roads.

Dietrich, the commander of the *Sixth Panzer Armee*, said of the failure "it was mainly bad preparation, lack of fuel, supplies and training, plus the time of year — in that order." But his able chief of staff, Genmaj. Krämer, gave other reasons more in line with Wagener's assessment: the quality of the men and leaders at the stage of the war, the diminished mobility of the German army, bad roads and bad driving and the effects of the U.S. air force. The rotund head of the Luftwaffe, Göring, perhaps put it most succinctly: "It was no longer 1940."

On the U.S. side, Dr. Cole's fine official U.S. account gives six reasons:

1) Unexpected tough American resistance
2) Supply failure
3) Denial of free German use of the road net such as at St. Vith and Bastogne
4) Failure to carry the shoulders of the offensive
5) Lack of depth to the attack due to the slow German commitment of reserves
6) A timely Allied reaction to the offensive.

German supply problems have been underrated by many historical accounts. The transport and fuel situation in *Heeresgruppe B* was such that the attack force was not really capable of getting much further than the Meuse River. The distance to Antwerp from the German start line varied somewhat, but was generally in excess of 125 miles. The Germans began the attack with only enough fuel to go about 50 miles in the Ardennes — the distance for Dietrich's *Sixth Panzer Armee* to reach the Meuse. The rest of the petrol was in dumps east of the Rhine River that could not be brought up fast enough to keep the panzer spearheads ahead of the infantry. From Christmas on, fuel was so short that panzer divisions sent officers on motorcycles scouting the frozen countryside in search of allotted gasoline, sometimes personally allocated by von Rundstedt himself. The transport failure also made ammunition and artillery movement tardy — a state of affairs quite different from the requirements of the *blitzkrieg*.

The German problem with committing reserves in the battle deserves further comment. On the modern battlefield, one area where army and army group commanders can influence the engagement is through the commitment of reserves at the right time and place. Two factors influenced the German release of reserves to the Ardennes. The first and major reason for the slow commitment was the failure to clear the panzer march routes so that there was maneuver room to deploy the oncoming panzer divisions. Failing to breakthrough the Americans in the Elsenborn area and clear important road centers in their path (Rocherath, Bütgenbach, St. Vith and Bastogne), the traffic situation in the German rear reached chaotic proportions. To compound the problem, the muddy conditions of the Ardennes ground made deployment off roads nearly impossible. So bad was the road situation, that moving more motorized units into the road net would have risked bringing everything to a standstill. The situation was made even worse on Christmas Eve when the Allied bombers began to strafe and bomb the few clear roads that the Germans did possess.

The other reason that the Germans hesitated to commit reserves was based on operational considerations. Once the Meuse was reached, fresh units would be required to exploit the crossing towards Antwerp. The general plan was to commit reserves as the panzer spearheads approached the river. As an example, the *9th Panzer* and *15th Panzer Grenadier Divisions* were brought up to reinforce the *2nd Panzer Division* when it neared the Meuse on December 22 - 24th. Likewise, the *9th SS Panzer Division* was brought up in response to Peiper's breakout on December 17th. No doubt, had the Germans been able to shake loose in their attack, they would have continued to have committed reserves to exploit their success. Under the circumstances as they developed, the Germans were correct in bringing up infantry formations as reserves when room for deployment of motorized units was not available.

Historians have long debated the effect of the Ardennes Campaign on the course of the final months of the war. The Battle of the Bulge was not a decisive engagement in the fashion of Kursk or Normandy. Nor did it represent a turning point in the conflict as with Rommel's defeat in North Africa or the surrender of Hitler's *Sixth Armee* at Stalingrad. The battle did, however, represent a late reversal of the Allied military dominance in the last year of the war. It was also the last serious expression of the tough military might that had terrorized Europe a scant two years before.

Post war speculation has considered the probable consequences for the war in Europe should *Wacht am Rhein* have succeeded. In the extremely unlikely event that Hitler had actually been able to take Antwerp, a serious situation would have arisen for the Western Allies. Montgomery would have been cutoff in the north. Even if the danger had been foreseen, and attempts made to evacuate the trap, much of the 21st Army Group might have been lost. The Americans, on the other hand, would have been forced to add another 100 miles to their lines losing perhaps half a dozen divisions. Although, this would have forced them entirely to the defensive, they probably could have accomplished this without overall collapse.

Many reserves that were in England and moving up from Normandy could have been used to shore up this line.[1] And, of course, Allied air power would still have to be reckoned with. Needless to say, Hitler's armies in far away Holland would be even more susceptible to air interdiction from the long supply lines that would have to come from Germany. Also, the inevitable attack by Patton from the south would have found the German southern flank even more vulnerable. A successful German offensive to Antwerp would have run even greater risk of total encirclement of the German spearhead. Eisenhower might have been sacked as scapegoat for such a disaster and the Western Allies would have been delayed in their attack on Germany by months. However, there is little reason to believe as Hitler did, that the Alliance would have collapsed. What is more likely is that the Russian forces would have met the Allies on the Rhine in summer rather than on the Elbe in May. At best Hitler might have won the Atom Bomb as an epitaph to a continued struggle for his Third Reich.[2]

In terms of Hitler's treatment of the war in the East, victory in the Ardennes would have made little difference. Hitler had promised Guderian that after success in the Ardennes and the "collapse of the Western Alliance" he would throw all his forces into the battle against Russia. His failure in the Ardennes changed his plans but little. By mid-January, the German leader was in the process of switching the *Sixth Panzer Armee* to the Eastern Front. Speculation as to whether the Germans could have halted the Russians with a total collapse of the Western Front seems rather pointless, for Hitler's very premise of such a success was based on his self-delusion regarding the political situation in the West. Short of a German atomic bomb, there seems little reason to believe that Hitler's desired separate peace could have been available under any circumstances in December 1944.

For the Third Reich, *Wacht am Rhein* was really Hitler's last choice between attack and the "barren rot of defense." The venerated von Moltke of German military tradition preached that "The offensive is the straight way to the goal." However, Germany did not now have the resources to maintain the initiative for long. It was this offensive that was to take Nazi Germany into the grueling seventh year of a war. "Only the offensive will enable us to give a successful turn to the war in the West," Hitler said. "If the German people are to be defeated in this struggle it will be because the people have been found incapable of withstanding the test of history. It will be ripe for destruction." With failure, Hitler washed his hands of the fate of Germany.

For the Allied intelligence services the Battle of the Bulge was an embarrassment. For all the sophistication of the UL-TRA code breaking system and other Allied intelligence, only two men foresaw a coming blow and they were too late and unsuccessful in convincing either themselves or their superiors. Part of the failing was not the fault of the intelligence officers in the Allied armies; a German winter offensive in the Ardennes was so desperate and ill-advised (even by Hitler's own generals), that Allied intelligence was rightfully inclined to discount the possibility. On the other hand, in painting a picture of an enemy feeble and near collapse in December 1944, the Allied ground commanders and their G-2s, particularly Bradley and the 12th Army Group, had committed the most grievous sin possible for an intelligence staff. They had totally underestimated the capabilities of their enemy.

---

1   By December 26th there was such a shortage of reserves and replacements that Lt. Gen. John C. H. Lee of the Communications Zone offered "a limited number of colored troops who have had infantry training, the privilege of joining our veteran units at the front." Eisenhower was forced to order Lee to abandon the idea for political reasons.

2   In an interview after the war Jodl explained that in the event that they had been able to capture Antwerp, "We would have... started concentric attacks on Aachen from Monschau, Maastricht and Central Holland and crushed your forces in the Aachen pocket, their supply lines having been cut...It is difficult to say whether we could have destroyed the forces in the pocket or whether you could have supplied them by air by using your entire air force. But such an event would have made a terrific impression on political, military and public opinion. But even with captured fuel and supplies I doubt if we could have reconquered France...All the same it would have been a big setback for you."

An Inventory

The damages wrought by the battle on either side were substantial. As one might expect, both opponents overestimated the casualties of their enemy. The Germans figured that the Allies had lost 150-200,000 men in the battle as well as 2,000 tanks. This gross overestimate detailed the total destruction of three American divisions and the mauling of twelve others. According to the German report:

> ...the enemy forces on the continent were rushed to the salient. After the airborne divisions had been smashed, the intended Allied assault toward Cologne and the Ruhr was impossible. The danger of a western offensive, coordinated with the huge Bolshevist drive was averted.

According to the official U.S. account, losses in the Ardennes Campaign totalled 80,987 men, with 10,276 killed, 47,493 wounded and 23,218 missing. Of these some 41,315 were lost from December 16th through January 2nd and the rest up to January 28th. The relative casualties among the Allies reflected the fact that it was primarily an American battle; of the total, 1,408 were British casualties including 200 dead. Most of the Allied missing were in the First U.S. Army, with some 21,000 casualties in the Third Army. Nearly 7,000 of the Allied losses were prisoners taken from the 106th Infantry Division.[3]

Although both sides committed large numbers of tanks

Grim duty. A U.S. graves registration company collects Allied and enemy dead from the Ardennes battlefield.

the Battle of the Bulge was resolved primarily as an infantry battle. Because of the forbidding terrain and weather, both armor and artillery could not be used to full advantage by either combatant. Consequently, responsibility for fighting the Germans most often fell on the shoulders of the individual American rifleman. It is then, not surprising that the U.S. infantry divisions suffered greatly in the fighting. For example at the end of the campaign, the U.S. First Army noted that of its total casualties over 90% came from the infantry in the regular infantry divisions or the infantry battalions in its armored divisions.

Ostensibly, the 106th Division was destroyed in the battle (one battered regiment, the 424th, survived). The 28th Division was totally decimated, although even the Bloody Bucket division would fight again. In the December fighting the 1st, 2nd, 4th, 30th, 78th, 80th, and 99th Infantry Divisions were badly damaged. Casualties mounted in January. Consequently, the 5th, 26th, 35th 75th, 83rd, 84th, 87th and 90th Divisions lost heavily in the grim frigid campaign to reduce the Bulge. Only the 9th Infantry Division escaped serious damage. But despite grave losses, most of the U.S. infantry divisions paused only briefly to reorganize before returning to combat. All, too, received replacements, unlike the enemy they were facing.

Losses to U.S. armor were also severe. Some 733 American tanks and tank destroyers were lost in the Ardennes. The 9th Armored Division was severely battered and Combat Command R was nearly annihilated. Even this division cannot be reckoned as having been destroyed, however, as was convincingly demonstrated with its capture of the Remagen River bridgehead on March 7th, 1945. Although suffering fewer casualties than the infantry, the 2nd, 3rd, 4th, 6th, 7th, 10th and 11th Armored Divisions, nonetheless, took severe losses in both men and equipment. Even

so, all would fight again after reorganization, and equipment losses were soon made good.

Both the 82nd and 101st Airborne Divisions sustained very heavy casualties in the Bulge; the elite 101st suffered more men killed in action than any other U.S. division in the campaign. The 17th Airborne was also mauled in heavy fighting around Bastogne during the terrible fight there in early January. Even though they were not knocked out, the airborne divisions were not available as paratroop forces for two months. Given the fear that the Arnhem operation had given the Nazi regime of airborne attacks, senior German officers could find some solace in this fact.

Allied aircraft losses from the beginning of the German offensive to mid-month January, 1945 were listed at 592 planes, a relatively small fraction of the total Allied air forces involved. Unlike their German foe, these losses were made up by newly arriving machines in less than two weeks.

All told the Battle of the Bulge probably reduced the Allied rifle strength in the West by ten percent. Weapon losses were perhaps double this fraction. The First Army alone reported the loss of 237 tanks, 1,284 machine guns, 542 mortars and 1,344 trucks as of the end of December. Taken as a whole, these losses had the effect of temporarily halting any Allied offensive plans. However, replacements in men and equipment for the Allied forces were ever increasing. By the beginning of January, Eisenhower had taken on some

Tactical Air Sorties during the Ardennes Campaign

Date	Weather	Allied	German
Dec. 16th	Overcast	359*	100+
17th	Fog	1,053**	650++
18th	Fog	519	849++
19th	Overcast	196	290
20th	Overcast	2	2
21st	Overcast	100	40+
22nd	Snow	94***	90+
23rd	Fog/Clear	619****	800
24th	Clear	1,138	1,088
25th	Clear	1,066*****	600
26th	Clear	937	404
27th	Clear	1,294	415
28th	Heavy Snow	23	15
29th	Fog	460	165
30th	Fog	690	200+
31st	Fog	700	613
Jan. 1st	Clear	1,000	1,035+++

* None of these were battlefield sorties
** 647 of these were battlefield sorties
*** 80 of these were 2nd TAF sorties
**** 294 were battlefield sorties
***** The British 2nd TAF flew an additional 1,099 sorties, but only 371 were battlefield sorties
+ Estimate +50%
++ A further 200 to 250 sorties were flown each night
+++ Perhaps only 100 sorties were over the battlefield

Allied Air Mission Summary
December 16, 1944 - January 16, 1945

Unit	Sorties	Bombs (Long Tons)	Aircraft Lost
U.S. 9th AF	23,264	10,371	286
U.S. 8th AF	28,330	36,326	128
British 2nd TAF	5,636	1,418	190
British RAF BC	6,511	23,072	43
TOTAL	63,741	71,187	647

3   These figures do not include other Allied losses associated with the other winter battles. Another 15,000 men were casualties in the fighting in the Alsace against Hitler's *Operation Nordwind* in Dever's 6th Army Group. Air force losses, the sinking of the troopship Leopoldville and the results of the terror bombing on Antwerp served to increase the numbers even further.

30,000 replacements and 351 new tanks. The flow of replacements and equipment was even greater in the following month. While the losses were temporarily serious, they were not crippling. Eisenhower, himself, later admitted that the German offensive delayed Allied aims in the West by some six weeks. However, after that point, the Americans and British met a foe both without the material and psychological means to fight.

The German High Command estimated that they lost between 81,834 and 98,024 men in the Bulge for the period December 16th to January 28th. The accepted figure was 81,834 of which 12,652 were killed; 38,600 wounded and 30,582 were missing. Dietrich estimated that his *Sixth Panzer Armee* alone had lost 37,000 men. Probably the best estimate has been made by Magna Bauer for the U.S. official history in which German losses for the same period were estimated at approximately 100,000 when Luftwaffe air and ground force losses are included. Prospects for replacing these losses were bleak. On December 26th *OB West* reported that 13,090 men were headed for *Heeresgruppe B* although "a further replacement supply beyond the communicated amount is not possible." Himmler's manpower comb-out had reached the bottom of the barrel.

German tank and assault gun losses were 600-800, close to half of the number employed in the Ardennes and nearly one-fourth of Hitler's remaining panzer force. Again, Bauer's careful study reveals that 324 of the losses occurred

Ever present danger. American GIs frantically dig for protection while under fire. The soldier in the foreground has just been killed.

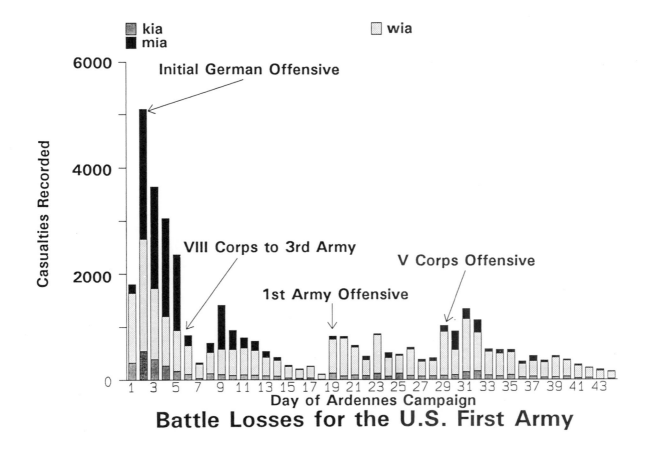

Battle Losses for the U.S. First Army

Panzer graveyard. Smashed German armor of the 116th Panzer Division *lies in quiet fields near Compogne, Belgium.*

in December with the larger balance in January. The *OKW War Diary* records the loss of 222 tanks (77 Mk IV, 132 Mk V, 13 Mk VI) and 102 assault guns for 16 through 31 December. More tanks were no doubt knocked out, although captured German panzer workshop personnel reported that when in possession of the battlefield "all but burnt out tanks were recovered." Even so, these crippled hulks were not available at the front. On January 12th, a tally of armored strength in *Heeresgruppe B* found only 143 operational armored vehicles in *Sixth Panzer Armee*, 167 in the *Fifth Panzer Armee* and 39 in the *Seventh Armee*. Given the initial panzer strength with which these formations began the offensive, this represented a loss in *Heeresgruppe B* of half of its armor.[4]

The losses to individual German divisions were shocking. The *Panzer Lehr Division* which went into battle with 3,000 grenadiers and 104 tanks and assault guns. They limped back across the Westwall a month later with just 16 armored

Upper right: *Representing Hitler's final comb out of available manpower, much of the German soldiery in the Ardennes was physically sub-standard. These two "boys" of the 12th SS* Panzer Division *look particularly diminutive beside their two strapping MP guards of the 6th Armored Division. Magaret, January, 1945.*

Right: *The price of failure. The frozen remains of a dead grenadier from the 6th SS Mountain Division. Schillersdorf, January 26th, 1945.*

vehicles and scarcely 400 rifles. Fifty-three of their tanks and assault guns had to be left behind due to lack of fuel or tank recovery vehicles. The *2nd SS Panzer Division* moved to the East after suffering 3,200 casualties and losing nearly sixty tanks and assault guns. The elite *Führer Begleit Brigade* lost 2,000 men and half of its seventy armored vehicles. Even the symbol of Hitler's military might, the famous *1st SS Panzer Division*, moved its shattered panzer regiment out of the battle near Bastogne on January 9th with only six combat ready tanks. German armor losses increased during the retreat later that month when large numbers of vehicles were lost due to mechanical failure, lack of tank retrievers and the chronic shortage of fuel. These problems were further aggravated by Hitler's "no retreat" policy during the

4   At the end of January 1945, *Heeresgruppe B* reported itself in possession of only 161 combat-ready armored vehicles, 192 artillery pieces and 170 heavy anti-tank guns. *OB West* reported total strength on the Western Front of only 1,502 armored vehicles on January 30th (813 were combat ready) as contrasted with the 2,567 on the strength roster for 16 December. Of this total, 800 had been shipped to the East and 324 reported lost in December although another 340 had been received in shipment.

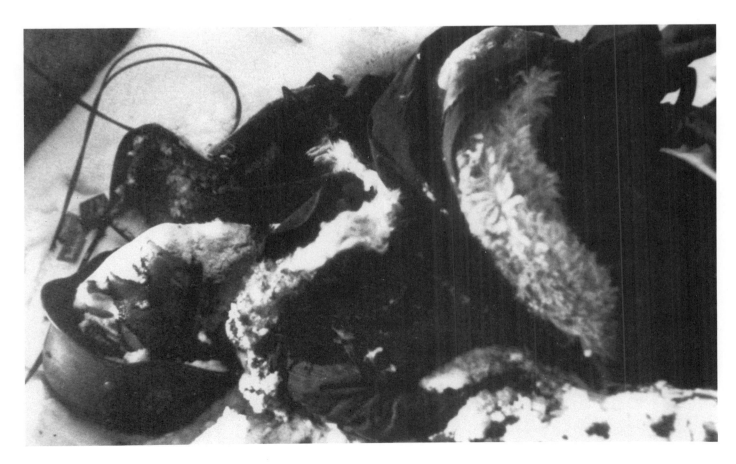

January campaign. As Gen. von Manteuffel, the commander of the *Fifth Panzer Armee* observed after the war, "In a tank battle, if you stand still you are lost."

The situation for the common German soldier was even worse. The *212th Volksgrenadier Division* emerged from December with less than thirty men in its rifle companies — a loss of over 3,000 men in two weeks of fighting. On January 5th the *326th Volksgrenadier Division* reported only 300 combat effectives. Losses in the *26th Volksgrenadiers* that invested the Bastogne garrison were severe — two of the three regimental commanders were killed. The *5th Fallschirmjäger Division* that had stoutly defended against Patton's counterattack in the south was thoroughly wrecked. According to the commander, "The 14th regiment was almost entirely de-stroyed." Other units like the *560th Volksgrenadier Division* ceased to exist as divisions — only 700 riflemen were available on New Year's Day.

The Luftwaffe had lost nearly 800 aircraft — ten percent of the total force available to the Germans. Over 500 planes were lost in the fighting in December and another 280 during the *Operation Bodenplatte* attack on Allied air fields on New Year's Day. Nearly 700 German pilots who participated (one in four) were now dead or taken prisoner. Although rapid production of new German fighters made replacement of aircraft possible, the lack of trained pilots and the steadily worsening poverty of aviation fuel stocks made for a very bleak outlook indeed. As Adolf Galland has said, "in the Ardennes the Luftwaffe received its death blow."

German volksgrenadiers, carrying their wounded, surrender to the 7th Armored Division on January 25th near Wallerode, Belgium. Within minutes, the combat photographer, T/5 Hugh F. McHugh, was himself killed in the swirling battle for the town.

The Place of the Ardennes Campaign in World War II

Historians have long asserted that the Ardennes battle shortened the war by months. This claim is difficult to substantiate. It is true that the Germans came out of hiding and used a powerful group of armies that would have been very difficult to overcome on the defensive. The last German reserve had been wasted before the Meuse. However, it must be kept in mind that the Allies had suffered greatly as well.

Wacht am Rhein postponed Allied offensive plans in the West by at least six weeks. It also made a difficult infantry replacement problem into a dilemma of drastic proportions. Likewise, the millions of gallons of fuel that had been so carefully stockpiled for the drive to the Rhine were consumed in a massive re-deployment of motorized forces. Over a million rounds of artillery were fired off and thousands of vehicles of all types were lost. Only a manufacturing giant like the U.S. could afford waste on such a grandiose scale and emerge without complete economic bankruptcy. But even for the Allies, it took time to make amends. Unlike the Allied losses, however, the German damages could no longer be made good.

In practical terms the Ardennes Campaign had been an important American victory. Caught completely unaware, the Germans had clobbered the U.S. forces with its best Sunday punch. Not only had the Americans thwarted the German effort and recovered from the blow, but they went over to the offensive on January 3rd with the knowledge that they had taken the worst that Hitler could muster and still come out fighting. This, too, gave lie to the German leader's vision of America as a weak foe; he had once sarcastically called the U.S. forces "the Italians of the Western Alliance."[5] But, perhaps no more fitting nor eloquent a comment has been made of the accomplishment of the U.S. soldier in the Ardennes than that bestowed by Sir Winston Churchill in an address to the House of Commons on January 18th:

This is undoubtedly the greatest American battle of the war and will, I believe, be regarded as an ever-famous American victory.

The clear political victor in the Ardennes Campaign was Soviet Russia. When Stalin's legions attacked Hitler's army in January, he found no respectable German forces with which to oppose his multitudes. The Ardennes Offensive had squandered the final German reserve that could have been used against the Russians in the East.[6] So the Allied command in the West was quiescent in the early winter, assimilating replacements in men and equipment while on January 12th the Soviet juggernaut collapsed the German front in the East and slammed across Poland and into East Prussia. Looking that direction, Gen. Jodl sarcastically remarked that the Allies in the Ardennes were "executing the artillery preparation for the Russians." The Soviet success in January provided a strong position for Stalin at the Yalta Conference in February; there he won important concessions from Churchill and Roosevelt.[7]

In the German camp, shocking losses coupled with the realization of certain defeat devastated German morale. If the Ardennes did shorten the war in the West, it was not because of men or material — both opponents were gravely hurt. The real benefit of the German failure for the Allies was the severe blow to the German soldier's will to fight. At a meeting on February 6th, *Heeresgruppe B* reported that "the German soldier is in general fed up." The entry for January 16th in a diary of a soldier of the *18th Volksgrenadier Division* is particularly telling in this regard: "Four weeks ago, our attack started. How quickly everything has changed! Now everything looks hopeless."

Even Hitler could see the handwriting on the wall, but chose to hide behind a fantasy that would become ever more psychotic as the end drew near. The dictator's delusion with

---

5   This is not to say, however, that American commanders were unconcerned about troop morale. This was clear from the confirmation by Eisenhower himself on December 23rd of the death sentence for Private Eddie Slovik. Eisenhower was determined to make an example out of Slovik, who was a repeat deserter from the 28th Division. AWOL soldiers were a problem of chronic proportions for the U.S. Army in the fall and winter of 1944—there had been 40,000 desertions since June 6th. Slovik was executed by firing squad on January 31st, 1945.

6   Generals Jodl and Keitel gave this joint assessment of the strategic question of the location of the German winter offensive just before their execution in 1945: "The criticism whether it would have been better to have employed our available reserves in the East rather than in the West, we submit to the judgment of history."

7   At the height of the German offensives in the Ardennes and in the Alsace, Eisenhower worried when the Russians might attack in the East and take off the pressure in the West. Thus, Churchill cabled Stalin on January 6th: "The battle in the West is very heavy...I shall be grateful if you can tell me whether we can count on a major Russian offensive on the Vistula front or elsewhere in January." Stalin replied that the weather was unfavorable, but that they would accelerate their plans for attack. As the Soviets interpreted it at Yalta, they bailed out the Allies from Hitler's offensive wrath.

The victor. The stalwart defense by the average U.S. soldier was perhaps the major reason for the German defeat in the Ardennes. T/5 John A. Lavoie stand ready for the enemy in St. Vith, Belgium on January 25, 1945.

numbers had begun to get out of control. For the remainder of the conflict he fought a "corporal's war" — ordering about panzer divisions that could muster no more than regimental strength. When Gen. Guderian, in charge of the Eastern Front, filed a report that warned of the impending disaster there, Hitler reprimanded the general in an angry outburst. "Who's responsible for producing all this rubbish?" the German leader demanded pointing to the estimates of Soviet military superiority. "It's the greatest imposture since Genghis Khan!"

Hitler, it would seem, entertained only facts that supported his optimistic fantasies of the future of the Third Reich. As Guderian has said, "He had a special picture of the world, and every fact had to fit into that fancied picture." In the fall of 1944, the dictator saw himself as a modern day Frederick the Great. That historical figure had boldly attacked a superior enemy forcing the alliance against him to split. As Hitler saw it, the British and the U.S. were the weak alliance and the Ardennes was his bold attack. He was resolved to "continue this struggle until one of our damned enemies give up. Only then shall we get a peace that will guarantee the future existence of the German nation."

But the end of the Third Reich was near. By the end of January 1945 it was apparent to all involved that *Wacht am Rhein* had failed. Although he continued to talk of a politi-

cal solution to the war, even the most fervent of the Führer's admirers could see the terrible end that was coming. Albert Speer, his Minister of Production and Armaments, said at the Nuremburg trials:

> He deceived us all...He raised hopes that, like Japan, we would start negotiations in this hopeless situation so that the people would be saved the worst consequences. To do this, however, it was necessary to stiffen resistance as much as possible. He deceived all of us by holding out to the military leaders false hopes in the success of diplomatic steps and by promising the political leaders fresh victories through the use of new troops and new weapons and by systematically spreading rumors to encourage the people to believe in the

Right: *"The dream is over." A German grenadier leaves a fitting comment on Hitler's Ardennes Offensive before departing the village of Rochefort.*

Upper right: *Ignominious defeat. The corpse of a German soldier of the 5th Fallschirmjäger Division lies where he was shot down.*

appearance of a miracle weapon — all for the purpose of keeping up resistance.

Although Hitler continued his pretense of winning the war, he must have known that it was lost.[8] Of course, he always professed to the contrary. On December 28th Hitler announced, "By no means am I entertaining the thought that the war will be lost. I have never in my life known the word 'capitulation'."

Whatever the nature of Hitler's delusion, it would not matter, for 130 days later it was all done. The Führer was dead in his Berlin bunker; the tanks, guns and planes of the Third Reich lay wrecked and broken from the Ardennes to Prussia in the East, along with graves of thousands of Ger-

man and Allied soldiers who had perished on the field of battle. The military machine of Nazi Germany faltered quickly after its defeat in the dark forest. As aging Prussian Field Marshal von Rundstedt observed after the war, the Ardennes Offensive for the German army was "Stalingrad number two."

8   Before his execution at Nuremberg, Gnfldm. Jodl said of his Führer's resolve that: "It is often said that Hitler's military advisors ought to have opened his eyes to the fact that the war was lost. This is a naive idea. Before any of us, he sensed and knew the war was lost. But can anyone give up a nation, particularly his own people, for lost if there is anyway out...Let those who so wish, condemn him—personally I cannot."

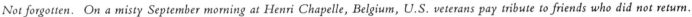

Not forgotten. On a misty September morning at Henri Chapelle, Belgium, U.S. veterans pay tribute to friends who did not return.

APPENDICES

ORGANIZATION OF COMBAT FORCES IN THE ARDENNES CAMPAIGN

THE U.S. ARMY

By the late fall of 1944, the U.S. Army was a formidable opponent. It was undoubtedly the best equipped and best trained fighting force in the world. And after hard battles in North Africa, the Mediterranean, Normandy and the Siegfried Line, the U.S. Army was an increasingly skilled adversary. Moreover, the American army was capable of a methodical and serious attritional style of warfare that the Germans fighting in the Ardennes could ill afford.

If there was a central American problem it was one of approach. American GIs were not professional soldiers; they generally considered the war as more of a "lousy" eight to five job than a struggle to decide the fate of Europe. The army was generally top heavy with a prodigious number of personnel in communication zone activities while the front line troops suffered from lack of infantry replacements.

The American officers were professionals, and while abundant they were not always in command for the right reasons. The Americans had tried to copy the German concept of flexibility in combined arms warfare but found that it did not work well for them. So while the Germans were theoretically organized in their component units, they improvised *Kampfgruppen* out of a mix of units styled to the mission. When the Americans tried it with their combat commands they found that mixing units up made things confused and less efficient. What the Americans never figured out from this lesson was that central authoritative leadership in charge of the battle group was the element that made it so successful in the enemy camp. But the Americans could never accept such a system since it smacked too much of Nazi totalitarianism.

In an operational sense the Americans were competent enough, but tended to rely more on prodigious expenditures of artillery ammunition, fighter-bomber ordnance, and gasoline to win battles than they did on small unit tactical ability and well-honed training. When they were without these commodities (and the Germans really relished those times), they tended to perform unevenly. Still, when it came to a war of material, the Americans could waste the Germans every time. This approach also had the side benefit of minimizing casualties at a time when the butchery of the battles in the Hürtgen forest and the Aachen area had the American army strapped for replacements.

An unheralded advantage of the American life-style was their consummate skill as drivers. Most GIs had driven their dad's Ford around the streets of Anytown, U.S.A., before coming to Europe. These recruits made some amazing truck, tank and tank destroyer drivers. General William E. DePuy, of Vietnam fame, remembers his training with the U.S. 90th Division:

> There wasn't much conviction about tactics. The regimental commander, for example, when he talked to us, didn't talk about tactics, he talked about movements...We were motorized by that time, and all the energy and imagination in the division was totally absorbed in how we could get a regiment mounted up in trucks, move down the road, not get lost, and get there on time. We spent months doing that, whereas, we should have spent months learning how to fight.

Meanwhile, most of the green German replacements were driving with new driver's licenses earned for a few minutes driving around Berlin. As a result, the Americans were able to move their ponderous army with deft driving skill and traffic control while the German army lurched forward in starts and stops plagued by traffic snarls and fuel outages. The huge communications tail that was such a drain on Allied manpower paid off handsomely in the Ardennes with the rapidity with which the Americans were able to reinforce the endangered salient.

Although the Americans stressed individuality, they neglected several aspects which might have increased esprit de corps. To begin with, the U.S. Army had dispensed with the idea of forming divisions from common geographic areas, primarily because it denuded certain regions of man power on the homefront. While a uniquely American idea ("we're all Americans"), there is evidence to indicate that keeping territorial units would have added to the cohesiveness in battle. As it was, U.S. infantry divisions that had maintained their complexion from their national guard upbringing, such as the U.S. 30th Infantry, did develop a special reputation for stamina in battle.

Even worse, due to the manpower shortage, forming infantry divisions were often cannibalized for infantry replacements and these units had their morale adversely affected (to say nothing of the replacements culled from them). The inspired idea of calling replacements "reinforcements" didn't fool anyone outside the newspapers. The Americans never developed a satisfactory reserve system. Instead they kept units in battle for months on end leading to utter exhaustion and loss of hope for many riflemen. Successful combat leaders were not typically promoted out of their squad, but were left there to keep winning or die. The only way to get out was either get killed or if lucky enough, get wounded. As it was, the American Army had a higher proportion of psychological casualties than any other army at the time.

The lack of an effective replacement policy led to a curious development in regards to U.S. divisional effectiveness. Normally divisions with greater combat experience were recognized as more dependable in battle. However, with the great numbers of casualties during the fall campaign along the German border, the complexion of the more experienced divisions such as the U.S. 1st, 4th and 28th Infantry Division became decidedly weighted towards the less trained replacements they were receiving. Unlike the Germans, who assimilated replacements over a period of time into a training detachment, the *Feldersatz* battalion, the American replacements were almost nameless warm bodies who suddenly showed up at the front with little indoctrination or sense of belonging. Since divisions were not kept out the line for more than a day or two at a time, these replacements never had much of an opportunity to train with the surviving veterans to increase operational cohesiveness. An avoidable situation, this nevertheless lead to a declining effectiveness in the most heavily engaged U.S. divisions.

On the other hand, many of the new, nominally "green" U.S. infantry divisions who were committed into battle in fall 1944 performed well from the very start. This was perhaps a consequence of the more realistic training the divisions were receiving within the U.S. based on American combat experiences in Europe. Also, there was the fact that the new divisions in late 1944 contained a greater proportion of men transferred from the Army Specialized Training Program (ASTP), which provided a college education for soldiers of high intelligence until the needs at the front lead to their reassignment with the infantry. To the extent that the divisions containing large quotients of ASTP men performed well from the start, this outcome called into question the usual American practice of only assigning the least promising soldier canidates to the infantry. A big qualification was whether these smarter, better trained divisions could be spared the travesty of being stripped for replacements to the line divisions. Some like the 99th Division lucked out in this regard; others like the 106th Division were stripped repeatedly before arriving at the front.

On the other hand, Hitler's belief that the Americans were too soft and too unrefined in cultural heritage to be capable of fighting was proved completely wrong. If not sticklers for march drill or fancy tactics, the scruffy looking Americans of varied origins proved a tough and resourceful enemy in the Ardennes. A soldier of the 99th Infantry Division wrote home on January 5th:

> I imagine you all have reading the newspapers about the big German counter-offensive. If I were a novelist, I could write a magnificent tale about a bunch of soda jerks and grocery clerks. After all, that's what all these American soldiers are. They're not professional military men, but just a bunch of guys over here doing a job, and a darn good one, and proving themselves much superior to the German, who has spent the better part of this life pursuing military training.

The American army's foe, the German training staff, published a series of "Battle Experiences" at the end of 1944 containing the official estimate of the American soldier.[1] Of course, this decidely biased appraisal must be examined with a critical eye. Nevertheless, when stripped of its overt propaganda, it does provide an interesting commentary from the enemy side of the hill.

Despite recognition that the American soldier was considerably more skilled than in the early weeks following the Normandy landings, the pronouncement of the superiority of the individual German soldier was unaltered from previous assessment. The American GI was portrayed as reliant on tremendous material superiority, disliking of close combat, night fighting and prone to surrender under adverse conditions. The German soldier was alerted to a number of peculiarities by American troops including slipshod security with radio communications, a tendency to start attacks in the late morning and stop all activity by midnight. Supposedly, American security during the hours of darkess was portrayed as negligent, particularly on rainy nights. Individually the American soldier was "more tenacious" on defense than attack and tended to stick to streets and roads, avoiding woods and underbrush.

Besides this long list of derogatory comments, the publications did describe certain American tactics and techniques believed to be worthy of emulation. High on the list was the coordination between infantry, tanks and air power. By far, however, the American artillery recieved the greatest praise, distinguished, as it was, by a rapid system of communication, accurate fire with air observation and a plentiful supply of ammunition. And of course, the extent of motorization in the American army was a source of constant envy within the German ranks.

Formations

There were three major type of divisions used by the Americans in the European theater of operations: infantry, armored and airborne. Additionally, there were two types of armored formations, a heavy 1942 version and the 1943 organization or light armored division.

---

1 OKH Gen. St. d. H., Abt. Fremde Heere West: Einzelnachrichten des IC Dienstes West.

Infantry

The 14,253-man U.S. infantry division was the backbone of the American army. It contained some 5,124 riflemen in 27 rifle companies with numerous support and artillery elements making up the other assigned personnel. The organization consisted of three infantry regiments of three battalions each. In theory the regimental anti-tank company provided organic protection against enemy armor. In reality, the 57mm guns were nearly worthless. Organic artillery support was very capable, however, with three 105mm howitzer battalions (12 guns each) and one 155mm battalion. Other support elements included a reconnaissance troop, an engineer combat battalion and anti-tank and cannon companies. Although they were not organic, divisions were seldom without attached tank, anti-aircraft, and tank destroyer (TD) battalions. About two-thirds of the TD battalions were self-propelled. Although many of the American divisions in the Ardennes had little combat experience — and some had inadequate training — they were still generally better off than the German Volksgrenadiers. Some divisions had been stripped repeatedly by the incessant demands for rifle replacements both in the U.S. and England. These troops were therefore denied prolonged training, this being particularly true for the higher numbered divisions in the sequence.

In the experienced divisions, the shortage of riflemen was acute due to the bloody autumn fighting. "Ninety-two percent of the casualties ocurr in the rifle companies," Patton wrote, "when an infantry division has 4,000 casualties it has no riflemen left." Some divisions, like the 28th, had suffered over 6,000 casualties in the Hürtgen Forest before coming to recuperate in the Ardennes.

Armor

The 1942 Armored Division organization was maintained by only two American units in the Bulge: the 2nd and 3rd Armored. Composition consisted of two armored regiments and an armored infantry regiment, loosely modeled after the early German panzer divisions. The heavy armored divisions contained 14,488 men and 232 M-4 Sherman tanks and 158 light Stuart tanks (the M-5s were little better than armored cars, however). Each armored regiment contained two M-4 battalions and one battalion of M-5s. There were only 2,600 infantry in the armored infantry regiment and the divisions tended to be tank heavy, working better if infantry from a neighboring unit was attached. Artillery was composed of three battalions of 105mm guns. Reconnaissance, engineer, anti-tank and anti-aircraft battalions were standard elements. Even though these divisions were organized as regiments; they often fought as combat commands like the 1943 version.

The 1943 Armored Division consisted of three "combat commands:" CC"A", CC"B" and CC "R"(Reserve). The adoption of the combat command organization was an attempt to emulate the German combined arms *Kampfgruppen* approach to mechanized warfare. The divisions had some 10,937 men assigned including an established strength of 186 M-4 tanks and 77 M-5s. Artillery and support battalions were identical to the 1942 formation. Each combat command was theoretically flexible in organization, make up of *ad hoc* task forces from the division. In practice this did not work too well. Each combat command usually consisted of one armored battalion and one armored infantry battalion with its leader reluctant to separate units that were used to fighting together. The U.S. armored division made up for the technical superiority of the German armored vehicles by commonly fielding a hundred vehicles more than a typical panzer division could find in December of 1944.

Airborne

The organization of the airborne division was not formulated until the war was already under way. Thus, it went through an evolution of sorts from 1942-1945. Basically, the airborne division was a lightly equipped infantry division trained for both offensive and defensive operations. Strong leadership, coupled with a high level of esprit de corps this made these units extremely tough and aggressive. However, without many of the necessary heavy weapons — particularly artillery, the airborne divisions suffered greatly when encountering an enemy ground force with tanks and artillery. This was convincingly shown in the encounters of the 82nd Airborne Division with the *1st SS Panzer Division* on the west bank of the Ambleve River. Total authorized personnel totalled 12,979 men, although the divisions in the Ardennes each had an extra attached airborne infantry regiment. A prime weakness was the small caliber 75mm Pack howitzers of the artillery battalions (some paratroopers called them "pop guns") and the lack of armored support. Three U.S airborne divisions fought in the Ardennes: the 82nd, 101st and the new 17th. There had been only two division sized drops during the war in Europe so far (D-Day and Arnhem) and the only jump experience that the airborne divisions gathered in the Bulge was out of the back of 2 1/2 ton trucks!

Independent Units

These included the tank and tank destroyer battalions. They were officially under the control of the Corps, but in practice were typically attached to the various divisions. The tank battalions had an established strength of 53 M-4 "Shermans" and another six assault M-4s armed with 105mm howitzers. Towed TD battalions included 36 3-inch guns. The self-propelled tank destroyer battalions consisted of 36 M-10 3-inch guns on motor carriages; or a like number of 76mm M-18s or 90mm M-36 TDs. The majority of the guns were M-10s, the M-36 TDs with their sought after guns, were just coming into service in Europe. In practice operational field strength of the tank and TD battalions seldom exceeded 85% — a number of vehicles being either down for maintenance or in the process of being requisitioned after being lost in combat.

Artillery battalions (12 guns each) were organized into field artillery groups of two to six battalions or were directly attached to divisions. The U.S. engineer battalions were often organized into engineer combat groups. The armored cavalry groups were specifically designed for reconnaissance or pursuit activities, yet in the Ardennes they often drew static defensive missions for which they were not trained or equipped.

Transportation and supply activities were organized at the corps or army level in numerous truck battalions possessing hundreds of vehicles and making the American forces extremely mobile. Extra corps and army level trucks were obtained during the Bulge by cannibalizing the transport from anti-aircraft units. Thus, all of these battalions were more or less immobile in the Ardennes with the AA guns being used as provost guards or to protect vital bridges or supply installations from enemy aircraft.

U.S. ORDER OF BATTLE IN THE ARDENNES CAMPAIGN

December 16, 1944

FIRST ARMY - Lt. Gen. Courtney H. Hodges
  526 Arm Inf Bn
  99 Inf Bn
  825 TD Bn [towed]
  61, 158, 299, 300, 1278 Eng Bns.
  Trp B, 125 Cav Rcn Sq
  9 Canadian Forestry Co.

V Corps - Maj. Gen. Leonard T. Gerow
  51, 112, 146, 202, 254, 291, 296 Eng Bns.
  186 FA Bn
  941 FA Bn
    78 Inf Div - Maj. Gen. Edwin P. Parker
      95 Arm FA Bn
      709 Tnk Bn
      893 TD Bn
    102 Cav. Grp
      62 AFA Bn
    99 Inf Div - Maj. Gen Walter E. Lauer
      196 FA Bn
      776 FA Bn
      924 FA Bn
      801 TD Bn [towed]
    2 Inf Div - Maj. Gen. Walter M. Robertson
      16 Arm FA Bn
      18 FA Bn
      200 FA Bn (-)
      955 FA Bn

  987 FA Bn (-)
  741 Tnk Bn
  644 TD Bn [M-10]
  612 TD Bn [towed]
  CCB, 9 Arm Div- Brig Gen. William M. Hoge
    811 TD Bn (-) [M-18]

VIII Corps - Maj. Gen. Troy H. Middleton
  35, 44, 159, 168 Eng Bns.
    106 Inf Div - Maj. Gen. Alan W. Jones
      333, 559, 561, 578, 740, 770, 771, 965, 969 FA Bns
      14 Cav Grp
        275 AFA Bn
      820 TD Bn [towed]
    28 Inf Div - Maj. Gen. Norman D. Cota
      630 TD Bn [towed]
      687 FA Bn
      707 Tnk Bn
    4 Inf Div - Maj. Gen. Raymond O. Barton
      802 TD Bn [towed]
      803 TD Bn [M-10]
      81 FA Bn
      174 FA Bn
      70 Tnk Bn
    9 Arm Div (less CCB) - Maj. Gen. John W. Leonard
      811 TD Bn (-) [M-18]

Organization of·the 9th U.S. Air Force:
December, 1944

Lt. Gen. Hoyt S. Vandenberg, commanding

IX TAC Brig. Gen. Elwood R. Quesada
  70th Fighter Wing
    365, 366, 367, 368, 370, 474 Fighter Groups (FG)
    67 Tactical Reconnaissance Group (TRG)
    422 Night Fighter Squadron (NFS)

XIX TAC Maj. Gen. Otto P. Weyland
  100th Fighter Wing
    354, 358, 362, 405, 406 FG
    10 Photo Reconnaissance Group (PRG)
    425 NFS

XXIX TAC Brig. Gen. Richard E. Nugent
  84th and 303 Fighter Wings
    36, 48, 373, 404, 363 FG

IX Bombardment Command Brig. Gen. Samuel E. Anderson
  97th Combat Bomb Wing (CB)

    409, 410, 416 Bomb Group (BG)
  98th CB
    323, 387, 394, 397 BG
    1 Pathfinder Squadron
  99th CB
    322, 344, 386, 391 BG

IX Troop Carrier Command Brig. Gen. Benjamin F. Giles
  52 Troop Carrier Command (TCC)
    61, 313, 314, 315, 349 Troop Carrier Group (TCG)
  53 TCC
    434 - 438 TCG
  50 TCC
    439 - 442 TCG

Plane types in the fighter and bomber groups:
  P-47: 36, 48, 50, 354, 358, 362, 365, 366, 368, 371, 373, 404, 405.
  P-38: 367, 370, 474.
  P-51: 363.
  B-26: 322, 323, 344, 387, 391, 394, 397, 1 PF
  A-20: 410, 416; A-26: 409

COMMITMENT OF REINFORCEMENTS TO THE ARDENNES:

16 Dec: N CCR, 5 Arm [in reserve]
       751 FA Bn
17 Dec: N 7 Arm Div – Brig. Gen. Robert W. Hasbrouck
       1 Inf Div – Brig. Gen. Clift Andrus
          745 Tnk Bn
          634 TD Bn [M-10]
       9 Inf Div (-) – Maj. Gen. Louis A. Craig
          47 Reg
             746 Tnk Bn (-)
             899 TD Bn (-)
          58 AFA Bn
      S 10 Arm Div – Maj. Gen. William H. Morris, Jr.
          609 TD Bn [M-18]
18 Dec: N 30 Inf Div – Maj. Gen. Leland S. Hobbs
          743 Tnk Bn
          823 TD Bn [towed, converting to M-10]
       703 TD Bn [M-36]
       254, 755 FA Bns
       400 AFA Bn
       705 TD Bn [M-18]
    W XVIII Abn Corps HQ – Maj. Gen. Matthew B. Ridgway
       82 Abn Div – Maj. Gen. James W. Gavin
       101 Abn Div – Brig. Gen. Anthony C. McAuliffe
       1/341 Eng GS Bn
19 Dec: N 3 Arm Div – Maj. Gen. Maurice Rose
       9 Inf/39 Reg.
       1340 Eng Bn
20 Dec: N 83 AFA Bn
       991 FA Bn
       1 Inf/18 Reg
       740 Tnk Bn
       20 Eng Bn
      S Third Army HQ – Lt. Gen. George S. Patton, Jr.
       III Corps HQ – Maj. Gen. John Millikin
       4 Arm Div – Maj. Gen. Hugh J. Gaffey
          704 TD Bn [M-18]
       80 Inf Div – Maj. Gen. Horace L. McBride
          702 Tnk Bn
          808 TD Bn [towed]
       26 Inf Div – Maj. Gen. Willard S. Paul
          735 Tnk Bn
          818 TD Bn [M-10]
       179, 731 FA Bns
       1303, 1306 Eng GS Rgts
       145, 178, 183, 188, 249 Eng Bns
    W 115 FA Bn
       643 TD Bn [towed]
21 Dec: N 84 Inf Div – Brig. Gen. Robert C. Macon
       771 Tnk Bn
       638 TD Bn [M-18]
       187, 172, 957, 980 FA Bns
      S 602 TD Bn [M-18]
       176, 177, 512, 752, 949 FA Bns
       253, 274, 696 AFA Bns
       XII Corps HQ – Maj. Gen. Manton S. Eddy
       5 Inf Div – Maj. Gen. Leroy Irwin
          610 TD Bn [M-36]
    W Br. 29 Arm Brig.
22 Dec: N VII Corps HQ – Maj. Gen. Lawton J. Collins
       2 Arm Div – Maj. Gen. Ernest N. Harmon
          702 TD Bn [M-36]
       4 Cav Grp
          759 Lt Tnk Bn [M-5]
          635 TD Bn [towed]
          195, 951 FA Bns
          207 Eng Bn

       750 Tnk Bn
       628 TD Bn [M-36]
       237, 238, 297 Eng Bns
    W 75 Inf Div – Maj. Gen. Fay B. Prickett
       517 Para Inf Regt
          509 Para Inf Bn
          460 Para FA Bn
       551 Para Inf Bn
       29 Inf Reg
       342, 366, 392 Eng GS Regs
       6/2, 4/20, 5/20, 12/30, 2/106, 5/106 Fr Lt Inf Bns
      S 191, 244, 255, 273, 802, 945, 974 FA Bns
       276, 695 AFA Bns
       5 Inf/2 Reg
       737 Tnk Bn
23 Dec: N 9 Inf/60 Reg
       183, 188, 190, 193, 953, 981 FA Bns
       49, 148, 164, 294, 298 Eng Bns
       87 AFA Bn
    W 203 Eng Bn
      S 654 TD Bn [M-10]
       775 FA Bn
24 Dec: N 5 Arm Div – Maj. Gen. Lunsford E. Oliver
       (held in V Corps Reserve)
       629 TD Bn [M-10]
       76, 240 FA Bns
    W 118 Inf Reg (-)
       1308 Eng GS Reg
       348 Eng Bn
      S 6 Cav Grp
25 Dec: W 11 Arm Div – Brig. Gen. Charles S. Kilbrun
      S 351 Eng GS Reg
26 Dec: N 83 Inf Div – Maj. Gen. Robert C. Macon
       772 TD Bn [towed]
       259, 268 FA Bns
      S 6 Arm Div – Maj. Gen. Robert W. Grow
       603 TD Bn [M18]
       35 Inf Div – Maj. Gen. Paul W. Baade
       10 Arm Div (withdraws less CCB)
    W 17 Airborne Div – Maj. Gen. William M. Miley
27 Dec: N 153, 266, 551 FA Bns
       774 Tnk Bn
28 Dec: N 552 FA Bn
      S 277, 736 FA Bns
29 Dec: W 243 Eng Bn
30 Dec: S 87 Inf Div – Maj. Gen. Frank L. Culin, Jr.
       761 Tnk Bn
31 Dec: N 264, 666, 809 FA Bns
2 Jan: W 466 Para FA Bn

6 Jan: S 691 TD Bn [towed]

7 Jan: S 90 Inf Div – Maj. Gen. James A. van Fleet
       3 Chem. Mortar Bn
       773 TD Bn [M-18]
8 Jan: S 712 Tnk Bn

THE BRITISH ARMY

The British Army, as one historian has commented, has always been a singular institution. The army of 1944 had several years of combat experience fighting the Germans. Its structure reflected the highly stratified class structure of Britain; officers and enlisted men were often from totally different backgrounds. Even so, the traditional territorial recruitment policy led to tough, extremely reliable combat formations with very high esprit de corps.

The British army had been molded by long standing historical traditions, which unlike in France, Prussia and Austria had not been greatly disturbed by great political and revolutionary upheavals. The British fighting men engaged in intense inter-regimental rivalry. A British soldier thought of himself as a Grenadier Guardsman, a member of the Black Watch or a Sherwood Forester first and foremost with little regard for his brigade or division. His loyalty was almost always to his own regiment, which, needless to say, he regarded as superior to any other!

In terms of fighting, the British had given up on emulating the German style of warfare although they had incorporated a number of important lessons (notably to increase infantry strength in tank units). This is not to say that the British did not respect the Germans. As the British were fond of saying, "He who has not fought the Germans does not know war." On the other hand, the British were not overly impressed with the Americans, which they characterized as "over paid, over sexed and over here."

An important advantage the British had was in the cohesiveness and skill of their infantry. Knowing that the "queen of battle" could often be decisive, the British lavished a good deal of training on its riflemen and this paid off handsomely. Leadership tended to be very good on the small unit level, but somewhat too cautious on the strategic level. The biggest problem for the U.K. forces in 1944 was the dire shortage of infantry replacements. Unlike the U.S. forces where the shortages were caused by the excesses of administrative fat elsewhere, the British were experiencing a real shortage of manpower caused by the losses of the war and the limited pool available from the island country. On this basis, the lack of aggressive combat behavior can be somewhat overlooked since all the British commanders knew of the serious nature of this problem and were attempting to minimize their casualties.

Formations

The British units fighting under XXX Corps in the Ardennes consisted chiefly of three divisional types: infantry, armor and airborne units. Independent armored brigades and reconnaissance regiments were also involved.

Infantry Division

The British infantry Division had three infantry brigades. These were similar in strength to the American infantry regiments, being composed of three infantry battalions each with an extra heavy weapons detachment. Artillery support consisted of three regiments (of what the Americans called battalion strength) with 72 25-pound guns and 32 17-pounders. Support elements included anti-tank, anti-aircraft battalions and reconnaissance squadrons. Although the divisions had an established strength in excess of their American infantry counterparts, this was seldom the case in actual practice due to the manpower shortage. The divisions lacked self-propelled guns or tanks and usually one of the independent armored brigades were attached for offensive operations.

Armored Division

The British Armored Division was a product of pre-war thinking and lacked necessary infantry support. It consisted of two maneuver brigades — one of armor and the other with armored infantry. Nominally, it had over 200 M-4 Sherman tanks including some M-4/A4 "Fireflys" and Cromwell tanks. Seldom did its actual strength reach the established numbers, however. Tank crew replacements were lacking and much of the British armor was in poor repair after the pursuit across France and the Arnhem debacle. The Guards Armored Division was the only such British formation alerted for commitment in the Ardennes. It saw no fighting there, however, remaining in reserve in the Namur-Huy region guarding the Meuse bridgeheads.

Airborne Division

These light infantry divisions were similar to the American divisions by the same name. Likewise, they often ended up fighting as infantry. The organization was very similar to the British infantry division, the main difference being the light 75mm pack howitzers used for artillery support. The main maneuver elements consisted of two parachute and one glider brigade. The British 6th Airborne Division, the only such formation in the Ardennes, fought against the Germans at the tip of the Bulge in early January.

Armored Brigades

The armored brigade theoretically possessed three armored regiments (battalion sized in strength) with a single armored infantry battalion. The ration armored strength consisted of 165 medium tanks, 33 light tanks and 18 anti-aircraft tanks. Seldom were these units near their established strength and the British armor in these units was in poor repair at the time the Germans opened their offensive on December 16th. Conceptually, the organization was outdated. Heavy with armor, short on infantry and without any artillery the brigades were not really functional on an independent basis. Thus, in practice, these brigades were most often attached to a British infantry division to the mutual benefit of both organizations.

Independent Units

The cavalry regiments were basically the equivalent of a U.S. reconnaissance battalion with an established strength of 67 Daimler and U.S. Staghound armored cars with 735 officers and men. The Army Group Royal Artillery groups generally contained one heavy regiment (7.2-inch howitzers or U.S. 155mm guns) and two medium artillery regiments (5.5-inch howitzers). Each British artillery regiment contained 16 guns. The anti-tank regiments contained 48 6-pdr and 17-pdr guns, all towed. Anti-aircraft brigades generally contained two heavy and two light AA regiments with 48 3.7-inch guns and 108 40-mm guns.

BRITISH ORDER OF BATTLE IN THE ARDENNES CAMPAIGN

January 1, 1945

21st ARMY GROUP - Field Marshal Sir Bernard L. Montgomery

XXX Corps - Lt. Gen. Brian G. Horrocks
    4th and 5th Army Group Royal Artillery
    2nd Household Cav. Reg.
    11th Hussars and Cav. Rgt.
    53rd and 61st Recon Reg.
    73st AT Reg.
    106th AA Brig.
    27th Lt. AA Reg.
    Belgian Special Air Service Sqn.

French 2nd Parachute Bn
    43rd (Wessex) Inf Div. - Maj. Gen. G.I. Thomas
    51st (Highland) Inf. Div - Maj. Gen. T.G. Rennie
    53rd (Welsh) Inf Div. - Maj. Gen. R.K. Ross
    Guards Armored Div - Maj. Gen. A.H.S. Adair
    6th Airborne Div - Maj. Gen. Eric L. Bols
    29th Arm Brig.- Brig. Gen. C.B.C. Harvey
    33rd Arm Brig. - Brig. Gen. H.B. Scott
    34th Army Tnk Brig. - Brig. Gen. W.S. Clarke

COMMITMENT OF BRITISH FORCES TO THE ARDENNES:

20 Dec: 2nd Household Cav. Reg.
21 Dec: 29th Arm Brig.
    French 2nd Parachute Reg.
25 Dec: 53rd (Welsh) Inf Div.
    33rd Arm Brig.

26 Dec: 6th Abn Div.
    34th Army Tnk Brig.
8 Jan: 51st (Highland) Inf Div.

THE GERMAN ARMY

The German Army was in a period of transition from good to bad in late 1944. Only two years before, it had undoubtedly been the best army in the world on a unit for unit basis. By the fall of 1944, however, German survival demanded improvisation. The Germans excelled in their training and small unit tactics. Although relatively poorly equipped, the Germans were masters of innovation, often doing much more with less than their Allied counterparts. The German concept of leadership and officer promotion was superior. Virtually anyone who could demonstrate leadership ability, no matter social class or economic status, was officer material. Leaders were encouraged to be solicitous of their men and units and their replacements were deliberately culled on a territorial basis. Senior commanders directly chose their officers which inspired loyalty, trust and cooperation. In battle, *Kampfkraft* or fighting ability was the sole judge of a soldier's character. The German soldier understood war as a clash of will to be conducted with maximum ferocity and efficiency as enumerated by Clausewitz over a century before:

He who uses force unsparingly, without reference against the bloodshed involved, must obtain a superiority if his adversary uses less vigour in its application. To introduce into a philosophy of war a principle of moderation would be an absurdity. War is an act of violence pushed to its utmost bounds.

By late 1944, however, the training edge that made the crucial difference in the German abilities could no longer be maintained. Then too, the SS were now appointing commanders based on their political reputation rather than battle competence. What the SS now lacked in leadership and administrative ability, they tried to make up for in *Härte,* best translated as "harshness" or "severity." It was no coincidence that rather than the traditional Wehrmacht motto, "*Gott mit uns* (God with us), the SS version "*Unsere Ehre heisst Treue*" (Our Honor is Loyalty) emphasized devotion to the Führer above all else. Although the SS were tenacious fighters, the concept of *Härte* as returned from the Eastern front made for a barbaric style of warfare where decency was reserved for comrades and death for all others — even civilians. Just as this beastly combat had increased the ferocity of both antagonists in Russia, it increased the resolve of the American soldier when confronted with its horror.

To be sure, the same highly trained and less bloodthirsty abilities were still nurtured in the more elite panzer formations, although many of the new *Volksgrenadier* divisions simply did not have the basic training with which to successfully carry out the difficult role of infantry assault forces. Many engaged the enemy even when ordered to bypass them. Small units often became lost and advantages that were gained were not exploited due to lack of experience. Still others, however, such as the *12th, 212th and 26th Volksgrenadiers,* still had the touch as they had maintained a veteran cadre that made all the difference. Considering the supply and material difficulties under which the Germans labored, the accomplishments of the German Army in the Ardennes is all the more remarkable.

Formations

Although production of weapons had actually increased in 1944 and a large contingent of replacements had been wrung out of Germany, the battle wastage of both commodities had been tremendous during the military catastrophes of summer 1944. Divisions had been totally destroyed and many others were at a quarter of their established strength by fall of 1944. Futhermore, Hitler was committed to a delusion of numbers that entailed creation of new divisions while existing ones fell apart from lack of replacements. To further confuse matters, the German ground armed forces now consisted of three separate field organizations: the regular army, the Luftwaffe and the Waffen SS. This lead to a bewildering array of different division types, a certain amount of duplication of effort and associated logistical problems with supply.

The German Army

The German Army of 1944 had come under a severe manpower squeeze and had dropped to second place in preference for new equipment — the best going to Hitler's more favored SS. Regardless, it was still the most capable force under German command, benefiting from superior experience and leadership.

The Volksgrenadier Division

The "People's Division" was the real beginning of the cannon fodder units that Hitler threw together in the closing months of the war. Lack of replacements necessitated that manpower be cut in infantry divisions from 12,000 to 10,000. This was done by using two battalion regiments rather than the preferred three battalion organization. This reduced the staying power of the volksgrenadier formations since regimental reserves were now hard to keep in battle. Front-line infantry strength was available from 25 grenadier companies with an authorized total of 3,616 men. Even worse, the replacements used to fill these divisions were often very young or old and only had two months of training on the average. Signal equipment was often lacking and many of these divisions went into battle missing their assault gun company (established strength: 14 guns) on which the German soldier had learned to lean heavily. Artillery support included three battalions of 105mm and one of 150mm, but all of it was horse drawn and ammunition was often in short supply. A *Fusilier* company or battalion of light motorized (or bicycled) infantry was usually available for reserve or pursuit duties. Performance in battle of these untried divisions was uneven. Some such as the experienced *12th Volksgrenadiers* fought like veterans, while others like the *276th*, were little more than armed mobs. In general, the increase in automatic weapons, such as machine guns, did not make up for the loss of personnel and training.

The Panzer Division

The panzer units represented the most capable attack forces available to the German army. The elite status of the panzer divisions meant that the best trained and most highly motivated individuals were usually found there. The 1944 panzer division had a good mix of infantry and armor consisting of one armored regiment and two armored infantry regiments and a total authorized strength of 13,725 men. The allotted armored strength was established at two battalions; one each of 51 Mk IV and Mk V tanks. In practice, these were always under strength. The panzer grenadier regiments each had two battalions. Only one battalion of the four panzergrenadier battalions was mounted on half-tracks. The rest were lucky to ride on trucks and several divisions — even the elite *2nd Panzer* — were forced to put some of their grenadiers on bicycles. Artillery consisted of three 105mm battalions — usually, but not always self-propelled. Tank destroyer, anti-aircraft and service elements were organic to the divisions. A shortage of tanks for *Wacht am Rhein* often lead to additional assault guns and tank destroyers being attached to the divisions to make up for their armored weakness. Even with fewer tanks and after long years of war, the German panzer divisions were still a match of their American armored foes.

The Panzer Grenadier Division

These formations were very similar in organization to the panzer divisions with two important exceptions. Firstly, their two armored infantry regiments each had an additional panzergrenadier battalion generally giving them more staying power in a defensive engagement and allowing them to hold a greater frontage. Secondly, they had an armored or assault gun battalion (often called a brigade) in the place of the panzer regiment — usually with 50-70 assault guns and tank destroyers. Authorized strenght was 13,876. Due to shortages in armored personnel carriers, all the grenadiers rode into battle on trucks. The two divisions in the Ardennes (*3rd and 15th Panzer Grenadier Divisions*) were rather run down, having recently been in combat. Both were missing armored cars in their reconnaissance battalions which had to make do with half-tracks. Regardless of their shortcomings, these divisions were well suited to the infantry fighting that was typical in the Ardennes Campaign.

The Waffen SS

Hitler's dictatorship necessitated a "private army" to ensure political obedience within his domain. The SS panzer divisions involved in the Battle of the Bulge enjoyed an elite status. Much of their reputation, however, was based on their equipment and ration strength, which included many extras which the regular panzer divisions did not possess: werfer battalions, Tiger tanks, and additional infantry and artillery. In general, it can be said that the training and leadership, even in the favored SS, was not outstanding at the close of 1944. The typical SS grenadier was a better Nazi than he was a soldier. Even so, each division usually had a *Kampfgruppe* of well equipped, battle-hardened veterans who proved exceedingly tough opponents for the American soldier. On the dark side, however, the criminal element that had always surrounded the SS made several brutal appearances in the Ardennes.

The SS Panzer Division

The four SS panzer divisions in the Ardennes (*1st SS, 2nd SS, 9th SS, 12th SS*) had six panzer grenadier battalions in two armored infantry regiments. The armored regiment had an established strength of 64 Mk IVs and 64 Mk Vs in two battalions, although even the favored SS divisions in the Ardennes usually possessed only 50% tank strength. A tank destroyer battalion organic to the divisions gave a further 22 Jagdpanzer IV tank destroyers. Also, in each SS division in the Ardennes another tank, tank destroyer or assault gun battalion was allocated to give the divisions more armored muscle. The artillery complement was very heavy including a 170mm gun battalion and a 150mm rocket battalion, although all of the artillery regiments in the four SS divisions was towed. Ration strength was 17,262 and, unlike the Wehrmacht, most the SS divisions were over strength at the beginning of the battle.

Luftwaffe Field Army

There was no real reason why the Luftwaffe had to maintain a ground force and Göring's early field divisions had been abject failures. By 1944, however, Hitler had lost confidence in airborne operations so it seemed expedient to use the parachute divisions in a ground role. They were considered elite units, although by the time of the Ardennes Offensive, so many infantry replacements had been absorbed into these divisions that they had begun to resemble the ragtag *Volksgrenadier* conscripts.

The Fallschirmjäger Division

The two parachute divisions in the Ardennes (the *3rd FJ* and the *5th FJ*) were similar to the old German infantry division with three infantry battalions in three regiments with theoretical strength of 15976 men. Limited motorization was available and strong anti-aircraft and anti-armor capability was available in their powerful flak battalions. The *5th FJ* did have an assault gun brigade attached, although the *3rd* had no armor at all. The other weakness in these divisions was in the small number of regular guns in the artillery regiment. Both divisions were poorly trained at the time they were committed to the Ardennes battle and the idea that the offensive would be won by the paratrooper's "usual audacity" rung hollow in their combat performance. In attack, they showed poor tactical know-how, although both divisions did distinguish themselves in the defensive phase of the fighting.

Independent Units

There were numerous independent organizations in the German army. These included panzer, jägdpanzer, sturmgeschütz, engineer and artillery battalions and brigades. The army tank and tank destroyer battalions were usually under strength with 10 to 50 operational vehicles. Assault gun battalions (called a *Sturmgeschütz Brigade* for propaganda purposes) usually had 15 to 30 vehicles. The army generally tried to keep the German engineers out of the fighting. Bridge columns and bridge construction engineers were both in short supply. However, during the defensive phase of the Ardennes Campaign, the German engineers were generally swept up into combat along with everyone else. German non-divisional artillery was organized into *Volksartillerie Korps* with four to six battalions (12-18 tubes each). The rocket units were formed into *Volkswerfer Brigades* with two werfer regiments of three battalions (18 launchers each). The Luftwaffe *III Flak Korps* wielded a powerful group of about 120 heavy flak guns of 88mm or greater. These guns served both in an anti-aircraft was well as anti-tank role.

GERMAN ORDER OF BATTLE FOR THE ARDENNES CAMPAIGN

December 16th, 1944

OKW Reserve - Adolf Hitler, Genobst. Alfred Jodl
  3 PzGr Div - Gen. Maj. Walter Denkert [25 JgIV, 20 StuG]
  9 VG Div - Obst. Werner Kolb [12 Jpz38t]
  10SS Pz Div - SS Brigadeführer Heinz Harmel
    [26 Mk IV, 33 Mk V, 33 JgIV & JgV]
    655 s. Pzjgr Bn [20 JgIV, 9 JgV]
  Fuh Bgt Brig - Obst. Otto Remer [23 Mk IV, 20 StuG]
    StuG Brig 200 [28 StuG]
  Fuh Gr Brig - Obst. Hans-Joachim Kahler
    [11 Mk IV, 37 Mk V, 10 Marder III]
    911 StuG Brig. [34 StuG]
  167 VG Div - Genlt. Hans-Kurt Höcker [12 Jpz38t]
  6SS Mtn Div - SS Gruppenführer Karl H. Brenner
  257 VG Div - Obst. Erich Seidel [6 Jpz38t]
  11 Pz Div - Genlt. Wend von Wietersheim
    [39 Mk IV, 56 Mk V, 19 Jg IVs]

OB West - Generalfeldmarschal Karl Gerd von Rundstedt

HERRESGRUPPE B - Generalfeldmarschal Walter Model
  79 VG Div - Obst. Alois Weber
  725 Rail Art Bn
  813 Pz Eng Co.

Fifteenth Armee - Gen. der Inf. Gustav von Zangen
  1076 Festung Art Bttr.
  1310 Festung Art Bn
  341 StuG Brig. [16 StuG]
  434 Construction Eng Bn

  9 Pz Div - Gen. Maj. Harald von Elverfeldt
    301 s. FKL Pz Bn [14 Mk VIa]
    [28 Mk IV, 37 Mk V, 10 JgIV]
  15 Pz Gr. Div - Obst. Hans-Joachim Deckert
    [14 Mk IV, 38 StuG, 20 JgIV]
  246 VG Div - Obst. Peter Körte [8 Jgpz38t]
  340 VG Div - Obst. Theodor Tolsdorf [9 Jgpz38t]

  LXXIV Armeekorps - Gen. der Inf. Karl Püchler
    III/139 sFH Bn
    628 Mortar Bttr
    992 LtFH Bn
    1193 sFH Bn
    1308 Fest.Art Bn
    843 H. Art Bn
    353 Inf Div - Genlt. Paul Mahlmann [8 Jpz38t]
      627 Ost Bn
    344 Inf Div - Gen. Maj. Erwin Jolasse [10 Jpz38t]
    85 Inf Div - Obst. Helmut Bechler
    89 Inf Div - Gen. Maj. Walter Bruns [9 StuG]

Sixth Panzer Armee - SS Obergruppenführer Josef Dietrich
2nd Flak Div: 2, 3, 4 Flak Sturm Regts.
519 s. Pzjgr Bn [7 JgV, 9 JglV, 17 StuG]
667 StuG Brig. [5 StuG]
217 Sturmpz Bn [8 Sturmpz IV]
653 s. Pzjgr Bn [9 Jg VI]
506 s. Pz Bn [8 Mk VI]
428 H. Mortar Bty
62, 73 and 253 Combat Eng Bns
59, 798 Construction Eng Bns
655 Bridge Construction Eng Bn

LXVII Armeekorps - Gen. der Inf. Otto Hitzfeld
17 VW Brig
405 VAK
1000 Sturm Mortar Co.
1001 Sturm Mortar Co.
902 StuG Brig. [20 StuG]
394 StuG Brig. [3 StuG]
683 Pzjgr Bn
1110 Mortar Bty
272 VG Div - Genlt. Eugen König [8 Jgpz 38t]
326 VG Div - Obst. Erwin Kaschner

ISS Panzerkorps - SS Gruppenführer Hermann Priess
9 VW Brig
4 VW Brig
402 VAK
388 VAK
501SS Art Bn
502SS Art Bn
1098 Mortar Bty
1120 Mortar Bty
1123 Fest. Art Bty
277 VG Div - Obst. Wilhelm Viebig [6 Jpz38t]
12 VG Div - Gen. Maj. Gerhard Engel [6 StuG]
1 SS Pz Div - SS Oberführer Wilhelm Mohnke
    [34 Mk IV, 37 Mk V, 20 JgIV]
    501SS Pz Bn [30 Mk VI]
    84 Lt Flak Bn
12SS Pz Div - SS Standartenführer Hugo Kraas
    [39 Mk IV, 38 Mk V, 22 Jg IV]
    560 s. Pzjr Bn [12 JgV, 25 JglV]
3 FJ Div - Gen. Maj. Walther Wadehn
150th Pz Brig - SS Obersturmbannführer Otto Skorzeny
    [5 Mk V, 5 StuG, 2 M-4]

IISS Panzerkorps - SS Obergruppenführer Willi Bittrich
2SS Pz Div - SS Brigadeführer Heinz Lammerding
    [28 Mk IV, 58 Mk V, 20 Jg IV, 28 StuG]
    508SS Werfer Bn
9SS Pz Div - SS Oberführer Sylvester Stadler
    [32 Mk IV, 49 Mk V, 21 Jg IV, 28 StuG]
    502SS Werfer Bn

Fifth Panzer Armee - Gen. der Pz Trp Hasso von Manteuffel
638 Mortar Bty
410 VAK
III/999 Construction Eng Bn

LXVI Armeekorps - Gen. der Art. Walther Lucht
460 Art. Bn
16 VW Brig.
10SS Pz Art Reg. [on loan]
244 StuG Brig. [14 StuG]
74 Lt. Flak Sturm Bn
1099 Mortar Bty
803 Construction Eng Bn
18 VG Div - Obst. Gunther Hoffmann-Schonborn
    [14 Jpz38t]
62 VG Div - Obst. Friedrich Kittel
    [14 Jpz38t]

LVIII Panzerkorps - Gen. der Pz Trp Walter Krüger
401 VAK
7 VW Brig
1121 H. Mortar Bty
1125 H. Mortar Bty
25/975 Festung Art. Bty
207 Combat Eng. Bn
1 Flak Sturm Reg.
560 VG Div - Obst. Rudolf Langhaeuser
116 Pz Div - Gen. Maj. Siegfried von Waldenburg
    [26 Mk IV, 43 Mk V, 13 Jg IV]

XLVII Panzerkorps - Gen. der Pz Trp Heinrich von Lüttwitz
766 VAK
15 VW Brig.
1124 H. Art Bty
1119 H. Mortar. Bty
600 Combat Eng Bn
182 Flak Sturm Reg.
2 Pz Div - Obst. Meinrad von Lauchert
    [26 Mk IV, 49 Mk V, 45 StuG]
Lehr Pz Div - Genlt. Fritz Bayerlein
    [30 Mk IV, 23 Mk V, 14 JgIV]
    559 s. Pzjgr Bn [19 JgIV & JglV]
    243 StuG Brig. [18 StuG]
26 VG Div - Obst. Heinz Kokott
    [14 Jgpz38t]

Seventh Armee - Gen. der Pz Trp Erich Brandenberger
660, 1092, 1093 H. Art. Btys
1122 H. Mortar Bty
47 Combat Eng. Brig.
501 Festung Pzjgr Bn
677 Eng. Bn
605 Bridge Construction Bn

LXXXV Armeekorps - Gen. der Inf. Baptist Kneiss
18 VW Brig.
406 VAK
15th Flak Reg.
668 s. Pzjgr Bn
1094 Art. Bty
5 FJ Div - Obst. Ludwig Heilmann
    11 StuG Brig. [27 StuG]
352 VG Div - Obst. Erich Schmidt [6 Jpz38t]

LXXX Armeekorps - Gen. der Inf. Franz Beyer
657 s. Pzjgr Bn
8 VW Brig.
408 VAK
1095 Art. Bty
276 VG Div - Gen. Maj. Kurt Möhring
212 VG Div - Genlt. Franz Sensfuss [5 StuG]

LIII Armeekorps - Gen. der Cav. Edwin von Rothkirch
44 Festung MG Bn
XIII/999 Festung Bn
7th Armee Service School

Organization of *Luftwaffenkommando West*: December 1944

Luftwaffenkommando West   Generalleutnant Josef Schmidt

II Jagdkorps   Generalmajor Dietrich Peltz

3rd Jagddivision	Generalmajor Walter Grabmann
geschwader	*gruppen*
JG 1	(3)
JG 3	(3)
JG 6	(3)
JG 26	(3)
JG 27	(4)
JG 77	(3)
JG 54/IV	(1)

Jagdabschnitt Mittelrhein	Oberst Trübenbach
JG 2	(3)
JG 4	(3)
JG 11	(3)
JG 53	(3)
JG 54/IV	(1)
SG 4	(3)

3rd Flieger Division
   KG 51, 66, 76
   NG 1, 2, 20
   NJG 2

Plane Types:
   Me-109: *JG 77, 53*
   FW-190: *SG 4, NG 20*
   Me-109 & FW-190: *JG 1, 2, 4, 6, 11, 26, 27*
   Ar-234: *KG 76*
   Me-262: *KG 51*
   Ju-87: *NG 1, 2*
   Ju-188 & Do-217: *KG 66*
   Ju-88: *NJG 2*

COMMITMENT OF REINFORCEMENTS TO THE ARDENNES:

17 Dec: von der Heydte parachute drop
   669 Ost Bn
   276 VG/1276 StuG Co. [4 Jpz38t]
18 Dec: IISS Panzerkorps HQ
   9SS Pz Div
   Fuh Bglt Brig.
   3 Pz Gr Div
   560 VG/1129 Reg.
      560 VG/1560 StuG Co. [12 Jpz38t]
19 Dec: Fuh Gr. Brig.
   2SS Pz Div.
   246 VG Div.
20 Dec: LXXIV Armeekorps HQ
   506 s. Pz Bn
21 Dec: 79 VG Div
22 Dec: 9 Pz Div.
   15 Pz Gr. Div.
   403 VAK

23 Dec: 741 Pzjgr Bn (20 Jpz38t]
24 Dec: XXXIX Panzerkorps HQ - Genlt. Karl Decker
   167 VG Div
   326 VG/1326 StuG Co. [12 Jpz38t]
25 Dec: 9 VG Div.
   410 VAK
28 Dec: 19 VW Brig
   167 VG/1167 StuG Co. [12 Jpz38t]
   Withdrawn: 150 Pz Brig. 7, 17 VW Brig, 410 VAK
      653 s. Pzjgr Bn
      394, 667 StuG Brig.
29 Dec: 340 VG Div
1 Jan: Korps Felber HQ - Genlt. Hans Felber
4 Jan: XXXIX Panzerkorps HQ withdrawn
5 Jan: 19 VW Brig withdrawn

RECOMMENDED READING

The Ardennes Campaign is one of those important military topics about which a lot has been written, although not always with a great degree of historical validity. This list will hopefully guide the interested reader to the better works.

Six references tower above the lot to cover the great battle. For completeness and sheer detail, the U.S. Army's official account, *The Ardennes Campaign: The Battle of the Bulge* (Washington D.C.: 1965), is vital. However, Dr. Cole's work is sometimes errs in its coverage of detail on the German side. To supplement Cole, I recommend Pallud's *The Battle of the Bulge: Then and Now* (London: 1986 2nd ed.). This monumental volume has excellent coverage of the German operations and intentions during the offensive as well

as an astonishing collection of "then and now" photographs of the battlefield. The closest to an official German account is Hermann Jung's *Die Ardennen Offensive,* (Zurich: 1971), written as the author's Ph.D. thesis at the University of Heidelberg. It is untranslated, but makes scholarly use of primary German sources. Russell Weigley's *Eisenhower's Lieutenants* (Bloomington: 1981), is another indispensible work covering the Ardennes operation as well as the rest of the war in Europe, focusing on the U.S. command.

Coverage of the "human" side of the battle is given exceptional treatment in two books. John Toland's *Battle: The Story of the Bulge* (New York: 1959) is skillful in recreating the emotional atmosphere surrounding the battle. The late Charles B. MacDonald's *A Time for Trumpets: The Untold*

Story of the Battle of the Bulge (New York: 1985) covers much the same ground. However, the MacDonald volume is also big on detail as well as human interest. The author was the former chief of the Office of Military History and a skillful writer who was intimately familiar with the Ardennes area and its inhabitants. All this promises good reading as well as solid history.

Other useful general accounts include John Eisenhower's *The Bitter Woods* (New York: 1969) and Merriam's *Dark December* (New York: 1947). A French account, Nobecourt's *Hitler's Last Gamble* (New York: 1967), contains a good retelling of the German parachute operation. Photographic accounts include Crookenden's *Battle of the Bulge 1944* (New York: 1980) and Goolrick and Tanner's *The Battle of the Bulge* (Alexandria: 1979), but both are readily exceeded by Pallud's book.

British accounts of the battle are sparse. Peter Elstob's *Hitler's Last Offensive* (New York: 1971) contains an account as well as some interesting observations in its epilogue. Strawson's *The Battle for the Ardennes* (New York: 1972) also contains some information as well as a good amount of armchair generaling. The official U.K. account is given in Ellis' *Victory in the West, Vol. I & II*, (London: 1968) but this does little for operational detail. This sort of information is found in Gill and Groves' *Club Route in Europe: The Story of 30 Corps in the European Campaign* (London: 1946).

The story of the air battle is less than complete — particularly for the U.S. forces. The official U.S. account, *The Army Air Forces in World War II* (Chicago: 1951) contains some detail in Chapter 19, although Craven and Cate would have us believe that the air force single-handedly won the battle! Another account is found in Ken Rust's *The Ninth Air Force in World War II* (Fallbrook, CA: 1970). By far the best German record is Werner Girbig's *Six Months to Oblivion: The Eclipse of the German Fighter Force* (New York: 1975).

A number of books cover individual engagements in greater detail. The Kampfgruppe Peiper operations and the infamous massacre is covered in Pallud's *Ardennes 1944: Peiper and Skorzeny* (London: 1987), Whiting's *Massacre at Malmedy* (New York: 1981), as well as Weingartner's scholarly *Crossroads of Death* (Berkeley: 1979). The Bastogne epic is best told in S.L.A. Marshall's *Bastogne: The First Eight Days* (Washington D.C.: 1946) and the battle for Clervaux and the "Skyline Drive" is recounted in Phillips' *To Save Bastogne* (New York: 1982). Cavanagh's *Rocherath-Krinkelt* (Norwell, MA: 1986) covers the less well known, but pivotal battle for the twin villages. A description of the turning-point Celles engagement is given in the 2nd Armored Division history, *Hell on Wheels* (Novato, CA: 1977) by Don Houston. The struggle for St. Vith is told in a biographical account of an important U.S. commander, *Clarke of St. Vith* (Cleveland: 1977).

Memoirs and biographic accounts have also been voluminous. For coverage of Hitler during the battle, Irving's *Hitler's War* (New York: 1977), Warlimont's *Inside Hitler's Headquarters* (New York: 1964) and Gilbert's *Hitler Directs His War* (New York: 1950) are best. Eisenhower tells his story in *Crusade in Europe* (New York: 1948), and Bradley in *A Soldier's Story* (New York: 1951) and *A General's Life*

(New York: 1983). Patton provides a particularly honest treatment in *War As I Knew It* (1947). Blair's *Ridgway's Paratroopers* (New York: 1986) gives a highly readable account of this controversial corps commander and Gavin recounts his memoirs in *On to Berlin* (New York: 1978). Montgomery tells his story in *Memoirs of the Field Marshal the Viscount Montgomery of Alamein* (Cleveland: 1958), but the discerning reader should consider Lamb's more recent *Montgomery in Europe* (New York: 1984) for some objectivity. On the German side, the commander of the *Fifth Panzer Army* has produced insightful records in Liddell Hart's *The German Generals Talk* (New York: 1979) and in *Decisive Battles of World War II: The German View* (New York: 1965). There are a number of others, but most are untranslated.

The story of the war as it was experienced by the average G.I. is probably best told in MacDonald's *Company Commander* (Washington D.C. 1947) and more recently in Leinbaugh and Campbell's excellent *The Men of Company K* (New York: 1985). William Breuer's *Bloody Clash at Sadzot* (St. Louis: 1981) provides a similar perspective. Front-line German grenadiers have their story recounted in Shulman's *Defeat in the West* (New York: 1948) and Whiting's *'44: In Combat from Normandy to the Ardennes* (New York: 1984).

Objective accounts of how World War II battle was fought include Marshall's *Men Against Fire* (New York: 1947), Ellis' *The Sharp End* (New York: 1980), English's *Perspective on Infantry* (New York: 1981), *Combat WWII* (New York: 1983) edited by Don Condon and the excellent *Six Armies in Normandy* (New York: 1982) by John Keegan. Again, a number of the German division histories offer the view from the other side, but are, as yet, untranslated.

Unit histories exist in quantity for both sides, and vary greatly in quality. These vary from detailed objective accounts to photographic volumes with more "unit pride" than substance. Coverage of the German side is greatly aided by after-war interviews of German commanders which are filed at the Foreign Military studies Branch at the National Archives.

What German records as survived the war's end are catalogued on microfilm both at the archives as well as at the Bundesarchiv in Freiburg, West Germany. The primary sources for U.S. combat units are the after-action reports, combat interview and journals that are filed at the depository in Suitland, Maryland.

Order of Battle information is available in Stanton's *Order of Battle WW II* (Novato, CA: 1984); for the U.S. units. Madej's *German Army Order of Battle* (Allentown: 1981) and Tessin's gargantuan *Verbande und Truppen der Deutschen Wehrmacht und Waffen SS Im Zweiten Weltkrieg* (Osnabruck: 1980) gives coverage for the other side. Joslen's *Orders of Battle* (London: 1960) gives composition for the British XXX Corps.

For the characteristics of the weapons and equipment used by both sides, see Kirk and Young's *Great Weapons of World War II*, (New York: 1966), Ellis' *Tanks of World War II* (London: 1981) and Hogg's *British and American Artillery of World War II* and the companion *German Artillery of World War II* (London: 1981). Chamberlain and Ganders' *WW II Fact Files* (New York: 1975) series covers a variety of weapons and is very useful. Also handy is Davies' *The German Army Handbook* (New York:1977) and the Ballantine series on weapons of WW II (New York: Various dates).

PERIODICALS AND INTEREST GROUPS

The official publication of Veterans of the Battle of the Bulge, *The Bulge Bugle*, is the only periodical on the Ardennes Campaign that is published in English. Published five times yearly, the *Bugle*, is available for $10 per year from Veterans of the Battle of the Bulge (P.O. Box 11129, Arlington, Virginia 22210-2129). It features historical articles, anecdotes from Bulge participants and announcements of meetings of associated veterans organizations.

The Bulge, an Luxembourg publication, is available from the interest group, Cercle D'Etudes sur La Bataille des Ardennes (C.C.P. 10609 - 36 C.E.B.A. Clervaux, Luxembourg). *The Bulge*, is published four times a year and the text is generally in German and French. The annual price is 200 Luxembourg Francs. The Belgian equivalent interest group is C.R.I.B.A. (Center for Research and Information of the Battle of the Ardennes), 22 Thier de la Chartreuse, 4020 Liège, Belgium.

FILM

The significance of the Ardennes Campaign has predictably led to a Hollywood version of the battle. The Warner Brothers production *The Battle of the Bulge* starring Henry Fonda, Charles Bronson and Robert Shaw, hardly does justice to this important historical event. Characters are Hollywood make-believe, the banal script only vaguely resembles the actual circumstances and the entire affair was filmed in Spain! Upon seeing this film in Munich the former German commander of the *Fifth Panzer Armee*, General Hasso von Manteuffel, told the press:

> The content of this film is completely fictional and has hardly anything to do with the events of those days....It also presents a distortion of the facts and actual conditions under which the battle took place....The film is an insult not only to the American soldier who fought in the Ardennes, but also a scandal for all soldiers including those on the *other* side.

Better than this Hollywood pap is an older film, *Battleground*, starring Van Johnson and Ricardo Montelban. The plot concerns U.S. GIs swept up in the Battle of the Bulge and surrounded in Bastogne. The story focuses on the human side of the war, in a similar fashion to *A Walk in the Sun*. It won Oscars in 1949 for its slick script and innovative cinematography.

Probably the best film on the Ardennes Campaign is a British documentary — *Battle of the Bulge*. Written and directed by Peter Batty, this hour-long film features vintage U.S. and captured German footage from the Imperial War Museum. A well written script with interviews of participants rounds out the presentation and makes for an entertaining history lesson.

Another hour long documentary, also titled *The Battle of the Bulge*, is available on video tape (Fusion Video 6730 North St., Dept WW 8808, Tinley Park, IL 60477). This presents a 1964 NBC black and white television production on the conflict. Although not so impressive as the British film, this piece features narratives from a number of key participants. There are at least two others: "The Battle of the Bulge" a 30-minute segment made in 1983 for the PBS *War Chronicles* series and a similar piece in the *Twentieth Century* hosted by Walter Cronkite.

SIMULATION GAMES

The most historically comprehensive wargame on the Ardennes Campaign is the author's own, *Hitler's Last Gamble*, published by 3W (P.O. Box F Cambria, CA 93428). The game is detailed and fairly complex presenting the Bulge on a regimental and battalion level with two maps, 800 playing pieces and historical notes. A computerized version of the game is also planned. Another less rigorous, but very playable version of the campaign is Avalon Hill's *The Battle of the Bulge, 2nd Edition- 1981* (4517 Harford Rd., Baltimore, Maryland 21214). This game is a vast improvement over it's predecessor, the 1965 Avalon Hill edition. Another interesting game on the Bulge is the author's *Battles for the Ardennes* (1978) which depicts both the German 1940 and 1944 offensives in the region. It is currently published by TSR Hobbies (P.O. Box 110, Lake Geneva, WI 53147). There are now two computer games on the Bulge: *Tigers in the Snow* (1980) on a division level and the more complex *Breakthrough in the Ardennes* (1984) both by Strategic Simulations, Inc. (1046 N. Rengstorff Ave, Mountain View, CA 94043).

The Bulge has been an immensely popular topic for historical games; there are probably more titles on this one battle than any other. Previous games on the Ardennes Campaign, many of which are out of print, include: *Bastogne* (1970), *Ardennes Offensive* (1973), *Hitler's Last Gamble* (1975), *Wacht Am Rhein* (1977), *Dark December* (1979), *Bulge* (1979) and *Attack in the Ardennes* (1982).

BATTLEFIELD MUSEUMS

A number of museums lie in the Ardennes area. By far the most famous is the Bastogne Nuts! museum, now redesignated the "Bastogne Historical Center." The center was the world's first WWII historical museum and features a very original presentation on the battle which can easily take hours for visitors to fully appreciate. The museum features life-size dioramas of battlefield scenes around Bastogne, free movies of the footage shot during the battle and a large collection of uniforms, weapons and memorabilia. Also, outside the historical center is a Sherman tank, a M-10 tank destroyer (with a 17 pounder gun) and a *Jagdpanzer 38t* tank destroyer—all carefully restored with markings of appropriate U.S. and German units that actually fought in the area. The museum souvenir shop has an interesting collection of books on the battle. The museum is open from February through mid-November.

The December '44 museum at La Gleize features the most famous Ardennes relic — a beautifully restored 70-ton King Tiger panzer that fought with *Kampfgruppe Peiper* during December 1944. The museum, assembled by curator Gérard Grégorie focuses on the German side of the battle. It features many battlefield relics from the area — a fuel drum parachuted to Peiper, a mapboard used by the famous SS colonel, a heavy 12 cm mortar, other weapons and SS uniforms. Captured German film of the Peiper *Kampfgruppe* is shown in an adjoining room. An impressive collection of German photographs is displayed. The museum is open from May to mid-September.

In the medieval castle in Wiltz, Luxembourg, is a museum created by the Amis de la Feerie du Genet. The facility features weapons, and other battlefield relics recovered by locals from the battlefields that surround the town. Outside is a memorial to General Eisenhower and the U.S. 28th Infantry Division which had its headquarters there on December 16th, 1944. The museum is open from mid-June through mid-September.

In the picturesque town of Clervaux the CEBA association (see interest groups) operates a museum out of the ancient castle that served as a modern day Alamo for defenders of the U.S. 110th Infantry Regiment on December 17th, 1944. Uniformed mannequins, restored weapons and other Bulge era equipment are on display. Outside the castle are two beautifully restored Ardennes era weapons — a 76mm Sherman tank complete with 707th Tank Battalion insignia, appropriately faced by a restored German 88mm Pak anti-tank gun with markings of the *2nd Panzer Division*. The museum is open from May 8th to September 18th.

Diekirch, Luxembourg, features the newest addition to the Bulge museums — and also the most impressive. Fostered by the young enthusiasts of the Diekirch Historical Society, the museum features some 150 uniforms on display — many in astonishingly detailed life-sized dioramas with fully equipped mannequins copiously adorned with restored weapons. Outside the museum, a carefully painted *Jagdpanzer 38t* (German tank destroyers of this type operated in the area from the *352nd Volksgrenadier Division*) a 75mm German towed anti-tank gun and a German 10.5 cm field howitzer form center pieces for the display. To top it off, the photo collection in the museum is remarkable. The Diekirch Historical Museum is open each day from May 1st to October 1st.

TOURS OF THE ARDENNES

Self-Guided Tours

Good roads, hotels, food and drink make a self-guided tour of the Ardennes region a pleasant vacation. Numerous battlefield museums, monuments and memorials dot the quaint countryside. For those looking for vistas of historical import on the battlefield, Jean Paul Pallud's book *The Battle of the Bulge: Then and Now* is highly recommended. This book locates many photographs of combat action taken during the battle where photographed in the Ardennes area today. Visitors can see how things have (and have not) changed since 1944.

Self-guided tours of the battlefield are arranged in a handy guide available free from the Luxembourg ministry of tourism, "The Battle of the Ardennes: Map of Historical and Touristical Tours." The guide features nine nicely organized motor tours of the battle area. Also provided is a guide to twenty "boundary stones" placed around the Ardennes area by the Belgian Touring Club. The boundary stones mark the furthest advance of the German invaders in December 1944 from Eupen to Martelange. Of particular interest are the numerous Bulge museums that are located in the area (see the guide to museums).

Roads are good and rental cars can be acquired for reasonable rates. Hotels vary considerably; the more expensive feature "*confort moderne*," whereas the more quaint facilities are often traditional. Sabena, the national airline of Belgium, offers packages featuring hotel accommodations and rental cars. Hotel reservations can be made free of charge through the Belgium or Luxembourg tourist offices.

Those with you not interested in the battle will find many other events and places of interest in the Ardennes: the caves of Remouchamps, the great basilica in St. Hubert at the Church of St. Giles and the Victor Hugo house in Vianden. Liège and Eupen feature thousands of high quality shops. Nature parks are in the Hürtgen area near Malmédy in Belgium. In Luxembourg, the Valley of the Wiltz and *Le Petite Suisse* near Berdorf features great hiking. For the outdoors minded, the area offers bicycling, fishing, golfing, kayaking and horseback riding. Clervaux, Vianden, Durbuy and La Roche feature picturesque castled towns from the 16th Century.

Many art museums are also available: the Museum of the Ancient Arts in Namur and the Archaeological Museum in Arlon. The famous Spa-Franchorchamps Formula I car race is held in mid-August. Of course, Spa has the famous watering place from which the name for all similar resorts is taken. Visitors can both take the cure from its mineral waters and gamble at the local casino. A number of festivals occur in the region during summer: the Ardennes Folk Festival at Stavelot in August, the Wine Festival in La Gleize on August 17th. International Day for Hunting and Nature along with a Grand Parade comes St. Hubert on September 6th.

The area is famous for its food and drink: delectable thinly sliced Ardennes ham, Belgian *Pommes Frites* and over 300 tasty local "pure malt and hop" beers (try *Köngisbacher Pils* in Clervaux) are available in the area. Lovers of the grape will find the Moselle region offering wines of particular distinction. The beautiful city of Dinant on the Meuse River (the most advanced German spearhead came to within 3 miles of the town on Christmas Eve 1944) boasts several gastronomic delights: *Escaveche de la Meuse* a fish specialty, and a cheese tart known locally as *Flamiche*. Other traditional dishes in Luxembourg include black pudding (*Treipen*) and smoked pork with broad beans.

There are at least three languages spoken in the area: Belgium features both French and German in the Ardennes region. German, French and Luxembourgeois (a sort of combination of French and German) is found in the Grand Duchy of Luxembourg. Many people are tri-lingual and it is not usually difficult to find someone who speaks some English. Weather in summer is moderate, but somewhat unpredictable so that a variety of different types of clothing are recommended for visitors.

Useful Addresses:
Belgian Tourist Office
745 Fifth Ave.
New York, N.Y. 10151

Luxembourg Office of Tourism
801 Second Ave.
New York, N.Y. 10017

Guided Battlefield Tours

Guided tours of the Ardennes are available to those interested. Veterans of the Battle of the Bulge (see interest groups for more information) usually has an annual tour. The author (139 W. Leon Lane, Cocoa Beach, FL 32931) can serve as a guide for small groups wanting to visit the area. William C.C. Cavanagh can provide battlefield "seminars" for those who want an education on the battle (10 Gundekarstr 8501 Rosstal/West Germany). The leading British company undertaking such tours is Major & Mrs. Holt's Battlefield Tours, Ltd. (Golden Key Building, 15 Market Street, Sandwich, Kent, CT13 9DA). Information on additional firms offering tours is available from the Belgian National Tourist Office (745 5th Ave., New York, N.Y. 10022). Most of the packaged tours take place in the summer from June through September.

TABLE OF EQUIVALENT RANKS

German Army	Waffen-SS	British Army	U.S. Army
Generalfeldmarschall	SS-Reichsführer	Field Marshal (5★)	-
Generaloberst	SS-Oberstgruppenführer und Generaloberst	General (4★)	General of the Army
General der Infanterie, Panzertruppen, etc.	SS-Gruppenführer und General	General (3★)	General (4★)
Generalleutnant	SS-Gruppenführer und Generalleutnant	Lt. General (3★)	Lt. (3★) General
Generalmajor	SS-Brigadeführer und Generalmajor	Maj. General (2★)	Maj. (2★) General
-	SS-Oberführer	Brigadier(1★)	Brig.(1★)General
Oberst	SS-Standartenführer	Colonel	Colonel
Oberstleutnant	SS-Obersturmbannführer	Lt. Colonel	Lt. Col.
Major	SS-Sturmbannführer	Major	Major
Hauptmann	SS-Hauptsturmführer	Captain	Captain
Oberleutnant	SS-Obersturmführer	Lieutnant	1st Lt.
Leutnant	SS-Untersturmführer	2nd Lt.	2nd Lt.
Feldwebel	SS-Oberscharführer	Sergeant	T. Sgt.
Unteroffizier	SS-Unterscharführer	Corporal	Sergeant
Oberschütze	SS-Oberschütze	-	Pvt. 1st Class
Schütze, Grenadier, Pionier etc.	SS-Schütze etc.	Private	Private

GLOSSARY OF TERMS AND ABBREVIATIONS

AA: Anti-aircraft artillery

AAAW: Anti-aircraft Automatic Weapons

Abteilung: battalion

Abwehrschlact im Westen: Defensive battle in the West

Adlerhorst: Eagle's Nest; Hitler's headquarters in the West

Armee: Army

Armeekorps: corps

Artillerie: artillery

AT: Anti-tank

BAR: Browning Automatic Rifle

Begleit: Escort

Blitzkrieg: Lightning War; German armored warfare

Bolshevik: derogatory term for Soviet Russia

CCA: Combat Command A

CCB: Combat Command B

CCR: Combat Command Reserve

CP: Command Post

Das Reich: The Reich

Einheit: unity principal for unit organization

Eisenbahn Artillerie: German heavy caliber rail guns

Eng: Engineer

Ersatz: replacement training

FA: Field Artillery

Fallschirmjäger: Parachute Infantry

Feldherr: Great general

Festung: fortress

Feuerwalze: rolling artillery barrage

FG: Fighter Group

FKL Panzer Battalion: Funklenk or radio controlled small demolition tanks operated from German panzers in the rear

Flak: Fliegerabwehrkanone; German anti-aircraft guns

Führer: leader, commander; Hitler when capitalized

Führersonderzug Brandenburg: Hitler's personal train

Füsilier battalion: light reconnaissance infantry battalion

G-2: intelligence section

G-3: operations section

G-4: supply section

Gebirgs: mountain

Gewehr: rifle

Grenadier: infantryman

Gruppe: group

Heersgruppe: Army Group

Hitler Jugend: Hitler Youth

Inf: Infantry

Infanterie: infantry

Jabo: German slang for Allied fighterbombers

Jagdgeschwader: German fighter wing

Jagdkorps: German fighter command corps

Jagdpanzer: hunting tank, Mk IV or Jg38t type

Jagdpanther: Panther type tank destroyer

Jagdtiger: Tiger type tank destroyer

Jägeraufmarsch: Fighter plane concentration

Kampfgruppe: battle group, typically named after its leader

Kampfraum: battle area

Kessel: surrounded pocket

Klein Losung: Small Solution

Königstiger: King Tiger tank

Kompanie: company

Kriegsmarine: German navy

Kriegstagebuch: KTB; German war diary

Lehr: training

Luftwaffe: German air force

Mk IV: German Panzer IV tank

Mk V: German Mk V, Panther tank

Mk VI: German Mk VI, Tiger tank

Mk VIb: German Mk VIb, King Tiger tank

Mörser: mortar, howitzer

Nacht: night

Nebelwerfer: Multiple tube rocket artillery

Ober: Over, first

Oberkommando: High Command

OB West: Obetbefehlshaber West; High Command of German forces in the West; von Rundstedt's headquarters

Ohren Abteilung: Infantry battalions composed of men with hearing disorders

OKL: Oberkommando der Luftwaffe, High Command of the Air Force

OKW: Oberkommando der Wehrmacht, High Command of the German armed forces

Operation 'Bodenplatte': Codename for Luftwaffe attack against Allied airfields, January 1, 1945.

Operation Grief: Codename for Skorzeny's commando operation

Operation Herbstnebel: Operation 'Autumn Fog;' Code name for Army Group B's alternative attack plan

Operation Nordwind: Codename for German attack in the Alsace, January 1, 1945

Operation Stösser: Codename for German parachute operation

O-Tag: Zero-day; Code for day of start of Ardennes Offensive

Ost Battalion: Non-German volunteer troops from East-European countries

Panzer: tank, armor

Panzer Grenadier: German armored infantry, motorized in halftracks trucks or bicycles

Panzerfaust: German recoilless anti-tank rocket launcher

Panzerjäger: tank destroyer

Panzerkorps: armored corps

Pionier: engineer

Plan Martin: Code name for offensive plan drawn up by OB West

POL: Petroleum, oil and lubricants

RCT: Regimental Combat Team

Reichsbahn: German state railroads

Rollbahn: panzer rolling road; tank division march route

Sicherheitsdienst: SD; security service of the SS

SS: Schutzstaffel; elite guard of the Nazi party

Schwere: heavy

SHAEF: Supreme Headquarters, Allied Expeditionary Force

Staffel: squadron

Sturm: assault

Sturmgeschütz: assault gun

TAC: Tactical Air Command

TCC: Troop Carrier Command

TD: Tank Destroyer

Third Reich: Hitler's National socialist state

T/O&E: Tables of Organization and Equipment

Treibstoff: fuel

Untermenschen: sub-humans; derogatory term for Russians

Verbrauchssätze: VS; German fuel issue; sufficient to take motorized formation 100 km over good terrain

Volks: people's

Volksgrenadier: People's Infantry divisions organized in late '44

Volksartillerie: People's Artillery organized in late '44

Volkswerfer: Peoples rocket artillery organized in late '44

Volksdeutsche: Citizens of a non-German country considered to be Germans racially.

Wacht am Rhein: Watch on the Rhine; Hitler's codename for the Ardennes Offensive

Wehrmacht: German armed forces

Wehrmachtführungsstab: Armed forces operations staff

Werfer: multiple-tube rocket artillery

Wolfschanze: Wolf's Lair; Hitler's headquarters in East Prussia

INDEX